SAT®
Prep
2020

Editor-in-Chief

Alexandra Strelka, MA

Contributing Editors

Dr. Brandon Deason, MD; M. Dominic Eggert; Kathryn Sollenberger, MEd; Glen Stohr, JD

Special thanks to our faculty authors and reviewers

Michael Cook; Christopher Cosci; Boris Dvorkin; John Evans; Jack Hayes; Rebecca Knauer; Jo L'Abbate; Bird Marathe; Karen McCulloch; Melissa McLaughlin; Gail Rivers; Anne Marie Salloum; Jason Selzer; Gordon Spector; Caroline Sykes; Bob Verini, MFA; Bonnie Wang; and Ethan Weber

Additional special thanks to

Laura Aitcheson; Matthew Callan; Paula L. Fleming, MA, MBA; Joanna Graham; Adam Grey; Rebekah Hawthorne; Rebecca Knauer; Abnia Loriston, MEd; Mandy Luk; Kristin Murner, PhD and the countless others who made this project possible.

SAT® is a trademark registered and/or owned by the College Board, which was not involved in the production of, and does not endorse, this product.

This publication is designed to provide accurate information in regard to the subject matter covered as of its publication date, with the understanding that knowledge and best practice constantly evolve. The publisher is not engaged in rendering medical, legal, accounting, or other professional service. If medical or legal advice or other expert assistance is required, the services of a competent professional should be sought. This publication is not intended for use in clinical practice or the delivery of medical care. To the fullest extent of the law, neither the Publisher nor the Editors assume any liability for any injury and/or damage to persons or property arising out of or related to any use of the material contained in this book.

Published by Kaplan Publishing, a division of Kaplan, Inc.
750 Third Avenue
New York, NY 10017

10 9 8 7 6 5 4 3 2

ISBN-13: 978-1-5062-3689-6

Kaplan Publishing print books are available at special quantity discounts to use for sales promotions, employee premiums, or educational purposes. For more information or to purchase books, please call the Simon & Schuster special sales department at 866-506-1949.

TABLE OF CONTENTS

GO ONLINE

*www.kaptest.com/
moreonline*

How to Use This Book

Congratulations on taking this important step in your college admissions process! By studying with Kaplan, you'll maximize your score on the SAT, a major factor in your overall college application.

Our experience shows that the greatest SAT score increases result from active engagement in the preparation process. Kaplan will give you direction, focus your preparation, and teach you the specific skills and effective test-taking strategies you need to know for the SAT. We will help you achieve your top performance on test day, but your effort is crucial. The more you invest in preparing for the SAT, the greater your chances of achieving your target score and getting into your top-choice college.

Are you registered for the SAT? Kaplan cannot register you for the official SAT. If you have not already registered for the upcoming SAT, talk to your high school guidance counselor or visit the College Board's website at www.collegeboard.org to register online and for information on registration deadlines, test sites, accommodations for students with disabilities, and fees.

Practice Tests

Kaplan's practice tests are just like the actual SAT. By taking a practice exam you will prepare yourself for the actual test day experience. One of your practice tests is included in this book and one more can be accessed online. See the "Digital Resources" section below to learn how to access your online practice test.

Chapter Organization

The chapters in this book follow a standard format to make this book as easy to use as possible. Most chapters in this book start with a section called "How Much Do You Know?" that allows you to get a sense of how comfortable you already are with the material in the chapter. Answers and explanations follow immediately in the "Check Your Work" section. Each lesson in a chapter starts with a question typical of the way the SAT tests a given topic and ends with a set of practice questions called "Try on Your Own." There is yet another practice set at the end of each chapter called "How Much Have You Learned?" to reinforce the concepts explained in the chapter. Answers and Explanations for the "Try on Your Own" and "How Much Have You Learned?" sections are provided at the end of each chapter for easy reference.

Smartpoints®

Different topics are worth different numbers of points on the SAT because they show up more or less frequently in questions. By studying the information released by the College Board, Kaplan has been able to determine how often certain topics are likely to appear on the SAT, and therefore how many points these topics are worth on test day. If you master a given topic, you can expect to earn the corresponding number of SmartPoints® on test day.

We have used a 600-point scale for Smartpoints® because that's the number of points you can earn within the Math and Verbal subscores: the SAT scoring scale is 200–800, so there are $800 - 200 = 600$ points to be earned within each major section of the test. The breakdown of SmartPoints® for Math, Reading, and Writing & Language are summarized in the following tables. Keep in mind that these values are approximate because testing administrations differ.

Math		
SmartPoints® Category	**# of Points**	**Sub-Categories**
Linear Equations	110	Linear equations, linear graphs, word problems
Functions	105	Functions, graphs of functions, functions in word problems
Ratios, Proportions, and Percents	70	Setting up a proportion to solve for an unknown, unit conversion, calculating percent and percent change
Geometry	65	Triangles, circles, 3-dimensional figures
Quadratics	60	Quadratic equations, parabolas, modeling data, mixed systems of equations
Statistics and Probability	50	Descriptive statistics, probability, tables and charts, data samples
Systems of Linear Equations	45	Systems of equations, number of possible solutions
Inequalities	35	Inequalities, graphical representations of inequalities
Scatterplots	25	Scatterplots, lines of best fit, modeling data
Exponents, Radicals, Polynomials, and Radical Expressions	25	Exponents, radicals, polynomial operations, graphs of polynomials, modeling growth and decay, rational expressions/equations
Imaginary Numbers	5	Adding, subtracting, multiplying, and dividing complex numbers
Trigonometry	5	Sine, cosine, tangent
TOTAL	**600**	

Reading		
SmartPoints® Category	**# of Points**	**Sub-Categories**
Inference questions	90	Making deductions
Command of Evidence questions	60	Citing evidence
Detail questions	45	Finding details in the text
Vocab-in-Context questions	45	Determining the meaning of a word as it is used in the passage
Function questions	40	Explaining *why* the author included a certain detail
Global questions	20	Determining Central Ideas and Themes, Summarizing
TOTAL	**300**	

Writing & Language		
SmartPoints® Category	# of Points	Sub-Categories
Sentence Structure	85	Correcting run-ons and fragments, using correct conjunctions, punctuation
Development	85	Precision, relevance, revising text
Agreement	60	Subject-verb agreement, verb tense, pronoun agreement, modifiers, idioms
Organization	40	Transitions, sentence placement
Conciseness	20	Avoiding wordiness and redundancy
Graphs	10	Drawing inferences from a graph included with a passage
TOTAL	**300**	

Digital Resources

To access the online resources that accompany this book, which include an extra practice test and study planning guidance, follow the steps below:

GO ONLINE

www.kaptest.com/ moreonline

1. Go to: kaptest.com/moreonline

2. Have this book available as you complete the on-screen instructions.

PART 1

The SAT and You

CHAPTER 1

Inside the SAT

LEARNING OBJECTIVES

After completing this chapter, you will be able to:

- Recall the timing and scope of each section in anticipation of section management
- State what the SAT scoring system means for you the test taker

---

SAT Structure

The SAT, like any standardized test, is predictable. The more comfortable you are with the test structure, the more confidently you will approach each question type, thus maximizing your score.

The SAT is 3 hours long, or 3 hours and 50 minutes long if you choose to complete the optional Essay Test. The SAT is made up of mostly multiple-choice questions that test two subject areas: Evidence-Based Reading and Writing, and Math. The former is broken into a Reading Test and a Writing and Language Test.

Test	Allotted Time (minutes)	Question Count
Reading	65	52
Writing and Language	35	44
Math	80	58
Essay (optional)	50	1
Total	180 OR 230 (w/Essay)	154 OR 155 (w/Essay)

If you choose not to write the essay, you may also see an additional 20-minute multiple-choice section, but this is fairly rare.

SAT Scoring

SAT scoring can be pretty complex. You will receive one score ranging from 200–800 for Evidence-Based Reading and Writing and another for Math. Your overall SAT score will range from 400–1600 and is calculated by adding these two scores together. You will receive a separate score for the Essay Test, if you choose to take it.

In addition to your overall scores, you will receive subscores that provide a deeper analysis of your SAT performance. The SAT also gives you a percentile ranking, which allows you to compare your scores with those of other test takers. For example, a student who scored in the 63rd percentile did better than 63 percent of all others who took that test.

The scores you need depend primarily on which colleges you are planning to apply to. For example, if you want to attend an engineering school, you'll typically need a higher math score than if you want to attend a liberal arts college. Research the colleges you are interested in, find out what scores they require, and structure your SAT studying accordingly.

How to Maximize Your Score

What is most important to remember while taking the test is that maximizing all the various scores and subscores depends on getting the most points you can out of every section. You'll find advice on test-taking strategies below and in the section management chapters in the online Appendix of this book. However, if you still have a meaningful amount of time to prepare for the SAT, the best advice we can give you is to improve the skills you need to answer Math and Verbal questions correctly and efficiently. That's what this book is for. Use it in any order you like; you don't need to start with Math. But do use it. Read the instructional text for those topics you feel weak in and work your way through the practice questions. There are hundreds of them in this book, and they are very similar to those that you will see on test day. Practice will not only improve your skills; it will also raise your confidence, and that's very important to test-day success.

Where and When to Take the SAT

The SAT is offered every year on multiple Saturday test dates. Typically, exams are offered in August, October, November, December, March, May, and June. You can take the SAT multiple times. Some states offer special administrations of the SAT on different dates. Sunday tests are available by request for students requiring religious or other exemptions. The SAT is administered at high schools around the country that serve as testing centers. Your high school may or may not be a testing center. Check www.collegeboard.org for a list of testing centers near you. Note that you must register for the SAT approximately one month in advance to avoid paying a late fee. Some SAT test dates also offer SAT Subject Tests. You may not take both the SAT and the Subject Tests in a single sitting.

The SAT Math Test

The SAT Math Test is broken down into a calculator section and a no-calculator section. Questions across the sections consist of multiple-choice, student-produced response (Grid-in), and more comprehensive multi-part question sets.

	No-Calculator Section	Calculator Section	Total
Duration (minutes)	25	55	80
Multiple-choice	15	30	45
Grid-in	5	8	13
Total Questions	20	38	58

The SAT Math Test is divided into four content areas: Heart of Algebra, Problem Solving and Data Analysis, Passport to Advanced Math, and Additional Topics in Math.

SAT Math Test Content Area Distribution	
Heart of Algebra (19 questions)	Analyzing and solving equations and systems of equations; creating expressions, equations, and inequalities to represent relationships between quantities and to solve problems; rearranging and interpreting formulas
Problem Solving and Data Analysis (17 questions)	Creating and analyzing relationships using ratios, proportions, percentages, and units; describing relationships shown graphically; summarizing qualitative and quantitative data
Passport to Advanced Math (16 questions)	Using function notation; creating, analyzing, and solving quadratic and higher-order equations; manipulating polynomials to solve problems
Additional Topics in Math (6 questions)	Making area and volume calculations in context; investigating lines, angles, triangles, and circles using theorems; working with trigonometric functions and complex numbers

A few math questions might look like something you'd expect to see on a science or history test. These "crossover" questions are designed to test your ability to use math in real-world scenarios. There are a total of 18 "crossover" questions that will contribute to subscores that span multiple tests. Nine of the questions will contribute to the Analysis in Science subscore, and 9 will contribute to the Analysis in History/Social Studies subscore.

The SAT Reading Test

The SAT Reading Test will focus on your comprehension and reasoning skills when you are presented with challenging extended prose passages taken from a variety of content areas.

SAT Reading Test Overview	
Timing	65 minutes
Questions	52 passage-based multiple-choice questions
Passages	4 single passages; 1 set of paired passages
Passage Length	500–750 words per passage or passage set

Passages will draw from U.S. and World Literature, History/Social Studies, and Science. One set of History/Social Studies or Science passages will be paired. History/Social Studies and Science passages can also be accompanied by graphical representations of data such as charts, graphs, tables, and so on.

Reading Test Passage Types	
U.S. and World Literature	1 passage with 10 questions
History/Social Studies	2 passages or 1 passage and 1 paired-passage set with 10–11 questions each
Science	2 passages or 1 passage and 1 paired-passage set with 10–11 questions each

The multiple-choice questions for each passage will be arranged with main idea questions at the beginning of the set so that you can consider the entire passage before answering questions about details.

Skills Tested by Reading Test Questions	
Reading for Detail	Finding details in the passage, citing textual evidence
Summarizing	Determining central ideas and themes, understanding how a passage is structured, understanding relationships
Drawing Inferences	Understanding relationships, drawing conclusions from facts stated in a passage, interpreting words and phrases in context
Rhetorical Analysis	Analyzing word choice, analyzing point of view, determining why a fact is included, analyzing arguments
Synthesis	Analyzing multiple texts, analyzing quantitative information

The SAT Writing and Language Test

The SAT Writing and Language Test will focus on your ability to revise and edit text from a range of content areas.

SAT Writing and Language Test Overview	
Timing	35 minutes
Questions	44 passage-based, multiple-choice questions
Passages	4 single passages with 11 questions each
Passage Length	400–450 words per passage

The SAT Writing and Language Test will contain four single passages, one from each of the following subject areas: Careers, Humanities, History/Social Studies, and Science.

Writing and Language Passage Types	
Careers	Hot topics in "major fields of work" such as information technology and health care
Humanities	Texts about literature, art, history, music, and philosophy pertaining to human culture
History/Social Studies	Discussion of historical or social sciences topics such as anthropology, communication studies, economics, education, human geography, law, linguistics, political science, psychology, and sociology
Science	Exploration of concepts, findings, and discoveries in the natural sciences including Earth science, biology, chemistry, and physics

Passages will also vary in the "type" of text. A passage can be an argument, an informative or explanatory text, or a nonfiction narrative.

Writing and Language Passage Text Type Distribution	
Argument	1–2 passages
Informative/Explanatory Text	1–2 passages
Nonfiction Narrative	1 passage

Some passages and/or questions will refer to one or more data tables or charts. Questions associated with these graphics will ask you to revise and edit the passage based on the data presented in the graphic.

The most prevalent question format on the SAT Writing and Language Test will ask you to choose the best of three alternatives to an underlined portion of the passage or to decide that the current version is the best option. You will be asked to improve the development, organization, and diction in the passages to ensure they conform to conventional standards of English grammar, usage, and style.

Skills Tested by Writing and Language Test Questions	
Expression of Ideas (24 questions)	Organization and development of ideas
Standard English Conventions (20 questions)	Sentence structure, conventions of usage, and conventions of punctuation

The SAT Essay Test (Optional)

The SAT Essay Test assesses your college and career readiness. The essay tests your ability to read and analyze a high-quality source document. Your goal is to write a coherent analysis for the source supported with critical reasoning and evidence from the given text.

The SAT Essay Test features an argumentative source text of 650–750 words aimed toward a large audience. Passages will examine ideas, debates, and shifts in the arts and sciences as well as civic, cultural, and political life. Rather than having a simple for/against structure, these passages will be nuanced and will relate views on complex subjects. These passages will also be logical in their structure and reasoning.

It is important to note that prior knowledge is not required.

The SAT Essay Test prompt will ask you to explain how the presented passage's author builds an argument to convince an audience. In writing your essay, you may analyze elements such as the author's use of evidence, reasoning, style, and persuasion; you will not be limited to those elements listed, however.

Rather than writing about whether you agree or disagree with the presented argument, you will write an essay in which you analyze *how* the author makes an argument.

The SAT Essay Test will be broken down into three categories for scoring: Reading, Analysis, and Writing. Each of these elements will be scored on a scale of 1–4 by two graders, for a total score of 2–8 for each category.

Test-Taking Strategies

You have already learned about the overall structure of the SAT as well as the structure of the three main areas it entails: Reading, Writing and Language, and Math. The strategies outlined in this section can be applied to any of these tests.

The SAT is different from the tests you are used to taking in school. The good news is that you can use the SAT's particular structure to your advantage.

For example, on a test given in school, you probably go through the questions in order. You spend more time on the harder questions than on the easier ones because harder questions are usually worth more points. You also probably show your work because your teacher tells you that how you approach a question is as important as getting the correct answer.

This approach is not optimal for the SAT. On the SAT, you benefit from moving around within a section if you come across tough questions, because the harder questions are worth the same number of points as the easier questions. Similarly, showing your work is unimportant. It doesn't matter how you arrive at the correct answer—only that you bubble in the correct answer choice.

Strategy #1: Triaging the Test

You do not need to complete questions on the SAT in order. Every student has different strengths and should attack the test with those strengths in mind. Your main objective on the SAT should be to score as many points as you can. While approaching questions out of order may seem counterintuitive, it is a surefire way to achieve your best score.

Just remember, you can skip around within each section, but you cannot work on a section other than the one you've been instructed to work on.

To triage a section effectively, do the following:

- First, work through all the easy questions that you can do quickly. Skip questions that are hard or time-consuming. For the Reading Test, start with the passage you find most manageable and work toward the one you find most challenging. You do not need to go in order.
- Second, work through the questions that are doable but time-consuming.
- Third, work through the hard questions.

A Letter of the Day is an answer choice letter (A, B, C, or D) that you choose before test day to select for questions you guess on.

Strategy #2: Elimination

Even though there is no wrong-answer penalty on the SAT, Elimination is still a crucial strategy. If you can determine that one or more answer choices are definitely incorrect, you can increase your chances of getting the right answer by paring the selection down.

To eliminate answer choices, do the following:

- Read each answer choice.
- Cross out the answer choices that are incorrect.
- There is no wrong-answer penalty, so take your best guess.

Strategy #3: Strategic Guessing

Each multiple-choice question on the SAT has four answer choices and no wrong-answer penalty. That means if you have no idea how to approach a question, you have a 25 percent chance of randomly choosing the correct answer. Even though there's a 75 percent chance of selecting the incorrect answer, you won't lose any points for doing so. The worst that can happen on the SAT is that you'll earn zero points on a question, which means you should *always* at least take a guess, even when you have no idea what to do.

When guessing on a question, do the following:

- Try to strategically eliminate answer choices before guessing.
- If you run out of time, or have no idea what a question is asking, pick a Letter of the Day.
- If a question is taking too long, skip it and guess. Spend your time on those questions that you know how to do; don't allow yourself to get bogged down in fighting it out with a question that is too time-consuming.

PART 2

SAT Math

CHAPTER 2

Prerequisite Skills and Calculator Use

LEARNING OBJECTIVES

After completing this chapter, you will be able to:

- Identify skills necessary to obtain the full benefits of the Math sections of this book
- Use efficiency tips to boost your test-day speed
- Distinguish between questions that need a calculator and questions in which manual calculations are more efficient

---

Math Fundamentals

LEARNING OBJECTIVES

After this lesson, you will be able to:

- Identify skills necessary to obtain the full benefits of the Math sections of this book
- Use efficiency tips to boost your test-day speed

Prerequisites

This book focuses on the skills that are tested on the SAT. It assumes a working knowledge of arithmetic, algebra, and geometry. Before you dive into the subsequent chapters where you'll try testlike questions, there are a number of concepts—ranging from basic arithmetic to geometry—that you should master. The following sections contain a brief review of these concepts.

Algebra and Arithmetic

Order of operations is one of the most fundamental of all arithmetic rules. A well-known mnemonic device for remembering this order is PEMDAS: Please Excuse My Dear Aunt Sally. This translates to Parentheses, Exponents, Multiplication/Division, Addition/Subtraction. Perform multiplication and division from left to right (even if it means division before multiplication) and treat addition and subtraction the same way:

$$(14 - 4 \div 2)^2 - 3 + (2 - 1)$$
$$= (14 - 2)^2 - 3 + (1)$$
$$= 12^2 - 3 + 1$$
$$= 144 - 3 + 1$$
$$= 141 + 1$$
$$= 142$$

Three basic properties of number (and variable) manipulation—commutative, associative, and distributive—will assist you with algebra on test day:

- **Commutative:** Numbers can swap places and still provide the same mathematical result. This is valid only for addition and multiplication:

$$a + b = b + a \rightarrow 3 + 4 = 4 + 3$$
$$a \times b = b \times a \rightarrow 3 \times 4 = 4 \times 3$$

BUT: $3 - 4 \neq 4 - 3$ and $3 \div 4 \neq 4 \div 3$

- **Associative:** Different number groupings will provide the same mathematical result. This is valid only for addition and multiplication:

$$(a + b) + c = a + (b + c) \rightarrow (4 + 5) + 6 = 4 + (5 + 6)$$
$$(a \times b) \times c = a \times (b \times c) \rightarrow (4 \times 5) \times 6 = 4 \times (5 \times 6)$$

BUT: $(4 - 5) - 6 \neq 4 - (5 - 6)$ and $(4 \div 5) \div 6 \neq 4 \div (5 \div 6)$

- **Distributive:** A number that is multiplied by the sum or difference of two other numbers can be rewritten as the first number multiplied by the two others individually. This does *not* work with division:

$$a(b + c) = ab + ac \rightarrow 6(x + 3) = 6x + 6(3)$$
$$a(b - c) = ab - ac \rightarrow 3(y - 2) = 3y + 3(-2)$$

BUT: $12 \div (6 + 2) \neq 12 \div 6 + 12 \div 2$

Note: When subtracting an expression in parentheses, such as in $4 - (x + 3)$, distribute the negative sign outside the parentheses first: $4 + (-x - 3) \rightarrow 1 - x$.

Subtracting a positive number is the same as adding its negative. Likewise, subtracting a negative number is the same as adding its positive:

$$r - s = r + (-s) \rightarrow 22 - 15 = 7 \text{ and } 22 + (-15) = 7$$
$$r - (-s) = r + s \rightarrow 22 - (-15) = 37 \text{ and } 22 + 15 = 37$$

You should be comfortable manipulating both proper and improper fractions.

- To add and subtract fractions, first find a common denominator, then add the numerators together:

$$\frac{2}{3} + \frac{5}{4} \rightarrow \left(\frac{2}{3} \times \frac{4}{4}\right) + \left(\frac{5}{4} \times \frac{3}{3}\right) = \frac{8}{12} + \frac{15}{12} = \frac{23}{12}$$

- Multiplying fractions is straightforward: multiply the numerators together, then repeat for the denominators. Cancel when possible to simplify the answer:

$$\frac{5}{8} \times \frac{8}{3} = \frac{5}{\cancel{8}} \times \frac{\cancel{8}^1}{3} = \frac{5 \times 1}{1 \times 3} = \frac{5}{3}$$

- Dividing by a fraction is the same as multiplying by its reciprocal. Once you've rewritten a division problem as multiplication, follow the rules for fraction multiplication to simplify:

$$\frac{3}{4} \div \frac{3}{2} = \frac{\cancel{3}^1}{\cancel{4}_2} \times \frac{\cancel{2}^1}{\cancel{3}_1} = \frac{1 \times 1}{2 \times 1} = \frac{1}{2}$$

Absolute value means the distance a number is from 0 on a number line. Because absolute value is a distance, it is always positive or 0. Absolute value can *never* be negative:

$$|-17| = 17, |21| = 21, |0| = 0$$

Whatever you do to one side of an equation, you must do to the other. For instance, if you multiply one side by 3, you must multiply the other side by 3 as well.

The ability to solve straightforward, one-variable equations is critical on the SAT. For example:

$$\frac{4x}{5} - 2 = 10$$

$$\frac{4x}{5} = 12$$

$$\frac{5}{4} \times \frac{4x}{5} = 12 \times \frac{5}{4}$$

$$x = 15$$

Note: $\frac{4x}{5}$ is the same as $\frac{4}{5}x$. You could see either form on the SAT.

You will encounter **irrational numbers**, such as common radicals and π, on test day. You can carry an irrational number through your calculations as you would a variable (e.g., $4 \times \sqrt{2} = 4\sqrt{2}$). Only convert to a decimal when you have finished any intermediate steps and when the question asks you to provide an *approximate* value.

Mental Math

Even if you're a math whiz, you need to adjust your thought process in terms of the SAT to give yourself the biggest advantage you can. Knowing a few extra things will boost your speed on test day.

- Don't abuse your calculator by using it to determine something as simple as $15 \div 3$ (we've seen it many times). Besides, what if you're in the middle of the no-calculator section? Save time on test day by reviewing multiplication tables. At a bare minimum, work up through the 10s. If you know them through 12 or 15, that's even better!
- You can save a few seconds of number crunching by memorizing **perfect squares**. Knowing perfect squares through 10 is a good start; go for 15 or even 20 if you can.
- **Percent** means "out of a hundred." For example, $27\% = \frac{27}{100}$. You can write percents as decimals, for example, $27\% = 0.27$.

Math

- The ability to recognize a few simple fractions masquerading in decimal or percent form will save you time on test day, as you won't have to turn to your calculator to convert them. Memorize the content of the following table.

Fraction	Decimal	Percent
$\frac{1}{10}$	0.1	10%
$\frac{1}{5}$	0.2	20%
$\frac{1}{4}$	0.25	25%
$\frac{1}{3}$	$0.333\overline{3}$	$33.3\overline{3}$%
$\frac{1}{2}$	0.5	50%
$\frac{3}{4}$	0.75	75%

Tip: If you don't have the decimal (or percent) form of a multiple of one of the fractions shown in the table memorized, such as $\frac{2}{5}$, just take the fraction with the corresponding denominator ($\frac{1}{5}$ in this case), convert to a decimal (0.2), and multiply by the numerator of the desired fraction to get its decimal equivalent:

$$\frac{2}{5} = \frac{1}{5} \times 2 = 0.2 \times 2 = 0.4 = 40\%$$

Graphing

- Basic two-dimensional graphing is performed on a **coordinate plane**. There are two **axes**, x and y, that meet at a central point called the **origin**. Each axis has both positive and negative values that extend outward from the origin at evenly spaced intervals. The axes divide the space into four sections called **quadrants**, which are labeled I, II, III, and IV. Quadrant I is always the upper-right section and the rest follow counterclockwise, as shown below:

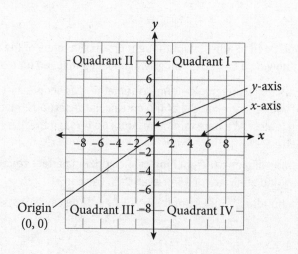

- To plot points on the coordinate plane, you need their coordinates. The ***x*-coordinate** is where the point falls along the *x*-axis, and the ***y*-coordinate** is where the point falls along the *y*-axis. The two coordinates together make an **ordered pair** written as (x, y). When writing ordered pairs, the *x*-coordinate is always listed first (think alphabetical order). Four points are plotted in the following figure as examples:

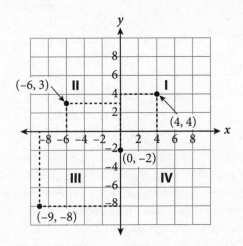

- When two points are vertically or horizontally aligned, calculating the distance between them is easy. For a horizontal distance, only the *x*-value changes; for a vertical distance, only the *y*-value changes. Take the positive difference of the *x*-coordinates (or *y*-coordinates) to determine the distance—that is, subtract the smaller number from the larger number so that the difference is positive. Two examples are presented here:

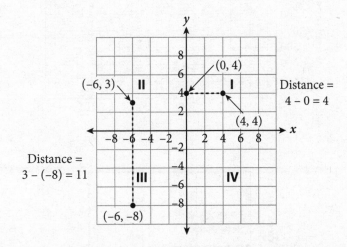

- Two-variable equations have an **independent variable** (input) and a **dependent variable** (output). The dependent variable (often *y*), depends on the independent variable (often *x*). For example, in the equation $y = 3x + 4$, *x* is the independent variable; any *y*-value depends on what you plug in for *x*. You can construct a table of values for the equation, which can then be plotted as shown on the next page.

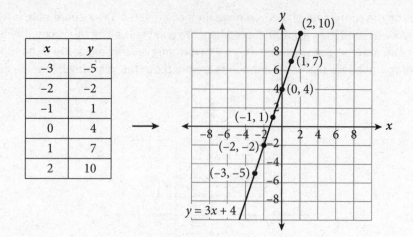

x	y
−3	−5
−2	−2
−1	1
0	4
1	7
2	10

- You may be asked to infer relationships from graphs. In the first of the following graphs, the two variables are year and population. Clearly, the year does not depend on how many people live in the town; rather, the population increases over time and thus depends on the year. In the second graph, you can infer that plant height depends on the amount of rain; thus, rainfall is the independent variable. Note that the independent variable for the second graph is the vertical axis; this can happen with certain nonstandard graphs. On the standard coordinate plane, however, the independent variable is always plotted on the horizontal axis as shown below:

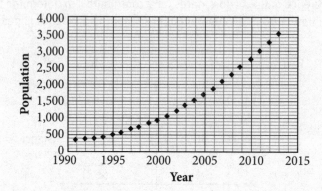

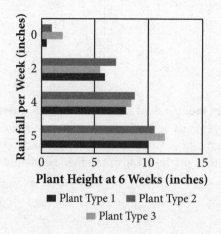

- When two straight lines are graphed simultaneously, one of three possible scenarios will occur:
  - The lines will not intersect at all (no solution).
  - The lines will intersect at one point (one solution).
  - The lines will lie on top of each other (infinitely many solutions).

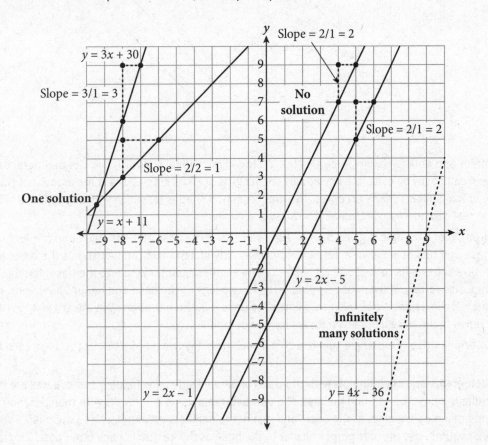

Geometry

- **Adjacent angles** can be added to find the measure of a larger angle. The following diagram demonstrates this:

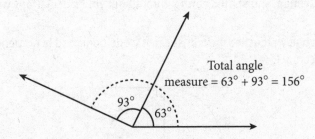

- Two angles that sum to 90° are called **complementary angles**. Two angles that sum to 180° are called **supplementary angles**.

- Two distinct lines in a plane will either intersect at one point or extend indefinitely without intersecting. If two lines intersect at a right angle (90°), they are **perpendicular** and are denoted with ⊥. If the lines never intersect, they are **parallel** and are denoted with ‖:

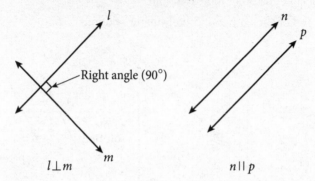

- **Perimeter** and **area** are basic properties that all two-dimensional shapes have. The perimeter of a polygon can easily be calculated by adding the lengths of all its sides. Area is the amount of two-dimensional space a shape occupies. The most common shapes for which you'll need these two properties on test day are triangles, parallelograms, and circles.

- The **area (A) of a triangle** is given by $A = \frac{1}{2}bh$, where b is the base of the triangle and h is its height. The base and height are always perpendicular. Any side of a triangle can be used as the base; just make sure you use its corresponding height (a line segment perpendicular to the base, terminating in the opposite vertex). You can use a right triangle's two legs as the base and height, but in non-right triangles, if the height is not given, you'll need to draw it in (from the vertex of the angle opposite the base down to the base itself at a right angle) and compute it.

- The **interior angles** of a triangle sum to 180°. If you know any two interior angles, you can calculate the third.

- **Parallelograms** are quadrilaterals with two pairs of parallel sides. Rectangles and squares are subsets of parallelograms. You can find the **area of a parallelogram** using $A = bh$. As with triangles, you can use any side of a parallelogram as the base, and again, the height is perpendicular to the base. For a rectangle or square, use the side perpendicular to the base as the height. For any other parallelogram, the height (or enough information to find it) will be given.

- A circle's perimeter is known as its **circumference (C)** and is found using $C = 2\pi r$, where r is the **radius** (distance from the center of the circle to its edge). The **area of a circle** is given by $A = \pi r^2$. The strange symbol is the lowercase Greek letter pi (π, pronounced "pie"), which is approximately 3.14. As mentioned in the algebra section, you should carry π throughout your calculations without rounding unless instructed otherwise.

- A **tangent line,** shown below, touches a circle at exactly one point and is perpendicular to a circle's radius at the point of contact:

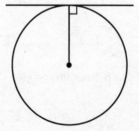

The presence of a right angle opens up the opportunity to draw otherwise hidden shapes, so pay special attention to tangents when they're mentioned.

- A shape is said to have **symmetry** when it can be split by a line (called an **axis of symmetry**) into two identical parts. Consider folding a shape along a line: if all sides and vertices align once the shape is folded in half, the shape is symmetrical about that line. Some shapes have no axis of symmetry, some have one, some have multiple axes, and still others can have infinite axes of symmetry (e.g., a circle):

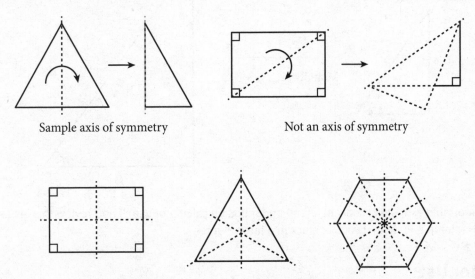

Sample axis of symmetry   Not an axis of symmetry

Sample shapes with corresponding axes of symmetry

- **Congruence** is simply a geometry term that means identical. Angles, lines, and shapes can be congruent. Congruence is indicated by using hash marks: everything with the same number of hash marks is congruent:

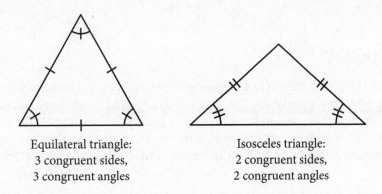

Equilateral triangle:
3 congruent sides,
3 congruent angles

Isosceles triangle:
2 congruent sides,
2 congruent angles

- **Similarity** between shapes indicates that they have identical angles and proportional sides. Think of taking a shape and stretching or shrinking each side by the same ratio. The resulting shape will have the same angles as the original. While the sides will not be identical, they will be proportional:

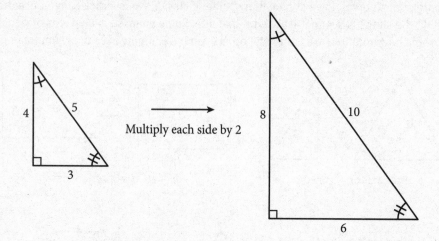

Multiply each side by 2

If you're comfortable with these concepts, read on for tips on calculator use. If not, review this lesson and remember to refer to it for help if you get stuck in a later chapter.

Calculator Use

LEARNING OBJECTIVE

After this lesson, you will be able to:

- Distinguish between questions that need a calculator and questions in which manual calculations are more efficient

Calculators and the SAT

Educators believe that calculators serve a role in solving Math questions, but they are sometimes concerned that students rely too heavily on calculators. They believe this dependence weakens students' overall ability to think mathematically. Therefore, the SAT has a policy on calculator use to promote the idea that students need to be able to analyze and solve math problems both with and without a calculator. The first Math section you see will require you to work without a calculator, while the second Math section will allow you to use one.

Many students never stop to ask whether using a calculator is the most efficient way to solve a problem. This chapter will show you how the strongest test takers use their calculators strategically; that is, they carefully evaluate when to use the calculator and when to skip it in favor of a more streamlined approach. As you will see, even though you can use a calculator, sometimes it's more beneficial to save your energy by approaching a question more strategically. Work smarter, not harder.

Which Calculator Should You Use?

The SAT allows four-function, scientific, and graphing calculators. No matter which calculator you choose, start practicing with it now. You don't want to waste valuable time on test day looking for the exponent button or figuring out how to correctly graph equations. Due to the wide range of mathematics topics you'll encounter on test day, **we recommend using a graphing calculator**, such as the TI-83/84. If you don't already own one, see if you can borrow one from your school's math department or a local library.

A graphing calculator's capabilities extend well beyond what you'll need for the test, so don't worry about memorizing every function. The next few pages will cover which calculator functions you'll want to know how to use for the SAT. If you're not already familiar with your graphing calculator, you'll want to get the user manual; you can find this on the Internet by searching for your calculator's model number. Identify the calculator functions necessary to answer various SAT Math questions, then write down the directions for each to make a handy study sheet.

When Should You Use a Calculator?

Some SAT question types are designed based on the idea that students will do some or all of the work using a calculator. As a master test taker, you want to know what to look for so you can identify when calculator use is advantageous. Questions involving statistics, determining roots of complicated quadratic equations, and other topics are generally designed with calculator use in mind.

Other questions aren't intentionally designed to involve calculator use. Solving some with a calculator can save you time and energy, but you'll waste both if you go for the calculator on others. You will have to decide which method is best when you encounter the following topics:

- Long division and other extensive calculations
- Graphing quadratics
- Simplifying radicals and calculating roots
- Plane and coordinate geometry

Practicing **long computations** by hand and with the calculator will not only boost your focus and mental math prowess, but it will also help you determine whether it's faster to do the work for a given question by hand or reach for the calculator on test day.

Graphing quadratic equations may be a big reason you got that fancy calculator in the first place; it makes answering these questions a snap! This is definitely an area where you need to have an in-depth knowledge of your calculator's functions. The key to making these questions easy with the calculator is being meticulous when entering the equation.

Another stressful area for many students is **radicals**, especially when the answer choices are written as decimals. Those two elements are big red flags that trigger a reach for the calculator. Beware: not all graphing calculators have a built-in radical simplification function, so consider familiarizing yourself with this process.

Geometry can be a gray area for students when it comes to calculator use. Consider working by hand when dealing with angles and lines, specifically when filling in information on complementary, supplementary, and congruent angles. You should be able to work fluidly through those questions without using your calculator.

If you choose to use **trigonometric functions** to get to the answer on triangle questions, make sure you have your calculator set to degrees or radians as required by the question.

To Use or Not to Use?

A calculator is a double-edged sword on the SAT: using one can be an asset for verifying work if you struggle when doing math by hand, but turning to it for the simplest computations will cost you time that you could devote to more complex questions. Practice solving questions with and without a calculator to get a sense of your personal style as well as your strengths and weaknesses. Think critically about when a calculator saves you time and when mental math is faster. Use the exercises in this book to practice your calculations so that by the time test day arrives, you'll be in the habit of using your calculator as effectively as possible!

The Method for SAT Math Questions

How to Do SAT Math

SAT Math questions can seem more difficult than they actually are, especially when you are working under time pressure. The method we are about to describe will help you answer SAT questions, whether you are comfortable with the math content or not. This method is designed to give you the confidence you need to get the right answers on the SAT by helping you think through a question logically, one piece at a time.

Take a look at this question and take a minute to think about how you would attack it if you saw it on test day:

> Building M is an apartment building in city Z. According to data kept by the housing commission in city Z, 24% of the 150 apartments in building M have at least 3 bedrooms. There are 1,350 apartment buildings in city Z and the average number of apartments in those buildings is 150. If building M is representative of the apartment buildings in city Z, then which of the following is the best estimate of how many apartments in city Z have fewer than 3 bedrooms?

A) 48,600

B) 67,500

C) 153,900

D) 202,500

Many test takers will see a question like this and panic. Others will waste a great deal of time reading and rereading without a clear goal. You want to avoid both of those outcomes.

Start by defining clearly for yourself **what the question is actually asking**. What do the answer choices represent? In this question, they represent *the number of apartments in city Z that have fewer than 3 bedrooms*.

Next, **examine the information** that you have and organize it logically. The question asks about the number of apartments with fewer than 3 bedrooms. Okay, then what information do you have about number of bedrooms? You know that 24% of the 150 building M apartments have *at least 3* bedrooms. That's the opposite of *fewer than 3*. You can deduce that 100% − 24% = 76% of the 150 apartments in building M have *fewer than 3* bedrooms.

Now **make a strategic decision** about how to proceed. The answer choices are far apart, so you might consider rounding 76% to $\frac{3}{4}$ and estimating. However, this question appears on the calculator section, and it's a quick calculation. Let's say that you decide to use your calculator. Plug the numbers into your calculator and jot down what you know so far:

Fewer than 3 in building M: $0.76 \times 150 = 114$

The question asks for the number of apartments *in city Z* with fewer than 3 bedrooms, so hunt for information tying building M to city Z. You're told that the average number of apartments in city Z buildings is 150, which is identical to the number of apartments in building M, and that building M is "representative" of the apartment buildings in city Z. Translation: what is true for building M is also true for all apartment buildings in city Z. You also know that there are 1,350 apartment buildings in city Z. You can deduce that the number of apartments with fewer than 3 bedrooms in building M (114) times the total number of apartment buildings in city Z (1,350) will give you the number of apartments with fewer than 3 bedrooms in all of city Z. Plug that into your calculator:

$$114 \times 1,350 = 153,900$$

Finally, **confirm** that you answered the right question: you want the number of apartments in city Z with fewer than 3 bedrooms. Great! You're done; the correct answer is **(C)**.

Here are the steps of the method we just used:

Method for SAT Math Questions	
Step 1.	State what the question is asking
Step 2.	Examine the given information
Step 3.	Choose your approach
Step 4.	Confirm that you answered the right question

You can think of these steps as a series of questions to ask yourself: What do they want? What are they giving me to work with? How should I approach this? Did I answer the right question?

Not all SAT Math questions will require time spent on all the steps. The question above, because it is a word problem, required a fair amount of analysis in steps 1 and 2, but choosing an approach (step 3) was straightforward; the calculations were quick to do on a calculator, so there was no need to estimate. Other questions will require very little thought in steps 1 and 2 but will benefit from a careful strategy decision in step 3. Step 4 is always quick, but you should always do it: just make sure you answered the question that was actually asked before you bubble in your response. Doing so will save you from speed mistakes on questions that you know how to do and should be getting credit for.

There are several approaches you can choose from in step 3: doing the traditional math, as we did in the question above; Picking Numbers; Backsolving; estimating; or taking a strategic guess. In the next two examples, you'll see Picking Numbers and Backsolving in action.

Here's another example. This one is not a word problem, so steps 1 and 2 require negligible mental energy, but pay attention when you get to step 3.

Which of the following is equivalent to the expression $\frac{8x-2}{x+1}$?

A) $8 - \frac{10}{x+1}$

B) $8 - \frac{2}{x+1}$

C) $8 + \frac{2}{x+1}$

D) $\frac{8-2}{1}$

Step 1: What do they want? An answer choice that is equal to $\frac{8x-2}{x+1}$.

Step 2: What do they give you? Only the expression $\frac{8x-2}{x+1}$.

Step 3: What approach will you use?

Here's where it gets interesting. The creator of this question may be expecting you to use polynomial long division to solve, and we'll cover that technique in chapter 11 because you may want to have it in your arsenal. But if you don't know how to do polynomial long division, there's no need to panic. You could use an alternate approach called **Picking Numbers** that will work just as well: choose a number to substitute for x in the question, then substitute the same number for x in the choices and see which one matches. Like this:

Pick a small number for x, say 2. When $x = 2$, the original expression becomes:

$$\frac{8x-2}{x+1} = \frac{8(2)-2}{2+1} = \frac{14}{3}$$

Now plug $x = 2$ into the choices:

(A) $8 - \frac{10}{x+1} = 8 - \frac{10}{3} = \frac{24}{3} - \frac{10}{3} = \frac{14}{3}$

This is a match. It is always possible that another answer choice can produce the same result, so check the rest to be sure there isn't another match when $x = 2$. (If there is, go back and pick another number to distinguish between the choices that match.)

(B) $8 - \frac{2}{x+1} = 8 - \frac{2}{3} = \frac{24}{3} - \frac{2}{3} = \frac{22}{3}$

Eliminate (B).

(C) $8 + \frac{2}{x+1} = 8 + \frac{2}{3} = \frac{24}{3} + \frac{2}{3} = \frac{26}{3}$

Eliminate (C).

(D) $\frac{8-2}{1} = 6$

Eliminate (D).

Step 4: Did you solve for the right thing? You found the equivalent expression, so yes. Only **(A)** is a match, so it is the correct answer.

When picking numbers, use numbers that are **permissible** and **manageable**. That is, use numbers that are allowed by the stipulations of the question and that are easy to work with. In this question, you could have picked any real number because x was not defined as positive, negative, odd, even, a fraction, etc. A small positive integer is usually the best choice in this situation. In other questions, other kinds of numbers may be more manageable. For example, in percents questions, 100 is typically a smart number to pick.

Try one more:

Mr. Dvorkin is distributing colored markers to a group of children. If he gives each child 4 markers, he will have 3 markers left over. In order to give each child 5 markers, with no markers left over, he will need 17 additional markers. How many markers does Mr. Dvorkin have?

A) 55

B) 68

C) 83

D) 101

Step 1: What do they want? The number of markers.

Step 2: What do they give you? Two unknowns (the number of children and the number of markers) and sufficient information to set up a system of equations.

Step 3: What approach will you use? You could set up the system of equations, but it might be faster to use a technique called **Backsolving**: plug the choices in for the unknown and see which one works. Here, you need an answer choice that will leave a remainder of 3 when divided by 4. Choices (B) and (D) don't meet this condition, so the answer must be (A) or (C).

(A) If Mr. Dvorkin has 55 markers, and gives each child 4 markers, he will indeed have 3 markers left over, since $55 \div 4 = 13\ R3$. Now, what happens in the other situation? With an extra 17 markers, Mr. Dvorkin should be able to give each child exactly 5 markers. But $55 + 17 = 72$, which is not evenly divisible by 5. Eliminate (A).

You've now eliminated every choice but **(C)**, so it must be correct—you don't even need to test it! For the record:

(C) If Mr. Dvorkin has 83 markers and gives each child 4 markers, he will indeed have 3 left over, since $83 \div 4 = 20\ R3$. With an extra 17 markers, Mr. Dvorkin should be able to give each child exactly 5 markers, and this is in fact what happens: $83 + 17 = 100$, which is evenly divisible by 5.

Step 4: Did you solve for the right thing? The question asked for the number of markers. You found that 83 markers satisfies all conditions of the problem. Choose **(C)** and move on.

Although it wasn't the case in this question, when backsolving it often makes sense to start with (B) or (C) in case you can tell from the context whether you'll need a larger or smaller answer choice if the one you're testing fails.

Now, it's your turn. Be deliberate with these questions. If there is analysis to do up front, do it. If there is more than one way to do a question, consider carefully before choosing your approach. And be sure to check whether you answered the right question. Forming good habits now, in slow and careful practice, will build your confidence for test day.

Try on Your Own

Directions: Take as much time as you need on these questions. Work carefully and methodically. There will be opportunities for timed practice in future chapters.

1. A cargo airplane has a maximum takeoff weight of 19,000 kilograms. The airplane, crew, and fuel have a combined weight of 14,750 kilograms. The airplane will be loaded with n identical cargo containers, each of which has a weight of 125 kilograms. What is the greatest value of n such that the airplane does not exceed its maximum takeoff weight?

   A) 28

   B) 34

   C) 118

   D) 152

2. A certain model of laptop computer is priced at $550 at a local electronics store. The same model laptop at an online retailer sells for $\frac{9}{10}$ of the electronics store's price. At a luxury department store, the same model laptop sells for $\frac{7}{5}$ of the electronics store's price. How many dollars more is the cost of the laptop at the luxury department store than at the online retailer?

   A) 198

   B) 220

   C) 275

   D) 495

3. A stack of 75 identical plastic plates forms a column approximately $9\frac{7}{8}$ inches tall. At this rate, which of the following is closest to the number of plates that would be needed to form a column 20 inches tall?

   A) 125

   B) 150

   C) 185

   D) 220

4. Last month, Kiera ran 22 more miles than Bianca did. If they ran a combined total of 86 miles, how many miles did Bianca run?

   A) 27

   B) 32

   C) 43

   D) 54

5. If $\frac{4x}{2y} = 4$, what is the value of $\frac{3y}{x}$?

   A) $\frac{3}{4}$

   B) $\frac{4}{3}$

   C) $\frac{3}{2}$

   D) 2

6.

x	2	4	6	8	10
y	$\frac{7}{5}$	$\frac{11}{5}$	$\frac{15}{5}$	$\frac{19}{5}$	$\frac{23}{5}$

Which of the following equations relates y to x according to the values shown in the table above?

   A) $y = \left(\frac{2}{5}\right)^x - \frac{7}{5}$

   B) $y = \left(\frac{3x}{5}\right)^2 - 2$

   C) $y = \frac{5}{2}x - \frac{3}{5}$

   D) $y = \frac{2}{5}x + \frac{3}{5}$

7. $n - \sqrt{c + 5} = 1$

In the equation above, c is a constant. If $n = 5$, what is the value of c ?

A) -1

B) 0

C) 3

D) 11

8. At a child's lemonade stand, p pitchers of lemonade are made by adding m packets of lemonade mix to cold water. If $m = 2p + 4$, how many more packets of lemonade mix are needed to make each additional pitcher of lemonade?

A) 0

B) 1

C) 2

D) 4

9. A health club charges a one-time membership fee of \$125 plus n dollars for each month. If a member pays \$515 dollars for the first six months, including the membership fee, what is the value of n ?

A) 55

B) 65

C) 75

D) 85

10. If $x > 0$, which of the following is equivalent to $\dfrac{2}{\dfrac{1}{x+6} + \dfrac{1}{x+2}}$?

A) $x^2 + 8x + 12$

B) $\dfrac{x+4}{x^2 + 8x + 12}$

C) $2x + 8$

D) $\dfrac{x^2 + 8x + 12}{x + 4}$

A Note About Grid-ins

You will see an occasional question without answer choices throughout the Math chapters of this book, starting in the next chapter. On the SAT, several of these Grid-in questions appear at the end of each Math section. Instead of bubbling in a letter, you'll enter your responses to these questions into a grid that looks like this:

If you are gridding a value that doesn't take up the whole grid, such as 50, you can enter it anywhere in the grid as long as the digits are consecutive; it doesn't matter which column you start in. Gridding mixed numbers and decimals requires some care. Anything to the left of the fraction bar will be read as the numerator of a fraction, so you must grid mixed numbers as improper fractions. For instance, say you want to grid the mixed fraction $5\frac{1}{2}$. If you enter 5 1/2 into the grid, your answer will be read as $\frac{51}{2}$. Instead, enter your response as 1 1/2, which will be read (correctly) as $\frac{11}{2}$. Alternatively, you could grid this answer as 5.5.

A repeating decimal can either be rounded or truncated, but it must be entered to as many decimal places as possible. This means it must fill the entire grid. For example, you can grid $\frac{1}{6}$ as .166 or .167 but not as .16 or .17.

Note that you cannot grid a minus sign or any value larger than 9,999, so if you get an answer that is negative or larger than 9,999 to a grid-in question, you've made a mistake and should check your work.

Reflect

Directions: Take a few minutes to recall what you've learned and what you've been practicing in this chapter. Consider the following questions, jot down your best answer for each one, and then compare your reflections to the expert responses on the following page. Use your level of confidence to to determine what to do next.

Think about your current habits when attacking SAT questions. Are you a strategic test taker? Do you take the time to think through what would be the fastest way to the answer?

_____

_____

_____

Do word problems give you trouble?

_____

_____

_____

What are the steps of the Method for SAT Math, and why is each step important?

_____

_____

_____

Expert Responses

Think about your current habits when attacking SAT questions. Are you a strategic test taker? Do you take the time to think through what would be the fastest way to the answer?

If yes, good for you! If not, we recommend doing questions more than one way whenever possible as part of your SAT prep. If you can discover now, while you're still practicing, that Picking Numbers is faster for you on certain types of questions but not on others, you'll be that much more efficient on test day.

Do word problems give you trouble?

If word problems are difficult for you, get into the habit of taking an inventory, before you do any math, of what the question is asking for and what information you have.

What are the steps of the Method for SAT Math, and why is each step important?

Here are the steps:

Step 1. *State what the question is asking*

Step 2. *Examine the given information*

(Taking an inventory is especially important in word problems.)

Step 3. *Choose your approach*

(Taking a moment to decide what approach will be the fastest way to the answer will ultimately save you time.)

Step 4. *Confirm that you answered the right question*

(Making sure you solved for the right thing will save you from losing points to speed mistakes on questions that you know how to do and should be getting credit for.)

Next Steps

If you answered most questions correctly in the "How Much Have You Learned?" section, and if your responses to the Reflect questions were similar to those of the SAT expert, then consider the Method for SAT Math Questions an area of strength and move on to the next chapter. Do keep using the method as you work on the questions in future chapters.

If you don't yet feel confident, review those parts of this chapter that you have not yet mastered and try the questions you missed again. As always, be sure to review the explanations closely.

Answers and Explanations

1. B

Difficulty: Medium

Category: Solving Equations

Strategic Advice: Break apart the question into its mathematical parts; determine what information you have and what value you need to find and then determine how you'll find that value.

Getting to the Answer: You're given the weight of everything on the airplane except the combined weight of the cargo containers and you're given the maximum takeoff weight of the plane. Therefore, the difference between the maximum takeoff weight and the weight of the plane, crew, and fuel must be the maximum combined weight of the cargo containers.

You're also told that n represents the number of cargo containers that will be loaded on the plane and that each container weighs 125 kilograms. You need to find the number of containers, n, that make up the difference in weights.

The maximum takeoff weight of the plane is 19,000 kilograms and the weight of the plane, crew, and fuel is 14,750 kilograms. Hence, the maximum number of cargo containers can have a combined weight no greater than $19,000 - 14,750 = 4,250$ kilograms. That means that the maximum number of containers, n, must be 4,250 kilograms ÷ 125 kilograms = 34 containers. Thus, **(B)** is correct.

2. C

Difficulty: Medium

Category: Solving Equations

Strategic Advice: Think about what you're being asked to find—the difference between the price of the laptop at the luxury department store and at the online retailer—and what information you're given—the actual price at a local electronics store and two fractions of that price that represent the prices at the online retailer and at the luxury department store.

Getting to the Answer: The price of the laptop at the electronics store is $550. You also know that the price at the online retailer is $\frac{9}{10}$ of this, so that price is $\frac{9}{10} \times \$550 = \$495$. The question also states that the price at the luxury store is $\frac{7}{5}$ of the price at the

electronics store, so that's $\frac{7}{5} \times \$550 = \$770$. Therefore, the difference between the price at the luxury department store and the price at the online retailer is $\$770 - \$495 = \$275$. Choice **(C)** is correct.

3. B

Difficulty: Easy

Category: Proportions

Strategic Advice: Because the answer choices are widely spaced apart, and the question asks for the answer that is "closest to the number," estimation will be a better approach than wading into unnecessarily detailed and tedious calculations.

Getting to the Answer: Notice the relationship between the height of the stack of 75 plates and the height of the unknown number of plates: $9\frac{7}{8}$ inches is *about half* of 20 inches. Put another way, a 20-inch stack of plates will be about twice as tall as a stack of 75 plates. Therefore, it's logical to deduce that approximately twice as many plates, or about $2 \times 75 = 150$, will be needed to form a stack 20 inches tall. Hence, **(B)** is correct.

4. B

Difficulty: Medium

Category: Heart of Algebra/Systems of Linear Equations

Strategic Advice: Use the answer choices to your advantage to quickly find Bianca's distance.

Getting to the Answer: The question gives two unknowns and enough information to create a system of equations; therefore, it could be solved with a traditional algebraic approach.

There is, however, a more efficient way: assess the answer choices to see which makes sense for Bianca's distance. Since Kiera ran 22 miles farther than Bianca, and the combined distance they ran is 86 miles, Bianca must have run less than half of 86 miles. Since one-half of 86 is 43, you can quickly eliminate (C) and (D), which are both too big.

Now check (B) against the known information. If Bianca ran 32 miles, then Kiera ran $32 + 22 = 54$ miles. Check if Bianca's distance and Kiera's distance add up to 86: $32 + 54 = 86$; thus, **(B)** is correct.

If you're curious about the algebraic approach, here it is: let b stand for the number of miles Bianca ran and k stand for the number of miles Kiera ran. Then $b + k = 86$, and $k = b + 22$. Now, substitute the value of k in terms of b into the first equation:

$$b + (b + 22) = 86$$
$$2b + 22 = 86$$
$$2b = 64$$
$$b = 32$$

Again, Bianca ran 32 miles, and **(B)** is correct.

5.　C

Difficulty: Medium

Category: Solving Equations

Strategic Advice: You have two variables, but only one equation, so solving for each variable will not be possible. Instead, pick numbers for x and y that will make the equation true.

Getting to the Answer: Pick a simple number for x, solve for y, and if y is also easy to work with, plug them into the expression you're trying to find. Say $x = 2$; then you have $\frac{4(2)}{2y} = 4$, which simplifies to $\frac{8}{2y} = 4$. Solving for y, you multiply both sides by $2y$ and get $8 = 8y$, so $y = 1$, another manageable number.

Now, plug these same values of x and y into $\frac{3y}{x}$ to get $\frac{3(1)}{(2)} = \frac{3}{2}$. Thus, **(C)** is correct.

6.　D

Difficulty: Medium

Category: Heart of Algebra/Linear Equations

Strategic Advice: The answer choices are split into two types: the first two are exponential and the second two are linear. Therefore, to quickly narrow down the answers, examine the table to determine whether the change in x-values versus y-values is exponential or linear.

Getting to the Answer: Notice that, for every increase of 2 in the x-value, the y-value increases by $\frac{4}{5}$. Therefore, you have a linear relationship, so you can eliminate (A) and (B), which are both exponential functions.

Now, plug values from the table into the remaining answers to see whether the math works out. Try the first column in the table and plug in 2 for x and $\frac{7}{5}$ for y:

(C): $\frac{7}{5} = \frac{5}{2} \times 2 - \frac{3}{5} = 5 - \frac{3}{5} = \frac{25}{5} - \frac{3}{5} = \frac{22}{5}$. This doesn't work out, so **(D)** must be correct. No need to check it. For the record:

(D): $\frac{7}{5} = \frac{2}{5} \times 2 + \frac{3}{5} = \frac{4}{5} + \frac{3}{5} = \frac{7}{5}$

7.　D

Difficulty: Medium

Category: Heart of Algebra/Linear Equations

Strategic Advice: Backsolve by plugging the answer choices in for c to determine which one makes the given equation true.

Getting to the Answer: The question provides a linear equation and the value of one of the variables.

Since you're told that $n = 5$, fill this value into the equation, and then simplify to find the root:

$$5 - \sqrt{c + 5} = 1$$
$$4 - \sqrt{c + 5} = 0$$
$$4 = \sqrt{c + 5}$$

Simplifying to this point makes it easier to see if the value of c you plug in works. Now check the answer choices, starting with (B) or (C). If the answer you choose is too large or too small, you'll know which direction to go when testing the next choice.

(B): $4 \neq \sqrt{0 + 5}$. This answer is too small, so try (C) next.

(C): $4 \neq \sqrt{3 + 5}$. This choice is still too small, so the correct choice must be **(D)**. No need to check it. For the record:

(D): $4 = \sqrt{11 + 5} = \sqrt{16} = 4$.

If you prefer the algebraic approach, here it is:

$$5 - \sqrt{c + 5} = 1$$
$$4 - \sqrt{c + 5} = 0$$
$$4 = \sqrt{c + 5}$$
$$4^2 = c + 5$$
$$16 = c + 5$$
$$11 = c$$

Again, **(D)** is correct.

8. C

Difficulty: Medium

Category: Heart of Algebra/Linear Equations

Strategic Advice: Pick a number for p to determine how many packets of mix will be needed, and then pick another number for p to see how the number of packets changes.

Getting to the Answer: Say $p = 2$, then $m = 2(2) + 4 = 8$, so there are 8 packets of mix needed to make 2 pitchers of lemonade. Now try $p = 3$: $m = 2(3) + 4 = 10$. For one additional pitcher, the packets needed increased from 8 to 10, which is a change of 2. Therefore, **(C)** is correct. You can confirm by trying $p = 4$, then $m = 2(4) + 4 = 12$.

9. B

Difficulty: Medium

Category: Heart of Algebra/Linear Equations

Strategic Advice: Backsolve by plugging the answer choices in for n to determine which one matches the given price of six months of membership.

Getting to the Answer: Check the answer choices, starting with (B) or (C). If the answer you choose is too large or too small, you'll know which direction to go when testing the next choice. Multiply the value in the answer choice by the six months and then add the $125 membership fee.

(B): $65 \times 6 = \$390$. $\$390 + \$125 = \$515$. This is a match, so **(B)** is correct. Since there can be only one correct answer, you're finished.

Alternatively, you can solve algebraically:

$$\$125 + 6n = \$515$$
$$6n = \$390$$
$$\frac{6n}{6} = \frac{\$390}{6}$$
$$n = \$65$$

(B) is correct.

10. D

Difficulty: Medium

Category: Heart of Algebra/Linear Equations

Strategic Advice: Pick a number for x to determine the numerical value of the given expression, then plug the same number into the answer choices to find the one that matches.

Getting to the Answer: To make calculations easy, say $x = 1$; then the given expression becomes $\dfrac{2}{\dfrac{1}{1+6} + \dfrac{1}{1+2}}$. Now, simplify this expression:

$$= \frac{2}{\dfrac{1}{7} + \dfrac{1}{3}}$$

$$= \frac{2}{\dfrac{3}{21} + \dfrac{7}{21}}$$

$$= \frac{2}{\left(\dfrac{10}{21}\right)}$$

$$= 2 \times \frac{21}{10}$$

$$= \frac{21}{5}$$

Next, plug 1 in for x in the answer choices to see which yields the same value:

(A): $1^2 + 8 \times 1 + 12 = 21$. Eliminate.

(B): $\dfrac{1+4}{1^2 + 8 \times 1 + 12} = \dfrac{5}{21}$. Eliminate.

(C): $2 \times 1 + 8 = 10$. Eliminate. You have eliminated three answer choices so the one left is correct; **(D)** is correct.

For the record: (D): $\dfrac{1^2 + 8 \times 1 + 12}{1 + 4} = \dfrac{21}{5}$. This is a match, which confirms that **(D)** is correct.

You might also have noticed that (B) gave you the reciprocal of the value you were looking for; therefore, the reciprocal of the expression in (B) must give you the correct answer, and that is **(D)**.

The Heart of Algebra

CHAPTER 4

Linear Equations and Graphs

LEARNING OBJECTIVES

After completing this chapter, you will be able to:

- Isolate a variable
- Translate word problems into equations
- Calculate the slope of a line given two points
- Write the equation of a line in slope-intercept form
- Discern whether the slope of a line is positive, negative, zero, or undefined based on its graph
- Describe the slopes of parallel and perpendicular lines

110/600 SmartPoints®

How Much Do You Know?

Directions: Try the questions that follow. Show your work so that you can compare your solutions to the ones found in the Check Your Work section immediately after this question set. The "Category" heading in the explanation for each question gives the title of the lesson that covers how to solve it. If you answered the question(s) for a given lesson correctly, and if your scratchwork looks like ours, you may be able to move quickly through that lesson. If you answered incorrectly or used a different approach, you may want to take your time on that lesson.

$$v = \frac{2\pi r}{T}$$

1. Uniform circular motion is used in physics to describe the motion of an object traveling at a constant speed in a circle. The speed of the object is called tangential velocity and it can be calculated using the formula above, where r is the radius of the circle and T is the time is takes for the object to make one complete circle, called a period. Which of the following formulas could be used to find the length of one period if you know the tangential velocity and the radius of the circle?

A) $T = \dfrac{v}{2\pi r}$

B) $T = \dfrac{2\pi r}{v}$

C) $T = 2\pi r v$

D) $T = \dfrac{1}{2\pi r v}$

$$F = \gamma \frac{m_1 m_2}{r^2}$$

2. The formula above is Newton's law of universal gravitation, where F is the attractive force, γ is the gravitational constant, m_1 and m_2 are the masses of the particles, and r is the distance between their centers of mass. Which of the following gives r in terms of F, γ, m_1, and m_2 ?

A) $r = \sqrt{\dfrac{(m_1)(m_2)}{F(\gamma)}}$

B) $r = \sqrt{\dfrac{F(m_2)}{\gamma(m_1)}}$

C) $r = \sqrt{\dfrac{\gamma(m_1)}{F(m_2)}}$

D) $r = \sqrt{\dfrac{\gamma(m_1)(m_2)}{F}}$

3. Andrew works at a travel agency. He gets paid $120 for a day's work, plus a bonus of $25 for each cruise he books. Which of the following equations represents the relationship between the total Andrew earns in a day, d, and the number of cruises he books, c ?

A) $c = 25d + 120$

B) $c = 120d + 25$

C) $d = 25c + 120$

D) $d = 120c + 25$

4. Vera is on her school's track and field team. In a practice long-jump competition against her teammates, she gets 5 points for landing over the nearer line and 10 points for landing over the more distant line. She gets a total of 7 jumps and lands x times over the more distant line and the rest of the times over the nearer line. Which of the following equations represents the relationship between Vera's total score, y, and the number of times she lands over the more distant line, x?

A) $y = 10x$

B) $y = 5x + 35$

C) $y = 10x + 5$

D) $y = 70 - 5x$

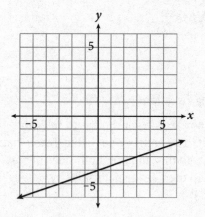

6. The graph shown represents which of the following equations?

A) $y = -3x + 4$

B) $y = -\frac{1}{3}x + 4$

C) $y = \frac{1}{3}x - 4$

D) $y = 3x - 4$

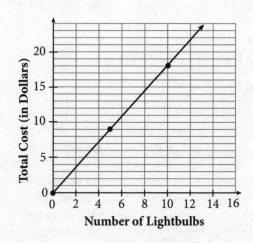

Number of Lightbulbs

5. A hardware store sells light bulbs in different quantities. The graph shows the cost of various quantities. According to the graph, what is the cost of a single light bulb?

A) $0.56

B) $1.80

C) $2.50

D) $3.60

Check Your Work

1.   B

Difficulty: Easy

Category: Solving Equations

Getting to the Answer: The goal here is to solve the equation for T. Start by getting T out of the denominator of the fraction. To do this, multiply both sides of the equation by T, and then divide both sides by v:

$$v = \frac{2\pi r}{T}$$

$$T \times v = \left(\frac{2\pi r}{T}\right) \times T$$

$$Tv = 2\pi r$$

$$T = \frac{2\pi r}{v}$$

Choice **(B)** is the correct answer.

2.   D

Difficulty: Medium

Category: Solving Equations

Strategic Advice: Even when the equation is entirely made up of variables, the process for isolating one variable is still the same.

Getting to the Answer: This equation needs to be rearranged to solve for r, so start by multiplying both sides by r^2 to get that expression out of the denominator:

$$\left(r^2\right)(F) = \gamma(m_1)(m_2)$$

Next, divide both sides by F:

$$r^2 = \frac{\gamma(m_1)(m_2)}{F}$$

Finally, take the square root of both sides to get r by itself:

$$r = \sqrt{\frac{\gamma(m_1)(m_2)}{F}}$$

(D) is correct.

3.   C

Difficulty: Easy

Category: Word Problems

Getting to the Answer: When writing a linear equation to represent a real-world scenario, a flat rate is a constant while a unit rate is always multiplied by the independent variable. You can identify the unit rate by looking for words like *per* or *for each*.

Because the amount Andrew gets paid daily, $120, is a flat rate that doesn't depend on the number of cruises he books, 120 should be the constant in the equation. This means you can eliminate (B) and (D). The question tells you to multiply $25 by the number of cruises he books, c, so the equation is *total pay* $= 25 \times$ *number of cruises* $+ 120$, or $d = 25c + 120$, making **(C)** correct.

4.   B

Difficulty: Hard

Category: Word Problems

Getting to the Answer: The key to answering this question is determining how many jumps land across each line. If Vera gets 7 jumps total and x jumps land over the more distant line, then the rest, or $7 - x$, must land over the nearer line. Now, write the expression in words: points per distant line (10) times number of jumps landing over the distant line (x), plus points per near line (5) times number of jumps landing over the near line ($7 - x$). Next, translate the words into numbers, variables, and operations: $10x + 5(7 - x)$. This is not one of the answer choices, so simplify the expression by distributing the 5 and combining like terms: $10x + 5(7 - x) = 10x + 35 - 5x = 5x + 35$, so the equation is $y = 5x + 35$. **(B)** is correct.

5. B

Difficulty: Easy

Category: Linear Graphs

Getting to the Answer: The x-axis represents the number of light bulbs, so find 1 on the x-axis and trace up to where it meets the graph of the line. The y-value is somewhere between \$1 and \$2, so the only possible correct answer choice is \$1.80. **(B)** is correct.

You could also find the unit rate by calculating the slope of the line using two of the points shown on the graph: the graph rises 9 units and runs 5 units from one point to the next, so the slope is $\frac{9}{5}$, or 1.8, which confirms that **(B)** is correct.

6. C

Difficulty: Medium

Category: Linear Graphs

Getting to the Answer: Use the graph to identify the y-intercept and the slope of the line and then write an equation in slope-intercept form, $y = mx + b$. Once you have your equation, look for the answer choice that matches. The line crosses the y-axis at $(0, -4)$ so the y-intercept, b, is -4. The line rises 1 unit for every 3 units that it runs to the right, so the slope, m, is $\frac{1}{3}$. The equation of the line is $y = \frac{1}{3}x - 4$, which matches **(C)**.

You could also graph each of the answer choices in your calculator to see which one matches the given graph, but this is not the most time-efficient strategy. You also have to be very careful when entering fractions—to graph **(C)**, for example, you would enter $(1/3)x - 4$.

Solving Equations

To answer a question like this:

$$\frac{1}{2}(3x + 14) = \frac{1}{6}(7x - 10)$$

Which value of x satisfies the equation above?

A) −26

B) 2

C) 8

D) 16

You need to know this:

Isolating a variable means getting that variable by itself on one side of the equation. To do this, use inverse operations to manipulate the equation, remembering that whatever you do to one side of the equation, you must do to *both* sides.

You need to do this:

It usually makes sense to proceed in this order:

- Eliminate any fractions
- Collect and combine like terms
- Divide to leave the desired variable by itself

Explanation:

Eliminate the fractions by multiplying both sides of the equation by 6:

$$\left(\frac{6}{1}\right)\frac{1}{2}(3x + 14) = \left(\frac{6}{1}\right)\frac{1}{6}(7x - 10)$$
$$3(3x + 14) = (7x - 10)$$

In order to collect all the x terms on one side, you'll first need to distribute the 3 on the left side of the equation:

$$9x + 42 = 7x - 10$$

Next, subtract 7x from both sides:

$$2x + 42 = -10$$

Now, subtract 42 from both sides:

$$2x = -52$$

Finally, divide both sides by 2 to leave *x* by itself:

$$x = -26$$

Choice **(A)** is correct.

If you find isolating a variable to be challenging, try these Drill questions before proceeding to the Try on Your Own set. Isolate the variable in each equation. Turn the page and look at the bottom of the page to see the answers.

Drill

a. $3(x + 2) = 14 - 2(3 - 2x)$

b. $5(6 - 3b) = 3b + 3$

c. $\dfrac{r}{6} - \dfrac{3r}{5} = \dfrac{1}{2}$

d. Isolate *F*: $C = \dfrac{5}{9}(F - 32)$

e. Isolate *b*: $A = \dfrac{1}{2}(a + b)h$

Math

Try on Your Own

Directions: Take as much time as you need on these questions. Work carefully and methodically. There will be an opportunity for timed practice at the end of the chapter.

HINT: For Q1, what do you need to do before you can collect all the *y* terms on one side?

$$3y + 2(y - 2) = \frac{3y}{2} + 1$$

1. What value of *y* satisfies the equation above?

    A) $-\dfrac{10}{7}$

    B) $-\dfrac{6}{13}$

    C) $\dfrac{7}{9}$

    D) $\dfrac{10}{7}$

$$S = \frac{C - \frac{1}{4}I}{C + I}$$

2. A teacher uses the formula above to calculate her students' scores, *S*, by subtracting $\frac{1}{4}$ of the number of questions the students answered incorrectly, *I*, from the number of questions they answered correctly, *C*, and dividing by the total number of questions. Which of the following expresses the number of questions answered incorrectly in terms of the other variables?

    A) $\dfrac{C(1 - 4S)}{4S + 1}$

    B) $\dfrac{C(1 + 4S)}{4S - 1}$

    C) $\dfrac{4C(1 - S)}{4S + 1}$

    D) $\dfrac{4C(1 + S)}{4S - 1}$

Drill answers from previous page:

a. $3x + 6 = 14 - 6 + 4x$
    $3x = 2 + 4x$
    $x = -2$

b. $30 - 15b = 3b + 3$
    $-18b = -27$
    $\dfrac{-18b}{-18} = \dfrac{-27}{-18}$
    $b = \dfrac{3}{2}$

c. $30 \times \left(\dfrac{r}{6} - \dfrac{3r}{5}\right) = \left(\dfrac{1}{2}\right) \times 30$
    $5r - 6(3r) = 15$
    $-13r = 15$
    $r = -\dfrac{15}{13}$

d. $\dfrac{9}{5} \times C = \dfrac{9}{5} \times \dfrac{5}{9}(F - 32)$
    $\dfrac{9}{5}C = F - 32$
    $\dfrac{9}{5}C + 32 = F$

e. $A = \dfrac{1}{2}(a + b)h$
    $2A = (a + b)h$
    $\dfrac{2A}{h} = a + b$
    $\dfrac{2A}{h} - a = b$

3. What value of n satisfies the equation $\frac{7}{8}(n-6) = \frac{21}{2}$?

HINT: For Q5, simplify the numerators before clearing
the equation of fractions.

$$\frac{4 + z - (3 + 2z)}{6} = \frac{-z - 3(5 - 2)}{7}$$

5. What is the value of z in the equation above?

A) -61

B) $-\frac{61}{27}$

C) $\frac{61}{27}$

D) 61

HINT: For Q4, use $\frac{a}{b}$ as your target and solve for that expression
rather than solving for a and b separately.

4. If $b \neq 0$ and $\frac{3a + b}{b} = \frac{11}{2}$, which of the following
could be the value of $\frac{a}{b}$?

A) $\frac{3}{2}$

B) $\frac{7}{2}$

C) $\frac{9}{2}$

D) It is not possible to determine a value of $\frac{a}{b}$.

Math

Word Problems

To answer a question like this:

A laser tag arena sells two types of memberships. One package costs $325 for one year of membership with an unlimited number of visits. The second package has a $125 enrollment fee, includes five free visits, and costs an additional $8 per visit after the first five. How many visits over a one-year period would a person who purchases the second package need to use for the cost to equal that of the one-year membership?

A) 20

B) 25

C) 30

D) 40

You need to know this:

The SAT likes to test your understanding of how to describe real-world situations using math equations. For some questions, it will be up to you to extract and solve an equation; for others, you'll have to interpret an equation in a real-life context. The following table shows some of the most common phrases and mathematical equivalents you're likely to see on the SAT.

Word Problems Translation Table	
English	**Math**
equals, is, equivalent to, was, will be, has, costs, adds up to, the same as, as much as	$=$
times, of, multiplied by, product of, twice, double	$\times$
divided by, out of, ratio	$\div$
plus, added to, sum, combined, increased by	$+$
minus, subtracted from, smaller than, less than, fewer, decreased by, difference between	$-$
a number, how much, how many, what	x, n, etc.

You need to do this:

When translating from English to math, *start by defining the variables,* choosing letters that make sense. Then, *break down the question into small pieces*, writing down the translation for one phrase at a time.

Explanation:

The phrase "how many visits" indicates an unknown, so you need a variable. Use an intuitive letter to represent the number of visits; call it v. The question asks when the two memberships will cost the "same amount," so write an equation that sets the total membership costs equal to each other.

The first membership type costs \$325 for unlimited visits, so write 325 on one side of the equal sign. The second type costs \$8 per visit (not including, or *except*, the first 5 visits), or $8(v - 5)$, plus a flat \$125 enrollment fee, so write $8(v - 5) + 125$ on the other side of the equal sign. That's it! Now solve for v:

$$325 = 8(v - 5) + 125$$
$$200 = 8v - 40$$
$$240 = 8v$$
$$30 = v$$

The answer is **(C)**.

Try on Your Own

Directions: Take as much time as you need on these questions. Work carefully and methodically. There will be an opportunity for timed practice at the end of the chapter.

6. A local restaurant is hosting a dance-a-thon for charity. Each couple must dance a minimum of three hours before earning any money for the charity. After the first three hours, couples earn $50 per half-hour of continuous dancing. Which expression represents the total amount earned by a couple who dance h hours, assuming they dance at least three hours?

    A) $25h$

    B) $100h$

    C) $50(h - 3)$

    D) $100h - 300$

HINT: For Q7, start with the most concrete information:
1 is the second value.

---

7. The final value, v, in a four-digit lock code is determined by multiplying the second value by two, subtracting that expression from the first value, and dividing the resulting expression by half of the third value. The first value is f, the second value is 1, and the third value is t. What is the final value, v, in terms of f and t ?

    A) $\dfrac{f - 2}{t}$

    B) $\dfrac{2f - 4}{t}$

    C) $\dfrac{t}{2f - 4}$

    D) $\dfrac{2t - 4}{f}$

HINT: For Q8, profit = sales − expenses

---

8. A pizzeria's top-selling pizzas are The Works and The Hawaiian. The Works sells for $17, and The Hawaiian sells for $13. Ingredient costs for The Works are $450 per week, and ingredient costs for The Hawaiian are $310 per week. If x represents the number of each type of pizza sold in one week, and the weekly profit from the sale of each type of pizza is the same, what is the value of x ?

    A) 30

    B) 35

    C) 140

    D) 145

9. A student opens a checking account when she starts a new job so that her paychecks can be directly deposited into the account. Her balance can be computed using the expression $10nw + 50$, where n is the number of hours she works every week and w is the number of weeks that she has worked so far. Assuming she does not withdraw any money from her account, which of the terms in the expression most logically will change if the student gets a raise?

    A) 10

    B) n

    C) w

    D) The expression will not change if the student gets a raise.

10. Malik starts a job at which his starting salary is $25,500 per year. He expects that his salary will increase by a constant dollar amount annually. In 12 years, his salary will be double his starting salary. Assuming salary increases take place only at the end of a full year, how many years must Malik wait until his salary is at least $40,000 annually?

Linear Graphs

LEARNING OBJECTIVES

After this lesson, you will be able to:

- Calculate the slope of a line given two points
- Write the equation of a line in slope-intercept form
- Discern whether the slope of a line is positive, negative, zero, or undefined based on its graph
- Describe the slopes of parallel and perpendicular lines

To answer a question like this:

What is the equation of the line that passes through the points $(-3, -1)$ and $(1, 3)$?

A) $y = -x + 2$

B) $y = -x - 2$

C) $y = x - 2$

D) $y = x + 2$

You need to know this:

The answer choices in this question are written in slope-intercept form: $y = mx + b$. In this form of a linear equation, m represents the **slope** of the line and b represents the **y-intercept**. You can think of the slope of a line as how steep it is. The y-intercept is the point at which the line crosses the y-axis and can be written as the ordered pair $(0, y)$.

You can calculate the slope of a line if you know any two points on the line. The formula is $m = \frac{y_2 - y_1}{x_2 - x_1}$, where (x_1, y_1) and (x_2, y_2) are the coordinates of the two points on the line.

A line that moves from the bottom left to the top right has a positive slope. A line that moves from the top left to the bottom right has a negative slope. A horizontal line has a slope of 0 and a vertical line has an undefined slope.

Some SAT questions ask about parallel or perpendicular lines. Parallel lines have the same slope, while perpendicular lines have negative reciprocal slopes.

You need to do this:

- Find the slope of the line
- Write the equation in slope-intercept form, substituting the value of the slope you found and one of the known points for x and y
- Solve for the y-intercept

Explanation:

In this question, $m = \dfrac{3-(-1)}{1-(-3)} = \dfrac{4}{4} = 1$. Of the answer choices, only (C) and (D) have a slope of 1, so rule out (A) and (B), which both have a slope of -1.

To find the y-intercept of the line, write the equation for the line in slope-intercept form and plug in one of the known points for x and y:

$$y = 1x + b$$
$$3 = 1(1) + b$$
$$2 = b$$

The correct answer is **(D)**. For the record, here is the graph of the line. Note that as you would expect from the fact that m is positive, the line moves from the lower left to upper right, and it crosses the y-axis at the y-intercept of $b = 2$.

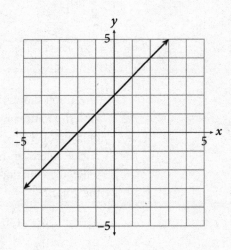

Try on Your Own

Directions: Take as much time as you need on these questions. Work carefully and methodically. There will be an opportunity for timed practice at the end of the chapter.

HINT: For Q11, what do you know about lines that never intersect?

---

11. Line A passes through the coordinate points $\left(-\frac{2}{5}, 0\right)$ and $(0, 1)$. Which of the following lines will line A never intersect?

A)

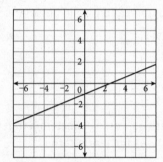

B)

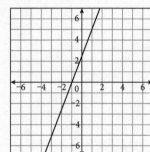

C)

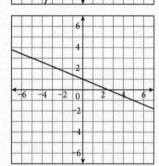

D)

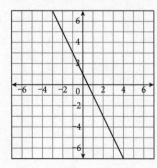

12. In the xy-plane, the point $(4, 7)$ lies on the line t, which is perpendicular to the line $y = -\frac{4}{3}x + 6$. What is the equation of line t?

A) $y = \frac{3}{4}x + 4$

B) $y = -\frac{4}{3}x + 4$

C) $y = \frac{3}{4}x + 7$

D) $y = -\frac{3}{4}x + 4$

HINT: For Q13, remember that at the y-intercept, $x = 0$.

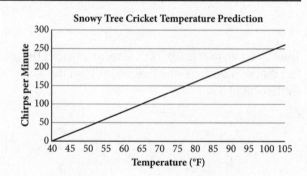

13. The graph shows the correlation between ambient air temperature, t, in degrees Fahrenheit and the number of chirps, c, per minute that a snowy tree cricket makes at that temperature. Which of the following equations represents the line shown in the graph?

A) $c = 4t - 160$

B) $c = \frac{1}{4}t - 160$

C) $c = \frac{1}{2}t - 40$

D) $c = 4t + 160$

HINT: For Q14, the starting point (flat fee) is the *y*-intercept.
The rate of change (price per pound) is the slope.

Minutes Charging	10	15	30
Percent Charged	34	41.5	64

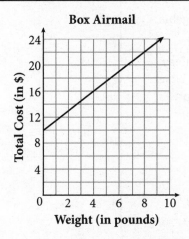

Box Airmail

15. Xia is charging her laptop. She records the battery charge for the first 30 minutes after she plugs it in to get an idea of when it will be completely charged. The table above shows the results. If *y* is the percent battery charge on Xia's laptop, which linear equation represents the correct relationship between *y* and *x* ?

A) $y = 1.5x + 19$

B) $y = 2x + 14$

C) $y = 2.5x + 9$

D) $y = 10x + 34$

14. A freight airline charges a flat fee to airmail a box, plus an additional charge for each pound the box weighs. The graph above shows the relationship between the weight of the box and the total cost to airmail it. Based on the graph, how much would it cost in dollars to airmail a 40-pound box?

On Test Day

Remember that the SAT doesn't ask you to show your work. If you find the algebra in a question challenging, there is often another way to get to the answer.

Try this question first using algebra and then using the Picking Numbers strategy you learned in chapter 3. Time yourself. Which approach do you find easier? Which one was faster? Did you get the correct answer both times? Remember your preferred approach and try it first if you see a question like this on test day.

$$\frac{2(a-3)}{b} = \frac{4}{7}$$

16. If the equation above is true, which of the following must NOT be true?

A) $\dfrac{b}{a-3} = \dfrac{7}{2}$

B) $\dfrac{2a}{b} = -\dfrac{10}{7}$

C) $14a - 4b = 42$

D) $\dfrac{a-3}{b} = \dfrac{2}{7}$

The correct answer and both ways of solving can be found at the end of this chapter.

How Much Have You Learned?

Directions: For testlike practice, give yourself 15 minutes to complete this question set. Be sure to study the explanations, even for questions you got right. They can be found at the end of this chapter.

17. Which value of x makes the equation

    $\frac{8}{5}\left(x + \frac{33}{12}\right) = 16$ true?

    A) 7.25

    B) 8.75

    C) 12.75

    D) 13.25

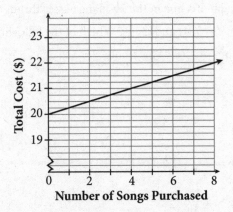

18. The graph above shows the cost of joining and buying music from a music subscription service. What does the y-intercept of the line most likely represent?

    A) The cost per song

    B) The cost to join the service

    C) The cost of buying 20 songs

    D) The cost of 20 subscriptions to the service

19. If $\frac{3}{4}y = 6 - \frac{1}{3}c$, then what is the value of $2c + \frac{9}{2}y$?

20. Three years ago, Madison High School started charging an admission fee for basketball games to raise money for new bleachers. The initial price was $2 per person; the school raised the price of admission to $2.50 this year. Assuming this trend continues, which of the following equations can be used to describe c, the cost of admission, y years after the school began charging for admission to games?

    A) $c = 6y + 2$

    B) $c = \frac{y}{6} + 2.5$

    C) $c = \frac{y}{6} + 2$

    D) $c = \frac{y}{2} + 2$

Price of One Pound	Projected Number of Pounds Sold
$1.20	15,000
$1.40	12,500
$1.60	10,000
$1.80	7,500
$2.00	5,000
$2.20	2,500

21. Which of the following equations best describes the linear relationship shown in the table, where g represents the number of pounds of grain sold and d represents the price in dollars of one pound of grain?

    A) $g = 1.2d + 12,500$

    B) $g = 12,500d + 15,000$

    C) $g = -12,500d + 17,500$

    D) $g = -12,500d + 30,000$

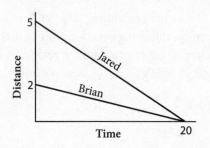

22. Brian and Jared live in the same apartment complex and both bike to and from work every day. The figure above shows a typical commute home for each of them. Based on the figure, which of the following statements is true?

    A) It takes Brian longer to bike home because his work is farther away.

    B) It takes Jared longer to bike home because his work is farther away.

    C) Jared and Brian arrive home at the same time, so they must bike at about the same rate.

    D) Jared bikes a longer distance than Brian in the same amount of time, so Jared must bike at a faster rate.

23. When graphing a linear equation that is written in the form $y = mx + b$, the variable m represents the slope of the line and b represents the y-intercept. Assuming that $b > 0$, which of the following best describes how reversing the sign of b will affect the graph?

    A) The new line will be shifted down b units.

    B) The new line will be shifted down $2b$ units.

    C) The new line will be a perfect reflection across the x-axis.

    D) The new line will be a perfect reflection across the y-axis.

24. The graph of a line in the xy-plane passes through the points $(5, 4)$ and $\left(3, \frac{1}{2}\right)$. Which of the following equations describes the line?

    A) $y = \frac{7}{4}x + \frac{19}{4}$

    B) $y = -\frac{7}{4}x - \frac{19}{4}$

    C) $y = \frac{7}{4}x - \frac{19}{4}$

    D) $y = \frac{4}{7}x + \frac{8}{7}$

25. Line f in the xy-plane passes through the origin and has a slope of $-\frac{2}{5}$. Line z is perpendicular to line f and passes through the point $(6, 2)$. Which of the following is the equation of line z?

    A) $y = -\frac{2}{5}x$

    B) $y = -\frac{2}{5}x - 13$

    C) $y = \frac{5}{2}x$

    D) $y = \frac{5}{2}x - 13$

$$V = \frac{1}{3}\pi\left(\frac{d}{2}\right)^2 h$$

26. A circle of rubber with a constant diameter d is placed on a table; its perimeter is anchored to the table and a string is attached to its center. When the string is pulled upwards, a cone is formed with height h and volume V. The relationship between d, h, and V is represented above. Which of the following statements must be true?

    I. As the volume of the cone decreases, the height also decreases.

    II. If the diameter of the base of the cone is 6 centimeters, the height can be determined by dividing the volume by 3π.

    III. If the height of the cone triples, the volume must also triple.

    A) I only

    B) I and II only

    C) II and III only

    D) I, II, and III

Reflect

Directions: Take a few minutes to recall what you've learned and what you've been practicing in this chapter. Consider the following questions, jot down your best answer for each one, and then compare your reflections to the expert responses on the following page. Use your level of confidence to to determine what to do next.

What should you do to isolate a particular variable in an equation?

_____

_____

_____

What types of key words should you look for when translating English into math?

_____

_____

_____

What is the most useful equation for a line in the coordinate plane? Why?

_____

_____

_____

When the SAT gives you two points on a line, what can you figure out?

_____

_____

_____

How are parallel and perpendicular lines related to each other?

_____

_____

_____

Expert Responses

What should you do to isolate a particular variable in an equation?

Perform inverse operations until the variable is by itself on one side of the equal sign. If the equation has fractions, make them disappear by multiplying both sides of the equation by the denominator(s). If like terms appear on different sides of the equation, collect them on the same side so that you can combine them.

What types of key words should you look for when translating English into math?

Look for key words that signal equality ("is," "has," "was"), variable names ("Marina's age," "the cost of one bathtub"), or one of the four arithmetic operations (addition, subtraction, multiplication, and division).

What is the most useful equation for a line in the coordinate plane? Why?

The best equation is slope-intercept form, $y = mx + b$, because it tells you the slope (m) and the y-intercept (b). Conversely, if you need to derive an equation yourself, you can plug the slope and y-intercept into slope-intercept form and you're done.

When the SAT gives you two points on a line, what can you figure out?

If you know two points, you can figure out the slope of the line with the equation $m = \dfrac{y_2 - y_1}{x_2 - x_1}$. From there, you can plug one of the points and the slope into slope-intercept form and find the y-intercept.

How are parallel and perpendicular lines related to each other?

Parallel lines never intersect and they have equal slopes. Perpendicular lines intersect at a 90° angle and they have negative reciprocal slopes.

Next Steps

If you answered most questions correctly in the "How Much Have You Learned?" section, and if your responses to the Reflect questions were similar to those of the SAT expert, then consider linear equations and graphs an area of strength and move on to the next chapter. Come back to this topic periodically to prevent yourself from getting rusty.

If you don't yet feel confident, review those parts of this chapter that you have not yet mastered. In particular, review the variable isolation drills in the Solving Equations lesson and the definition of slope-intercept form in the Linear Graphs lesson. Then try the questions you missed again. As always, be sure to review the explanations closely.

Answers and Explanations

1. D

Difficulty: Easy

Getting to the Answer: Distribute the factor of 2, combine like terms, multiply both sides of the equation by 2 to clear the fraction, and then solve for y:

$$3y + 2y - 4 = \frac{3y}{2} + 1$$

$$5y - 4 = \frac{3y}{2} + 1$$

$$10y - 8 = 3y + 2$$

$$7y = 10$$

$$y = \frac{10}{7}$$

Choice **(D)** is correct.

2. C

Difficulty: Hard

Strategic Advice: Complicated-looking equations appear difficult, but they always succumb to the steps of solving an equation. First, clear the equation of fractions, then collect like terms, and solve for the desired variable.

Getting to the Answer: Clear the equation of the fraction in the numerator by multiplying both sides by 4 to yield:

$$4S = \frac{4C - I}{C + I}$$

Now, multiply both sides by the denominator $C + I$ to clear the equation of fractions:

$$4S(C + I) = 4C - I$$

Distribute the $4S$:

$$4SC + 4SI = 4C - I$$

To solve for I, collect all the terms that include I on one side of the equation:

$$4SI + I = 4C - 4SC$$

Factor out the I:

$$I(4S + 1) = 4C - 4SC$$

Divide to isolate I, and factor out $4C$ from the numerator:

$$I = \frac{4C - 4SC}{4S + 1} = \frac{4C(1 - S)}{4S + 1}$$

(C) is correct.

3. 18

Difficulty: Easy

Getting to the Answer: First, clear the fractions by multiplying both sides of the equation by 8. Then solve for x using inverse operations:

$$\frac{7}{8}(n - 6) = \frac{21}{2}$$

$$8\left[\frac{7}{8}(n - 6)\right] = 8\left[\frac{21}{2}\right]$$

$$7(n - 6) = 4(21)$$

$$7n - 42 = 84$$

$$7n = 126$$

$$n = 18$$

Grid in **18**.

4. A

Difficulty: Medium

Strategic Advice: Noticing key information about the answer choices and using that information to pick numbers saves time by eliminating algebra.

Getting to the Answer: Rearranging the terms of the equation such that $\frac{a}{b}$ is on one side and the constants are all on the other will work for this problem. First, cross-multiply to get rid of the fractions. Then, use inverse operations to isolate $\frac{a}{b}$:

$$\frac{3a + b}{b} \nearrow \frac{11}{2}$$

$$2(3a + b) = 11b$$

$$6a + 2b = 11b$$

$$6a = 9b$$

$$a = \frac{9}{6}b$$

$$\frac{a}{b} = \frac{3}{2}$$

The answer is **(A)**.

There is a faster approach. Notice that 2 shows up in the denominator in most of the choices, indicating that it is likely that b equals 2. If $b = 2$, then a must be 3 for the numerator to equal 11. Test this by plugging the numbers into the equation:

$$\frac{3(3) + 2}{2} = \frac{11}{2}$$

Thus, $\frac{a}{b} = \frac{3}{2}$, confirming **(A)** as the answer. You can avoid a lot of work by using key information in the answer choices to pick numbers.

5. D

Difficulty: Medium

Getting to the Answer: Simplify the numerators as much as possible, then isolate the variable. Begin by combining like terms on both sides of the equation. Then cross-multiply and solve for z:

$$\frac{4 + z - (3 + 2z)}{6} = \frac{-z - 3(5 - 2)}{7}$$
$$\frac{1 - z}{6} = \frac{-z - 9}{7}$$
$$7 - 7z = -6z - 54$$
$$-z = -61$$
$$z = 61$$

Choice **(D)** is correct.

6. D

Difficulty: Medium

Getting to the Answer: Use the information in the question to write your own expression, then look for the answer choice that matches. Simplify your expression only if you don't find a match. If a couple earns $50 *per half-hour* that they dance, then they earn $50 \times 2 = \$100$ *per hour*. Multiply this amount by the number of hours (not including the first 3 hours). This can be expressed as $100(h - 3)$. This is not one of the answer choices, so simplify by distributing the 100 to get $100h - 300$, which is **(D)**.

If you're struggling with the algebra, try Picking Numbers. Pick a number of hours a couple might dance, like 5. They don't earn anything for the first 3 hours, but they earn $50 per half-hour for the last 2 hours, which is 50 times 4 half-hours, or $200. Now, find the expression that gives you an answer of $200 when $h = 5$ hours: $100(5) - 300 = 500 - 300 = 200$. If you use Picking Numbers, remember that it is possible that the number

you choose satisfies more than one answer choice, so plug it in to the other three choices. In this case, $h = 5$ does not give a value of 200 in any other equation, which confirms that **(D)** is correct.

7. B

Difficulty: Medium

Getting to the Answer: Translate piece by piece to get a final expression for the final value, v. Multiply the second value by 2 to get $2(1) = 2$. Subtract that from the first value to get $f - 2$. Divide this expression by half of the third value to get $\dfrac{f - 2}{\frac{t}{2}}$, which you can simplify by multiplying by the reciprocal: $\left(\dfrac{f - 2}{1}\right)\left(\dfrac{2}{t}\right) = \left(\dfrac{2f - 4}{t}\right)$. Choice **(B)** matches the final expression. Watch out for (D), the trap answer choice that switches the variables.

8. B

Difficulty: Medium

Getting to the Answer: Write expressions to represent the profit generated by selling each type of pizza. You're told The Works sells for $17 each and that its ingredients cost the pizzeria $450 per week. This means the weekly profit generated by this pizza's sales can be represented by the expression $17x - 450$. Do the same for The Hawaiian: Each one sells for $13, but the pizzeria loses $310 to pay for ingredients each week. Therefore, the weekly profit from this pizza can be represented by $13x - 310$. To determine the value of x at which the profit from the sale of each type of pizza is the same, set the two profit expressions equal to each other and solve:

$$17x - 450 = 13x - 310$$
$$4x = 140$$
$$x = 35$$

Thus, **(B)** is correct. Always be sure you're answering the right question; choice (D), 145, is the profit when $x = 35$.

9. A

Difficulty: Easy

Getting to the Answer: When faced with a question that includes abstract expressions, it is helpful to pick concrete numbers to work with. These numbers don't have to be realistic; just choose numbers that are easy to work with. Suppose the student checks her balance after 2 weeks working 3 hours each week. She would have worked a total of 6 hours, which would have to be multiplied by the amount she is paid per hour to get her total pay. In the expression, plugging in $w = 3$ and $n = 2$ demonstrates that the number 10 in the expression must be the amount that she is paid per hour, and thus is the term that would change if the student got a raise. **(A)** is correct. Although 50 is not an answer choice, you can deduce that it must have been her checking account's original balance because it is a constant.

10. 7

Difficulty: Medium

Getting to the Answer: First, notice that the actual dollar amount of the increase each year is unknown, so assign a variable like d. After 12 increases, his salary will rise by $25,500, so write a formula $12d = 25,500$. Solve for d to find that Malik will receive an increase of $2,125 per year.

The question asks how many years must go by until Malik's salary is at least $40,000; the number of years is another unknown, so assign it a variable like n. Multiplying n by the amount of each increase will give you the total increase of dollars over n years, but don't forget to add in the starting salary to reflect his total salary amount:

$$25,500 + 2,125n = 40,000$$
$$2,125n = 14,500$$
$$n \approx 6.8$$

The question asks you to assume that salary increases only take place at the end of a full year. If you are unsure and want to prove that the answer is not 6, check by using $n = 6$ to calculate the total dollar amount: $25,500 + 2,125(6) = 38,250$. Six years is not long enough; grid in **7**.

11. B

Difficulty: Easy

Getting to the Answer: You're asked to identify the line that the one described in the question stem will never intersect. Lines that never intersect are parallel and therefore have identical slopes, so start by finding the slope of the line whose two coordinate pairs are given. You'll find:

$$m = \frac{1 - 0}{0 - \left(-\frac{2}{5}\right)} = \frac{1}{\frac{2}{5}} = \frac{5}{2}$$

Choices (C) and (D) have negative slopes, so eliminate them. Next, find the slopes of (A) and (B). No need to use the slope formula; counting units on the graphs will be faster. The slope of (A) is $\frac{2}{5}$ because for every 2 units the line rises, it runs 5 units to the right. The slope of (B) is $\frac{5}{2}$ because when the line goes up 5 units, it goes 2 units to the right. Therefore, **(B)** is correct.

12. A

Difficulty: Medium

Strategic Advice: Remember that parallel lines have the same slope and perpendicular lines have opposite sign reciprocal slopes.

Getting to the Answer: The first useful piece of information is that the slope of the line perpendicular to line t is $-\frac{4}{3}$. Perpendicular lines have negative reciprocal slopes, so the slope of line t is $\frac{3}{4}$. Eliminate (B) and (D) because they have the incorrect slopes.

Plug the values for the slope and the coordinate point $(4, 7)$ into the slope-intercept equation to solve for b:

$$7 = \frac{3}{4}(4) + b$$
$$7 = 3 + b$$
$$7 - 3 = b$$
$$b = 4$$

Eliminate (C) because it does not have the correct y-intercept. Choice **(A)** is correct.

13. A

Difficulty: Medium

Getting to the Answer: Start by finding the slope of the line by picking a pair of points, such as $(40, 0)$ and $(65, 100)$: $m = \dfrac{100 - 0}{65 - 40} = \dfrac{100}{25} = 4$. Choices (B) and (C) have slopes other than 4, so eliminate them. Choices (A) and (D) have y-intercepts of -160 and 40, respectively. Now, read the axis labels carefully: the horizontal axis begins at 40 (not 0). The line is trending downward as x-values get smaller, so the y-intercept (when $x = 0$) must be well below 0 on the vertical axis. Therefore, the answer must be **(A)**.

14. 70

Difficulty: Hard

Getting to the Answer: Because 40 pounds is not shown on the graph, you need more information. In a real-world scenario, the y-intercept of a graph usually represents a flat fee or a starting amount. The slope of the line represents a unit rate, such as the cost per pound to airmail the box.

The y-intercept of the graph is 10, so the flat fee is \$10. To find the cost per pound (the unit rate), substitute two points from the graph into the slope formula. Using the points $(0, 10)$ and $(4, 16)$, the cost per pound is $\dfrac{16 - 10}{4 - 0} = \dfrac{6}{4} = 1.5$, which means it costs \$1.50 per pound to airmail a box. The total cost to airmail a 40-pound box is $\$10 + 1.50(40) = \$10 + \$60 = \$70$. Grid in **70**.

15. A

Difficulty: Hard

Getting to the Answer: The question tells you that the relationship is linear, so start by finding the rate of change (the slope, m) using any two pairs of values from the table and the slope formula. Next, substitute the slope and any pair of values from the table, such as $(10, 34)$, into the equation $y = mx + b$ and solve for b. Finally, use the values of m and b to write the function.

$$m = \frac{y_2 - y_1}{x_2 - x_1} = \frac{64 - 34}{30 - 10} = \frac{30}{20} = 1.5$$

You can stop right there! Only **(A)** has a slope of 1.5, so it must be the correct answer. For the record:

$$34 = 10(1.5) + b$$
$$34 = 15 + b$$
$$19 = b$$

16. B

Difficulty: Hard

Strategic Advice: Watch out for the "NOT" keyword in the question stem. Picking numbers based on clues in the equation is faster than doing the algebra.

Getting to the Answer: To find the answer using Picking Numbers, take advantage of the fact that the equation is a proportion (that is, two fractions equal to each other). If $b = 7$ and $2(a - 3) = 4$, then both fractions will be the same and the numbers you've picked will be valid. Solve for a: $a - 3 = 2$, and $a = 5$. Now plug $b = 7$ and $a = 5$ into the choices, looking for the one that ISN'T true:

(A) $\dfrac{b}{a - 3} = \dfrac{7}{5 - 3} = \dfrac{7}{2}$, eliminate.

(B) $\dfrac{2a}{b} = \dfrac{2(5)}{7} = \dfrac{10}{7} \neq -\dfrac{10}{7}$

You're done; pick **(B)** and move on. For the record:

(C) $14a - 4b = 14(5) - 4(7) = 70 - 28 = 42$, eliminate.

(D) $\dfrac{a - 3}{b} = \dfrac{5 - 3}{7} = \dfrac{2}{7}$, eliminate.

To solve this question using algebra, first cross-multiply and simplify the original equation:

$$\frac{2(a - 3)}{b} = \frac{4}{7}$$
$$14(a - 3) = 4b$$
$$7(a - 3) = 2b$$
$$7a - 21 = 2b$$
$$7a - 2b = 21$$

Then, repeat this entire process for each answer choice, looking for the one that *doesn't* yield the same equation:

(A) $\dfrac{b}{a - 3} = \dfrac{7}{2}$, $2b = 7a - 21$, $21 = 7a - 2b$, eliminate.

(B) $\dfrac{2a}{b} = -\dfrac{10}{7}$, $14a = -10b$, $7a = -5b$, $7a + 5b = 0$

This equation is different from the one in the question, so **(B)** is correct. For the record:

(C) $14a - 4b = 42$, $7a - 2b = 21$, eliminate.

(D) $\dfrac{a - 3}{b} = \dfrac{2}{7}$, $7a - 21 = 2b$, $7a - 2b = 21$, eliminate.

17. A

Difficulty: Medium

Category: Solving Equations

Getting to the Answer: This question has multiple fractions, so clear the $\frac{8}{5}$ by multiplying both sides of the equation by its reciprocal, $\frac{5}{8}$. Then, because the answers are given in decimal form, change the other fraction to a decimal by dividing the numerator by the denominator.

$$\frac{8}{5}\left(x + \frac{33}{12}\right) = 16$$

$$\frac{\cancel{5}}{\cancel{8}} \times \left[\frac{\cancel{8}}{\cancel{5}}\left(x + \frac{33}{12}\right)\right] = \frac{5}{8} \times 16$$

$$x + 2.75 = 10$$

$$x = 7.25$$

(A) is correct.

18. B

Difficulty: Easy

Category: Linear Graphs

Getting to the Answer: Read the axis labels carefully. The y-intercept is the point at which $x = 0$, which means the number of songs purchased is 0. The y-intercept is (0, 20), so the cost is $20 before buying any songs and therefore most likely represents a flat membership fee for joining the service. **(B)** is correct.

19. 36

Difficulty: Medium

Category: Solving Equations

Getting to the Answer: When you're asked to find an expression rather than a variable value, it means there's likely a shortcut: try to make the expression you have look like the expression you want. Start by eliminating the fractions. A common multiple of 4 and 3 is 12, so multiply both sides of the equation by that. Once the fractions are gone, move both variable terms to the same side:

$$12\left(\frac{3}{4}y = 6 - \frac{1}{3}c\right)$$

$$9y = 72 - 4c$$

$$4c + 9y = 72$$

$$2c + \frac{9}{2}y = 36$$

The expression on the left side is precisely what you're looking for, so grid in **36**.

20. C

Difficulty: Medium

Category: Word Problems

Getting to the Answer: Look closely; buried in the text are two sets of coordinates you can use. The question states that admission was $2 when the admission charge was first implemented and increased to $2.50 after 3 years, making your coordinates (0, 2) and (3, 2.5). The slope of the line passing through these is $m = \frac{2.5 - 2}{3 - 0} = \frac{0.5}{3} = \frac{1}{6}$. Eliminate (A) and (D). Because the admission fee started at $2, 2 is the y-intercept, so the full equation is $y = \frac{c}{6} + 2$. **(C)** is correct.

Because the question says "three years ago," it may be tempting to use (−3, 2) and (0, 2.5) as your coordinates. Think about what that would mean: the first admission charge would be $2.50, as it's impossible to have a negative year. This contradicts the question stem, so (B) is incorrect.

21. D

Difficulty: Medium

Category: Word Problems

Getting to the Answer: Take a quick peek at the answer choices. The equations are given in slope-intercept form, so start by finding the slope. Substitute two pairs of values from the table (try to pick easy ones, if possible) into the slope formula, $m = \frac{y_2 - y_1}{x_2 - x_1}$. Keep in mind that the projected number of pounds sold *depends* on the price, so the price is the independent variable (x) and the projected number is the dependent variable (y). Using the points (1.2, 15,000) and (2.2, 2,500), you can find the slope:

$$m = \frac{2,500 - 15,000}{2.2 - 1.2}$$

$$m = \frac{-12,500}{1}$$

$$m = -12,500$$

This means you can eliminate (A) and (B) because the slope is not correct. Don't let (B) fool you—the projected number of pounds sold goes *down* as the price goes *up*, so there is an inverse relationship, which means the slope must be negative. To choose between (C) and (D), you could find the y-intercept of the line. Pick a point with easy values, such as (2, 5,000), and plug in 5,000 for y and 2 for x:

$$y = mx + b$$
$$5,000 = -12,500(2) + b$$
$$5,000 = -25,000 + b$$
$$30,000 = b$$

(D) is correct. Another option is to substitute (2, 5,000) into (C) and (D) only. Again, **(D)** is correct because $5,000 = -12,500(2) + 30,000$ is a true statement.

22. D

Difficulty: Medium

Category: Word Problems

Getting to the Answer: Consider each choice systematically, using the numbers on the figure to help you evaluate each statement.

It takes Brian and Jared each 20 minutes to bike home, so (A) and (B) are false. Jared bikes 5 miles in 20 minutes, while Brian only bikes 2 miles in 20 minutes; their rates are not the same, so (C) is false. This means **(D)** must be true. Jared starts out farther away than Brian, so Jared must bike at a faster rate to arrive home in the same amount of time.

23. B

Difficulty: Hard

Category: Linear Graphs

Getting to the Answer: You aren't given any numbers in this question, so make some up. Sketch a quick graph of any simple linear equation that has a positive y-intercept (because it is given that $b > 0$). Then, change the sign of the y-intercept and sketch the new graph on the same coordinate plane. Pick a simple equation that you can sketch quickly, such as $y = x + 3$, and then change the sign of b. The new equation is $y = x - 3$. Sketch both graphs. The second line is shifted down 6 units, and because $b = 3$, 6 is $2b$ units. **(B)** is correct. The graph that follows illustrates this. If you're still unsure, try another pair of equations.

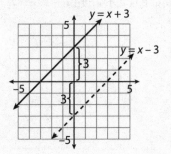

24. C

Difficulty: Medium

Category: Linear Graphs

Strategic Advice: Be careful when the answer choices look very similar to each other. Eliminating incorrect answers during intermediate steps lowers your odds of making a careless mistake.

Getting to the Answer: The question provides two coordinate points, which means that the best approach is to find the slope using the formula $m = \dfrac{y_2 - y_1}{x_2 - x_1}$, then use the slope-intercept equation for a line to find b, the y-intercept. Plugging the results into the slope formula results in:

$$\frac{\frac{1}{2} - 4}{3 - 5} = \frac{\frac{1}{2} - \frac{8}{2}}{-2} = \frac{-\frac{7}{2}}{-2} = -\frac{7}{2} \times -\frac{1}{2} = \frac{7}{4}$$

Eliminate (B) and (D) because they do not have the slope $\frac{7}{4}$. Plug the slope and one of the given points (5, 4) into the slope-intercept equation to solve for b:

$$4 = \frac{7}{4}(5) + b$$
$$4 = \frac{35}{4} + b$$
$$\frac{16}{4} - \frac{35}{4} = b$$
$$b = -\frac{19}{4}$$

Eliminate (A) because it does not have the correct y-intercept; therefore only **(C)** is left and is correct. Plugging the calculated values for the slope and the y-intercept into the slope-intercept equation indeed gives you choice **(C)**: $y = \frac{7}{4}x - \frac{19}{4}$.

After eliminating (B) and (D), you can save time by noticing that the two possible y-intercepts are $\frac{19}{4}$ and $-\frac{19}{4}$. You really only need to determine if b is positive or negative.

Math

25. D

Difficulty: Easy

Category: Linear Graphs

Getting to the Answer: This question provides an equation for a line perpendicular to line z and a coordinate point for line z, $(6, 2)$. The opposite sign reciprocal of the slope of the perpendicular line, $\frac{5}{2}$, is the slope of line z. Eliminate (A) and (B) because they have the incorrect slope.

Plug the values for the slope and the coordinate point $(6, 2)$ into the slope-intercept equation to solve for b:

$$2 = \frac{5}{2}(6) + b$$
$$2 = 15 + b$$
$$2 - 15 = b$$
$$b = -13$$

Plug the values for the slope and the y-intercept into the slope-intercept equation to get $y = \frac{5}{2}x - 13$. **(D)** is correct.

You can save a little time if you eliminate (C) as soon as you see that $b \neq 0$, which you should be able to tell as soon as you see that $2 = 15 + b$.

26. D

Difficulty: Hard

Category: Word Problems

Strategic Advice: In problems that include verifying statements marked with roman numerals, start with the easiest statement to verify and work to the hardest, eliminating answer choices along the way. This may save you time on test day.

Getting to the Answer: The key to this problem is to see that because the question stem states that d is constant, the cumbersome expression $\frac{1}{3}\pi\left(\frac{d}{2}\right)^2$ is just a constant that is the coefficient of the variable h. The formula is really $V = (\text{some constant}) \times h$. In any formula written such that $y = ax$, where a is a constant, as one amount increases (or decreases), the other amount must increase (or decrease) at the same rate. So if V decreases, h must have decreased. Statement I is true; eliminate (C).

Pick the next easiest statement to verify; in this case, statement III. If h increases by tripling, V must also increase by the same rate; it must triple, too. Test this statement if you like by picking a number for h and solving for V, then tripling h and solving for V again. Statement III is true; eliminate (A) and (B). That leaves **(D)** as the correct answer.

On test day, you'd stop here. For the sake of learning, though, you can verify whether statement II is true. Plug $d = 6$ into the formula and solve for h in terms of V:

$$V = \frac{1}{3}\pi\left(\frac{6}{2}\right)^2 h$$
$$V = \frac{(3)^2}{3}\pi h$$
$$\frac{V}{3\pi} = \frac{3\pi h}{3\pi}$$
$$h = \frac{V}{3\pi}$$

Thus, statement II is indeed true.

CHAPTER 5

Systems of Linear Equations

LEARNING OBJECTIVES

After completing this chapter, you will be able to:

- Solve systems of linear equations by substitution
- Solve systems of linear equations by combination
- Determine the number of possible solutions for a system of linear equations, if any

45/600 SmartPoints®

How Much Do You Know?

Directions: Try the questions that follow. Show your work so that you can compare your solutions to the ones found in the Check Your Work section immediately after this question set. The "Category" heading in the explanation for each question gives the title of the lesson that covers how to solve it. If you answered the question(s) for a given lesson correctly, and if your scratchwork looks like ours, you may be able to move quickly through that lesson. If you answered incorrectly or used a different approach, you may want to take your time on that lesson.

$$-7x + 2y = 18$$
$$x + y = 0$$

1. In the system of equations above, what is the value of x?

   A) -2

   B)   0

   C)   2

   D)   4

2. At a certain movie theater, there are 16 rows and each row has either 20 or 24 seats. If the total number of seats in all 16 rows is 348, how many rows have 24 seats?

   A)   7

   B)   9

   C)   11

   D)   13

3. If $17x - 5y = 8$ and $14x - 7y = -7$, what is the value of $3x + 2y$?

   A) -15

   B) -5

   C)   5

   D)   15

4. If $0.2x = 10 - 0.5y$, then $10y + 4x =$

$$\frac{1}{2}x - \frac{2}{3}y = 7$$
$$ax - 8y = -1$$

5. If the system of linear equations above has no solution, and a is a constant, then what is the value of a?

   A) -2

   B) $-\dfrac{1}{2}$

   C)   2

   D)   6

Answers and explanations are on the next page. ▶ ▶ ▶

Check Your Work

1. A

Difficulty: Easy

Category: Substitution

Getting to the Answer: Solve the second equation for y in terms of x, then substitute into the first equation and solve:

$$y = -x$$
$$-7x - 2x = 18$$
$$-9x = 18$$
$$x = -2$$

(A) is correct.

2. A

Difficulty: Hard

Category: Substitution

Getting to the Answer: Create a system of equations in which x represents the number of rows with 20 seats and y represents the number of rows with 24 seats. The first equation should represent the total *number of rows*, each with 20 or 24 seats, or $x + y = 16$. The second equation should represent the total *number of seats*. Because x represents rows with 20 seats and y represents rows with 24 seats, the second equation should be $20x + 24y = 348$. Now solve the system using substitution. Solve the first equation for either variable and substitute the result into the second equation:

$$x + y = 16$$
$$x = 16 - y$$
$$20(16 - y) + 24y = 348$$
$$320 - 20y + 24y = 348$$
$$320 + 4y = 348$$
$$4y = 28$$
$$y = 7$$

So 7 rows have 24 seats, which means **(A)** is correct. This is all the question asks for, so you don't need to find the value of x.

3. D

Difficulty: Medium

Category: Combination

Getting to the Answer: Subtract the second equation from the first to find that $3x + 2y = 15$, making **(D)** the correct answer.

4. 200

Difficulty: Medium

Category: Number of Possible Solutions

Getting to the Answer: Rearrange the equation so that the y and x terms appear, in that order, on the left side: $0.5y + 0.2x = 10$. What number do you need to multiply $0.5y$ by to get $10y$? Twenty. Notice that $10y + 4x$ is 20 times $0.5y + 0.2x$. Multiply both sides of the equation by 20 to find that $10y + 4x = $ **200**. Note that both of these equations describe the same line.

5. D

Difficulty: Hard

Category: Number of Possible Solutions

Getting to the Answer: Graphically, a system of linear equations that has no solution indicates two parallel lines—that is, two lines that have the same slope but different y-intercepts. To have the same slope, the x- and y-coefficients must be the same. To get from $-\frac{2}{3}$ to -8, you multiply by 12, so multiply $-\frac{1}{2}x$ by 12 as well to yield $6x$. Because the other x-coefficient is a, it must be that $a = 6$, and **(D)** is correct. Note that, even though it is more work, you could also write each equation in slope-intercept form and set the slopes equal to each other to solve for a.

Substitution

LEARNING OBJECTIVE

After this lesson, you will be able to:

- Solve systems of linear equations by substitution

To answer a question like this:

If $3x + 2y = 15$ and $x + y = 10$, what is the value of y?

A) -15

B) -5

C) 5

D) 15

You need to know this:

A **system** of two linear equations simply refers to the equations of two lines. "Solving" a system of two linear equations usually means finding the point where the two lines intersect. (However, see the lesson titled "Number of Possible Solutions" later in this chapter for exceptions.)

There are two ways to solve a system of linear equations: substitution and combination. For some SAT questions, substitution is faster; for others, combination is faster. We'll cover combination in the next lesson.

You need to do this:

To solve a system of two linear equations by substitution:

- Isolate a variable (ideally, one whose coefficient is 1) in one of the equations
- Substitute the result into the other equation

Explanation:

Isolate x in the second equation, then substitute the result into the first equation:

$$x = 10 - y$$
$$3(10 - y) + 2y = 15$$
$$30 - 3y + 2y = 15$$
$$-y = -15$$
$$y = 15$$

If you needed to know the value of x as well, you could now substitute 15 for y into either equation to find that $x = -5$. The correct answer is **(D)**.

Try on Your Own

Directions: Solve these questions by substitution. Take as much time as you need on these questions. Work carefully and methodically. There will be an opportunity for timed practice at the end of the chapter.

HINT: For Q1, which equation is the easier one to solve for one variable in terms of the other?

---

1. If $7c + 8b = 15$ and $3b - c = 2$, what is the value of b?

HINT: For Q2, the second equation is in a convenient form for substitution. But look at the first equation: what can you learn quickly about x and y?

$$\begin{cases} 3x - 3y = 0 \\ y = 2x + 5 \end{cases}$$

2. Given the system of equations above, what is the sum of x and y?

A) -10

B) -5

C) 0

D) 5

$$\begin{cases} 4x + 3y = 14 - y \\ x - 5y = 2 \end{cases}$$

3. If (x, y) is a solution to the system of equations above, then what is the value of $x - y$?

A) $\dfrac{1}{4}$

B) 1

C) 3

D) 18

4. If $5a = 6b + 7$ and $a - b = 3$, what is the value of $\dfrac{b}{2}$?

A) 2

B) 4

C) 5.5

D) 11

5. Marisol is selling snacks at her school's soccer games to raise money for a service project. She buys nuts in cases that contain 24 bags and granola bars in cases that contain 20 packages. She sells the nuts for $1.25 a bag and the granola bars for $1.75 a package. If she raised $160 and sold 112 items, how many cases of granola bars did Marisol buy?

A) 2

B) 3

C) 40

D) 72

Combination

To answer a question like this:

$$\begin{cases} 4x - 5y = 10 \\ 2x + 3y = -6 \end{cases}$$

If the solution to the system of equations above is (x, y), what is the value of y?

A) -2

B) -1

C) 1

D) 2

You need to know this:

Combining two equations means adding or subtracting them, usually with the goal of either eliminating one of the variables or solving for a combination of variables (e.g., $5n + 5m$).

You need to do this:

To solve a system of two linear equations by combination:

- Make sure that the coefficients for one variable have the same absolute value. (If they don't, multiply one equation by an appropriate constant. Sometimes, you'll have to multiply both equations by constants.)
- Either add or subtract the equations to eliminate one variable
- Solve for the remaining variable, then substitute its value into either equation to solve for the variable you eliminated in the preceding step

Explanation:

Both variables have different coefficients in the two equations, but you can convert the $2x$ in the second equation to $4x$ by multiplying the entire second equation by 2:

$$2(2x + 3y = -6)$$
$$4x + 6y = -12$$

Now that the coefficients for one variable are the same, subtract the second equation from the first to eliminate the x variable. (Note that if the x-coefficients were 4 and -4, you would add the equations instead of subtracting.)

$$4x - 5y = 10$$
$$\underline{-(4x + 6y = -12)}$$
$$0x - 11y = 22$$

Solve this equation for y:

$$-11y = 22$$
$$y = -2$$

(A) is the correct answer. If the question asked for x instead of y, you would now substitute -2 into either of the original equations and solve for x. (For the record, $x = 0$.)

Try on Your Own

Directions: Solve these questions using combination. Take as much time as you need on these questions. Work carefully and methodically. There will be an opportunity for timed practice at the end of the chapter.

HINT: For Q6, there's no need to solve for *x* and *y* separately.

$$\begin{cases} 3x + 2y = 15 \\ 2x + 3y = 10 \end{cases}$$

6. Given the system of equations above, what is the value of $5x + 5y$?

HINT: For Q7, should you add or subtract these equations to eliminate a variable?

---

7. If $2x - 3y = 14$ and $5x + 3y = 21$, what is the value of x?

   A) -1

   B) 0

   C) $\dfrac{7}{3}$

   D) 5

8. If $7c - 2b = 15$ and $3b - 6c = 2$, what is the value of $b + c$?

   A) -27

   B) -3

   C) 8

   D) 17

9. If $y = -x - 15$ and $\dfrac{5y}{2} - 37 = -\dfrac{x}{2}$, then what is the value of $2x + 6y$?

10. If $2x + 2y = 22$ and $3x - 4y = 12$, what is the value of $\dfrac{y}{x}$?

Math

Number of Possible Solutions

LEARNING OBJECTIVE

After this lesson, you will be able to:

- Determine the number of possible solutions for a system of linear equations, if any

To answer a question like this:

$$\begin{cases} 5x - 3y = 10 \\ 6y = kx - 42 \end{cases}$$

In the system of linear equations above, k represents a constant. If the system of equations has no solution, what is the value of $2k$?

A) $\dfrac{5}{2}$

B)   5

C)   10

D)   20

You need to know this:

The solution to a system of linear equations consists of the values of the variables that make both equations true.

A system of linear equations may have one solution, infinitely many solutions, or no solution.

If a system of equations represents two lines that intersect, then the system will have exactly **one solution** (in which the x- and y-values correspond to the point of intersection).

If a system of equations has **infinitely many solutions**, the two equations actually represent the same line. For example, $2x + y = 15$ and $4x + 2y = 30$ represent the same line. If you divide the second equation by 2, you arrive at the first equation. Every point along this line is a solution.

If a system of equations has **no solution**, as in the question above, the lines are parallel: there is no point of intersection.

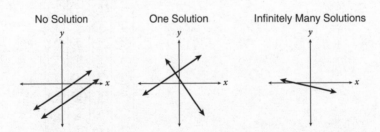

You need to do this:

- If the question states that the system has no solution, manipulate the equations to make the x-coefficients equal to each other and the y-coefficients equal to each other, but be sure that the y-intercepts (or constant terms, if the equations are in $ax + by + c$ form) are different.
- If the question states that the system has infinitely many solutions, make the x-coefficients equal to each other, the y-coefficients equal to each other, and the y-intercepts (or constant terms) equal to each other.
- If the question states that the system has one solution and provides the point of intersection, substitute the values at that point of intersection for x and y in the equations.

Explanation:

Start by recognizing that for two lines to be parallel, the coefficients for x must be identical in the two equations; ditto for the coefficients for y. Manipulate the second equation so that it is in the same format as the first one:

$$kx - 6y = 42$$

The y-coefficient in the first equation, $5x - 3y = 10$, is 3. Divide the second equation by 2 in order to make the y-coefficients in both equations equal:

$$\frac{k}{2}x - 3y = 21$$

Now set the x-coefficient equal to the x-coefficient in the first equation:

$$\frac{k}{2} = 5$$
$$k = 10$$

Note that the question asks for the value of $2k$, so the correct answer is **(D)**, 20.

Try on Your Own

Directions: Take as much time as you need on these questions. Work carefully and methodically. There will be an opportunity for timed practice at the end of the chapter.

$$\begin{cases} 21x - 6y = 54 \\ 9 + y = 3.5x \end{cases}$$

11. The system of equations shown above has how many solutions?

   A) Zero

   B) One

   C) Two

   D) Infinitely many

HINT: For Q12, if a system of equations has infinitely many solutions, what do you know about the two equations?

$$\begin{cases} 6x + 3y = 18 \\ qx - \dfrac{y}{3} = -2 \end{cases}$$

12. In the system of linear equations above, q is a constant. If the system has infinitely many solutions, what is the value of q?

   A) -9

   B) $-\dfrac{2}{3}$

   C) $\dfrac{2}{3}$

   D) 9

HINT: For Q13, the point of intersection is the solution to the system of equations. Use those concrete x- and y-values.

$$\begin{cases} hx - 4y = -10 \\ kx + 3y = -15 \end{cases}$$

13. If the graphs of the lines in the system of equations above intersect at $(-3, 1)$, what is the value of $\dfrac{k}{h}$?

   A) $\dfrac{1}{3}$

   B) 2

   C) 3

   D) 6

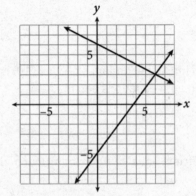

14. What is the y-coordinate of the solution to the system shown above?

   A) -5

   B) 3

   C) 5

   D) 6

$$\begin{cases} 3x - 9y = -6 \\ \dfrac{1}{2}x - \dfrac{3}{2}y = c \end{cases}$$

15. If the system of linear equations above has infinitely many solutions, and c is a constant, what is the value of c?

   A) -6

   B) -3

   C) -2

   D) -1

On Test Day

Many SAT Math questions can be solved in more than one way. A little efficiency goes a long way in helping you get through the Math sections on time, so it's useful to try solving problems more than one way to learn which way is fastest.

Try this question using two approaches: both substitution and combination. Time yourself on each attempt. Which approach allowed you to get to the answer faster?

16. If $28x - 5y = 36$ and $15x + 5y + 18 = 68$, what is the value of x?

    A)   1

    B)   2

    C)   3

    D)   4

The answer and both ways of solving can be found at the end of this chapter.

How Much Have You Learned?

Directions: For testlike practice, give yourself 15 minutes to complete this question set. Be sure to study the explanations, even for questions you got right. They can be found at the end of this chapter.

17. If $8x - 2y = 10$ and $3y - 9x = 12$, then what is the value of $y - x$?

    A) -8
    B) 2
    C) 12
    D) 22

18. A state college has separate fee rates for resident students and nonresident students. Resident students are charged $421 per semester and nonresident students are charged $879 per semester. The college's sophomore class of 1,980 students paid a total of $1,170,210 in fees for the most recent semester. Which of the following systems of equations represents the number of resident (r) and nonresident (n) sophomores and the amount of fees the two groups paid?

    A) $r + n = 1{,}170{,}210$
       $421r + 879n = 1{,}980$

    B) $r + n = 1{,}980$
       $879r + 421n = 1{,}170{,}210$

    C) $r + n = 1{,}980$
       $421r + 879n = 1{,}170{,}210$

    D) $r + n = 1{,}170{,}210$
       $879r + 421n = 1{,}980$

19. A sofa costs $50 less than three times the cost of a chair. If the sofa and chair together cost $650, how much more does the sofa cost than the chair?

    A) $175
    B) $225
    C) $300
    D) $475

Equation 1	
x	y
-2	6
0	4
2	2
4	0

Equation 2	
x	y
-8	-8
-4	-7
0	-6
4	-5

20. The tables above represent data points for two linear equations. If the two equations form a system, what is the x-coordinate of the solution to that system?

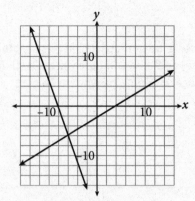

21. If (A, B) is the solution to the system of equations shown above, and A and B are integers, then what is the value of $A + B$?

    A) -12

    B) -6

    C) 0

    D) 6

$$\begin{cases} -16 = 7y + 4x \\ k = \dfrac{7}{8}y + \dfrac{1}{2}x \end{cases}$$

22. If the system of linear equations above has infinitely many solutions, and k is a constant, what is the value of k ?

    A) -8

    B) -4

    C) -2

    D) -1

$$\begin{cases} -13 = ay + 24x \\ 9 + 6bx = 5y \end{cases}$$

23. If the system of equations above has no solution, and a and b are constants, then what is the value of $|a + b|$?

    A) 0

    B) 1

    C) 4

    D) 9

24. If $\dfrac{1}{4}x + 2y = \dfrac{11}{4}$ and $-6y - x = 7$, what is half of y ?

25. At a certain toy store, tiny stuffed pandas cost \$3.50 and giant stuffed pandas cost \$14. If the store sold 29 panda toys and made \$217 in revenue in one week, how many tiny stuffed pandas and giant stuffed pandas were sold?

    A) 18 tiny stuffed pandas, 11 giant stuffed pandas

    B) 11 tiny stuffed pandas, 18 giant stuffed pandas

    C) 12 tiny stuffed pandas, 17 giant stuffed pandas

    D) 18 tiny stuffed pandas, 13 giant stuffed pandas

26. A bead shop sells wooden beads for \$0.20 each and crystal beads for \$0.50 each. If a jewelry artist buys 127 beads total and pays \$41 for them, how much more did she spend on crystal beads than wooden beads?

    A) \$11

    B) \$15

    C) \$23

    D) \$26

Reflect

Directions: Take a few minutes to recall what you've learned and what you've been practicing in this chapter. Consider the following questions, jot down your best answer for each one, and then compare your reflections to the expert responses on the following page. Use your level of confidence to determine what to do next.

When is substitution a good choice for solving a system of equations?

_____

_____

_____

When is combination a good choice for solving a system of equations?

_____

_____

_____

What does it mean if a system of equations has no solution? Infinitely many solutions?

_____

_____

_____

Expert Responses

When is substitution a good choice for solving a system of equations?

Substitution works best when at least one of the variables has a coefficient of 1, making the variable easy to isolate. This system, for example, is well suited for substitution:

$$a + 3b = 5$$
$$4a - 6b = 21$$

That's because in the first equation, you can easily isolate a as a = 5 − 3b *and plug that in for* a *in the other equation. By contrast, substitution would not be a great choice for solving this system:*

$$2a + 3b = 5$$
$$4a - 6b = 21$$

If you used substitution now, you'd have to work with fractions, which is messy.

When is combination a good choice for solving a system of equations?

Combination is always a good choice. It is at its worst in systems such as this one:

$$2a + 3b = 5$$
$$3a + 5b = 7$$

Neither a coefficient is a multiple of the other, and neither b coefficient is a multiple of the other, so to solve this system with combination you'd have to multiply both equations by a constant (for example, multiply the first equation by 3 and the second equation by 2 to create a 6a term in both equations). But substitution wouldn't be stellar in this situation, either.

Note that combination may be particularly effective when the SAT asks for a variable expression. For example, if a question based on the previous system of equations asked for the value of 5a + 8b, then you could find the answer instantly by adding the equations together.

What does it mean if a system of equations has no solution? Infinitely many solutions?

A system of equations with no solution represents two parallel lines, which never cross. The coefficient of a variable in one equation will match the coefficient of the same variable in the other equation, but the constants will be different. For example, this system has no solution:

$$2x + 3y = 4$$
$$2x + 3y = 5$$

Subtracting one equation from the other yields the equation 0 = −1, which makes no sense.

If a system of equations has infinitely many solutions, then the two equations represent the same line. For example, this system has infinitely many solutions:

$$2x + 3y = 4$$
$$4x + 6y = 8$$

Dividing the second equation by 2 yields 2x + 3y = 4, so although the two equations look different, they are actually the same.

Next Steps

If you answered most questions correctly in the "How Much Have You Learned?" section, and if your responses to the Reflect questions were similar to those of the SAT expert, then consider Systems of Equations an area of strength and move on to the next chapter. Come back to this topic periodically to prevent yourself from getting rusty.

If you don't yet feel confident, review those parts of this chapter that you have not yet mastered. In particular, review the mechanics for solving a system of equations by substitution and by combination. Then try the questions you missed again. As always, be sure to review the explanations closely.

Answers and Explanations

1.   1

Difficulty: Medium

Getting to the Answer: Start by isolating c in the second equation: $c = 3b - 2$. Then substitute into the first equation and solve:

$$7(3b - 2) + 8b = 15$$
$$21b - 14 + 8b = 15$$
$$29b - 14 = 15$$
$$29b = 29$$
$$b = 1$$

Grid in **1**.

2.   A

Difficulty: Easy

Getting to the Answer: The quickest way to solve is to realize that you can rearrange the first equation to find that $x = y$. Then substitute y in for x in the second equation: $y = 2y + 5$. Solve to find that $y = -5$. Because $x = y$, x also equals -5, and $x + y = -10$. **(A)** is correct.

3.   C

Difficulty: Medium

Getting to the Answer: Because x has a coefficient of 1 in the second equation, solve the system using substitution. Before you select your answer, make sure you found the right quantity (the difference between x and y).

First, solve the second equation for x and substitute:

$$x - 5y = 2$$
$$x = 2 + 5y$$
$$4(2 + 5y) + 3y = 14 - y$$
$$8 + 20y + 3y = 14 - y$$
$$8 + 23y = 14 - y$$
$$24y = 6$$
$$y = \frac{6}{24} = \frac{1}{4}$$

Next, substitute this value back into $x = 2 + 5y$ and simplify:

$$x = 2 + 5\left(\frac{1}{4}\right)$$
$$x = \frac{8}{4} + \frac{5}{4}$$
$$x = \frac{13}{4}$$

Finally, subtract $x - y$ to find the difference:

$$\frac{13}{4} - \frac{1}{4} = \frac{12}{4} = 3$$

(C) is correct.

4.   B

Difficulty: Medium

Getting to the Answer: It's equally easy to solve the second equation for either variable. The question asks for $\frac{b}{2}$, so solve for a and substitute to create an equation in only one variable:

$$a = b + 3$$
$$5(b + 3) = 6b + 7$$
$$5b + 15 = 6b + 7$$
$$8 = b$$

So $\frac{b}{2} = 4$, and **(B)** is correct.

5.   A

Difficulty: Medium

Getting to the Answer: Set up two equations: one for the number of items sold and one for the money collected. Let N = the number of bags of nuts sold and G = the number of packages of granola bars sold.

The equation for the total items is $N + G = 112$.

The equation for the money collected is $1.25N + 1.75G = 160$.

Even though this is a calculator question, quickly converting the second equation to fractions is an efficient way to save time and prevent an entry mistake: $\frac{5}{4}N + \frac{7}{4}G = 160$.

Multiply by 4 to clear the equation of fractions to get $5N + 7G = 640$.

At this point, you could solve by either combination or substitution. If you use substitution, solve the first equation for N, the number of bags of nuts, because the question asks for G, the number of packages of granola bars. Solving the first equation for N yields $N = 112 - G$.

Substituting that equation into the second equation gives:

$$5(112 - G) + 7G = 640$$
$$560 - 5G + 7G = 640$$
$$560 + 2G = 640$$
$$2G = 80$$
$$G = 40$$

Remember the question asks for the number of *cases* of granola bars Marisol purchased, so divide 40 by 20, the number of packages of granola bars per case. **(A)** is correct.

As an alternative approach, if you read the question carefully and recognized you're solving for the number of *cases*, not packages, the correct answer would have to be either (A) or (B), since (C) and (D) are way too big. You could then test one of those choices, say (A) 2, by multiplying by 20 packages of granola bars per case: $2 \times 20 = 40$. Subtract that number from 112 to get the number of bags of nuts: $112 - 40 = 72$. Multiply each quantity by the price per package: $72 \times 1.25 = 90$ and $40 \times 1.75 = 70$. Then add the sales of the two items together: $90 + 70 = 160$. You've now confirmed the correct answer because $160 is how much Marisol raised. If you had tested (B) instead, then you could have eliminated it and still arrived at the correct answer with no more work because you eliminated all choices except **(A)**.

If you chose any of the other options, you likely answered the wrong question. (B) is the number of cases of nuts Marisol purchased, (C) is the number of packages of granola bars sold, and (D) is the number of bags of nuts sold.

6.   25
Difficulty: Easy

Getting to the Answer: Often, when the SAT asks for a sum or difference of variables, solving by combination yields the answer very quickly. Add the equations:

$$2x + 3y = 15$$
$$\underline{+\quad 3x + 2y = 10}$$
$$5x + 5y = 25$$

Grid in **25** and move on.

7.   D
Difficulty: Easy

Getting to the Answer: This system is already set up perfectly to solve using combination because the y terms ($-3y$ and $3y$) are opposites. Add the two equations to cancel $-3y$ and $3y$. Then solve the resulting equation for x:

$$2x - 3y = 14$$
$$\underline{+\, 5x + 3y = 21}$$
$$7x \qquad = 35$$
$$x \qquad = 5$$

Choice **(D)** is correct. The question asks only for the value of x, so you don't need to substitute x back into either equation to find the value of y.

8.   D
Difficulty: Easy

Getting to the Answer: If you're not asked to find the value of an individual variable, the question may lend itself to combination. This question asks for $b + c$, so don't waste your time finding the variables individually if you can avoid it. After rearranging the equations so that variables and constants are aligned, you can add the equations together:

$$-2b + 7c = 15$$
$$\underline{+3b - 6c = 2}$$
$$b + c = 17$$

This matches **(D)**.

9. 59

Difficulty: Hard

Getting to the Answer: You're asked for the value of an expression rather than the value of one of the variables, so try combination. Start by rearranging the two equations so that variables and constants are aligned:

$$x + y = -15$$
$$\frac{x}{2} + \frac{5y}{2} = 37$$

Clear the fractions in the second equation and then add the equations:

$$2\left(\frac{x}{2} + \frac{5y}{2} = 37\right) \rightarrow x + 5y = 74$$

$$\begin{array}{r} x + y = -15 \\ +\ \ x + 5y = 74 \\ \hline 2x + 6y = 59 \end{array}$$

This is precisely what the question asks for, so you're done. Grid in **59**.

10. $\frac{3}{8}$

Difficulty: Medium

Getting to the Answer: None of the coefficients in either equation is 1, so using combination is a better strategy than substitution here. Examine the coefficients of x: they don't share any factors, so multiply each equation by the coefficient from the other equation:

$$3(2x + 2y = 22) \rightarrow 6x + 6y = 66$$
$$2(3x - 4y = 12) \rightarrow 6x - 8y = 24$$

Subtract the second equation from the first:

$$\begin{array}{r} 6x + 6y = 66 \\ -\ (6x - 8y = 24) \\ \hline 14y = 42 \\ y = 3 \end{array}$$

Next, you need x so you can determine the value of $\frac{y}{x}$. Substitute 3 for y in one of the original equations:

$$2x + 2(3) = 22$$
$$2x + 6 = 22$$
$$2x = 16$$
$$x = 8$$

Plug your x- and y-values into $\frac{y}{x}$ to get $\frac{3}{8}$. Grid in $\frac{3}{8}$.

11. D

Difficulty: Medium

Strategic Advice: Note that (C) is impossible. There are only three possibilities: the lines intersect, in which case there is one solution; the lines are parallel, in which case there are no solutions; or the equations describe the same line, in which case there are infinitely many solutions.

Getting to the Answer: Get the two equations into the same format so that you can distinguish among these possibilities:

$$21x - 6y = 54$$
$$3.5x - y = 9$$

Now it's easier to see that the first equation is equivalent to multiplying every term in the second equation by 6. Both equations describe the same line, so there are infinitely many solutions; **(D)** is correct.

12. B

Difficulty: Hard

Getting to the Answer: A system of equations that has infinitely many solutions describes a single line. Therefore, manipulation of one equation will yield the other. Look at the constant terms: to turn the 18 into a -2, divide the first equation by -9:

$$\frac{(6x + 3y = 18)}{-9} \rightarrow -\frac{6}{9}x - \frac{3}{9}y = -2$$
$$\rightarrow -\frac{2}{3}x - \frac{1}{3}y = -2$$

The y terms and constants in the second equation now match those in the first; all that's left is to set the coefficients of x equal to each other: $q = -\frac{2}{3}$. Choice **(B)** is correct.

Note that you could also write each equation in slope-intercept form and set the slopes equal to each other to solve for q.

13. C

Difficulty: Medium

Getting to the Answer: If the graphs intersect at $(-3, 1)$, then the solution to the system is $x = -3$ and $y = 1$. Substitute these values into both equations and go from there:

$$hx - 4y = -10 \qquad kx + 3y = -15$$
$$h(-3) - 4(1) = -10 \quad k(-3) + 3(1) = -15$$
$$-3h - 4 = -10 \qquad -3k + 3 = -15$$
$$-3h = -6 \qquad\quad -3k = -18$$
$$h = 2 \qquad\qquad k = 6$$

So, $\frac{k}{h} = \frac{6}{2} = 3$, making **(C)** correct.

14. B

Difficulty: Easy

Getting to the Answer: The solution to a system of linear equations represented graphically is the point of intersection. If the lines do not intersect, the system has no solution.

According to the graph, the lines intersect, or cross each other, at $(6, 3)$. The question asks for the y-coordinate of the solution, which is 3, so **(B)** is correct.

15. D

Difficulty: Hard

Getting to the Answer: A system of linear equations has infinitely many solutions if both lines in the system have the same slope and the same y-intercept (in other words, they are the same line).

To have the same slope, the x- and y-coefficients of the two equations must be the same. Use the x-coefficients here: to turn $\frac{1}{2}$ into 3, multiply by 6. So c becomes $6c$, and $6c = -6$, or $c = -1$, which is **(D)**.

Note that you could also write each equation in slope-intercept form and set the y-intercepts equal to each other to solve for c.

16. B

Difficulty: Medium

Strategic Advice: The numbers here are fairly large, so substitution is not likely to be convenient. Moreover, the y-coefficients have the same absolute value, so combination will probably be the faster way to solve.

Getting to the Answer: Start by writing the second equation in the same form as the first, then use combination to solve for x:

$$\begin{array}{r} 28x - 5y = 36 \\ + 15x + 5y = 50 \\ \hline 43x \quad\quad = 86 \\ x \quad\quad = 2 \end{array}$$

Choice **(B)** is correct.

If you feel more comfortable using substitution, you can maximize efficiency by solving one equation for $5y$ and substituting that value into the other equation:

$$15x + 5y = 50$$
$$5y = 50 - 15x$$
$$28x - (50 - 15x) = 36$$
$$43x - 50 = 36$$
$$43x = 86$$
$$x = 2$$

Note that the arithmetic is fundamentally the same, but the setup using combination is quicker and visually easier to follow.

17. D

Difficulty: Medium

Category: Combination

Strategic Advice: When a question asks for a sum or difference of variables, consider solving by combination.

Getting to the Answer: Rearrange the equations to be in the same form, with the y terms before the x terms, and then add:

$$\begin{array}{r} -2y + 8x = 10 \\ +(3y - 9x = 12) \\ \hline y - x = 22 \end{array}$$

The correct answer is **(D)**.

18. C

Difficulty: Medium

Category: Substitution/Combination

Getting to the Answer: Because you're given the variables (*r* for resident and *n* for nonresident), the only thing left for you to do is to break the wording apart into phrases and translate into math. Add together both student types to get the first equation: $r + n = 1{,}980$. This eliminates (A) and (D). Residents pay $421 in fees (421*r*), which eliminates (B). Only **(C)** is left, so it has to be the answer.

19. C

Difficulty: Medium

Category: Substitution

Getting to the Answer: Write a system of equations where $c =$ the cost of the chair in dollars and $s =$ the cost of the sofa in dollars. A sofa costs $50 less than three times the cost of the chair, or $s = 3c - 50$; together, a sofa and a chair cost $650, so $s + c = 650$.

The system is:

$$\begin{cases} s = 3c - 50 \\ s + c = 650 \end{cases}$$

The top equation is already solved for *s*, so substitute $3c - 50$ into the bottom equation for *s* and solve for *c*:

$$3c - 50 + c = 650$$
$$4c - 50 = 650$$
$$4c = 700$$
$$c = 175$$

Remember to check if you solved for the right thing! The chair costs $175, so the sofa costs $3(175) - 50 = 525 - 50 = \$475$. This means the sofa costs $\$475 - \$175 = \$300$ more than the chair. Therefore, **(C)** is correct.

20. 8

Difficulty: Medium

Category: Number of Possible Solutions

Strategic Advice: The solution to the system is the point that both tables will have in common, but the tables, as given, do not share any points. You could use the data to write the equation of each line and then solve the system, but this will use up valuable time on test day. Instead, look for patterns that can be extended.

Getting to the Answer: In the table for Equation 1, the *x*-values increase by 2 each time and the *y*-values decrease by 2. In the table for Equation 2, the *x*-values increase by 4 each time and the *y*-values increase by 1. Use these patterns to continue the tables.

Equation 1	
x	y
−2	6
0	4
2	2
4	0
6	−2
8	**−4**

Equation 2	
x	y
−8	−8
−4	−7
0	−6
4	−5
8	**−4**
12	−3

The point $(8, -4)$ satisfies both equations, so the *x*-coordinate of the solution to the system is **8**.

21. A

Difficulty: Easy

Category: Number of Possible Solutions

Getting to the Answer: The solution to a system of equations shown graphically is the point of intersection. Read the axis labels carefully. Each grid line represents 2 units. The two lines intersect at the point $(-6, -6)$, so $A + B = -6 + (-6) = -12$, which means **(A)** is correct.

22. C

Difficulty: Hard

Category: Number of Possible Solutions

Getting to the Answer: The system has infinitely many solutions, so both equations must describe the same line. Notice that if you multiply the x- and y-coefficients in the second equation by 8, you arrive at the x- and y-coefficients in the first equation. The constant k times 8 must then equal the constant in the first equation, or -16:

$$8k = -16$$
$$k = -2$$

The correct answer is **(C)**.

23. B

Difficulty: Hard

Category: Number of Possible Solutions

Getting to the Answer: Rearrange the equations and write them on top of each other so that the x and y variables line up:

$$\begin{cases} 24x + ay = -13 \\ 6bx - 5y = -9 \end{cases}$$

In a system of equations that has no solution, the x-coefficients must equal each other and the y-coefficients must equal each other. Thus, for the x-coefficients, $24 = 6b$, which means that $b = 4$. For the y-coefficients, $a = -5$. The question asks for the value of $|a + b|$, which is $|-5 + 4| = |-1| = 1$, choice **(B)**. (Note that if you used the equation $-6bx + 5y = 9$, you would get $a = 5$ and $b = -4$, which would still result in the correct answer.)

24. $\frac{9}{2}$ or 4.5

Difficulty: Medium

Category: Substitution/Combination

Getting to the Answer: Start by clearing the fractions from the first equation (by multiplying by 4) to make the numbers easier to work with. Then use combination to solve for y:

$$\begin{array}{r} x + 8y = 11 \\ + \quad -x - 6y = 7 \\ \hline 2y = 18 \\ y = 9 \end{array}$$

Take half of 9 to get $\frac{9}{2}$, then grid in $\frac{9}{2}$ or **4.5**.

25. A

Difficulty: Medium

Category: Substitution/Combination

Getting to the Answer: Choose intuitive letters for the variables: t for tiny pandas, g for giant pandas. You're given the cost of each as well as the number of each sold and the total revenue generated. Then write the system of equations that represents the information given:

$$t + g = 29$$
$$3.5t + 14g = 217$$

Multiplying the top equation by -14 allows you to solve for t using combination:

$$\begin{array}{r} -14t - 14g = -406 \\ + \quad 3.5t + 14g = 217 \\ \hline -10.5t \quad\quad = -189 \\ t \quad\quad = 18 \end{array}$$

Solving for t gives 18, which eliminates (B) and (C). Plugging 18 into t in the first equation allows you to find g, which is 11. Choice **(A)** is correct.

26. A

Difficulty: Hard

Category: Substitution/Combination

Getting to the Answer: Choose letters that make sense for the variables: w for wooden and c for crystal. You know the jewelry artist bought 127 beads total. You're also told each wooden bead costs \$0.20 ($0.2w$) and each crystal bead costs \$0.50 ($0.5c$), as well as the fact that she spent \$41 total. You'll have two equations: one relating the number of wooden beads and crystal beads and a second relating the costs associated with each:

$$w + c = 127$$
$$0.2w + 0.5c = 41$$

Either combination or substitution is a good choice for solving this system. Both are shown here:

Combination:

$$2(0.2w + 0.5c = 41) \rightarrow 0.4w + c = 82$$
$$w + c = 127$$
$$-\quad 0.4w + c = 82$$
$$\overline{\quad 0.6w \quad\quad = 45}$$
$$w \quad\quad = 75$$

Substitution:

$$w + c = 127 \rightarrow c = 127 - w$$
$$0.2w + 0.5(127 - w) = 41$$
$$0.2w + 63.5 - 0.5w = 41$$
$$-0.3w = -22.5$$
$$w = 75$$
$$75 + c = 127 \rightarrow c = 52$$

The question asks for the difference in the amount spent on each type of bead, not the difference in the quantity of each type. Multiply the bead counts by the correct pricing to get $75 \times \$0.2 = \$15$ for the wooden beads and $52 \times \$0.5 = \$26$ for the crystal beads. Take the difference to get $\$26 - \$15 = \$11$, which is **(A)**.

CHAPTER 6

Inequalities

LEARNING OBJECTIVES

After completing this chapter, you will be able to:

- Solve an inequality for a range of values
- Identify the graph of an inequality or a system of inequalities
- Solve for the point of intersection of the boundary lines of a system of inequalities
- Solve algebraically a system of one inequality with two variables and another inequality with one variable
- Identify one or more inequalities that match a real-life situation

35/600 SmartPoints®

How Much Do You Know?

Directions: Try the questions that follow. Show your work so that you can compare your solutions to the ones found in the Check Your Work section immediately after this question set. The "Category" heading in the explanation for each question gives the title of the lesson that covers how to solve it. If you answered the question(s) for a given lesson correctly, and if your scratchwork looks like ours, you may be able to move quickly through that lesson. If you answered incorrectly or used a different approach, you may want to take your time on that lesson.

1. If $\frac{3}{5}p - 2 \geq 5$, what is the least possible value of $\frac{6}{5}p + 2$?

   A) 7

   B) 10

   C) 16

   D) 18

2. If $-3 < \frac{4}{3}h + \frac{1}{6} < 1$, then what is one possible value of $12h - 4$?

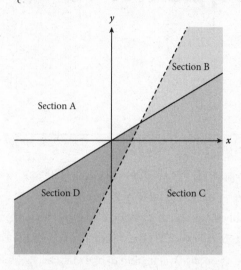

$$\begin{cases} y > 2x - 3 \\ 5y \leq 3x \end{cases}$$

3. The graph above depicts the system of inequalities shown. Which of the labeled section or sections of the graph could represent all of the solutions of the system?

   A) Sections A and D

   B) Section B

   C) Sections C and D

   D) Section D

4. A bowling alley charges a flat $6.50 fee for shoe and ball rental plus $3.75 per game and 6.325 percent sales tax. If each person in a group of seven people has $20 to spend on a bowling outing, and at least some members of the group must rent shoes and a ball, which inequality best describes this situation, given that the number of shoe and ball rentals is represented by r and the number of games is represented by g?

   A) $1.06325(6.5r + 3.75g) \leq 140$

   B) $1.06325(6.5r + 3.75g) \leq 20$

   C) $1.06325\left(\dfrac{6.5}{r} + \dfrac{3.75}{g}\right) \leq 140$

   D) $0.06325(6.5r + 3.75g) \leq 20$

5. Marco is paid $80 per day plus $15 per hour for overtime. If he works five days per week and wants to make a minimum of $520 this week, what is the fewest number of hours of overtime he must work?

6. An architect in an arid region determines that a building's current landscaping uses $1,640 worth of water monthly. The architect plans to replace the current landscaping with arid-zone landscaping at a cost of $15,900, which will reduce the monthly watering cost to $770. Which of the following inequalities can be used to find m, the number of months after replacement that the savings in water costs will be at least as much as the cost of replacing the landscaping?

A) $15,900 \geq (1,640 - 770)m$

B) $15,900 > 770m$

C) $15,900 \leq (1,640 - 770)m$

D) $15,900 \leq 770m$

Check Your Work

1. C

Difficulty: Medium

Category: Linear Inequalities

Getting to the Answer: You might be tempted to solve for p, but some critical thinking and algebra make that unnecessary. First, get $\frac{3}{5}p$ by itself by adding 2 to both sides: $\frac{3}{5}p \geq 7$. Next, multiply both sides by 2 to get the value range of $\frac{6}{5}p \geq 14$. Finally, add 2 to both sides to get $\frac{6}{5}p + 2 \geq 14 + 2$. Thus, $\frac{6}{5}p + 2 \geq 16$, so **(C)** is correct.

2. Any value greater than or equal to 0 and less than 3.5

Difficulty: Hard

Category: Linear Inequalities

Getting to the Answer: Don't automatically start solving the two inequalities separately. Instead, look for a series of quick manipulations to convert $\frac{4}{3}h + \frac{1}{6}$ to $12h - 4$. Start by multiplying the entire inequality by 9 to yield $-27 < 12h + \frac{3}{2} < 9$. Next, subtract $\frac{3}{2}$ and then 4 more (to get the desired -4) from all parts of the inequality (converting the fraction component to a decimal will make this step easier), which will become $-32.5 < 12h - 4 < 3.5$. Because grid-in answers cannot be negative, pick any value that is **greater than or equal to 0 but less than 3.5**.

3. D

Difficulty: Medium

Category: Systems of Inequalities

Getting to the Answer: Sections A and D are all the y values greater than $2x - 3$, so those sections are the solution set for the inequality $y > 2x - 3$. Similarly, Sections C and D are the solution set for $5y \leq 3x$. The solutions for a system of inequalities are all the points that satisfy all (both, in this case) of the inequalities. The points in Section D are in the solution set for both inequalities, so **(D)** is correct.

4. A

Difficulty: Medium

Category: Modeling Real-Life Situations with Inequalities

Getting to the Answer: The question has defined the variables for you (r and g). The bowling alley charges $6.50 for shoe and ball rental and $3.75 per game. Sales tax is 6.325% (0.06325 in decimal form). Rental and game costs are given by $6.5r$ and $3.75g$, respectively. To incorporate sales tax into the total cost, multiply the sum of $6.5r$ and $3.75g$ by 1.06325 (not 0.06325, which gives the cost of sales tax only). The question asks for an inequality that represents the amount that the group can spend, which can be no more than $7 \times 20 = 140$; therefore, the correct inequality is $1.06325(6.5r + 3.75g) \leq 140$. This matches **(A)**.

5. 8

Difficulty: Medium

Category: Modeling Real-Life Situations with Inequalities

Getting to the Answer: Translate from English into math to create an inequality in which h represents the number of hours of overtime Marco must work. Marco gets paid a daily wage plus an hourly rate for overtime, so his weekly pay is his daily rate ($80) times 5 days, plus the number of hours of overtime he works (h) times his overtime rate ($15). If he wants to make *at least* $520, which means that much or more, the inequality is $(80 \times 5) + 15h \geq 520$. Solve for h:

$$400 + 15h \geq 520$$
$$15h \geq 120$$
$$h \geq 8$$

Marco must work at least 8 hours of overtime to make $520 or more this week. Grid in **8**.

6. C

Difficulty: Medium

Category: Modeling Real-Life Situations with Inequalities

Getting to the Answer: The question asks for the point at which the savings will be *at least as much* as the cost of replacing the landscaping, so the value range could include a value equal to the exact cost of replacement; eliminate the strict inequality in (B). Because you need a value range that is at least as much as the cost of landscaping, you need the cost of landscaping, $15,900, to be *less than* or equal to the value range. Eliminate (A).

The value range will be the value of the monthly savings times the number of months, which will be *m* times the difference between the old monthly water cost and the new monthly water cost: $(1,640 - 770)m$. Therefore, the entire inequality expression is $15,900 \leq (1,640 - 770)m$, so **(C)** is correct.

Linear Inequalities

LEARNING OBJECTIVES

After this lesson, you will be able to:

- Solve an inequality for a range of values
- Identify the graph of an inequality

To answer a question like this:

Which of the following graphs represents the solution set for $5x - 10y > 6$?

A)
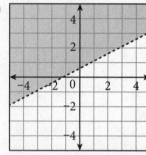

B)
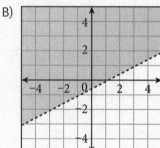

C)
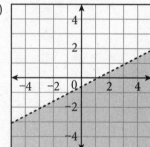

D)
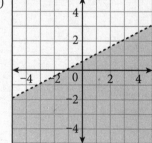

You need to know this:

Linear inequalities are similar to linear equations but have two differences:

- You are solving for a **range of values** rather than a single value.
- If you multiply or divide both sides of the inequality by a negative, you must **reverse the inequality sign**.

While linear equations graph as simple lines, inequalities graph as shaded regions. Use solid lines for inequalities with $\leq$ or $\geq$ signs because the line itself is included in the solution set. Use dashed lines for inequalities with $<$ or $>$ signs because, in these cases, the line itself is not included in the solution set. The shaded region represents all points that make up the solution set for the inequality.

You need to do this:

To graph an inequality, start by writing the inequality in slope-intercept form, then graph the solid or dashed line. Finally, add shading:

- For $y > mx + b$ and $y \geq mx + b$, shade the region *above* the line.
- For $y < mx + b$ and $y \leq mx + b$, shade the region *below* the line.

If it's hard to tell which region is above/below the line (which can happen when the line is steep), compare the y-values on both sides of the line.

Explanation:

Rewrite the inequality in slope-intercept form and then identify which half-plane should be shaded. Subtract $5x$ from both sides of the inequality, divide both sides by -10, and flip the inequality symbol to yield $y < \frac{1}{2}x - \frac{3}{5}$. Eliminate (A) and (D) because they have positive y-intercepts. The "less than" symbol indicates that the half-plane below the line should be shaded, making **(C)** the correct answer.

Try on Your Own

Directions: Take as much time as you need on these questions. Work carefully and methodically. There will be an opportunity for timed practice at the end of the chapter.

$$-\frac{a}{6} - a > -\frac{4}{3}$$

1. Which of the following is equivalent to the inequality above?

   A) $a < \frac{7}{8}$

   B) $a > \frac{7}{8}$

   C) $a < \frac{8}{7}$

   D) $a > \frac{8}{7}$

HINT: For Q2, save time by solving for the entire expression, not *c*.

---

2. If $-5c - 7 \leq 8$, what is the least possible value of $15c + 7$?

   A) -38

   B) -4

   C) 15

   D) 22

HINT: For Q3, be careful not to "lose" a negative sign.

$$-\frac{1}{8}(8 - 10x) > 3x - 2$$

3. Which of the following describes all possible values of x?

   A) $x < -\frac{12}{7}$

   B) $x > -\frac{4}{7}$

   C) $x < \frac{4}{7}$

   D) $x > \frac{4}{7}$

$$\frac{1}{4}a - \frac{1}{16}b + 3 < 5$$

4. Which of the following is equivalent to the inequality above?

   A) $4a - b < 8$

   B) $4a - b < 32$

   C) $a - 4b < 32$

   D) $4b - a < 4$

5. If $4c + 20 \geq 31$, what is the least possible value of $12c + 7$?

   A) 18

   B) 40

   C) 51

   D) 58

Systems of Inequalities

To answer a question like this:

If $12x - 4y > 8$ and $\frac{2}{3}x + 6y \geq 14$ form a system of inequalities, which of the following graphs shows the solution set for the system?

A)

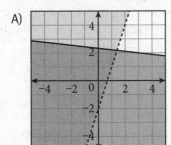

B)

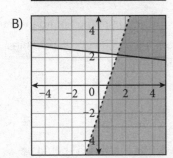

C)

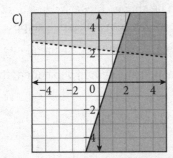

D)

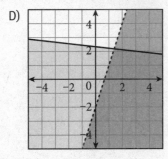

You need to know this:

The solution set for a system of inequalities is not a single point (a single *x*-value and *y*-value) but a region of overlap between the two inequalities: that is, a range of *x*-values and *y*-values. It is easiest to see this graphically.

Systems of inequalities can be presented graphically with multiple boundary lines and multiple shaded regions. Follow the same rules as for graphing single inequalities, but keep in mind that **the solution set is the region where the shading overlaps**.

Note that you generally cannot use substitution or combination to solve a system of two inequalities where both have two variables. That said, the SAT may ask for the maximum or minimum *x*- or *y*-value of a system of inequalities. These questions are actually asking about the intersection of the **boundary lines** of the system. If you see one of these questions, use substitution or combination to solve for the point of intersection, as you learned to do in chapter 5. For an example of this type of question (which is rare on the SAT), see question number 8 in the Try on Your Own set for this lesson.

You may also see an occasional question without a graph asking you to solve a system of one inequality in two variables and another inequality in one variable. As long as both inequalities have the same symbol, you can do this by substitution. Question number 6 in this lesson's Try on Your Own set is an example of this rare question type.

You need to do this:

- To identify the graph of a system of inequalities, follow the same rules as for single inequalities. The solution set is the region where the shading overlaps.
- For a question asking for a maximum or minimum, solve for the intersection point of the boundary lines.
- For a question asking for the range of values that satisfies a system of one inequality in two variables and one inequality in one variable (both with the same sign), solve by substitution.

Explanation:

Rewrite the inequalities in slope-intercept form. Once complete, determine whether each line should be solid or dashed and which half of the plane (above or below the line) should be shaded for each. The correct graph should have a dashed line with a positive slope ($y < 3x - 2$) and a solid line with a negative slope $\left(y \geq -\frac{1}{9}x + \frac{7}{3}\right)$; eliminate (C) because the dashed and solid lines are incorrect. According to the inequality symbols, the half-plane above the solid line and the half-plane below the dashed line should be shaded; the only match is **(B)**.

Try on Your Own

Directions: Take as much time as you need on these questions. Work carefully and methodically. There will be an opportunity for timed practice at the end of the chapter.

$$a < 6b + 4$$
$$3b < 8$$

6. Which of the following consists of all the a-values that satisfy the system of inequalities above?

   A) $a < 20$

   B) $a < 16$

   C) $a < 12$

   D) $a < \dfrac{8}{3}$

HINT: For Q7, remember that the solution set is the overlap between both inequalities. Make a sketch or use a graphing calculator.

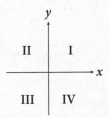

7. If the system of inequalities $y \le -x + 1$ and $y < \dfrac{1}{2}x$ is graphed on the above plane, which of the quadrants contain(s) no solutions to the system?

   A) Quadrant I

   B) Quadrant II

   C) Quadrant III

   D) Quadrants I and II

$$-y \le 6x - 2200$$
$$3y \ge 9x - 1500$$

8. Given the system of inequalities above, if point (a, b) lies within the solution set, what is the minimum possible value of b ?

$$x < 4 - 2y$$
$$y \le -2x + 1$$

9. Which of the following ordered pairs satisfies both of the inequalities above?

   A) $(-1, 3)$

   B) $(1, 1)$

   C) $(2, -3)$

   D) $(4, 4)$

HINT: For Q10, remember that *solution* means "an (x, y) pair that is true for both inequalities."

$$y \; > \; x + r$$
$$y \; < \; s - x$$

10. If $x = y = 1$ is a solution to the system of inequalities above, which of the following ordered pairs could correspond to (r, s) ?

    A) $(-1, 1)$

    B) $\left(-\dfrac{1}{2}, 2\right)$

    C) $\left(-\dfrac{1}{10}, 3\right)$

    D) $(3, -1)$

Modeling Real-Life Situations with Inequalities

LEARNING OBJECTIVE

After this lesson, you will be able to:

- Identify one or more inequalities that match a real-life situation

To answer a question like this:

To make its sales goals for the month, a toy manufacturer must sell at least $10,400 of toy hoops and basketballs. Toy hoops sell for $8 and basketballs sell for $25. The company hopes to sell more than three times as many basketballs as toy hoops. If h represents the number of toy hoops and b represents the number of basketballs, where h and b are positive integers, which of the following systems of inequalities best describes this situation?

A) $8h + 25b \geq 10,400$
$b > 3h$

B) $8h + 25b \geq 10,400$
$h > 3b$

C) $25h + 8b \geq 10,400$
$b > 3h$

D) $25h + 8b \geq 10,400$
$h > 3b$

You need to know this:

Word problems involving inequalities require you to do the same sort of translation that you learned in chapter 4. They also require you to get the direction of the inequality sign right. The following table shows which symbols correspond to which words.

English	Symbol
more, greater, longer, heavier	$>$
less, fewer, shorter, lighter	$<$
no less than, no fewer than, at least	$\geq$
no more than, no greater than, at most	$\leq$

You need to do this:

Break down the word problem one inequality at a time. For each one:

- Identify the correct symbol based on the table above
- Put the value that follows the word "than" or "as" on the right and the other value on the left
- If the sentence does not use the words "than" or "as," use logic to determine the relationship between the values

Explanation:

"At least $10,400" means $\geq 10,400$. It's the money from the sales of toy hoops and basketballs that has to be greater than or equal to $10,400, so that's what needs to go on the left of the $\geq$ sign. Each toy hoop costs $8, so the cash generated by sales of toy hoops will be $8h$. Each basketball costs $25, so basketballs will generate $25b$. Add them: $8h + 25b \geq 10,400$. Eliminate (C) and (D).

The company wants to sell "*more than* three times as many basketballs as toy hoops," so write down $>$ and work out what needs to go on each side. The company wants to sell more basketballs than toy hoops, so b should go on the left. Specifically, they want basketball sales to be more than 3 times toy hoop sales, so the final statement is $b > 3h$. **(A)** is correct.

Try on Your Own

Directions: Take as much time as you need on these questions. Work carefully and methodically. There will be an opportunity for timed practice at the end of the chapter.

HINT: For Q11, set up one inequality for the number of ads and a second inequality for the money the ads bring in.

---

11. Ariel enters a contest to sell advertisements in her school's yearbook. To qualify for a prize, she has to sell at least $1,500 worth of advertisements consisting of no fewer than 15 individual ads. Each full-page ad costs $110, each half-page ad costs $70, and each quarter-page ad costs $50. Which of the following systems of inequalities represents this situation, where x is the number of full-page ads she sells, y is the number of half-page ads she sells, and z is the number of quarter-page ads she sells?

    A) $110x + 70y + 50z \geq 1{,}500$
       $x + y + z \leq 15$

    B) $110x + 70y + 50z \leq 1{,}500$
       $x + y + z \leq 15$

    C) $110x + 70y + 50z \geq 1{,}500$
       $x + y + z \geq 15$

    D) $110x + 70y + 50z \leq 1{,}500$
       $x + y + z \geq 15$

12. A farmer sells watermelons, cantaloupes, and tomatoes from a small cart at a county fair. He needs to sell at least $200 of produce each day. His watermelons are priced at $0.50 per pound, his cantaloupes at $1 per pound, and his tomatoes at $2.50 per pound. His cart can hold no more than 250 pounds. Which of the following inequalities represents this scenario, if w is the number of pounds of watermelons, c is the number of pounds of cantaloupes, and t is the number of pounds of tomatoes?

    A) $0.5w + 1c + 2.5t \geq 200$
       $w + c + t \leq 250$

    B) $0.5w + 1c + 2.5t \leq 200$
       $w + c + t \leq 250$

    C) $0.5w + 1c + 2.5t \geq 200$
       $w + c + t \geq 250$

    D) $0.5w + 1c + 2.5t \leq 200$
       $w + c + t \geq 250$

Math

13. Allison is planting a garden with at least 15 trees. There will be a combination of apple trees, which cost $120 each, and pear trees, which cost $145 each. Allison's budget for purchasing the trees is no more than $2,050. She must plant at least 5 apple trees and at least 3 pear trees. Which of the following systems of inequalities represents the situation described if x is the number of apple trees and y is the number of pear trees?

A) $120x + 145y \geq 2,050$
$x + y \leq 15$
$x \geq 5$
$y \geq 3$

B) $120x + 145y \geq 2,050$
$x + y \geq 15$
$x \leq 5$
$y \leq 3$

C) $120x + 145y \leq 2,050$
$x + y \geq 15$
$x \leq 5$
$y \leq 3$

D) $120x + 145y \leq 2,050$
$x + y \geq 15$
$x \geq 5$
$y \geq 3$

14. A utility shelf in a warehouse is used to store containers of paint and containers of varnish. Containers of paint weigh 50 pounds each and containers of varnish weigh 35 pounds each. The shelf can hold up to 32 containers, the combined weight of which must not exceed 1,450 pounds. Let x be the number of containers of paint and y be the number of containers of varnish. Which of the following systems of inequalities represents this relationship?

A) $50x + 35y \leq 32$
$x + y \leq 1,450$

B) $50x + 35y \leq 1,450$
$x + y \leq 32$

C) $85(x + y) \leq 1,450$
$x + y \leq 32$

D) $50x + 35y \leq 1,450$
$x + y \leq 85$

HINT: For Q15, read carefully. *At least* is a minimum, so which way should the inequality sign point?

---

15. A bakery is buying flour and sugar from its supplier. The supplier will deliver no more than 750 pounds in a shipment. Each bag of flour weighs 50 pounds and each bag of sugar weighs 20 pounds. The bakery wants to buy at least three times as many bags of sugar as bags of flour. If f represents the number of bags of flour and s represents the number of bags of sugar, where f and s are nonnegative integers, which of the following systems of inequalities represents this situation?

A) $50f + 60s \leq 750$
$f \leq 3s$

B) $50f + 20s \leq 750$
$f \leq 3s$

C) $50f + 20s \leq 750$
$3f \leq s$

D) $150f + 20s \leq 750$
$3f \leq s$

On Test Day

Modeling real life situations with inequalities can be tricky, especially when there are multiple inequalities involved or when a question doesn't state the information in the most straightforward way. The good news is that you can often make use of the answer choices to get to the answer quickly.

Try the question below. If you use the choices, you shouldn't have to do any calculations. Just pay close attention to the direction of the inequality signs.

16. A florist is organizing a sale that offers carnations at a price of $4 for 10 and daisies at a price of $7 for 5. The florist plans to order a maximum of 500 flowers for the sale and wants the revenue from the sale to be at least $400. If x is the number of carnations and y is the number of daisies, and the florist sells all the flowers ordered, which system of inequalities best describes this situation?

A) $0.4x + 1.4y \geq 400$
$x + y \leq 500$

B) $0.4x + 1.4y \leq 400$
$x + y \leq 500$

C) $0.4x + 1.4y \geq 400$
$x + y \geq 500$

D) $0.4x + 1.4y \leq 400$
$x + y \geq 500$

The answer and explanation can be found at the end of this chapter.

How Much Have You Learned?

Directions: For testlike practice, give yourself 15 minutes to complete this question set. Be sure to study the explanations, even for questions you got right. They can be found at the end of this chapter.

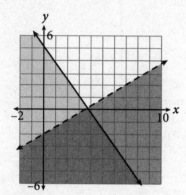

17. The figure above shows the solution set for this system of inequalities:

$$\begin{cases} y < \dfrac{3}{5}x - 2 \\ y \le -\dfrac{4}{3}x + 5 \end{cases}$$

Which of the following is NOT a solution to this system?

A) $(-1, -4)$

B) $(1, -1)$

C) $(4, -1)$

D) $(6, -3)$

18. Ezekiel has $5.00 to spend on snacks. Candy bars cost $0.60 each, gum costs $0.50 per pack, and nuts are priced at $1.29 per small bag. If c represents the number of candy bars, g represents the number of packs of gum, and n represents the number of bags of nuts, which of the following inequalities correctly describes Ezekiel's choices?

A) $\dfrac{c}{0.60} + \dfrac{g}{0.50} + \dfrac{n}{1.29} \le \dfrac{1}{5}$

B) $c + g + n \le 5$

C) $0.60c + 0.50g + 1.29n \le 5.00$

D) $0.60c + 0.50g + 1.29n \ge 5.00$

19. A shipping company employee is in charge of packing cargo containers for shipment. He knows a certain cargo container can hold a maximum of 50 microwaves or a maximum of 15 refrigerators. Each microwave takes up 6 cubic feet of space, and each refrigerator takes up 20 cubic feet. The cargo container can hold a maximum of 300 cubic feet. The employee is trying to figure out how to pack a container containing both microwaves and refrigerators. Which of the following systems of inequalities can the employee use to determine how many of each item (microwaves, m, and refrigerators, r) he can pack into one cargo container?

A) $m \le 6$
   $r \le 20$
   $50m + 15r \le 300$

B) $m \le 50$
   $r \le 15$
   $m + r \le 300$

C) $m \le 50$
   $r \le 15$
   $6m + 20r \le 300$

D) $m \le 50$
   $r \le 15$
   $50m + 15r \le 300$

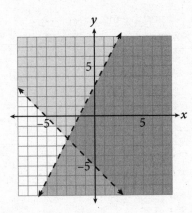

$$\begin{cases} y > -x - 5 \\ y < 2x + 3 \end{cases}$$

$$y \geq -3x + 18$$
$$y \geq 9x$$

22. In the xy plane, the point (a, b) lies in the solution set of the system of inequalities above. What is the minimum possible value of b ?

A) $1\frac{1}{2}$

B) 3

C) $7\frac{1}{2}$

D) $13\frac{1}{2}$

20. The figure above shows the solution for the system of inequalities shown. Suppose (a, b) is a solution to the system. If $a = 0$, what is the greatest possible integer value of b ?

23. Francine sells advertising time packages for a local television station. She is able to make up to 15 sales calls per week offering potential advertisers either a prime time package for \$12,000 or a non prime time package for \$8,000. Her weekly sales goal is to sell more than \$20,000 worth of advertising. Which of the following systems of inequalities represents this situation in terms of p, the number of prime time packages Francine sells in a week, n, the number of non prime time packages, and u, the number of unsuccessful sales calls for which she sells neither offering?

A) $p + n + u \leq 15$
    $12,000p + 8,000n > 20,000$

B) $p + n + u \geq 15$
    $12,000p + 8,000n > 20,000$

C) $p + n + u \leq 15$
    $12,000p + 8,000(n + u) > 20,000$

D) $p + n + u \leq 15$
    $12,000p + 8,000n < 20,000$

$$3x + 2 > 5$$
$$-2x + 8 > -10$$

21. Which of the following describes the range of x ?

A) $x > 1$

B) $x > 9$

C) $-1 < x < 9$

D) $9 > x > 1$

24. Luis has $25 to spend on school supplies. Pencils (p) cost $1.25 per package, notebooks (n) are priced at $2.50 each, and markers ($m$) sell for $4 per pack. He must buy exactly one calendar/planner for $5.75. Which of the following describes how many markers Luis can buy?

    A) $m \leq \dfrac{1.25p + 2.5n + 5.75}{25}$

    B) $m \leq \dfrac{19.25 - 1.25p - 2.5n}{4}$

    C) $m \leq \dfrac{25 - 1.25p - 2.5n}{4} - 5.75$

    D) $m \leq 19.25 - 1.25p - 2.5n$

25. Let a and b be numbers such that $-a < b + 1 < a$. Which of the following must be true?

    I. $a > 0$

    II. $|b| < a$

    III. $b > a + 1$

    A) I only

    B) I and II

    C) II only

    D) I, II, and III

26. The variable x is a positive integer. If $3(x - 1) + 5 > 11$ and $-5x + 18 \geq -12$, how many possible values are there for x?

Reflect

Directions: Take a few minutes to recall what you've learned and what you've been practicing in this chapter. Consider the following questions, jot down your best answer for each one, and then compare your reflections to the expert responses on the following page. Use your level of confidence to determine what to do next.

What is the difference between a linear inequality and a linear equation?

_____

_____

_____

The rules for manipulating an inequality are very similar to those for manipulating an equation. What is the major difference?

_____

_____

_____

When two lines cross in the coordinate plane, they create four regions. How many regions will be shaded if the system of inequalities uses the word "and"? The word "or"?

_____

_____

_____

Expert Responses

What is the difference between a linear inequality and a linear equation?

A linear equation is solved for a single value, whereas a linear inequality is solved for a range of values.

The rules for manipulating an inequality are very similar to those for manipulating an equation. What is the major difference?

When solving an inequality, you can do the same thing to both sides, just as you could for an equation. The big difference is that if you divide or multiply both sides of an inequality by a negative number, you have to flip the inequality sign.

When two lines cross in the coordinate plane, they create four regions. How many regions will be shaded if the system of inequalities uses the word "and"? The word "or"?

Of the four regions, one represents values that satisfy neither inequality. One represents values that satisfy both inequalities. The other two regions represent values that satisfy one inequality but not the other. For an "and" inequality, only the region of values that satisfy both inequalities will be shaded. For an "or" inequality, the only region not shaded will be the one that satisfies neither inequality; the other three regions will be shaded.

Next Steps

If you answered most questions correctly in the "How Much Have You Learned?" section, and if your responses to the Reflect questions were similar to those of the SAT expert, then consider inequalities an area of strength and move on to the next chapter. Come back to this topic periodically to prevent yourself from getting rusty.

If you don't yet feel confident, review those parts of this chapter that you have not yet mastered and try the questions you missed again. As always, be sure to review the explanations closely.

Answers and Explanations

1.   C

Difficulty: Easy

Getting to the Answer: Begin by multiplying all parts of the inequality by 6 to clear the fractions: $-a - 6a > -\frac{24}{3}$, which, when simplified, is $-7a > -8$. Divide both sides by -7, remembering to switch the direction of the sign: $a < \frac{8}{7}$. Therefore, **(C)** is correct.

2.   A

Difficulty: Medium

Getting to the Answer: Don't solve for c on autopilot. Instead, solve for $15c$, then add 7 to both sides. To do this, first multiply both sides of the inequality by -1 to get $5c + 7 \geq -8$. (Notice that the inequality sign had to be flipped due to multiplication by a negative number.) Then subtract 7 from both sides to yield $5c \geq -15$. Multiply both sides by 3: $15c \geq -45$. Finally, add 7 to both sides: $15c + 7 \geq -38$. Choice **(A)** is correct.

3.   C

Difficulty: Medium

Getting to the Answer: First, to clear the fraction, multiply both sides of the inequality by -8, remembering to flip the direction of the inequality sign: $8 - 10x < -24x + 16$.

Next, subtract 8 from both sides, and then add $24x$ to both sides. Divide both sides by 14, and then simplify the fraction.

$$-10x < -24x + 8$$
$$14x < 8$$
$$x < \frac{8}{14}$$
$$x < \frac{4}{7}$$

Thus, **(C)** is correct.

4.   B

Difficulty: Medium

Getting to the Answer: Begin by subtracting 3 from both sides of the inequality to get $\frac{1}{4}a - \frac{1}{16}b < 2$. Next, clear the fractions in that inequality by multiplying all terms by 16: $16 \times \left(\frac{1}{4}a - \frac{1}{16}b < 2\right) = 4a - b < 32$. **(B)** is correct.

5.   B

Difficulty: Medium

Strategic Advice: Because the given inequality contains $4c$ and the value you're solving for has $12c$ (a multiple of $4c$), solve for $4c$ and then multiply by 3 to find $12c$.

Getting to the Answer: Subtract 20 from both sides of the inequality to find that $4c \geq 11$. Multiply by 3: $12c \geq 33$. Finally, add 7 to both sides: $12c + 7 \geq 40$. So the least permissible value for $12c + 7$ is 40. **(B)** is correct.

6.   A

Difficulty: Easy

Getting to the Answer: The question offers a value range of a in terms of $6b$ and a value range for $3b$. Therefore, use the known value range of $3b$ to find the value range of $6b$.

Since $6b$ is two times $3b$, multiply both sides of the second inequality by 2 to find the value range of $6b$: $2 \times 3b < 2 \times 8$, so $6b < 16$.

Because the signs are the same in the two inequalities (both are less-than signs), you can plug 16 in for b in the first inequality: $a < 16 + 4$, or $a < 20$. Hence, **(A)** is correct.

7.   B

Difficulty: Medium

Getting to the Answer: Draw a sketch of the two lines to help visualize the system of inequalities.

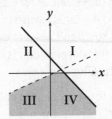

Clearly, quadrants III and IV contain solutions to the system. Eliminate (C). Quadrant II contains no solutions, so you can also eliminate (A). Look closely at quadrant I. The line for $y \leq -x + 1$ intersects both the x and y axes at $+1$. The line for $y < \frac{1}{2}x$ passes through the origin and upward into quadrant I. Thus, there is a very small triangle of solutions to both inequalities that lies in quadrant I. Therefore, **(B)** is correct.

8. 400

Difficulty: Medium

Getting to the Answer: The first task is to express both inequalities in terms of y. Multiply $-y \leq 6x - 2200$ by -1 to get $y \geq -6x + 2200$; don't forget to flip the sign since you are multiplying by a negative number. Divide $3y \geq 9x - 1500$ by 3 to get $y \geq 3x - 500$.

The solution set for these inequalities is the area of the coordinate plane on or above both lines. Thus, the minimum y-value will occur at the intersection of the two lines, whose equations are $y = -6x + 2200$ and $y = 3x - 500$. To find the point of intersection, set these two equations equal to each other: $-6x + 2200 = 3x - 500$. Isolate the x-values on one side to yield $-9x = -2700$ and $x = 300$. Plug this value into one of the equations (it doesn't matter which one because $x = 300$ is where they intersect) to obtain the y-coordinate at the point of intersection: $3(300) - 500 = 400$. The y-coordinate at the point of intersection is the minimum possible value of b that the question was asking for, so grid in **400**.

9. C

Difficulty: Medium

Getting to the Answer: You could plot the two lines and identify the solution set on a graph, but testing the choices to see if they satisfy both inequalities is a more efficient approach, particularly since one inequality is "less than" and the other is "less than or equal to." If you take this approach, you don't even need to rearrange the inequalities to isolate y on one side.

(A): Substituting these values for x and y in $x < 4 - 2y$ gives you $(-1) < 4 - 2(3)$, which is $-1 < -2$ (not a true statement). You don't need to evaluate the other inequality since this ordered pair is not in the solution set for $x < 4 - 2y$. Eliminate (A).

(B): Substituting these values for x and y in $x < 4 - 2y$ gives you $(1) < 4 - 2(1)$, which is $1 < 2$. The ordered pair is in the solution set for this inequality, so plug the values into $y \leq -2x + 1$ to get $(1) \leq -2(1) + 1$, which simplifies to $1 \leq -1$. Thus, this ordered pair is not in the solution set for the second inequality. Eliminate (B).

(C): Substituting these values for x and y in $x < 4 - 2y$ gives you $(2) < 4 - 2(-3)$, which is $2 < 10$. The ordered pair is in the solution set for this inequality, so plug the values into $y \leq -2x + 1$ to get $(-3) \leq -2(2) + 1$, which

simplifies to $-3 \leq -3$. Since the sign for this inequality is "less than or equal to," this ordered pair is in the solution set. **(C)** is correct.

(D): Since you already identified the correct choice, you do not need to check this pair.

10. C

Difficulty: Hard

Getting to the Answer: Since the question states that $x = y = 1$ is a solution to the system, plug those values in to get $1 > 1 + r$ and $1 < s - 1$. These inequalities further simplify to $r < 0$ and $s > 2$. Check each pair of values in the answer choices to see which complies with these limitations. Only **(C)** has both $r < 0$ and $s > 2$, and is correct. (B) is incorrect because s must be greater than 2, and (D) reverses r and s.

11. C

Difficulty: Medium

Getting to the Answer: Translate each part of the word problem into its mathematical equivalent. Because x, y, and z represent the numbers of each of the three ad sizes, the total number of ads will be $x + y + z$. "No fewer than 15 ads" means $x + y + z \geq 15$, so eliminate (A) and (B).

The total cost of the ads Ariel sells will be represented by the number of each size ad sold times the respective cost of each size ad. Thus, $110x + 70y + 50z$ represents the total cost of all of the ads; "at least 1,500" means that $110x + 70y + 50z \geq 1,500$. Therefore, **(C)** is correct.

12. A

Difficulty: Medium

Getting to the Answer: Translate each part of the word problem into its mathematical equivalent. The total weight of produce will be represented by the combined pounds of watermelons, w, cantaloupes, c, and tomatoes, t. This combined weight cannot exceed 250 pounds, so the inequality is $w + c + t \leq 250$. Eliminate (C) and (D).

The total money for the produce sold is represented by the price per pound of each type of produce times the number of pounds of that type. This must be at least (greater than or equal to) \$200, so the inequality is $0.5w + 1c + 2.5t \geq 200$. **(A)** is correct.

13. D

Difficulty: Medium

Getting to the Answer: Translate each part of the word problem into its mathematical equivalent, beginning with the easiest-to-translate components. Allison needs at least 5 apple trees and at least 3 pear trees, so the correct inequalities are $x \geq 5$ and $y \geq 3$. Eliminate (B) and (C). The total number of apple and pear trees combined that Allison purchases must be at least 15, so the correct inequality is $x + y \geq 15$. Eliminate (A). Only **(D)** is left and is correct.

Note that, by being strategic, you never even have to determine the first, most complicated inequality in each of the answer choices. For the record: apple trees cost $120 and pear trees cost $145, so the total amount Allison will spend on trees is $120x + 145y$. This total amount cannot go above $2,050, which means it must be less than or equal to $2,050. Therefore: $120x + 145y \leq 2,050$.

14. B

Difficulty: Medium

Getting to the Answer: First, define the relationship between the weight of each kind of container and the weight the shelf can hold. Since x is the number of 50-pound containers of paint and y is the number of 35-pound containers of varnish, the combined weight of the containers will be represented by $50x + 35y$. This needs to be no more than 1,450 pounds, so the inequality that represents this is $50x + 35y \leq 1,450$. Eliminate (A) and (C).

The question also states that the total number of containers the shelf can hold is no more than 32, so the combined number of containers of paint and containers of varnish must be no more than 32. This is represented by the inequality $x + y \leq 32$. Thus, **(B)** is correct.

15. C

Difficulty: Hard

Getting to the Answer: Begin by translating the weight of the combined bags of flour and sugar. The weight of each bag of flour times the number of bags of flour—plus the weight of each bag of sugar times the number of bags of sugar—will yield the total. Thus, $50f + 20s$ will describe the weight of all of the bags combined. Since

the weight that the supplier can deliver is no more than 750 pounds, the inequality that describes this situation is $50f + 20y \leq 750$. Eliminate (A) and (D).

The question also specifies that the bakery needs to buy at least three times as many bags of sugar as bags of flour. In other words, the number of bags of sugar must be equal to or greater than three times the number of bags of flour. This is represented by $s \geq 3f$, which can be rewritten as $3f \leq s$. **(C)** is correct.

16. A

Difficulty: Hard

Strategic Advice: All the numbers in the answer choices are the same, so you don't actually have to calculate the cost of one carnation or one daisy. The answer choices have done that for you.

Getting to the Answer: Focus on the keywords that tell you the direction of the inequality signs. The florist plans to order a "maximum" of 500 flowers, so that's ≤ 500. Eliminate (C) and (D). The florist wants to earn "at least" $400, or ≥ 400. The correct answer is **(A)**.

17. B

Difficulty: Medium

Category: Systems of Inequalities

Getting to the Answer: The intersection (overlap) of the two shaded regions is the solution to the system of inequalities. Check each point to see whether it lies in the region where the shading overlaps. Be careful—you are looking for the point that is *not* a solution to the system. Choices (A) and (C) lie in the overlap, so you can eliminate them. Choice (D), which is the point $(6, -3)$, lies on a boundary line, and because the line is solid, the point *is* included in the solution region. The only point that does not lie within the overlap must be (B). To check this, plug $(1, -1)$ into the first inequality:

$$y < \frac{3}{5}x - 2$$
$$-1 < \frac{3}{5}(1) - 2$$
$$-1 \not< -\frac{7}{5}$$

Because -1 is not less than $-\frac{7}{5}$, **(B)** is correct.

18. C

Difficulty: Easy

Category: Modeling Real-Life Situations with Inequalities

Getting to the Answer: The fact that Ezekiel has exactly $5.00 means that he can spend up to and including $5.00, so use the less than or equal symbol ($\leq$) for the limit on how much he can spend. For that reason alone you can eliminate (D). The amount of money Ezekiel spends on each type of snack is the number of units of that snack times its price. So, $0.60c + 0.50g + 1.29n \leq 5.00$. **(C)** is correct.

19. C

Difficulty: Medium

Category: Modeling Real-Life Situations with Inequalities

Getting to the Answer: The clue "holds a maximum" means the container can hold exactly that much or less, so use the less than or equal to symbol ($\leq$) throughout. The cargo container can hold a maximum of 50 micro-waves, so the first inequality is $m \leq 50$. Eliminate (A). The container can hold a maximum of 15 refrigerators, so the second inequality is $r \leq 15$. The third inequality deals with the size of each appliance. The cargo container can hold m microwaves multiplied by the size of the microwave, which is 6 cubic feet; it can hold r refrigerators multiplied by the size of the refrigerator, which is 20 cubic feet; and it can hold a maximum of 300 cubic feet total. Put these together to write the final inequality: $6m + 20r \leq 300$, which is **(C)**.

20. 2

Difficulty: Hard

Category: Systems of Inequalities

Getting to the Answer: If (a, b) is a solution to the system, then a is the x-coordinate of any point in the region where the shading overlaps, and b is the corresponding y-coordinate. When $a = 0$ (or $x = 0$), the maximum possible value for b lies on the upper boundary line, $y < 2x + 3$. It looks like the y-coordinate is 3, but to be sure, substitute $x = 0$ into the equation and simplify. You can replace the inequality symbol with an equal sign to make it an equation because you are finding a point on the boundary line, not a range:

$$y = 2(0) + 3$$
$$y = 3$$

The point on the boundary line is (0, 3). The boundary line is dashed (because the inequality is strictly less than), so (0, 3) is *not* a solution to the system. This means 2 is the greatest possible *integer* value for b when $a = 0$. Grid in **2**.

21. D

Difficulty: Medium

Category: Linear Inequalities

Getting to the Answer: Isolate x in each of the given inequalities, then consider the results in combination. For $3x + 2 > 5$, subtract 2 from each side to get $3x > 3$, which means that $x > 1$. For $-2x + 8 > -10$, subtract 8 from each side to get $-2x > -18$. Divide each side by -2, which means that you have to flip the inequality sign to get $x < 9$. Taking the two inequalities together, x must be greater than 1 but less than 9. This can be expressed as $1 < x < 9$ or, alternatively, $9 > x > 1$. **(D)** is correct.

22. D

Difficulty: Medium

Category: Systems of Inequalities

Strategic Advice: If the given inequalities are graphed in the xy-plane, the solution set is the portion of the plane on or above both lines. Since the value of y for both lines increases moving away from the point where they intersect, the minimum value of y will occur at the intersection of these lines, which is the point (a, b).

Getting to the Answer: The boundary lines of this system of inequalities are $y = -3x + 18$ and $y = 9x$. To find their intersection point, set them equal to each other to get $9x = -3x + 18$. So, $12x = 18$ and $x = 1\frac{1}{2}$. That represents a, but the question asks for the value of b. Substitute $1\frac{1}{2}$ for x in either equation, preferably the simpler one: use $y = 9x$ to get $y = 9\left(1\frac{1}{2}\right) = 13\frac{1}{2}$. Therefore, **(D)** is correct.

23. A

Difficulty: Medium

Category: Modeling Real-Life Situations with Inequalities

Strategic Advice: Translating English into math, set up one inequality for Francine's number of sales calls and another for the dollar amount of sales in terms of her goal.

Getting to the Answer: Since Francine can make *up to* 15 sales calls per week and there are three categories of the results of her efforts, you can write the inequality $p + n + u \leq 15$. Eliminate (B). For the monetary goal, that is *more than* \$20,000, so this inequality is $12,000p + 8,000n > 20,000$. Note that the unsuccessful sales calls are not included in this inequality since they do not generate any revenue. **(A)** is correct.

24. B

Difficulty: Medium

Category: Modeling Real-Life Situations with Inequalities

Getting to the Answer: The amount Luis spends on each item is that item's price times the quantity he buys. The total amount must be less than or equal to \$25. Thus, you can write the inequality $1.25p + 2.50n + 4.00m + 1(5.75) \leq 25.00$. Since the question asks for the number of markers, isolate m on one side of the inequality: $4m \leq 25 - 1.25p - 2.5n - 5.75$. Therefore, $m \leq \dfrac{19.25 - 1.25p - 2.5n}{4}$. **(B)** is correct.

25. B

Difficulty: Hard

Category: Linear Inequalities

Getting to the Answer: Examine each of the roman numeral choices individually, determine which one or ones must be true, then select the correct choice. Subtract 1 from all terms in the given inequality to get $-a - 1 < b < a - 1$, so that b stands alone.

I. Ignoring the middle term, b, the given inequality tells you that $-a < a$. The only way this can be true is if a is a positive number, so statement I must be true. If you have a hard time seeing this, pick a negative number for a. For example, if $a = -1$, then the inequality would say $-(-1) < -1$, which is $1 < -1$, which is false. Note that if $a = 0$, then the inequality becomes $0 < 0$, which is also false. Because statement I must be true, you can eliminate (C).

II. Recall that the absolute value of any number is its distance from 0 on the number line, which is its value without a sign. If b is positive or 0, then, since $b < a - 1$, the value of b, which is the same as $|b|$, must also be less than a. However, if b is negative, the relationship is not directly clear. Pick some numbers that satisfy the original inequality, such as $a = 4$ and $b = -2$. For these numbers, $-a - 1 = -5$, $|b| = 2$, $a - 1 = 3$. Thus, $-5 < 2 < 3$, so $-a - 1 < |b| < a - 1$, which means that a must be more than 1 greater than $|b|$. Because a must be positive (as determined by statement I) and because a must be more than 1 greater than b (from the original inequality), the value of $-a - 1$ must be less than b. Thus, statement II must be true. Eliminate (A). If the logic here is difficult, plug in more numbers for a and b to find a pattern.

III. Since a must be positive and any positive value of b is less than $a - 1$, there is no way that $b > a + 1$. Statement III is not true, so eliminate (D).

Because I and II must be true, and III cannot be true, **(B)** is correct.

26. 3

Difficulty: Medium

Category: Linear Inequalities

Strategic Advice: Isolate x in each of the two inequalities to determine a range for x.

Getting to the Answer: Expand the first inequality to get $3x - 3 + 5 > 11$, so $3x > 9$ and $x > 3$. Multiply the second inequality by -1, so that $5x - 18 \leq 12$. This simplifies to $x \leq 6$. Combine the two results: $3 < x \leq 6$. There are 3 allowable integer values for x: 4, 5, and 6. Grid in **3**.

Data Analysis

CHAPTER 7

Ratios, Proportions, and Percents

LEARNING OBJECTIVES

After completing this chapter, you will be able to:

- Set up and solve a proportion for a missing value
- Use ratios to perform unit conversions
- Calculate percents and percent change

70/600 SmartPoints®

How Much Do You Know?

Directions: Try the questions that follow. Show your work so that you can compare your solutions to the ones found in the Check Your Work section immediately after this question set. The "Category" heading in the explanation for each question gives the title of the lesson that covers how to solve it. If you answered the question(s) for a given lesson correctly, and if your scratchwork looks like ours, you may be able to move quickly through that lesson. If you answered incorrectly or used a different approach, you may want to take your time on that lesson.

1. Leonardo da Vinci asserted that a person's height is proportional to the length of the person's palm. Don's palm is 5 centimeters in length and he is 120 centimeters tall. Mateo's palm is 7.5 centimeters in length. Assuming that da Vinci's theory is correct, how tall, in centimeters, is Mateo?

   A) 60 centimeters

   B) 80 centimeters

   C) 160 centimeters

   D) 180 centimeters

2. As of 2009, there were about 225 quarters for every 2 fifty-cent coins in circulation. If there were 380 million quarters in circulation that year, approximately how many total quarters and fifty-cent coins, in millions, were there in circulation?

   A) 383

   B) 415

   C) 493

   D) 605

3. If $\dfrac{5}{7a} = \dfrac{1}{b-a}$, which of the following proportions is equivalent?

   A) $\dfrac{a}{b} = \dfrac{5}{12}$

   B) $\dfrac{a}{b} = \dfrac{5}{2}$

   C) $\dfrac{b-a}{a} = \dfrac{5}{7}$

   D) $\dfrac{b-a}{a} = -\dfrac{7}{5}$

4. British Thermal Units (BTUs) and calories are two measures of heat energy. If there are 2,016 calories in 8 British Thermal Units, how many calories are in 3 British Thermal Units?

5. Sai's car is leaking engine oil at a rate of 2.5 milliliters per hour. If his car's engine contains 6 liters of oil, what will be the amount of oil, in milliliters, remaining in Sai's engine after 24 hours? (Note: There are 1,000 milliliters in 1 liter.)

6.

Category	Percentage
Completely satisfied	
Somewhat satisfied	
Somewhat dissatisfied	15%
Completely dissatisfied	25%

A company conducts a customer satisfaction survey. The results are partly summarized in the table. If 240 customers responded to the survey, how many customers were either completely or somewhat satisfied?

A) 60

B) 96

C) 144

D) 204

7. In a week, a light bulb factory produces 12,500 light bulbs. The ratio of light emitting diodes (LED bulbs) to compact fluorescent lamps (CFL bulbs) is 2:3. Of the LED bulbs produced, 3 percent were defective. If the factory produces no other kind of bulbs, how many LED bulbs were NOT defective?

A) 2,425

B) 4,850

C) 7,275

D) 8,083

8. In 1950, scientists estimated a certain animal population in a particular geographical area to be 6,400. In 2000, the population had risen to 7,200. If this animal population experiences the same percent increase over the next 50 years, what will the approximate population be?

A) 8,000

B) 8,100

C) 8,400

D) 8,600

Check Your Work

1. D

Difficulty: Easy

Category: Proportions

Getting to the Answer: Since you are given the palm-to-height ratio for Don's as well as Mateo's palm length, set up a proportion using M to represent Mateo's height:

$$\frac{5\ cm}{120\ cm} = \frac{7.5\ cm}{M}$$

Cross-multiply to solve for M:

$$5M = 7.5(120)$$
$$M = \frac{7.5(120)}{5}$$
$$M = 180$$

The correct answer is **(D)**.

2. A

Difficulty: Easy

Category: Proportions

Getting to the Answer: Notice that the question asks you for the total number of coins in millions, but the ratio given specifies only the parts. Set up a proportion using the given ratio:

$$\frac{225\ quarters}{2\ fifty\text{-}cent\ coins} = \frac{380\ million\ quarters}{x\ fifty\text{-}cent\ coins}$$

Cross-multiply: $225x = 2 \times 380$ million. Solve for x to find that $x = 3.3\overline{7}$ million fifty-cent coins in circulation. To calculate the total number of fifty-cent coins and quarters in circulation in millions in 2009, add the number of fifty-cent coins to the number of quarters: $3.3\overline{7}$ million $+ 380$ million ≈ 383 million. Choice **(A)** is correct.

3. A

Difficulty: Medium

Category: Proportions

Getting to the Answer: Since the answer choices are expressed as $\frac{a}{b} =$ and $\frac{b-a}{a} =$, cross-multiply the proportion and rewrite it to get an expression that matches one of the answer choices. Solving for $\frac{b-a}{a}$, you get the following:

$$\frac{5}{7a} = \frac{1}{b-a}$$
$$5(b-a) = 7a$$
$$\frac{b-a}{a} = \frac{7}{5}$$

This does not match (C) or (D), so eliminate them. Now solve for $\frac{a}{b}$:

$$5(b-a) = 7a$$
$$5b - 5a = 7a$$
$$5b = 12a$$
$$\frac{5}{12} = \frac{a}{b}$$

This matches **(A)**.

4. 756

Difficulty: Easy

Category: Unit Conversion

Getting to the Answer: Let x represent the number of calories in 3 BTUs, and set up a proportion equating the ratio of 8 BTUs to 2,016 calories to the ratio of 3 BTUs to x calories: $\frac{8\ BTU}{2,016\ CAL} = \frac{3\ BTU}{x\ CAL}$. Solving for x gives 756 calories. Grid in **756**.

5. 5940

Difficulty: Medium

Category: Unit Conversion

Getting to the Answer: First, determine the amount of oil that will leak out of Sai's engine after 24 hours: $\frac{2.5\,\text{mL}}{1\,\text{hr}} \times 24\,\text{hr} = 60\,\text{mL}$. Then, use the conversion to determine the amount of oil, in milliliters, initially in the engine: $6\,\text{L} \times \frac{1{,}000\,\text{mL}}{1\,\text{L}} = 6{,}000\,\text{mL}$. Calculate the difference between the two to find the amount of oil remaining in the engine after 24 hours: $6{,}000\,\text{mL} - 60\,\text{mL} = \mathbf{5{,}940}\,\text{mL}$. Grid in **5940**.

6. C

Difficulty: Easy

Category: Percents

Getting to the Answer: According to the table, 25% of the customers are completely dissatisfied and 15% are somewhat dissatisfied. So, 100% − 25% − 15% = 60% of the customers are completely or somewhat satisfied. Thus, the number of customers who are completely or somewhat satisfied is 60% of 240, or $0.6 \times 240 = 144$ customers, making **(C)** correct.

7. B

Difficulty: Hard

Category: Percents

Getting to the Answer: Approach the question as a series of steps. Before you bubble in your answer, check that you answered the right question (the number of LED bulbs that were *not* defective).

First, find the total number of LED bulbs produced. Since the ratio of LED to CFL is 2:3 and a total of 12,500 of both kinds of bulbs were produced, two parts LED plus three parts CFL equals 12,500. Let x be the number of LED bulbs produced and use the part to whole ratio to set up a proportion:

$$\frac{2}{5} = \frac{x}{12{,}500}$$

Solve for x by cross-multiplying:

$$2(12{,}500) = 5x$$
$$25{,}000 = 5x$$
$$5{,}000 = x$$

Now find the number of LED bulbs that were not defective: $5{,}000 \times 97\% = 5{,}000 \times 0.97 = 4{,}850$. Choice **(B)** is correct.

8. B

Difficulty: Medium

Category: Percent Change

Getting to the Answer: Find the percent increase in the population from 1950 to 2000 using this formula: % increase $= \dfrac{\text{amount of increase}}{\text{original amount}} \times 100\%$. Then apply the same percent increase to the animal population in 2000.

The amount of increase is $7{,}200 - 6{,}400 = 800$, so the percent increase is $\dfrac{800}{6{,}400} \times 100\% = 0.125 \times 100\% = 12.5\%$ between 1950 and 2000. If the total percent increase over the next 50 years is the same, the animal population should be about

$$7{,}200 \times (100\% + 12.5\%) = 7{,}200 \times (112.5\%) =$$
$$7{,}200 \times 1.125 = 8{,}100.$$

(B) is correct.

Ratios and Proportions

> **LEARNING OBJECTIVE**
>
> After this lesson, you will be able to:
>
> - Set up and solve a proportion for a missing value

To answer a question like this:

The World War II aircraft carrier *Essex* was 872 feet long with a beam (width) of 147 feet. A museum wishes to build an exact replica scale model of the Essex that is 8 feet long. Approximately how many <u>inches</u> wide will the scale model's beam be? (1 foot = 12 inches)

A) 13

B) 16

C) 26

D) 109

You need to know this:

A **ratio** is a comparison of one quantity to another. When writing ratios, you can compare one part of a group to another part of that group or you can compare a part of the group to the whole group. Suppose you have a bowl of apples and oranges: you can write ratios that compare apples to oranges (part to part), apples to total fruit (part to whole), and oranges to total fruit (part to whole).

Keep in mind that ratios convey *relative* amounts, not necessarily actual amounts, and that they are typically expressed in lowest terms. For example, if there are 10 apples and 6 oranges in a bowl, the ratio of apples to oranges would likely be expressed as $\frac{5}{3}$ on the SAT rather than as $\frac{10}{6}$. However, if you know the ratio of apples to oranges and either the actual number of apples or the total number of pieces of fruit, you can find the actual number of oranges by setting up a proportion (see below).

Note that the SAT may occasionally use the word "proportion" to mean "ratio."

A **proportion** is simply two ratios set equal to each other, such as, $\frac{a}{b} = \frac{c}{d}$. Proportions are an efficient way to solve certain problems, but you must exercise caution when setting them up. Noting the units of each piece of the proportion will help you put each piece of the proportion in the right place. Sometimes the SAT may ask you to determine whether certain proportions are equivalent—check this by cross-multiplying. You'll get results that are much easier to compare.

$$\text{If } \frac{a}{b} = \frac{c}{d}, \text{ then: } ad = bc, \frac{a}{c} = \frac{b}{d}, \frac{d}{b} = \frac{c}{a}, \frac{b}{a} = \frac{d}{c}, \text{ BUT } \frac{a}{d} \neq \frac{c}{b}$$

Each derived ratio shown except the last one is simply a manipulation of the first, so all except the last are correct. You can verify this via cross-multiplication ($ad = bc$ in each case except the last).

Alternatively, you can pick equivalent fractions $\frac{2}{3}$ and $\frac{6}{9}$ ($a = 2$, $b = 3$, $c = 6$, $d = 9$). Cross-multiplication gives $2 \times 9 = 3 \times 6$, which is a true statement. Dividing 2 and 3 by 6 and 9 gives $\frac{2}{6} = \frac{3}{9}$, which is also true, and so on. However, attempting to equate $\frac{2}{9}$ and $\frac{3}{6}$ will not work.

If you know any three numerical values in a proportion, you can solve for the fourth. For example, say a fruit stand sells 3 peaches for every 5 apricots, and you are supposed to calculate the number of peaches sold on a day when 20 apricots were sold. You would use the given information to set up a proportion and solve for the unknown:

$$\frac{3}{5} = \frac{p}{20}$$

You can now solve for the number of peaches sold, p, by cross-multiplying:

$$60 = 5p$$
$$p = 12$$

Alternatively, you could use the common multiplier to solve for p: the numerator and denominator in the original ratio must be multiplied by the same value to arrive at their respective terms in the new ratio. To get from 5 to 20 in the denominator, you multiply by 4, so you also have to multiply the 3 in the numerator by 4 to arrive at the actual number of peaches sold: $4(3) = 12$.

You need to do this:

- Set up a proportion and solve for the unknown, either by cross-multiplying or by using the common multiplier

Explanation:

The ratio of the length of the real Essex to that of the scale model is $\frac{872\,\text{ft}}{8\,\text{ft}}$. You know the actual beam width (147 feet), so set up a proportion and solve for the scale model's beam width:

$$\frac{872\,\text{ft}}{8\,\text{ft}} = \frac{147\,\text{ft}}{x\,\text{ft}}$$
$$872x = 1{,}176\,\text{ft}$$
$$x \approx 1.349\,\text{ft}$$

The question asks for the answer in inches, not feet, so multiply by 12 inches per foot: $1.349\,\text{ft} \times 12\,\text{in/ft} = 16.188$ inches. The correct answer is **(B)**.

Try on Your Own

Directions: Take as much time as you need on these questions. Work carefully and methodically. There will be an opportunity for timed practice at the end of the chapter.

1. Teachers at a certain school know that, when reviewing for exams, the number of topics they can cover is directly proportional to the length of time they have to review. If teachers can cover 9 topics in a single 45-minute period, how many topics can they cover in a 1-hour period?

    A)   5

    B)   7

    C)   10

    D)   12

2. Objects weigh less on the Moon because the Moon's gravitational pull is less than Earth's. In general, 1 pound on Earth is equal to approximately 0.166 pounds on the Moon. If a person weighs 29 pounds on the Moon, approximately how much, in pounds, does the person weigh on Earth?

    A)   21

    B)   48

    C)   175

    D)   196

3. A machine produces 6 defective parts out of every 3,500 it makes. How many total parts were made during the time the machine produced 27 defective parts?

    A)   14,000

    B)   15,750

    C)   17,500

    D)   21,000

4. The ratio of freshmen to sophomores in an auditorium was 3 to 10. After an additional 270 freshmen and 120 sophomores entered the auditorium, the ratio of freshmen to sophomores was 6 to 5. No other students entered or left the auditorium. How many freshmen were in the auditorium before the additional students entered?

    A)   15

    B)   42

    C)   140

    D)   182

5.   Riding her bicycle, Reyna can travel 1 mile in 5.5 minutes. If she rides at a constant rate, which of the following is closest to the distance she will travel in 1.5 hours?

A)   9 miles

B)   11 miles

C)   13 miles

D)   16 miles

7.   All of the attendees at a symposium are either physicists or biologists. If there are 123 physicists and 270 biologists, then how many additional physicists must arrive at the symposium in order for the ratio of physicists to total attendees to become 2 to 5 ?

A)   25

B)   50

C)   57

D)   114

6.   If $\dfrac{x + y}{x} = \dfrac{4}{9}$, which of the following proportions is equivalent?

A) $\dfrac{y}{x} = -\dfrac{5}{9}$

B) $\dfrac{y}{x} = \dfrac{13}{9}$

C) $\dfrac{y - x}{x} = -\dfrac{4}{9}$

D) $\dfrac{y - x}{x} = -\dfrac{9}{4}$

Unit Conversion

LEARNING OBJECTIVE

After this lesson, you will be able to:

- Use ratios to perform unit conversions

To answer a question like this:

The nearest star to the Sun, Proxima Centauri, is approximately 4.3 light years away. Another star, Sirius A, is twice that distance from the Sun. If one light year equals 63,000 astronomical units (AU), and 1 AU equals 150 million kilometers, approximately how far is Sirius A from the Sun in trillions of kilometers? (1 trillion = 1,000,000,000,000)

A) 2.2

B) 20

C) 41

D) 81

You need to know this:

You can use ratios to perform unit conversions. This is especially useful when there are multiple conversions or when the units are unfamiliar.

For example, though these units of measurement are no longer commonly used, there are 8 furlongs in a mile and 3 miles in a league. Say you're asked to convert 4 leagues to furlongs. A convenient way to do this is to set up the conversion ratios so that equivalent units cancel:

$$4 \text{ leagues} \times \frac{3 \text{ miles}}{1 \text{ league}} \times \frac{8 \text{ furlongs}}{1 \text{ mile}} = 4 \times 3 \times 8 = 96 \text{ furlongs}$$

Notice that all the units cancel out except the furlongs, which is the one you want.

You need to do this:

Set up a series of ratios to make equivalent units cancel. (Keep track of the units by writing them down next to the numbers in the ratios.) You should be left with the units you're converting into.

Explanation:

Sirius A is twice as far from the Sun as Proxima Centauri, so it is $2(4.3) = 8.6$ light years away from the Sun. Set up a series of ratios to convert to trillion kilometers:

$$8.6 \ \cancel{\text{light years}} \times \frac{63,000 \ \cancel{\text{AU}}}{1 \ \cancel{\text{light year}}} \times \frac{150 \ \text{million km}}{1 \ \cancel{\text{AU}}} = 8.6 \times 63,000 \times 150 \ \text{million km}$$

$$= 81,270,000 \ \text{million km}$$

$$= 81.27 \ \text{trillion km}$$

Because there are 6 zeroes in a million, 81,270,000 million is 81,270,000,000,000. There are 12 zeroes in a trillion, so this number equals 81.27 trillion. The correct answer is **(D)**.

Try on Your Own

Directions: Take as much time as you need on these questions. Work carefully and methodically. There will be an opportunity for timed practice at the end of the chapter.

HINT: For Q8, *cubic feet* means ft^3 or ft × ft × ft.

---

8. Quinn wants to rent a self-storage unit for her college dorm room furniture for the summer. She estimates that she will need 700 cubic feet of storage space, but the self-storage provider measures its units in cubic meters. If 1 meter is approximately 3.28 feet, about how many cubic meters of space will Quinn need?

   A) 19.84

   B) 25.93

   C) 65.07

   D) 213.41

9. Because court reporters must type every word at a trial or hearing, they must be able to type at a minimum rate of 3.75 words per second in order to be certified. Suppose a trial transcript contains 25 pages with an average of 675 words per page. Assuming the court reporter typed the transcript at the minimum rate, how long was he actively typing?

   A) 1 hour, 15 minutes

   B) 1 hour, 45 minutes

   C) 2 hours, 30 minutes

   D) 3 hours

HINT: For Q10, *how many more* means you're solving for a difference. Subtract, then convert pounds/hour to ounces/minute.

---

10. At 350°F, an oven can cook approximately 3 pounds of turkey per hour. At 450°F, it can cook approximately 4.5 pounds per hour. How many more ounces of turkey can the oven cook at 450°F than at 350°F in 10 minutes? (1 pound = 16 ounces)

    A) 4

    B) 6

    C) 8

    D) 12

11. An emergency room doctor prescribes a certain pain medication to be delivered through an IV drip. She prescribes 800 milliliters of the medication to be delivered over the course of 8 hours. The IV delivers 1 milliliter of medication over the course of 30 drips. How many drips per minute are needed to deliver the prescribed dosage?

12. Botanists studying a particular coastal redwood tree determined that the tree grew 46 meters in the first 50 years of its life. On average, how many centimeters per day did it grow during this period? Assume that there are 365 days in a year and round your answer to the nearest hundredth of a centimeter.

Percents

To answer a question like this:

Political canvassers polled voters in two locations on whether they viewed a particular candidate for governor favorably. At the first location, they asked 125 people and of those, 22.4 percent responded favorably. At the second location, 37.5 percent of 272 people responded favorably. Approximately what percent of all the people surveyed responded favorably?

A) 25.7%

B) 30.0%

C) 31.5%

D) 32.7%

You need to know this:

To calculate percents, use this basic equation:

$$\text{Percent} = \frac{\text{part}}{\text{whole}} \times 100\%$$

Alternatively, use this statement: [blank] percent of [blank] is [blank]. Translating from English into math, you get [blank]% × [blank] = [blank].

You need to do this:

- Plug in the values for any two parts of the formula and solve for the third
- In some calculations, you may find it convenient to express percents as decimals. To do this, use the formula above but stop before you multiply by 100% at the end.

Explanation:

Use a variation of the three-part percent formula to answer this question: whole $\times$ percent = part, where the percent is expressed as a decimal.

First, find the number of people at each location who responded favorably using the formula. Start with the first location: $125 \times 0.224 = 28$. Move on to the second location: $272 \times 0.375 = 102$. Next, find the total number of people who were surveyed at both locations, which is $125 + 272 = 397$, and the total number who responded favorably, $28 + 102 = 130$. Finally, find the percent of people who responded favorably by using the formula one more time:

$$397 \times \text{percent} = 130 \times 100\%$$
$$\text{percent} = \frac{130}{397} \times 100\%$$
$$\approx 0.327 \times 100\%$$
$$= 32.7\%$$

Of all the people surveyed, about 32.7% responded favorably, making **(D)** the correct answer.

Try on Your Own

Directions: Take as much time as you need on these questions. Work carefully and methodically. There will be an opportunity for timed practice at the end of the chapter.

13. A college athletics program found that approximately 3 percent of 308 runners were injured during workouts and that approximately 6 percent of 237 weightlifters were injured during workouts. Which of the following is the closest to the total number of runners and weightlifters who were injured?

    A) 50

    B) 39

    C) 26

    D) 23

HINT: For Q14, what percent of the attendees are teachers?

---

14. At a high school conference, 15 percent of the attendees are sophomores, 30 percent are juniors, 25 percent are seniors, and the remaining 18 attendees are teachers. How many more juniors are there than seniors?

HINT: For Q15, how many gallons of *pigment* is the painter starting with? How many gallons of *pigment* are needed for the final mix? How many gallons of the final paint will it take to provide the needed pigment?

---

15. A painter has 20 gallons of a paint mixture that is 15 percent blue pigment. How many gallons of a mixture that is 40 percent blue pigment would the painter need to add to achieve a mixture that is 20 percent blue pigment?

    A) 4

    B) 5

    C) 8

    D) 12

16. On August 1, the price of one share of a company's stock was $75. On September 1, the price of one share was $10 more than it was on August 1 and 80 percent of the price of one share on October 1. To the nearest dollar, what was the price of one share on October 1?

    A) $68

    B) $99

    C) $102

    D) $106

Percent Change

LEARNING OBJECTIVE

After this lesson, you will be able to:

- Calculate percent change

To answer a question like this:

On a particular day, a power company makes several changes in the power allocated to a neighborhood. First, it increases the power by 20 percent. Then, it decreases the power by 10 percent. Finally, it increases the power by 30 percent. What is the net percent increase in this neighborhood's power allocation, to the nearest tenth of a percent? (The percent sign is understood after your answer. For example, if the answer is 15.1%, grid in 15.1.)

You need to know this:

You can determine the **percent change** in a given situation by applying this formula:

$$\text{Percent increase or decrease} = \frac{\text{amount of increase or decrease}}{\text{original amount}} \times 100\%$$

Sometimes, more than one change will occur. Be careful here, as it can be tempting to take a "shortcut" by just adding two percent changes together (which will almost always lead to an incorrect answer). Instead, you'll need to find the total amount of the increase or decrease and then apply the formula.

You need to do this:

- Calculate the actual increase or decrease
- Divide by the *original* amount (not the new amount!)
- Multiply by 100%

Explanation:

The question does not give an initial value for power allocation, so pick 100 (often the best number to use when picking numbers for questions involving percents) and then calculate the actual change. A 20% increase from 100 is $100 + 100 \times 0.2$ and brings the power allocation to $100 + 20 = 120$. A 10% decrease from 120 is $120 - 120 \times 0.1$ and brings the power allocation to $120 - 12 = 108$. Lastly, an increase of 30% puts the final power allocation at $108 + 0.3 \times 108 = 108 + 32.4 = 140.4$. The actual increase, then, is $140.4 - 100 = 40.4$. (Again, note that simply combining the percents would get you the wrong answer: $10\% - 20\% + 30\% = 40\%$.)

Plugging this increase into the percent change formula yields the following (remember to divide by the *original* amount, 100, rather than by the new amount, 140.4):

$$\text{Percent change} = \frac{40.4}{100} \times 100\% = 40.4\%$$

Grid in **40.4**.

Math

Try on Your Own

Directions: Take as much time as you need on these questions. Work carefully and methodically. There will be an opportunity for timed practice at the end of the chapter.

HINT: For Q17, remember to divide by the *original* value.

17. A homeowner's annual property tax payment was $1,494. Due to a property value reassessment, the tax payment was increased to $1,572. To the nearest tenth of a percent, by what percent was the home-owner's property tax payment increased?

   A)   0.1%

   B)   5.0%

   C)   5.2%

   D)   7.9%

18. The price of a single share of a certain corporation's stock was $35. Six months later, the price of a single share of the corporation's stock had risen to $49. To the nearest percent, what was the percent increase in the price per share?

   A)   14%

   B)   29%

   C)   40%

   D)   48%

HINT: For Q19, how does the wording of the question help you determine which container of coins is the original amount?

19. The number of coins in jar X is 75. The number of coins in jar Y is 54. By what percent is the number of coins in jar Y less than the number of coins in jar X?

   A)   21%

   B)   28%

   C)   39%

   D)   72%

HINT: For Q20, if you have 75% more senior than juniors, you have all the juniors (100%) plus 75%, or 175%. Adding the percents at the start saves a calculation step.

20. At a school rally, there are 50 sophomores, 80 juniors, and 75 percent more seniors than juniors. By what percent is the number of seniors greater than the number of sophomores?

   A)   80%

   B)   140%

   C)   150%

   D)   180%

HINT: For Q21, the final 25% discount is applied to an already reduced price. You *cannot* add the percent discounts together.

21. The original price of a newly released smart phone was y dollars. A year later, the original price of the phone was discounted by 36 percent. After another six months, an online retailer was selling the phone at a price that was 25 percent less than the previously discounted price. By what percent was the online retailer's price less than y ?

   A)   27%

   B)   48%

   C)   52%

   D)   61%

On Test Day

When a question features multiple percentages, you have to make a key strategic decision: can I do the arithmetic on the percentages themselves and get the answer right away, or do I have to calculate each percentage individually and do the arithmetic on the actual values?

For example, suppose a car traveling 50 miles per hour increases its speed by 20 percent and then decreases its speed by 20 percent. Can you just say that its final speed is 50 miles per hour since $+20\% - 20\% = 0$? No, because after a 20% increase, the car's speed becomes 120% of the original: $1.2(50) = 60$. When the car "decreases its speed by 20 percent," that 20 percent is calculated based on the new speed, 60, not the original speed, and 20 percent of 60 is greater than 20 percent of 50. Thus, the car's final speed is lower than its starting speed: $50(1.2)(0.8) = 48$ miles per hour.

By contrast, suppose you have to find how many more non-smokers than occasional smokers live in a certain region where there are 13,450 residents, given that 62 percent of them don't smoke, and 8 percent of them do smoke occasionally. It may be tempting to find 62 percent of 13,450 ($0.62 \times 13,450 = 8,339$), then find 8 percent of 13,450 ($0.08 \times 13,450 = 1,076$), and finally subtract those two numbers to get the answer ($8,339 - 1,076 = 7,263$). This is a waste of time, though. Instead, you can quickly find the difference between the two percentages ($62 - 8 = 54$) and take 54 percent of the total to get the answer in one step: $13,450 \times 0.54 = 7,263$, the same answer.

If you *can* do arithmetic using the percentages but choose to do arithmetic on the raw numbers instead, you'll waste time doing unnecessary work. But if you *can't* do arithmetic on the percentages (as in the first example) but do anyway, then you'll get the wrong answer. So, being able to tell whether you can or can't do the arithmetic on the percentages is a useful skill.

Luckily, the fundamental principle is simple: you can always do arithmetic on the percentages as long as the percentages are out of the same total. If the totals are different, then you must convert the percentages into actual values. Practice applying this principle on the following question.

22. Flanders Corporation has 250 full-time and 250 part-time employees. If 92 percent of the full-time employees qualify for health insurance benefits, and 74 percent of the part-time employees do not qualify for health insurance benefits, then how many more full-time than part-time employees at Flanders Corporation qualify for health insurance benefits?

   A)   45

   B)   90

   C)   165

   D)   330

The answer and explanation can be found at the end of this chapter.

How Much Have You Learned?

Directions: For testlike practice, give yourself 15 minutes to complete this question set. Be sure to study the explanations, even for questions you got right. They can be found at the end of this chapter.

Undergraduate Costs at a State University

2014–15	2015–16	2016–17	2017–18	2018–19	2019–20
$12,192	$12,804	$13,446	$14,118	$14,820	$15,564

23. The table above summarizes the total cost per undergraduate student per year at a state university for each academic year from 2014–15 to 2019–20.

    If fees account for 8.75 percent of one year's total costs, what is the average fee increase per academic year? Round your answer to the nearest dollar.

24. A gardener planted a 20-inch tall sapling in his yard. Four months later, the sapling was 27 inches tall. By what percent did the height of the sapling increase over the four months?

    A) 7%

    B) 26%

    C) 35%

    D) 74%

25. From 1997 to 1998, company T's profits increased by 25 percent. From 1998 to 1999, company T's profits rose from $375 million to $483 million. By what percent did company T's profits increase from 1997 to 1999?

    A) 38%

    B) 49%

    C) 54%

    D) 61%

26. At a certain store, the price of a calculator is $150, the price of a radio is $75, and the price of a printer is 16 percent less than the price of a radio. By what percent is the price of a printer less than the price of a calculator?

    A) 39%

    B) 58%

    C) 63%

    D) 87%

27. A car that is traveling at a constant speed of 9 miles per hour is traveling at a constant speed of how many feet per second? (1 mile = 5,280 feet)

    A) 1.5

    B) 6.1

    C) 13.2

    D) 79.2

28. In a certain music store, every guitar is either a dreadnought or a parlor guitar. The ratio of dreadnoughts to parlor guitars in the music store is 4 to 15, and there is a total of 114 guitars in the music store. How many guitars in the music store are dreadnoughts?

    A) 24

    B) 29

    C) 34

    D) 46

29. The population of a town was 84,600 on January 1, 2016, and 74,025 on January 1, 2017. By what percent did the population of the town decrease from January 1, 2016, to January 1, 2017?

    A) 10.5%

    B) 12.5%

    C) 14.5%

    D) 17%

30. The perimeter of regular pentagon *P* is half the perimeter of regular hexagon *H*. What is the ratio of the length of a side of the pentagon to a side of the hexagon?

    A) 1:2

    B) 3:5

    C) 5:6

    D) 5:3

31. A jar contains red, white, and yellow candy pieces in the ratio of 9:5:4, respectively. When 7 pieces of red candy and 5 pieces of white candy are removed from the jar and 3 pieces of yellow candy are added, the ratio of red to white to yellow becomes 4:2:3. If the jar contains only these three colors of candy, how many pieces were originally in the jar?

32. Juan's air mattress deflates at a constant rate of 100 milliliters per minute. If Juan's air mattress contains 300 liters of air, how long will it take, in hours, for the air mattress to completely deflate? (Note: there are 1,000 milliliters in 1 liter).

Reflect

Directions: Take a few minutes to recall what you've learned and what you've been practicing in this chapter. Consider the following questions, jot down your best answer for each one, and then compare your reflections to the expert responses on the following page. Use your level of confidence to determine what to do next.

What is a ratio and how is it different from a proportion?

_____

_____

_____

If you're given a ratio of one quantity to another, what can you say about the total number of quantities?

_____

_____

_____

When doing unit conversions, how can you make sure you're doing them correctly?

_____

_____

_____

Suppose the value of something increases by 20 percent. How can you calculate the final value in the fewest number of steps? What if the value decreases by 20 percent?

_____

_____

_____

What is the percent change formula and what is the biggest pitfall to avoid when using it?

_____

_____

_____

Expert Responses

What is a ratio and how is it different from a proportion?

A ratio is the relative comparison of one quantity to another. For example, if the ratio of dogs to cats in an animal shelter is 3 to 5, then there are 3 dogs for every 5 cats. A proportion is two ratios set equal to each other.

If you're given a ratio of one quantity to another, what can you say about the total number of quantities?

Given a ratio, you know that the total must be a multiple of the sum of the ratio's parts. For example, if the ratio of dogs to cats is 3 to 5, then the total number of dogs and cats must be a multiple of 3 + 5, or 8. This means that when the SAT gives you one ratio, it's actually giving you several. If you're told that dogs:cats = 3:5, then you also know that dogs:total = 3:8 and cats:total = 5:8. You can use this "hidden" knowledge to your advantage.

When doing unit conversions, how can you make sure you're doing them correctly?

To do unit conversions correctly, set up the conversion in whichever way makes units cancel. For example, to convert 3 feet into inches, you multiply 3 feet by 12 inches per foot, because it cancels out the feet unit. If instead you multiplied 3 feet by 1 foot per 12 inches, then the resulting units would be "feet squared per inch," which makes no sense.

Suppose the value of something increases by 20 percent. How can you calculate the final value in the fewest number of steps? What if the value decreases by 20 percent?

The fastest way to increase a value by 20 percent is to multiply it by 1.2, which is 100% + 20% = 120%. Similarly, to decrease something by 20 percent, you multiply it by 0.8, as that is 100% − 20% = 80%.

What is the percent change formula and what is the biggest pitfall to avoid when using it?

The percent change formula is as follows:

$$\text{Percent change} = \frac{\text{amount of increase or decrease}}{\text{original amount}} \times 100\%$$

A common mistake is to put the new amount on the bottom of the fraction rather than the original amount.

Next Steps

If you answered most questions correctly in the "How Much Have You Learned?" section, and if your responses to the Reflect questions were similar to those of the SAT expert, then consider ratios and the related topics in this chapter to be an area of strength and move on to the next chapter. Come back to this topic periodically to prevent yourself from getting rusty.

If you don't yet feel confident, review those parts of this chapter that you have not yet mastered and try the questions you missed again. As always, be sure to review the explanations closely.

Answers and Explanations

1. D

Difficulty: Easy

Getting to the Answer: To answer a question that says "directly proportional," set two ratios equal to each other and solve for the missing amount. Be sure to match the units in the numerators and in the denominators on both sides of the proportion.

Because the first rate is given in minutes, write 1 hour as 60 minutes. Let t equal the number of topics the teachers can cover in a 60-minute period. Set up a proportion and solve for t:

$$\frac{9 \text{ topics}}{45 \text{ minutes}} = \frac{t \text{ topics}}{60 \text{ minutes}}$$
$$9(60) = 45(t)$$
$$540 = 45t$$
$$12 = t$$

Choice **(D)** is correct.

2. C

Difficulty: Easy

Getting to the Answer: Think about how your answer should look. A person weighs *less* on the Moon, so that person should weigh *more* on Earth. This means your answer must be greater than 29, so you can eliminate (A) right away.

Now, set up a proportion:

$$\frac{0.166 \text{ lb on Moon}}{1 \text{ lb on Earth}} = \frac{29 \text{ lb on Moon}}{p \text{ lb on Earth}}$$
$$0.166p = 29(1)$$
$$p \approx 174.7$$

The person weighs about 175 pounds on Earth. Choice **(C)** is correct.

3. B

Difficulty: Easy

Getting to the Answer: This is a typical proportion question. Use words first to write the proportion. Then translate from English into math. Let n equal the total number of parts made. Set up a proportion and solve for n. Be sure to match the units in the numerators and in the denominators on both sides of the proportion:

$$\frac{\text{defective parts}}{\text{number made}} = \frac{\text{defective parts}}{\text{number made}}$$
$$\frac{6}{3,500} = \frac{27}{n}$$
$$6n = 27(3,500)$$
$$6n = 94,500$$
$$n = 15,750$$

This means **(B)** is correct.

4. B

Difficulty: Hard

Getting to the Answer: This question has two unknowns: you don't know the starting number of either freshmen or sophomores. To solve for two unknowns, you need two equations. Let f represent the original number of freshmen in the auditorium and s represent the original number of sophomores. The starting ratio is $\frac{f}{s} = \frac{3}{10}$. Cross-multiplying yields $10f = 3s$. This is your first equation.

Set up a second equation to represent the adjusted number of freshmen and sophomores:

$$\frac{f + 270}{s + 120} = \frac{6}{5}$$
$$5(f + 270) = 6(s + 120)$$
$$5f + 1,350 = 6s + 720$$

You've determined from the first ratio that $10f = 3s$, and if you multiply this equation by 2, you get $20f = 6s$. Now substitute $20f$ for $6s$ in the above equation:

$$5f + 1,350 = 20f + 720$$
$$630 = 15f$$
$$42 = f$$

There were 42 freshmen in the auditorium to start, so **(B)** is correct.

5. D

Difficulty: Medium

Getting to the Answer: Use the known time of 5.5 minutes it takes Reyna to travel 1 mile to calculate the distance she can cover in 1.5 hours. So that you're working with the same units, first convert 1.5 hours to minutes: $1.5 \times 60 = 90$ minutes. Let d be the unknown distance and then set up a proportion to solve for d:

$$\frac{1}{5.5} = \frac{d}{90}$$
$$90 = 5.5d$$
$$\frac{90}{5.5} = d$$
$$d \cong 16$$

Therefore, **(D)** is correct.

6. A

Difficulty: Medium

Getting to the Answer: Since the answer choices are expressed as $\frac{y}{x} =$ and $\frac{y-x}{x} =$, cross-multiply the proportion and rewrite it to get an expression that matches the form of one of the answer choices. Solve for $\frac{y}{x}$:

$$\frac{x+y}{x} = \frac{4}{9}$$
$$9(x+y) = 4x$$
$$9x + 9y = 4x$$
$$9y = -5x$$
$$\frac{y}{x} = -\frac{5}{9}$$

This matches **(A)**.

Alternatively, you could rewrite the proportion as follows:

$$\frac{x}{x} + \frac{y}{x} = \frac{4}{9}$$
$$1 + \frac{y}{x} = \frac{4}{9}$$
$$\frac{y}{x} = \frac{4}{9} - 1$$
$$\frac{y}{x} = -\frac{5}{9}$$

Note that multiplying both sides of the proportion by -1 would give $-\frac{(x+y)}{x} = -\frac{4}{9}$ or $\frac{-x-y}{x} = -\frac{4}{9}$, which does not match (C) or (D).

7. C

Difficulty: Hard

Getting to the Answer: The ratio of physicists to total attendees is the number of physicists divided by the number of all attendees. Suppose x new physicists arrive at the symposium. The new number of physicists will be $123 + x$, and the new number of all attendees will be the original physicists (123) + biologists (270) + the newcomer physicists (x). The ratio of the first number over the second equals 2 to 5, so set up a proportion and solve for x:

$$\frac{123+x}{123+270+x} = \frac{2}{5}$$
$$\frac{123+x}{393+x} = \frac{2}{5}$$
$$5(123+x) = 2(393+x)$$
$$615 + 5x = 786 + 2x$$
$$3x = 171$$
$$x = 57$$

Therefore, **(C)** is correct.

8. A

Difficulty: Medium

Getting to the Answer: Map out your route from starting units to ending units, being mindful of the fact that the question deals with units of volume (cubic units). The starting quantity is in ft^3, and the desired quantity is in m^3. The only conversion factor you need is 1 m $\approx$ 3.28 ft, but you'll need to use it three times. Setting up your route to m^3, you get:

$$\frac{700 \text{ ft}^3}{1} \times \frac{1 \text{ m}}{3.28 \text{ ft}} \times \frac{1 \text{ m}}{3.28 \text{ ft}} \times \frac{1 \text{ m}}{3.28 \text{ ft}} = \frac{700}{(3.28)^3} \text{m}^3$$
$$\approx 19.84 \text{ m}^3$$

This matches **(A)**.

9. A

Difficulty: Hard

Getting to the Answer: Whenever multiple rates are given, pay very careful attention to the units. Starting with the number of pages the reporter typed, set up your ratios so that equivalent units cancel. Be sure your units match those in the answer choices:

$$25 \text{ pages} \times \frac{675 \text{ words}}{1 \text{ page}} \times \frac{1 \text{ second}}{3.75 \text{ words}}$$

$$\times \frac{1 \text{ minute}}{60 \text{ seconds}} \times \frac{1 \text{ hour}}{60 \text{ minutes}} = 1.25 \text{ hours}$$

Because 1.25 hours is not an answer choice, convert 0.25 to minutes: $0.25 \times 60 \text{ minutes} = 15 \text{ minutes}$, making **(A)** the correct answer.

10. A

Difficulty: Medium

Getting to the Answer: The 450° oven cooks $4.5 - 3 = 1.5$ more pounds per hour than the 350° oven. However, the question asks for the answer in ounces per 10 minutes, so convert from pounds per hour to ounces per minute, then multiply by 10 minutes:

$$\frac{1.5 \text{ lb}}{1 \text{ hr}} \times \frac{16 \text{ oz}}{1 \text{ lb}} \times \frac{1 \text{ hr}}{60 \text{ min}} \times 10 \text{ min} = 4 \text{ oz}$$

In 10 minutes, the oven at 450° can cook 4 ounces more than the oven at 350°, making **(A)** the correct answer.

11. 50

Difficulty: Medium

Getting to the Answer: Starting with the prescribed dosage, set up your ratios so that equivalent units cancel and you get drips per minute:

$$\frac{800 \text{ mL}}{8 \text{ hours}} \times \frac{30 \text{ drips}}{1 \text{ mL}} \times \frac{1 \text{ hour}}{60 \text{ minutes}} = 50 \frac{\text{drips}}{\text{minute}}$$

Grid in **50**.

12. 0.25

Difficulty: Easy

Getting to the Answer: The question provides the growth rate, in meters, over a 50-year period. You need to convert this to a rate of centimeters per day. Set up your ratios so that the units cancel:

$$\frac{46 \text{ meters}}{50 \text{ years}} \times \frac{100 \text{ centimeters}}{1 \text{ meter}} \times \frac{1 \text{ year}}{365 \text{ days}}$$

$$\cong 0.252 \frac{\text{centimeters}}{\text{day}}$$

You're told to round to the nearest hundredth of a centimeter, so grid in **.25**.

13. D

Difficulty: Easy

Getting to the Answer: The question asks for the approximate combined number of runners and weightlifters who were injured. Calculate the approximate number from each group who were injured and then add the numbers together:

$$3\% \times 308 = 0.03 \times 308 \cong 9$$
$$6\% \times 237 = 0.06 \times 237 \cong 14$$
$$9 + 4 = 23$$

Therefore, **(D)** is correct.

14. 3

Difficulty: Medium

Strategic Advice: First find the total number of attendees; then calculate the difference in the actual number of juniors and seniors.

Getting to the Answer: The question gives you the percents of sophomores, juniors, and seniors attending the conference, as well as the actual number of teachers. Add up all of the percents to find the total percent of the attendees who are *not* teachers: $15\% + 25\% + 30\% = 70\%$. Therefore, the 18 teachers account for $100\% - 70\% = 30\%$ of the attendees.

You can solve for the total number of attendees (the whole) by plugging in the corresponding values for percent and part into the equation part = percent × whole. Say the total number of attendees is *t*:

$$18 = 0.30t$$
$$\frac{18}{0.30} = t$$
$$t = 60$$

So the total number of attendees is 60. Juniors are 30% of this number and seniors are 25%, so the difference between juniors and seniors is 30% − 25% = 5%. Now calculate 5% of the total: 60 × 0.05 = 3. Thus, there are 3 more juniors than seniors. Grid in **3**.

15. B
Difficulty: Hard

Getting to the Answer: The question gives you the amount of 15% mixture and the desired concentration (20%) that the painter wants to achieve by adding an unknown quantity of 40% mixture. In effect, the question is asking you to calculate a weighted average where the desired average is known.

Let *x* represent the unknown number of gallons of the 40% mixture that the painter needs to add. Set up a weighted average equation using the known amount (20 gallons) of the 15% mixture and the unknown amount of the 40% mixture to equal the desired mixture concentration of 20%:

$$\frac{0.15(20) + 0.40(x)}{20 + x} = 0.20$$

Next, multiply both sides of the equation by the denominator and then solve for *x*:

$$0.15(20) + 0.40x = 0.20(20 + x)$$
$$3 + 0.40x = 4 + 0.20x$$
$$0.20x = 1$$
$$x = 5$$

Thus, the painter needs to add 5 gallons of the 40% mixture to achieve the desired 20% concentration of blue pigment. **(B)** is correct.

16. D
Difficulty: Medium

Getting to the Answer: You need to find the price of a share of the stock on October 1. You know that the price of a share was $75 on August 1 and that on September 1 the price was $10 higher than it was on August 1. Thus, on September 1, it was $75 + $10 = $85.

The question also states that the September 1 price is 80% of the October 1 price. Set up an equation where *p* represents the October 1 price:

$$0.8p = \$85$$
$$p = \frac{\$85}{0.8}$$
$$p = \$106.25$$

The question asks for the price to the nearest dollar, so **(D)** is correct.

17. C
Difficulty: Easy

Getting to the Answer: The formula for percent increase or decrease is $\frac{\text{actual change}}{\text{original amount}} \times 100\%$. In this case, that's $\frac{1,572 - 1,494}{1,494} \times 100\% \cong 5.2\%$. Therefore, **(C)** is correct.

If you chose (B), you likely divided by the new amount, $1,572, instead of the original amount, $1,494.

18. C
Difficulty: Easy

Getting to the Answer: The formula for percent increase or decrease is $\frac{\text{actual change}}{\text{original amount}} \times 100\%$. Since the price per share of stock started at $35 and ended up at $49, that's $\frac{49 - 35}{35} \times 100\% = 40\%$.

Therefore, **(C)** is correct.

19. B

Difficulty: Medium

Getting to the Answer: The question asks for a percent decrease in the number of coins from the larger jar to the smaller one. The formula for percent decrease is $\frac{\text{actual change}}{\text{original amount}} \times 100\%$. Jar X has 75 coins and jar Y has 54 coins. The phrase "less than" means that you're calculating percent decrease from a starting value of 75 coins (the "original amount"); the calculation is $\frac{75 - 54}{75} \times 100\% = \frac{21}{75} \times 100\% = 28\%$. Therefore, **(B)** is correct.

20. D

Difficulty: Medium

Strategic Advice: Begin by calculating the number of seniors and then figure out what percent greater this number is than the number of sophomores.

Getting to the Answer: The number of seniors is 75% greater than the number of juniors, so that is $80 + (0.75 \times 80)$, or $1.75 \times 80 = 140$.

The formula for percent increase is $\frac{\text{actual change}}{\text{original amount}} \times 100\%$. In this case, the actual change is the number of seniors minus the number of sophomores, $140 - 50$. The original amount is the number of sophomores because the question asks for a percent "greater than"—greater than the original amount, which is sophomores, or 50: $\frac{140 - 50}{50} \times 100\% = \frac{90}{50} \times 100\% = 180\%$. Thus, **(D)** is correct.

21. C

Difficulty: Hard

Strategic Advice: When presented with a two-part percent change scenario, you cannot simply add the two percents; you have to calculate the second percent change on the adjusted value that results from the first percent change.

Getting to the Answer: The price of the phone goes through two different changes: an initial discount of 36% and a second reduction of 25% from that discounted price. Because you don't know y, the original price of the phone, you can pick a number to make calculations easier.

Usually, the best number to pick when calculating the percent change of an unknown value is 100, so assume that the initial price of the phone was $100 (the numbers don't have to be realistic, just easy to work with). Now, calculate the resulting price after the first discount: 36% of $100 is $0.36 \times \$100 = \$36$, so the new price of the phone will be $\$100 - \$36 = \$64$.

Next, calculate the change in price after an additional 25% off of the current price of $64: 25% of $64 is $0.25 \times \$64 = \$16$, so the final price will be $\$64 - \$16 = \$48$. (Note you could have also calculated the new price by subtracting the percent discount from 100 percent: $100\% - 25\% = 75\%$, so $0.75 \times \$64 = \$48$.)

The formula for percent change is $\frac{\text{actual change}}{\text{original amount}} \times 100\%$.

Use the starting price of $100 and the final price of $48:

$\frac{100 - 48}{100} \times 100\% = \frac{52}{100} \times 100\% = 52\%$.

Thus, **(C)** is correct.

22. C

Difficulty: Hard

Getting to the Answer: Although the full-time and part-time employees are separate groups, the total number of employees in each group is the same. Thus, you don't need to calculate the individual number of full- and part-time employees who have benefits. Instead, find the difference as a percent, then find that percent of 250 to get the answer in one step.

Be careful: 74 percent of part-time employees *don't* qualify for benefits. This means that $100\% - 74\% = 26\%$ of them do qualify. Since 92 percent of full-time employees qualify for benefits, the percent difference is $92 - 26 = 66$. Find 66 percent of 250: $250 \times 0.66 = 165$. **(C)** is correct.

23. 59

Difficulty: Hard

Category: Percents

Getting to the Answer: Don't switch on autopilot and do five separate cost increase calculations because you can do just one and save time. First, determine the total increase from 2014–15 through 2019–20: $15,564 − $12,192 = $3,372. Dividing $3,372 by 5 (the number of increases) gives $674.40, the average increase per year. To determine what portion of this amount is fees, find 8.75% of $674.40: 0.0875 × $674.40 = $59.01. Rounded to the nearest dollar, the correct answer is 59. Grid in **59**.

24. C

Difficulty: Easy

Category: Percent Change

Getting to the Answer: The formula for percent increase or decrease is $\dfrac{\text{actual change}}{\text{original amount}} \times 100\%$.
In this case, that works out to

$$\frac{27-20}{20} \times 100\% = \frac{7}{20} \times 100\% = 0.35 \times 100\% = 35\%.$$

Hence, **(C)** is correct.

25. D

Difficulty: Hard

Category: Percent Change

Strategic Advice: Begin by determining how much profit company T made in 1997 so that you can calculate the percent increase in profit from 1997 to 1999.

Getting to the Answer: The question indicates that the 1998 profit of $375 million was 25% greater than the 1997 profit. Therefore, you can set up this equation: 125% × 1997 profit = $375 million. This can be written as $1.25p = \$375$ million, where p represents the 1997 profit. Divide both sides by 1.25 to find that $p = \$300$ million. Thus, the actual change in profit from 1997 to 1999 was $483 million − $300 million = $183 million. The formula for percent increase or decrease is $\dfrac{\text{actual change}}{\text{original amount}} \times 100\%$. In this scenario, that's $\dfrac{183}{300} \times 100\% = 61\%$. **(D)** is correct.

26. B

Difficulty: Medium

Category: Percent Change

Strategic Advice: Before you can calculate the percent difference between the price of a printer and the price of a calculator, you need to determine the price of the printer.

Getting to the Answer: The question indicates that the price of the printer is 16% less than the price of the radio, or 16% less than $75. Therefore, the price of the printer is $(100 − 16)\% \times \$75 = 0.84 \times \$75 = \$63$. Thus, the difference in price between the calculator and the printer is $150 − $63 = $87. With this value, you can determine what percent less this is than $150.

The formula for percent increase or decrease is $\dfrac{\text{actual change}}{\text{original amount}} \times 100\%$. Hence, the price of the printer is $\dfrac{87}{150} \times 100\% = 58\%$ less than the price of the calculator, so **(B)** is correct.

27. C

Difficulty: Easy

Category: Unit Conversions

Getting to the Answer: The question provides the speed of a car in miles per hour and asks for the speed in feet per second. Set up a ratio so that the units cancel:

$$\frac{9 \text{ miles}}{1 \text{ hour}} \times \frac{5,280 \text{ feet}}{1 \text{ mile}} \times \frac{1 \text{ hour}}{60 \text{ minutes}} \times \frac{1 \text{ minute}}{60 \text{ seconds}}$$
$$= 13.2 \frac{\text{feet}}{\text{second}}$$

Hence, **(C)** is correct.

28. A

Difficulty: Medium

Category: Proportions

Getting to the Answer: This is a proportions question that requires you to relate the total known number of guitars to the given ratio in order to find the unknown number of dreadnoughts, a type of guitar. First, define the relationship in the proportion with words. Then, translate from English into math. Let d equal the unknown number of dreadnoughts. Set up a proportion and cross-multiply to solve for d:

$$\frac{\text{number of dreadnoughts in the ratio}}{\text{total number of guitars in the ratio}}$$
$$= \frac{\text{actual number of dreadnoughts}}{\text{actual number of guitars}}$$
$$\frac{4}{4+15} = \frac{d}{114}$$
$$4 \times 114 = (4+15)d$$
$$456 = 19d$$
$$24 = d$$

Thus, **(A)** is correct.

Here's another way to approach this question. The total of the two values in the ratio 4:15 is 19. The total number of guitars is 114, which is 6 × 19. Thus, the number of dreadnoughts is 6 × 4 = 24.

29. B

Difficulty: Easy

Category: Percent Change

Getting to the Answer: The formula for percent increase or decrease is $\frac{\text{actual change}}{\text{original amount}} \times 100\%$.

In this case, that works out to

$$\frac{84,600 - 74,025}{84,600} \times 100\% = \frac{10,575}{84,600} \times 100\% = 12.5\%.$$

Choice **(B)** is correct.

30. B

Difficulty: Medium

Category: Proportions

Getting to the Answer: Call the length of each side of the pentagon p and the length of each side of the hexagon h. The perimeter of the pentagon is 5 × p and the perimeter of the hexagon is 6 × h, so you can write

the proportion $\frac{5p}{6h} = \frac{1}{2}$. Rather than cross-multiplying, multiply both sides by $\frac{6}{5}$ which is $\frac{6}{5} \times \frac{5p}{6h} = \frac{6}{5} \times \frac{1}{2}$. This simplifies to $\frac{p}{h} = \frac{6}{10} = \frac{3}{5}$. This is another way of expressing 3:5, so **(B)** is correct.

31. 54

Difficulty: Hard

Category: Proportions

Getting to the Answer: Since you are given both the initial values of the different-colored candies and their values after additions and deletions in terms of ratios, you can express these as amounts relative to each other. There are the least amount of yellow candies, so you can write that the initial number of yellow candies is y, the number of white candies is $\frac{5}{4}y$, and the number of red ones is $\frac{9}{4}y$.

Now you can compare the "before and after" quantities of the red or white candies in terms of y. If you choose to look at the red candies, after the deletions and additions, the number of red candies is $\frac{4}{3}(y+3)$ because 3 yellow candies were added. But, 7 reds were removed, so the equation is $\frac{9}{4}y - 7 = \frac{4}{3}(y+3)$. Multiply both sides by 12 to clear the fractions: $27y - 84 = 16y + 48$. So, $11y = 132$, and $y = 12$.

The original number of white candies is $\frac{5}{4}(12) = 15$, and the original number of red is $\frac{9}{4}(12) = 27$. So, the total number of all three colors before the changes is $12 + 15 + 27 = 54$. Grid in **54**.

Another way to solve this question is by picking numbers, making sure they are permissible according to the ratios. You know that the ratio of red to white is 9 to 5, and that after 7 red and 5 white are removed, the ratio will be 4 to 2—in other words, there will be twice as many red as white. Start with 9 red and 5 white candies and work up from there until you find a multiple that works:

9 red, 5 white
2 red, 0 white: doesn't work

18 red, 10 white
11 red, 5 white: doesn't work

27 red, 15 white
20 red, 10 white: this works!

The common multiplier is 3, and there are
$4 \times 3 = 12$ yellow candies. The total is
$27 + 15 + 12 = $ **54** candies.

32. 50

Difficulty: Medium

Category: Unit Conversion

Getting to the Answer: Since the rate of deflation is

$100 \frac{mL}{min}$, convert the initial volume of 300 liters of air to

milliliters: $300 \, \cancel{L} \times \frac{1{,}000 \text{ mL}}{1 \, \cancel{L}} = 300{,}000 \text{ mL}$.

Then, to determine the number of hours it will take
for the air mattress to completely deflate, set up
the calculation so that equivalent units cancel:

$300{,}000 \, \cancel{mL} \times \frac{1 \, \cancel{min}}{100 \, \cancel{mL}} \times \frac{1 \text{ hr}}{60 \, \cancel{min}} = 50 \text{ hr}$

Grid in **50**.

CHAPTER 8

Tables, Statistics, and Probability

LEARNING OBJECTIVES

After completing this chapter, you will be able to:

- Draw inferences about data presented in a variety of graphical formats
- Find an unknown value given the average
- Calculate mean, median, mode, and range
- Describe standard deviation and margin of error
- Determine whether a survey is valid or biased
- Draw inferences about surveys and data samples
- Calculate probabilities based on data sets

50/600 SmartPoints®

How Much Do You Know?

Directions: Try the questions that follow. Show your work so that you can compare your solutions to the ones found in the Check Your Work section immediately after this question set. The "Category" heading in the explanation for each question gives the title of the lesson that covers how to solve it. If you answered the question(s) for a given lesson correctly, and if your scratchwork looks like ours, you may be able to move quickly through that lesson. If you answered incorrectly or used a different approach, you may want to take your time on that lesson.

Questions 1 and 2 refer to the following information.

The amount of glucose, or sugar, in a person's blood is the primary indicator of diabetes. When a person without diabetes fasts (doesn't eat) for eight hours prior to taking a blood sugar test, that person's glucose level will be below 100 milligrams per deciliter. An individual is considered at risk for diabetes, but is not diagnosed as diabetic, when fasting glucose levels are between 100 and 125. If the level is above 125, the person is considered to have diabetes. The following table shows the ages and glucose levels of a group of study participants.

Study Results				
Age Group	<100 mg/dL	100–125 mg/dL	>125 mg/dL	Total
18–25	9	22	17	48
26–35	16	48	34	98
36–45	19	35	40	94
Older than 45	12	27	21	60
Total	56	132	112	300

1. According to the data, which age group had the smallest percentage of people with a healthy blood sugar level?

   A) 18–25

   B) 26–35

   C) 36–45

   D) Older than 45

2. Based on the table, if a single participant is selected at random from all the participants, what is the probability that he or she will be at risk for diabetes and be at least 36 years old?

   A) $\dfrac{7}{60}$

   B) $\dfrac{11}{25}$

   C) $\dfrac{31}{77}$

   D) $\dfrac{31}{150}$

History Majors Declared at College X

Year	Number of History Majors
2010	225
2011	287
2012	162
2013	240
2014	s

3. The table above shows the number of history majors declared each year at a certain college from 2010 to 2014. If the median number of history majors declared for the five years was 225, what is the greatest possible value of s ?

A) 161

B) 225

C) 239

D) 288

4. A writers association sponsored a nationwide convention attended by 1,650 nonfiction writers. Before the convention, the association surveyed 150 of the writers who were planning to attend (chosen at random) about their lunch preferences. Thirty-eight said they preferred salads, 23 preferred pizza, 59 preferred sandwiches, and 30 preferred grilled chicken. Based on the results of this survey, how many of the writers attending the convention can be expected to want sandwiches for lunch?

5. A researcher conducted a poll to determine how many people in a city of 100,000 residents enjoy the taste of non-dairy milks such as coconut milk or almond milk. The researcher polled 800 city residents who are allergic to dairy. Of those polled, 72 percent responded that they enjoyed the taste of non-dairy milks.

Which of the following indicates why the survey results would not allow for a reliable conclusion about the taste preferences of the city's residents?

A) The researcher did not ask people if they prefer the taste of dairy milk to non-dairy milks.

B) The survey sample is not representative of the city's residents.

C) The population of the city is too large to get a reliable survey sample.

D) The survey sample likely consisted of only adults and did not consider the opinion of children.

Cookies Baked

	Chocolate Chip	Oatmeal Raisin	Total
With Nuts		40	
Without Nuts			104
Total			186

6. A baker makes 186 cookies. Some are chocolate chip and some are oatmeal raisin, and both kinds are made with and without nuts, as shown in the table above. Because they are more popular, the baker makes $\frac{2}{3}$ of the cookies chocolate chip. If a chocolate chip cookie is chosen at random, what is the probability that it will have nuts?

A) $\frac{21}{93}$

B) $\frac{21}{62}$

C) $\frac{41}{93}$

D) $\frac{21}{41}$

Check Your Work

1. B

Difficulty: Medium

Category: Tables and Graphs

Getting to the Answer: To calculate the percentage of people in each age group with a healthy blood sugar level (<100 mg/dL), divide the number of people in that age group with a healthy blood sugar level by the total number of participants in that same age group and multiply by 100%. Choice **(B)** is correct because $\frac{16}{98} \times 100\% \approx 0.1633 \times 100\% = 16.33\%$, which is a lower percentage than in the other age groups (18.75% for 18–25; 20.21% for 36–45; and 20% for Older than 45).

2. D

Difficulty: Medium

Category: Probability

Getting to the Answer: This question requires careful reading of the table. The first criterion is fairly straight-forward—you're looking for a participant with a blood sugar level in the 100–125 mg/dL range, so focus on that column in the table. The second criterion is a bit trickier—*at least 36 years old* means you'll need to use the values in both the row for 36–45 and the row for Older than 45. Within the 100–125 mg/dL range, there are 35 in the 36–45 age group and 27 in the Older than 45 age group, resulting in a total of $35 + 27 = 62$ out of 300 total participants overall. The probability of randomly selecting one participant who fits the criteria, therefore, is $\frac{62}{300}$, which reduces to $\frac{31}{150}$, or **(D)**.

3. B

Difficulty: Medium

Category: Statistics

Getting to the Answer: The median is the middle number in a series of numbers. Arrange the number of history majors from least to greatest, making sure that 225 is in the middle. Use s to balance out the number of history majors on either side of 225. Because there are already two numbers above the median (240 and 287), there must be two numbers below the median, 162 and s:

s, 162, 225, 240, 287

or

162, s, 225, 240, 287

Because s could be on either side of 162, it could be anything less than or equal to 225. Its greatest possible value is therefore 225, which is **(B)**.

4. 649

Difficulty: Medium

Category: Surveys and Data Samples

Getting to the Answer: The question indicates that of the 150 survey respondents, 59 wanted sandwiches. To find the number of the writers attending the convention who can be expected to want sandwiches for lunch, set up a proportion using the number of survey respondents who want sandwiches, the total number of survey respondents, and the total number of writers attending the convention: $\frac{59}{150} = \frac{x}{1,650}$. Cross-multiply to find that $x = 649$. Grid in **649**.

5. B

Difficulty: Medium

Category: Surveys and Data Samples

Getting to the Answer: Determine who is being surveyed and what results are intended. In this question, the intended result is to determine whether people in a large city like non-dairy milks. To obtain a representative sample of the population, the survey should randomly select individuals from the population. However, the researcher polled only people who have a dairy allergy. Those people may have acquired tastes and may not be representative of the general population of the city, making **(B)** the correct answer.

6. B

Difficulty: Medium

Category: Probability

Getting to the Answer: The table is not complete, so your first step is to fill in the missing values. Start with what you know and work from there. It may not be necessary to complete the entire table, so stop when you have enough information to answer the question.

There are 186 cookies total and 104 are without nuts, which means $186 - 104 = 82$ have nuts. Because the table already indicates that 40 of those cookies are oatmeal raisin, $82 - 40 = 42$ are chocolate chip. Recall that $\frac{2}{3}$ of the total number of cookies are chocolate chip, which means there are $\frac{2}{3} \times 186 = 124$ chocolate chip cookies, so you can fill this number in the "Total" row of the chocolate chip column. You do not need to fill in any more of the table because the question asks only about chocolate chips cookies with nuts. There are 124 chocolate chip cookies total and 42 of them have nuts, so the probability of randomly choosing one with nuts is $\frac{42}{124}$, or $\frac{21}{62}$, which is **(B)**.

Tables and Graphs

LEARNING OBJECTIVES

After this lesson, you will be able to:

● Draw inferences about data presented in a variety of graphical formats

● Find an unknown value given the average

To solve a question like this:

Appliance Sales

```
            X       X
        X   X       X               X
        X   X   X   X   X   X        X
    ─────────────────────────────────────
    1   2   3   4   5   6   7   8   9   10
```

Number Sold

An appliance salesperson sets a goal to sell an average of 6 appliances per day for the first two weeks of his new job. The dot plot shows the number he sold each day during the first 13 days. What is the minimum number of appliances he must sell on the 14th day in order to reach his goal?

A) 5

B) 6

C) 7

D) 8

You need to know this:

The SAT uses some straightforward methods of representing data sets that you are certainly already familiar with. You likely don't need to review, for example, how to look up information in a table or read a bar chart. There are, however, some less common types of plots that show up from time to time that can be confusing at first glance.

● **Tables, bar charts, and line graphs** show up all the time in the Math sections (and in the Reading and Writing & Language sections, too). They shouldn't be difficult to interpret, but it's helpful to keep in mind that the test maker often includes more information than you actually need. It's important to consider what the question asks for so that you find only the information that you need.

● **Frequency tables and dot plots** are ways of representing how many times a data point appears within a data set. The sample problem presents its data as a dot plot:

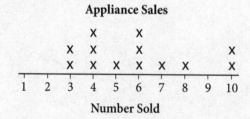

Appliance Sales

```
            X       X
        X   X       X               X
        X   X   X   X   X   X        X
    ─────────────────────────────────────
    1   2   3   4   5   6   7   8   9   10
```

Number Sold

Each "X" represents one instance in the data set of each "number sold." So, for example, there were two different days on which this person sold 3 appliances, three different days on which this person sold 4 appliances, and so on. The data could just as easily be written as a data set: {3, 3, 4, 4, 4, 5, 6, 6, 6, 7, 8, 10, 10}, or placed in a frequency table:

Number Sold	Frequency
1	0
2	0
3	2
4	3
5	1
6	3
7	1
8	1
9	0
10	2

- **Histograms** look a lot like bar charts and can be read in the same way, but they are similar to frequency tables and dot plots in that they show how many times a certain value shows up in a data set for a variable. The histogram for the appliances data set would look like this:

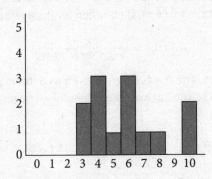

Notice that the histogram is basically the same as the dot plot for this data set. Histograms are better for representing larger data sets for which individual dots would be difficult to count.

You need to do this:

- When presented with a question that uses a graph or table to present information, first inspect the format of the graph or table. What kind of graph or table is it? What information is presented on each axis? What information do you need to find in order to answer the question?

- Find the information you need from the table or graph and then use the information for any calculation the question might require, such as taking the average, finding the median, or thinking about standard deviation.

- Use the average formula, average $= \dfrac{\text{sum}}{\text{number of items}}$, to find unknowns. For example, if you know that the average of 5 terms is 7, and you know that 4 of the terms are 3, 6, 8, and 9, you can call the last term x and plug into the equation, then solve for x:

$$7 = \frac{3+6+8+9+x}{5}.$$
$$35 = 26 + x$$
$$x = 9$$

Explanation

This question gives you an average and asks for a missing value, which is a kind of calculation that shows up in word problems all the time. First, set up a general equation for the average:

$$\text{Average} = \frac{\text{sum}}{\text{number of items}}$$

The scenario takes place over 14 days, and the average is given as 6 items per day. Let a represent the unknown number of appliances sold on the 14th day and then fill in the number of appliances sold the previous days from the dot plot:

$$6 = \frac{3+3+4+4+4+5+6+6+6+7+8+10+10+a}{14}$$

Multiply both sides by 14 to get rid of the fraction and simplify the addition on the right before isolating a:

$$84 = 3+3+4+4+4+5+6+6+6+7+8+10+10+a$$
$$84 = 76 + a$$
$$a = 8$$

Choice **(D)** is correct.

Try on Your Own

Directions: Take as much time as you need on these questions. Work carefully and methodically. There will be an opportunity for timed practice at the end of the chapter.

Questions 1 and 2 refer to the following information.

	Bob's Bookshop	Clara's Bookshop	Derek's Bookshop	Evelyn's Bookshop	Total
Monday	14	7	15	12	48
Tuesday	8	13	15	13	49
Wednesday	10	13	12	14	49
Thursday	8	15	14	10	47
Friday	13	7	10	9	39
Total	53	55	66	58	232

HINT: For Q1, fraction $= \frac{part}{whole}$. Which *part* is the question asking for? Out of which *whole*?

---

1. Which of the four bookshops made the greatest fraction of its total sales on Tuesday?

    A) Bob's Bookshop

    B) Clara's Bookshop

    C) Derek's Bookshop

    D) Evelyn's Bookshop

2. What fraction of all the books sold on Monday, Wednesday, and Friday were sold at Derek's Bookshop and Evelyn's Bookshop?

    A) $\frac{9}{29}$

    B) $\frac{11}{32}$

    C) $\frac{9}{17}$

    D) $\frac{18}{31}$

Questions 3 and 4 refer to the following information.

Numerous health studies have found that people who eat breakfast are generally healthier and weigh less than people who skip this meal. The following table shows the results of a study related to this topic.

Breakfast Study Results

	Breakfast ≤1 Time per Week	Breakfast 2–4 Times per Week	Breakfast 5–7 Times per Week	Total
Within Healthy Weight Range	6	15	36	57
Outside Healthy Weight Range	38	27	9	74
Total	44	42	45	131

3. What percent of the participants who were outside a healthy weight range ate breakfast one or fewer times per week?

    A) 29.01%

    B) 51.35%

    C) 56.49%

    D) 86.36%

HINT: For Q4, which group in the study is of interest to this company?

---

4. A large company that provides breakfast for all its employees wants to determine how many of them are likely to be within a healthy weight range, given that all the employees take advantage of the free breakfast all five weekdays. If the company has 3,000 employees, and assuming the participants in the study are a good representative sample, about how many of the employees are likely to be within a healthy weight range?

    A) 825

    B) 1,030

    C) 1,900

    D) 2,400

Questions 5 and 6 refer to the following information.

When people sleep, they experience various types of brain activity. Scientists have classified these types of activity into four sleep stages: 1, 2, 3, and 4 (also known as REM). Stage 3 is the only stage considered to be deep sleep. Suppose a person went to a sleep clinic to have his or her sleeping brainwaves analyzed. A technician monitored the person's brainwaves in 15-minute intervals, for 8 continuous hours, and categorized them into one of the four stages. The bar graph below shows the results of the one-night study.

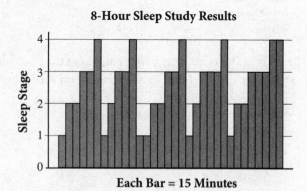

8-Hour Sleep Study Results

Sleep Stage

Each Bar = 15 Minutes

6. After the completion of the one-night study, the patient was monitored an additional four nights. Over the total number of nights that the patient spent at the clinic, he spent an average of 180 minutes in stage 3 sleep per night. If the patient spent an average of 175 minutes in stage 3 sleep on the second, third, and fourth nights, how many minutes did he spend in stage 3 sleep on the last night?

5. Based on the graph, how many minutes did the patient spend in non-deep sleep over the course of the entire night?

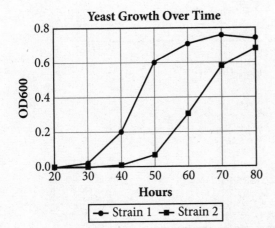

7. A microbiologist is comparing the growth rates of two different yeast strains. She indirectly measures the number of yeast cells by recording the optical density (OD600) of each strain every 10 hours. The measurements are presented in the graph above. Based on the data, which of the following is NOT a true statement?

A) Between hours 30 and 80, Strain 1 had a higher OD600 reading than Strain 2.

B) The growth rate of Strain 2 was less than the growth rate of Strain 1 until hour 50, at which point Strain 1's growth rate became the lesser one.

C) Between hours 50 and 70, Strain 2's OD600 reading increased by approximately 0.03 every hour.

D) The growth rate of Strain 1 was greater than the growth rate of Strain 2 throughout the monitored period.

Statistics

To answer a question like this:

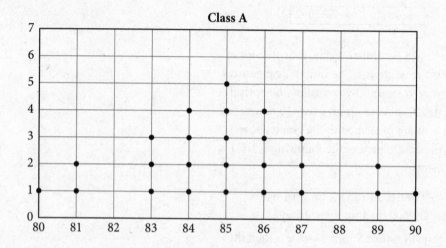

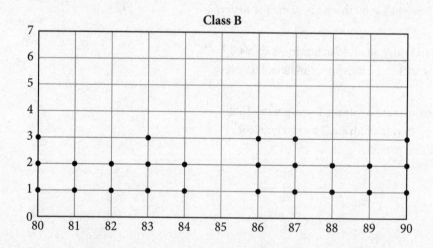

Two classes of 25 students each took an identical exam. Their percent correct scores are shown in the dot plots above. If M_A and S_A are the median and standard deviation, respectively, of class A, and M_B and S_B are the median and standard deviation, respectively, of class B, then which of the following statements is true?

A) $M_A < M_B$ and $S_A < S_B$

B) $M_A > M_B$ and $S_A < S_B$

C) $M_A > M_B$ and $S_A > S_B$

D) $M_A < M_B$ and $S_A > S_B$

You need to know this:

Suppose a nurse took a patient's pulse at different times of day and found it to be 75, 78, 71, 71, and 68. Here are six fundamental statistics figures you can determine for this data set:

- **Mean (also called arithmetic mean or average):** The sum of the values divided by the number of values. For this data set, the mean pulse is $\frac{75+78+71+71+68}{5} = \frac{363}{5} = 72.6$.

- **Median:** The value that is in the middle of the set *when the values are arranged in ascending order*. The pulse values in ascending order are 68, 71, 71, 75, and 78. The middle term is the third term, making the median 71. (If the list consists of an even number of values, the median is the average of the middle two values.)

- **Mode:** The value that occurs most frequently. The value that appears more than any other is 71, which appears twice (while all other numbers appear only once), so it is the mode. If more than one value appears the most often, that's okay; a set of data can have multiple modes. For example, if the nurse took the patient's pulse a sixth time and it was 68, then both 71 and 68 would be modes for this data set.

- **Range:** The difference between the highest and lowest values. In this data set, the lowest and highest values are 68 and 78, respectively, so the range is $78 - 68 = 10$.

- **Standard deviation:** A measure of how far a typical data point is from the mean. A low standard deviation means most values in the set are fairly close to the mean; a high standard deviation means there is much more spread in the data set. On the SAT, *you will need to know what standard deviation is and what it tells you about a set of data, but you won't have to calculate it.*

- **Margin of error:** A description of the maximum expected difference between a true statistics measure (for example, the mean or median) for a data pool and that same statistics measure for a random sample from the data pool. A lower margin of error is achieved by increasing the size of the random sample. As with standard deviation, *you will need to know what a margin of error is on the SAT, but you won't be asked to calculate one.*

You need to do this:

- To compare two standard deviations, look at how spread out the data set is. The more clustered the data, the lower the standard deviation.

- To find the median, arrange *all* values in order. In a dot plot or frequency distribution table, that means finding the group with the middle value.

Explanation:

Start with the standard deviation. The scores in class A are more clustered around the mean, so the standard deviation for class A will be smaller than that for class B, where the scores are more spread out. Eliminate (B) and (C).

To calculate the medians of the two classes, you need to find the middle value in each data set. Each class has 25 students, so the middle score will be the 13th term. Count from the left of each dot plot to find that the 13th score for class A is 85 and for class B is 86. So the median for class B is greater. **(A)** is correct.

Try on Your Own

Directions: Take as much time as you need on these questions. Work carefully and methodically. There will be an opportunity for timed practice at the end of the chapter.

Questions 8 and 9 refer to the following information.

An anthropologist chose 250 citizens at random from each of two European countries and separated them into groups based on how many languages they spoke. The results are shown in the table below.

Number of Languages	Country A	Country B
1	55	70
2	80	30
3	50	20
4	40	70
5	25	60

There are a total of 550,000 citizens in country A and 1.3 million citizens in country B.

8. What is the median number of languages spoken by the sample of citizens from country B?

A) 1

B) 2

C) 3

D) 4

9. Based on the data in the table, which of the following statements most accurately reflects the estimated total number of citizens who speak multiple languages in both countries?

A) Half as many citizens in both countries combined speak exactly five languages as citizens who speak exactly four languages.

B) Twice as many citizens in both countries combined speak exactly five languages as citizens who speak exactly four languages.

C) The number of citizens in both countries combined who speak exactly two languages is less than the number of citizens who speak exactly four languages.

D) The number of citizens in both countries combined who speak exactly two languages is greater than the number of citizens who speak exactly four languages.

HINT: For Q10, when you see the word *consistent,* think "standard deviation."

	Charles	Gautam	Brin
Run 1	8.3	8.5	8.4
Run 2	7.7	8.0	8.0
Run 3	7.1	8.5	7.5
Run 4	6.6	7.8	9.0
Run 5	8.0	8.1	7.5
Run 6	6.6	7.5	7.2
Mean Score	7.38	8.07	7.93
Standard Deviation	0.73	0.39	0.67

10. Charles, Gautam, and Brin participated in a snowboarding competition. The scores for each of their six qualifying runs are shown in the table above. According to the data, which of the following is a valid conclusion?

A) Charles had the smallest mean score, so his performance was the least consistent.

B) Gautam had the smallest standard deviation, so his performance was the most consistent.

C) Charles had the largest standard deviation, so his performance was the most consistent.

D) Brin had the highest score on any one run, so her performance was the most consistent.

Ages of Used Cars in Dealer Inventory

Age (Model Years)	Number of Cars
1	3
2	5
3	18
4	17
5	11
6	6
7	2

11. The table above shows the distribution of the ages (in model years) of the cars in a certain dealer's inventory. Which of the following correctly lists the mean, median, and mode of the ages of the cars in ascending order?

A) Mean, Median, Mode

B) Median, Mode, Mean

C) Mode, Mean, Median

D) Mode, Median, Mean

HINT: For Q12, start with the most definite information. What
do you know, given the average of the first 12 days?

12. A company produces an equal number of a certain
    product each working day in the month. The daily
    reject rates for the first 12 days of this month
    ranged from 0.0 percent to 1.5 percent with an
    average of 0.4 percent. If there are 22 working
    days this month and the company's monthly reject
    goal is 0.5 percent or less, what is the maximum
    reject rate, as a percent, for the 13th day that would
    still enable the company to attain its goal for the
    month? (Round your answer to the nearest tenth
    and ignore the percent sign when gridding your
    response.)

Surveys and Data Samples

LEARNING OBJECTIVES

After this lesson, you will be able to:

- Determine whether a survey is valid or biased
- Draw inferences about surveys and data samples

To answer a question like this:

A book club wanted to determine the average number of books read each year by residents of a certain town, so it conducted a survey of 100 patrons of the town's public library. The average number of books read per year by these 100 patrons was 51.5. Which of the following statements must be true based on this information?

A) The survey is biased due to a poor choice of sampling method.

B) The survey is not biased and will likely produce a correct estimate of the number of books read annually by the town's residents.

C) The average number of books read annually by all the town's residents is 51.5.

D) The average number of books read per town resident per year cannot be determined from such a small sample.

You need to know this:

You will see occasional questions on the SAT Math sections that do not test any calculation or even your ability to interpret numerical data. Instead, these questions test your ability to draw logical conclusions about surveys and data sampling methods.

Answering these questions correctly hinges on your ability to tell whether a data sample is **representative** of the larger population. A representative sample is a small group that shares key characteristics with a larger group you are trying to draw conclusions about.

A sample that is selected truly at random is generally representative of the larger group. For example, a scientist who wants to learn the average height of the penguins in a colony of 200 might measure the heights of a random sample of only 20 penguins. As long as the 20 penguins are selected at random, their average height will approximate the average height of the birds in the entire colony.

On the other hand, a sample that is not selected at random may not be representative and may lead to a biased conclusion. For instance, imagine that a small town uses volunteer firefighters and that a stipulation for becoming a volunteer firefighter is living within a mile of the fire station. If you wanted to know what percent of households in the town include at least one volunteer firefighter, you would need to survey a random sample of households from the entire town, not just a sample of households within a mile of the fire station. A sample of households within a mile of the fire station would be a biased sample and would lead to an erroneous conclusion (namely, that the percent of households in the town that include at least one volunteer firefighter is higher than it actually is).

You need to do this:

- Check whether the data sample represents the larger population. If it doesn't, the survey is biased.
- In questions that ask you to draw a conclusion from a random (unbiased) sample, look for the answer choice for which the representative sample accurately reflects the larger population. For example, in a question asking for a conclusion based on a sample of librarians, the correct answer will match the sample to a larger population of librarians, not to a population of, say, accountants.

Explanation:

The sample in this question includes 100 public library patrons. This is not a randomly selected sample. It's a good bet that frequent readers of books will be overrepresented at a public library. Thus, the survey is biased, so **(A)** is correct.

Try on Your Own

Directions: Take as much time as you need on these questions. Work carefully and methodically. There will be an opportunity for timed practice at the end of the chapter.

HINT: For Q13, who is in the survey group? Who is in the larger population? Are these groups different? If so, the survey is likely biased.

---

13. A railroad company is planning to build a new station along one of its busiest lines into the downtown area where many commuters work. The company chooses a town where it plans to build the new station. To assess the opinion of the town's residents, the company surveys a sample of 200 residents who commute to the downtown area for work. Over 80 percent of those surveyed are in favor of building the new station.

    Which of the following is true about the survey's reliability?

    A) It is unreliable because the survey sample is not representative of the entire town.

    B) It is unreliable because the survey sample is too small.

    C) It is reliable because nobody in the survey sample works for the railroad company.

    D) It is reliable because the survey sample excludes people who do not ride the train.

14. A bottled water company conducts a survey to find out how many bottles of water people consume per day. If a representative and random sample of 500 people is chosen from a population estimated to be 50,000, which of the following accurately describes how the mean of the sample data relates to the estimated mean of the entire population?

    A) The mean of the sample data is equal to the estimated mean of the population.

    B) The mean of the sample data cannot be used to estimate the mean of the much larger population.

    C) The mean of the sample data should be multiplied by 100 to get the estimated mean of the population.

    D) The mean of the sample data should be multiplied by 1,000 to get the estimated mean of the population.

15. A department store manager wants to determine why customers return the products they buy. The manager surveyed randomly selected customers and asked them to explain why they were returning their products. This sample included 70 customers who were returning dinnerware, of whom 80 percent indicated that at least one piece of dinnerware was chipped or broken.

    Which of the following conclusions is best supported by the sample data?

    A) Most of the products returned to the store contain chipped or broken pieces.

    B) Dinnerware products are more likely to contain chipped or broken pieces than other products.

    C) Most customers returning dinnerware returned products containing chipped or broken pieces.

    D) At least 80 percent of the products sold at the store contain chipped or broken pieces.

16. The owner of a miniature golf course wants to determine what color golf ball is most popular at the course. The owner asked 150 randomly surveyed children what color they prefer. Approximately 60 percent of them said they prefer red, while approximately 30 percent of them said blue.

    This data best supports which of the following conclusions?

    A) Most people prefer a red golf ball when playing miniature golf.

    B) Red golf balls are used twice as often for miniature golf as blue golf balls.

    C) Most children at the miniature golf course prefer a red golf ball.

    D) Approximately 10 percent of miniature golf players prefer a white golf ball.

HINT: For Q17, find the result of the sample in the chart, and then apply that result to the larger group.

---

17. A candy company sells jelly beans in five colors: black, green, orange, red, and yellow. The company sells boxes of jelly beans, each of which contains 20 individual bags. Each individual bag contains 75 jelly beans. A customer purchased 5 boxes of jelly beans and selected one bag at random from each box. The customer counted the number of each color in each bag. The results are shown in the chart below.

Color	Bag 1	Bag 2	Bag 3	Bag 4	Bag 5
Black	10	12	8	11	9
Green	13	11	13	12	12
Orange	22	20	21	21	21
Red	20	21	23	21	22
Yellow	10	11	10	10	11

Which of the following is the closest approximation of the total number of green jelly beans in the customer's purchase?

A)   60

B)   240

C) 1,200

D) 4,500

Probability

To answer a question like this:

Number of Cyclists in Regional Race, by Age and Town

Town	Age (years)					Total
	15 to 18	19 to 25	26 to 34	35 to 46	47 and Older	
Pine Falls	9	52	31	26	29	147
Greenville	14	38	42	53	30	177
Salem	5	17	18	13	10	63
Fairview	19	41	32	34	27	153
Total	47	148	123	126	96	540

The table above shows the number of participants in a regional bicycle race, categorized by town and age group. Based on the table, if a cyclist from Fairview is chosen at random, which of the following is closest to the probability that the cyclist was 35 or older at the time of the race?

A) 0.40

B) 0.18

C) 0.11

D) 0.05

You need to know this:

Probability is a fraction or decimal between 0 and 1 comparing the number of desired outcomes to the number of total possible outcomes. A probability of 0 means that an event will not occur; a probability of 1 means that it definitely will occur. The formula is as follows:

$$\text{Probability} = \frac{\text{number of desired outcomes}}{\text{number of total possible outcomes}}$$

For instance, if you roll a six-sided die, each side showing a different number from 1 to 6, the probability of rolling a number higher than 4 is $\frac{2}{6} = \frac{1}{3}$, because there are two numbers higher than 4 (5 and 6) and six numbers total (1, 2, 3, 4, 5, and 6).

To find the probability that an event will *not* happen, subtract the probability that the event will happen from 1. Continuing the previous example, the probability of *not* rolling a number higher than 4 would be:

$$1 - \frac{1}{3} = \frac{2}{3}$$

The SAT tends to test probability in the context of data tables. Using a table, you can find the probability that a randomly selected data value (be it a person, object, etc.) will fit a certain profile. For example, the following table summarizing a survey on water preference might be followed by a question asking for the probability that a person randomly selected for a follow-up survey falls into a given category.

	Tap	Carbonated	Bottled	Total
Female	325	267	295	887
Male	304	210	289	803
Total	629	477	584	1,690

If the question asked for the probability of randomly selecting a female who prefers tap water from all the participants of the original survey, you would calculate it using the same general formula as before:

$$\frac{\text{\# female, tap}}{\text{\# total}} = \frac{325}{1{,}690} = \frac{5}{26} \approx 0.192.$$

If the question asked for the probability of randomly selecting a female for the follow-up survey, given that the chosen participant prefers tap water, the setup is a little different. This time, the number of possible outcomes is the total participants *who prefer tap water*, which is 629, not the grand total of 1,690. The calculation is now $\frac{\text{\# female, tap}}{\text{\# total, tap}} = \frac{325}{629} \approx 0.517.$

Conversely, if you needed to find the probability of selecting someone who prefers tap water for the follow-up survey, given that the chosen participant is female, the new number of possible outcomes would be the female participant total (887). The calculation becomes $\frac{\text{\# female, tap}}{\text{\# total, females}} = \frac{325}{887} \approx 0.366.$

You need to do this:

- Determine the number of desired and total possible outcomes by looking at the table.
- Read the question carefully when determining the number of possible outcomes: do you need the entire set or a subset?

Explanation:

The number of desired outcomes is the number of cyclists from Fairview who are 35 or older. That means you need to add the "35 to 46" and "47 and Older" categories: $34 + 27 = 61$. The number of possible outcomes is the total number of cyclists from Fairview. The number is given in the totals column: 153. Plug these numbers into the probability formula and divide:

$$\text{Probability} = \frac{\text{\# Fairview, 35 and Older}}{\text{\# Fairview, Total}} = \frac{61}{153} \approx 0.40$$

The correct answer is **(A)**.

Try on Your Own

Directions: Take as much time as you need on these questions. Work carefully and methodically. There will be an opportunity for timed practice at the end of the chapter.

	Marked Defective	Not Marked Defective	Total
Defective Bearing	392	57	449
Non-defective Bearing	168	49,383	49,551
Total	560	49,440	50,000

18. A manufacturing plant produces 50,000 bearings per week. Of these, 449 will be defective. The manager of the plant installs a new quality control device that is designed to detect defective bearings and mark them with a laser. The device is allowed to run for a week and the results are tallied as shown in the table above. According to these results, to the nearest percent, what is the probability that a part that is marked defective will actually be defective?

    A) 30%

    B) 43%

    C) 70%

    D) 87%

HINT: For Q19, what percentage of the fish at the hatchery are salmon? How many salmon are there? How many of those were tested?

19. The table below shows the distribution of four species of fish at a hatchery that has approximately 6,000 fish.

Species	Percent of Total
Carp	50
Salmon	25
Tilapia	15
Tuna	10

A biologist randomly tests 5 percent of each species of fish for mercury content. Her findings are shown in the following table.

Mercury Content Test Results

Species	Number of Fish with Dangerous Mercury Levels
Carp	11
Salmon	6
Tilapia	5
Tuna	8

Based on the biologist's findings, if a single salmon is randomly selected from those that were tested, what is the probability that this particular fish would have a dangerous mercury level?

    A) 0.001

    B) 0.004

    C) 0.02

    D) 0.08

Type of Engineer	Specialization		Total
	Robotics	AV	
Mechanical	198	245	443
Electrical	149	176	325
Total	347	421	768

20. In a research study, a group of mechanical and electrical engineers indicated their specialization preference between robotics and autonomous vehicles (AV). The results are shown in the table above. What is the probability that a randomly selected engineer will be a mechanical engineer specializing in autonomous vehicles?

A) 0.229

B) 0.319

C) 0.553

D) 0.582

HINT: For Q21, how many groups have *at least* 8 days vacation?

21. **Yearly Paid Vacation Days at Excor Manufacturing**

	0–7	8–14	14–30	Total
Hourly	79	183	38	300
Salaried	8	27	65	100
Total	87	210	103	400

The human resources department at Excor Manufacturing decided to collect data on the paid vacation days accrued by hourly and salaried employees. The table above shows the results of the data collection. If an employee has at least 8 paid vacation days, what is the probability that the person is a salaried employee?

A) $\dfrac{92}{313}$

B) $\dfrac{221}{300}$

C) $\dfrac{313}{400}$

D) $\dfrac{92}{100}$

Engine Type	Fuel Economy (miles per gallon)	
	0–45 mpg	45+ mpg
Hybrid		
Internal Combustion (IC)		
Total	53	258

22. The daily engine production goals of an automobile manufacturer are summarized in the incomplete table above. The factory produced six times as many hybrid engines that achieve 45+ miles per gallon as it did hybrid engines that achieve 0–45 miles per gallon, and the factory produced four times as many internal combustion (IC) engines that achieve 45+ miles per gallon as it did IC engines that achieve 0–45 miles per gallon. If the factory produced 53 engines that achieve 0–45 miles per gallon and 258 engines that achieve 45+ miles per gallon, which of the following is the approximate probability that a 45+ miles per gallon engine selected at random is IC?

A) 0.566

B) 0.535

C) 0.465

D) 0.386

On Test Day

The SAT tests the concept of average fairly heavily. The average formula will serve you well on questions that ask about a sum of values or the average of a set of values, but for questions that give you the average and ask for a missing value in the data set, there is an alternative that can be faster: the balance approach.

The balance approach is based on the the idea that if you know what the average is, you can find the totals on both sides of the average and then add the missing value that makes both sides balance out. This approach is especially helpful if the values are large and closely spaced. Imagine that a question gives you the set $\{976, 980, 964, 987, x\}$ and tells you that the average is 970. You would reason as follows: 976 is 6 over the average, 980 is 10 over, 964 is 6 under, and 987 is 17 over. That's a total of $6 + 10 - 6 + 17 = 27$ over, so x needs to be 27 under the average, or $970 - 27 = 943$.

Try solving the question below both ways, using first the average formula and then the balance approach. If you find the latter to be fast and intuitive, add it to your test-day arsenal.

	Height Change in Inches						
Plant Type	Week 3	Week 4	Week 5	Week 6	Week 7	Week 8	Week 9
Zinnia	3	2	1	4	2	1	1
Sunflower	3		8	6	7	2	5
Marigold	1	1	3	2	4	4	3

23. The table above summarizes the height change (inches) over a seven-week period of three different plants grown by Ms. Walker's biology class. If the mean height change for the sunflower plant over the seven-week period is 5 inches, what was the height change in week 4?

The correct answer and both ways of solving can be found at the end of the chapter.

How Much Have You Learned?

Directions: For testlike practice, give yourself 15 minutes to complete this question set. Be sure to study the explanations, even for questions you got right. They can be found at the end of this chapter.

Question 24 refers to the following information.

The table below summarizes the results of a survey about favorite leisure activities for a group of high school students. Assume that every student has a favorite leisure activity and that each student could select only one favorite.

	Freshmen	Sophomores	Juniors	Seniors	Total
Sports	144	122	134	115	515
Video Games	126	140	152	148	566
Music	120	117	153	148	538
Reading	110	114	63	98	385
Total	500	493	502	509	2,004

24. The research group that conducted the survey wants to select one sophomore at random for a follow-up survey. What is the probability that the student selected will prefer a type of leisure activity other than video games?

A) $\dfrac{140}{493}$

B) $\dfrac{140}{2,004}$

C) $\dfrac{353}{493}$

D) $\dfrac{353}{2,004}$

Questions 25 and 26 refer to the following information.

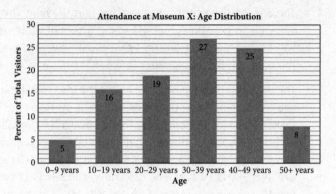

Attendance at Museum X: Age Distribution

The bar graph above shows the age distribution of visitors to museum X in 2014. Visitors aged 0–9 years get into museum X for free, visitors aged 50 and older pay $5 for admission and everyone else pays $10.

25. If 553 people aged 20 years and older visited museum X in 2014, then approximately how many people visited museum X in 2014?

26. Assuming, as before, that 553 people aged 20 years and older visited museum X in 2014, how much revenue did museum X collect from tickets sold to people aged 40 and older in 2014? (Ignore the dollar sign when gridding your response.)

27. According to the table, what percent of all the board games sold by the boutique have a "bad" average customer rating? Round to the nearest tenth of a percent and ignore the percent sign when entering your answer.

Questions 27 and 28 refer to the following information.

	1	2	3	4	5	Total
Strategy	5	17	24	10	5	61
Trivia	3	12	28	8	3	54
Role-playing	3	10	30	14	2	59

A small boutique sells board games online. The boutique specializes in strategy, trivia, and role-playing games. Any customer who purchases a game is invited to rate the game on a scale of 1 to 5. A rating of 1 or 2 is considered "bad," a rating of 3 is considered "average," and a rating of 4 or 5 is considered "good." The table above shows the distribution of average customer ratings of the games sold. For example, 24 of the strategy games sold have an average customer rating of 3.

28. The boutique decides to stop selling 50 percent of the games that have a "bad" average customer rating to make room for promising new stock. Assuming no significant changes in ratings in the foreseeable future, what should the difference be between the percentages of games with a "bad" average customer rating before and after the games are removed? Round to the nearest tenth of a percent and ignore the percent sign when entering your answer.

29. Fit and Fab, a membership-only gym, is hoping to open a new branch in a small city in Pennsylvania that currently has no fitness centers. According to the gym management's research, approximately 12,600 residents live within driving distance of the gym. Fit and Fab sends out surveys to a sample of 300 randomly selected residents in this area (all of whom respond) and finds that 40 residents say they would visit a gym if one were located in their area. Based on past survey research, Fit and Fab estimates that approximately 30 percent of these respondents would actually join the gym if one were opened in the area. Based on this information and the results of the sample survey, about how many residents should Fit and Fab expect to join its new branch?

A) 134

B) 504

C) 1,680

D) 3,780

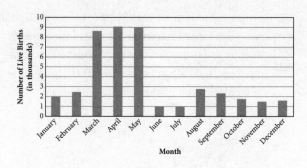

30. Most animals give birth during a general time of year. This is because animals naturally breed so that their young will be born at the time of year when there will be an adequate food supply. The bar graph shows the number of live births in California of a particular jackrabbit species, the black-tailed jackrabbit, over the course of year X. Based on the data, which of the following would be an appropriate conclusion?

A) In general, rabbits give birth during March, April, and May.

B) In general, rabbits give birth during June, July, and August.

C) In general, black-tailed jackrabbits in California give birth during March, April, and May.

D) In general, black-tailed jackrabbits in California give birth during June, July, and August.

31. Soil contains a wide variety of nutrients, including nitrogen, phosphorous, potassium, magnesium, sulfur, and iron. A fertilizer company conducted an experimental study to determine which of five additives is most effective in helping soil retain nutrients. If, after application of the additives, the fertilizer company tested only for the soil nutrients nitrogen and potassium, which of the following is a valid conclusion?

A) The additive that is found to be the most effective will work for all nutrients in the soil.

B) The additive that is found to be the most effective will work only for nitrogen and potassium.

C) The study is biased and therefore not significantly relevant to determining which additive is most effective.

D) The study will be able to produce results concerning only the effects of the additives on nitrogen and potassium.

32. As part of its market research, a company sent out a survey to see how much consumers would be willing to pay for a certain product. The survey distinguished between a store brand version of the product and a brand name version, and people participating in the survey received questions about only one of the versions. A summary of the survey results is shown in the following bar graph.

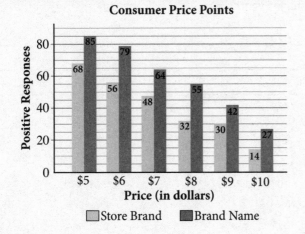

Consumer Price Points

If a consumer is chosen at random from the 600 respondents, what is the probability that the consumer is willing to pay at least $8 for the product?

33. The average (arithmetic mean) of $p + 12t - 5$, $q + 16t + 4$, and $r - 7t + 25$ is $10t + 34$. In terms of t, what is the average of p, q, and r?

A) $3t + 26$

B) $4t + 16$

C) $6t + 16$

D) $8t - 37$

Reflect

Directions: Take a few minutes to recall what you've learned and what you've been practicing in this chapter. Consider the following questions, jot down your best answer for each one, and then compare your reflections to the expert responses on the following page. Use your level of confidence to determine what to do next.

What are some common ways the SAT may present data?

_____

_____

_____

What is the difference between median, mode, and range?

_____

_____

_____

What does the standard deviation of a data set tell you?

_____

_____

_____

When can you generalize the results of a survey of a small group to a larger group?

_____

_____

_____

What are two ways to calculate the probability of a single event?

_____

_____

_____

Expert Responses

What are some common ways the SAT may present data?

The SAT may present data in tables, bar charts, line graphs, dot plots, and histograms.

What is the difference between median, mode, and range?

The median of a set is the middle value, whereas the mode is the most common value. The range of a set is the distance between the smallest value and the largest one.

What does the standard deviation of a data set tell you?

A data set's standard deviation reflects how far apart the numbers are from each other. The standard deviation of a set whose numbers are all the same—for example, {5, 5, 5, 5}—is 0. The greater the distance between the numbers, the greater the standard deviation.

When can you generalize the results of a survey of a small group to a larger group?

A survey can be generalized to a larger population if the data sample is representative. To be representative, the data sample needs to be drawn at random from the larger population.

What are two ways to calculate the probability of a single event?

One way is to use the basic probability formula:

$$\text{Probability} = \frac{\text{number of desired outcomes}}{\text{number of total outcomes}}$$

Alternatively, the probability that an event happens is 1 minus the probability that it doesn't happen.

Next Steps

If you answered most questions correctly in the "How Much Have You Learned?" section, and if your responses to the Reflect questions were similar to those of the SAT expert, then consider tables, statistics, and probability an area of strength and move on to the next chapter. Come back to this topic periodically to prevent yourself from getting rusty.

If you don't yet feel confident, review those parts of this chapter that you have not yet mastered, then try the questions you missed again. In particular, make sure that you understand the six terms explained in the Statistics lesson and the probability formulas explained in the Probability lesson. As always, be sure to review the explanations closely.

Math

Answers and Explanations

1. B

Difficulty: Easy

Getting to the Answer: The trickiest part of this question is understanding what is being asked. You need to find the shop that had the most Tuesday sales *as a fraction of its total sales*, so focus only on those rows in the table. For each shop, divide the number of books it sold on Tuesday by the number of books it sold all week. Use your calculator to speed up this step.

$$\text{Bob's Bookshop: } \frac{\text{Tuesday total}}{\text{weekly total}} = \frac{8}{53} \approx 0.1509$$

$$\text{Clara's Bookshop: } \frac{\text{Tuesday total}}{\text{weekly total}} = \frac{13}{55} \approx 0.2364$$

$$\text{Derek's Bookshop: } \frac{\text{Tuesday total}}{\text{weekly total}} = \frac{15}{66} \approx 0.2273$$

$$\text{Evelyn's Bookshop: } \frac{\text{Tuesday total}}{\text{weekly total}} = \frac{13}{58} \approx 0.2241$$

The greatest portion of Tuesday sales belongs to Clara's Bookshop, so **(B)** is correct.

2. C

Difficulty: Medium

Getting to the Answer: Add the number of books sold by Derek and Evelyn on Monday, Wednesday, and Friday; then divide the result by the total number of books sold on those days.

Derek's and Evelyn's M/W/F sales:
$(15 + 12) + (12 + 14) + (10 + 9) = 72$

Total M/W/F sales: $48 + 49 + 39 = 136$

Divide Derek's and Evelyn's M/W/F sales by total M/W/F sales to get $\frac{72}{136}$, which simplifies to $\frac{9}{17}$. Choice **(C)** is correct.

3. B

Difficulty: Easy

Getting to the Answer: The question asks only about participants who were outside a healthy weight range, so focus on this row: 38 out of the 74 participants who were outside a healthy weight range ate breakfast one or fewer times per week. This expressed as a percent is $\frac{38}{74} \times 100\% = 0.51351 \times 100\% = 51.35\%$, which matches **(B)**.

4. D

Difficulty: Medium

Getting to the Answer: The question asks about employees who eat breakfast every weekday, so focus on the "5–7 times per week" column in the table. Assuming the participants in the study were a good representative sample, 36 out of 45, or 80%, of the 3,000 employees are likely to be within a healthy weight range. Multiply $0.8 \times 3,000$ to arrive at 2,400, which is **(D)**.

5. 300

Difficulty: Easy

Getting to the Answer: Read the graph carefully, including the key at the bottom indicating that each bar represents 15 minutes. The question states that only stage 3 is considered deep sleep, and the question asks how much time was spent in non-deep sleep. You could count all of the bars that don't represent stage 3, but it would be faster to count the bars that do and then subtract that number from the total. There are 12 bars that represent stage 3, which means the person spent $12 \times 15 = 180$ minutes in deep sleep. The study was for 8 hours, or 480 minutes, so the person spent $480 - 180 = 300$ minutes in non-deep sleep.

6. 195

Difficulty: Medium

Strategic Advice: In multi-part Math question sets, the second question often uses information that you had to calculate in the first question. Keep track of your computations and reuse information so that you don't waste time repeating calculations.

Getting to the Answer: Set up the average formula and start filling in the values to find the missing night's stage 3 sleep. You're given two of the three quantities needed for the average formula: the total number of nights is 5 and the average over all the nights is 180 minutes. You know from your work in the previous question that the patient spent 180 minutes in stage 3 sleep on the first night. The following 3 nights, as given in the questions stem, average out to 175 minutes each, so even though you don't know their precise values, you can represent them as 175 three times. Use a variable, x, for the unknown number of minutes in stage 3 sleep on the fifth night and solve:

$$180 = \frac{180 + 175 + 175 + 175 + x}{5}$$

$$900 = 705 + x$$

$$x = 195$$

Grid in **195**.

7.   D

Difficulty: Medium

Getting to the Answer: Compare each statement to the line graph one at a time, eliminating true statements as you work. Start with (A): at every reading after 20 hours, Strain 1 has a higher OD600 level than Strain 2, so this statement is true. Eliminate (A). Choice (B) states that Strain 2's growth rate (slope) overtook Strain 1's at hour 50, which is consistent with the line graph; eliminate it. It looks as though (C) requires time-consuming calculations, so skip it for now. Choice (D) states that Strain 1's growth rate was greater than Strain 2's over the entire period. This statement contradicts what you already confirmed in (B), which makes **(D)** false and, therefore, correct. There's no need to check (C).

8.   D

Difficulty: Medium

Strategic Advice: The median is the middle value when all of the values are in numerical order, so you'll need to find the total number of values in the set and figure out which one is the middle value.

Getting to the Answer: The note above the chart says that the total number of people who were surveyed in country B is 250. Since it is an even set of values, the median will be the average of the 125th and 126th values. To get to those values, add the number of citizens who speak one or two languages: $70 + 30 = 100$. The hundredth value falls within the group that speaks two languages. Keep going because this group does not include the 125th and 126th values. Add the citizens who speak three languages: $100 + 20 = 120$. Still not quite there, so add the citizens who speak four languages: $120 + 70 = 190$. This means that the 125th and 126th values are both 4, so the median is 4. **(D)** is correct.

9.   C

Difficulty: Hard

Getting to the Answer: The answer choices compare the number of citizens who speak different numbers of languages. (A) and (B) compare the number of citizens who speak exactly five languages to the number of citizens who speak exactly four languages. Notice that in both countries, the fraction that speaks exactly five languages is smaller than the fraction that speaks exactly four languages, so (B) can be eliminated.

To evaluate (A), you need to calculate the number of citizens who speak five languages and the number of citizens who speak four languages. Take the population in each country and multiply it by the fraction of citizens surveyed who speak the specified number of languages (the denominator of the fraction will be the total number surveyed, 250):

Country A: $(550,000)\left(\frac{25}{250}\right) = (550,000)\left(\frac{1}{10}\right) = 55,000$

Country B: $(1,300,000)\left(\frac{60}{250}\right) = (1,300,000)\left(\frac{6}{25}\right) = 312,000$

This means that $55,000 + 312,000 = 367,000$ citizens speak five languages. Next, calculate how many citizens speak exactly four languages:

Country A: $(550,000)\left(\frac{40}{250}\right) = (550,000)\left(\frac{4}{25}\right) = 88,000$

Country B: $(1,300,000)\left(\frac{70}{250}\right) = (1,300,000)\left(\frac{7}{25}\right) = 364,000$

This means that $88,000 + 364,000$, or $452,000$, citizens speak exactly four languages. Because 312,000 is not half of 364,000, eliminate (A).

Use logic to decide between (C) and (D). Notice that the fraction of citizens who speak four languages in country B, which has a larger population, is more than twice the fraction of citizens in country B who speak two languages—while in country A, which has a smaller population, the fraction of citizens who speak two languages is exactly twice the fraction of citizens who speak four languages. Country B's larger population means that overall, more citizens of both countries combined will speak four languages than two languages. Choice **(C)** is correct.

For the record, here are the calculations for **(C)** and (D):

Country A: $(550,000)\left(\frac{80}{250}\right) = (550,000)\left(\frac{8}{25}\right) = 176,000$

Country B: $(1,300,000)\left(\frac{30}{250}\right) = (1,300,000)\left(\frac{3}{25}\right) = 156,000$

The number of citizens who speak two languages in both countries is $176,000 + 156,000$, or $332,000$, which is fewer than the 452,000 who speak four languages.

10. B

Difficulty: Easy

Getting to the Answer: Consider the definitions of mean and standard deviation: mean is a measure of center, while standard deviation is a measure of spread. The closer the data points for a given snowboarder are to the mean, the more consistent that snowboarder's performance, so the explanation should involve standard deviation. Based on this, you can eliminate (A) and (D). Greater consistency means lower standard deviation (and vice versa); the only choice that reflects this—and correctly represents the data in the table—is **(B)**.

11. C

Difficulty: Medium

Getting to the Answer: You'll have to determine the values of all three measurements so that you can place them in ascending order. Start with the easiest, the mode. That is 3 because there are 18 cars of that age, which is the most of any age. Next, calculate the total number of cars, since you'll need that to compute both the mean and median. Adding the total in the right-hand column gives you $3 + 5 + 18 + 17 + 11 + 6 + 2 = 62$ cars in inventory. Since this is an even number, the median age will be the average of the 31st and 32nd values. The are $3 + 5 + 18 = 26$ cars that are 1, 2, and 3 years old and 17 that are 4 years old. Thus, the 27th through 43rd ($26 + 17 = 43$) values are 4, and that is the median.

Calculating the mean is more complex since it is a weighted average. Multiply each value by its frequency, total those values, and divide by 62. So, $1 \times 3 = 3$, $2 \times 5 = 10$, $3 \times 18 = 54$, $4 \times 17 = 68$, $5 \times 11 = 55$, $6 \times 6 = 36$, and $7 \times 2 = 14$, and $3 + 10 + 54 + 68 + 55 + 36 + 14 = 240$. You could divide 240 by 62 to get approximately 3.87, or you could recognize that 240 divided by 60 is 4, so the result when divided by 62 is just less than 4, which is all you need to know to answer this question. The ascending order of the three values is mode (3), mean (3.87), and median (4), so **(C)** is correct.

12. 6.2

Difficulty: Hard

Getting to the Answer: Read this question carefully, since it is rather unusual. In order to meet a goal of a 0.5% reject rate for the month, use the average formula,
$$0.5\% = \frac{\text{maximum allowable sum of the daily reject rates}}{22}.$$
Thus, the sum of the daily reject rates for a 0.5% average is $22 \times 0.5\% = 11.0\%$. Since 12 days have already passed with an average reject rate of 0.4%, the sum of the daily rates so far is $12 \times 0.4\% = 4.8\%$. So, the sum of the daily rates for the next 10 days cannot exceed $11.0\% - 4.8\% = 6.2\%$ if the monthly average is to be 0.5% or less.

The question doesn't ask for the total or average of the next 10 days, however. Instead, it asks for the maximum reject rate on the next single day that could still conceivably allow the company to meet its monthly goal. If the other 9 remaining days all had a 0.0% reject rate, then the 10-day total would be the reject rate for that 13th day. This is 6.2%, so grid in **6.2**.

13. A

Difficulty: Easy

Getting to the Answer: Any sample used to determine a general opinion needs to be representative and unbiased. The railroad company fails to meet that requirement, surveying only people who commute to work and who would probably benefit from the station. This potentially leaves out a large portion of the population who may not share the commuters' favorable opinion. The use of a biased sample group makes the survey unreliable and not representative, which makes **(A)** the correct answer.

14. A

Difficulty: Medium

Getting to the Answer: As long as a sample is representative, without bias, and relatively large, inferences can be drawn from the sample data about the population from which the sample was taken. The sample here meets all of these requirements. If the mean number of bottles of water consumed per person each day were 2.5, then it could be assumed that the average number consumed in the general population would also be approximately 2.5. The mean of the sample equals the estimated mean of the general population, and **(A)** is the correct answer.

15. C

Difficulty: Medium

Getting to the Answer: As the customers were selected at random, it is reasonable to assume that the survey results will be representative of what is true for customers in general. However, the data provided refers only to people who bought dinnerware. So, an inference can be drawn only about dinnerware returns. Based on the 80% of surveyed customers who returned dinnerware items because of damage, it is reasonable to infer that this statistic will be similar for all customers who return dinnerware. That makes **(C)** the correct answer. Choices (A), (B), and (D) are incorrect because they are not confined to dinnerware.

16. C

Difficulty: Medium

Getting to the Answer: To make a reliable inference from a survey, the survey sample needs to be representative, unbiased, and relatively large. In this case, the miniature golf course owner surveyed only children who played at that course. Thus, any inference drawn from the data must be about such children. Since 60% of the surveyed children prefer a red golf ball, it is reasonable to infer that a similar percentage of total children at that golf course would prefer red golf balls. Thus, **(C)** is the correct answer.

17. C

Difficulty: Hard

Getting to the Answer: The customer purchased 5 boxes, each of which contains 20 bags, which means the customer bought a total of $5 \times 20 = 100$ bags. In each bag tested, there were between 11 and 13 green jelly beans. As the bags were chosen at random, it's reasonable to expect that the results will be consistent for all 100 bags. With 11–13 beans per bag, the total number of green jelly beans will likely be between $11 \times 100 = 1{,}100$ and $13 \times 100 = 1{,}300$. Right in the middle of that range is 1,200, making **(C)** the correct answer.

Note that if you chose (A) 60, you might have been thinking of the total green jelly beans in just the five randomly selected bags. Similarly, if you chose (B) 240, you calculated the approximate number in just one box of 20 bags. Incorrect answer choices often try to anticipate minor mistakes you might make in your calculations. Be sure to confirm that you answered the question being asked.

18. C

Difficulty: Medium

Getting to the Answer: The number of desired outcomes is 392 (marked bearings that are defective). The number of total possible outcomes is 560 (all the bearings that are marked defective). Thus, the probability that a bearing marked defective is in fact defective is $\frac{392}{560} \times 100\% = 0.70 \times 100\% = 70\%$. **(C)** is correct.

19. D

Difficulty: Hard

Getting to the Answer: The probability that one randomly selected salmon from those that were tested would have a dangerous level of mercury is equal to the number of salmon that had dangerous mercury levels divided by the total number of salmon that were tested. This means you need only two numbers to answer this question. One of those numbers is in the second table—6 salmon had dangerous mercury levels. Finding the other number is the tricky part. Use information from the question stem and the first table. The biologist tested 5% of the total number of each species of fish, and 25% of the 6,000 fish are salmon. So the biologist tested 5% of 25% of 6,000 fish. Multiply to find that $0.05 \times 0.25 \times 6{,}000 = 75$ salmon were tested. This means the probability is $\frac{6}{75} = 0.08$, which matches **(D)**.

20. B

Difficulty: Medium

Strategic Advice: Recognizing which value goes in the denominator, whether it is the entire total or the total of a subgroup, is essential for probability questions that are based on data in a table.

Getting to the Answer: The question indicates that the random selection is from all the engineers, or the entire total of 768. The specific engineer to be selected is a mechanical engineer who specializes in autonomous vehicles, and the table indicates that there are 245 such engineers. Therefore, the probability of selecting a mechanical engineer specializing in autonomous vehicles from all the engineers is $\frac{245}{768}$, which is ≈ 0.319. **(B)** is correct.

Note that the incorrect answer choices often reflect common misunderstandings and simple table-reading errors. For example, (C) and (D) both use the wrong total and (A) is the probability of choosing an electrical engineer specializing in autonomous vehicles.

21. A

Difficulty: Medium

Strategic Advice: Be on the lookout for "at least" language. It will usually require adding data from multiple rows or columns.

Getting to the Answer: The probability of choosing an employee with "at least" 8 paid vacation days who is salaried is the number of salaried employees with 8 or more paid vacation days divided by the total number of employees with 8 or more paid vacation days. Find the number of salaried employees with 8 or more paid vacation by adding the salaried employees with 8–14 paid vacation days, 27, and the salaried employees with 15–30 paid vacation days, 65. That means there are $27 + 65$, or 92, salaried employees with 8 or more paid vacation days. The total number of employees with 8 or more paid vacation days is 210 (the total number of employees with 8–14 paid vacation days) plus 103 (the total number of employees with 15–30 paid vacation days), or 313. The probability is $\frac{92}{313}$. **(A)** is correct.

22. C

Difficulty: Hard

Strategic Advice: If totals and the relationships between the data are the only information provided, write out a system of equations.

Getting to the Answer: The question gives the relationships between unknown values in the table, so fill them in accordingly. For hybrid engines, let h be the number that are rated 0–45 miles per gallon. There are 6 times as many hybrid engines that achieve 45+ miles per gallon, so that is $6h$. Similarly, for IC, let c be the number of IC engines that are 0–45 miles per gallon. Because the factory produced four times as many IC engines that achieve 45+ miles per gallon, fill in that blank with $4c$:

	Fuel Economy (miles per gallon)	
Engine Type	**0–45 mpg**	**45+ mpg**
Hybrid	h	$6h$
Internal Combustion (IC)	c	$4c$
Total	53	258

Write a system of equations based on the two miles per gallon columns:

$$h + c = 53$$
$$6h + 4c = 258$$

Solve the first equation for h and substitute the result into the second equation to solve for c:

$$h = 53 - c$$
$$6(53 - c) + 4c = 258$$
$$318 - 6c + 4c = 258$$
$$-2c = -60$$
$$c = 30$$

If c is 30, then there are 4×30, or 120, IC engines that achieve 45+ miles per gallon. The probability of choosing one of those 120 engines out all 258 engines that achieve 45+ miles per gallon is $\frac{120}{258}$, or 0.465. **(C)** is correct. Notice that there is no need to actually calculate h to answer this question.

23. 4

Difficulty: Medium

Category: Statistics

Strategic Advice: When the goal is to find a missing value in a set of data and the average is given, consider using the balance approach. We'll demonstrate both approaches starting with the average formula.

Getting to the Answer: The question is about the height change for the sunflower plant, so ignore the data for the other plants. The given height changes for the other six weeks are: 3, 8, 6, 7, 2, and 5. The average change in height for the sunflower plant is given as 5. If you call the missing value x, plugging the known values into the average formula results in the following:

$$\frac{3 + x + 8 + 6 + 7 + 2 + 5}{7} = 5$$

$$\frac{3 + x + 8 + 6 + 7 + 2 + 5}{7} = 5$$

$$\frac{31 + x}{7} = 5$$

$$31 + x = 35$$

$$x = 4$$

Grid in **4** as the correct answer.

Alternatively, to use the balance approach, write down how much each value is above or below the average of 5. For example, the Week 3 value of 3 is 2 below the average: $3 - 5 = -2$.

Week 3	Week 5	Week 6	Week 7	Week 8	Week 9
3: −2	8: +3	6: +1	7: +2	2: −3	5: +0

Now observe that, excluding Week 4, the values are $-2 + 3 + 1 + 2 - 3 = 1$. Without Week 4, the total is 1 more than what you'd expect based on the average. So for the values to balance out to the average, the Week 4 value must be one less than the average of 5, or $5 - 1 = 4$. Grid in **4**.

24. C

Difficulty: Medium

Category: Probability

Getting to the Answer: The research firm is choosing one student from among the sophomores, so you need the total number of sophomores, 493, in the denominator of the probability formula, not the total number of students. There are $493 - 140 = 353$ sophomores who prefer activities other than video games, so the probability of choosing a sophomore who doesn't prefer video games is $\frac{353}{493}$. Choice **(C)** is correct.

25. 700

Difficulty: Medium

Category: Tables and Graphs

Getting to the Answer: Identify the pieces of the graph you need and then convert from the percent to the total. You know from the graph that 21% (5% + 16%) of the visitors are *not* aged 20 or older. This means that $100\% - 21\% = 79\%$ were aged 20+. Given that the number of visitors aged 20+ is 553, use the three-part percent formula to calculate the total:

$$\text{total} \times 79\% = 553$$
$$\text{total} = \frac{553}{0.79} = 700$$

26. 2030

Difficulty: Medium

Category: Tables and Graphs

Getting to the Answer: From the previous question, you know that the total number of visitors in 2014 was 700. According to the bar graph, 25% of all the visitors were aged 40–49, and 8% were aged 50+. This means that $0.25 \times 700 = 175$ attendees were aged 40–49, and $0.08 \times 700 = 56$ were aged 50+. The visitors aged 40–49 paid $175 \times \$10 = \$1,750$ for their tickets, and the visitors aged 50+ paid $56 \times \$5 = \$280$ for their tickets. The total revenue for the two groups was therefore $\$1,750 + \$280 = \$2,030$. Grid in **2030**.

27. 28.7

Difficulty: Medium

Category: Tables and Graphs

Getting to the Answer: To be considered "bad," a game must have a rating of 1 or 2. Begin by counting the number of "bad" games. There are $5 + 3 + 3 = 11$ games with a rating of 1 and $17 + 12 + 10 = 39$ games with a rating of 2. That's a total of $11 + 39 = 50$ games. Divide this by the total number of games and multiply by 100%: $\frac{50}{61 + 54 + 59} \times 100\% \approx 28.7\%$. Grid in **28.7**.

28. 12

Difficulty: Medium

Category: Tables and Graphs

Getting to the Answer: You know from the previous question that 50 games are "bad." Reducing this number by 50% is the same as halving it, meaning there will be 25 remaining "bad" games after the removal. Subtract this from the original total game count ($61 + 54 + 59 = 174$) to get the new total, $174 - 25 = 149$. Divide the new "bad" count by this total, and then multiply by 100% as you did before: $\frac{25}{149} \times 100\% \approx 16.7785\%$. Subtracting the new percentage from the old one (rounded to a minimum of 4 decimal places just to be safe) gives $28.7356\% - 16.7785\% = 11.9571\%$. This rounds to 12.0%. Grid in **12**.

Math

29. B

Difficulty: Medium

Category: Surveys and Data Samples

Getting to the Answer: According to the sample survey, $\frac{40}{300}$ *say* they would join the gym. But the gym estimates that only 30% of these respondents would *actually* join, so multiply 40 by 30% to find that the gym can expect $\frac{12}{300} = 0.04 = 4\%$ of the respondents to join. Multiply this by the total number of residents: $12{,}600 \times 0.04 = 504$ residents, so **(B)** is correct.

30. C

Difficulty: Easy

Category: Tables and Graphs

Getting to the Answer: The question states that the data collected was about black-tailed jackrabbits in California, so any conclusion drawn can be generalized only to that particular species of rabbit in California, not to all rabbits generally. According to the data, the California jackrabbit gives birth mostly during March, April, and May, so **(C)** is correct.

31. D

Difficulty: Medium

Category: Surveys and Data Samples

Getting to the Answer: The question indicates that there are a wide variety of nutrients in the soil, but the study only tests for nitrogen and potassium, so the sample is limited. You can eliminate (A) and (B) because all nutrients were not included in the sample, so you can't say anything about them one way or the other. The additives may or may not help the soil retain other types of nutrients, and you certainly don't know which of the five additives would produce the best results. You can eliminate (C) because the question doesn't tell you anything about the data collection methods, so you can't determine whether the study was biased. This means that the study will only be able to produce results concerning the effects of the additives on soil retention of nitrogen and potassium. Thus, **(D)** is correct.

32. 1/3 or .333

Difficulty: Medium

Category: Probability

Getting to the Answer: First, find the number of respondents willing to pay at least $8 (which means $8 or more). Be careful—the question doesn't specify store brand or brand name, so use both versions of the product:

$$32 + 55 + 30 + 42 + 14 + 27 = 200$$

Now, find the total number of people in the survey. Again, the question doesn't specify store brand or brand name. The question stem states that there is a total of 600 respondents. This means the probability that a randomly chosen respondent is willing to pay at least $8 is $\frac{200}{600}$, or $\frac{1}{3}$. Grid in **1/3** or **.333**.

33. A

Difficulty: Hard

Category: Statistics

Getting to the Answer: The number of variables may look daunting, but the question is just asking you to find an average. The average of a set of terms is equal to the sum of the terms divided by the number of terms; thus, the average of p, q, and r is $\frac{p + q + r}{3}$.

Use the average formula to set up an equation using the rest of the information in the problem. Even though you are given expressions with lots of variables, the average formula is still the sum of the terms divided by the number of terms. Notice that the question states that the average of these expressions is $10t + 34$, which translates to "$= 10t + 34$." So you can set up an equation like this:

$$\frac{(p + 12t - 5) + (q + 16t + 4) + (r - 7t + 25)}{3} = 10t + 34$$

Because the question asks for the average of p, q, and r in terms of t, solve the equation above for $\frac{p + q + r}{3}$:

$$\frac{p + 12t - 5 + q + 16t + 4 + r - 7t + 25}{3} = 10t + 34$$

$$\frac{p + q + r + 21t + 24}{3} = 10t + 34$$

$$\frac{p + q + r}{3} + \frac{21t}{3} + \frac{24}{3} = 10t + 34$$

$$\frac{p + q + r}{3} = 10t + 34 - 7t - 8$$

$$\frac{p + q + r}{3} = 3t + 26$$

(A) is correct.

CHAPTER 9

Scatterplots

LEARNING OBJECTIVES

After completing this chapter, you will be able to:

- Determine the average rate of change
- Write an equation for a line of best fit
- Extrapolate values from the line of best fit
- Determine whether a linear, a quadratic, or an exponential model describes the data presented in a scatterplot

25/600 SmartPoints®

How Much Do You Know?

Directions: Try the questions that follow. Show your work so that you can compare your solutions to the ones found in the Check Your Work section immediately after this question set. The "Category" heading in the explanation for each question gives the title of the lesson that covers how to solve it. If you answered the question(s) for a given lesson correctly, and if your scratchwork looks like ours, you may be able to move quickly through that lesson. If you answered incorrectly or used a different approach, you may want to take your time on that lesson.

Questions 2 and 3 refer to the following stimulus.

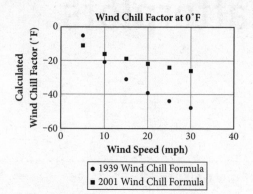

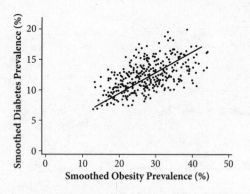

Source: CDC

1. The scatterplot shows the prevalence of obesity plotted against the prevalence of diabetes in various areas of the United States. Which of the following best estimates the average rate of change in the prevalence of diabetes as compared to the prevalence of obesity?

    A)   0.3

    B)   0.9

    C)   1.1

    D)   3

2. Wind chill, a measurement that reflects the temperature that one feels when outside based on the actual temperature and the wind speed, was first introduced in 1939, and the formula was revised in 2001. If the outside temperature is 0°F, what is the approximate wind chill at 40 miles per hour based on the 2001 formula?

    A)   −20°F

    B)   −30°F

    C)   −40°F

    D)   −50°F

3. What wind speed would produce the same wind chill using the 1939 formula as the wind chill produced using the 2001 formula when the outside temperature is 0°F and the wind speed is 40 miles per hour?

    A)   10 miles per hour

    B)   15 miles per hour

    C)   20 miles per hour

    D)   40 miles per hour

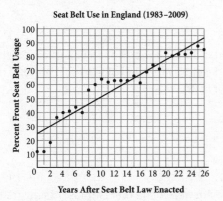

Seat Belt Use in England (1983–2009)

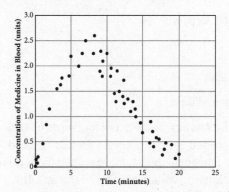

4. The scatterplot above shows data collected each year after the British Parliament enacted a mandatory seat belt law and the line of best fit to the data. Which of the following equations best represents the trend of the data shown in the figure?

A) $y = 0.4x + 25$

B) $y = 1.8x + 15$

C) $y = 2.1x + 35$

D) $y = 2.6x + 25$

6. Scientists measured the concentration of an experimental medication in blood samples over time. If a quadratic function is used to model the data, which of the following best explains the meaning of the vertex?

A) The average maximum medicine concentration in the blood sample is 7.5 units.

B) The average maximum medicine concentration is more than 20 units.

C) The average maximum medicine concentration in the blood samples occurs around 2.5 minutes.

D) The average maximum medicine concentration in the blood sample occurs between 5 and 10 minutes.

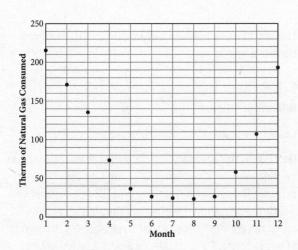

5. The scatterplot above shows the average therms of natural gas used by residential customers over a 12-month period. Of the following equations, which best models the data in the scatterplot?

A) $y = 1.061^x + 312.9$

B) $y = -1.061^x - 312.9$

C) $y = 6.1x^2 - 85.1x + 312.9$

D) $y = -6.1x^2 + 85.1x - 312.9$

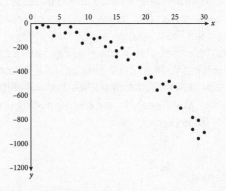

7. For which of the following values of a and b does the equation $y = ax^b$ model the data in the scatterplot above?

A) $a < 0, b < 0$

B) $a < 0, b > 0$

C) $a > 0, b < 0$

D) $a > 0, b > 0$

Check Your Work

1. A

Difficulty: Easy

Category: Line of Best Fit

Getting to the Answer: The scatterplot shows obesity prevalence plotted against diabetes prevalence, and because the line goes up as it moves to the right, there is a positive linear correlation between the two. The phrase "rate of change" is the same as the slope of the line of best fit, so pick two points to plug into the slope formula. Estimating, the endpoints appear to be $(14, 7)$ and $(44, 17)$. (If your estimate is different, that's okay—whenever the SAT requires you to make an estimate, the answer choices will be spread far enough apart that you'll get the right answer as long as you're looking in the right place and thinking the right way.) Calculate the slope, m:

$$m = \frac{y_2 - y_1}{x_2 - x_1} = \frac{17 - 7}{44 - 14} = \frac{10}{30} = 0.3$$

This matches **(A)**.

2. B

Difficulty: Medium

Category: Line of Best Fit

Getting to the Answer: The 2001 formula plot has a slight curve that straightens as wind speed increases. Extend the line to reflect this trend; once complete, draw a straight line from 40 mph on the x-axis to the extended 2001 formula plot (a straight edge such as an extra pencil will help). Then draw a horizontal line from the intersection of the 2001 formula line and the vertical line to the y-axis; you'll see that the corresponding wind chill is $-30°F$. **(B)** is correct.

3. B

Difficulty: Medium

Category: Line of Best Fit

Getting to the Answer: Since the conditions mentioned are the same as those in the previous question, start with the wind chill calculated using the 2001 formula for that question, $-30°F$.

Draw a horizontal line from $-30°F$ on the y-axis until it intersects a data point on the 1939 formula plot. Draw a vertical line from that point down to the x-axis;

you'll find that in 1939, a wind speed of approximately 15 mph would yield a wind chill of $-30°F$. Therefore, the correct answer is **(B)**.

4. D

Difficulty: Medium

Category: Line of Best Fit

Getting to the Answer: A line that "represents the trend of the data" is another way of referring to the line of best fit, which is linear in this diagram. Use the y-intercept and slope of the line of best fit to eliminate the choices.

Start by finding the y-intercept. For this graph, it's about 25, so eliminate (B) and (C). To choose between (A) and (D), find the approximate slope using two points that lie on (or very close to) the line of best fit. Use the y-intercept, $(0, 25)$, as one of the points to save time (it's easy to subtract 0) and estimate the second, such as $(21, 80)$. Then, use the slope formula to find the slope:

$$m = \frac{y_2 - y_1}{x_2 - x_1} = \frac{80 - 25}{21 - 0} = \frac{55}{21} = 2.62$$

The result is very close to the slope in **(D)**, making it the correct answer.

5. C

Difficulty: Medium

Category: Scatterplot Modeling

Getting to the Answer: The data in the scatterplot can be modeled by a parabola opening upward. (A) is an exponential growth equation, and (B) is an exponential decay equation. Neither will graph as a parabola, so eliminate both. Recall that a parabola is the graph of a quadratic. For a quadratic equation in the form $ax^2 + bx + c$, a determines whether the parabola opens upward or downward and c is the y-intercept. When $a > 0$, the parabola opens upward, so **(C)** is correct. (D) is a quadratic equation, but $a < 0$, so this equation would graph as a parabola that opens downward.

6.   D

Difficulty: Medium

Category: Scatterplot Modeling

Getting to the Answer: The vertex of a parabola opening downward, like this one, is at the maximum. For this scatterplot, the medicine concentration is measured on the y-axis, and the maximum value (the vertex) is about 2.6 units, so the average maximum medicine concentration cannot be above 2.6 units. Eliminate (A) and (B). The x-value of the vertex occurs between 5 and 10 minutes; therefore, **(D)** is correct.

7.   B

Difficulty: Hard

Category: Scatterplot Modeling

Getting to the Answer: The shape of the data is concave down with an increasingly negative slope as x increases. The y-values of the data are negative, which indicates $a < 0$. Eliminate (C) and (D). As x increases, the magnitude of the y-values increases. This indicates $b > 0$. Note that If $b < 0$, the y-values would approach 0 as x increases. Thus, **(B)** is correct.

Line of Best Fit

To answer a question like this:

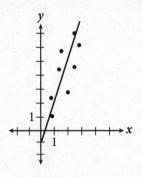

Which of the following equations corresponds to the line of best fit for the data set shown above?

A) $y = 0.4x - 1$

B) $y = 0.4x + 1$

C) $y = 2.5x + 1$

D) $y = 2.5x - 1$

You need to know this:

A **scatterplot** is a visual representation of a set of data points. The data points are plotted on the x- and y-axes such that each axis represents a different characteristic of the data set. For example, in the scatterplot below, each data point represents a dachshund. The x-axis represents the dog's length and the y-axis represents its height.

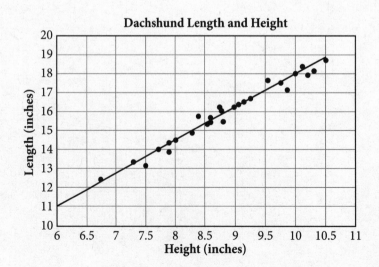

The **line of best fit**, or trend line, is drawn through the **data points** to describe the relationship between the two variables as an equation. This line does not necessarily go through any single data point, but it does accurately reflect the trend shown by the data with about half the points above the line and half below.

The **equation of the line of best fit** is the equation that describes the line of best fit algebraically. On test day, you'll most likely encounter this equation as linear, quadratic, or exponential, though it can also be other types of equations. The next lesson will cover these various forms.

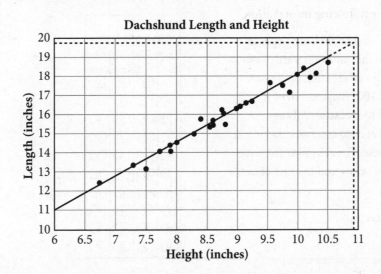

Some SAT questions will require you to extrapolate from the line of best fit. (Question 1 in the Try on Your Own set is an example of this type of question.) For example, you might be asked to predict the length of a dachshund that is 10.9 inches in height. Trace your way up to the line of best fit from the given *x*-value and trace over to find the corresponding *y*-value, in this case about 19.75 inches.

You need to do this:

To determine the equation of the line of best fit for a linear equation, like the one in the dachshund scatterplot, start by finding the slope, also called the **average rate of change**. Watch out for the units when you do this. In the dachshund example, using the points (6, 11) and (10, 18), the slope is $\frac{y_2 - y_1}{x_2 - x_1} = \frac{18 - 11}{10 - 6} = \frac{7}{4} = 1.75$. Next, find the *y*-intercept. Using the point (10, 18) and plugging those values into slope-intercept form yields $18 = 1.75(10) + b$. Thus, $b = 0.5$ in the dachshund example. So the equation in slope-intercept form is length $= (1.75 \times \text{height}) + 0.5$.

You can also extrapolate using the equation for the line of best fit. For a dachshund that is 11 inches tall, the calculation would be: length $= 1.75(11) + 0.5 = 19.75$.

Explanation:

Knowing where the *y*-intercept of the line of best fit falls will help you eliminate answer choices. Because the line of best fit intersects the *y*-axis below the *x*-axis, you know that the *y*-intercept is negative, so eliminate (B) and (C) (the *y*-intercept is +1 for each of those lines). Now, look at the slope. The line rises along the *y*-axis much faster than it runs along the *x*-axis, so the slope must be greater than 1, making **(D)** correct.

Math

Try on Your Own

Directions: Take as much time as you need on these questions. Work carefully and methodically. There will be an opportunity for timed practice at the end of the chapter.

Questions 1 and 2 refer to the following information.

Most chickens reach maturity and begin laying eggs at around 20 weeks of age. From this point forward, however, as the chicken ages, its egg production decreases. A farmer was given a flock of 100 chickens (all of which were the same age) and asked to measure daily egg output for the entire flock at random intervals starting at maturity until the chickens were 70 weeks old. The data are recorded in the scatterplot below and the line of best fit has been drawn.

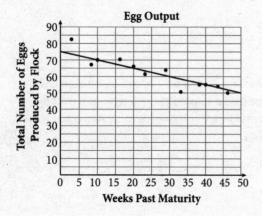

1. Based on the line of best fit, what is the predicted number of eggs that will be produced by the flock when it is 33 weeks past maturity?

   A) 33

   B) 50

   C) 58

   D) 64

HINT: For Q2, how many tick marks on the y-axis represent 5 eggs?

2. How many times did the farmer's data differ by more than 5 eggs from the number of eggs predicted by the line of best fit?

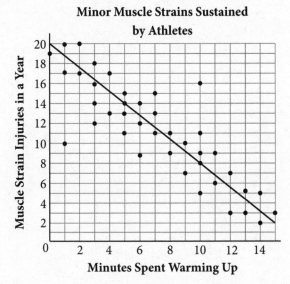

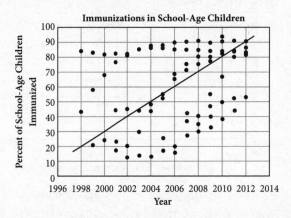

3. The scatterplot above shows the number of minor muscle strain injuries sustained in a year by athletes, plotted against their self-reported amount of time spent stretching and doing other "warm up" activities before engaging in rigorous physical activity. Which of the following best estimates the average rate of change in the number of injuries compared with the number of minutes spent warming up?

    A) −1.2

    B) −0.8

    C) 2

    D) 20

4. The graph above shows the percent of school-age children in the United States who received immunizations for various illnesses between 1996 and 2012. What was the average rate of increase in the percent of children immunized per year over the given time period?

    A) 5 percent per year

    B) 10 percent per year

    C) 25 percent per year

    D) 70 percent per year

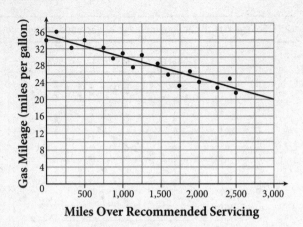

Miles Over Recommended Servicing

5. A car manufacturer compiled data that indicated gas mileage decreased as the number of miles driven between recommended servicing increased. The manufacturer used the equation $y = -\dfrac{1}{200}x + 35$ to model the data. Based on the information, how many miles per gallon could be expected if this particular car is driven 3,400 miles over the recommended miles between servicing?

Scatterplot Modeling

LEARNING OBJECTIVE

After this lesson, you will be able to:

- Determine whether a linear, quadratic, or exponential model describes the data presented in a scatterplot

To solve a question like this:

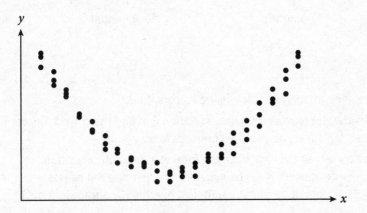

Given that *a*, *b*, and *c* are constants and that $a > 0$, which of the following is the equation for the line of best fit for the above scatterplot?

A) $y = ax + b$

B) $y = a^{bx}$

C) $y = -ax^2 + bx + c$

D) $y = ax^2 + bx + c$

You need to know this:

There are several patterns that are common forms for the line of best fit. Scatterplots are typically constructed so that the variable on the *x*-axis is the independent variable (input) and the variable on the *y*-axis is the dependent variable (output). The equation for the line of best fit quantifies the relationship between the variables represented by the two axes. The patterns that you are most likely to encounter on the SAT are shown in the table below.

Best Fit Description	Relationship Between Variables
Upward-sloping straight line	Linear and positive
Downward-sloping straight line	Linear and negative
Upward-opening parabola	Quadratic with a positive coefficient in front of the squared term
Downward-opening parabola	Quadratic with a negative coefficient in front of the squared term
Upward-sloping curve with an increasing slope	Exponential and positive (e.g., compound interest)
Downward-sloping curve with a flattening slope	Exponential and negative (e.g., radioactive decay)

Here are visual representations of linear, quadratic, and exponential models:

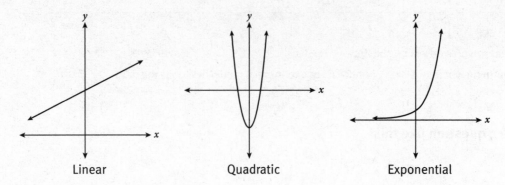

Linear   Quadratic   Exponential

You need to do this:

- Examine the line of best fit (draw it in, if necessary) and determine its curvature.
- If the line of best fit is straight, the scatterplot represents a linear relationship and the correct answer choice will not contain any exponents. It will likely be in slope-intercept form, $y = mx + b$.
- If the line of best fit is a parabola, the correct answer will be in the form of a quadratic equation, $y = ax^2 + bx + c$. If the parabola opens downward, a will be negative; if upward, a will be positive. (Chapter 12 presents more detailed information about parabolas, but this will suffice for now.)
- If the line of best fit starts with a gradual rate of change that steepens over time, the correct answer will represent an exponential relationship in the form $y = ab^x + c$.

Explanation:

The line of best fit for this scatterplot is curved, so it is not a straight line as would be created by the linear equation $y = ax + b$. Eliminate (A).

The exponential equation $y = a^{bx}$ would result in a curve that opens upward in one direction. The line of best fit of the scatterplot opens upward in two directions, so (B) is incorrect.

Quadratic equations create parabolas when graphed, but the negative coefficient of the x^2 term means that (C) would be a downward-opening parabola rather than the upward-opening parabola of the scatterplot. Thus, **(D)** is correct since that equation would be graphed as an upward-opening parabola.

Try on Your Own

Directions: Take as much time as you need on these questions. Work carefully and methodically. There will be an opportunity for timed practice at the end of the chapter.

6. Which of the following is best modeled using a linear regression equation, $y = ax + b$, where $a < 0$?

A)

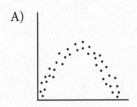

B)

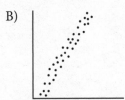

C)

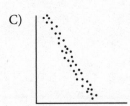

D)

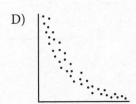

HINT: For Q7, in an exponential equation, you're taking a starting value and multiplying repeatedly by some other value.

7. Adriana used the data from a scatterplot she found on the U.S. Census Bureau's website to determine a regression model showing the relationship between the population in the area where she lived and the number of years, x, after she was born. The result was an exponential growth equation of the form $y = x_0(1 + r)^x$. Which of the following does x_0 most likely represent in the equation?

A) The population in the year that she was born

B) The rate of change of the population over time

C) The maximum population reached during her lifetime

D) The number of years after her birth when the population reached its maximum

8. Suppose a scatterplot shows a weak negative linear correlation. Which of the following statements is true?

A) The slope of the line of best fit will be a number less than -1.

B) The slope of the line of best fit will be a number between -1 and 0.

C) The data points will follow, but not closely, the line of best fit, which has a negative slope.

D) The data points will be closely gathered around the line of best fit, which has a negative slope.

Math

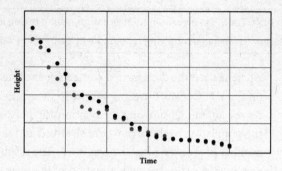

9. A drain at the bottom of a cylindrical water tank
    is opened and the height of the water is meas-
    ured at regular time intervals. The tank is refilled
    and the process is then repeated. The scatterplot
    above shows the measured height on the y-axis
    and time on the x-axis for the two trials. Which of
    the following conclusions can be drawn from the
    observations in the scatterplot?

    A) Water flows out of the drain at a constant rate.

    B) The flow rate from the tank decreases as the
        height of the water in the tank decreases.

    C) The drain is inefficiently designed.

    D) The is no relationship between the height of
        the water in the tank and time.

On Test Day

The SAT often tests your understanding of the real-world implications of the *y*-intercept of the line of best fit. The *y*-intercept indicates the starting value of the item measured on the *y*-axis before any time has passed. Scatterplots will test your ability to recognize the meaning of the *y*-intercept in various ways:

- For linear lines of best fit, common examples include the flat fee for renting an item before the hourly rate begins or the down payment on an item before the monthly payments begin.

- For quadratic lines of best fit, the most common example is the path of a projectile where the *y*-intercept is the starting height of the projectile.

- For exponential lines of best fit, common examples include the principal when calculating compound interest, the starting amount of an isotope with a specific half-life (radioactive decay), or the initial population when calculating population growth over time.

Keep in mind that lines of best fit are only approximate based on the given data, but the logic is straightforward: the *y*-intercept is directly related to the approximate initial amount of what is measured on the *y*-axis. Try the following question to see if you can recognize the real-world implication of the *y*-intercept of the line of best fit.

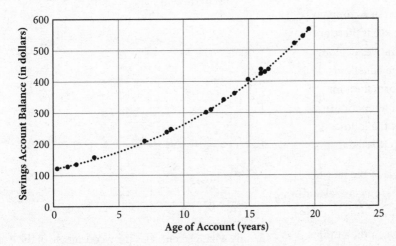

10. Students in a finance class surveyed 20 percent of the account holders at Docen Bank to determine whether the bank's "Stock Market Special" savings account actually paid account holders the promised 10 percent annual interest rate. The scatterplot above shows the data the students collected from account holders about how long ago they opened their accounts and their current balances. The students calculated a line of best fit with the equation $y = 120\left(1 + \frac{.08}{12}\right)^{12x}$, which means that the bank was actually paying account holders only an 8 percent annual interest rate. Which of the following best explains how the number 120 in the equation relates to the scatterplot?

A) A "Stock Market Special" account with $120 initially will likely have less than $350 after 15 years.

B) All "Stock Market Special" accounts started with a $120 initial investment.

C) The difference between the promised 10 percent annual interest rate and the actual 8 percent rate is $120 a year.

D) A "Stock Market Special" account with $120 initially will likely have more than $350 after 15 years.

How Much Have You Learned?

Directions: For testlike practice, give yourself 15 minutes to complete this question set. Be sure to study the explanations, even for questions you got right. They can be found at the end of this chapter.

Employee Sick Day Usage

11. The Human Resources department of a company tracks employee sick day usage to see if there are patterns. One of the HR representatives decides to check employee sick day usage against outside temperature. He compiles the information for the employees' sick day usage and temperature in the scatterplot above. Which of the following conclusions can he draw based on this data?

A) There is no relationship between the number of sick days used by employees in general and outside temperature.

B) There is no relationship between the number of sick days used by this company's employees and outside temperature.

C) No conclusions can be drawn about the number of sick days used by this company's employees and outside temperature.

D) There is a relationship, but not a causal link, between the number of sick days used by this company's employees and outside temperature.

12. Scientists plotted data for two animal populations on a scatterplot: population A, which they graphed along the *x*-axis, and population B, which they graphed along the *y*-axis. The data showed a strong negative correlation. Which of the following statements is justified?

A) The rise in population A caused the decline in population B.

B) The decline in population B caused the rise in population A.

C) Because the correlation is negative, there cannot be causation between the two populations.

D) The rise in population A is correlated to the decline in population B, but causation is unknown.

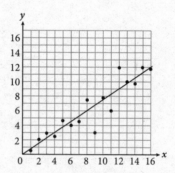

13. By what percent does the *y*-coordinate of the data point (12, 12) deviate from the *y*-value predicted by the line of best fit for an *x*-value of 12 ? (Ignore the percent sign and grid your response to the nearest percent.)

14. The scatterplot below compares the average gasoline prices in Boston, per gallon, to the average gasoline prices across the United States, per gallon, during a one-year period from 2017 to 2018.

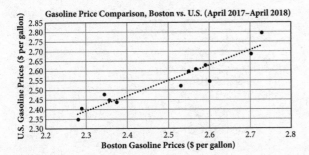

Of the following equations, which best models the data in the scatterplot?

A) $y = -1.7848x + 0.5842$

B) $y = 1.7848x + 1.5842$

C) $y = 0.7848x + 0.5842$

D) $y = -0.7848x + 0.5842$

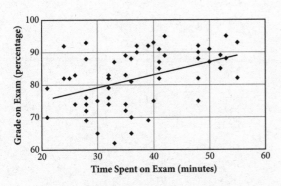

15. A physics professor presented the scatterplot above to her first-year students. What is the significance of the slope of the line of best fit?

A)   The slope represents the rate at which time spent on an exam increases based on a student's exam performance.

B)   The slope represents the average grade on the exam.

C)   The slope represents the rate at which a student's exam grade increases based on time spent on the exam.

D)   The slope has no significance.

16. Which of the following is the most accurate statement about the scatterplot above?

A)   The data in the scatterplot has a weak positive correlation.

B)   The data in the scatterplot has a strong positive correlation.

C)   The data in the scatterplot has a negative correlation.

D)   There is no correlation in the data set.

Questions 17 and 18 refer to the following information.

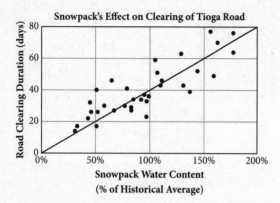

Snowpack's Effect on Clearing of Tioga Road

(Data source: www.nps.gov/yose/planyourvisit/tiogaopen.htm)

Tioga Road is a mountain pass that crosses the Sierra Nevada through northern Yosemite National Park. The road is closed from about November through late May. This time period can change depending on the quantity and nature of the season's snowfall, as well as unforeseen obstacles such as fallen trees or rocks. The scatterplot above compares the snowpack water content on April 1 (for years 1981–2014) as a percent of the historical average to the time it takes the National Park Service to fully clear the road and open it to traffic.

17. For every 5 percent increase in snowpack water content, how many more days does it take the National Park Service to clear Tioga Road?

18. Assuming no unforeseen obstacles or machinery issues, if the road's snowpack water content on April 1 is 248 percent of the historical average, based on the prior experience shown on the graph, how many days will it take to fully clear Tioga Road?

19. Which of the following scatterplots shows a relationship that is appropriately modeled with the equation $y = -ax^2 + bx - c$, where a and c are negative and b is positive?

A)

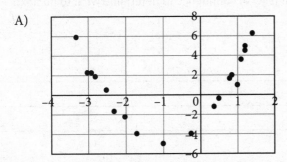

B)

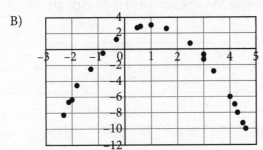

C)

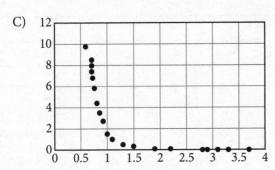

D)

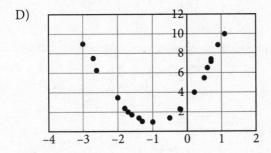

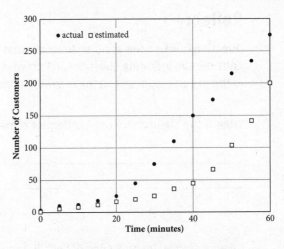

20. The scatterplot above shows the actual and estimated number of customers visiting a new shopping plaza within the first hour of opening. Which of the following statements correctly compares the rates of increase for the actual and estimated numbers of customers?

A) The rate of increase for the actual number of customers is greater than that of the estimated number in every 20-minute interval.

B) The rate of increase for the actual number of customers is less than that of the estimated number in every 20-minute interval.

C) The rate of increase for the actual number of customers is greater than that of the estimated number in the interval from 20 to 40 minutes and less in the interval 40 to 60 minutes.

D) The rate of increase for the actual number of customers is less than that of the estimated number in the interval from 20 to 40 minutes and greater in the interval 40 to 60 minutes.

Reflect

Directions: Take a few minutes to recall what you've learned and what you've been practicing in this chapter. Consider the following questions, jot down your best answer for each one, and then compare your reflections to the expert responses on the following page. Use your level of confidence to determine what to do next.

What is the significance of a scatterplot's line of best fit?

_____

_____

_____

Given a scatterplot and a line of best fit, how can you tell whether the line of best fit is an accurate one?

_____

_____

_____

What are the three most common patterns for modeling scatterplots that you'll see on test day?

_____

_____

_____

Expert Responses

What is the significance of a scatterplot's line of best fit?

The line of best fit describes the relationship between the two variables of the scatterplot. For example, if the line of best fit is linear and has a positive slope, then the two variables have a linear and positive relationship: as one variable increases, the other one also increases and at a constant rate.

Given a scatterplot and a line of best fit, how can you tell whether the line of best fit is an accurate one?

A line of best fit should be drawn such that approximately half the points are above it and half are below it.

What are the three most common patterns for modeling scatterplots that you'll see on test day?

Most test day scatterplots can be modeled by a linear $(y = mx + b)$, quadratic $(y = ax^2 + bx + c)$, or exponential $(y = ab^x + c)$ relationship.

Next Steps

If you answered most questions correctly in the "How Much Have You Learned?" section, and if your responses to the Reflect questions were similar to those of the SAT expert, then consider scatterplots an area of strength and move on to the next chapter. Come back to this topic periodically to prevent yourself from getting rusty.

If you don't yet feel confident, review those parts of this chapter that you have not yet mastered, then try the questions you missed again. In particular, make sure that you feel comfortable extrapolating data from a line of best fit. As always, be sure to review the explanations closely.

Answers and Explanations

1.   C

Difficulty: Easy

Getting to the Answer: In this case, you merely need to match the y-value on the line of best fit with the x-value of 33, since the x-axis of the graph represents the number of weeks after maturity. Take care to use the line of best fit rather than an individual point on the graph; (B) is a trap answer. At $x = 33$, the y-value of the line of best fit seems to be just shy of 60. Thus, **(C)** is correct.

2.   2

Difficulty: Easy

Getting to the Answer: Examine the graph, including the axis labels and numbering. Each vertical grid line represents 5 eggs, so look to see how many data points are more than a complete grid space away from the line of best fit. Only 2 data points meet this requirement—the first data point at about 3 weeks and the one between 30 and 35 weeks, making **2** the correct answer.

3.   A

Difficulty: Medium

Getting to the Answer: Examine the graph, paying careful attention to units and labels. The average rate of change is the same as the slope of the line of best fit. The data is decreasing (going down from left to right), so eliminate (C) and (D). To choose between (A) and (B), find the slope of the line of best fit using the slope formula, $m = \dfrac{y_2 - y_1}{x_2 - x_1}$, and any two points that lie on (or very close to) the line. Using the two points (5, 14) and (10, 8), the average rate of change is about $\dfrac{8 - 14}{10 - 5} = \dfrac{-6}{5} = -1.2$, which matches **(A)**.

4.   A

Difficulty: Easy

Getting to the Answer: The question asks for a rate of change, which means you'll need the slope of the line of best fit. Pick a pair of points to use in the slope formula, such as (1998, 20) and (2012, 90):

$$m = \frac{y_2 - y_1}{x_2 - x_1} = \frac{90 - 20}{2012 - 1998} = \frac{70}{14} = 5$$

Choice **(A)** is correct.

5.   18

Difficulty: Medium

Getting to the Answer: Because the y-value of the graph when $x = 3,400$ is not shown, this question requires a mathematical solution; extending the line of best fit will not provide an accurate enough answer. The equation of the model is given as $y = -\dfrac{1}{200}x + 35$. Miles over recommended servicing are graphed along the x-axis, so substitute 3,400 for x to find the answer:

$$y = -\frac{1}{200}(3,400) + 35 = -17 + 35 = 18$$

Grid in **18**.

6.   C

Difficulty: Easy

Getting to the Answer: A regression equation is the equation of the line (or curve) that best fits the data. A *linear* regression is used to model data that follows the path of a straight line. In the equation given, a represents the slope of the linear regression (the line of best fit), so you are looking for data that is linear and is decreasing, or falling from left to right, which happens with a is negative, or as the question states, when $a < 0$. You can eliminate (A), which is a quadratic curve, and (D), an exponential curve. You can also eliminate (B) because it is increasing (rising from left to right) instead of decreasing (falling from left to right). **(C)** is correct.

7.   A

Difficulty: Easy

Getting to the Answer: When an exponential equation is written in the form $y = x_0(1 + r)^x$, the value of x_0 gives the y-intercept of the equation's graph. To answer this question, you need to think about what the y-intercept would represent in the context described.

Whenever time is involved in a relationship that is modeled by an equation or a graph, it is almost always the independent variable and therefore graphed on the x-axis. Therefore, for this question, population would be graphed on the y-axis, so x_0 most likely represents the population when the time elapsed was zero, or in other words, in the year that Adriana was born, making **(A)** correct.

8. C

Difficulty: Medium

Getting to the Answer: "Correlation" simply means relationship. The word "weak" refers to the strength of the relationship (how close the data lies to the line of best fit), which has no effect on slope. Be careful not to confuse slope and strength. The fact that a data set shows a weak correlation does not give you any information about the magnitude of the slope. This means you can eliminate (A) and (B). Also, keep in mind that the terms "weak" and "negative" are not related, but rather are two independent descriptors of the correlation. So the fact that the rate of change is negative has nothing to do with the strength of the correlation. In a weak correlation, the data points will loosely follow the line of best fit, which makes **(C)** the correct answer.

9. B

Difficulty: Easy

Getting to the Answer: A line of best fit for the scatterplot would show that the measured height of the water decreases over time, but the slope becomes less steep over time, too. The slope, change in height divided by change in time, represents the flow rate of water out of the tank. Since the flow changes as the height of the water changes, (A) is incorrect. Because the slope of the line of best fit becomes less steep as the height of the water decreases, it follows that the flow rate decreases as the height of the water decreases. **(B)** is correct. (D) is incorrect because the height of the water decreases (though at an ever slower rate) as time progresses, so there is a relationship between the height of the water and time. (C) is incorrect because the data presented doesn't imply anything about the efficiency of the drain design.

10. D

Difficulty: Medium

Strategic Advice: Lines of best fit only approximate trends based on a given data set.

Getting to the Answer: In the line of best fit equation that the students calculated, the initial principal is $120, but that does not necessarily mean that *all* of the account holders had that much in the account initially. Eliminate (B).

To test (A) and (D), sketch in the line of best fit:

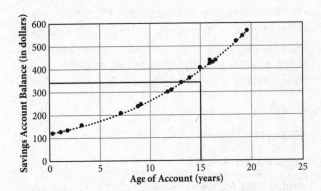

Notice that the line of best fit, which is based on an initial principal of $120, is definitely above $350 at the 15 year mark, so **(D)** is correct. Since the line of best fit is exponential, not linear, there will not be a consistent difference between the 10 percent annual rate and 8 percent annual rate, which makes (C) incorrect.

11. B

Difficulty: Medium

Category: Scatterplot Modeling

Getting to the Answer: There are two things to keep in mind for a question like this: correlation does not prove causation, and as a general rule, conclusions can be drawn only about the population studied, not about all populations. The population in the study is only the employees at the company, not all employees in general, so eliminate (A). The data points are scattered and do not form any discernible pattern. This means there is no correlation, which is another way of saying the two variables aren't related, so you can eliminate (D). You can also eliminate (C) because the HR representative *is* able to draw a conclusion—that there is no relationship. Therefore, **(B)** is correct.

12. D

Difficulty: Medium

Category: Scatterplot Modeling

Getting to the Answer: The fact that the two variables are strongly correlated, whether it be negatively or positively, shows only that there is a relationship between the variables. It does not indicate whether the change in one variable caused the change in the other. For example, population A might thrive in wet climates, while population B does not, and in the years studied, rainfall may have increased, which caused the changes in the populations. Eliminate (A) and (B). Conversely, the negative correlation does not discount the possibility of causation; rather, the data does not allow you to draw a conclusion about causation, so eliminate (C). This means **(D)** is the correct answer.

13. 33

Difficulty: Medium

Category: Line of Best Fit

Getting to the Answer: The point (12, 12) is 3 full grid lines away from the line of best fit, which goes through (12, 9). To find the percent difference between the expected and actual y-values, use the percent change formula. Note that the phrasing of the question indicates that the original value to use is 9, the y-value on the line of best fit: $\frac{12-9}{9} \times 100\% = \frac{3}{9} \times 100\% = 33.3\%$. Grid in **33**.

14. C

Difficulty: Medium

Category: Scatterplot Modeling

Strategic Advice: For scatterplot questions, it is important to determine whether using logic or plugging in values is more efficient.

Getting to the Answer: Notice that the answer choices involve very precise coefficients, which is a good indicator that logic is the best way to get to the correct answer. The slope of the line of best fit is positive, so eliminate (A) and (D), which have negative slopes. It is also important to note that the lower-left corner of the graph is not the origin, which means that the y-intercept needs to be extrapolated. With only two choices left, you can test only one of them. If the equation you test works, then it is correct. If the equation you test does not work, the other is correct. To test (B), choose one of the values

from the scatterplot that is close to the line of best fit, for example (2.7, 2.7). Plugging 2.7 in for x should mean that $y = 2.7$, but with the equation in choice (B) you get:

$$y = 1.7848(2.7) + 1.5842$$
$$y = 4.81896 + 1.5842$$
$$y = 6.40316$$

This does not match the coordinate point, so **(C)** is correct.

15. C

Difficulty: Medium

Category: Line of Best Fit

Getting to the Answer: The slope of a line is always a rate of change of some sort, so you can eliminate (B) and (D). The graph indicates that time spent on the exam is the independent variable, so exam performance depends on it. The choice that correctly describes this relationship is **(C)**.

16. C

Difficulty: Medium

Category: Scatterplot Modeling

Strategic Advice: Correlation refers to how closely values on the scatterplot match the line of best fit.

Getting to the Answer: Since correlation is related to the best-fit line, it is important to sketch one on the graph. Here's a rough approximation:

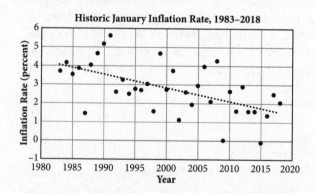

A strong correlation means that the data points are closely gathered around the line of best fit; a weak correlation means that the data points are farther from the line of best fit. The line of best fit has a definite negative slope, so eliminate (A) and (B). When there is no correlation, the data set is distributed evenly over the entire graph, but that is not the case here, so (D) can be eliminated as well. **(C)** is correct.

17. 2

Difficulty: Medium

Category: Line of Best Fit

Getting to the Answer: You're asked for a rate; this means finding the slope of the line of best fit. Start by picking a pair of points, preferably where the line of best fit passes through a grid line intersection to minimize error. The points (0, 0) and (50, 20) are good choices to make the calculation easy. Determine the slope:

$$m = \frac{y_2 - y_1}{x_2 - x_1} = \frac{20 - 0}{50 - 0} = \frac{20}{50} = \frac{2}{5}$$

Don't grid in $\frac{2}{5}$, though. Remember what you're being asked: you need the road clearing duration increase for a 5% increase in snowpack water content, not a 1% increase. Therefore, multiply $\frac{2}{5}$ by 5, which yields 2. Grid in **2**.

18. 99.2

Difficulty: Medium

Category: Line of Best Fit

Getting to the Answer: The slope you found in the previous question will save you some time here. The line of best fit on the scatterplot intersects the y-axis at (0, 0). Therefore, the equation of the line of best fit is $y = \frac{2}{5}x$. Plug 248 in for x and simplify:

$$y = \frac{2}{5}(248) = \frac{496}{5} = 99.2$$

The road clearing time at 248% snowpack water content will take **99.2** days.

19. D

Difficulty: Medium

Category: Line of Best Fit

Strategic Advice: Think about how the graphs of different equations look and eliminate the choices that don't match.

Getting to the Answer: Sketch in the lines of best fit for the answer choices. (A) and (D) are parabolas that open up, (B) is a parabola that opens down, and (C) is an exponential curve. The equation that needs to be modeled is $y = -ax^2 + bx - c$, which is quadratic and graphs as a parabola. Eliminate (C). Pay careful attention to the details "*a* and *c* are negative and *b* is positive." The coefficient in front of the x^2 term determines whether the parabola opens up or down. The negative sign in front of the *a* multiplies by the negative value for *a* to create a positive coefficient in front of the x^2 term, which means that the parabola opens up. Eliminate (B). Finally, the *c* coefficient in the equation determines the y-intercept for the graph. Again, the negative sign in front of *c* multiplies by the negative value for *c* to create a positive y-intercept. Eliminate (A) because the best-fit parabola has a negative y-intercept. **(D)** is correct.

20. C

Difficulty: Hard

Category: Scatterplot Modeling

Getting to the Answer: For every 20-minute interval, draw a line of best fit through the data for the actual number of customers and similarly for the estimated number of customers. Then compare the slopes of the lines of best fit for actual and estimated for each 20-minute interval to compare the rates of increase.

In the interval from 0 to 20 minutes, the slope of the line of best fit for the actual number of customers is slightly greater (steeper) than that of the estimated model. In the interval from 20 to 40 minutes, the slope of the line of best fit for the actual data is greater than that of the estimated data. In the interval from 40 to 60 minutes, the slope of the line of best fit for the actual data is less than that of the estimated data. Thus, **(C)** is correct.

Passport to Advanced Math

CHAPTER 10

Functions

LEARNING OBJECTIVES

After completing this chapter, you will be able to:

- Apply function notation
- Define the domain and range of a function
- Evaluate the output of a function for a given input
- Interpret the graph of a function
- Write a function to describe a rule or data set

105/600 SmartPoints®

Math

How Much Do You Know?

Directions: Try the questions that follow. Show your work so that you can compare your solutions to the ones found in the Check Your Work section immediately after this question set. The "Category" heading in the explanation for each question gives the title of the lesson that covers how to solve it. If you answered the question(s) for a given lesson correctly, and if your scratchwork looks like ours, you may be able to move quickly through that lesson. If you answered incorrectly or used a different approach, you may want to take your time on that lesson.

$$p(x) = 7x + 4$$
$$s(x) = 7 - p(x)$$

1. What is the value of $s(-1)$?

    A)   −3

    B)   4

    C)   10

    D)   17

2. A function is defined by the equation 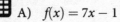 $f(x) = \dfrac{x^2}{4} - 11$. For this function, which of the following domain values corresponds to a range value of 14 ?

    A)   −4

    B)   10

    C)   38

    D)   100

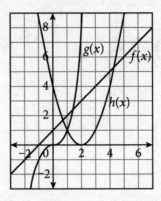

3. In the figure above, what is the value of $h(0) - 3(g(1) - f(2))$?

    A)   −2

    B)   5

    C)   10

    D)   12

x	2	3	4	5
$f(x)$	7	13	19	25

4. Some values of the function f are shown in the table above. Which of the following defines f?

    A) $f(x) = 7x - 1$

    B) $f(x) = 6x - 5$

    C) $f(x) = 5x + 1$

    D) $f(x) = 4x + 5$

5. Briana is writing a 60-page paper for a law school class. She estimates that she will average 45 words per minute while typing. If one page contains approximately 500 words, which of the following correctly estimates the number of pages, p, remaining as a function of the number of minutes, m, that Briana types?

A) $p(m) = 60 - \dfrac{9m}{100}$

B) $p(m) = \dfrac{60 - 100}{9m}$

C) $p(m) = 60 - \dfrac{100}{9m}$

D) $p(m) = \dfrac{60 - 9m}{100}$

Math

Check Your Work

1. C

Difficulty: Medium

Category: Function Notation

Getting to the Answer: To evaluate a function at any value, substitute that value for the variable in the function definition. The question asks for the value of $s(-1)$, so replace the x in the s function with -1: $s(-1) = 7 - p(-1)$. To find the value of $p(-1)$, replace the x in the p function with -1: $p(-1) = 7(-1) + 4 = -3$. Replace $p(-1)$ with its value, -3, in the s function: $s(-1) = 7 - (-3) = 10$. **(C)** is correct.

2. B

Difficulty: Medium

Category: Function Notation

Getting to the Answer: In this question, you are given a range value (14), which means $f(x) = 14$, and you are asked for the corresponding domain value (x-value). This means you are solving for x, not substituting for x. Set the function equal to 14 and solve using inverse operations:

$$14 = \frac{x^2}{4} - 11$$
$$25 = \frac{x^2}{4}$$
$$100 = x^2$$
$$\pm 10 = x$$

Because -10 is not one of the answer choices, you know the answer is 10. **(B)** is correct.

3. C

Difficulty: Medium

Category: Graphs of Functions

Getting to the Answer: Start with $h(0)$, which means the y-value when $x = 0$. Based on the graph of the h function, $h(0) = 4$. Repeat with $g(1)$, which is 1, and $f(2)$, which is 3. Manipulate these values as instructed: $4 - 3(1 - 3) = 4 + 6 = 10$. Choice **(C)** is correct.

4. B

Difficulty: Easy

Category: Graphs of Functions

Getting to the Answer: Use one of the given points to test the functions. Choose the point that is easiest for you to test. When $x = 2$, $y = 7$, so plug $x = 2$ into the choices and find the one that yields $y = 7$.

Test (A): $f(2) = 7(2) - 1 = 13$. Eliminate (A).

Test (B): $f(2) = 6(2) - 5 = 7$. Keep (B).

Test (C): $f(2) = 5(2) + 1 = 11$. Eliminate (C).

Test (D): $f(2) = 4(2) + 5 = 13$. Eliminate (D).

Only **(B)** remains, and it is correct.

Since all the choices have different slopes, an alternative approach would be to find the slope of the line by using two points.

Use the formula Slope $= \frac{\text{rise}}{\text{run}}$ to get $\frac{13 - 7}{3 - 2} = 6$. **(B)** is correct.

5. A

Difficulty: Hard

Category: Describing Real-Life Situations with Functions

Getting to the Answer: Use the two given rates to determine Briana's typing rate in pages per minute. She types 45 words per minute, which becomes:

$$\frac{45 \text{ words}}{1 \text{ minute}} \times \frac{1 \text{ page}}{500 \text{ words}} = \frac{45 \text{ pages}}{500 \text{ minutes}} = \frac{9 \text{ pages}}{100 \text{ minutes}}$$

Multiplying this rate by m gets you the number of pages typed after m minutes, which can then be subtracted from the starting page count, 60, to get the number of pages Briana has left to type. The function should read $p(m) = 60 - \frac{9m}{100}$, which matches **(A)**.

Function Notation

LEARNING OBJECTIVES

After this lesson, you will be able to:

- Apply function notation
- Define the domain and range of a function
- Evaluate the output of a function for a given input

To answer a question like this:

$$h(x) = \frac{2x + 7}{x - 4}$$

Which of the following must be true about $h(x)$?

I. $h(14) = 3.5$

II. The domain of $h(x)$ is all real numbers

III. $h(x)$ may be positive or negative

A) I and II only

B) I and III only

C) II and III only

D) I, II, and III

You need to know this:

A **function** is a rule that generates one unique output for a given input. In function notation, the *x*-value is the input and the *y*-value, designated by $f(x)$, is the output. (Note that other letters besides *x* and *f* may be used.)

For example, a linear function has the same form as the slope-intercept form of a line; $f(x)$ is equivalent to *y*:

$$f(x) = mx + b$$

In questions that describe real-life situations, the *y*-intercept will often be the starting point for the function. You can think of it as $f(0)$, or that value of the function where $x = 0$.

The set of all possible *x*-values is called the **domain** of the function, while the set of all possible *y*-values is called the **range**.

You need to do this:

- To find $f(x)$ for some value of x, substitute the concrete value in for the variable and do the arithmetic.
- For questions that ask about the domain of a function, check whether any inputs are not allowed, for example, because they cause division by 0.
- For questions that ask about a function of a function, for example, $g(f(x))$, start on the inside and work your way out.

Explanation:

Check each statement. For the first statement, plug in 14 for x:

$$\frac{2(14)+7}{14-4} = \frac{28+7}{10} = \frac{35}{10} = 3.5$$

So the first statement is true. Eliminate choice (C).

For the second statement, you need to determine the set of all permitted x-values for this function. Note that the function will be undefined at $x = 4$ (because at $x = 4$, the denominator would be 0.) Thus, 4 is not a permitted x-value, and the domain is not all real numbers. The second statement is false. Eliminate (A) and (D).

By process of elimination, the answer is **(B)**, and on test day, you would stop here. For the record, here's why the third statement is true: you've already established that $h(x) = 3.5$ is a permitted value. If you plug in a smaller value, such as 0, you get: $h(0) = \frac{2(0)+7}{0-4} = \frac{7}{-4} = -\frac{7}{4}$, so $f(x)$ can be negative as well.

Try on Your Own

Directions: Take as much time as you need on these questions. Work carefully and methodically. There will be an opportunity for timed practice at the end of the chapter.

HINT: For Q1, replace every x in the function definition with -2.

1. If $g(x) = -2x^2 + 7x - 3$, what is the value of $g(-2)$?

    A) -25

    B) -9

    C) -1

    D) 3

2. If $k(x) = 5x + 2$, what is the value of $k(4) - k(1)$?

    A) 15

    B) 17

    C) 19

    D) 21

HINT: For Q3, work from the inside parentheses out.

x	$g(x)$
-6	-3
-3	-2
0	-1
3	0
6	1

x	$h(x)$
0	6
1	-4
2	2
3	0
4	-2

3. Several values for the functions $g(x)$ and $h(x)$ are shown in the tables above. What is the value of $g(h(3))$?

    A) -1

    B) 0

    C) 3

    D) 6

4. If $p(x) = x^2 - 4x + 8$ and $q(x) = x - 3$, what is the value of $\dfrac{q(p(5))}{p(q(5))}$?

    A) 0

    B) 0.4

    C) 1

    D) 2.5

n	$f(n)$	$g(n)$
2	11.6	1.5
3	13.9	1
4	16.2	0.5

5. The table above shows some values of the linear functions f and g. If $h(n) = 2 \times f(n) - g(n)$, what is the value of $h(6)$?

    A) 21.3

    B) 35.0

    C) 41.1

    D) 42.1

Graphs of Functions

To answer a question like this:

x	$h(x)$
0	-3
1	-2
2	1
3	6
4	13
5	22
6	33

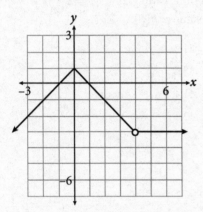

The maximum value of function g, whose graph is shown above, is m. Values for the function h are shown in the table. What is the value of $h(m)$?

A) -3

B) -2

C) 2

D) 4

You need to know this:

Interpreting graphs of functions is similar to interpreting graphs of equations. For example:

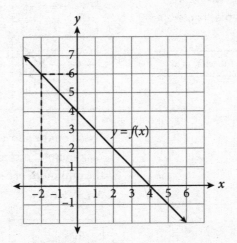

Say the graph above represents the function $f(x)$ and you're asked to find the value of x for which $f(x) = 6$. Because $f(x)$ represents the output value, or range, you can translate this to, "When does the y value equal 6?" To answer the question, find 6 on the y-axis, then trace over to the function (the line). Read the corresponding x-value: it's -2, so when $f(x) = 6$, x must be -2.

The SAT may sometimes ask about a function's **maximum** or **minimum**. These terms mean the greatest and least value of the function, respectively. This graph of $f(x)$ does not have a maximum or minimum, as the arrows on the line indicate that it continues infinitely in both directions. The question above, however, does show a function with a maximum.

You need to do this:

- Treat $f(x)$ as the y-coordinate on a graph.
- The maximum and minimum refer to a function's greatest and least y-coordinates, respectively.

Explanation

Start by identifying m, which occurs at the apex of the function at $(0, 1)$. The "maximum value of function g" means the greatest y-value, so $m = 1$. Next, use the table to find $h(1)$, which is the y-value when $x = 1$. According to the table, when $x = 1$, $h(x) = -2$. **(B)** is correct.

Try on Your Own

Directions: Take as much time as you need on these questions. Work carefully and methodically. There will be an opportunity for timed practice at the end of the chapter.

HINT: For Q6, $p(x)$ means the y-value of the function at x.

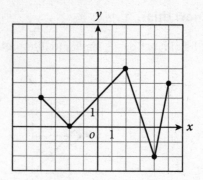

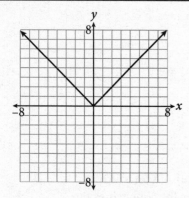

6. The above figure shows the function $p(x) = |x|$. Which statement about the function is NOT true?

A) $p(0) = 0$

B) $p(-4) = 4$

C) $p(4) = -4$

D) The domain of $p(x)$ is all real numbers.

8. Based on the above graph, if the coordinates of the maximum of $f(x)$ are (a, b) and the coordinates of the minimum of $f(x)$ are (c, d), what is the value of $a + b + c + d$?

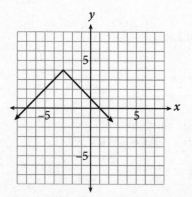

7. The graph of $f(x)$ is shown above. Which of the following represents the domain and range of the function?

A) Domain: $f(x) \geq 4$; range: all real numbers

B) Domain: $f(x) \leq 4$; range: all real numbers

C) Domain: all real numbers; range: $f(x) \geq 4$

D) Domain: all real numbers; range: $f(x) \leq 4$

9. The graph of the linear function f has intercepts at $(c, 0)$ and $(0, d)$ in the xy-plane. If $2c = d$ and $d \neq 0$, which of the following is true about the slope of the graph of f?

A) It is positive.

B) It is negative.

C) It equals zero.

D) It is undefined.

HINT: For Q10, which roman numeral statement appears the most often in the answer choices? What advantage would you have if you knew that statement was not part of the correct answer?

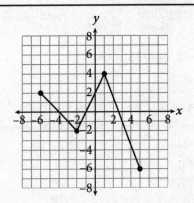

10. The complete graph of the function f is shown in the figure above. Which of the following is equal to -1 ?

I. $f(-4)$

II. $f(0)$

III. $f(3)$

A) I and II

B) II only

C) I, II, and III

D) III only

Describing Real-Life Situations with Functions

LEARNING OBJECTIVE

After this lesson, you will be able to:

- Write a function to describe a rule or data set

To answer a question like this:

Type of Ingredient	Number of Cookies per Box	Profit per Box (dollars)
Walnuts	22	1.26
Pecans	20	1.10
Butterscotch	24	1.42
Mint	18	0.94
Macadamias	12	0.46
Hazelnuts	16	0.78

A certain cookie company sells several varieties of chocolate cookies, each with an added ingredient. The company sells the different varieties in differently sized boxes. The number of cookies per box and the profit per box for the different varieties is shown in the table above. The relationship between the number of cookies per box and the profit, in dollars, that the company makes per box can be represented by a linear function. Which of the following functions correctly represents the relationship?

A) $p(n) = 0.11n - 0.25$

B) $p(n) = 0.1n - 0.35$

C) $p(n) = 0.09n - 0.45$

D) $p(n) = 0.08n - 0.5$

You need to know this:

Modeling real-life situations using functions is the same as modeling them using equations; the only difference is the function notation and the rule that each input has only one output.

For example, suppose a homeowner wants to determine the cost of installing a certain amount of carpet in her living room. Say that the carpet costs \$0.86 per square foot, the installer charges a \$29 installation fee, and sales tax on the total cost is 7%. Using your algebra and function knowledge, you can describe this situation in which the cost, c, is a function of square footage, f. The equation would be $c = 1.07(0.86f + 29)$. In function notation, this becomes $c(f) = 1.07(0.86f + 29)$, where $c(f)$ is shorthand for "cost as a function of square footage." The following table summarizes what each piece of the function represents in the scenario.

English	Overall cost	Square footage	Material cost	Installation fee	Sales tax
Math	c	f	$0.86f$	29	1.07

You need to do this:

In word problems involving function notation, translate the math equations exactly as you learned in chapter 4 in the Word Problems lesson, but substitute $f(x)$ for y.

Explanation:

Note that the question asks for the relationship between the number of cookies per box and the profit per box and that the answer choices all start with $p(n)$. Given the context, this translates to the relationship "profit as a function of the number of cookies." All the choices express a linear relationship, so you can't rule out any of them on that basis.

There are several approaches you could take to find the correct answer. One would be to recognize that all the choices are in the form $p(n) = kn + b$ (a variation of the slope-intercept form $y = mx + b$) and that you can set up a system of linear equations using the data from any two rows of the table to solve for k and b. That approach would look like this:

$$1.26 = 22k + b$$
$$- \quad (1.10 = 20k + b)$$
$$\overline{0.16 = 2k}$$
$$0.08 = k$$

$$1.10 = 20(.08) + b$$
$$1.10 = 1.60 + b$$
$$b = -0.5$$

Because $k = 0.08$ and $b = -0.5$, the correct function is $p(n) = 0.08k - 0.5$, so **(D)** is correct.

Another approach would be to use two of the pairs of data points from the table to calculate a slope; for example, using the "pecans" and "macadamias" rows would yield $\frac{1.10 - 0.46}{20 - 12} = \frac{0.64}{8} = 0.08$. Because only one answer has a slope of 0.08, you can pick **(D)**.

Finally, you could backsolve. Plug any one of the rows of data from the table into all four answer choices. The second row has the easiest numbers to work with, so use those. You are checking which equation will produce a profit of \$1.10 per box given 20 cookies per box:

A) $0.11(20) - 0.25 = 1.95 \neq 1.10$

B) $0.1(20) - 0.35 = 1.65 \neq 1.10$

C) $0.09(20) - 0.45 = 1.35 \neq 1.10$

D) $0.08(20) - 0.5 = 1.10$

Again, **(D)** is correct.

Try on Your Own

Directions: Take as much time as you need on these questions. Work carefully and methodically. There will be an opportunity for timed practice at the end of the chapter.

HINT: For Q11, pick the easiest number of days from the chart, plug that into the choices, and eliminate any that don't give you the correct vote count. Repeat if necessary until only one choice is left.

Day	Vote Count
3	21
4	35
5	53
6	75
7	101

11. Paulo is one of five contest finalists in the running for a year's worth of college book expenses. The winner is the finalist with the highest number of votes on the contest host's website. Paulo recorded his vote total each day of the contest; data for five days are in the table above. Which of the following represents Paulo's vote count, v, as a function of time, t, in days?

A) $v(t) = 2t^2 + 3$

B) $v(t) = \dfrac{t^2}{2} + 3$

C) $v(t) = 2t^2 + 21$

D) $v(t) = \dfrac{t^2}{2} + 21$

HINT: For Q12, the faster the rate of change, the steeper the slope.

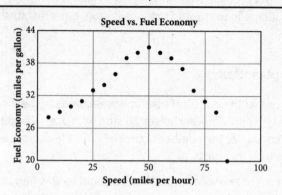

12. The graph above shows a compact car's fuel economy as a function of speed. Which of the following is true?

A) The rate of increase in fuel economy below 50 miles per hour is greater than the rate of decrease in fuel economy above 50 miles per hour.

B) The rate of increase in fuel economy below 50 miles per hour is equal to the rate of decrease in fuel economy above 50 miles per hour.

C) The rate of increase in fuel economy below 50 miles per hour is less than the rate of decrease in fuel economy above 50 miles per hour.

D) Fuel economy peaks at 50 miles per hour, but nothing can be said about the rates of change in fuel economy above and below 50 miles per hour.

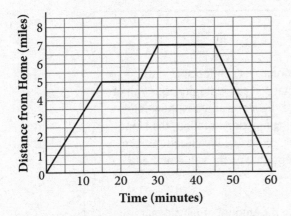

HINT: For Q14, which two readings will be easiest to use to find the number of visitors admitted every 15 minutes?

Time	Total Number of Visitors for the Day
10:10 am	140
12:30 pm	420
2:00 pm	600
2:50 pm	700

13. The graph above shows Carmel's distance from home over a one-hour period, during which time she first went to the library, then went to the grocery store, and then returned home. Which of the following statements must be true?

A) The grocery store is about 5 miles from Carmel's house.

B) Carmel traveled a total of 7 miles from the time she left home until she returned.

C) The grocery store is 7 miles farther from Carmel's house than the library is.

D) Carmel spent 10 minutes at the library and 15 minutes at the grocery store.

14. The entrance gates at a museum allow a constant number of visitors to enter every 15 minutes. A supervisor records the cumulative number of visitors for the day at various times as shown in the table above. The museum does not admit any visitors after 4:45 pm. What is the projected total number of visitors for the day, assuming that the same number of visitors are granted entrance each 15-minute period throughout the day?

A) 810

B) 895

C) 930

D) 960

On Test Day

The SAT likes to test the modeling of real-life situations. Get comfortable with function notation in these questions. Remember that you can write the equation of a line as $y = mx + b$ or as $f(x) = mx + b$, where m is the slope and b is the y-intercept. Both mean the same thing. In the formula using function notation, the slope indicates rate of change. Often, in questions asking about real-life situations, the x-variable indicates time. In that case, the y-intercept (that is, the value of the function at $x = 0$, or $f(0)$) indicates the starting point.

15. An environmental agency is working to reduce the amount of plastic that a community discards in the ocean. Currently, the community discards 6.2 million pounds of plastic annually, and the agency's goal is to eliminate that amount by collecting and recycling the plastic. If the agency increases its collection and recycling capacity at a constant rate, and meets its goal at the end of the eighth year, which of the following linear functions, f, could the agency use to model the amount of plastic being added to the ocean t years into the program?

    A) $f(t) = -\dfrac{62}{40}t + 6.2$

    B) $f(t) = -\dfrac{31}{40}t + 6.2$

    C) $f(t) = \dfrac{31}{40}t + 6.2$

    D) $f(t) = \dfrac{62}{40}t + 6.2$

The correct answer and explanation can be found at the end of the chapter.

How Much Have You Learned?

Directions: For testlike practice, give yourself 15 minutes to complete this question set. Be sure to study the explanations, even for questions you got right. They can be found at the end of this chapter.

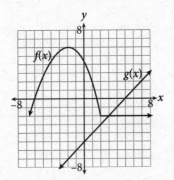

16. Based on the figure above, what is the value of $f(-2) + g(2)$?

    A) -3

    B) 0

    C) 3

    D) 6

17. A company uses the function $P(x) = 150x - x^2$ to determine how much profit the company will make when it sells 150 units of a certain product that sells for x dollars per unit. How much more profit per unit, in dollars, will the company make if it charges $25 for the product than if it charges $20? (Ignore the dollar sign when gridding your response.)

18. The customer service department of a wireless cellular provider has found that on Wednesdays, the polynomial function $C(t) = -0.0815t^4 + t^3 + 12t$ approximates the number of calls received by any given time, where t represents the number of hours that have passed during the workday. Based on this function, how many calls can be expected by the end of one 10-hour workday?

19. A biologist is studying the effect of pollution on the reproduction of a specific plant. She uses the function $n(p)$ to represent these effects, where p is the number of seeds germinated by the test group of the plant over a given period of time. Which of the following lists could represent a portion of the domain for the biologist's function?

    A) $\{\ldots -150, -100, -50, 0, 50, 100, 150 \ldots\}$

    B) $\{-150, -100, -50, 0, 50, 100, 150\}$

    C) $\{0, 0.25, 0.5, 0.75, 1, 1.25, 1.5 \ldots\}$

    D) $\{0, 20, 40, 60, 80 \ldots\}$

Math

20. If $f(x) = 3 - x$ and $g(x) = \dfrac{x^2}{2}$, which of the following is NOT in the range of $f(g(x))$?

A) -3

B) 0

C) 2

D) 4

$$g(x) = -3x - 5$$

21. The function g is defined above. What is the value of $g(-4x)$?

A) 7

B) $-12x - 5$

C) $12x - 5$

D) $12x^2 - 20x$

$$r(x) = 3x - 7$$
$$t(x) = 3x + r(x)$$

22. The functions r and t are defined above. What is the value of $t(2)$?

A) -3

B) -1

C) 0

D) 5

$$f(x) = ax^2 + 3x + 5$$

23. The function f is defined above, and $f(3) = -4$. If a is a constant, what is the value of $f(2)$?

A) -2

B) 3

C) 5

D) 19

24. A function a satisfies $a(-2) = 3$ and $a(3) = 8$. A function b satisfies $b(3) = 4$ and $b(7) = -2$. What is the value of $a(b(7))$?

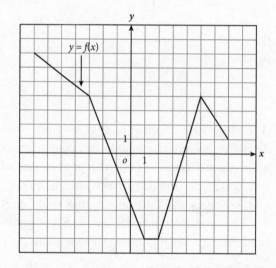

25. The function f, shown in the graph above, is defined for $-7 \le x \le 7$. For which of the following values of x does $f(x) = 4$?

I. -4

II. -3

III. 5

A) III only

B) I and II only

C) II and III only

D) I, II, and III

Reflect

Directions: Take a few minutes to recall what you've learned and what you've been practicing in this chapter. Consider the following questions, jot down your best answer for each one, and then compare your reflections to the expert responses on the following page. Use your level of confidence to determine what to do next.

What are the domain and range of a function?

What is another way to write the function $f(x) = x + 4$?

In the function in question 2, what does x represent? What does $f(x)$ represent?

What will the function in question 2 look like when graphed?

In a function whose x-value represents time, what does the y-intercept represent?

Expert Responses

What are the domain and range of a function?

The domain of a function indicates the possible x-values and the range of a function indicates the possible y-values. For example, in the function $f(x) = x^2$, the domain is all real numbers because any number can be squared, and the range is any number greater than or equal to 0, because x^2 can't be negative.

What is another way to write the function $f(x) = x + 4$?

When you graph the function on the xy-coordinate plane, you can replace f(x) with y. This function is equivalent to $y = x + 4$.

In the function in question 2, what does x represent? What does $f(x)$ represent?

In this function, x is the input and f(x) is the output.

What will the function in question 2 look like when graphed?

The slope of the line is 1 and its y-intercept is 4, so it will move from the lower left to the upper right and cross the y-axis at $y = 4$.

In a function whose x-value represents time, what does the y-intercept represent?

The y-intercept represents the initial quantity when $t = 0$. Say a function represents the progress of a machine manufacturing widgets at a rate of 6 widgets per hour. The machine adds the widgets it makes to a growing pile that consisted of 12 widgets when the machine started working. If this function were graphed as a function of time, the y-intercept would be 12—the pile of 12 widgets that were there when the machine started its task.

Next Steps

If you answered most questions correctly in the "How Much Have You Learned?" section, and if your responses to the Reflect questions were similar to those of the SAT expert, then consider functions an area of strength and move on to the next chapter. Come back to this topic periodically to prevent yourself from getting rusty.

If you don't yet feel confident, review those parts of this chapter that you have not yet mastered. All three lessons in this chapter cover question types that are fairly common on the SAT, and it is to your advantage to have a firm grasp on this material, so go back over it until you feel more confident. Then try the questions you missed again. As always, be sure to review the explanations closely.

Answers and Explanations

1.   A

Difficulty: Easy

Getting to the Answer: The notation $g(-2)$ is asking for the value of $g(x)$ when x is -2, so substitute -2 for x and simplify. Don't forget to use the correct order of operations as you work:

$$\begin{aligned} g(-2) &= -2(-2)^2 + 7(-2) - 3 \\ &= -2(4) + (-14) - 3 \\ &= -8 - 14 - 3 \\ &= -25 \end{aligned}$$

(A) is correct.

2.   A

Difficulty: Easy

Getting to the Answer: The notation $k(4)$ is equivalent to the output value of the function when 4 is substituted for the input x, and $k(1)$ is the output value of the function when 1 is substituted for the input x. Substitute 4 and 1 into the function, one at a time, and then subtract the results:

$$\begin{aligned} k(4) &= 5(4) + 2 = 20 + 2 = 22 \\ k(1) &= 5(1) + 2 = 5 + 2 = 7 \\ k(4) - k(1) &= 22 - 7 = 15 \end{aligned}$$

Choice **(A)** is correct. Caution—subtracting 1 from 4 and then substituting 3 into the function will give a different and incorrect result.

3.   A

Difficulty: Medium

Getting to the Answer: The notation $g(h(x))$ can be read "g of h of x." It means that the output when x is substituted in $h(x)$ becomes the input for $g(x)$. First, use the table on the right to find that $h(3)$ is 0. This is your new input. Now, use the table on the left to find $g(0)$, which is -1, making **(A)** the correct answer.

4.   D

Difficulty: Medium

Getting to the Answer: Evaluate the numerator and denominator separately:

$$\begin{aligned} p(5) &= 5^2 - 4(5) + 8 = 13 \\ q(p(5)) &= q(13) = 13 - 3 = 10 \\ q(5) &= 5 - 3 = 2 \\ p(q(5)) &= p(2) = 2^2 - 4(2) + 8 = 4 \end{aligned}$$

Then combine to get $\dfrac{q(p(5))}{p(q(5))} = \dfrac{10}{4} = 2.5$. The correct answer is **(D)**.

5.   D

Difficulty: Hard

Getting to the Answer: Determine the linear change of the functions relative to the change in n, then extrapolate to get the values of $f(6)$ and $g(6)$. You don't need to determine the actual expressions for the functions. As a shortcut, find the changes per 2 unit increase of n and apply that to the values of the functions when $n = 4$. For $f(n)$, the increase from $n = 2$ to $n = 4$ is $16.2 - 11.6 = 4.6$. Thus, the value of $f(6)$ is $f(4) + 4.6 = 16.2 + 4.6 = 20.8$. The change in $g(n)$ for $n = 2$ to $n = 4$ is $0.5 - 1.5 = -1$. So the value of $g(6)$ is $g(4) + (-1) = 0.5 - 1 = -0.5$. Now, calculate $h(6)$: $h(6) = 2 \times f(6) - g(6) = 2(20.8) - (-0.5) = 41.6 + 0.5 = 42.1$. **(D)** is correct.

6.   C

Difficulty: Easy

Getting to the Answer: The function graphed is the absolute value function, and all of the values in its range (the y-values) are positive. That makes any negative value as an output impossible. Because you're looking for the statement that is *not* true, **(C)** is correct.

7.   D

Difficulty: Easy

Getting to the Answer: To determine the domain, look at the *x*-values. To determine the range, look at the *y*-values. For the domain, the graph is continuous (no holes or gaps in the graph) and has arrows on both sides, so the domain is all real numbers. This means you can eliminate (A) and (B). For the range, the function's maximum (the vertex) is located at $(-3, 4)$, which means that the greatest possible *y*-value of $f(x)$ is 4. The graph is continuous and opens downward, so the range of the function is $y \leq 4$, which is the same as $f(x) \leq 4$, making **(D)** correct.

8.   8

Difficulty: Medium

Getting to the Answer: The maximum of $f(x)$ occurs at the point where the *y*-value is the greatest, which in this case is $(2, 4)$. So, $a = 2$ and $b = 4$. The point with the smallest *y*-value is $(4, -2)$. Thus, $c = 4$ and $d = -2$. The total of the four values is $2 + 4 + 4 + (-2) = 8$. Grid in **8**.

9.   B

Difficulty: Medium

Strategic Advice: Quickly sketching the different possibilities can be helpful.

Getting to the Answer: Because $2c = d$, both the *x*-intercept, c, and the *y*-intercept, d, must have the same sign. If both are positive, then d would be greater than c, and the graph of f would look something like this:

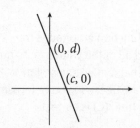

This is all you need to do to solve the problem. According to the choices, the slope is always the same regardless of the sign of c and d. In other words, if the slope is negative at one point, then it must be negative all the time. Therefore, **(B)** is correct. On test day, you would move on to the next question without needing to check what the line looks like when c and d are negative. For the record, if c and d are negative, then d will be less than c, and the graph would look like this:

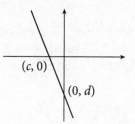

If you're curious to see the algebra, plug $(0, d)$ and $(c, 0)$ into the slope formula:

$$m = \frac{y_2 - y_1}{x_2 - x_1} = \frac{d - 0}{0 - c} = -\frac{d}{c}$$

The question states that $d = 2c$, so sub in $2c$ for d:

$$-\frac{d}{c} = -\frac{(2c)}{c} = -2$$

Therefore, the slope is -2, and the answer is indeed **(B)**.

10.   D

Difficulty: Easy

Strategic Advice: Save time on questions with roman numerals in the choices by testing the roman numeral that appears most often in the choices first. Here, check statement II first because it appears in three of the four choices.

Getting to the Answer: Plug each of the *x*-values into the function and see which produces a *y*-value of -1. Statement II is $f(0)$. When $x = 0$, the function's *y*-value is 2. Statement II is not equal to -1, so any answer choices that include statement II are incorrect. Eliminate (A), (B), and (C). Only **(D)** is left and is correct. On test day, you would stop here and move on to the next question. For the record, statement I is $f(-4) = 0$ and statement III is $f(3) = -1$. Also note that there are two other places where the function's output is -1: $f(-3)$ and $f(-1.5)$, neither of which is an answer choice.

11. A

Difficulty: Medium

Getting to the Answer: Thinking about the *y*-intercept (the starting amount) for the function will reduce the amount of work you need to do. The table indicates that Paulo had 21 votes on day 3, when $t = 3$, not at the start of the contest, when $t = 0$. This means that (C) and (D) are incorrect. To evaluate the remaining answer choices, pick a point, try it in a function, and if it works, then you've found the correct answer. If it doesn't work, then you can confidently select the other answer choice without any further work:

$$(A): 35 = 2(4)^2 + 3$$
$$35 = 2(16) + 3$$
$$35 = 32 + 3$$
$$35 = 35$$

(A) is correct. On test day, you would stop here. For the record, here is the reason (B) is incorrect:

$$(B): 35 = \frac{1}{2}(4)^2 + 3$$
$$35 = \frac{1}{2}(16) + 3$$
$$35 = 8 + 3$$
$$35 \neq 11$$

12. C

Difficulty: Medium

Getting to the Answer: Examine the graph and look for trends in the rate of increase and decrease of fuel economy before and after 50 mph. Note the increase below 50 mph (to the left of 50 on the horizontal axis) and the decrease above 50 mph (to the right of 50): the decreasing part of the graph is steeper than the increasing part. In other words, the rate of increase below 50 mph is less than the rate of increase above 50 mph. Choice **(C)** is correct.

13. D

Difficulty: Medium

Getting to the Answer: Compare each answer choice to the graph, eliminating false statements as you go.

(A): Carmel went to the library first, so the library (not the grocery store) is about 5 miles from her home. Eliminate (A).

(B): Carmel traveled 7 miles away from her home (between $t = 0$ minutes and $t = 30$ minutes), but then also traveled 7 miles back (between $t = 45$ minutes and $t = 60$ minutes), so she traveled a total of 14 miles. Eliminate (B).

(C): When Carmel reached the library, she was 5 miles from home; when she reached the grocery store, she was 7 miles from home. This means the grocery store must be $7 - 5 = 2$ miles farther away. Eliminate (C).

(D) must be correct. Carmel is the same distance from home (5 miles) between $t = 15$ minutes and $t = 25$ minutes, so she spent 10 minutes at the library. She is stopped once again (at the grocery store) between $t = 30$ minutes and $t = 45$ minutes, so she spent 15 minutes at the grocery store.

14. C

Difficulty: Medium

Strategic Advice: The fact that the number of visitors each 15 minutes is constant means that the cumulative number of visitors is a linear function.

Getting to the Answer: Because the time between the numbers of cumulative visitors in the table varies, pick an interval that is easy to work with to determine the number of visitors who enter every 15 minutes. Next, use that value to find how many entered by 4:45 p.m. There are six 15-minute periods between 12:30 p.m. and 2:00 p.m. The number of visitors admitted during that time was $600 - 420 = 180$. So, $\frac{180}{6} = 30$ visitors enter every 15 minutes.

In order to project the cumulative, or total, number of visitors for a specific time, set up a function, $f(v)$. Pick a time that is convenient, such as 2:00 pm. Since you know that there were 600 visitors by 2:00 pm, you can write $f(v) = 600 + 30v$, where v is the number of 15-minute periods after 2:00 pm. The question asks for the cumulative visitors admitted by 4:45 pm. Thus, v is the number of 15-minute periods between 2:00 and 4:45, which is 11. So, $f(11) = 600 + 30(11) = 930$. **(C)** is correct.

15. B

Difficulty: Medium

Strategic Advice: When modeling a real-life situation with a linear function, the starting point in the description is the y-intercept of the equation and the rate of change is the slope. Eliminate choices as you go; you may find that you are able to answer the question after only one or two steps. Never do more math than necessary to answer the question.

Getting to the Answer: In this question, the agency is reducing the amount of plastic disposed annually, so the slope must be negative. Eliminate (C) and (D) because their positive slopes indicate an *increasing* function.

The starting point, or y-intercept, is the amount of plastic the community is now discarding, or 6.2 million pounds. Unfortunately, this value is the same in (A) and (B), so you will need to find the slope.

The agency wants to eliminate the total amount of plastic in 8 years, so to find the amount of reduction per year, divide 6.2 by 8.

Because $-\frac{6.2}{8}$ does not appear in the choices, and the slopes in the choices do not have decimal points, multiply the fraction by 1 in the form of $\frac{10}{10}$ to get $-\frac{6.2}{8} \times \frac{10}{10} = -\frac{62}{80} = -\frac{31}{40}$. Choice **(B)** is correct.

16. C

Difficulty: Medium

Category: Graphs of Functions

Getting to the Answer: Graphically, the notation $f(-2)$ means the y-value when x is -2. Pay careful attention to which graph is which. It may help to draw dots on the graph. Find $x = -2$ along the horizontal axis, trace up to the graph of $f(x)$, and draw a dot on the graph. Do the same for $g(2)$, as shown here:

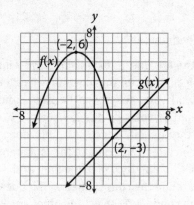

Now, read the y-coordinates from the graph and add: $f(-2)$ is 6 and $g(2)$ is -3, so $f(-2) + g(2) = 6 + (-3) = 3$, which is **(C)**.

17. 3.5 or 3.50

Difficulty: Medium

Category: Describing Real-Life Situations with Functions

Getting to the Answer: Start by evaluating the function at $x = 25$ and at $x = 20$. Make sure you follow the correct order of operations as you simplify:

$$P(25) = 150(25) - (25)^2$$
$$= 3{,}750 - 625$$
$$= 3{,}125$$
$$P(20) = 150(20) - (20)^2$$
$$= 3{,}000 - 400$$
$$= 2{,}600$$

The question asks how much more profit *per unit* the company makes, so find the difference in the amounts of profit and divide by the number of units (150) to get $\frac{3{,}125 - 2{,}600}{150} = \frac{525}{150} = \$3.50$. Grid in **3.5**.

18. 305

Difficulty: Easy

Category: Describing Real-Life Situations with Functions

Getting to the Answer: At the end of one workday, 10 hours have passed, so evaluate the function at $t = 10$. Make sure you follow the correct order of operations as you simplify:

$$C(t) = -0.0815t^4 + t^3 + 12t$$
$$C(10) = -0.0815(10)^4 + 10^3 + 12(10)$$
$$= -0.0815(10,000) + 1,000 + 120$$
$$= -815 + 1,000 + 120$$
$$= 305$$

Grid in **305**.

19. D

Difficulty: Easy

Category: Describing Real-Life Situations with Functions

Getting to the Answer: The domain of a function includes every possible input value, which is usually represented by x. In this function, instead of x, the input is represented by p, which is the number of seeds germinated by the plants over a given period of time. Because there cannot be a negative number of seeds germinated or a fraction of a seed germinated, the list in **(D)** is the only one that could represent a portion of the function's domain.

20. D

Difficulty: Hard

Category: Graphs of Functions

Getting to the Answer: When working with a composition (also called nested functions), the range of the inner function becomes the domain of the outer function, which in turn produces the range of the composition. In the composition $f(g(x))$, the function $g(x) = \frac{x^2}{2}$ is the inner function. Every value of x, when substituted into this function, will result in a non-negative value because the result of squaring a number is always a positive number. This means the smallest possible range value of $g(x)$ is 0. If you don't see this relationship, try plugging in various values for x and look for a pattern. Now look at $f(x)$. Substituting large positive values of x in the function will result in large negative numbers. Consequently, substituting the smallest value from the range of g, which is 0, results in the largest range value for the composition, which is $3 - 0 = 3$. Therefore, 4 is not in the range of $f(g(x))$. **(D)** is correct.

21. C

Difficulty: Medium

Category: Function Notation

Getting to the Answer: To evaluate a function at a particular value, replace the variable in the function with the value. In this question, replace x in the function definition with $-4x$ to get $g(-4x) = -3(-4x) - 5 = 12x - 5$. **(C)** is correct.

Note that you can replace one variable with another. In this question, $-4x$ replaces x. If you chose (A), you likely replaced x in the function definition with -4. If you chose (B), you may have "lost" a negative sign. Finally, (D) results if you multiply each term in the definition by $-4x$ instead of replacing x with $-4x$.

22. D

Difficulty: Medium

Category: Function Notation

Getting to the Answer: To evaluate the value of a function, replace the variable in the definition with the given value. Since the question asks for $t(2)$, and the definition of the t function includes the r function, evaluate $r(2)$ first, then use that result to evaluate $t(2)$:

$$r(2) = 3(2) - 7 = 6 - 7 = -1$$

Because $t(2) = 3(2) + r(2) = 6 - 1 = 5$, **(D)** is correct.

Math

23. B

Difficulty: Medium

Category: Function Notation

Getting to the Answer: To evaluate a function for a particular value, substitute the value for the variable in the function. In this case, substitute 3 for x and then use the given value for $f(3)$ to solve for the value of a:

$$f(3) = a(3)^2 + 3(3) + 5$$
$$-4 = 9a + 9 + 5$$
$$-4 = 9a + 14$$
$$-18 = 9a$$
$$-2 = a$$

Next, use the known value of a to find $f(2)$:

$$f(2) = -2(2)^2 + 3(2) + 5$$
$$f(2) = -2(4) + 6 + 5$$
$$f(2) = -8 + 11$$
$$f(2) = 3$$

(B) is correct.

24. 3

Difficulty: Medium

Category: Function Notation

Getting to the Answer: To evaluate a composite function (a set of nested functions), start with the innermost function and work outward. For this question, begin by evaluating $b(7)$. Because $b(7) = -2$, you know that $a(b(7)) = a(-2)$, so next, evaluate $a(-2)$. The question tells you that $a(-2) = 3$, which makes **(B)** correct.

25. C

Difficulty: Easy

Category: Graphs of Functions

Getting to the Answer: The term $f(x)$ is equivalent to the y-value of the function at x. So this question is asking, "Which values of x produce a y-value of 4?" Draw a horizontal line at the point $y = 4$ and identify where that line intercepts the function. The two points of intersection are -3 and 5. **(C)** is correct.

CHAPTER 11

Exponents, Radicals, Polynomials, and Rational Expressions

LEARNING OBJECTIVES

After completing this chapter, you will be able to:

- Apply exponent rules
- Apply radical rules
- Add, subtract, multiply, and factor polynomials
- Divide polynomials
- Define root, solution, zero, and *x*-intercept and identify them on the graph of a nonlinear function
- Determine whether the growth or decay described in a question is linear or exponential
- Apply the linear and exponential equations to answer growth and decay questions
- Simplify rational expressions
- Isolate a variable in a rational equation

25/600 SmartPoints®

Math

How Much Do You Know?

Directions: Try the questions that follow. Show your work so that you can compare your solutions to the ones found in the Check Your Work section immediately after this question set. The "Category" heading in the explanation for each question gives the title of the lesson that covers how to solve it. If you answered the question(s) for a given lesson correctly, and if your scratchwork looks like ours, you may be able to move quickly through that lesson. If you answered incorrectly or used a different approach, you may want to take your time on that lesson.

1. Which expression is equivalent to $2(-4\,j^3k^{-4})^{-3}$?

   A) $-\dfrac{k^{12}}{512j^9}$

   B) $-\dfrac{k^{12}}{32j^9}$

   C) $-\dfrac{j^9}{32k^{12}}$

   D) $-\dfrac{k^{12}}{128j^9}$

$$T = 2\pi\sqrt{\dfrac{L}{g}}$$

2. The formula above was created by Italian scientist Galileo Galilei in the early 1600s to demonstrate that the time it takes for a pendulum to complete a swing—called its period, T—can be found using only the length of the pendulum, L, and the force of gravity, g. He proved that the mass of the pendulum did not affect its period. Based on the equation above, which of the following equations could be used to find the length of the pendulum given its period?

   A) $L = \dfrac{gT}{2\pi}$

   B) $L = \dfrac{gT^2}{4\pi^2}$

   C) $L = \dfrac{T^2}{4\pi^2 g}$

   D) $L = \dfrac{g}{4\pi^2 T^2}$

3. Which of the following represents $\dfrac{\sqrt[6]{x^{10}y^{12}}}{\sqrt[3]{x^5y^6}}$ written in simplest form, given that $x > 0$ and $y > 0$?

   A) 1

   B) 2

   C) $x^2y^3\sqrt{x}$

   D) $xy^2\sqrt[3]{x^2}$

4. What is the result when $4x^3 - 5x^2 + x - 3$ is divided by $x - 2$?

   A) $4x + 3 + \dfrac{11}{x-2}$

   B) $4x^2 + 3x - 6$

   C) $4x^2 + 3x + 18$

   D) $4x^2 + 3x + 7 + \dfrac{11}{x-2}$

5. The function f is a parabolic function that intersects the x-axis. Which of the following statements must be true?

   A) The function has at least one real root.

   B) The function has no real roots.

   C) The function intersects the positive y axis.

   D) The function has two zeros.

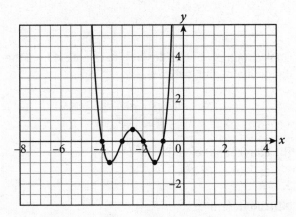

Age (months)	Height (centimeters)
15	80
18	82.5
21	85
24	87.5
27	90

6. The function $f(x) = (x + 1)(x + 2)(x + 3)(x + 4)$ is graphed above. If k is a constant such that $g(x) = k$ and the system of functions f and g have exactly two real solutions, which of the following could be a value of k?

A) -2

B) 0

C) 0.5

D) 1

8. The growth of a young child is given in the chart above. If t represents the number of months after 15 and $f(t)$ represents the child's height, which of the following equations is the best model for the data in the age range shown?

A) $f(t) = 80t + 3$

B) $f(t) = \frac{5}{6}t + 80$

C) $f(t) = 80\left(\frac{5}{6}\right)^t$

D) $f(t) = \frac{5}{6}(80)^t$

7. In the equation $ax^4 + bx^3 + cx^2 - dx = 0$, a, b, c, and d are constants. If the equation crosses the x-axis at 0, -2, 3, and 5, which of the following is a factor of $ax^4 + bx^3 + cx^2 - dx$?

A) $x - 2$

B) $x + 3$

C) $x - 5$

D) $x + 5$

$$\frac{8x}{3(x - 5)} + \frac{2x}{3x - 15} = \frac{50}{3(x - 5)}$$

9. What value(s) of x satisfy the equation above?

A) 0

B) 5

C) No solution

D) Any value such that $x \neq 5$

10. If $\dfrac{6}{2x - 3} + 6a = \dfrac{10}{2x - 3} + 4b$ and $3a - 2b = 2$, what is the value of x?

A) $\dfrac{1}{2}$

B) 2

C) No solution

D) The value cannot be determined from the information given.

Check Your Work

1. B

Difficulty: Easy

Category: Exponents

Getting to the Answer: Move the expression in parentheses to the denominator to make the sign of the exponent outside positive; do not change the signs of the exponents inside the parentheses. Next, distribute the exponent as usual. Divide the 2 into -64, and move k^{-12} back to the numerator and change the sign of its exponent. Work for these steps is shown below:

$$2\left(-4j^3k^{-4}\right)^{-3} = \frac{2}{\left(-4j^3k^{-4}\right)^3}$$

$$= \frac{2}{(-4)^3\left(j^3\right)^3\left(k^{-4}\right)^3}$$

$$= \frac{2}{-64\,j^9k^{-12}}$$

$$= -\frac{k^{12}}{32j^9}$$

Choice **(B)** is the correct answer.

2. B

Difficulty: Medium

Category: Radicals

Getting to the Answer: The question asks you to solve the equation for L. Use inverse operations to accomplish the task. Divide both sides of the equation by 2π and then square both sides. You'll need to apply the exponent to all the terms on the left side of the equation, including the π:

$$T = 2\pi\sqrt{\frac{L}{g}}$$

$$\frac{T}{2\pi} = \sqrt{\frac{L}{g}}$$

$$\left(\frac{T}{2\pi}\right)^2 = \left(\sqrt{\frac{L}{g}}\right)^2$$

$$\frac{T^2}{4\pi^2} = \frac{L}{g}$$

Finally, multiply both sides by g to remove g from the denominator and isolate L:

$$L = \frac{gT^2}{4\pi^2}$$

The correct answer is **(B)**.

3. A

Difficulty: Hard

Category: Radicals

Getting to the Answer: You can't simplify an expression that has different roots (in this case, sixth and third), so rewrite the expression with fraction exponents first, and then use exponent rules to simplify it. The rule for fraction exponents is "power over root"; use this to rewrite the expression:

$$\frac{\sqrt[6]{x^{10}y^{12}}}{\sqrt[3]{x^5y^6}} = \frac{x^{\frac{10}{6}}y^{\frac{12}{6}}}{x^{\frac{5}{3}}y^{\frac{6}{3}}}$$

When dividing like bases, subtract the exponents. Find common denominators as needed:

$$x^{\frac{10}{6}-\frac{5}{3}}y^{\frac{12}{6}-\frac{6}{3}} = x^{\frac{10}{6}-\frac{10}{6}}y^{\frac{12}{6}-\frac{12}{6}} = x^0y^0$$

Any number raised to the zero power becomes 1, so the expression becomes $1 \times 1 = 1$. Choice **(A)** is correct.

4. D

Difficulty: Medium

Category: Polynomial Division

Getting to the Answer: Since factoring the numerator does not appear to be practical, use polynomial division to find the result:

$$x - 2 \overline{)4x^3 - 5x^2 + x - 3}$$

The first number in this process will be $4x^2$ since $4x^2 \cdot x = 4x^3$:

$$
\begin{array}{r}
4x^2 \\
x - 2 \overline{)4x^3 - 5x^2 + x - 3} \\
-\left(4x^3 - 8x^2\right) \\
\hline
3x^2
\end{array}
$$

Next, complete the rest of the polynomial division process:

$$
\begin{array}{r}
4x^2 + 3x + 7 \\
x - 2 \overline{)4x^3 - 5x^2 + x - 3} \\
-\left(4x^3 - 8x^2\right) \\
\hline
3x^2 + x \\
-\left(3x^2 - 6x\right) \\
\hline
7x - 3 \\
-(7x - 14) \\
\hline
11
\end{array}
$$

Remember that you are dividing by $x - 2$, so the remainder of 11 is actually $\frac{11}{x - 2}$. **(D)** is correct.

5. A

Difficulty: Easy

Category: Graphs of Polynomial Functions

Getting to the Answer: The key to this question is knowing that an x-intercept is another word for root, or zero; those three terms are synonyms. Even though the question stem does not say how many roots f has, you know it must have at least one if it intersects the x-axis. **(A)** is correct. Watch out for trap answer (D), which does not consider the case when a parabola touches the x-axis at one point but does not cross it.

6. D

Difficulty: Medium

Category: Graphs of Polynomial Functions

Strategic Advice: Working backward from the answer choices saves time.

Getting to the Answer: The solution or solutions of a system of functions, like a system of equations, can be found at the points of intersection. Because the function $g(x)$ is equal to a constant, all x-values produce the same output—it must represent a horizontal line. A horizontal line and a 4th degree function could intersect 0, 1, 2, 3, or 4 times. Set each of the answer choices equal to k and sketch the resulting functions on the graph. You'll see that only $g(x) = 1$ intersects f exactly twice, so **(D)** is correct. Pay special attention to the scale of the axes to avoid trap answers like (A).

7. C

Difficulty: Medium

Category: Graphs of Polynomial Functions

Getting to the Answer: The question is asking for a factor of the function and tells you where the function crosses the x-axis. The roots are the y-values where the graph crosses the x-axis. To find the factors from the roots, consider what expressions would produce a value of zero. Thus, if the roots are at 0, -2, 3, and 5, then the factored form of this equation must be $x(x + 2)(x - 3)(x - 5)$ because plugging in any one of the four roots will equal zero. The only factor that appears in the answer choices is $x - 5$, so **(C)** is correct.

8.   B

Difficulty: Easy

Category: Modeling Growth and Decay

Strategic Advice: Determining the type of growth represented by the data will help to eliminate half of the choices immediately. Look at what happens to the height from each measurement to the next. From 15 to 18 months, the child's height increases by 2.5 centimeters. The same is true for 18 to 21 months, and for 21 to 24 months, and so on. Since 2.5 centimeters are added each equal time interval, the best model for this data would be linear.

Getting to the Answer: Because this growth is linear, eliminate choices (C) and (D) immediately because they represent exponential growth. The remaining two choices differ in both the coefficient of t and the value being added. When linear growth is modeled with the equation $y = mx + b$, m represents the rate of growth and b represents the starting amount. In this case, the starting height is 80 centimeters and the growth rate is 2.5 centimeters every 3 months, or $\frac{5}{6}$ centimeter per month, so choice **(B)** is correct.

9.   C

Difficulty: Hard

Category: Rational Expressions and Equations

Getting to the Answer: Because the denominators are the same (just written in different forms), multiplying both sides of the equation by $3x - 15$ will immediately clear all the fractions, the result of which is a much easier equation to solve:

$$8x + 2x = 50$$
$$10x = 50$$
$$x = 5$$

Because there are variables in the denominator, you must check the solution to make sure it is not extraneous. When $x = 5$, each of the denominators is equal to 0, and division by 0 is not possible. Therefore, there is no solution to the equation, making **(C)** the correct answer.

10. B

Difficulty: Hard

Category: Rational Expressions and Equations

Getting to the Answer: Begin by putting the x terms on one side and the a and b terms on the other for the first equation:

$$6a - 4b = \frac{10}{2x - 3} - \frac{6}{2x - 3} = \frac{10 - 6}{2x - 3} = \frac{4}{2x - 3}$$

Now note that the left side of the equation is $6a - 4b$, which is equivalent to $2(3a - 2b)$. The question states that $3a - 2b = 2$. So $6a - 4b = 2(3a - 2b) = 2(2) = 4$. Substitute 4 for $6a - 4b$, multiply both sides by $2x - 3$ to clear the fractions, and solve for x:

$$4 = \frac{4}{2x - 3}$$
$$4(2x - 3) = 4$$
$$2x - 3 = 1$$
$$2x = 4$$
$$x = 2$$

Because "No solution" is an answer choice, make sure that $x = 2$ is not an extraneous solution before selecting choice (B). When $x = 2$, the denominator $2x - 3 \neq 0$. Thus, $x = 2$ is a valid solution, and the answer is **(B)**.

Exponents

LEARNING OBJECTIVE

After this lesson, you will be able to:

- Apply exponent rules

To answer a question like this:

The expression $x\left(x^3y^2\right)^{-4}$ is equivalent to which of the following?

A) $\dfrac{1}{y^2}$

B) $\dfrac{1}{x^4}$

C) $\dfrac{1}{x^{11}y^8}$

D) $\dfrac{1}{x^{16}y^8}$

You need to know this:

Rule	Example
When multiplying two terms with the same base, add the exponents.	$a^b \cdot a^c = a^{(b+c)} \rightarrow 4^2 \cdot 4^3 = 4^{2+3} = 4^5$
When dividing two terms with the same base, subtract the exponents.	$\dfrac{a^b}{a^c} = a^{(b-c)} \rightarrow \dfrac{4^3}{4^2} = 4^{3-2} = 4^1$
When raising a power to another power, multiply the exponents.	$(a^b)^c = a^{(bc)} \rightarrow (4^3)^2 = 4^{3 \cdot 2} = 4^6$; $(2x^2)^3 = 2^3 x^{2 \cdot 3} = 8x^6$
When raising a product to a power, apply the power to all factors in the product.	$(ab)^c = a^c \cdot b^c \rightarrow (2m)^3 = 2^3 \cdot m^3 = 8m^3$
Any non-zero term raised to the zero power equals 1.	$a^0 = 1 \rightarrow 4^0 = 1$
A base raised to a negative exponent can be rewritten as the reciprocal raised to the positive of the original exponent.	$a^{-b} = \dfrac{1}{a^b}$; $\dfrac{1}{a^{-b}} = a^b \rightarrow 4^{-2} = \dfrac{1}{4^2}$; $\dfrac{1}{4^{-2}} = 4^2$
A negative number raised to an even exponent will produce a positive result; a negative number raised to an odd exponent will produce a negative result.	$(-2)^4 = 16$, but $(-2)^3 = -8$

You need to do this:

- Identify the appropriate rule by looking at the operation
- Apply the rule
- Repeat as necessary

SAT exponent questions should be quick points. Make sure you memorize the rules in the table above before test day.

Explanation:

You'll need several exponent rules to answer the question at the beginning of this lesson. The order of operations dictates that you start with the negative exponent. When one power is raised to another, multiply the exponents:

$$x\left(x^3y^2\right)^{-4} = x\left(x^{3(-4)}y^{2(-4)}\right) = x\left(x^{-12}y^{-8}\right)$$

The x out front has no exponent, which means it is raised to the power of 1. To do the multiplication, add the exponents:

$$x^1\left(x^{-12}y^{-8}\right) = x^{-11}y^{-8}$$

Finally, because this expression is not among the choices, you'll need the rule for negative exponents: you can write them as the reciprocal of the positive exponent. Like this:

$$x^{-11}y^{-8} = \frac{1}{x^{11}y^8}$$

The correct answer is **(C)**.

If exponents give you trouble, study the rules in the table above and try these Drill questions before completing the Try on Your Own questions that follow. Simplify each expression (without using a calculator). Turn the page to see the answers.

Drill

a. 3^4

b. $(-5)^3$

c. $4^2 \times 2^{-4}$

d. $\dfrac{2^4}{2^3}$

e. $\left(\dfrac{1}{3}\right)^{-2}$

f. $\left(2^2\right)^3$

g. $(7x)^2$

h. $\left(-\dfrac{1}{2}\right)^{-2}$

i. $\left(a^2\right)^5$

j. $\left(b^3\right)^{-6}$

Try on Your Own

Directions: Take as much time as you need on these questions. Work carefully and methodically. There will be an opportunity for timed practice at the end of the chapter.

HINT: For Q1, how can you get all three bases to have the same value?

---

1. What is the value of $\dfrac{3^5 \times 27^3}{81^3}$?

HINT: For Q2, look for common factors in the numerator and denominator.

$$\frac{18x^4 + 27x^3 - 36x^2}{9x^2}$$

2. If $x \neq 0$, which of the following is equivalent to the expression above?

    A) $2x^2 + 3x - 4$

    B) $2x^2 + 3x - 6$

    C) $2x^4 + 3x^3 - 4x^2$

    D) $2x^6 + 3x^5 - 4x^4$

3. Human blood contains three primary cell types: red blood cells (RBC), white blood cells (WBC), and platelets. In an adult male, a single microliter (1×10^{-3} milliliters) of blood contains approximately 5.4×10^6 RBC, 7.5×10^3 WBC, and 3.5×10^5 platelets on average. What percentage of an adult male's total blood cell count is comprised of red blood cells?

    A) 1.30%

    B) 6.21%

    C) 60.79%

    D) 93.79%

4. If $n^3 = -8$, what is the value of $\dfrac{\left(n^2\right)^3}{\dfrac{1}{n^2}}$?

HINT: For Q5, how can you get rid of the fraction on the left side?

$$\frac{x^{5r}}{x^{3r-2s}} = x^t$$

5. If $r + s = 6$, what is the value of t in the equation above?

    A) 6

    B) 12

    C) 18

    D) 30

Math

Radicals

To answer a question like this:

$$\frac{\sqrt[3]{x} \cdot x^{\frac{5}{2}} \cdot x}{\sqrt{x}}$$

If x^n is the simplified form of the expression above, what is the value of n ?

Drill answers:

a. $3^4 = 3 \times 3 \times 3 \times 3 = 81$

b. $(-5)^3 = (-5) \times (-5) \times (-5) = -125$

c. $4^2 \times 2^{-4} = \frac{16}{16} = 1$

d. $\frac{2^4}{2^3} = 2^1 = 2$

e. $\left(\frac{1}{3}\right)^{-2} = \left(\frac{3}{1}\right)^2 = 9$

f. $\left(2^2\right)^3 = 2^{2\times3} = 2^6 = 64$

g. $(7x)^2 = 49x^2$

h. $\left(-\frac{1}{2}\right)^{-2} = (-2)^2 = 4$

i. $\left(a^2\right)^5 = a^{10}$

j. $\left(b^3\right)^{-6} = b^{-18} = \frac{1}{b^{18}}$

You need to know this:

Rule	Example
When a fraction is under a radical, you can rewrite it using two radicals: one containing the numerator and the other containing the denominator.	$\sqrt{\dfrac{a}{b}} = \dfrac{\sqrt{a}}{\sqrt{b}} \rightarrow \sqrt{\dfrac{4}{9}} = \dfrac{\sqrt{4}}{\sqrt{9}} = \dfrac{2}{3}$
Two factors under a single radical can be rewritten as separate radicals multiplied together.	$\sqrt{ab} = \sqrt{a} \times \sqrt{b} \rightarrow \sqrt{75} = \sqrt{25} \times \sqrt{3} = 5\sqrt{3}$
A radical can be written using a fractional exponent.	$\sqrt{a} = a^{\frac{1}{2}} \rightarrow \sqrt{289} = 289^{\frac{1}{2}}$ $\sqrt[3]{a} = a^{\frac{1}{3}} \rightarrow \sqrt[3]{729} = 729^{\frac{1}{3}}$
When you have a fractional exponent, the numerator is the power to which the base is raised, and the denominator is the root to be taken.	$a^{\frac{b}{c}} = \sqrt[c]{a^b} \rightarrow 5^{\frac{2}{3}} = \sqrt[3]{5^2}$
When a number is squared, the original number can be positive or negative, but the square root of a number can only be positive.	If $a^2 = 81$, then $a = \pm 9$, BUT $\sqrt{81} = 9$ only.
Cube roots of negative numbers are negative.	$\sqrt[3]{-27} = -3$

You need to do this:

- Identify the appropriate rule by looking at the answer choices. What form do you need to get the expression into? What rule do you need to apply to get there?
- Apply the rule
- Repeat as necessary

SAT Radicals questions should be quick points. Make sure you memorize the rules in the table above before test day.

Explanation:

Write each factor in the expression in exponential form (using fractional exponents for the radicals). Next, use exponent rules to simplify the expression:

$$\frac{\sqrt[3]{x} \cdot x^{\frac{5}{2}} \cdot x}{\sqrt{x}} = \frac{x^{\frac{1}{3}} \cdot x^{\frac{5}{2}} \cdot x^{1}}{x^{\frac{1}{2}}}$$

Now add the exponents of the factors that are being multiplied and subtract the exponent of the factor that is being divided, find common denominators, and simplify:

$$= x^{\frac{1}{3}+\frac{5}{2}+\frac{1}{1}-\frac{1}{2}} = x^{\frac{2}{6}+\frac{15}{6}+\frac{6}{6}-\frac{3}{6}}$$
$$= x^{\frac{20}{6}} = x^{\frac{10}{3}}$$

The question states that n is the power of x, so the value of n is $\frac{10}{3}$.

If radicals give you trouble, study the rules in the table above and try these Drill questions before completing the following Try on Your Own questions. Simplify each expression (without using a calculator). Turn the page to see the answers.

Drill

a. $\sqrt{\dfrac{121}{9}}$

b. $\sqrt{225}$

c. $\sqrt{\dfrac{16\times125}{5}}$

d. $\sqrt{\dfrac{50}{288}}$

e. $\sqrt[3]{-27}$

f. $\dfrac{\sqrt{5}\sqrt{60}}{\sqrt{3}}$

g. $\dfrac{4\sqrt{21}\times5\sqrt{2}}{10\sqrt{7}}$

h. $9^{\frac{1}{2}}\times\sqrt{4}\times81^{\frac{1}{4}}$

i. $\dfrac{\sqrt{81x^2}}{\sqrt{64y^4}}$

j. $\sqrt{\dfrac{x^8}{y^{12}}}$

Try on Your Own

Directions: Take as much time as you need on these questions. Work carefully and methodically. There will be an opportunity for timed practice at the end of the chapter.

$$8 + \frac{\sqrt{2x + 29}}{3} = 9$$

6. What do you need to do before squaring both sides?

For what value of x is the equation above true?

   A) -10

   B) -2

   C) 19

   D)   No solution

$$3x = x + 14$$

$$\sqrt{3z^2 - 11} + 2x = 22$$

7. If $z > 0$, what is the value of z?

   A)   1

   B)   3

   C)   5

   D)   8

8. Which of the following expressions is equivalent to $-x^{\frac{1}{4}}$?

   A) $-\dfrac{1}{4x}$

   B) $-\dfrac{1}{x^4}$

   C) $-\sqrt[4]{x}$

   D) $\dfrac{1}{\sqrt[4]{-x}}$

For Q9, remember that the denominator of the exponent becomes the root, and the numerator remains the exponent.

9. When simplified, $8^{\frac{4}{3}}$ is what number?

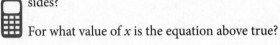

HINT: For Q10, which approach is faster for you? Algebra or Backsolving?

$$\sqrt{3a + 16} - 3 = a - 1$$

10. In the equation above, if $a > 0$, which of the following is a possible value of a?

   A)   3

   B)   2

   C)   1

   D) -4

Math

Polynomials

LEARNING OBJECTIVE

After this lesson, you will be able to:

- Add, subtract, multiply, and factor polynomials

To answer a question like this:

If $-2x^2 + 5x - 8$ is multiplied by $4x - 9$, what is the coefficient of x in the resulting polynomial?

A) -77

B) -45

C) -32

D) -13

You need to know this:

A **polynomial** is an expression composed of variables, exponents, and coefficients. By definition, a polynomial cannot have a variable in a denominator, and all exponents must be integers. Here are some examples of polynomial and non-polynomial expressions:

Polynomial	$23x^2$	$\frac{x}{5} - 6$	$y^{11} - 2y^6 + \frac{2}{3}xy^3 - 4x^2$	$z + 6$
NOT a Polynomial	$\frac{10}{z} + 13$	$x^3 y^{-6}$	$x^{\frac{1}{2}}$	$\frac{4}{y - 3}$

Drill answers:

a. $\frac{\sqrt{121}}{\sqrt{9}} = \frac{11}{3}$

b. $\sqrt{25} \times \sqrt{9} = 5 \times 3 = 15$

c. $\frac{4 \times 5\sqrt{5}}{\sqrt{5}} = 20$

d. $\frac{5\sqrt{2}}{12\sqrt{2}} = \frac{5}{12}$

e. -3

f. $\frac{\sqrt{5} \times 2\sqrt{3}\sqrt{5}}{\sqrt{3}} = 2 \times 5 = 10$

g. $\frac{4\sqrt{3}\sqrt{7} \times 5\sqrt{2}}{10\sqrt{7}} = \frac{20\sqrt{6}}{10} = 2\sqrt{6}$

h. $3 \times 2 \times 3 = 18$

i. $\frac{9|x|}{8y^2}$

j. $\frac{x^4}{y^6}$

You need to do this:

To add and subtract polynomials, start by identifying like terms—that is, terms in which the types of variables and their exponents match. For example, x^2 and $3x^2$ are like terms; adding them would give $4x^2$ and subtracting them would give $x^2 - 3x^2 = -2x^2$. Note that you cannot add or subtract unlike terms. For example, there is no way to simplify $x^2 + y$. You can, however, multiply unlike terms: $x^2 \cdot y = x^2 y$.

To multiply two polynomials, multiply each term in the first factor by each term in the second factor, then combine like terms.

To factor a polynomial, find a value or variable that divides evenly into each term, for example: $2x^3 + 2x^2 + 2x = 2x\left(x^2 + x + 1\right)$. (Factoring quadratics into binomials is discussed in chapter 12.)

Explanation:

Multiply each term in the first factor by each term in the second factor, then combine like terms:

$$\left(-2x^2 + 5x - 8\right)(4x - 9)$$
$$= -2x^2(4x - 9) + 5x(4x - 9) - 8(4x - 9)$$
$$= -8x^3 + 18x^2 + 20x^2 - 45x - 32x + 72$$
$$= -8x^3 + 38x^2 - 77x + 72$$

The coefficient of x is -77, so **(A)** is correct.

Try on Your Own

Directions: Take as much time as you need on these questions. Work carefully and methodically. There will be an opportunity for timed practice at the end of the chapter.

11. What is the sum of the polynomials $6a^2 - 17a - 9$ and $-5a^2 + 8a - 2$?

    A) $a^2 - 9a - 11$

    B) $a^2 - 25a - 7$

    C) $11a^2 - 9a - 11$

    D) $11a^2 - 25a - 7$

12. What is the difference when $3x^3 + 7x - 5$ is subtracted from $8x^2 + 4x + 10$?

    A) $5x^2 - 3x + 15$

    B) $-3x^3 - 3x + 5$

    C) $3x^3 - 8x^2 + 3x - 15$

    D) $-3x^3 + 8x^2 - 3x + 15$

HINT: For Q13, as you calculate each term, eliminate choices. Stop when there's only one choice left.

---

13. If $A = 4x^2 + 7x - 1$ and $B = -x^2 - 5x + 3$, then what is $\frac{3}{2}A - 2B$?

    A) $4x^2 + \frac{31}{2}x - \frac{9}{2}$

    B) $4x^2 + \frac{41}{2}x - \frac{15}{2}$

    C) $8x^2 + \frac{31}{2}x - \frac{9}{2}$

    D) $8x^2 + \frac{41}{2}x - \frac{15}{2}$

HINT: Which is more efficient for you? Math or backsolving the choices?

---

14. If $x^3 - 9x = 9 - x^2$, which of the following CANNOT be the value of x ?

    A) -3

    B) -1

    C) 1

    D) 3

$$(2x^2 + 3x - 4)(3x + 2) = 6x^3 + ax^2 - 6x - 8$$

15. In the above equation, a is a constant. If the equation is true for all values of x, what is the value of a ?

    A) 4

    B) 9

    C) 13

    D) 16

Polynomial Division

To answer a question like this:

Which of the following is equivalent to $\dfrac{x^2 + 3x + 7}{x + 4}$?

A) $\dfrac{3 + 7}{4}$

B) $x + \dfrac{3}{4}$

C) $3 + \dfrac{7}{x + 4}$

D) $x - 1 + \dfrac{11}{x + 4}$

You need to know this:

To divide polynomials, you can use an approach called **polynomial long division**. This process is similar to ordinary long division, except that you use polynomials instead of numbers. In the process described below, the *dividend* is the polynomial to be divided, the *divisor* is the polynomial you are dividing the dividend by, and the *quotient* is the result of the division.

You need to do this:

- Start with the dividend arranged so that the powers are in descending order, for example: $x^4 + x^3 + x + 1$. If any terms are missing, put in zeros, like this: $x^4 + x^3 + 0x^2 + x + 1$. Write the problem using a long division sign.
- Divide the first term of the dividend by the first term of the divisor to yield the first term of the quotient.
- Multiply the divisor by the first term of the quotient.
- Subtract the product you got in the last step from the dividend, then bring down the next term, just as you would in ordinary long division. Use the result as the new dividend.
- Repeat the process until you arrive at the remainder.

Explanation:

To divide $x^2 + 3x + 7$ by $x + 4$, set up a long division problem:

$$x + 4 \overline{)\, x^2 + 3x + 7}$$

Start by dividing the first term of the dividend, x^2, by the first term of the divisor, x. Multiply the entire divisor by x and subtract this product from the dividend:

$$
\begin{array}{r}
x \\
x + 4 \overline{)\, x^2 + 3x + 7} \\
-\left(x^2 + 4x\right) \\
\hline
-x + 7
\end{array}
$$

Next, divide the first term of the result of this subtraction, $-x$, by the first term of the divisor, x, to get -1. Repeat the process of multiplying and subtracting:

$$
\begin{array}{r}
x - 1 \\
x + 4 \overline{)\, x^2 + 3x + 7} \\
-\left(x^2 + 4x\right) \\
\hline
-x + 7 \\
-(-x - 4) \\
\hline
+11
\end{array}
$$

You're left with a remainder of 11. Put this over the divisor, $x + 4$, and you're done. The result of the division is $x - 1 + \dfrac{11}{x + 4}$, which is choice **(D)**.

Try on Your Own

Directions: Take as much time as you need on these questions. Work carefully and methodically. There will be an opportunity for timed practice at the end of the chapter.

> HINT: For Q16, because $a - 3$ is not a factor of the numerator, you'll have to use polynomial long division.

16. Which of the following is equivalent to $\dfrac{2a^2 - 5a - 1}{a - 3}$?

    A) $2a - 2$

    B) $2a + 1 - \dfrac{2}{a - 3}$

    C) $2a + \dfrac{2}{a - 3}$

    D) $2a + 1 + \dfrac{2}{a - 3}$

> HINT: For Q17, if the fraction simplifies to $ax + b$, the denominator divides evenly into the numerator. Does that suggest another approach?

$$\dfrac{6x^2 + 19x + 10}{2x + 5}$$

17. If $ax + b$ represents the simplified form of the expression above, then what is the value of $a + b$?

    A) 2

    B) 3

    C) 5

    D) 6

18. Which of the following is equivalent to $\dfrac{4x^2 - 6x}{2x + 2}$?

    A) $2x - \dfrac{10}{2x + 2}$

    B) $2x - 5 + \dfrac{10}{2x + 2}$

    C) $2x - 3$

    D) $2x + 5 - \dfrac{10}{2x + 2}$

> HINT: The quotient (result of division) times the divisor (the denominator) equals the dividend (the numerator.) For Q19, stop as soon as you have the value of t.

19. The equation $\dfrac{36x^2 + 16x - 21}{tx - 4} = -9x + 5 - \dfrac{1}{tx - 4}$ is true for all values of x for which $x \neq \dfrac{4}{t}$, where t is a constant. What is the value of t ?

    A) -20

    B) -4

    C) 4

    D) 12

20. If the polynomial $f(x)$ is evenly divisible by $x - 5$ and the polynomial $g(x) = f(x) + 4$, what is the value of $g(5)$?

    A) -4

    B) 0

    C) 4

    D) 9

Graphs of Polynomial Functions

LEARNING OBJECTIVE

After this lesson, you will be able to:

- Define root, solution, zero, and *x*-intercept and identify them on the graph of a nonlinear function

To answer a question like this:

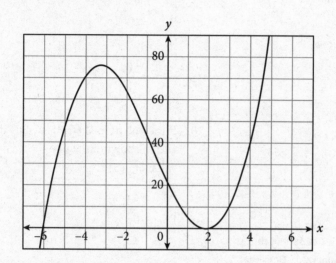

Which of the following could be the function whose graph is shown above?

A) $f(x) = (x - 6)(x + 2)^2$

B) $f(x) = (x + 6)(x - 2)^2$

C) $f(x) = 3x + 23$

D) $f(x) = 6x + 23$

You need to know this:

When applied to polynomial functions, the words **root**, **solution**, **zero**, and *x-intercept* all mean the same thing: the *x*-values on the function's graph where the function touches or crosses the *x*-axis. You can find the roots of a polynomial function by setting each factor of the polynomial equal to zero. For example, the polynomial function $f(x) = x^2 + x$ factors into $f(x) = x(x + 1)$. Set each factor equal to zero to find that $x = 0$ and $x = -1$. These are the function's solutions, also known as zeros. A solution can be represented using the coordinate pair $(x, 0)$.

Note that if a function crosses the *x*-axis, the factor associated with that *x*-intercept will have an odd exponent. If the function touches but does not cross the *x*-axis, the factor associated with that zero will have an even exponent. For example, the function $f(x) = x(x + 1)$ will cross the *x*-axis at $x = 0$ and $x = -1$, while the function $f(x) = x^2(x + 1)$ will cross the *x*-axis at $x = -1$ but only touch the *x*-axis at $x = 0$.

You need to do this:

- Identify the *x*-values where the function crosses or touches the *x*-axis.
- For each *x*-intercept, change the sign of the *x*-value and add it to the variable *x* to find the associated factor. For example, if the function crosses the *x*-axis at $x = -1$, then the factor associated with that root must be $x + 1$ (since $x + 1 = 0$ will produce the solution $x = -1$).
- Recognize that if the function only touches the *x*-axis without crossing it, the factor must have an even exponent.

Explanation:

Start by looking at the answer choices. The function is clearly not linear, so rule out (C) and (D). Next, look at the *x*-intercepts on the graph: the function crosses the *x*-axis at $x = -6$ and touches the *x*-axis at $x = 2$. Remember that the *x*-intercepts occur where the factors of the function equal zero. For the *x*-intercepts to be -6 and 2, the factors of the function must be $(x + 6)$ and $(x - 2)$. Because the function touches, but does not cross, the *x*-axis at $x = 2$, the $(x - 2)$ factor must have an even exponent. **(B)** is correct.

Try on Your Own

Directions: Take as much time as you need on these questions. Work carefully and methodically. There will be an opportunity for timed practice at the end of the chapter.

> HINT: For Q21, set each factor equal to 0 and solve for *x* to find the *x*-intercepts.

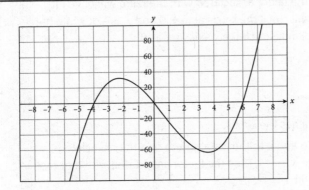

21. Which of the following could be the equation of the graph above?

    A) $y = x^2(x + 4)(x - 6)$

    B) $y = x(x + 4)(x - 6)$

    C) $y = x^2(x - 4)(x + 6)$

    D) $y = x(x - 4)(x + 6)$

x	h(x)
−3	6
−1	0
0	−5
2	−8

22. The function *h* is defined by a polynomial. The table above gives some of the values of *x* and *h(x)*. Which of the following must be a factor of *h(x)* ?

    A) $x - 8$

    B) $x - 1$

    C) $x + 1$

    D) $x + 5$

> HINT: In Q23, the definition of the *b* function has a variable in the denominator. What does this tell you about the value of *x*?

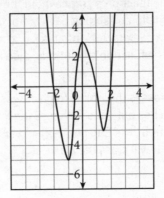

23. The graph of the function *a(x)* is shown above. If $b(x) = \frac{1}{x}$, which of the following is a true statement about $b(a(x))$?

    A) $b(a(x))$ is defined for all real numbers.

    B) $b(a(x))$ is undefined for exactly one real value of *x*.

    C) $b(a(x))$ is undefined for exactly four real values of *x*.

    D) $b(a(x))$ is undefined for all real numbers.

24. If function f has exactly two distinct real zeros, which of the following graphs could be the complete graph of $f(x)$?

A)

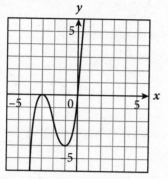

B)

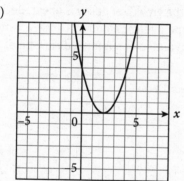

C)

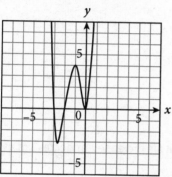

D)

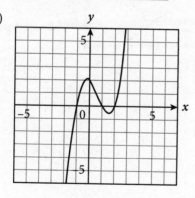

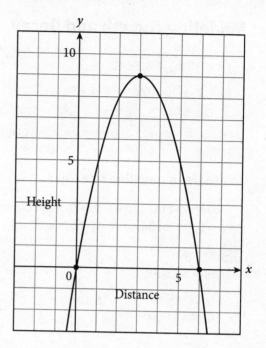

25. The graph of $f(x) = -(x-3)^2 + 9$ above approximates the trajectory of a water balloon shot from a cannon at ground level. In terms of the trajectory, what information is represented by a root of this function?

A) The maximum height achieved by the balloon.

B) The total horizontal distance traveled by the balloon.

C) The maximum speed of the balloon.

D) The initial acceleration of the balloon.

Modeling Growth and Decay

LEARNING OBJECTIVES

After this lesson, you will be able to:

- Determine whether the growth or decay described in a question is linear or exponential
- Apply the linear and exponential equations to answer growth and decay questions

To answer a question like this:

A certain car costs $20,000. If the car loses 15 percent of its value each year, approximately how much will the car be worth after 5 years?

A) $5,000

B) $8,900

C) $11,200

D) $15,000

You need to know this:

The terms **growth** and **decay** refer to situations in which some quantity is increased or decreased over time according to a rule.

- If the rule is to add or subtract the same amount each time, then the growth or decay is **linear**. Because the graph of linear growth and decay is a line, you can use the slope-intercept form of a line—$y = mx + b$—to describe it, where b is the starting amount and m is the amount added or subtracted each time.

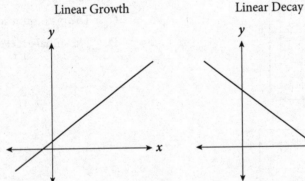

Linear Growth   Linear Decay

- If the rule is to multiply or divide by the same amount each time, then the growth or decay is **exponential**. The general form of an exponential function is $y = ab^x$, where a is the y-intercept and b is the amount multiplied or divided each time. Given that $a > 0$ and $b > 1$, when x is positive, the equation describes exponential growth, and when x is negative, the equation describes exponential decay.

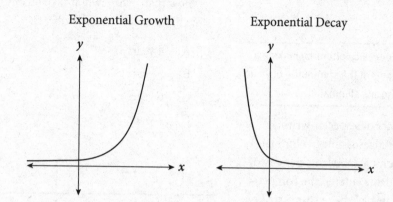

Exponential Growth   Exponential Decay

- When an exponential growth or decay question gives you a growth rate over time, you can use a modified version of the exponential function, $f(x) = f(0)(1 + r)^t$, where $f(0)$ is the amount at time $t = 0$ and r is the growth rate (or decay rate, if negative) expressed as a decimal.

You need to do this:

- First, determine whether the situation described is linear or exponential. If an amount is added or subtracted each time, then the growth is linear; if the original quantity is multiplied or divided by some amount each time, then the growth is exponential.
- Plug the values from the question into the appropriate equation and solve for the missing quantity.
- When the numbers are manageable, you might be able to avoid using the equations by simply carrying out the operations described. For example, if the question says that an amount doubles each day and asks for the amount after three days, then doubling the initial quantity three times will likely be more efficient than plugging the numbers into the exponential growth equation.

Explanation:

The question says that the car loses value at a certain rate per year, which means the question involves exponential decay. The question gives three pieces of important information: the initial value $f(0) = \$20{,}000$, the rate $r = -0.15$, and the time $t = 5$. The question asks for the approximate value of the car after 5 years, which is $f(5)$. The rate must be expressed as a decimal, and since the value of the car is decreasing, the rate is also negative. Plug these values into the equation $f(t) = f(0)(1 + r)^t$ and use your calculator to solve:

$$f(t) = 20{,}000(1 - 0.15)^5$$

$$= 20{,}000(0.85)^5 \approx \$8{,}900$$

Choice **(B)** is correct.

Try on Your Own

Directions: Take as much time as you need on these questions. Work carefully and methodically. There will be an opportunity for timed practice at the end of the chapter.

HINT: For Q26, keep track of your calculations by making a chart with the number of applicants at the start of the day and the number of applicants eliminated.

---

26. In determining the winner of a speech-writing competition, a panel of judges is able to eliminate one-quarter of the remaining applicants per day of deliberations. If 128 students entered the competition, how many applicants have been eliminated by the end of the third day of deliberations?

27. The manager of a health club determines that the club's membership has increased at a rate of 16 percent per year for the past four years. The club currently has 42 members. If this trend continues, how many years will it take for the club's membership to exceed 100 members?

    A)   4 years

    B)   5 years

    C)   6 years

    D)   7 years

HINT: For Q28, no original amount is given. What would be a good number to pick for that amount?

---

28. Radioactive carbon dating can determine how long ago an organism lived by measuring how much of the ^{14}C in the sample has decayed. ^{14}C is an isotope of carbon that has a half-life of 5,600 years. Half-life is the amount of time it takes for half of the original amount to decay. If a sample of a petrified tree contains 6.25 percent of its original ^{14}C, how long ago did the tree die?

    A)   22,400 years

    B)   28,000 years

    C)   35,000 years

    D)   89,600 years

HINT: For Q29, is she saving more, the same, or less each month? What does that tell you about the function?

29. Penelope receives the same amount of money each month for her allowance. Each month she spends half of her allowance and puts the rest in a piggy bank. On Penelope's 8th birthday, the piggy bank contains $40. If the piggy bank contains $244 after 2 years, what is her monthly allowance? (Ignore the dollar sign when gridding your response.)

30. At a certain bank, money held in account X earns a monthly interest equal to 2 percent of the original investment, while account Y earns a monthly interest equal to 2 percent of the current value of the account. If $500 is invested into each account, what is the positive difference between the value of account X and account Y after three years? (Round your answer to the nearest dollar and ignore the dollar sign when gridding your response.)

Rational Expressions and Equations

LEARNING OBJECTIVES

After this lesson, you will be able to:

- Simplify a rational expression
- Isolate a variable in a rational equation

To answer a question like this:

$$\frac{5y + 7}{(y + 4)^2} - \frac{5}{(y + 4)}$$

If the expression above is equal to $\frac{-b}{(y + 4)^2}$, where b is a positive constant and $y \neq -4$, what is the value of b ?

A) 4

B) 7

C) 13

D) 27

You need to know this:

A **rational expression** is a ratio expressed as a fraction with a polynomial in the denominator. A **rational equation** is an equation that includes at least one rational expression.

- Factors in a rational expression can be canceled when simplifying, but under no circumstances can you do the same with individual terms. Consider, for instance, the expression $\frac{x^2 - x - 6}{x^2 + 5x + 6}$. Some test takers will attempt to cancel the x^2, x, and 6 terms to give $\frac{1 - 1 - 1}{1 + 5 + 1} = \frac{-1}{7}$, which is *never* correct. Instead, factor the numerator and denominator: $\frac{(x + 2)(x - 3)}{(x + 2)(x + 3)}$. Cancel the $x + 2$ factors to get $\frac{x - 3}{x + 3}$.

- If a rational expression has a higher-degree numerator than denominator $\left(e.g., \frac{x^2 + 3}{1 - x}\right)$, it can be simplified using polynomial long division. If a rational expression has a lower-degree numerator than denominator $\left(e.g., \frac{1 - x}{x^2 + 3}\right)$, it cannot.

- Because rational expressions have polynomial denominators, they will often be undefined for certain values. For example, the expression $\frac{x - 4}{x + 2}$ is defined for all values of x except -2. This is because when $x = -2$, the denominator of the expression is 0, which would make the expression undefined.

- Beware of undefined expressions when solving rational equations. Take the equation $\frac{1}{x + 4} + \frac{1}{x - 4} = \frac{8}{(x + 4)(x - 4)}$, for instance. After multiplying both sides by the common denominator $(x + 4)(x - 4)$, you have $(x - 4) + (x + 4) = 8$. Solving for x yields $2x = 8$, which simplifies to $x = 4$. When 4 is substituted for x, however, you get 0 in the denominator of both the second and third terms of the equation. Therefore, this equation is said to have no solution. (A value that causes a denominator to equal 0 is called an extraneous solution.)

You need to do this:

- Find a common denominator
- Multiply each term by the common denominator and simplify
- Make sure you haven't found an extraneous solution

Explanation:

Start by setting the two expressions equal:

$$\frac{5y+7}{(y+4)^2} - \frac{5}{y+4} = \frac{-b}{(y+4)^2}$$

Next, get rid of the fractions. To do this, multiply both sides of the equation by the common denominator, $(y+4)^2$:

$$\left(\frac{5y+7}{(y+4)^2} - \frac{5}{y+4} = \frac{-b}{(y+4)^2}\right)(y+4)^2$$

$$5y+7-5(y+4) = -b$$

Now all that remains is to solve for b:

$$5y+7-5y-20 = -b$$
$$-13 = -b$$
$$b = 13$$

The correct answer is **(C)**.

Try on Your Own

Directions: Take as much time as you need on these questions. Work carefully and methodically. There will be an opportunity for timed practice at the end of the chapter.

HINT: For Q31, multiply both sides by a common denominator or cross-multiply. (They are the same thing.)

---

31. Given the equation $\frac{6}{x} = \frac{3}{k+2}$ and the constraints $x \neq 0$ and $k \neq -2$, what is x in terms of k?

    A) $x = 2k + 4$
    B) $x = 2k + 12$
    C) $x = 2k - \frac{1}{4}$
    D) $x = \frac{1}{4}k + 12$

HINT: For Q32, how do you add fractions with different denominators?

$$\frac{3a+9}{(a-3)^2} + \frac{-9}{3a-9}$$

32. In the expression above, $(a-3)^2 = 6$. What is the value of the expression?

33. If $a > 6$, which of the following is equivalent to
$$\frac{\frac{2}{a}}{\frac{1}{a-2} + \frac{1}{a-6}}?$$

    A) $2a^2 - 16a + 24$
    B) $a(2a - 8)$
    C) $\frac{a^2 - 8a + 12}{a^2 - 4a}$
    D) $\frac{2a - 8}{a^2 - 8a + 12}$

34. If $\frac{5}{x+2} = \frac{2}{x+1} + \frac{1}{2}$ and $x > 1$, what is the value of x?

    A) 2
    B) 3
    C) 6
    D) 9

35. If $\frac{16}{7x+4} + A$ is equivalent to $\frac{49x^2}{7x+4}$, what is A in terms of x?

    A) $7x + 4$
    B) $7x - 4$
    C) $49x^2$
    D) $49x^2 + 4$

HINT: A common denominator is possible, but messy. Is there another approach to Q36?

$$\frac{c+5}{6c} + \frac{2}{2c-4} = 0$$

36. The equation above is true for all values of c such that $c \neq -6$ and $c \neq 2$. If $c < 0$, what is the value of c?

    A) -20
    B) -10
    C) 1
    D) 10

On Test Day

Remember that the SAT doesn't ask you to show your work. If you find the algebra in a question challenging, there is often another way to get to the answer.

Try this question first using algebra and then using the Picking Numbers strategy from chapter 3. Which approach do you find easier? There's no right or wrong answer—just remember your preferred approach and try it first if you see a question like this on test day.

37. The expression $\dfrac{3x-1}{x-4}$ is equivalent to which of the following?

    A) $\dfrac{1}{2}$

    B) $3x - \dfrac{1}{x-4}$

    C) $3 - \dfrac{11}{x-4}$

    D) $3 + \dfrac{11}{x-4}$

The correct answer and both ways of solving can be found at the end of this chapter.

How Much Have You Learned?

Directions: For testlike practice, give yourself 18 minutes to complete this question set. Be sure to study the explanations, even for questions you got right. They can be found at the end of this chapter.

38. An object launched upwards at an angle has parabolic motion. The height, h, of a projectile at time t is given by the equation $h = \frac{1}{2}at^2 + v_v t + h_0$, where a is the acceleration due to gravity, v_v is the vertical component of the velocity, and h_0 is the initial height. Which of the following equations correctly represents the object's acceleration due to gravity in terms of the other variables?

A) $a = \dfrac{h - v_v t - h_0}{t}$

B) $a = \dfrac{h - v_v t - h_0}{2t^2}$

C) $a = \dfrac{2(h - v_v t - h_0)}{t^2}$

D) $a = t\sqrt{2(h - v_v t - h_0)}$

39. If $\left(16^{3x}\right)\left(32^x\right)\left(8^{3x}\right) = \dfrac{\left(4^{6x}\right)\left(32^{3x}\right)}{4}$, then what is the value of x?

A) -2

B) -1

C) 1

D) 2

40. Given that $\dfrac{y}{\sqrt{x} - 3} = \dfrac{\sqrt{x} + 3}{3}$ and $2x + 42 = 9x - 63$, what is the value of y?

		/	/	
.	.	.	.	

$y = \dfrac{3x^2 + 7}{x - 3}$

41. Which of the following expressions is equivalent to y?

A) $3x + 9 - \dfrac{20}{x - 3}$

B) $3x + 9 + \dfrac{34}{x - 3}$

C) $3x + 43$

D) $3x^2 + \dfrac{9}{x - 3}$

$z = 15x^2 + 10xy - 6x - 4y$

42. For which of the ordered pairs, (x, y), below is $z \neq 0$?

A) $(-3, 2)$

B) $(-2, 3)$

C) $\left(\dfrac{2}{5}, 0\right)$

D) $\left(\dfrac{2}{5}, 10\right)$

43. $\sqrt{27^{\frac{2}{3}} + 128^{\frac{4}{7}}} =$

$$x^3 + 4 = 3x^2 - 7x + 25$$

46. For what real value of x is the above equation valid?

A) 0

B) 3

C) 4

D) 7

47. Which of the following equations has a graph for which all roots are greater than 0 ?

A) $y = 4|x|$

B) $y = x^2 - 4$

C) $y = (x - 2)^2$

D) $y = x(x - 2)^2$

44. Which of the following is equivalent to $\dfrac{4x^2 - 8}{2x + 3}$?

A) $2x - 3 + \dfrac{1}{2x + 3}$

B) $2x - 2$

C) $2x + 3 - \dfrac{1}{2x + 3}$

D) $2x + 4$

$$g(x) = \frac{2}{2x^3 - 12x^2 - 14x}$$

45. For which of the following values of x is the function $g(x)$ defined?

A) -1

B) 0

C) 1

D) 7

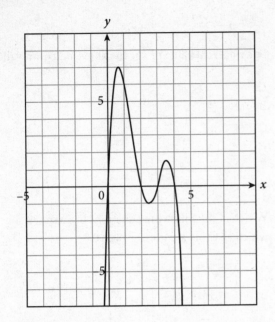

49. A marketing team conducted a study on the use of smartphones. In a certain metropolitan area, there were 1.6 million smartphone users at the end of 2018. The marketing team predicted that the number of smartphone users would increase by 35 percent each year beginning in 2019. If y represents the number of smartphone users in this metropolitan area after x years, then which of the following equations best models the number of smartphone users in this area over time?

A) $y = 1,600,000(1.35)^x$

B) $y = 1,600,000(35)^x$

C) $y = 35x + 1,600,000$

D) $y = 1.35x + 1,600,000$

48. The graph of the function
$f(x) = -x(x - 4)(x - 3)(x - 2)$ is shown above.
If $f(x) = 0$, how many real solutions exist?

A) 0

B) 2

C) 3

D) 4

Reflect

Directions: Take a few minutes to recall what you've learned and what you've been practicing in this chapter. Consider the following questions, jot down your best answer for each one, and then compare your reflections to the expert responses on the following page. Use your level of confidence to determine what to do next.

How do you multiply two polynomials?

_____

_____

_____

What are the zeros of a polynomial function?

_____

_____

_____

Describe the difference between linear and exponential growth.

_____

_____

_____

Name two ways to simplify rational expressions.

_____

_____

_____

Expert Responses

How do you multiply two polynomials?

Distribute each term in the first set of parentheses to each term in the second set, then combine like terms.

What are the zeros of a polynomial function?

The zeros are the points at which the value of the function (that is, the y-value) is zero. Think of the zeros as the x-intercepts of the function. The words "roots" and "solutions" mean the same thing.

Describe the difference between linear and exponential growth.

Linear growth is modeled by a linear function, with the equation $y = mx + b$, such that the slope of the line is positive. You're essentially adding the same amount over and over again. (In linear decay, the slope of the line is negative, and you're subtracting the same amount over and over again.)

Exponential growth is modeled by an exponential function in the form $y = ab^x$, where a is the y-intercept and b is the amount multiplied each time, over and over. The slope of an exponential growth function steepens with increasing x-values. (In exponential decay, b is the amount divided by each time, and the slope starts out steeply negative and flattens with increasing x-values.)

Name two ways to simplify rational expressions.

One way is to use polynomial long division, though this will work only if the higher-order polynomial is in the numerator. Another way is to cancel factors that appear in both the numerator and denominator.

Next Steps

If you answered most questions correctly in the "How Much Have You Learned?" section, and if your responses to the Reflect questions were similar to those of the SAT expert, then consider exponents and polynomial functions an area of strength and move on to the next chapter. Come back to this topic periodically to prevent yourself from getting rusty.

If you don't yet feel confident, review those parts of this chapter that you have not yet mastered. In particular, review the lessons covering Exponents, Modeling Growth and Decay, and Rational Expressions and Equations as these are high-yield topics on the SAT. Then try the questions you missed again. As always, be sure to review the explanations closely.

Answers and Explanations

1. 9

Difficulty: Medium

Getting to the Answer: You are not allowed to use your calculator on this question, so look for ways to rewrite the larger numbers as the same base. Memorizing the values of small integers up to the fourth or fifth power will help you see these patterns: $27 = 3^3$ and $81 = 3^4$. Now, rewrite the expression as $\dfrac{3^5 \times \left(3^3\right)^3}{\left(3^4\right)^3}$, which becomes $\dfrac{3^5 \times 3^9}{3^{12}} = \dfrac{3^{14}}{3^{12}}$. Subtract the exponents to get 3^2, which equals **9**, the correct answer.

2. A

Difficulty: Easy

Getting to the Answer: Find the greatest common factor (GCF) of both the numerator and the denominator, which in this question happens to be the denominator. Factor out the GCF, $9x^2$, from the numerator and denominator and then cancel what you can:

$$\frac{18x^4 + 27x^3 - 36x^2}{9x^2} = \frac{\cancel{9x^2}\left(2x^2 + 3x - 4\right)}{\cancel{9x^2}}$$

$$= 2x^2 + 3x - 4$$

This matches **(A)**. As an alternate method, you could split the expression up and reduce each term, one at a time:

$$\frac{18x^4 + 27x^3 - 36x^2}{9x^2} = \frac{18x^4}{9x^2} + \frac{27x^3}{9x^2} - \frac{36x^2}{9x^2}$$

$$= 2x^2 + 3x - 4$$

3. D

Difficulty: Medium

Getting to the Answer: Start by setting up a ratio that compares RBC count to total blood cell count. Manipulate the quantities to make all the exponents the same (to convert 7.5×10^3 to a product of 10^6 and another number, move the decimal point in 7.5 three places to the left and write "$\times 10^6$" after it), factor out 10^6, and then add the quantities in parentheses together. Once there, you can use exponent rules to simplify your equation. Divide through and multiply by 100 to get the RBC component as a percentage:

$$RBC = \frac{5.4 \times 10^6}{5.4 \times 10^6 + 7.5 \times 10^3 + 3.5 \times 10^5}$$

$$= \frac{5.4 \times \cancel{10^6}}{5.4 \times \cancel{10^6} + 0.0075 \times \cancel{10^6} + 0.35 \times \cancel{10^6}}$$

$$= \frac{5.4 \times \cancel{10^6}}{\cancel{10^6}\,(5.4 + 0.0075 + 0.35)}$$

$$= \frac{5.4}{5.7575}$$

Note that the answer choices are, for the most part, far apart. Because 5.4 is relatively close to 5.7575, you can conclude with confidence that the correct answer is likely close to 100%. Therefore, **(D)** is the correct answer. If this question is in the calculator section, you can plug the numbers into your calculator to check:

$$\%RBC = \frac{5.4}{5.7575} \times 100 \approx 93.79\%$$

Choice **(D)** is still correct.

4. 256

Difficulty: Medium

Getting to the Answer: If $n^3 = -8$, then $n = -2$. Simplify the given expression via exponent rules and then plug -2 in for n:

Grid in **256**.

5. B

Difficulty: Hard

Getting to the Answer: To simplify the division on the left side of the equation, subtract the powers and combine:

$$\frac{x^{5r}}{x^{3r-2s}} = x^{5r-(3r-2s)}$$

$$= x^{5r-3r+2s}$$

$$= x^{2r+2s}$$

Note that in the expression $2r + 2s$, it is possible to factor out a 2. Thus, $x^{2r+2s} = x^{2(r+s)}$. The question indicates that $r + s = 6$, so $x^{2(r+s)} = x^{2(6)} = x^{12}$. This is equal to x^t, so $t = 12$. The answer is **(B)**.

6. A

Difficulty: Medium

Getting to the Answer: Solve equations containing radical expressions the same way you solve any other equation: isolate the variable using inverse operations. Start by subtracting 8 from both sides of the equation, and then multiply by 3. Then, square both sides to remove the radical.

$$8 + \frac{\sqrt{2x + 29}}{3} = 9$$
$$\frac{\sqrt{2x + 29}}{3} = 1$$
$$\sqrt{2x + 29} = 3$$
$$2x + 29 = 9$$

Now you have a simple linear equation that you can solve using more inverse operations: subtract 29 and divide by 2 to find that $x = -10$. Be careful—just because the equation started with a radical and the answer is negative, it does not follow that *"No solution"* is the correct answer. If you plug -10 into the expression under the radical, the result is a positive number, which means -10 is a perfectly valid solution. Therefore, **(A)** is correct.

7. C

Difficulty: Medium

Getting to the Answer: First, solve for x and plug that value into the second equation. Subtract x from both sides of the equation to get $2x = 14$, so $x = 7$. Plugging this into the second equation gives you $\sqrt{3z^2 - 11} + 2(7) = 22$. Thus, $\sqrt{3z^2 - 11} = 8$. Square both sides of this equation and solve for z:

$$3z^2 - 11 = 64$$
$$3z^2 = 75$$
$$z^2 = 25$$
$$z = \pm 5$$

Since the question specifies that $z > 0$, **(C)** is correct.

8. C

Difficulty: Easy

Getting to the Answer: Follow the standard order of operations—deal with the exponent first and then attach the negative sign (because a negative in front of an expression means multiplication by -1). The variable x is being raised to the $\frac{1}{4}$ power, so rewrite the term as a radical expression with 4 as the degree of the root and 1 as the power to which the radicand, x, is being raised:

$$x^{\frac{1}{4}} = \sqrt[4]{x^1} = \sqrt[4]{x}$$

Now attach the negative to arrive at the correct answer, $-\sqrt[4]{x}$, which is **(C)**.

9. 16

Difficulty: Medium

Getting to the Answer: Because this is a no-calculator question, you need to rewrite the exponent in a way that makes it easier to evaluate: use exponent rules to rewrite $\frac{4}{3}$ as a unit fraction raised to a power. Then write the expression in radical form and simplify:

$$8^{\frac{4}{3}} = \left(8^{\frac{1}{3}}\right)^4$$
$$= \left(\sqrt[3]{8}\right)^4$$
$$= 2^4$$
$$= 2 \times 2 \times 2 \times 2$$
$$= 16$$

10. A

Difficulty: Medium

Getting to the Answer: Start by isolating the radical on the left side of the equation by adding 3 to both sides to get $\sqrt{3a + 16} = a + 2$. Now you can square both sides to get rid of the radical: $3a + 16 = (a + 2)^2 = a^2 + 4a + 4$. Since the right side of this equation is a quadratic, set it equal to 0 in order to determine the solutions: $0 = a^2 + 4a + 4 - (3a + 16) = a^2 + a - 12$. Next, factor the quadratic using reverse FOIL. The two factors of -12 that add up to 1 are -3 and 4, so $(a - 3)(a + 4) = 0$. Thus, a can be either 3 or -4, but the question says $a > 0$, so the only permissible value is 3. **(A)** is correct.

11. A

Difficulty: Easy

Getting to the Answer: Add polynomial expressions by combining like terms. Be careful of the signs of each term. It may help to write the sum vertically, lining up the like terms:

$$6a^2 - 17a - 9$$
$$\underline{+ -5a^2 + 8a - 2}$$
$$a^2 - 9a - 11$$

The correct choice is **(A)**.

12. D

Difficulty: Medium

Getting to the Answer: First, write the question as a subtraction problem. Pay careful attention to which expression is being subtracted so that you distribute the negative sign correctly:

$$8x^2 + 4x + 10 - \left(3x^3 + 7x - 5\right)$$
$$= -3x^3 + 8x^2 - 3x + 15$$

This expression matches **(D)**.

13. D

Difficulty: Medium

Getting to the Answer: Multiply each term in the first expression by $\frac{3}{2}$ and each term in the second expression by -2. Then add the two polynomials by writing them vertically and combining like terms. You'll have to find a common denominator to combine the x-coefficients and to combine the constant terms:

$$\frac{3}{2}A = \frac{3}{2}\left(4x^2 + 7x - 1\right) = 6x^2 + \frac{21}{2}x - \frac{3}{2}$$
$$-2B = -2\left(-x^2 - 5x + 3\right) = 2x^2 + 10x - 6$$

$$6x^2 + \frac{21}{2}x - \frac{3}{2}$$
$$\underline{+ 2x^2 + \frac{20}{2}x - \frac{12}{2}}$$
$$8x^2 + \frac{41}{2}x - \frac{15}{2}$$

This means **(D)** is correct. Notice that if you are simplifying the expression from left to right, after you find the x^2 coefficient, you can eliminate (A) and (B). After you find the x coefficient, you can eliminate (C) and stop your work.

14. C

Difficulty: Hard

Getting to the Answer: In order to solve the equation, move all the terms to one side of the equation and set them equal to 0, then factor the expression. Thus, the given equation becomes $x^3 + x^2 - 9x - 9 = 0$. Think of this as two pairs of terms, $(x^3 + x^2)$ and $(-9x - 9)$. The first pair of terms share a common factor of x^2, so they can be written as $x^2(x + 1)$. The second pair share the common factor of -9, so they are equivalent to $-9(x + 1)$. So, the equation becomes $x^2(x + 1) - 9(x + 1) = 0$. Now, factor out the $(x + 1)$ term: $(x^2 - 9)(x + 1) = 0$.

In order for the product of two terms to be 0, either one or both must be 0. If $x^2 - 9 = 0$, then $x^2 = 9$ and $x = \pm 3$. Eliminate (A) and (D). If $x + 1 = 0$, then $x = -1$. Eliminate (B), so **(C)** is correct. You could also answer the question using Backsolving by plugging in each answer choice until you found the value for x that did *not* satisfy the equation.

15. C

Difficulty: Medium

Strategic Advice: To multiply two polynomials, multiply each term in the first factor by each term in the second factor, then combine like terms.

Getting to the Answer: Multiply each part of the trinomial expression by each part of the binomial one piece at a time and then combine like terms:

$$\left(2x^2 + 3x - 4\right)(3x + 2)$$
$$= 2x^2(3x + 2) + 3x(3x + 2) - 4(3x + 2)$$
$$= 6x^3 + 4x^2 + 9x^2 + 6x - 12x - 8$$
$$= 6x^3 + 13x^2 - 6x - 8$$

Because a represents the coefficient of x^2, $a = 13$. Hence, **(C)** is correct.

16. D

Difficulty: Medium

Getting to the Answer: Use polynomial long division to simplify the expression:

$$\begin{array}{r} 2a + 1 \\ a - 3 \overline{\smash{\big)}\ 2a^2 - 5a - 1} \\ \underline{-\left(2a^2 - 6a\right)} \\ a - 1 \\ \underline{-(a - 3)} \\ 2 \end{array}$$

The quotient is $2a + 1$ and the remainder is 2, which will be divided by the divisor in the final answer: $2a + 1 + \dfrac{2}{a - 3}$. Thus, **(D)** is correct.

17. C

Difficulty: Hard

Getting to the Answer: A fraction is the same as division, so you can use polynomial long division to simplify the expression:

$$\begin{array}{r} 3x + 2 \\ 2x + 5 \overline{\smash{\big)}\ 6x^2 + 19x + 10} \\ \underline{-\left(6x^2 + 15x\right)} \\ 4x + 10 \\ \underline{-(4x + 10)} \\ 0 \end{array}$$

The simplified expression is $3x + 2$, so $a + b = 3 + 2 = 5$, which is **(C)**. As an alternate approach, you could factor the numerator of the expression and cancel common factors:

$$\frac{6x^2 + 19x + 10}{2x + 5} = \frac{\cancel{(2x + 5)}(3x + 2)}{\cancel{(2x + 5)}} = 3x + 2$$

18. B

Difficulty: Medium

Getting to the Answer: Use polynomial long division to simplify the expression:

$$\begin{array}{r} 2x - 5 \\ 2x + 2 \overline{\smash{\big)}\ 4x^2 - 6x} \\ \underline{-\left(4x^2 + 4x\right)} \\ -10x \\ \underline{-(-10x - 10)} \\ +10 \end{array}$$

The quotient is $2x - 5$ and the remainder is 10. Put the remainder over the divisor and add this to the quotient: $2x - 5 + \dfrac{10}{2x + 2}$; **(B)** is correct.

19. B

Difficulty: Hard

Getting to the Answer: The question provides the quotient of $-9x + 5$ of a division problem and asks you to find the coefficient of the first term of the divisor $tx - 4$. Set this up in polynomial long division form to better understand the relationship between t and the other terms:

$$\begin{array}{r} -9x + 5 \\ tx - 4 \overline{\smash{\big)}\ 36x^2 + 16x - 21} \end{array}$$

Note that, although the quotient of $-9x + 5$ leaves a remainder of $-\dfrac{1}{tx - 4}$, it's not necessary to consider the remainder when determining the value of t.

Viewed this way, it becomes apparent that $36x^2 \div tx = -9x$. Multiplying both sides by tx gives you $tx(-9x) = 36x^2$; therefore, $t(-9) = 36$, so $t = -4$. **(B)** is correct.

20. C

Difficulty: Hard

Getting to the Answer: Because $f(x)$ is divisible by $x - 5$, the value $x - 5$ must be a factor of $f(x)$. Therefore, you can define $f(x)$ as $(x - 5)(n)$, where n is some unknown polynomial. Since $g(x)$ is $f(x) + 4$, you can say that $g(x)$ must be $(x - 5)(n) + 4$.

Thus, $g(5)$ will be $(5 - 5)(n) + 4 = 0(n) + 4 = 0 + 4 = 4$. Therefore, **(C)** is correct.

21. B

Difficulty: Medium

Getting to the Answer: The solutions, or x-intercepts, of a polynomial are the factors of that polynomial. This polynomial has x-intercepts of −4, 0, and 6. The factors that generate those solutions are $(x + 4)$, x, and $(x − 6)$. Eliminate (C) and (D) because they do not include those three factors. Because the graph *crosses* the x-axis at each x-intercept (rather than merely touching the x-axis), none of the factors can be raised to an even exponent. Therefore, the x^2 term in (A) means it is incorrect. **(B)** is correct.

22. C

Difficulty: Medium

Getting to the Answer: To find the solutions to a polynomial function, factor the polynomial and set each factor equal to 0. The solutions of a function are the x-intercepts, so $h(x)$ or the y-coordinate of the solution must equal 0. From the chart, the only point with $h(x) = 0$ is at $x = −1$. If $x = −1$, the factor that generates that solution is $x + 1 = 0$ because $(−1) + 1 = 0$. **(C)** is correct.

23. C

Difficulty: Hard

Getting to the Answer: Translate the notation: $b(a(x))$ means b of $a(x)$. This tells you to use $a(x)$ as the input for $b(x)$. You can rewrite this as $\frac{1}{a(x)}$, which is the reciprocal of $a(x)$. This new function will be undefined anywhere that $a(x) = 0$ because a denominator of 0 is not permitted. Looking at the graph, you can see that $a(x)$ crosses the x-axis four times, at which point the value of $a(x)$ is 0. Since division by 0 is undefined, **(C)** is correct.

24. A

Difficulty: Easy

Getting to the Answer: The phrase "exactly 2 distinct real zeros" means that the graph must have exactly two different x-intercepts on the graph. An x-intercept is indicated any time that the graph either crosses or touches the x-axis. (B) and (D) have three distinct zeros, and (C) has two zeros, but because the graph only touches the x-axis, they are the same, not distinct. The only graph with exactly 2 distinct zeros is **(A)**.

25. B

Difficulty: Easy

Getting to the Answer: The keyword "root" in the question stem means that you should examine the places at which the graph intersects the x-axis. Thus, this graph has roots at $(0, 0)$ and $(6, 0)$. The x-axis, according to the graph, represents the distance traveled by the balloon. When $x = 0$, the distance the water balloon has traveled is 0, which is the balloon's starting position. The initial location of the balloon is not an answer choice, so the correct answer must be what the other root represents. When $x = 6$, the balloon's height is 0, which is the end point of the balloon's trajectory. This value, 6, is a root that represents the total horizontal distance traveled. **(B)** is correct.

26. 74

Difficulty: Easy

Strategic Advice: The goal is to find the number of applicants *eliminated* after four days, not the number remaining.

Getting to the Answer: The question describes the decay as the result of removing a certain fraction of the remaining applicants each day. The situation involves repeated division, so this is an example of exponential decay. You could use the exponential decay formula for a given rate, but without a calculator, raising a decimal to an exponent might create time-consuming calculations. Instead, determine how many applicants are eliminated each day and tally them up.

After the first day, the judges eliminate one-fourth of 128, or 32 applicants. This leaves $128 − 32 = 96$ applicants. On the second day, one-fourth of 96, or 24 applicants are eliminated, leaving $96 − 24 = 72$. Finally, on the third day, one-fourth are eliminated again; one-fourth of 72 is 18, so there are $72 − 18 = 54$ applicants remaining. If 54 applicants remain, then $128 − 54 = 74$ applicants have been eliminated.

27. C

Difficulty: Medium

Strategic Advice: This question gives you a percent increase per year, so use the exponential growth equation to solve for the number of years. Note that the question provides unnecessary information. It doesn't matter that the trend has been happening for the last four years because the question asks only about the number of years after the present.

Getting to the Answer: Use the formula for exponential growth and plug in the values from the question. The rate is 16%, which as a decimal is 0.16. The rate will remain positive because the question asks about increase, or growth; therefore, $r = 0.16$. The current number of members is 42, so this will be $f(0)$. The goal is at least 100 members so that will be the output, or $f(t)$. Put it all together:

$$f(t) = f(0)(1 + r)^t$$
$$100 = 42(1 + 0.16)^2$$
$$100 = 42(1.16)^t$$

At this point, Backsolving is the best approach. Plug in the number of years for t. Because the answer choices are in ascending order, try one of the middle options first. You might be able to eliminate more than one choice at a time. Choice (B) is $t = 5$:

$$42(1.16)^5 \approx 88$$

Since (B) is too small, (A) must be as well. Eliminate them both. Unfortunately, 88 is not close enough to 100 to be certain that (C) is the correct answer, so test it:

$$42(1.16)^6 \approx 102$$

Six years is enough to put the club over 100 members. (C) is correct.

28. A

Difficulty: Hard

Strategy Advice: The term "half-life" signals exponential decay because it implies repeated division by 2. Using the exponential decay formula here would be complicated. Instead, you can use the percentage given in the problem, along with the Picking Numbers strategy, to figure out how many half-lives have elapsed.

Getting to the Answer: Instead of providing an actual amount of ^{14}C, this question tells you what percent is left. For questions involving percentages of unknown values, it is often a good idea to pick 100. So, assume that the amount of ^{14}C in the sample when the tree died is 100. (Fortunately, there is no need to worry about the units here.) After one half-life, the amount of ^{14}C is halved to 50. A second half-life leaves 25, a third leaves 12.5, and a fourth leaves 6.25, which is 6.25% of 100. So four half-lives have elapsed. Since each half-life is 5,600 years, the tree died $4 \times 5,600$ or 22,400 years ago. Choice (A) is correct.

29. 17

Difficulty: Medium

Strategic Advice: The question describes a situation with linear growth since Penelope is adding the same amount of money to her piggy bank each month. Note: the question is asking for her monthly allowance, but she puts in only half that amount each month.

Getting to the Answer: Use the linear growth equation $y = mx + b$. The question gives you the starting amount b ($40), the final amount y ($244), and the amount of time x (2 years, which is 24 months). Plug these values into the equation and solve for m, which is the slope, or the rate of change—or in this case, how much Penelope puts in her piggy bank each month:

$$y = mx + b$$
$$244 = m(24) + 40$$
$$24m = 204$$
$$m = 8.5$$

Remember that what she puts in the piggy bank is only half of her allowance, so her total monthly allowance is twice $8.50. Grid in **17**.

30. 160

Difficulty: Hard

Strategic Advice: This question describes both types of growth. Account X adds a percentage of the original amount, which never changes, so the same amount of money is added each month. Account X grows linearly. Account Y, however, adds a percentage of the current balance, which grows monthly, so account Y grows exponentially.

Getting to the Answer: Account X begins with $500 (the y-intercept, or b) and adds 2% of $500, or $500 \times 0.02 = \$10$ (the rate of change, or m), each month for 3 years, which is 36 months (the input, or x). Plug these values into the linear growth equation to solve for the final value of the account:

$$y = mx + b$$
$$y = 10(36) + 500$$
$$y = 360 + 500 = \$860$$

Account Y begins with $500 ($f(0)$) and adds 2%, or 0.02, (r) each month for 36 months (t). Plug these values into the exponential growth equation to solve for the final value of the account:

$$f(t) = f(0)(1 + r)^t$$
$$f(t) = 500(1 + 0.02)^{36}$$
$$f(t) = 500(1.02)^{36} \approx \$1{,}019.94$$

The positive difference between the two accounts is therefore $1,019.94 - \$860 = \$159.94$. Round up, and grid in **160**.

31. A

Difficulty: Medium

Getting to the Answer: There are two variables and only one equation, but because you're asked to solve for one of the variables *in terms of* the other, you solve the same way you would any other equation, by isolating x on one side of the equation. Cross-multiplying is a quick route to the solution:

$$\frac{6}{x} = \frac{3}{k + 2}$$
$$6(k + 2) = 3x$$
$$6k + 12 = 3x$$
$$\frac{6k}{3} + \frac{12}{3} = \frac{3x}{3}$$
$$2k + 4 = x$$

Switch x to the left side of the equation and the result matches **(A)**.

32. 3

Difficulty: Hard

Getting to the Answer: Because the expression is adding fractions with different denominators, you'll need to establish a common denominator. Note that the second fraction is divisible by 3, so you can simplify the expression and then create the common denominator:

$$\frac{3a + 9}{(a - 3)^2} + \frac{-3}{a - 3}$$
$$= \frac{3a + 9}{(a - 3)^2} + \frac{-3}{a - 3} \times \frac{a - 3}{a - 3}$$
$$= \frac{3a + 9}{(a - 3)^2} + \frac{-3a + 9}{(a - 3)^2}$$
$$= \frac{18}{(a - 3)^2}$$

The question specifies that $(a - 3)^2 = 6$, so $\frac{18}{(a - 3)^2} = \frac{18}{6} = 3$. Therefore, the expression equals 3. Grid in **3**.

33. C

Difficulty: Medium

Getting to the Answer: The denominator of the expression contains the sum of two fractions that themselves have different denominators, so start by finding a common denominator:

$$\frac{\dfrac{2}{a}}{\dfrac{a-6}{(a-2)(a-6)} + \dfrac{a-2}{(a-2)(a-6)}} = \frac{\dfrac{2}{a}}{\dfrac{2a-8}{a^2-8a+12}}$$

Next, multiply the numerator of the expression by the reciprocal of the denominator and simplify:

$$\frac{2}{a} \times \frac{a^2-8a+12}{2a-8}$$

$$= \frac{2\left(a^2-8a+12\right)}{2a^2-8a}$$

$$= \frac{a^2-8a+12}{a^2-4a}$$

This expression matches **(C)**.

34. B

Difficulty: Hard

Getting to the Answer: First, subtract $\dfrac{2}{x+1}$ from both sides to consolidate the two rational expressions on the same side of the equation. Next, multiply the left side of the equation by $\dfrac{(x+1)(x+2)}{(x+1)(x+2)}$ to establish a common denominator to enable subtraction of fractions. Next, combine like terms and cross-multiply:

$$\frac{5}{x+2} - \frac{2}{x+1} = \frac{1}{2}$$

$$\frac{5x+5}{x^2+3x+2} - \frac{2x+4}{x^2+3x+2} = \frac{1}{2}$$

$$\frac{3x+1}{x^2+3x+2} = \frac{1}{2}$$

$$6x+2 = x^2+3x+2$$

Next, set the equation equal to zero by subtracting $6x+2$ from both sides: $0 = x^2 - 3x$. Now, factor the right side to yield $0 = x(x-3)$.

Therefore, either $x = 0$ or $x = 3$. Since the question specifies that $x > 1$, x must equal 3, and **(B)** is correct.

Note that, if you wanted to avoid the algebra, you could backsolve this question by plugging in the answer choices to find which works in the original equation.

35. B

Difficulty: Hard

Getting to the Answer: Because the question states that the expressions are equivalent, set up the equation $\dfrac{16}{7x+4} + A = \dfrac{49x^2}{7x+4}$ and solve for A. Start by subtracting the first term from both sides of the equation to isolate A. Then, simplify if possible (usually by cancelling common factors). The denominators of the rational terms are the same, so they can be combined:

$$\frac{16}{7x+4} + A = \frac{49x^2}{7x+4}$$

$$A = \frac{49x^2}{7x+4} - \frac{16}{7x+4}$$

$$A = \frac{49x^2-16}{7x+4}$$

$$A = \frac{\cancel{(7x+4)}(7x-4)}{\cancel{7x+4}}$$

$$A = 7x-4$$

The correct choice is **(B)**.

36. B

Difficulty: Medium

Getting to the Answer: While you might be tempted to establish a common denominator in order to add the fractions together, that would be extremely cumbersome. Instead, move the second fraction over to the other side of the equation by subtracting it from both sides. Then cross-multiply to simplify:

$$\frac{c+5}{6c} = \frac{-2}{2c-4}$$

$$(c+5)(2c-4) = -12c$$

$$2c^2+6c-20 = -12c$$

$$2c^2+18c-20 = 0$$

$$c^2+9c-10 = 0$$

$$(c+10)(c-1) = 0$$

Therefore, either $c = -10$ or $c = 1$. The question specifies that $c < 0$, so c must equal -10. **(B)** is correct.

37. D

Difficulty: Medium

Getting to the Answer: The first thought at seeing this question may be to try to break the expression into two separate fractions or see if some expression can be factored out. Unfortunately, that does not help with simplifying the expression. You'll need polynomial long division if you're going to use algebra:

$$
\begin{array}{r}
3 \\
x-4 \overline{)\, 3x-1} \\
\underline{-(3x-12)} \\
11
\end{array}
$$

That results in the expression $3 + \dfrac{11}{x-4}$, so the correct answer is **(D)**.

Another effective alternative for solving this question is to use Picking Numbers. Choose a small, permissible value like $x = 2$ to find a value for the original expression:

$$\frac{3(2)-1}{(2)-4} = \frac{6-1}{-2} = -\frac{5}{2}$$

Now check each answer choice to see which one is equal to $-\dfrac{5}{2}$ when you plug in $x = 2$:

(A): $\dfrac{3-1}{4} = \dfrac{2}{4} = \dfrac{1}{2} \ldots$, eliminate.

(B): $3(2) - \dfrac{1}{(2)-4} = 6 - \dfrac{1}{-2} =$

$6 - \left(-\dfrac{1}{2}\right) = 6 + \dfrac{1}{2} = 6\dfrac{1}{2} = \dfrac{13}{2} \ldots$, eliminate.

(C): $3 - \dfrac{11}{(2)-4} = 3 - \dfrac{11}{-2} = 3 - \left(-\dfrac{11}{2}\right) = 3 + \dfrac{11}{2} = \dfrac{17}{2}$ $\ldots$, eliminate.

(D): $3 + \dfrac{11}{(2)-4} = 3 + \dfrac{11}{-2} = 3 + \left(-\dfrac{11}{2}\right) = -\dfrac{5}{2}$

38. C

Difficulty: Medium

Category: Rational Expressions and Equations

Getting to the Answer: When solving polynomial equations for one variable, begin by moving all terms that don't contain that variable (in this case a) to one side of the equation. Once there, multiply both sides by 2 to eliminate the fraction, and then divide by t^2 to isolate a:

$$h = \frac{1}{2}at^2 + v_0 t + h_0$$
$$h - v_0 t - h_0 = \frac{1}{2}at^2$$
$$at^2 = 2(h - v_0 t - h_0)$$
$$a = \frac{2(h - v_0 t - h_0)}{t^2}$$

Choice **(C)** is the correct answer.

39. D

Difficulty: Medium

Category: Exponents

Getting to the Answer: In order to combine terms with exponents by multiplication or division, the terms must all have the same base. All the bases in the given equation are powers of 2, so restate that equation with all the terms in base two: $\left(2^4\right)^{3x}\left(2^5\right)^{x}\left(2^3\right)^{3x} = \dfrac{\left(2^2\right)^{6x}\left(2^5\right)^{3x}}{2^2}$.

When a base with an exponent is raised to a power, multiply the exponents. An exponent in a denominator is equivalent to the same exponent in the numerator with the sign flipped, so $(2^{12x})(2^{5x})(2^{9x}) = (2^{12x})(2^{15x})(2^{-2})$.

When the numbers with exponents and the same base are multiplied, add the exponents. Thus, the equation further simplifies to $2^{12x+5x+9x} = 2^{12x+15x-2}$. Because the base on each side of the equation is the same, the total of the exponents on both sides must be equal. Therefore, $12x + 5x + 9x = 12x + 15x - 2$. This further simplifies to $26x = 27x - 2$, so $x = 2$. **(D)** is correct.

40. 2

Difficulty: Medium

Category: Radicals

Getting to the Answer: Conveniently, the conjugate of the denominator, $\sqrt{x} - 3$, is the numerator of the other fraction, $\sqrt{x} + 3$, so cross-multiplying will rationalize the fraction.

Cross-multiplying the first equation yields $(y)(3) = \left(\sqrt{x} + 3\right)\left(\sqrt{x} - 3\right)$, which simplifies to $3y = x - 9$. (If this is a difficult simplification for you, study FOIL and the classic quadratics in chapter 12.) In the second equation, you are given that $2x + 42 = 9x - 63$, so $7x = 105$, and $x = 15$. Therefore, $3y = 15 - 9 = 6$, and $y = 2$. Grid in **2**.

You could have chosen to solve the second equation for the value of x, then substituted the result into the proportion and solved for y. Either approach would be equally effective.

41. B

Difficulty: Medium

Category: Polynomial Division

Getting to the Answer: Since there's no common factor in the numerator and denominator, you'll need to resort to using polynomial long division. Notice that the numerator does not have an x term, so include $0x$ in the long division so that the fraction can be shown as $x - 3 \overline{)3x^2 + 0x + 7}$. Next, do the long division:

$$
\begin{array}{r}
3x + 9 \\
x - 3 \overline{)3x^2 + 0x + 7} \\
\underline{3x^2 - 9x} \\
9x + 7 \\
\underline{9x - 27} \\
34
\end{array}
$$

The result of the long division is $3x + 9$ with a remainder of 34. The remainder is the "leftover" part that hasn't yet been divided by $x - 3$, so it can be expressed as $\frac{34}{x - 3}$.

Thus, **(B)** is correct.

42. A

Difficulty: Hard

Category: Polynomials

Strategic Advice: You could plug the x- and y-values from each choice into the given equation to see which does not equal zero. However, if you factor the polynomial, you'll save time by avoiding extra calculations.

Getting to the Answer: Look for common factors in the polynomial by groups. The first two terms, $15x^2$ and $10xy$, share the common factor $5x$. The third and fourth terms share a common factor of -2, so you can write the equation as $z = 5x(3x + 2y) - 2(3x + 2y)$. Next, factor out the $(3x + 2y)$ to regroup this as $z = (5x - 2)(3x + 2y)$. Since z is the product of two factors, if either factor equals 0, then $z = 0$.

If $(5x - 2) = 0$, then $x = \frac{2}{5}$. You can immediately eliminate (C) and (D) because, if $x = \frac{2}{5}$, $z = 0$ no matter what the value of y might be. If $(3x + 2y) = 0$, then $x = -\frac{2}{3}y$, as it is in (B). Thus, **(A)** is the only ordered pair for which $z \neq 0$.

43. 5

Difficulty: Hard

Category: Radicals

Getting to the Answer: Remember that the rules for combining terms under a radical are different for addition and multiplication. Although $\sqrt{xy}$ can be written as $\sqrt{x} \times \sqrt{y}$, terms that are added under a radical, such as $\sqrt{x + y}$, must be combined before taking the root. Now, find the value of each term in the radical above, add them, and then take the square root of the sum.

The term, $27^{\frac{2}{3}}$, is the square of the cube root of 27. Since $3 \times 3 \times 3 = 27$, the cube root of 27 is 3, which squared is $3^2 = 9$. The denominator of the exponent in $128^{\frac{4}{7}}$ quite likely means that 128 is some number to the seventh power. A good place to start would be to try 2 because it is small and easy to raise to high powers. Indeed, you'll find that $2 \times 2 \times 2 \times 2 \times 2 \times 2 \times 2 = 128$. So $128^{\frac{4}{7}} = \left(2^7\right)^{\frac{4}{7}} = 2^4 = 16$. Thus,

$$\sqrt{27^{\frac{2}{3}} + 128^{\frac{4}{7}}} = \sqrt{9 + 16} = \sqrt{25} = 5. \text{ Grid in } \mathbf{5}.$$

44. A

Difficulty: Medium

Category: Rational Expressions and Equations

Strategic Advice: Since there is no common factor in the numerator and denominator, you might be tempted to dive into polynomial long division. However, if you noticed that the numerator, $4x^2 - 8$, is very close to being the difference of two squares, $4x^2 - 9$, there is a more efficient way to unravel this fraction.

Getting to the Answer: Restate the fraction as $\frac{4x^2 - 9}{2x + 3} + \frac{1}{2x + 3}$. Now factor the numerator and cancel like terms: $\frac{(2x + 3)(2x - 3)}{2x + 3} + \frac{1}{2x + 3}$. **(A)** is correct.

45. C

Difficulty: Medium

Category: Rational Expressions and Equations

Strategic Advice: Recall that a denominator equal to zero results in an undefined value for the fraction. To answer this question, determine which of the choices does *not* result in the denominator being equal to zero.

Getting to the Answer: You could plug each of the answer choices into the denominator to see which three equal zero, or you could factor the denominator first to simplify the identification of those values. Start by factoring out $2x$ to show the denominator as $2x(x^2 - 6x - 7)$. The denominator is the product of the two factors, so if either one is 0, the denominator will be 0. If $2x = 0$, $x = 0$, so eliminate (B) because $x = 0$ makes $g(x)$ undefined.

Next, you could either plug the remaining choices into $x^2 - 6x - 7$ to see which choice does not produce a result of zero, or you could factor the expression into $(x - 7)(x + 1)$. Thus, either $x = 7$ or $x = -1$ results in the denominator of $g(x)$ equal to zero. Eliminate (A) and (D); **(C)** is correct. For the record, $g(1) = \frac{2}{-24}$.

46. B

Difficulty: Medium

Category: Polynomials

Getting to the Answer: In order to solve for possible values of x, first group all the terms on one side of the equation and set the other side to 0. Thus, $x^3 + 4 = 3x^2 - 7x + 25$ can be written as $x^3 - 3x^2 + 7x - 21 = 0$. Factor this by grouping the terms into two pairs. The first pair, $x^3 - 3x^2$, contains the common factor x^2, so it is equivalent to $x^2(x - 3)$. The second pair, $7x - 21$, factors to $7(x - 3)$. Thus, another form of the entire equation is $x^2(x - 3) + 7(x - 3) = 0$. Factor out $(x - 3)$ to get $(x^2 + 7)(x - 3) = 0$.

If the product of two factors is zero, one or both of the factors must be zero. If $(x^2 + 7) = 0$, then $x^2 = -7$. Since the square root of a negative number is not a real number, move on to $x - 3 = 0$. In this case, $x = 3$, so **(B)** is correct.

47. C

Difficulty: Medium

Category: Graphs of Polynomial Functions

Strategic Advice: Equations with roots of 0 as well as roots that are less than 0 will be incorrect and can be eliminated. When using elimination, start with the easiest looking choice first, then proceed to the next easiest, and so forth.

Getting to the Answer: Roots on a graph are the points at which $y = 0$. Start by plugging in 0 for y in each choice and solving for x, and then eliminate those choices for which x could be 0 or less. For (A), you would plug in 0 such that $0 = 4|x|$, which is true only for $x = 0$. Eliminate (A). For (B), plug in 0 for y and solve for x:

$$0 = x^2 - 4$$
$$x^2 = 4$$
$$\sqrt{x^2} = \sqrt{4}$$
$$x = \pm 2$$

Since x could equal -2, eliminate (B) as well. Choices (C) and (D) are the products of two factors. If the product of 2 factors is 0, then one of the factors must be 0. In (C), the only value for x that would make the equation equal to 0 is 2, which is greater than 0, so **(C)** is correct. On test day, you would move on, but for the record, in choice (D), $x = 0$ is a root, so (D) is incorrect.

48. D

Difficulty: Medium

Category: Graphs of Polynomial Functions

Getting to the Answer: The notation $f(x) = 0$ is another way of describing the x-axis, so this question is asking how many times the graph intersects or touches the x-axis. This graph crosses the x-axis four times, once each at $x = 0$, $x = 4$, $x = 3$, and $x = 2$, so **(D)** is correct.

49. A

Difficulty: Easy

Category: Modeling Growth and Decay

Getting to the Answer: If the number of smartphone users increases by 35% each year, then the amount of the increase is variable (because it's 35% of a bigger number each time), which means exponential growth. Eliminate (C) and (D). Consider the two remaining equations in terms of the exponential growth function, $f(x) = f(0)(1 + r)^x$. Note that the only difference between the two remaining choices is the r value. Recall that when assembling an exponential growth model, r (the rate) must be in decimal form. Therefore, the number raised to the power of x should be $1 + 0.35$, or 1.35. Choice **(A)** is the only one that fits these criteria.

CHAPTER 12

Quadratics

LEARNING OBJECTIVES

After completing this chapter, you will be able to:

- Solve a quadratic equation by factoring
- Recognize the classic quadratics
- Solve a quadratic equation by completing the square
- Solve a quadratic equation by applying the quadratic formula
- Relate properties of a quadratic function to its graph and vice versa
- Solve a system of one quadratic and one linear equation

60/600 SmartPoints®

How Much Do You Know?

Directions: Try the questions that follow. Show your work so that you can compare your solutions to the ones found in the Check Your Work section immediately after this question set. The "Category" heading in the expla- nation for each question gives the title of the lesson that covers how to solve it. If you answered the ques- tion(s) for a given lesson correctly, and if your scratch- work looks like ours, you may be able to move quickly through that lesson. If you answered incorrectly or used a different approach, you may want to take your time on that lesson.

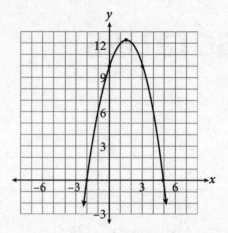

1. Which of the following linear expressions divides evenly into $6x^2 + 7x - 20$?

   A) $3x - 10$

   B) $3x - 5$

   C) $3x - 4$

   D) $3x - 2$

   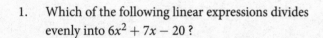

$$x^2 - 10x - 7$$

2. Which of the following expressions is equivalent to the expression above?

   A) $(x - 5)^2 - 32$

   B) $(x - 5)^2 + 32$

   C) $(x + 5)^2 - 32$

   D) $(x + 5)^2 + 32$

   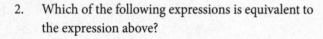

$$3x^2 - 5x = -k$$

3. In the equation above, k is a constant. For which of the following values of k does the equation have at least one real solution?

   A) 2

   B) 3

   C) 4

   D) 5

4. Which of the following could be the equation of the graph shown?

   A) $y = 2x + 10$

   B) $y = -x^2 + \frac{3}{2}x + 10$

   C) $y = -(x - 2)(x + 5)$

   D) $y = -(x + 2)(x - 5)$

5. The x-coordinates of the solutions to a system of equations are 3.5 and 6. Which of the following could be the system?

   A) $\begin{cases} y = x + 3.5 \\ y = x^2 + 6 \end{cases}$

   B) $\begin{cases} y = 2x - 7 \\ y = -(x - 6)^2 \end{cases}$

   C) $\begin{cases} y = \frac{1}{2}x + 3 \\ y = -(x - 5)^2 + 7 \end{cases}$

   D) $\begin{cases} y = \frac{1}{2}x + 7 \\ y = -(x - 6)^2 + 3.5 \end{cases}$

Answers and explanations are on the next page. ▶ ▶ ▶

Check Your Work

1. C

Difficulty: Medium

Category: Solving Quadratics by Factoring

Getting to the Answer: Understanding that in algebra "divides evenly" means "is a factor" is the key to answering the question. You could use polynomial long division, but in most cases, factoring is quicker. The leading coefficient of the equation is not 1, so you'll need to use grouping to factor the equation. The general form of a quadratic is $ax^2 + bx + c$. To find the factors, multiply a by c, $6 \times -20 = -120$, and then look for two factors of that product whose sum is equal to b, the coefficient of the middle term. The two factors of -120 that add up to 7 are 15 and -8:

$$6x^2 + 7x - 20 = 6x^2 + 15x - 8x - 20$$
$$= \left(6x^2 + 15x\right) - (8x + 20)$$
$$= 3x(2x + 5) - 4(2x + 5)$$
$$= (2x + 5)(3x - 4)$$

Therefore, $3x - 4$ divides evenly into the expression, so **(C)** correct.

2. A

Difficulty: Medium

Category: Completing the Square

Getting to the Answer: There are no integer factors of $x^2 - 10x - 7$, since no two integers whose product is -7 add up to -10. Note that the answer choices are stated in vertex format, the same as you would obtain by completing the square of the given expression. Half of the x-coefficient, -10, is -5, so the constant term needed to complete the square is $(-5)^2 = 25$. Thus, you can rewrite and group the given expression as $(x^2 - 10x + 25) - 25 - 7$. This simplifies to $(x - 5)^2 - 32$, which is **(A)**. Noticing that $x^2 - 10x + 25$ is a classic quadratic makes the process of factoring very quick.

3. A

Difficulty: Medium

Category: The Quadratic Formula

Getting to the Answer: Restate the equation in "standard" quadratic form, $3x^2 - 5x + k = 0$. Recall that a quadratic equation has two real solutions if the discriminant, $b^2 - 4ac$, is positive. The equation has one real solution if the discriminant is 0. For the given equation, $a = 3$, $b = -5$, and $c = k$, so you can set up the inequality $(-5)^2 - 4(3)k \geq 0$. This simplifies to $25 \geq 12k$. The only choice for which this is true is **(A)**.

If you didn't recall the shortcut about the discriminant, consider the quadratic formula, $x = \dfrac{-b \pm \sqrt{b^2 - 4ac}}{2a}$. If the term inside the radical, $b^2 - 4ac$, is negative, then there are no real solutions.

4. D

Difficulty: Easy

Category: Graphs of Quadratics

Getting to the Answer: The graph is a parabola, so you can eliminate (A) because its equation is linear. The x-intercepts of the graph are -2 and 5, so the factors of the quadratic are $(x + 2)$ and $(x - 5)$. These factors make $y = 0$ when $x = -2$ and $x = 5$. Eliminate (B) and (C). Only (D) is left, so it must be correct. On test day, you would move on. For the record, the parabola opens downward, so there should be a negative sign in front of the factors. **(D)** is correct.

Chapter 12
Quadratics

Math

5. C

Difficulty: Hard

Category: Systems of Quadratic and Linear Equations

Getting to the Answer: You don't actually need to solve each system. Instead, plug 3.5 or 6 into each answer choice and eliminate each one whose y-values don't come out the same. (If the same x-value produces different y-values in two equations, then it is not the x-coordinate of the solution to the system.) Because 3.5 is a decimal, doing arithmetic with it is likely to be messy. So start with 6:

(A): $y = 6 + 3.5 = 9.5$

$y = 6^2 + 6 = 36 + 6 = 42$

Different y-values; eliminate.

(B): $y = 2(6) - 7 = 12 - 7 = 5$

$y = -(6 - 6)^2 = -(0)^2 = 0$

Different y-values; eliminate.

(C): $y = \frac{1}{2}(6) + 3 = 3 + 3 = 6$

$y = -(6 - 5)^2 + 7 = -(1)^2 + 7 = -1 + 7 = 6$

Keep for now. You need to test (D) because it's possible that (D) is the right answer and (C) just happens to work for $x = 6$ (but not for $x = 3.5$).

(D): $y = \frac{1}{2}(6) + 7 = 3 + 7 = 10$

$y = -(6 - 6)^2 + 3.5 = -(0)^2 + 3.5 = 3.5$

Different y-values; eliminate.

(C) is correct.

Solving Quadratics by Factoring

LEARNING OBJECTIVE

After this lesson, you will be able to:

- Solve a quadratic equation by factoring

To answer a question like this:

If $x^2 - 7x = 30$ and $x > 0$, what is the value of $x - 5$?

A) 5

B) 6

C) 10

D) 25

You need to know this:

A quadratic expression is a second-degree polynomial—that is, a polynomial containing a squared variable. You can write a quadratic expression as $ax^2 + bx + c$.

The **FOIL** acronym (which stands for First, Outer, Inner, Last) will help you remember how to multiply two binomials: multiply the first terms together (ac), then the outer terms (ad), then the inner terms (bc), and finally the last terms (bd):

$$(a + b)(c + d) = ac + ad + bc + bd$$

FOIL can also be done in reverse if you need to go from a quadratic to its factors.

To solve a quadratic equation by factoring, the quadratic must be set equal to 0. For example:

$$x^2 + x - 56 = 0$$
$$(x + 8)(x - 7) = 0$$

From the binomial factors, you can find the **solutions**, also called **roots** or **zeros**, of the equation. For two factors to be multiplied together and produce zero as the result, one or both those factors must be zero. In the example above, either $x + 8 = 0$ or $x - 7 = 0$, which means that $x = -8$ or $x = 7$.

You need to do this:

Here are the steps for solving a quadratic equation by factoring:

- Set the quadratic equal to zero.
- Factor the squared term. (For factoring, it's easiest when a, the coefficient in front of x^2, is equal to 1.)
- Make a list of the factors of c. Remember to include negatives.
- Find the factor pair that, when added, equals b, the coefficient in front of x.
- Write the quadratic as the product of two binomials.
- Set each binomial equal to zero and solve.

Explanation:

Set the equation equal to zero and factor the first term:

$$x^2 - 7x = 30$$
$$x^2 - 7x - 30 = 0$$
$$(x \pm ?)(x \pm ?) = 0$$

Next, consider factors of -30, keeping in mind that they must sum to -7, so *the factor with the greater absolute value must be negative*. The possibilities are: -30×1, -15×2, -10×3, and -6×5. The factor pair that sums to -7 is -10×3. Write that factor pair into your binomials:

$$(x - 10)(x + 3) = 0$$

Set each factor equal to zero and solve:

$$(x - 10) = 0 \qquad (x + 3) = 0$$
$$x = 10 \qquad\qquad x = -3$$

The question says that $x > 0$, so $x = 10$. Now that you solved for x, you can answer the question, which asks for $x - 5$: $10 - 5 = 5$. **(A)** is correct.

If factoring quadratics gives you trouble, study the steps in the table above and try these Drill questions before completing the following Try on Your Own questions. Factor each quadratic expression (without using a calculator). Turn the page to see the answers.

Drill

a. $a^2 + 8a + 15$

b. $x^2 + 4x - 21$

c. $b^2 - 7b - 18$

d. $y^2 - 10y + 24$

e. $x^2 + \dfrac{1}{2}x - \dfrac{1}{2}$

f. $5x^2 + 10x + 5$

g. $2x^2 + 12x - 54$

h. $3x^2 - 6x + 3$

i. $x^2 + 3xy + 2y^2$

j. $4a^2 + 4ab - 8b^2$

Try on Your Own

Directions: Take as much time as you need on these questions. Work carefully and methodically. There will be an opportunity for timed practice at the end of the chapter.

1. Which of the following is an equivalent form of the expression $(6 - 5x)(15x - 11)$?

    A) $-75x^2 + 35x - 66$

    B) $-75x^2 + 145x - 66$

    C) $90x^2 - 141x + 55$

    D) $90x^2 + 9x + 55$

HINT: For Q2, what is the easiest way to factor the denominator?

2. Which of the following is equivalent to
    $\dfrac{x^2 - 10x + 25}{3x^2 - 75}$?

    A) $\dfrac{3(x - 5)}{(x + 5)}$

    B) $\dfrac{3(x + 5)}{(x - 5)}$

    C) $\dfrac{(x - 5)}{3(x + 5)}$

    D) $\dfrac{(x + 5)}{3(x - 5)}$

HINT: For Q3, what value in the denominator would make the fraction undefined?

3. For what positive value of x is the equation
    $\dfrac{3}{2x^2 + 4x - 6} = 0$ undefined?

$3x^2 + 9x = 54$

4. What is the sum of the roots of the equation above?

    A) -6

    B) -3

    C) 3

    D) 6

Drill answers from previous page:

a. $a^2 + 8a + 15 = (a + 3)(a + 5)$

b. $x^2 + 4x - 21 = (x - 3)(x + 7)$

c. $b^2 - 7b - 18 = (b + 2)(b - 9)$

d. $y^2 - 10y + 24 = (y - 4)(y - 6)$

e. $x^2 + \frac{1}{2}x - \frac{1}{2} = (x + 1)\left(x - \frac{1}{2}\right)$

f. $5x^2 + 10x + 5 = 5(x + 1)(x + 1)$

g. $2x^2 + 12x - 54 = 2(x - 3)(x + 9)$

h. $3x^2 - 6x + 3 = 3(x - 1)(x - 1)$

i. $x^2 + 3xy + 2y^2 = (x + y)(x + 2y)$

j. $4a^2 + 4ab - 8b^2 = 4(a - b)(a + 2b)$

$$f(x) = (1.3x - 3.9)^2 - \left(0.69x^2 - 0.14x - 9.79\right)$$

5. Which of the following functions is equivalent to the function above?

A) $f(x) = (x - 5)^2$

B) $f(x) = x^2 + 10.28x + 5.42$

C) $f(x) = 0.61x^2 + 0.14x + 25$

D) $f(x) = 1.3(x - 3)^2 - 0.69x^2 + 0.14x + 9.79$

Classic Quadratics

> **LEARNING OBJECTIVE**
>
> After this lesson, you will be able to:
>
> - Recognize the classic quadratics

To answer a question like this:

Which of the following expressions is equivalent to $25x^2y^4 - 1$?

A) $5(x^2y^4 - 1)$

B) $-5(xy^2 + 1)$

C) $(5xy - 1)(5xy + 1)$

D) $(5xy^2 - 1)(5xy^2 + 1)$

You need to know this:

Memorizing the following classic quadratics will save you time on test day:

- $x^2 - y^2 = (x + y)(x - y)$
- $x^2 + 2xy + y^2 = (x + y)^2$
- $x^2 - 2xy + y^2 = (x - y)^2$

You need to do this:

When you see a pattern that matches either the left or the right side of one of the above equations, simplify by substituting its equivalent form. For example, say you need to simplify the following:

$$\frac{a^2 - 2ab + b^2}{a - b}$$

You would substitute $(a - b)(a - b)$ for the numerator and cancel to find that the expression simplifies to $a - b$:

$$\frac{a^2 - 2ab + b^2}{a - b} = \frac{(a - b)(a - b)}{a - b} = \frac{a - b}{1} = a - b$$

Explanation:

The expression $25x^2y^4 - 1$ is a difference of perfect squares. It corresponds to the first of the three classic quadratic patterns above. The square root of $25x^2y^4$ is $5xy^2$ and the square root of 1 is 1, so the correct factors are $(5xy^2 - 1)(5xy^2 + 1)$. Choice **(D)** is correct.

Try on Your Own

Directions: Take as much time as you need on these questions. Work carefully and methodically. There will be an opportunity for timed practice at the end of the chapter.

6. For all a and b, what is the sum of $(a-b)^2$ and $(a+b)^2$?

    A) $2a^2$

    B) $2a^2 - 2b^2$

    C) $2a^2 + 2b^2$

    D) $2a^2 + 4ab + 2b^2$

HINT: For Q7, how can you remove the fraction to make factoring easier?

---

7. What is the positive difference between the roots of the equation $y = \frac{1}{3}x^2 - 2x + 3$?

HINT: For Q8, look for a classic quadratic in the denominator.

$$f(x) = \frac{3}{(x-7)^2 + 6(x-7) + 9}$$

8. For which value of x is the function $f(x)$ undefined?

9. Suppose $a^2 + 2ab + b^2 = c^2$ and $c - b = 4$. Assuming $c > 0$, what is the value of a?

$$2x^2 - 28x + 98 = a(x-b)^2$$

10. In the expression above, $a > 1$ and both a and b are constants. Which of the following could be the value of b?

    A) -7

    B) 7

    C) 14

    D) 49

Math

Completing the Square

To answer a question like this:

Which of the following equations has the same solutions as the equation $40 - 6x = x^2 - y$?

A) $y = (x - 6)^2 - 40$

B) $y = (x - 6)^2 + 40$

C) $y = (x + 3)^2 - 49$

D) $y = (x + 3)^2 + 49$

You need to know this:

For quadratics that do not factor easily, you'll need one of two strategies: completing the square or the quadratic formula (taught in the next lesson). To complete the square, you'll create an equation in the form $(x + h)^2 = k$, where h and k are constants.

As with factoring, completing the square is most convenient when the coefficient in front of the x^2 term is 1.

You need to do this:

Here are the steps for completing the square, demonstrated with a simple example.

Step	Scratchwork
Starting point:	$x^2 + 8x - 8 = 0$
1. Move the constant to the opposite side.	$x^2 + 8x = 8$
2. Divide b, the x-coefficient, by 2 and square the quotient.	$b = 8; \left(\frac{b}{2}\right)^2 = \left(\frac{8}{2}\right)^2 = (4)^2 = 16$
3. Add the number from the previous step to both sides of the equation and factor.	$x^2 + 8x + 16 = 8 + 16$ $(x + 4)(x + 4) = 24$ $(x + 4)^2 = 24$
4. Take the square root of both sides.	$\sqrt{(x + 4)^2} = \pm\sqrt{24} \rightarrow x + 4 = \pm\sqrt{24}$ $= \pm\sqrt{4}\sqrt{6} \, x + 4 = \pm 2\sqrt{6}$
5. Split the result into two equations and solve each one.	$x + 4 = 2\sqrt{6} \rightarrow x = 2\sqrt{6} - 4$ $x + 4 = -2\sqrt{6} \rightarrow x = -2\sqrt{6} - 4$

Explanation:

First, write the equation in standard form: $y = x^2 + 6x - 40$. Add 40 to both sides and complete the square on the right-hand side. Find $\left(\frac{b}{2}\right)^2 = \left(\frac{6}{2}\right)^2 = 3^2 = 9$, and add the result to both sides of the equation:

$$y = x^2 + 6x - 40$$
$$y + 40 = x^2 + 6x$$
$$y + 40 + 9 = x^2 + 6x + 9$$
$$y + 49 = x^2 + 6x + 9$$

Note that all of the answer choices are in factored form. The right side of the equation is a classic quadratic that factors as follows:

$$y + 49 = (x + 3)(x + 3)$$
$$y + 49 = (x + 3)^2$$

Finally, solve for y to get $y = (x + 3)^2 - 49$, which means **(C)** is correct.

If you find completing the square to be challenging, study the steps in the table above and try these Drill questions before completing the following Try on Your Own questions. Turn the page to see the answers.

Drill

a. $x^2 = 10x + 2$

b. $-9 = 2x^2 + 16x + 3$

c. $x^2 - x - 11 = 0$

d. $x^2 + \frac{x}{2} = 4$

e. $-x^2 + 6ax = 2a^2$

Try on Your Own

Directions: Take as much time as you need on these questions. Work carefully and methodically. There will be an opportunity for timed practice at the end of the chapter.

11. Which of the following is a value of x that satisfies the equation $x^2 + 2x - 5 = 0$?

    A) -1

    B) $1 - \sqrt{6}$

    C) $1 + \sqrt{6}$

    D) $-1 - \sqrt{6}$

HINT: For Q12, the algebra will be easier if you substitute another variable for a^2.

$$a^4 - 12a^2 - 72 = 0$$

12. Which of the following is the greatest possible value of a?

    A) $\sqrt{6 + \sqrt{3}}$

    B) $\sqrt{6(1 + \sqrt{3})}$

    C) 12

    D) $6(1 + \sqrt{3})$

HINT: For Q13, treat the square root in the b term just like any other: divide it by 2, then square it.

$$x^2 - (6\sqrt{5})x = -40$$

13. What is the sum of the possible values of x given the above equation?

    A) 15

    B) $5\sqrt{5}$

    C) $6\sqrt{5}$

    D) 60

$$x^2 + 7x + 1 = 2x^2 - 4x + 3$$

14. Which of the following is a value of x that is valid in the above equation?

    A) $5.5 - \sqrt{28.25}$

    B) $\sqrt{5.5}$

    C) $\sqrt{30.25}$

    D) $5.5 + \sqrt{30.25}$

Drill answers from previous page:

a. $x = 5 \pm 3\sqrt{3}$

b. $x = -4 \pm \sqrt{10}$

c. $x = \dfrac{1 \pm 3\sqrt{5}}{2}$

d. $x = \dfrac{-1 \pm \sqrt{65}}{4}$

e. $x = 3a \pm a\sqrt{7}$

The Quadratic Formula

LEARNING OBJECTIVE

After this lesson, you will be able to:

- Solve a quadratic equation by applying the quadratic formula

To answer a question like this:

Which of the following are the real values of x that satisfy the equation $2x^2 - 5x - 2 = 0$?

A) 1 and 4

B) $-\dfrac{5}{4} + \dfrac{\sqrt{41}}{4}$ and $-\dfrac{5}{4} - \dfrac{\sqrt{41}}{4}$

C) $\dfrac{5}{4} + \dfrac{\sqrt{41}}{4}$ and $\dfrac{5}{4} - \dfrac{\sqrt{41}}{4}$

D) No real solutions

You need to know this:

The quadratic formula can be used to solve any quadratic equation. It yields solutions to a quadratic equation that is written in standard form, $ax^2 + bx + c = 0$:

$$x = \frac{-b \pm \sqrt{b^2 - 4ac}}{2a}$$

The $\pm$ sign that follows $-b$ indicates that you will have two solutions, so remember to find both.

The expression under the radical $(b^2 - 4ac)$ is called the **discriminant**, and its value determines the *number* of real solutions. If the discriminant is positive, the equation has two distinct real solutions. If the discriminant is equal to 0, there is only one distinct real solution. If the discriminant is negative, there are no real solutions because you cannot take the square root of a negative number.

The arithmetic can get complicated, so reserve the quadratic formula for equations that cannot be solved by factoring and those in which completing the square is difficult because a $\neq$ 1.

You need to do this:

Get the quadratic equation into the form $ax^2 + bx + c = 0$. Then substitute a, b, and c into the quadratic formula and simplify.

Math

Explanation:

In the given equation, $a = 2$, $b = -5$, and $c = -2$. Plug these values into the quadratic formula and simplify:

$$x = \frac{-b \pm \sqrt{b^2 - 4ac}}{2a}$$

$$x = \frac{-(-5) \pm \sqrt{(-5)^2 - 4(2)(-2)}}{2(2)}$$

$$x = \frac{5 \pm \sqrt{25 - (-16)}}{4}$$

$$x = \frac{5 \pm \sqrt{41}}{4}$$

$$x = \frac{5}{4} + \frac{\sqrt{41}}{4} \text{ or } x = \frac{5}{4} - \frac{\sqrt{41}}{4}$$

The correct answer is **(C)**.

If you find the quadratic formula to be challenging, study the formula and try these Drill questions before completing the following Try on Your Own questions. Turn the page to see the answers.

Drill

a. $x^2 - 2x - 20 = 0$

b. $3x^2 - 5x - 2 = 0$

c. $-7x^2 + 14x + 24 = -4$

d. $0.3x^2 + 0.7x - 1 = 0$

e. $\frac{x^2}{2} - x\sqrt{2} - 2 = 0$

Try on Your Own

Directions: Take as much time as you need on these questions. Work carefully and methodically. There will be an opportunity for timed practice at the end of the chapter.

HINT: For Q15, use the discriminant.

---

15. Given the equation $2x^2 + 8x + 4 + 2z = 0$, for what value of z is there exactly one solution for x ?

16. The product of all the solutions to the equation $3v^2 + 4v - 2 = 0$ is M. What is the value of M ?

    A) -3

    B) $-\dfrac{2}{3}$

    C) $-\dfrac{1}{3}$

    D) $\dfrac{4}{3}$

17. What are the solutions to the equation $4x^2 - 24x + 16 = 0$?

    A) $x = 3 \pm \sqrt{5}$

    B) $x = 4 \pm \sqrt{6}$

    C) $x = 5 \pm \sqrt{3}$

    D) $x = 5 \pm 2\sqrt{2}$

$$3x^2 = m(5x + v)$$

18. What are the values of x that satisfy the equation above, where m and v are constants?

    A) $x = -\dfrac{5m}{6} \pm \dfrac{\sqrt{25m^2 + 12mv}}{6}$

    B) $x = \dfrac{5m}{6} \pm \dfrac{\sqrt{25m^2 + 12mv}}{6}$

    C) $x = -\dfrac{5m}{3} \pm \dfrac{\sqrt{12m^2 + 25mv}}{3}$

    D) $x = \dfrac{5m}{3} \pm \dfrac{\sqrt{25m^2 + 12mv}}{3}$

HINT: For Q19, start with the standard form of a quadratic equation.

$$x(dx + 10) = -3$$

19. The equation above, where d is a constant, has no real solutions. The value of d could be which of the following?

    A) -12

    B) 4

    C) 8

    D) 10

20. Which of the following equations does NOT have any solutions that are real numbers?

    A) $x^2 + 8x - 12 = 0$

    B) $x^2 - 8x + 12 = 0$

    C) $x^2 - 9x + 21 = 0$

    D) $x^2 + 100x - 1 = 0$

Graphs of Quadratics

LEARNING OBJECTIVE

After this lesson, you will be able to:

- Relate properties of a quadratic function to its graph and vice versa

To answer a question like this:

Given the equation $y = -(2x - 4)^2 + 7$, which of the following statements is NOT true?

A) The vertex is $(4, 7)$.

B) The y-intercept is $(0, -9)$.

C) The parabola opens downward.

D) The graph crosses the x-axis at least one time.

You need to know this:

A quadratic function is a quadratic equation set equal to y or $f(x)$ instead of 0. Remember that the solutions (also called "roots" or "zeros") of any polynomial function are the same as the x-intercepts. To solve a quadratic function, substitute 0 for y, or $f(x)$, then solve algebraically. Alternatively, you can plug the equation into your graphing calculator and read the x-intercepts from the graph.

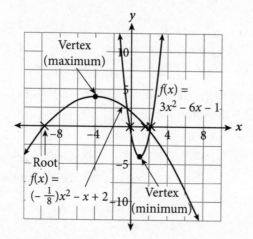

The graph of every quadratic equation (or function) is a **parabola**, which is a symmetric U-shaped graph that opens either upward or downward. To determine which way a parabola will open, examine the value of a in the equation. If a is positive, the parabola will open upward. If a is negative, it will open downward. Take a look at the examples above to see this graphically.

Drill answers:

a. $x = 1 \pm \sqrt{21}$

b. $x = 2, x = -\frac{1}{3}$

c. $1 \pm \sqrt{5}$

d. $x = -\frac{10}{3}, x = 1$

e. $\sqrt{2} \pm \sqrt{6}$

Like quadratic equations, quadratic functions will have zero, one, or two distinct real solutions, corresponding to the number of times the parabola touches or crosses the *x*-axis. Graphing is a powerful way to determine the number of solutions a quadratic function has.

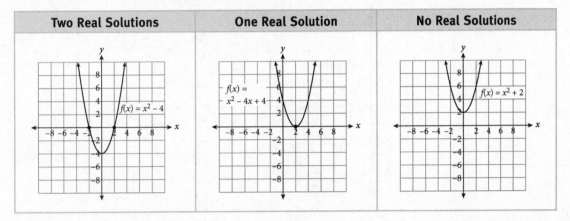

Two Real Solutions	One Real Solution	No Real Solutions

There are three algebraic forms that a quadratic equation can take: standard, factored, and vertex. Each is provided in the following table along with the graphical features that are revealed by writing the equation in that particular form.

Standard	Factored	Vertex
$y = ax^2 + bx + c$	$y = a(x - m)(x - n)$	$y = a(x - h)^2 + k$
y-intercept is *c*	Solutions are *m* and *n*	Vertex is (h, k)
In real-world contexts, starting quantity is *c*	*x*-intercepts are *m* and *n*	Minimum/maximum of function is *k*
Format used to solve via quadratic formula	Vertex is halfway between *m* and *n*	Axis of symmetry is given by $x = h$

You've already seen standard and factored forms earlier in this chapter, but vertex form might be new to you. In vertex form, *a* is the same as the *a* in standard form, and *h* and *k* are the coordinates of the **vertex** (h, k). If a quadratic function is not in vertex form, you can still find the *x*-coordinate of the vertex by plugging the appropriate values into the equation $h = \frac{-b}{2a}$, which is also the equation for the axis of symmetry (see graph that follows). Once you determine *h*, plug this value into the quadratic function and solve for *y* to determine *k*, the *y*-coordinate of the vertex.

The equation of the **axis of symmetry** of a parabola is $x = h$, where h is the x-coordinate of the vertex.

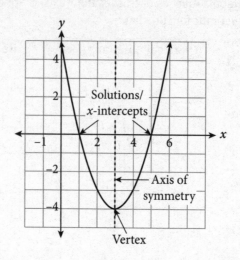

You need to do this:

- To find the vertex of a parabola, get the function into vertex form: $y = a(x - h)^2 + k$ or use the formula $h = \frac{-b}{2a}$.

- To find the y-intercept of a quadratic function, plug in 0 for x.

- To determine whether a parabola opens upward or downward, look at the coefficient of a. If a is positive, the parabola opens upward. If negative, it opens downward.

- To determine the number of x-intercepts, set the quadratic function equal to 0 and solve or examine its graph. (Quadratic function questions show up on both the no-calculator and calculator sections of the SAT.)

Explanation

Be careful—the equation looks like vertex form, $y = a(x - h)^2 + k$, but it's not quite there because of the 2 inside the parentheses. You could rewrite the equation in vertex form, but this would involve squaring the quantity in parentheses and then completing the square, which would take quite a bit of time. Alternatively, you could notice that the greatest possible value for y in this function is 7, which happens when the squared term, $-(2x - 4)^2$, equals zero. To check (A), find the x-value when $y = 7$:

$$2x - 4 = 0$$
$$2x = 4$$
$$x = 2$$

For the record:

Choice (B): Substitute 0 for x and simplify to find that the y-intercept is indeed $(0, -9)$.

Choice (C): There is a negative in front of the squared term, so the parabola *does* open downward.

Choice (D): Because the parabola opens downward and the vertex is at $y = 7$, above the x-axis, the parabola must cross the x-axis twice. This statement is true as well, which confirms that **(A)** is correct.

Try on Your Own

Directions: Take as much time as you need on these questions. Work carefully and methodically. There will be an opportunity for timed practice at the end of the chapter.

HINT: For Q21, which form of a quadratic equation tells you the *x*-intercepts? Consult the table given earlier if you can't remember.

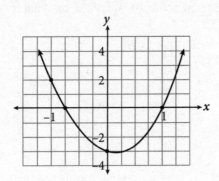

21. The following quadratic equations are all representations of the graph above. Which equation clearly represents the exact values of the *x*-intercepts of the graph?

    A) $y = 4x^2 - x - 3$

    B) $y = (4x + 3)(x - 1)$

    C) $y = 4(x - 0.125)^2 - 3.0625$

    D) $y + 3.0625 = 4(x - 0.125)^2$

HINT: For Q22, through which point on a parabola does the axis of symmetry pass?

---

22. Which equation represents the axis of symmetry for the graph of the quadratic function
    $f(x) = -\dfrac{11}{3}x^2 + 17x - \dfrac{43}{13}$?

    A) $x = -\dfrac{102}{11}$

    B) $x = -\dfrac{51}{22}$

    C) $x = \dfrac{51}{22}$

    D) $x = \dfrac{102}{11}$

23. How many times do the parabolas given by the equations $f(x) = 3x^2 - 24x + 52$ and $g(x) = x^2 + 12x - 110$ intersect?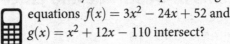

    A) Never

    B) Once

    C) Twice

    D) More than twice

24. What is the positive difference between the *x*-intercepts of the parabola given by the equation $g(x) = -2.5x^2 + 10x - 7.5$?

HINT: For Q25, what does "maximum height" correspond to on the graph of a quadratic equation?

---

25. A toy rocket is fired from ground level. The height of the rocket with respect to time can be represented by a quadratic function. If the toy rocket reaches a maximum height of 34 feet 3 seconds after it was fired, which of the following functions could represent the height, *h*, of the rocket *t* seconds after it was fired?

    A) $h(t) = -16(t - 3)^2 + 34$

    B) $h(t) = -16(t + 3)^2 + 34$

    C) $h(t) = 16(t - 3)^2 + 34$

    D) $h(t) = 16(t + 3)^2 + 34$

Systems of Quadratic and Linear Equations

To answer a question like this:

In the xy-plane, the graph of $y + 3x = 5x^2 + 6$ and $y - 6 = 2x$ intersect at points $(0, 6)$ and (a, b). What is the value of b?

You need to know this:

You can solve a system of one quadratic and one linear equation by substitution, exactly as you would for a system of two linear equations. Alternatively, if the question appears on the calculator section, you can plug the system into your graphing calculator.

You need to do this:

- Isolate y in both equations
- Set the equations equal to each other
- Put the resulting equation into the form $ax^2 + bx + c = 0$
- Solve this quadratic by factoring, completing the square, or using the quadratic formula. (You are solving for the x-values at the points of intersection of the original two equations.)
- Plug the x-values you get as solutions into one of the original equations to generate the y-values at the points of intersection. (Usually, the linear equation is easier to work with than the quadratic.)

Explanation:

Start by isolating y in both equations to get $y = 2x + 6$ and $y = 5x^2 - 3x + 6$. Next, set the right sides of the equations equal and solve for x:

$$2x + 6 = 5x^2 - 3x + 6$$
$$5x^2 - 5x = 0$$
$$5x(x - 1) = 0$$
$$x = 0 \text{ or } x = 1$$

The question says that $(0, 6)$ is one point of intersection for the two equations and asks for the y-value at the other point of intersection, so plug $x = 1$ into either of the original equations and solve for y. Using the linear equation will be faster:

$$y = 2(1) + 6$$
$$y = 8$$

Therefore, the point (a, b) is $(1, 8)$. Grid in **8**.

Try on Your Own

Directions: Take as much time as you need on these questions. Work carefully and methodically. There will be an opportunity for timed practice at the end of the chapter.

HINT: For Q26, note that both equations are equal to *a*.

$$\begin{cases} a = b^2 + 4b - 12 \\ a = -12 + b \end{cases}$$

26. The ordered pair (a, b) satisfies the system of equations above. What is one possible value of b ?

    A) -6

    B) -3

    C) 2

    D) 3

27. In the xy-coordinate plane, the graph of $y = 5x^2 - 12x$ intersects the graph of $y = -2x$ at points $(0, 0)$ and (a, b). What is the value of a ?

$$\begin{cases} y + 3x = 10 \\ y - x^2 + 7x = 13 \end{cases}$$

28. How many real solutions are there to the system of equations above?

    A)   Exactly 4 real solutions

    B)   Exactly 2 real solutions

    C)   Exactly 1 real solution

    D)   No real solutions

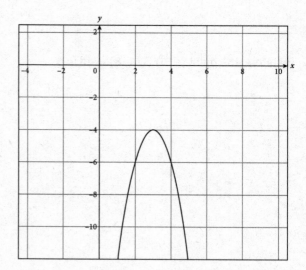

29. The graph of the function f, defined by $f(x) = -2(x - 3)^2 - 4$, is shown in the xy-plane above. The function g (not shown) is defined by $g(x) = 2x - 10$. If $f(c) = g(c)$, what is one possible value of c ?

    A) -6

    B) -4

    C) 2

    D) 4

HINT: For Q30, solve for the points of intersection, then use
the formula for distance in the coordinate plane.

30. On the xy-plane, points P and Q are the two
points where the parabola with the equation
$y = 3x^2 + \dfrac{14}{3}x - \dfrac{73}{3}$ and the line with the
equation $y = -\dfrac{4}{3}x - \dfrac{1}{3}$ meet. What is the distance
between point P and point Q ?

A)   5

B)   8

C)   10

D)   12

On Test Day

On the SAT, there is often more than one strategy that will get you to the answer. When a question involves a graph of two functions of x intersecting, you can either set the two functions equal to each other and solve for x, or you can use the coordinates of an intersection of the functions and set the values of both functions for that point equal to each other.

Try out this question using both approaches. Which approach do you find easier? There's no right or wrong answer—just remember your preferred approach and use it if you see a question like this on test day.

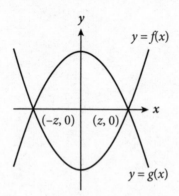

31. The functions $f(x) = 4x^2 - 25$ and $g(x) = -4x^2 + 25$ are graphed in the xy-plane above. The points where the two functions intersect are $(z, 0)$ and $(-z, 0)$. What is the value of z?

A) 0.5

B) 1.0

C) 2.5

D) 4.0

The correct answer and both ways of solving can be found at the end of this chapter.

How Much Have You Learned?

Directions: For testlike practice, give yourself 18 minutes to complete this question set. Be sure to study the explanations, even for questions you got right. They can be found at the end of this chapter.

32. The equation $\frac{1}{4}\left(4x^2 - 8x - k\right) = 30$ has two solutions: $x = -5$ and $x = 7$. What is the value of $2k$?

33. The maximum value of the data shown in the scatterplot above occurs at $x = 25$. If the data is modeled using a quadratic regression and the correlation coefficient is 1.0 (the fit is exact), then what is the y-value when $x = 35$?

A)   10

B)   15

C)   22

D)   27

Questions 34 and 35 refer to the following information.

The height of a boulder launched from a Roman catapult can be described as a function of time according to the following quadratic equation: $h(t) = -16t^2 + 224t + 240$.

34. What is the maximum height that the boulder attains?

A)   240

B)   784

C)   1,024

D)   1,696

35. How much time elapses between the moment the boulder is launched and the moment it hits the ground, assuming that the ground is at a height of 0?

A)   7

B)   12

C)   14

D)   15

X	Y
7.5	18.75
10.0	22.0
12.5	24.75
15.0	27.0
17.5	28.75
X =	

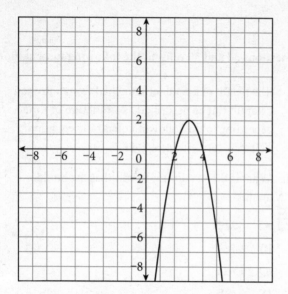

36. If the function shown in the graph is represented by $f(x) = a(x - h)^2 + k$, which of the following statements is NOT true?

A) The value of a is negative.

B) $f(x)$ is symmetrical across the line $y = 3$.

C) The function $g(x) = \dfrac{2x}{3}$ intersects $f(x)$ at its vertex.

D) The value of h is positive.

$$\begin{cases} y = 2x \\ 2x^2 + 2y^2 = 240 \end{cases}$$

37. If (x, y) is a solution to the system of equations above, what is the value of x^2 ?

38. What are the x-intercepts of the parabolic function $f(x) = x^2 - 7x + 8\dfrac{1}{4}$?

A) $-1\dfrac{1}{2}$ and $3\dfrac{1}{2}$

B) 1 and $8\dfrac{1}{4}$

C) $1\dfrac{1}{4}$ and $5\dfrac{3}{4}$

D) $1\dfrac{1}{2}$ and $5\dfrac{1}{2}$

39. If $g(x) = (x - 2)^2 - 5$, which of the following statements is true?

A) The function $g(x)$ is increasing over the entire domain.

B) The function $g(x)$ is decreasing over the entire domain.

C) The function $g(x)$ is increasing for $x < 2$ and decreasing for $x > 2$.

D) The function $g(x)$ is decreasing for $x < 2$ and increasing for $x > 2$.

40. What is the sum of the solutions of $(6x + 5)^2 - (3x - 2)^2 = 0$?

A) $-\dfrac{8}{3}$

B) $-\dfrac{1}{6}$

C) $\dfrac{7}{3}$

D) 3

$$4x - 12\sqrt{x} + 9 = 16$$

41. If the equation above is true, then what is the positive value of the expression $10\sqrt{x} - 15$?

A) 20

B) 25

C) 30

D) 35

42. In the equation $x - 2 = \dfrac{3}{x - 2}$, which of the following is a possible value of $x - 2$?

    A) $\sqrt{3}$

    B) 2

    C) $2 + \sqrt{3}$

    D) 3

43. If $\dfrac{z^{x^2 + y^2}}{z^{-2xy}} = \left(z^3\right)^3$, x and y are positive integers, and $x > y$, what is the value of $x - y$?

    A) 1

    B) 2

    C) 3

    D) 8

Math

Reflect

Directions: Take a few minutes to recall what you've learned and what you've been practicing in this chapter. Consider the following questions, jot down your best answer for each one, and then compare your reflections to the expert responses on the following page. Use your level of confidence to determine what to do next.

What features in a quadratic equation should you look for to decide whether to factor, complete the square, or apply the quadratic formula?

_____

_____

_____

Which constant in the vertex form of a quadratic function gives its maximum or minimum?

_____

_____

_____

Which form of a quadratic equation gives its y-intercept?

_____

_____

_____

Which form of a quadratic equation gives its x-intercepts, assuming the equation has two real roots?

_____

_____

_____

How do you solve a system of one linear and one quadratic equation?

_____

_____

_____

Expert Responses

What features in a quadratic equation should you look for to decide whether to factor, complete the square, or apply the quadratic formula?

Get the equation into standard form. If the coefficient in front of the squared term is 1, try factoring, but don't spend longer than about 15 seconds on the attempt. If you can't get the quadratic factored quickly, look at the coefficient on the middle term: if it is even, completing the square will be an efficient approach. Finally, the quadratic formula will work for any quadratic, no matter what the coefficients are.

Which constant in the vertex form of a quadratic function gives its maximum or minimum?

The vertex form is $y = a(x - h)^2 + k$. The constant k is the y-value at the vertex, which occurs at the maximum or minimum.

Which form of a quadratic equation gives its y-intercept?

The standard form, $y = ax^2 + bx + c$. The y-intercept is given by c.

Which form of a quadratic equation gives its x-intercepts, assuming the equation has two real roots?

The factored form, $y = a(x - m)(x - n)$. The x-intercepts are at $x = m$ and $x = n$.

How do you solve a system of one linear and one quadratic equation?

Put the linear equation in the form $y = mx + b$ and the quadratic in the form $y = ax^2 + bx + c$. Set the right sides of the equations equal to each other and solve.

Next Steps

If you answered most questions correctly in the "How Much Have You Learned?" section, and if your responses to the Reflect questions were similar to those of the SAT expert, then consider quadratics an area of strength and move on to the next chapter. Come back to this topic periodically to prevent yourself from getting rusty.

If you don't yet feel confident, review those parts of this chapter that you have not yet mastered. In particular, study the table describing the different forms of quadratics in the Graphs of Quadratics lesson. Then try the questions you missed again. As always, be sure to review the explanations closely.

Answers and Explanations

Try on Your Own

1. B

Difficulty: Easy

Getting to the Answer: FOIL the binomials $(6 - 5x)(15x - 11)$: First, Outer, Inner, Last. First: $(6)(15x) = 90x$. Outer: $(6)(-11) = -66$. Inner: $(-5x)(15x) = -75x^2$. Last: $(-5x)(-11) = 55x$. Add all the terms together and combine like terms: $90x - 66 - 75x^2 + 55x = -75x^2 + 145x - 66$. The correct answer is **(B)**.

2. C

Difficulty: Easy

Getting to the Answer: First, factor out a 3 in the denominator to make that quadratic a bit simpler. Then factor the numerator and denominator using reverse-FOIL to reveal an $x - 5$ term that will cancel out:

$$\frac{x^2 - 10x + 25}{3x^2 - 75} = \frac{x^2 - 10x + 25}{3(x^2 - 25)}$$

$$= \frac{(x - 5)(x - 5)}{3(x - 5)(x + 5)} = \frac{x - 5}{3(x + 5)}$$

The correct answer is **(C)**.

3. 1

Difficulty: Medium

Getting to the Answer: An expression is undefined when it involves division by 0, so the key to the problem is to recognize that the denominator will be 0 if either of the factors of the quadratic are zero. Factoring 2 out of the denominator leaves a relatively easy-to-factor quadratic:

$$\frac{3}{2x^2 + 4x - 6} = 0$$

$$\frac{3}{2(x^2 + 2x - 3)} = 0$$

$$\frac{3}{2(x + 3)(x - 1)} = 0$$

The denominator will be zero if the value of x is either 1 or -3. Because the question asks for a positive value of x, grid in **1**.

4. B

Difficulty: Medium

Getting to the Answer: Set the equation equal to zero, then divide through by 3 on both sides to remove the x^2-coefficient:

$$3x^2 + 9x - 54 = 0$$

$$x^2 + 3x - 18 = 0$$

$$(x - 3)(x + 6) = 0$$

$$x = 3 \text{ or } -6$$

The question asks for the sum of the roots, which is $3 + (-6) = -3$. The correct answer is **(B)**.

5. A

Difficulty: Hard

Strategic Advice: The question asks for an equivalent expression, so ignore the function notation and focus on manipulating the polynomial into standard form so it matches most of the answer choices.

Getting to the Answer: Expand the polynomial and distribute as necessary so that all of the parentheses are eliminated:

$$(1.3x - 3.9)^2 - \left(0.69x^2 - 0.14x - 9.79\right)$$

$$(1.3x - 3.9)(1.3x - 3.9) - 0.69x^2 + 0.14x + 9.79$$

$$1.69x^2 - 10.14x + 15.21 - 0.69x^2 + 0.14x + 9.79$$

Decimals are harder to work with than integers, so multiply by 100. Then combine like terms. Factor 100 back out and check to see if the result matches any of the answer choices:

$$169x^2 - 1,014x + 1,521 - 69x^2 + 14x + 979$$

$$100x^2 - 1,000x + 2,500$$

$$\frac{100x^2 - 1,000x + 2,500}{100}$$

$$x^2 - 10x + 25$$

Factor the polynomial: $x^2 - 10x + 25 = (x - 5)^2$. **(A)** is correct.

6. C

Difficulty: Easy

Getting to the Answer: Expand both classic quadratics and combine like terms to find the sum:

$$(a - b)^2 + (a + b)^2$$
$$= \left(a^2 - 2ab + b^2\right) + \left(a^2 + 2ab + b^2\right)$$
$$= 2a^2 + 2b^2$$

This matches **(C)**.

7. 0

Difficulty: Medium

Getting to the Answer: To find the roots, set the equation equal to 0, factor it, and then solve. Clear the fraction the same way you do when solving equations and multiply both sides of the equation by the denominator of the fraction:

$$0 = \tfrac{1}{3}x^2 - 2x + 3$$
$$3(0) = 3\left(\tfrac{1}{3}x^2 - 2x + 3\right)$$
$$0 = x^2 - 6x + 9$$
$$0 = (x - 3)(x - 3)$$

The equation only has one unique solution $(x = 3)$, so the positive difference between the roots is $3 - 3 = \mathbf{0}$.

8. 4

Difficulty: Hard

Getting to the Answer: A fraction is undefined when the denominator equals 0. To find the value of x where $f(x)$ is undefined, set the denominator to 0 and solve for x.

The equation $(x - 7)^2 + 6(x - 7) + 9 = 0$ is the expansion of the classic quadratic $a^2 + 2ab + b^2 = (a + b)^2$, where $a = (x - 7)$ and $b = 3$, so the denominator will factor as $\left[(x - 7) + 3\right]^2$. That's equivalent to $(x - 4)^2$. Set this expression equal to zero to find that the function is undefined when $x - 4 = 0$, or $x = \mathbf{4}$.

9. 4

Difficulty: Hard

Strategic Advice: Look for classic quadratics so you can avoid reverse-FOIL and save time:
$x^2 + 2xy + y^2 = (x + y)^2$

Getting to the Answer: Recognize that $a^2 + 2ab + b^2$ is a classic quadratic that simplifies to $(a + b)^2$. Factor the polynomial and take the square root of both sides to simplify the result:

$$(a + b)^2 = c^2$$
$$\sqrt{(a + b)^2} = \sqrt{c^2}$$
$$a + b = \pm c$$

The question says that c is positive. Subtracting b from both sides gives $a = c - b$. Plugging in 4 for $c - b$ gives $a = \mathbf{4}$.

10. B

Difficulty: Medium

Strategic Advice: Recognizing the classic quadratic $(x - y)^2 = x^2 + 2xy + y^2$ will save you time in factoring.

Getting to the Answer: In this question, the goal is to manipulate the polynomial so that it matches the factored form given. First, recognize that 2, the coefficient of x^2, can be factored out. The resulting expression is then $2\left(x^2 - 14x + 49\right)$. Notice that $\sqrt{49} = 7$ and factor the quadratic to get $2(x - 7)(x - 7) = 2(x - 7)^2$. Now the expression is in the same form as $a(x - b)^2$. Therefore, $b = 7$, so **(B)** is correct.

11. D

Difficulty: Medium

Getting to the Answer: Factoring won't work here because no two factors of -5 sum to 2. However, the coefficient of x^2 is 1, so try completing the square:

$$x^2 + 2x - 5 = 0$$
$$x^2 + 2x = 5$$
$$\left(\frac{b}{2}\right)^2 = \left(\frac{2}{2}\right)^2 = 1^2 = 1$$
$$x^2 + 2x + 1 = 5 + 1$$
$$(x+1)^2 = 6$$
$$x + 1 = \pm\sqrt{6}$$
$$x = -1 \pm \sqrt{6}$$

(D) matches one of the two possible values of x, so it's correct.

12. B

Difficulty: Hard

Getting to the Answer: Even though the given equation contains the value a^4, this is a quadratic-style question. You can say that $x = a^2$, so $x^2 - 12x - 72 = 0$. To complete the square, restate this as $x^2 - 12x = 72$. One-half of the x-coefficient is 6, which, when squared, becomes 36. So, $x^2 - 12x + 36 = 108$. Factor to find that $(x - 6)^2 = 108$ and then take the square root of both sides to get $x - 6 = \pm\sqrt{108}$. Since $108 = 36 \times 3$, the radical simplifies to $6\sqrt{3}$.

Now substitute a^2 back in for x: $a^2 - 6 = \pm 6\sqrt{3}$ and $a^2 = 6 \pm 6\sqrt{3}$. Since the question asks for the root with the greatest value, you can ignore the root with the minus sign, so $a^2 = 6 + 6\sqrt{3} = 6(1 + \sqrt{3})$. Take the square root of both sides, and ignore the root with the negative sign to get $a = \sqrt{6(1 + \sqrt{3})}$. **(B)** is correct.

13. C

Difficulty: Hard

Getting to the Answer: The radical looks as if it will make the calculation difficult, but it will drop out when you complete the square. The coefficient, b, is $6\sqrt{5}$, so $\left(\frac{6\sqrt{5}}{2}\right)^2 = \left(\frac{36 \times 5}{4}\right) = 45$. Adding 45 to both sides of the equation gives you $x^2 - \left(6\sqrt{5}\right)x + 45 = 5$, so the factored form is $\left(x - 3\sqrt{5}\right)^2 = 5$. Take the square root of both sides to get $x - 3\sqrt{5} = \pm\sqrt{5}$. The two possible values of x are $3\sqrt{5} + \sqrt{5} = 4\sqrt{5}$ and $3\sqrt{5} - \sqrt{5} = 2\sqrt{5}$. The question asks for the sum of these values, which is $4\sqrt{5} + 2\sqrt{5} = 6\sqrt{5}$. **(C)** is correct.

14. A

Difficulty: Hard

Getting to the Answer: Subtract the left side of the equation from the right side: $0 = 2x^2 - x^2 - 4x - 7x + 3 - 1 = x^2 - 11x + 2$. Combine like-terms to get $x^2 - 11x = -2$. So, $b = -11$, and $\left(\frac{b}{2}\right)^2 = \left(\frac{11}{2}\right)^2 = 30.25$. Thus, completing the square gives you $x^2 - 11x + 30.25 = 28.25$. (This is a calculator-allowed question, so feel free to use the calculator if you need to do so. You could also have used the calculator to backsolve to find the correct choice.) Factor the left side to get $(x - 5.5)^2 = 28.25$ and $x - 5.5 = \pm\sqrt{28.25}$. Therefore, x can be either $5.5 + \sqrt{28.25}$ or $5.5 - \sqrt{28.25}$. The latter solution matches **(A)**.

15. 2

Difficulty: Hard

Strategic Advice: Recall that when the value of the discriminant, $b^2 - 4ac$, is 0, there is exactly one solution to the quadratic equation.

Getting to the Answer: The given equation is $2x^2 + 8x + 4 + 2z = 0$, but there is a common factor of 2 in all the terms, so this becomes $x^2 + 4x + 2 + z = 0$. So $a = 1$, $b = 4$, and $c = 2 + z$. Set the discriminant $4^2 - 4(1)(2 + z)$ equal to 0 so that there is only one solution. Expand the equation to $16 - 8 - 4z = 0$. Thus, $8 = 4z$, and $z = 2$. Grid in **2**.

16. B

Difficulty: Hard

Getting to the Answer: The question presents a quadratic equation that cannot be easily factored. Therefore, use the quadratic formula to solve. The quadratic formula states that $x = \frac{-b \pm \sqrt{b^2 - 4ac}}{2a}$.

In this case, $a = 3$, $b = 4$, and $c = -2$. Plug in these values to get:

$$x = \frac{-4 \pm \sqrt{4^2 - 4(3)(-2)}}{6}$$
$$= \frac{-4 \pm \sqrt{16 - (-24)}}{6}$$
$$= \frac{-4 \pm \sqrt{40}}{6}$$

Thus, the solutions to the equation are $\frac{-4 + \sqrt{40}}{6}$ and $\frac{-4 - \sqrt{40}}{6}$. The question asks for their product:

$$\left(\frac{-4 + \sqrt{40}}{6}\right)\left(\frac{-4 - \sqrt{40}}{6}\right)$$
$$= \frac{16 + 4\sqrt{40} - 4\sqrt{40} - 40}{36}$$
$$= \frac{-24}{36}$$
$$= -\frac{2}{3}$$

(B) is correct.

17. A

Difficulty: Medium

Strategic Advice: When all of the coefficients in a quadratic equation are divisible by a common factor, simplify the equation by dividing all terms by that factor before solving.

Getting to the Answer: The given equation is $4x^2 - 24x + 16 = 0$, but there is a common factor of 4 in all the terms, so this becomes $x^2 - 6x + 4 = 0$. Therefore, $a = 1$, $b = -6$, and $c = 4$.

The radicals in the answer choices are a strong clue that the quadratic formula is the way to solve this equation. The quadratic formula is $x = \frac{-b \pm \sqrt{b^2 - 4ac}}{2a}$, and after you plug in the coefficients, you get:

$$x = \frac{6 \pm \sqrt{-6^2 - 4(1)(4)}}{2(1)}$$
$$= \frac{6 \pm \sqrt{36 - 16}}{2}$$
$$= \frac{6 \pm \sqrt{20}}{2}$$

This doesn't resemble any of the answer choices, so continue simplifying:

$$\frac{6 \pm \sqrt{20}}{2}$$
$$= \frac{6 \pm \sqrt{4}\sqrt{5}}{2}$$
$$= \frac{6 \pm 2\sqrt{5}}{2}$$
$$= \frac{6}{2} \pm \frac{2\sqrt{5}}{2}$$
$$= 3 \pm \sqrt{5}$$

Hence, **(A)** is correct.

18. B

Difficulty: Hard

Getting to the Answer: The question presents a variation of a quadratic equation. A glance at the radicals in the answer choices suggests that using the quadratic formula to solve is appropriate. Because there are so many variables, it might help to write down the quadratic formula in your notes as a guide $x = \frac{-b \pm \sqrt{b^2 - 4ac}}{2a}$.

Begin by reorganizing the quadratic into the standard form $ax^2 + bx + c = 0$:

$$3x^2 = m(5x + v)$$
$$3x^2 = 5mx + mv$$
$$3x^2 - 5mx - mv = 0$$

In this case, $a = 3$, $b = -5m$, and $c = -mv$. Now solve:

$$x = \frac{-(-5m) \pm \sqrt{(-5m)^2 - 4(3)(-mv)}}{6}$$
$$= \frac{5m \pm \sqrt{25m^2 - (-12mv)}}{6}$$
$$= \frac{5m \pm \sqrt{25m^2 + 12mv}}{6}$$
$$= \frac{5m}{6} \pm \frac{\sqrt{25m^2 + 12mv}}{6}$$

Therefore, **(B)** is correct.

19. D

Difficulty: Medium

Getting to the Answer: Get the equation $x(dx + 10) = -3$ into the form $ax^2 + bx + c = 0$. Multiply out the left side of the equation $x(dx + 10) = -3$ to get $dx^2 + 10x = -3$. Add 3 to both sides to yield $dx^2 + 10x + 3 = 0$.

When a, b, and c are all real, the equation $ax^2 + bx + c = 0$ (when $a \neq 0$) does not have real solutions only if the discriminant, which is $b^2 - 4ac$, is negative. In the equation $dx^2 + 10x + 3 = 0$, $a = d$, $b = 10$, and $c = 3$. The discriminant in this question is $10^2 - 4(d)(3) = 100 - 12d$.

Since you're looking for a negative discriminant, that is, $b^2 - 4ac < 0$, you need $100 - 12d < 0$. Solve the inequality $100 - 12d < 0$ for d:

$$100 - 12d < 0$$
$$100 < 12d$$
$$\frac{100}{12} < d$$
$$\frac{25}{3} < d$$
$$8\frac{1}{3} < d$$

Among the answer choices, only 10 is greater than $8\frac{1}{3}$, so **(D)** is correct.

20. C

Difficulty: Medium

Getting to the Answer: Recall that when a quadratic equation has no real solutions, its discriminant, which is $b^2 - 4ac$, will be less than 0. Calculate the discriminant of each answer choice and pick the one that's negative. You don't need to actually solve for x:

(A) $8^2 - 4(1)(-12) = 64 + 48 > 0$. Eliminate.

(B) $(-8)^2 - 4(1)(12) = 64 - 48 > 0$. Eliminate.

(C) $(-9)^2 - 4(1)(21) = 81 - 84 = -3 < 0$. Pick **(C)** and move on. For the record:

(D) $(100)^2 - 4(1)(-1) = 10,000 + 4 > 0$. Eliminate.

21. B

Difficulty: Easy

Getting to the Answer: Quadratic equations can be written in several different forms that tell various pieces of important information about the equation. For example, the constant k in the vertex form of a quadratic equation, $y = a(x - h)^2 + k$, gives the minimum or maximum value of the function. The standard form, $y = ax^2 + bx + c$, gives the y-intercept as c. The factored form of a quadratic equation makes it easy to find the solutions to the equation, which graphically represent the x-intercepts. Choice **(B)** is the only equation written in factored form and therefore is correct. You can set each factor equal to 0 and quickly solve to find that the x-intercepts of the graph are $x = -\frac{3}{4}$ and $x = 1$, which agree with the graph.

22. C

Difficulty: Medium

Getting to the Answer: An axis of symmetry splits a parabola in half and travels through the vertex. Use the formula to find h, plug in the correct values from the equation, and simplify:

$$x = -\frac{b}{2a}$$
$$= -\frac{17}{2\left(\frac{-11}{3}\right)}$$
$$= -\frac{17}{\left(\frac{-22}{3}\right)}$$
$$= -17 \cdot \frac{-3}{22}$$
$$= \frac{51}{22}$$

The correct answer is **(C)**.

23. B

Difficulty: Hard

Getting to the Answer: To find where the two functions intersect, set them equal to each other and solve for x:

$$f(x) = g(x)$$
$$3x^2 - 24x + 52 = x^2 + 12x - 110$$
$$2x^2 - 36x + 162 = 0$$
$$2(x^2 - 18x + 81) = 0$$
$$x^2 - 18x + 81 = 0$$

Notice that this is a classic quadratic:

$$x^2 - 18x + 81 = 0$$
$$(x - 9)^2 = 0$$
$$x = 9$$

Since there is only one solution for x, there must be only one point of intersection. **(B)** is correct.

24. 2

Difficulty: Medium

Getting to the Answer: An x-intercept of a function is a point at which the y-coordinate equals 0. Set the equation equal to zero, simplify, and factor:

$$g(x) = -2.5x^2 + 10x - 7.5$$
$$0 = -2.5x^2 + 10x - 7.5$$
$$0 = -2.5(x^2 - 4x + 3)$$
$$0 = x^2 - 4x + 3$$
$$0 = (x - 1)(x - 3)$$
$$x = 1 \text{ or } x = 3$$

The question asks for the *difference* between the x-intercepts, not for the x-intercepts themselves. Thus, $3 - 1 = $ **2**.

25. A

Difficulty: Hard

Getting to the Answer: The answer choices are all similar, so pay special attention to their differences and see if you can eliminate any choices logically. A rocket goes up and then comes down, which means that the graph will be a parabola opening downward. The equation, therefore, should have a negative sign in front. Eliminate (C) and (D).

To evaluate the two remaining choices, recall the *vertex form* of a quadratic, $y = a(x - h)^2 + k$, and what it tells you: the vertex of the graph is (h, k). The h is the x-coordinate of the maximum (or minimum) and k is the y-coordinate of the maximum (or minimum). In this situation, x has been replaced by t, or time, and y is now $h(t)$, or height. The question says that the maximum height occurs at 3 seconds and is 34 feet, so h is 3 and k is 34. Substitute these values into vertex form to find that the correct equation is $y = -16(x - 3)^2 + 34$. The function that matches is **(A)**.

26. B

Difficulty: Medium

Strategic Advice: Because each of the two expressions containing b is equal to a, the two expressions must be equal to each other.

Getting to the Answer: Set the two expressions equal to each other and then solve for b:

$$b^2 + 4b - 12 = -12 + b$$
$$b^2 + 4b = b$$
$$b^2 + 3b = 0$$
$$b(b + 3) = 0$$

If b $b(b + 3) = 0$, then $b = 0$ or $b = -3$. Of these two values, only -3 is among the answer choices, so **(B)** is correct.

27. 2

Difficulty: Medium

Getting to the Answer: The points of intersection of the graphs are the points at which the equations are equal. Since (a, b) is the label for an (x, y) point, set the two equations equal to each other and solve for the value of x to find the value of a:

$$-2x = 5x^2 - 12x$$
$$0 = 5x^2 - 10x$$
$$0 = 5x(x - 2)$$

Thus, $x = 0$ or $x = 2$. The question states that the intersection points are $(0, 0)$ and (a, b), so a must equal 2. Grid in **2**.

28. B

Difficulty: Medium

Getting to the Answer: The solutions to a system of equations are the points at which the equations intersect, which occurs when they are equal. Begin by setting both equations equal to y:

$$\begin{cases} y = -3x + 10 \\ y = x^2 - 7x + 13 \end{cases}$$

Because both equations are equal to y, they are also equal to each other. Set them equal and solve for x:

$$-3x + 10 = x^2 - 7x + 13$$
$$-3x = x^2 - 7x + 3$$
$$0 = x^2 - 4x + 3$$
$$0 = (x - 1)(x - 3)$$

Thus, there are 2 solutions, $x = 1$ and $x = 3$. **(B)** is correct.

Note that you could also use the discriminant, $b^2 - 4ac$, to determine how many solutions there are. If the discriminant is greater than 0, there are two real solutions; if it's equal to 0, there is one real solution; and if it's less than 0, there are no real solutions. In this case, $b^2 - 4ac = (-4)^2 - 4(1 \times 3) = 16 - 12 = 4$. Because $4 > 0$, there are 2 real solutions. **(B)** is correct.

29. C

Difficulty: Hard

Getting to the Answer: Because the question states that $f(c) = g(c)$, set the two functions equal to each other and solve for x. To make calculations easier, begin by converting $f(x)$ into standard form:

$$-2(x - 3)^2 - 4$$
$$= -2(x - 3)(x - 3) - 4$$
$$= -2(x^2 - 6x + 9) - 4$$
$$= -2x^2 + 12x - 18 - 4$$
$$= -2x^2 + 12x - 22$$

Now set the two functions equal:

$$-2x^2 + 12x - 22 = 2x - 10$$

Simplify by dividing all terms by -2:

$$x^2 - 6x + 11 = -x + 5$$

Next, combine like terms and solve for x:

$$x^2 - 6x + 11 = -x + 5$$
$$x^2 - 5x + 6 = 0$$
$$(x - 2)(x - 3) = 0$$

Therefore, $x = 2$ or $x = 3$, which means that c could also be either 2 or 3. Because 3 is not an answer choice, the answer must be 2. **(C)** is correct.

30. C

Difficulty: Hard

Strategic Advice: When you need to find the points of intersection of two equations, set the equations equal to each other.

Getting to the Answer: The question indicates that points P and Q are the points of intersection of the two equations, so set the two equations equal to each other, consolidate terms to get a single quadratic equation equal to 0, and simplify:

$$3x^2 + \frac{14}{3}x - \frac{73}{3} = -\frac{4}{3}x - \frac{1}{3}$$
$$3x^2 + \frac{18}{3}x - \frac{72}{3} = 0$$
$$3x^2 + 6x - 24 = 0$$
$$x^2 + 2x - 8 = 0$$

Factor the equation to find the values of x:

$$x^2 + 2x - 8 = 0$$
$$(x + 4)(x - 2) = 0$$
$$x = -4 \text{ or } 2$$

You can plug each value of x into either of the original equations to find the corresponding values of y. (The linear equation appears easier to work with.) For $x = -4$:

$$y = -\frac{4}{3}(-4) - \frac{1}{3}$$
$$y = \frac{16}{3} - \frac{1}{3}$$
$$y = \frac{15}{3} = 5$$

Therefore, one of the points of intersection is $(-4, 5)$. Find the other point of intersection by plugging in 2 for x into the linear equation:

$$y = -\frac{4}{3}(2) - \frac{1}{3}$$

$$y = -\frac{8}{3} - \frac{1}{3}$$

$$y = -\frac{9}{3} = -3$$

Thus, the other point of intersection is $(2, -3)$.

The question asks for the distance between these two points. The formula for the distance, d, between the points (x_1, y_1) and (x_2, y_2) is $d = \sqrt{(x_2 - x_1)^2 + (y_2 - y_1)^2}$. Thus, find the distance between points P and Q:

$$\sqrt{(-4 - 2)^2 + (5 - (-3))^2}$$

$$= \sqrt{(-6)^2 + 8^2}$$

$$= \sqrt{36 + 64}$$

$$= \sqrt{100}$$

$$= 10$$

Therefore, the distance between points P and Q is 10. **(C)** is correct.

31. C

Difficulty: Medium

Getting to the Answer: The first approach is to set $f(x)$ equal to $g(x)$: $4x^2 - 25 = -4x^2 + 25$. Isolate the x^2 terms on one side to get $8x^2 = 50$, so $4x^2 = 25$. Take the square root of both sides to see that $2x = \pm 5$, which means that the two intersections of the functions occur where $x = -2.5$ and $x = 2.5$. From the graph, you can see that these are the values of $\pm z$, so $z = 2.5$. **(C)** is correct. (Note that even if you had not been given the y-coordinates of the points of intersection, you could have calculated them from knowing their corresponding x-coordinates.)

The second approach is to plug in the coordinates of one of the intersections into either function. Using $f(x)$, the y-coordinate is 0 and the x-coordinate is z. So, $0 = 4z^2 - 25$. The math works out exactly the same as the first method: $4z^2 = 25$, so $z = \pm 2.5$, and, from the graph, you can determine that $z = 2.5$.

32. 40

Difficulty: Medium

Category: Graphs of Quadratics

Getting to the Answer: Since the given equation is valid for both $x = -5$ or $x = 7$, you can plug in either of those values and solve for k. Using 7 as the value of x gives you $\frac{1}{4}\left(4(7)^2 - 8(7) - k\right) = 30$. Multiply both sides by 4 to get $4(49) - 56 - k = 120$. Thus, $-k = 120 - 196 + 56 = -20$, so $k = 20$ and $2k = 40$. Grid in **40**.

33. D

Difficulty: Hard

Category: Graphs of Quadratics

Getting to the Answer: Because the quadratic regression is an exact fit of the data, you can treat the data points as a quadratic function.

The graph of a quadratic function is symmetric with respect to its axis of symmetry, which passes through the x-value of the vertex, or the maximum (or minimum) of the function. The question tells you the maximum occurs at $x = 25$, which makes it the line of symmetry. Because 35 is $35 - 25 = 10$ units to the right of the axis of symmetry, you know that the y-value will be the same as the point that is 10 units to the left of the axis of symmetry, which is $x = 25 - 10 = 15$. Find the corresponding y-value in the table: 27. Therefore, **(D)** is correct.

34. C

Difficulty: Hard

Category: Graphs of Quadratics

Getting to the Answer: Because the height of the boulder is expressed as a quadratic equation with a negative t^2 coefficient, the path of the boulder is a downward-facing parabola. Therefore, the maximum height occurs at the vertex of the parabola. The t-coordinate (generally called the x-coordinate) of the vertex of a parabola is given by $t = \frac{-b}{2a} = \frac{-224}{2(-16)} = 7$. Plug the result into the function to get the h-coordinate: $h(7) = -16(7)^2 + 224(7) + 240 = 1{,}024$. **(C)** is correct.

35. D

Difficulty: Medium

Category: Graphs of Quadratics

Getting to the Answer: Set the quadratic expression for the height of the boulder equal to 0 and solve for t:

$$-16t^2 + 224t + 240 = 0$$
$$-16\left(t^2 - 14t - 15\right) = 0$$
$$t^2 - 14t - 15 = 0$$
$$(t - 15)(t + 1) = 0$$
$$t = 15 \text{ or } t = -1$$

Because time can't be negative, $t = 15$. **(D)** is correct.

36. B

Difficulty: Medium

Category: Graphs of Quadratics

Getting to the Answer: Keep in mind that the question asks for the statement that's false, so eliminate the true choices as you go. The parabola opens downward, so the a term should be negative. Eliminate (A). The parabola's vertex is in quadrant I, so h and k are both positive. That makes choice (D) true as well; eliminate it. The axis of symmetry is $x = h$, so $x = 3$. According to the graph, the vertex is $(3, 2)$. Choice (B), however, claims that the axis of symmetry is $y = 3$. Choice **(B)** is false and is therefore the correct answer.

For the record, (C) is a true statement because the line $g(x) = \frac{2x}{3}$ passes through the point $(3, 2)$, which is indeed the vertex of $f(x)$.

37. 24

Difficulty: Medium

Category: Systems of Quadratic and Linear Equations

Getting to the Answer: The question tells you that $y = 2x$, so solving the system using substitution is a good option. Divide the second equation by 2 and plug in $2x$ for y:

$$2x^2 + 2y^2 = 240$$
$$x^2 + y^2 = 120$$
$$x^2 + (2x)^2 = 120$$
$$x^2 + 4x^2 = 120$$
$$5x^2 = 120$$
$$x^2 = 24$$

The question asks for the value of x^2, not x, so stop here. Grid in **24**.

38. D

Difficulty: Medium

Category: Completing the Square

Getting to the Answer: The x-intercepts of a function are the values of x that make the function equal to 0. Factoring this function would be cumbersome because you would need to determine two numbers whose product is $8\frac{1}{4}$ and whose sum is -7. This is a good candidate for completing the square.

Start with $x^2 - 7x + 8\frac{1}{4} = 0$, then subtract $8\frac{1}{4}$ from each side to get $x^2 - 7x = -8\frac{1}{4}$. Half of the b coefficient, -7, is $-3\frac{1}{2}$, which, when squared, is $12\frac{1}{4}$. Add that to both sides to get $x^2 - 7x + 12\frac{1}{4} = 4$.
So $\left(x - 3\frac{1}{2}\right)^2 = 4$. Take the square root of both sides to get $x - 3\frac{1}{2} = \pm 2$. Therefore, the x-intercepts are $3\frac{1}{2} \pm 2$, or $1\frac{1}{2}$ and $5\frac{1}{2}$. **(D)** is correct.

39. D

Difficulty: Medium

Category: Graphs of Quadratics

Getting to the Answer: Draw a quick sketch of the equation (or graph it in your graphing calculator):

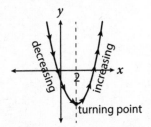

Based on the equation, the graph is a parabola that opens upward with a vertex of $(2, -5)$. A parabola changes direction at the x-coordinate of its vertex. You can immediately eliminate (A) and (B). To the left of 2 on the x-axis (or $x < 2$), the parabola is decreasing, and to the right of 2 on the x-axis (or $x > 2$), it is increasing. **(D)** is correct.

40. A

Difficulty: Medium

Category: Solving Quadratics by Factoring

Getting to the Answer: Rearrange the given equation to read $(6x + 5)^2 = (3x - 2)^2$. Given that the square of a number is the same value as the square of its negative counterpart, you can write that $\pm(6x + 5) = \pm(3x - 2)$. Therefore, either $6x + 5 = 3x - 2$ or $6x + 5 = (-1)(3x - 2) = -3x + 2$.

Solve the first case by subtracting $3x$ and 5 from both sides of the equation: $6x + 5 - 3x - 5 = 3x - 2 - 3x - 5$. Thus, $3x = -7$ and $x = -\frac{7}{3}$. For the alternative equation, add $3x$ to and subtract 5 from both sides:

$6x + 5 + 3x - 5 = -3x + 2 + 3x - 5$. Thus, $9x = -3$, so $x = -\frac{1}{3}$.

The question asks for the sum of the two solutions which is $-\frac{7}{3} + \left(-\frac{1}{3}\right) = -\frac{8}{3}$. **(A)** is correct.

41. A

Difficulty: Hard

Category: Classic Quadratics

Strategic Advice: Technically, this isn't a quadratic equation because the highest power on the variable isn't 2. However, it is a "quadratic-type" equation because the square of the variable part of the middle term is equal to the variable in the leading term. In other words, squaring $\sqrt{x}$ gives you x. You can use factoring techniques you learned for quadratics to answer the question.

Getting to the Answer: The presence of 4, 9, and 16—all perfect squares—is a big clue. Note that $4x - 12\sqrt{x} + 9$ is an instance of the classic quadratic $(a - b)^2 = a^2 - 2ab + b^2$. Use this shortcut to factor the equation and see where that leads you:

$$4x - 12\sqrt{x} + 9 = 16$$
$$\left(2\sqrt{x} - 3\right)^2 = 16$$
$$2\sqrt{x} - 3 = \pm 4$$

The question asks for $10\sqrt{x} - 15$, which happens to be 5 times the quantity on the left side of the last equation above, so multiply the positive result, 4, by 5 to get 20. The correct answer is **(A)**.

42. A

Difficulty: Medium

Category: Solving Quadratics by Factoring

Strategic Advice: When a question asks for a value of an expression, isolate that expression on one side of the equation, if possible, rather than solving for the variable.

Getting to the Answer: Notice that the question asks for a possible value of $x - 2$, not x. Isolate $x - 2$ on one side of the equation by multiplying both sides by $x - 2$ and taking the square root of both sides:

$$(x - 2)(x - 2) = \frac{3}{x - 2}(x - 2)$$
$$(x - 2)^2 = 3$$
$$\sqrt{(x - 2)^2} = \sqrt{3}$$
$$x - 2 = \pm\sqrt{3}$$

Thus, **(A)** is correct.

An alternative strategy is to backsolve, plugging each choice in for $x - 2$ to see which results in a true statement.

43. A

Difficulty: Hard

Category: Classic Quadratics

Getting to the Answer: Use exponent rules to simplify the fraction. Since the terms in the numerator and denominator have the same base, z, subtract the exponent of the denominator from that of the numerator: $z^{x^2+y^2-(-2xy)} = z^{x^2+2xy+y^2}$. When a value with an exponent is raised to another exponent, multiply the exponents. So, for the term on the right side, $\left(z^3\right)^3 = z^9$. Now the equation is $z^{x^2+2xy+y^2} = z^9$. Since both sides have the common base, z, their exponents must be equal and you can write $x^2 + 2xy + y^2 = 9$.

Factor $x^2 + 2xy + y^2$, a classic quadratic, to get $(x+y)^2 = 9$. Thus, $x + y$ must be either 3 or -3. However, the question limits x and y to positive integers, so they must be 1 and 2. Furthermore, since $x > y$, x must be 2 and y must be 1. Consequently, $x - y = 2 - 1 = 1$. **(A)** is correct.

PART 3

SAT Reading

CHAPTER 13

The Method for SAT Reading Questions

LEARNING OBJECTIVES

After completing this chapter, you will be able to:

- Read SAT Reading passages strategically
- Apply the Method for SAT Reading Questions efficiently and effectively to SAT Reading questions

---

300/600 SmartPoints®

How to Do SAT Reading

The SAT Reading section is made up of four passages and one set of paired passages, each approximately 500–750 words long and accompanied by 10–11 questions for a total of 52 questions in the section. To tackle all of this effectively in 65 minutes, the most successful test takers

- read the passages strategically to zero in on the text that leads to points, and
- approach the questions with a method that minimizes rereading and leads directly to correct answers.

The key to maximizing correct answers is learning in advance the kinds of questions that the test asks. SAT Reading questions focus more on the author's purpose (*why* she wrote this passage) and the passage's structure (*how* the author makes and supports her points) than on the details or facts of the subject matter (*what* this passage is about).

Knowing that the SAT rewards your attention to *how* and *why* the author wrote the passage or chose to include certain words or examples puts you in the driver's seat. You can read more effectively and answer the questions more quickly and confidently.

In this chapter, we'll give you an overview of how to tackle Reading passages and questions. The other chapters in this unit will help you become a stronger reader and present the five SAT Reading question types, as well as tips for improving your approach for paired passages and literature passages.

Try the passage and questions that follow on your own. Then, compare your approach to our recommendations for how to approach SAT Reading and reflect on how you can become a more efficient test taker.

Questions 1-10 refer to the following passage.

This passage describes the varying and changing scientific theories surrounding sunspots.

Astronomers noted more than 150 years ago that sunspots wax and wane in number in an 11-year cycle. Ever since, people have speculated that the solar cycle might exert some influence on
5 the Earth's weather. In this century, for example, scientists have linked the solar cycle to droughts in the American Midwest. Until recently, however, none of these correlations has held up under close scrutiny.
10 One problem is that sunspots themselves have been poorly understood. Observation revealed that the swirly smudges represent areas of intense magnetic activity where the sun's radiative energy has been blocked and that they are considerably
15 cooler than bright regions of the sun. Scientists had not been able, however, to determine just how sunspots are created or what effect they have on the solar constant (a misnomer that refers to the sun's total radiance at any instant).
20 The latter question, at least, seems to have been resolved by data from the *Solar Maximum Mission* satellite, which has monitored the solar constant since 1980, which was the peak of a solar cycle. As the number of sunspots decreased
25 through 1986, the satellite recorded a gradual dimming of the sun. Over the next year, as sunspots proliferated, the sun brightened. These data suggest that the sun is 0.1 percent more luminous at the peak of the solar cycle, when
30 the number of sunspots is greatest, than at its nadir, according to Richard C. Willson of the Jet Propulsion Laboratory and Hugh S. Hudson of the University of California at San Diego.
The data show that sunspots do not
35 themselves make the sun shine brighter. Quite the contrary. When a sunspot appears, it initially causes the sun to dim slightly, but then after a period of weeks or months islands of brilliance called faculas usually emerge near the sunspot
40 and more than compensate for its dimming effect. Willson says faculas may represent regions where energy that initially was blocked beneath a sunspot has finally breached the surface.

Does the subtle fluctuation in the solar
45 constant manifest itself in the Earth's weather? Meteorological reports offer statistical evidence that it does, albeit rather indirectly. The link seems to be mediated by a phenomenon known as the quasi-biennial oscillation (QBO), a 180-degree
50 shift in the direction of stratospheric winds above the Tropics that occurs about every two years.
Karin Labitzke of the Free University of Berlin and Harry van Loon of the National Center for Atmospheric Research in Boulder, Colorado, were
55 the first to uncover the QBO link. They gathered temperature and air-pressure readings from various latitudes and altitudes over the past three solar cycles. They found no correlation between the solar cycle and their data until they sorted the
60 data into two categories: those gathered during the QBO's west phase (when the stratospheric winds blow west) and those gathered during its east phase. A remarkable correlation appeared: temperatures and pressures coincident with the
65 QBO's west phase rose and fell in accordance with the solar cycle.
Building on this finding, Brian A. Tinsley of the National Science Foundation discovered a statistical correlation between the solar cycle and
70 the position of storms in the North Atlantic. The latitude of storms during the west phase of the QBO, Tinsley found, varied with the solar cycle: storms occurring toward the peak of a solar cycle traveled at latitudes about six degrees nearer the
75 Equator than storms during the cycle's nadir.
Labitzke, van Loon, and Tinsley acknowledge that their findings are still rather mysterious. Why does the solar cycle seem to exert more of an influence during the west phase of the QBO
80 than it does during the east phase? How does the 0.1 percent variance in solar radiation trigger the much larger changes—up to six degrees Celsius in polar regions—observed by Labitzke and van Loon? Van Loon says simply, "We can't explain it."
85 John A. Eddy of the National Center for Atmospheric Research, nonetheless, thinks these QBO findings as well as the Solar Maximum

Mission data "look like breakthroughs" in
the search for a link between the solar cycle
90 and weather. With further research into how
the oceans damp the effects of solar flux,
for example, these findings may lead to models
that have some predictive value. The next few
years may be particularly rich in solar flux.

1. Which one of the following best describes the main idea of the passage?

A) The scientific advances provided by the research of Labitzke and van Loon have finally cleared up some of the mysteries that long plagued the study of sunspots.

B) Recent research combining astronomical and climate data provides a promising foundation for better understanding the relationship between sunspots and Earth's weather.

C) Despite recent breakthroughs, scientists are unlikely to ever fully explain correlations between sunspot activity and Earth's weather patterns.

D) Scientists have used data from the *Solar Maximum Mission* satellite to explain how sunspots affect Earth's climate during the quasi-biennial oscillation's west phase.

2. The author's point of view can best be described as that of

A) a meteorologist voicing optimism that the findings of recent solar research will improve weather forecasting.

B) an astronomer presenting a digest of current findings to a review board of other astronomers.

C) a science writer explaining the possible influence of a solar phenomenon on terrestrial weather patterns.

D) a historian listing the contributions to climate science made by the *Solar Maximum Mission.*

3. The passage indicates which of the following about the sun's luminosity and the solar cycle?

A) Scientists have found no correlation between the sun's brightness and the solar cycle.

B) The sun is brightest at the nadir of the solar cycle.

C) The sun is brightest at the peak and again at the nadir of the solar cycle.

D) The sun is brightest at the peak of the solar cycle.

4. Which one of the following provides the best evidence for the answer to the previous question?

A) Lines 10–11 ("One problem . . . understood")

B) Lines 15–18 ("Scientists had . . . constant")

C) Lines 20–24 ("The latter . . . cycle")

D) Lines 27–31 ("These data . . . nadir")

5. Based on information in the passage, it can most reasonably be inferred that faculas

A) are directly responsible for increased temperatures on Earth.

B) have a dimming effect on the sun's luminescence during sunspot activity.

C) are mostly likely to appear at the peak of the solar cycle.

D) grow in number as the number of sunspots decreases.

6. Which one of the following provides the best evidence for the answer to the previous question?

A) Lines 20–24 ("The latter . . . cycle")

B) Lines 34–35 ("The data . . . brighter")

C) Lines 36–41 ("When a . . . effect")

D) Lines 46–47 ("Meteorological . . . indirectly")

7. As used in line 45, "manifest" most nearly means

A) impact.

B) disguise.

C) itemize.

D) reveal.

8. According to the passage, Labitzke and van Loon's research on the quasi-biennial oscillation (QBO) shows that

A) the QBO's west phase correlates to the solar cycle.

B) the QBO's west phase has a longer duration than that of its east phase.

C) the QBO shows no correlation with the solar cycle.

D) the reasons for the QBO's correlation to the solar cycle are now well understood.

9. The main purpose of the questions in the second-to-last paragraph (lines 76–84) is to

A) emphasize how little scientists know about the solar constant.

B) explain more fully the mysterious nature of the scientists' findings.

C) question the basis upon which these scientists built their hypotheses.

D) express doubts about the scientists' interpretations of their findings.

10. The use of the quoted phrase "look like breakthroughs" in line 88 is primarily meant to convey the idea that

A) information about the solar cycle has allowed scientists to predict changes in Earth's complex climate system.

B) additional analysis of the link between the solar cycle and Earth's weather may yield useful models.

C) despite the associated costs, space missions can lead to important discoveries.

D) an alternative interpretation of the data may contradict the initial findings.

Strategic Reading

The SAT Reading Test is an open-book test; the passage is right there for you to reference. Moreover, the SAT actively tests your skill in looking up details; there are Command of Evidence questions that actually ask you to cite the line numbers for the evidence you used to answer a question. Because of the way the test is constructed, it is in your best interest to read fairly quickly, noting the outline of the passage as you go, marking up the page as you read with margin notes, getting a solid understanding of the main idea, but not taking the time to memorize details.

Be sure to read the prepassage blurb, the short introduction that comes before the passage. Identify any information that helps you to understand the topic of the passage or to anticipate what the author will discuss. For the previous passage, the blurb states the topic (sunspots) and announces that the passage will discuss "varying and changing theories" about them. That's an invitation to keep your eye out for multiple theories as you read.

You'll learn all the skills you need to read strategically in chapter 14, but for now, here's an example of an expert's passage map. Don't worry if yours doesn't look exactly like this (or even anything like this, yet). Follow the expert's thought process in the discussion that follows the passage to see what he was thinking and asking as he read the passage.

Questions 1-10 refer to the following passage.

This passage details the varying and changing scientific theories surrounding sunspots.

Sunspots Passage Map

Astronomers noted more than 150 years ago that sunspots wax and wane in number in an 11-year cycle. Ever since, people have speculated that the solar cycle might exert some influence on
5   the Earth's weather. In this century, for example, scientists have linked the solar cycle to droughts in the American Midwest. Until recently, however, none of these correlations has held up under close scrutiny.

sunspot cycle & earth weather

10 One problem is that sunspots themselves have been poorly understood. Observation revealed that the swirly smudges represent areas of intense magnetic activity where the sun's radiative energy has been blocked and that they are considerably
15 cooler than bright regions of the sun. Scientists had not been able, however, to determine just how sunspots are created or what effect they have on the solar constant (a misnomer that refers to the sun's total radiance at any instant).

sunspots poorly understood

20 The latter question, at least, seems to have been resolved by data from the *Solar Maximum Mission* satellite, which has monitored the solar constant since 1980, which was the peak of a solar cycle. As the number of sunspots decreased
25 through 1986, the satellite recorded a gradual dimming of the sun. Over the next year, as sunspots proliferated, the sun brightened. These data suggest that the sun is 0.1 percent more luminous at the peak of the solar cycle, when
30 the number of sunspots is greatest, than at its nadir, according to Richard C. Willson of the Jet Propulsion Laboratory and Hugh S. Hudson of the University of California at San Diego.

SMM satellite

Sunspot cycle and sun's brightness

The data show that sunspots do not
35 themselves make the sun shine brighter. Quite the contrary. When a sunspot appears, it initially causes the sun to dim slightly, but then after a period of weeks or months islands of brilliance called faculas usually emerge near the sunspot
40 and more than compensate for its dimming effect. Willson says faculas may represent regions

sunspots dim, but faculas even brighter

ANALYSIS

Pre-passage blurb: The passage addresses various and changing theories about sunspots. Keep track of the different ideas and how they've evolved.

¶1: The author introduces the passage's topic—*sunspots*—and zeroes in on a more specific question: *how do they affect Earth's weather?* People have been investigating this for 150 years, but (note the contrast word "however" in line 7) only recently have they gotten some answers. The author will say more about these answers in coming paragraphs.

¶2: The author defines sunspots: areas where magnetic activity blocks some of the sun's energy. However (again, there's a contrast where the author wants to make a point), scientists still have questions: *how are sunspots created and how do they affect the sun's brightness?*

¶3: Here's the first recent discovery. The SMM satellite shows that the sun gets brighter with more sunspots (the solar cycle peak) and dimmer with fewer sunspots (the solar cycle nadir). This sets up a question that the author will have to answer: *If sunspots block and cool the sun's energy, how can the sun be brighter with more sunspots?*

¶4: The author clears up the paradox from the previous paragraph. Sunspots *initially* block the sun's energy, but (this author loves contrasts) then faculas—super bright hot spots—pop up around the sunspots. Faculas are so bright that they "more than compensate" for the sunspots' dimming effect. That's a lot about sunspots, but the author still needs to tie this to Earth's weather.

where energy that initially was blocked beneath a sunspot has finally breached the surface.

Does the subtle fluctuation in the solar
45   constant manifest itself in the Earth's weather? Meteorological reports offer statistical evidence that it does, albeit rather indirectly. The link seems to be mediated by a phenomenon known as the quasi-biennial oscillation (QBO), a 180-degree
50   shift in the direction of stratospheric winds above the Tropics that occurs about every two years.

indirect weather effects (QBO)

Karin Labitzke of the Free University of Berlin and Harry van Loon of the National Center for Atmospheric Research in Boulder, Colorado, were
55   the first to uncover the QBO link. They gathered temperature and air-pressure readings from various latitudes and altitudes over the past three solar cycles. They found no correlation between the solar cycle and their data until they sorted the
60   data into two categories: those gathered during the QBO's west phase (when the stratospheric winds blow west) and those gathered during its east phase. A remarkable correlation appeared: temperatures and pressures coincident with the
65   QBO's west phase rose and fell in accordance with the solar cycle.

sunspot correlation to temp and air pressure

Building on this finding, Brian A. Tinsley of the National Science Foundation discovered a statistical correlation between the solar cycle and
70   the position of storms in the North Atlantic. The latitude of storms during the west phase of the QBO, Tinsley found varied with the solar cycle: storms occurring toward the peak of a solar cycle traveled at latitudes about six degrees nearer the
75   Equator than storms during the cycle's nadir.

link to storm patterns

Labitzke, van Loon, and Tinsley acknowledge that their findings are still rather mysterious. Why does the solar cycle seem to exert more of an influence during the west phase of the QBO
80   than it does during the east phase? How does the 0.1 percent variance in solar radiation trigger the much larger changes—up to six degrees Celsius in polar regions—observed by Labitzke and van Loon? Van Loon says simply, "We can't explain it."

scientists can't fully explain links

85   John A. Eddy of the National Center for Atmospheric Research, nonetheless, thinks these QBO findings as well as the Solar Maximum

¶5: Here, the author starts to connect sunspots to the weather. It introduces something called the QBO that makes winds in the atmosphere change direction every two years. The next paragraph has to tie this to sunspots.

¶6: This paragraph discusses the research of two scientists, Labitzke and van Loon. They found that when the winds are moving westward, temperatures and air pressure correlate to the solar cycle (the cycle of more and fewer sunspots).

¶7: A different scientist—Tinsley—also correlated the sunspot cycle to the position of storms in the Atlantic Ocean. So far, the studies suggest that sunspots do affect the weather, but they don't say how or why.

¶8: This is a little disappointing: the scientists still don't know how or why sunspots seem to affect temperature and air pressure or the location of storms.

¶9: The author ends by citing one more scientist—Eddy—who is optimistic. He calls the research and the SMM satellite data a breakthrough and thinks we can learn a lot more about sunspots and the weather in the next few years.

90 Mission data "look like breakthroughs" in the search for a link between the solar cycle and weather. With further research into how the oceans damp the effects of solar flux, for example, these findings may lead to models that have some predictive value. The next few years may be particularly rich in solar flux.

break-throughs, but more research needed

BIG PICTURE

Main Idea: Scientists have learned quite a bit about sunspots and Earth's weather recently (faculas, the QBO, and storms are all evidence for that) and hope to learn more soon.

Author's Purpose: To outline the recent data and research suggesting that there is a connection between sunspots and the weather (but she doesn't go too far or say that all the mysteries have been solved)

SAT READING STRATEGY

A good rule of thumb for summarizing a passage's main idea is to boil down the author's takeaway to the reader to a single sentence. If the author had only a few seconds to make her point, what would she like the reader to remember?

Notice that the SAT expert reads actively, consistently summing up and paraphrasing what the author has said, asking what must come next, and never getting too caught up in details. The expert reader is not thrown off by encountering a new or unfamiliar term. He uses context to understand what it must mean and remembers that he can always consult the passage if he needs to remember a name or a definition. Finally, before turning to the questions, the expert takes a few seconds to summarize the "Big Picture," the Main Idea and Author's Purpose. This will help him answer questions about the passage's main idea and the author's purpose or point of view.

The Method for SAT Reading Questions

The best-prepared SAT test takers know that time is one of the SAT Reading section's biggest challenges. They also know that trying to speed up and cut corners can lead to sloppy mistakes, or worse, to reading a paragraph over and over because it just isn't sinking in. So, after setting themselves up for success with helpful passage notes and clear big picture summary, SAT experts use a simple four-step method to tackle each question quickly and confidently.

For example, take a look at this question from the set above:

The passage indicates which of the following about the sun's luminosity and the solar cycle?

A) Scientists have found no correlation between the sun's brightness and the solar cycle.

B) The sun is brightest at the nadir of the solar cycle.

C) The sun is brightest at the peak and again at the nadir of the solar cycle.

D) The sun is brightest at the peak of the solar cycle.

Because different question types require different strategies, start by *unpacking* the information in the question stem and identifying the question type. You'll learn to name and characterize six SAT Reading question types in chapter 15. The word "indicates" tells you that this is a Detail question, which means that you should be able to find the correct answer in the passage almost verbatim.

Next, based on the type of question, *research* the passage or consult your passage map to get the information you need. For this question, you have a margin note for paragraph 3 that says, "SMM sat data: more sunspots = brighter," so direct your research to paragraph 3. Here's the sentence you need: "These data suggest that the sun is 0.1 percent more luminous at the peak of the solar cycle, when the number of sunspots is greatest, than at its nadir."

Now, with the relevant part of the passage in mind, *predict* what the correct answer will say. In this case, you're looking for an answer choice that says that the sun is either brighter at the peak of the solar cycle or dimmer at its nadir.

Finally, use your prediction to evaluate the choices and *find* the one correct answer. Only choice **(D)** is a match for the prediction based on the research you did: the sun is indeed brightest at the peak of the solar cycle.

Notice that experts don't merely read or look at the answers; they *evaluate* them, knowing that only one of them answers the question correctly and that the other three are demonstrably incorrect in some way. Because SAT experts arm themselves with strong predictions in step 3, they can often zero in on the correct response without wasting time by rereading or hunting around in the passage to check each answer. You'll learn the strategies and tactics that experts use for steps 2–4 in chapter 16.

The steps are shown in the table below:

Method for SAT Reading Questions	
Step 1.	Unpack the question stem
Step 2.	Research the answer
Step 3.	Predict the answer
Step 4.	Find the one correct answer

Take a look at our expert's application of the SAT Reading Question Method to the questions from the *Sunspots* passage. Look for questions on which your own approach could have been faster and more confident.

Question	Analysis
1. Which one of the following best describes the main idea of the passage? A) The scientific advances provided by researchers such as Labitzke and van Loon have finally cleared up some of the mysteries that long plagued the study of sunspots. B) Recent research combining astronomical and climate data provides a promising foundation for better understanding the relationship between sunspots and Earth's weather. C) Despite recent breakthroughs, scientists are unlikely to ever fully explain correlations between sunspot activity and Earth's weather patterns. D) Scientists have used data from the *Solar Maximum Mission* satellite to explain how sunspots affect Earth's climate during the quasi-biennial oscillation's west phase.	**Step 1: Unpack the question stem.** Questions that ask for the main idea or primary purpose of a passage are Global questions. With a strong big picture summary, these can be answered quickly and confidently. **Step 2: Research the answer.** The main idea of this passage was that scientists have learned quite a bit about sunspots and Earth's weather patterns (e.g., faculas, the QBO, and storms) and are optimistic that they will soon be able to provide more answers. **Step 3: Predict the correct answer.** The correct answer will match the Main Idea summary. **Step 4: Find the one correct answer.** Choice **(B)** is correct; it matches the scope of the passage without being too broad or too narrow. (A) is too narrow (Labitzke and van Loon were only two of the scientists cited in the passage) and distorts the passage by suggesting that they have "cleared up" the mysteries, when they admit, they're still baffled by some of what they've found. (C) presents a pessimistic tone at odds with the optimism that closes the passage. (D) distorts what the passage said about the solar cycle and the QBO; scientists discovered a correlation between the two, but have not yet explained how or why this happens.

Question	Analysis
2. The author's point of view can best be described as that of A) a meteorologist voicing optimism that the findings of recent solar research will improve weather forecasting. B) an astronomer presenting a digest of current findings to a review board of other astronomers. C) a science writer explaining the possible influence of a solar phenomenon on terrestrial weather patterns. D) a historian listing the contributions to climate science made by the *Solar Maximum Mission*.	**Step 1: Unpack the question stem.** Questions that ask about the passage's main idea or the author's overall purpose or point of view are called Global questions. **Step 2: Research the answer.** This question covers the passage as a whole, so the Big Picture summaries will help predict the answer. **Step 3: Predict the answer.** The author's purpose is to outline recent developments in sunspot research, and the tone and language suggest a general readership. The correct answer will reflect this. **Step 4: Find the one correct answer.** Choice **(C)** matches the prediction. (A) goes outside the scope of the passage; the author focuses on the science behind the discoveries, not on applications like weather forecasting. (B) suggests an expert presentation to an academic peer group; this passage is more journalistic than that. (D) is too narrow; the *Solar Maximum Mission* is mentioned only in the third paragraph.
3. The passage indicates which of the following about the sun's luminosity and the solar cycle? A) Scientists have found no correlation between the sun's brightness and the solar cycle. B) The sun is brightest at the nadir of the solar cycle. C) The sun is brightest at the peak and again at the nadir of the solar cycle. D) The sun is brightest at the peak of the solar cycle.	**Step 1: Unpack the question stem.** A question asking what the passage "indicates" is a Detail question. The correct answer will paraphrase something stated explicitly in the passage. Research paragraph 3 where the author discusses the solar cycle. **Step 2: Research the answer.** Data gathered by the SMM satellite shows that the sun is brightest at the peak of the solar cycle and dimmest at its nadir. **Step 3: Predict the answer.** Your research provides clear-cut criteria for the correct answer: the sun is brightest at the peak of the solar cycle and dimmest at its nadir. **Step 4: Find the one correct answer.** Choice **(D)** matches your prediction and is correct. (A) is contradicted by the passage, though this choice may have been tempting if you stopped after paragraph 2, which says that, until relatively recently, scientists did not know how the two were correlated. (B) says the opposite of what the passage says on this subject. (C) misstates the passage by claiming that the sun brightens again at the nadir of the solar cycle.

Question	Analysis
4. Which one of the following provides the best evidence for the answer to the previous question?	**Step 1: Unpack the question stem.** This is a Command of Evidence question that asks you to locate a piece of text stated in the passage that supports another statement, most often, as it is in this case, the correct answer to the preceding question.
A) Lines 10–11 ("One problem . . . understood")	**Step 2: Research the answer.** In Command of Evidence questions, the answer choices all designate specific sentences or statements in the passage and indicate their precise locations by line numbers. Use the choices to conduct your research, keeping in mind that the correct answer here must support the correct answer to the preceding question.
B) Lines 15–18 ("Scientists had . . . constant")	
C) Lines 20–24 ("The latter . . . cycle")	**Step 3: Predict the answer.** The answer to the preceding question came directly from the final sentence in paragraph 3, lines 27–33.
D) Lines 27–31 ("These data . . . nadir")	**Step 4: Find the one correct answer.** Choice **(D)** cites the evidence for the correct answer to the preceding question, making it the correct choice for this Command of Evidence question. (A) summarizes the problems that scientists studying sunspots had in the past. (B) comes from paragraph 2 and describes the questions scientists still had before the SMM satellite data. (C) comes from the beginning of paragraph 3; it describes the source of the data but does not support the answer to the preceding question.

Question	Analysis
5. Based on information in the passage, it can most reasonably be inferred that faculas A) are directly responsible for increased temperatures on Earth. B) have a dimming effect on the sun's luminescence during sunspot activity. C) are mostly likely to appear at the peak of the solar cycle. D) grow in number as the number of sunspots decreases.	**Step 1: Unpack the question stem.** Questions that ask you for a statement that is "based on" the passage are Inference questions. The correct answer may combine two statements to reach a conclusion. **Step 2: Research the answer.** Faculas are discussed in paragraph 4. The passage says they are likely areas where the energy blocked by sunspots breaks through the sun's surface, and that they are probably why the sun is brightest when sunspot activity is high even though sunspots slightly dim the sun. **Step 3: Predict the answer.** In most Inference questions, you won't be able to predict the correct answer word-for-word, but you can characterize the correct answer as the only one that will follow directly from the relevant text (in this case, paragraph 4). **Step 4: Find the one correct answer.** Choice **(C)** is correct; if faculas are caused by sunspots, there will likely be more of them when there are more sunspots, in other words, at the peak of the solar cycle. (A) is too strong; scientists have found an indirect relationship between sunspot activity and Earth's weather (line 47). (B) is the opposite of what the passage states; faculas are so bright that they "more than compensate" for sunspots' dimming effect. (D) is the direct opposite of the correct answer.

Question	Analysis
6. Which one of the following provides the best evidence for the answer to the previous question? A) Lines 20–24 ("The latter . . . cycle") B) Lines 34–35 ("The data . . . brighter") C) Lines 36–41 ("When a . . . effect") D) Lines 46–47 ("Meteorological . . . indirectly")	**Step 1: Unpack the question stem.** This is a Command of Evidence question that asks you to locate a piece of text stated in the passage that supports another statement, most often, as it is in this case, the correct answer to the preceding question. **Step 2: Research the answer.** Because the previous question was about faculas, the correct answer to this question supports the fact that sunspots are most likely to appear at the peak of the solar cycle. **Step 3: Predict the answer.** For Command of Evidence questions asking for the text that supports the previous answer, use that answer to evaluate the excerpt in each choice. **Step 4: Find the one correct answer.** Choice **(C)** is correct; this is the sentence that explains the relationship between sunspots and faculas, and thus supports the correct answer to the previous question. (A) cites text that provides background information about the SMM. (B) contains a sentence that sets up the introduction of faculas but does not support the correct answer from the previous question. (D) is from the paragraph in which the author begins discussing the relationship between the solar cycle and Earth's weather.
7. As used in line 45, "manifest" most nearly means A) impact. B) disguise. C) itemize. D) reveal.	**Step 1: Unpack the question stem.** This is a Vocabulary-in-Context question. The correct answer will be a word that could take the place of the word in the question stem without changing the meaning of the sentence. **Step 2: Research the answer.** For Vocab-in-Context, read the full sentence containing the word cited in the question stem. **Step 3: Predict the answer.** The scientists in the passage are studying whether the influence of sunspots can be seen in Earth's weather, so manifest must mean something like *show* or *display*. **Step 4: Find the one correct answer.** The prediction leads to the correct answer, **(D)**. Choice (A) does not fit the context; the solar cycle might impact the weather, but wouldn't impact itself. (B) means the opposite of the correct answer. (C) suggests another meaning of the word manifest, which could also refer to a list of items in a shipment.

Question	Analysis
8. According to the passage, Labitzke and van Loon's research on the quasi-biennial oscillation (QBO) shows that A) the QBO's west phase correlates to the solar cycle. B) the QBO's west phase has a longer duration than that of its east phase. C) the QBO shows no correlation with the solar cycle. D) the reasons for the QBO's correlation to the solar cycle are now well understood.	**Step 1: Unpack the question stem.** "According to the passage" signals a Detail question. The answer will be contained in the passage text. **Step 2: Research the answer.** The QBO is introduced in paragraph 5, and Labitzke and van Loon's research is discussed in detail in paragraph 6. **Step 3: Predict the answer.** In a question like this one, it's difficult to predict the exact language of the correct answer choice, but we know it will conform to one of the facts presented in paragraph 6. The researchers tried to correlate temperature and air pressure to the solar cycle. At first, they saw no connection, but when they broke down the QBO into its east and west phases, they found a correlation to the west phase. **Step 4: Find the one correct answer.** Choice **(A)** matches the last sentence of paragraph 6 and is correct. (B) contradicts the passage; the shift from east to west and back occurs roughly every two years. (C) misuses a detail from the passage; the two researchers found no correlation *until* they split the QBO into its east and west phases. (D) contradicts paragraph 8, in which the scientists reveal that they still aren't sure why the QBO's west phase correlates to sunspot activity.

Question	Analysis
9. The main purpose of the questions in the second-to-last paragraph (lines 76–84) is to A) emphasize how little scientists know about the solar constant. B) explain more fully the mysterious nature of the scientists' findings. C) question the basis upon which these scientists built their hypotheses. D) express doubts about the scientists' interpretations of their findings.	**Step 1: Unpack the question stem.** A question that asks why the author included something in the text is a Function question. The correct answer will explain the author's purpose for including questions in paragraph 8. **Step 2: Research the answer.** This question stem leads you directly to paragraph 8. Determine what the author was trying to achieve by including questions there. **Step 3: Predict the answer.** The author uses the questions in paragraph 8 to illustrate why the scientists consider some of their findings "rather mysterious": despite all that they've learned to date, there are still several questions they can't answer. **Step 4: Find the one correct answer.** The prediction leads to the correct answer, **(B)**; the questions are included to explain why the scientists would consider their finding *mysterious*. (A) doesn't match the context of paragraph 8, which follows several paragraphs about how much scientists have recently learned. (C) runs counter to the author's purpose; the author doesn't try to call the scientist's findings into question. (D) is also out of step with the author's position; the author doesn't say or imply that the scientists have misunderstood the discoveries.

Question	Analysis
10. The use of the quoted phrase "look like breakthroughs" in line 88 is primarily meant to convey the idea that A) information about the solar cycle has allowed scientists to predict changes in Earth's complex climate system. B) additional analysis of the link between the solar cycle and Earth's weather may yield useful models. C) despite the associated costs, space missions can lead to important discoveries. D) an alternative interpretation of the data may contradict the initial findings.	**Step 1: Unpack the question stem.** A question that asks how an author supports a point made in the passage, or that asks why the author included something, is a Function question. **Step 2: Research the answer.** This question stem contains a line number. Examine the text immediately before and after the cited line to determine the context of the quote. The quote from the question stem was given by John A. Eddy who believes that the recent findings will lead to additional exciting discoveries about the relationship between sunspots and Earth's weather patterns **Step 3: Predict the answer.** The author includes the quote to show optimism about the potential for further research. **Step 4: Find the one correct answer.** The prediction matches correct answer **(B)**. Choice (A) is too strong; scientists may create predictive models in the near future, but they haven't yet. (C) appears to refer to the *Solar Maximum Mission*, but Eddy's quote refers to that *and* the subsequent research; the author doesn't include Eddy's quote to make a point just about space missions. (D) runs contrary to Eddy's optimism.

Putting It All Together

That's the expert's approach to SAT Reading in action. Take a moment to go over the steps one more time. Imagine applying them to the next question set you'll try. As you use the Method for Reading Questions repeatedly, it will become second nature. You won't have to say "Step 1, step 2, . . . " in your head; you'll just be performing them, and you'll be improving your score in the SAT Reading section as you do.

As you consider the purpose of strategic reading and the steps of the Method for Reading Questions, think back to what you saw the SAT expert accomplish in each step as he tackled the Sunspots passage and its questions.

SAT READING PASSAGE STRATEGY
• Extract everything you can from the pre-passage blurb
• Read each paragraph actively
• Summarize the passage's big picture

- SAT experts never skip the pre-passage blurb. They quickly process any information that it provides for the context of the passage or that helps them anticipate what the author will cover.

- Great test takers read *actively*, asking what the author's purpose is in writing each paragraph. They also anticipate where the passage will go. Experts "*map*" the passage by jotting down summaries for each paragraph. They might also circle or underline keywords that indicate the author's opinion, details she wishes to highlight or emphasize, and the comparisons and contrasts she makes in the text. You will focus on active reading and passage mapping in chapter 14.

- Experts pause for a moment after actively reading the passage to summarize the big picture by noting the passage's main idea and the author's primary purpose in writing it.

SAT Method for Reading Questions	
Step 1.	Unpack the question stem
Step 2.	Research the answer
Step 3.	Predict the answer
Step 4.	Find the one correct answer

- **Step 1**. Great test takers determine the kind of question being asked, which indicates the kind of thinking and research the question requires. They also look for clues in the question stem to tell them where in the passage to find the correct answer. In chapter 15, you'll learn the characteristics of six types of questions found in the SAT Reading section and you'll learn to spot the most common research clues.

- **Step 2**. SAT experts never answer a question on a whim. Instead they turn to the passage text or to their summaries of it. Here's where a good passage map becomes invaluable. If you're unsure where in the passage a detail or opinion was mentioned, many SAT Reading questions could lead you to reread all or most of the passage. That's a huge waste of time. With practice, you'll learn to use the research clues from the question stem to zero in on the relevant lines of text or paragraph summary.

- **Step 3**. Before reading the answer choices, top scorers predict (or at least characterize) what the correct answer will say. This allows them to evaluate each choice against the prediction. It's not always possible to predict the correct answer word for word, but you should be able to use your research to establish the criteria for the correct answer.

- **Step 4**. In SAT Reading questions, there is *one* correct answer. The other choices are demonstrably incorrect. Test takers who start reading the answer choices before completing steps 2 (Research) and 3 (Predict) often find themselves rereading portions of the passage after each answer choice, or worse, comparing the answer choices to each other instead of testing them against a strong prediction. If you find yourself struggling with two or more answer choices, stop. Rephrase your prediction to establish what the correct answer must say and evaluate the choices against that prediction.

By reading strategically and using the Method for SAT Reading Questions every time you practice, you'll internalize the steps. By test day, you'll be attacking this section efficiently and accurately without even thinking about it.

In the next section, you'll see another SAT Reading passage accompanied by 11 questions. Map the passage and apply the Method for SAT Reading Questions presented in this lesson to answer the questions as quickly and confidently as possible.

Reading

How Much Have You Learned?

Directions: Take 15 minutes to map this passage and answer the questions. Assess your work by comparing it to the expert responses at the end of the chapter.

Questions 1-11 refer to the following passage.

This passage is adapted from Carrie Chapman Catt's 1917 "Address to the United States Congress." Catt served as president of the National American Woman Suffrage Association, which advocated giving women the right to vote; the closing arguments from her speech are excerpted below.

Your party platforms have pledged woman suffrage. Then why not be honest, frank friends of our cause, adopt it in reality as your own, make it a party program and "fight with us"? As
5 a party measure—a measure of all parties—why not put the amendment through Congress and the Legislatures? We shall all be better friends, we shall have a happier nation, we women will be free to support loyally the party of our choice,
10 and we shall be far prouder of our history.

"There is one thing mightier than kings and armies"—aye, than Congresses and political parties—"the power of an idea when its time has come to move." The time for woman suffrage has
15 come. The woman's hour has struck. If parties prefer to postpone action longer and thus do battle with this idea, they challenge the inevitable. The idea will not perish; the party which opposes it may. Every delay, every trick, every political
20 dishonesty from now on will antagonize the women of the land more and more, and when the party or parties which have so delayed woman suffrage finally let it come, their sincerity will be doubted and their appeal to the new voters will
25 be met with suspicion. This is the psychology of the situation. Can you afford the risk? Think it over.

We know you will meet opposition. There are a few "woman haters" left, a few "old males
30 of the tribe," as Vance Thompson calls them, whose duty they believe it to be to keep women in the places they have carefully picked out for them. Treitschke, made world famous by war literature, said some years ago: "Germany, which
35 knows all about Germany and France, knows

far better what is good for Alsace-Lorraine than that miserable people can possibly know." A few American Treitschkes we have who know better than women what is good for them.
40 There are women, too. . . . But the world does not wait for such as these, nor does Liberty pause to heed the plaint of men and women with a grouch. She does not wait for those who have a special interest to serve, nor a selfish reason for
45 depriving other people of freedom. Holding her torch aloft, Liberty is pointing the way onward and upward and saying to America, "Come."

To you the supporters of our cause, in Senate and House, and the number is large, the
50 suffragists of the nation express their grateful thanks. This address is not meant for you. We are more truly appreciative of all you have done than any words can express. We ask you to make a last, hard fight for the amendment during the
55 present session. Since last we asked for a vote on this amendment your position has been fortified by the addition to suffrage territory of Great Britain, Canada, and New York.

Some of you have been too indifferent to give
60 more than casual attention to this question. It is worthy of your immediate consideration—a question big enough to engage the attention of our Allies in war time, is too big a question for you to neglect. . . .
65 Gentlemen, we hereby petition you, our only designated representatives, to redress our grievances by the immediate passage of the influence to secure its ratification in your own state, in order that the women of our nation
70 may be endowed with political freedom that our nation may resume its world leadership in democracy.

Woman suffrage is coming—you know it. Will you, Honorable Senators and Members of the
75 House of Representatives, help or hinder it?

1. What was Carrie Chapman Catt's primary purpose in giving this speech?

    A) To assert that women will vote for the party that supports their cause

    B) To demand more women candidates on political party tickets

    C) To persuade lawmakers to pass an amendment ensuring women's right to vote

    D) To rally support for women's equal representation in Congress

2. The stance that Catt takes in her speech is best described as that of

    A) a historian reflecting on historical events.

    B) an official campaigning for political office.

    C) an activist advocating for legislative reform.

    D) a reporter investigating a current controversy.

3. What counterclaim does Catt offer to the argument that some men and women still oppose suffrage?

    A) They are not voicing their opinions in Congress.

    B) They cannot stop the inevitable.

    C) They do have just cause for opposition.

    D) They have no legal basis for their claims.

4. Which choice provides the best evidence for the answer to the previous question?

    A) Lines 7–10 ("We shall all . . . our history")

    B) Lines 48–51 ("To you . . . grateful thanks")

    C) Lines 55–58 ("Since last . . . New York")

    D) Lines 60–64 ("It is worthy . . . to neglect")

5. As used in line 20, "antagonize" most nearly means

    A) dishearten.

    B) embitter.

    C) humiliate.

    D) inhibit.

6. The phrase in lines 21–25 ("when the party . . . with suspicion") implies that

    A) women voters will not support lawmakers who have resisted suffrage.

    B) women will not run for office because they do not trust politicians.

    C) women will vote more women into political office.

    D) women's influence on Congress will be minimal and is not a threat.

7. Catt most likely discusses Treitschke (lines 33–37) for which of the following reasons?

    A) To demonstrate support for women's suffrage in Europe

    B) To remind her audience of what happened to a politician who supported unpopular legislation

    C) To contrast his views on Alsace-Lorraine with the American values of freedom and democracy

    D) To draw an analogy between his views and the views of those who believe they know better than women what is best for women

8. The passage indicates which one of the following about the status of women's suffrage at the time of Catt's speech?

    A) At the time, only a minority of the U.S. population supported women's right to vote.

    B) Women already had the right to vote in at least one state in the United States.

    C) An earlier amendment to grant women the right to vote had been defeated.

    D) The women's suffrage movement was a recent development in American politics.

9. Which choice provides the best evidence for the answer to the previous question?

    A) Lines 14–17 ("The time . . . inevitable")

    B) Lines 28–33 ("There are . . . them")

    C) Lines 55–58 ("Since last . . . New York")

    D) Lines 65–72 ("Gentlemen . . . democracy")

10. As used in line 66, "redress" most nearly means

    A) appeal.

    B) communicate.

    C) implement.

    D) remedy.

11. What can you most reasonably infer from the thoughts expressed in lines 69–72 ("in order that . . . in democracy")?

    A) No citizen in our democracy is free as long as women cannot vote.

    B) Other nations have demanded that our government grant woman suffrage.

    C) A nation needs more women in positions of leadership.

    D) Woman suffrage is essential to true democracy.

Answers and Explanations

Carrie Chapman Catt Passage Map

This passage is adapted from Carrie Chapman Catt's 1917 "Address to the United States Congress." Catt served as president of the National American Woman Suffrage Association, which advocated giving women the right to vote; the closing arguments from her speech are excerpted below.

Your party platforms have pledged woman suffrage. Then why not be honest, frank friends of our cause, adopt it in reality as your own, make it a party program and "fight with us"? As
5 a party measure—a measure of all parties—why not put the amendment through Congress and the Legislatures? We shall all be better friends, we shall have a happier nation, we women will be free to support loyally the party of our choice,
10 and we shall be far prouder of our history.

"There is one thing mightier than kings and armies"—aye, than Congresses and political parties—"the power of an idea when its time has come to move." The time for woman suffrage has
15 come. The woman's hour has struck. If parties prefer to postpone action longer and thus do battle with this idea, they challenge the inevitable. The idea will not perish; the party which opposes it may. Every delay, every trick, every political
20 dishonesty from now on will antagonize the women of the land more and more, and when the party or parties which have so delayed woman suffrage finally let it come, their sincerity will be doubted and their appeal to the new voters will
25 be met with suspicion. This is the psychology of the situation. Can you afford the risk? Think it over.

We know you will meet opposition. There are a few "woman haters" left, a few "old males
30 of the tribe," as Vance Thompson calls them, whose duty they believe it to be to keep women in the places they have carefully picked out for them. Treitschke, made world famous by war literature, said some years ago: "Germany, which
35 knows all about Germany and France, knows far better what is good for Alsace-Lorraine than

Call for both parties to support women's vote

Time for women's suffrage is NOW

Those who oppose will be suspect in the future

Still have opponents

Examples

ANALYSIS

Pre-passage blurb: You learn a lot here. Catt is speaking to Congress in 1917. She represents an organization pushing for women's suffrage, that is, the right to vote. The passage represents her closing arguments, so you can expect her to offer evidence and reasoning in support of this cause.

¶1: Catt reminds the members of Congress that their parties have supported women's suffrage in their platforms and encourages them, as individuals, to support it as well. It will make the U.S. a happier, prouder nation.

¶2: Catt asserts that women *will* get the right to vote and, as a warning to congressmen opposing suffrage, she argues that women with the vote will most likely not support the congressmen who tried to delay or undermine their right.

¶3: Catt admits that there will still be some who oppose women's suffrage, but argues that their ideas are out-of-date. She is trying to persuade congressmen who might be swayed by a vocal opposition. She uses a moral argument by equating suffrage with liberty.

Reading

that miserable people can possibly know." A
few American Treitschkes we have who know
better than women what is good for them.

40 There are women, too…But the world does not
wait for such as these, nor does Liberty pause
to heed the plaint of men and women with a
grouch. She does not wait for those who have a
special interest to serve, nor a selfish reason for

45 depriving other people of freedom. Holding her
torch aloft, Liberty is pointing the way onward
and upward and saying to America, "Come."

To you the supporters of our cause, in
Senate and House, and the number is large, the

50 suffragists of the nation express their grateful
thanks. This address is not meant for you We
are more truly appreciative of all you have done
than any words can express. We ask you to make
a last, hard fight for the amendment during the

55 present session. Since last we asked for a vote on
this amendment your position has been fortified
by the addition to suffrage territory of Great
Britain, Canada, and New York.

Some of you have been too indifferent to give

60 more than casual attention to this question. It
is worthy of your immediate consideration—a
question big enough to engage the attention of
our Allies in war time, is too big a question for
you to neglect…

65 Gentlemen, we hereby petition you, our
only designated representatives, to redress our
grievances by the immediate passage of the
influence to secure its ratification in your own
state, in order that the women of our nation

70 may be endowed with political freedom that
our nation may resume its world leadership in
democracy.

Woman suffrage is coming—you know it. Will
you, Honorable Senators and Members of the

75 House of Representatives, help or hinder it?

BUT— liberty will overcome

Thanks to supporters- Help us fight

Other countries have suffrage

Suffrage— big/immediate issue

Petition to pass suffrage— then U.S. can again lead in freedom

Final appeal to Congress

¶4: Catt thanks members who already support her cause and encourages them to vote during the present session. She makes this appeal timely by referring to other countries and states that have adopted women's suffrage already.

¶5: Catt chastises those who have ignored the debate over suffrage—it's too big an issue—equating it with war.

¶6: Catt encourages lawmakers to support the suffrage amendment in their various states. She argues that only by granting suffrage can the U.S. once again be a leader of democracy in the world.

¶7: Catt's final appeal is for members of Congress to pick a side: are you with us or against us?

BIG PICTURE

Main Idea: Women's suffrage is inevitable; lawmakers should support it now for reasons both moral (making America freer and more democratic) and practical (better political prospects in the future).

Author's Purpose: To persuade members of Congress to pass a bill sending a proposed amendment to the Constitution (to grant women the right to vote) to the states

---

1. C

Difficulty: Medium

Category: Global

Strategic Advice: A question asking for an author's or speaker's primary purpose is a Global question. Consult your big picture summary to predict the correct answer.

Getting to the Answer: The pre-passage blurb tells you that Carrie Chapman Catt is speaking to Congress on behalf of the National American Woman Suffrage Association. In the first paragraph, she asks lawmakers to support a constitutional amendment. Additional context provided in the passage makes clear that the amendment would grant women suffrage, making **(C)** correct. While (A) captures a key part of Catt's reasoning, it does not reflect her purpose in giving the speech. (B) distorts the passage; Catt is calling for suffrage, not necessarily for female candidates. Similarly, (D) goes beyond the scope of Catt's speech.

2. C

Difficulty: Easy

Category: Global

Strategic Advice: Some Global questions ask about an author's overall attitude or the perspective from which the passage was written. Use your big picture summary of the main idea and the author's purpose to predict the correct answer.

Getting to the Answer: In the passage, Catt gives a speech in which she appeals to legislators to pass a constitutional amendment, or legislative reform, to grant women suffrage. She is speaking as a political activist. **(C)** is correct. The other three answers all distort Catt's purpose and main point.

3. B

Difficulty: Medium

Category: Detail

Strategic Advice: A question calling for a claim the author or speaker makes explicitly in the text is a Detail question. The research clue in the question stem points to paragraph 3.

Getting to the Answer: In paragraph 3, Catt acknowledges the opposition to woman suffrage, citing "woman haters" (line 29), "old males of the tribe" (lines 29–30), and "women, too" (line 40). She suggests that the argu-

ments against suffrage are dated and ineffectual, and goes on to state that the world will not slow down and that the cause of liberty will continue. Her underlying message is that suffrage is unavoidable, which echoes her earlier statement in line 17. All of this leads to **(B)** as the correct answer. (A) distorts Catt's response; whether opponents continue to speak out is almost irrelevant in her opinion. (C) is contradicted by Catt's rhetoric; suffrage is just, and it will prevail. (D) distorts Catt's argument; she addresses the moral and sociological reasons for endorsing suffrage.

4. C

Difficulty: Medium

Category: Command of Evidence

Strategic Advice: This is a Command of Evidence question. The correct answer to this question will cite text that provides evidence, either in reasoning or in fact, to support the claim in the answer to the previous question. Each answer choice contains line numbers that help focus your research as you evaluate the choices.

Getting to the Answer: The answer to the previous question asserts that woman suffrage is inevitable. Evidence to support this claim would show that suffrage is advancing, as demonstrated by **(C)**. (A) provides practical reasons to support suffrage but does not support a claim of its inevitability. (B) offers thanks to lawmakers who already support suffrage. (D) is an exhortation to immediate action, not evidence of inevitable victory for the women's suffrage movement.

5. B

Difficulty: Medium

Category: Vocab-in-Context

Strategic Advice: The correct answer to a Vocab-in-Context question like this one will reflect the specific meaning of the word in the context of the surrounding sentence and text.

Getting to the Answer: The text states, "Every delay, every trick, every political dishonesty from now on will antagonize the women of the land more and more" (lines 19–21). The surrounding text suggests that women will become only more resolved to their purpose as a result of delay, as well as more angry—or bitter—with politicians who forestall them, making **(B)** correct. (A) implies that women will give up; Catt clearly argues the opposite. (C) distorts the meaning of the sentence;

tricks and delays will anger women and encourage them to punish deceitful politicians at the polls. (D) sounds plausible (after all, the delays and tricks are meant to impede suffrage), but it doesn't fit the context of the sentence, which predicts a backlash from these tactics.

6. A

Difficulty: Medium

Category: Inference

Strategic Advice: The word "implies" identifies this as an Inference question. The correct answer will reflect the underlying or implied meaning of the excerpted line within the context of the surrounding text. The research clue points to the second half of paragraph 2.

Getting to the Answer: The text cited in the question stem asserts that new voters (the women enfranchised by suffrage) will mistrust political parties whose members have resisted suffrage; this leads to **(A)** as the correct answer. The message of choice (B) runs counter to Catt's argument. (C) goes too far; Catt asserts that women voters will flee the parties who have resisted suffrage, and not that they will vote for female candidates. (D) states the opposite of what Catt implies here.

7. D

Difficulty: Hard

Category: Function

Strategic Advice: A question that asks why an author included a detail or reference in her text is a Function question. Research the referenced detail (in this case, Treitschke) to see the author's purpose for including it in the passage.

Getting to the Answer: For Catt, Treitschke is an example of an outsider who thought he knew better than the residents of an area what was best for them. She analogizes that to male politicians who think they know what's best for women. Choice **(D)** describes Catt's use of the analogy. (A) conflates Treitschke with Catt's later statement that women's suffrage had passed in the United Kingdom. (B) misapplies the Treitschke example to a different argument Catt makes in her speech. (C) distorts Catt's point about Treitschke; she used him as an example of someone whose reasoning was misguided reasoning, not as someone who was anti-democratic.

8. B

Difficulty: Medium

Category: Detail

Strategic Advice: The word "indicates" signals a Detail question. The correct answer will clearly restate or paraphrase something stated in the passage.

Getting to the Answer: The entire speech is, of course, about women's suffrage, but Catt addresses the current status of women's right to vote explicitly near the end of paragraph 4. There, she tells Congress that suffrage laws have recently been passed in Great Britain, Canada, and New York. That directly supports choice **(B)**. (A) is too extreme; in paragraph 3, Catt admits that suffrage still had opponents, but she does not state that only a minority of voters support it. (C) is not supported anywhere in Catt's speech. (D) is a distortion of Catt's claim that momentum for women's suffrage was on the rise.

9. C

Difficulty: Medium

Category: Command of Evidence

Strategic Advice: This is a Command of Evidence question asking you to locate the line in the passage that supports the correct answer to the preceding question. Use the line references in each answer choice to research the passage text.

Getting to the Answer: The correct answer to the preceding question asserted that, at the time of Catt's speech, at least one state in the Union had already granted women the right to vote. That is directly supported by the text cited in choice **(C)**, where Catt encourages suffrage advocates in Congress with the fact that New York recently gave women the right to vote. (A) is Catt's warning to the members of Congress about a potential backlash for their failure to support the suffrage amendment, which is unrelated to the fact that women in New York can vote. (B) cites text in which Catt describes the opponents of women's suffrage; that might have tempted a test taker who chose (A) for the preceding question. (D) contains Catt's call to action in paragraph 6; that does not support the answer to the preceding question.

10. D

Difficulty: Medium

Category: Vocab-in-Context

Strategic Advice: This is a Vocab-in-Context question; the correct answer will correctly replace the original word and retain the meaning of the original sentence.

Getting to the Answer: The text states that Catt and her supporters want congressional lawmakers to "redress our grievances" (lines 66–67), meaning to set right—or to remedy—the ills committed against women. **(D)** reflects this meaning. None of the other choices fits logically into the sentence.

11. D

Difficulty: Medium

Category: Inference

Strategic Advice: The word "implied" signals an Inference question. The correct answer will follow from Catt's statement in the excerpted line. The research clue points you to paragraph 6.

Getting to the Answer: The excerpted line states that once women have the political freedom granted by suffrage, then the nation will resume its leadership in democracy. The implication is that the nation is not a leader in democracy as long as it denies women the right to vote. Therefore, **(D)** is correct. (A) is too extreme for the specific statement cited in the question stem. (B) misuses a detail from paragraph 4; other countries have adopted women's suffrage, but Catt doesn't say they've called on the United States to do the same. (C) is too broad; the quoted statement focuses specifically on the right to vote, not on electing women.

Reflect

Directions: Take a few minutes to recall what you've learned and what you've been practicing in this chapter. Consider the following questions, jot down your best answer for each one, and then compare your reflections to the expert responses on the following page. Use your level of confidence to to determine what to do next.

Describe active, or strategic, reading on SAT passages.

_____

What do SAT experts mean by summarizing the big picture of a passage?

_____

How can writing brief "margin notes" help you answer SAT Reading questions more effectively?

_____

What does an SAT expert look for in the question stem of an SAT Reading question?

_____

Why do expert test takers predict or characterize the correct answer to each SAT Reading question before assessing the answer choices?

_____

What will you do differently on future passages and their questions?

_____

Expert Responses

Describe active, or strategic, reading on SAT passages.

Because the SAT asks many questions about why an author has written the passage or about how the author makes a point, expert test takers read for the author's purpose and main idea. Noting keywords that indicate a shift or contrast in points of view or that indicate opinions and emphasis help keep SAT experts on point, as they anticipate where the passage will go.

What do SAT experts mean by summarizing the big picture of a passage?

To read for the big picture means being able to accurately summarize the main idea of a passage and to note the author's purpose for writing it. The big picture summary helps you answer Global questions and questions that ask about the author's opinion or point of view.

How can writing brief "margin notes" help you answer SAT Reading questions more effectively?

Jotting down margin notes provides a reference "map" to the subject or purpose of each paragraph in the passage. It helps locate specific subjects or opinions expressed in the passage when they are called out in the questions.

What does an SAT expert look for in the question stem of an SAT Reading question?

Each question stem indicates the type of question and contains clues as to whether the answer will come from researching the passage text or from the big picture summary. Many question stems have specific clues (for example, line numbers or references to details from the passage) that tell you precisely where to research.

Why do expert test takers predict or characterize the correct answer to each SAT Reading question before assessing the answer choices?

Predicting or characterizing the correct answer allows you to evaluate each answer choice one time and to avoid rereading for every answer choice. Wrong answers often distort what the passage said or misuse details from the passage, so it's best to research the passage once to know what the correct answer must say before diving into the choices.

What will you do differently on future passages and their questions?

There is no one-size-fits-all answer to this question. Each student has his or her own initial strengths and opportunities in the Reading section. What's important here is that you're honestly self-reflective. Take what you need from the expert's examples and strive to apply it to your own performance. Many test takers convince themselves that they'll never get faster or more confident in SAT Reading, but the truth is, many test takers who now routinely ace the Reading section were much slower and more hesitant before they learned to approach this section systematically and strategically.

Next Steps

If you answered most questions correctly in the "How Much Have You Learned?" section, and if your responses to the Reflect questions were similar to those of the SAT expert, then consider the Method for SAT Reading Questions an area of strength and move on to the next chapter. Come back to this topic periodically to prevent yourself from getting rusty.

If you don't yet feel confident, review the material in this chapter, then try the questions you missed again. As always, be sure to review the explanations closely.

CHAPTER 14

SAT Reading Passage Strategies

LEARNING OBJECTIVES

After completing this chapter, you will be able to:

- Identify keywords that promote active reading and relate passage text to the questions
- Create short, accurate margin notes that help you research the text efficiently
- Summarize the big picture of the passage

How Much Do You Know?

Directions: In this chapter, you'll learn how SAT experts actively read the passage, take notes, and summarize the main idea to prepare themselves to answer all of the passage's questions quickly and confidently. You saw this kind of reading modeled in the previous chapter. To get ready for the current chapter, take five minutes to actively read the following passage by 1) noting the keywords that indicate the author's point of view and the passage's structure, 2) jotting down a quick description next to each paragraph, and 3) summarizing the big picture (the passage's main idea and the author's purpose for writing it). When you're done, compare your work to the passage map on the following page.

Questions 1-11 refer to the following passage.

This passage is adapted from a 2018 article summarizing two different proposals for solving problems with maintaining New York City's mass transit system.

The history of the New York City subway system, quickly told: the first stations opened in 1904, and over the next century, it expanded to 472 stations,
5 more than any other subway system in the world, with 850 miles of track. Operating 24 hours a day seven days a week, with an average weekday ridership of approximately 5.7 million, it is the
10 planet's 7th-busiest rapid transit system. While the system is, on many levels, an amazing achievement, it is also beset by a problem that harms both quality of life and economic activity. Such a
15 large system must inevitably suffer from service interruptions and delays; normal wear and tear combined with the sheer age of the system necessitates regular maintenance. However, there
20 is no consensus as to the best way to accomplish the required repairs.

The current maintenance scheme is designed to minimize service interruptions. A subway line in need
25 of repair will be taken out of service during a comparatively less busy time, such as nights or weekends, while another line is re-routed to cover as many as possible of the missing line's
30 stops. The main advantage to this approach is that trains are not taken out of service during rush hour, when

most subway trips occur; subway service generally remains predictable
35 and commuters are, for the most part, able to use the system to get to their destinations on time.

But critics are quick to point out the disadvantages to this approach. Perhaps
40 most obvious is the confusion caused by trains switching lines. The labyrinthine system is hard enough to navigate at the best of times, especially for tourists. A subway rider on the A train naturally
45 expects the train to make stops on the A line. If, instead, it is diverted temporarily to the F line, the rider may find herself miles from her intended destination.
50 While annoying, the confusion arising from route switching is hardly the most serious problem with the current approach to repairs. Because the system runs 24 hours a
55 day, routine maintenance can generally be done only during the temporary closures on nights and weekends. This means that more serious repair and crucial preventative maintenance is
60 often neglected. Problems that could have been fixed or prevented reasonably expeditiously given a slightly longer closure wind up leading to major breakdowns and service interruptions
65 later on.

On rare occasions, such breakdowns have resulted in entire subway lines being shut down for months or even a year. Beginning in 2019, for
70 example, the L Train connecting lower

Manhattan to parts of Brooklyn was scheduled to close for as much as 15 months for long overdue service and upgrades. In a city fewer than half

75 of whose households own a car, this can have serious economic impacts. Residents of the affected area may face a much longer commute via an alternate subway line if one is available;

80 or, if there is no alternate subway service, they may need to take other, potentially more expensive, modes of transportation, such as taxis or ferries. Moreover, studies indicate that

85 increased stress from the commute to work can lead to lower productivity, and that businesses near the impacted lines may see decreased revenue as potential customers have a harder time getting to

90 them.

One controversial proposal for reducing breakdowns and the resulting transit interruptions is to end the subway's 24-hour service and to shut

95 down for several hours each night. Proponents of this plan argue that this would allow time, on a regular rather than sporadic basis, for more preventative maintenance. This, they

100 claim, would ultimately lead to more consistent service; rather than shutting down entire lines for long periods of a time, there would merely be shorter service outages overnight, when fewer

105 people use the subway system. While this may seem a preferable outcome to the economic consequences of a total shutdown resulting from a breakdown, it has its liabilities as well. While most

110 subway trips may occur during rush hour, not everyone works during the daytime. New York is famously known as the "the city that never sleeps." Doctors, nurses, bartenders, police

115 officers, and firefighters are just a few examples of occupations whose workers

need transportation at all hours of the day and night. Rather than be subjected to a relatively short period

120 of inconvenience, these workers would find their commutes irrevocably altered. One thing, at least, is clear: the city must carefully consider many economic and social factors in designing a subway

125 maintenance plan.

Reading

Check Your Work

Questions 1-11 refer to the following passage.

This passage is adapted from a 2018 article summarizing two different proposals for solving problems with maintaining New York City's mass transit system.

The history of the New York City subway system, quickly told: the first stations opened in 1904, and over the next century, it expanded to 472 stations,
5 more than any other subway system in the world, with 850 miles of track. Operating 24 hours a day seven days a week, with an average weekday ridership of approximately 5.7 million, it is the
10 planet's 7th-busiest rapid transit system. While the system is, on many levels, an amazing achievement, it is also beset by a problem that harms both quality of life and economic activity. Such a
15 large system must inevitably suffer from service interruptions and delays; normal wear and tear combined with the sheer age of the system necessitates regular maintenance. However, there
20 is no consensus as to the best way to accomplish the required repairs.

The current maintenance scheme is designed to minimize service interruptions. A subway line in need
25 of repair will be taken out of service during a comparatively less busy time, such as nights or weekends, while another line is re-routed to cover as many as possible of the missing line's
30 stops. The main advantage to this approach is that trains are not taken out of service during rush hour, when most subway trips occur; subway service generally remains predictable
35 and commuters are, for the most part, able to use the system to get to their destinations on time.

But critics are quick to point out the disadvantages to this approach. Perhaps

NYC subway: how to repair? diff. views

Current approach – night and weekend repairs

Critics: line switch confusion

ANALYSIS

Pre-passage blurb: This tells you that the topic of the passage is a debate over the New York City subway system. Expect to see at least two sides in the debate. Note where each different position is discussed.

SAT Reading Strategy: On the SAT, the blurb almost always contains the title of the book or article from which the passage was adapted. Sometimes the test maker will provide additional context as well. Always take advantage of it.

¶1: The author introduces the New York City subway system by highlighting its age and size. Those two factors are the reason maintenance is such a big issue. The scope of the passage comes at the end of the paragraph: there is no agreement on *how* best to perform upkeep on the massive system.

¶2: This paragraph outlines the current maintenance schedule. Repairs happen mostly on nights and weekends. The main advantage is that subway lines are not down during rush hours.

¶3: Here comes the opposing view. One disadvantage of the current system is that trains are re-routed causing confusion for riders.

40 most obvious is the ⟨confusion caused by⟩
trains switching lines. The labyrinthine
system is hard enough to navigate at the
best of times, especially for tourists. A
subway rider on the A train naturally
45 expects the train to make stops on
the A line. If, instead, it is diverted
temporarily to the F line, the rider may
find herself miles from her intended
destination.
50   While annoying, the confusion
arising from route switching is
⟨hardly the most serious⟩ problem
with the current approach to repairs.
⟨Because⟩ the system runs 24 hours a
55 day, routine maintenance can generally
be done only during the temporary
closures on nights and weekends. This
means that more serious repair and
crucial preventative maintenance is
60 often neglected. Problems that could
have been fixed or prevented reasonably
expeditiously given a slightly longer
closure wind up leading to ⟨major⟩
breakdowns and service interruptions
65 later on.
       On rare occasions, such breakdowns
have resulted in entire subway lines
being shut down for months or
even a year. Beginning in 2019, ⟨for⟩
70 ⟨example,⟩ the L Train connecting lower
Manhattan to parts of Brooklyn was
scheduled to close for as much as 15
months for long overdue service and
upgrades. In a city fewer than half
75 of whose households own a car, this
can have ⟨serious economic impacts⟩
Residents of the affected area may
face a much longer commute via an
alternate subway line if one is available;
80 or, if there is no alternate subway
service, they may need to take other,
potentially more expensive, modes
of transportation, such as taxis or
ferries. ⟨Moreover,⟩ studies indicate that
85 increased stress from the commute to

Even worse
– major
breakdowns

¶4: A second, worse problem with the current system is that it doesn't allow enough time for preventative maintenance. That leads to big problems down the line.

¶5: These big problems can shut down subway lines for weeks or months causing grave economic impact to affected riders and businesses.

Econ. & Soc.
harms of
shutdowns

work can lead to lower productivity, and that businesses near the impacted lines may see decreased revenue as potential customers have a harder time getting to
90 them.

One (controversial) proposal for reducing breakdowns and the resulting transit interruptions is to end the subway's 24-hour service and to shut
95 down for several hours each night. (Proponents) of this plan (argue) that this would allow time, on a regular rather than sporadic basis, for more preventative maintenance. This, they
100 claim, would (ultimately lead to) more consistent service; rather than shutting down entire lines for long periods of a time, there would merely be shorter service outages overnight, when fewer
105 people use the subway system. (While) this may seem a preferable outcome to the economic consequences of a total shutdown resulting from a breakdown, it has its liabilities as well. While most
110 subway trips may occur during rush hour, not everyone works during the daytime. New York is famously known as the "the city that never sleeps." Doctors, nurses, bartenders, police
115 officers, and firefighters are just a few examples of occupations whose workers need transportation at all hours of the day and night. Rather than be subjected to a relatively short period
120 of inconvenience, these workers would find their commutes irrevocably altered. (One thing, at least, is clear:) the city must carefully consider many economic and social factors in designing a subway
125 maintenance plan.

Alt proposal – stop 24-hour service

Pros

Cons

¶6: This paragraph opens with a controversial proposal: stop running the subway 24/7. While this would make more time for preventative maintenance, it too has a big disadvantage: many workers need to commute overnight. The author's conclusion is neutral: New York City has to weigh both sides to make the best decision.

BIG PICTURE

Main Idea: New York City must weigh different economic and social factors to design an effective subway maintenance plan.

Author's Purpose: To explain advantages and disadvantages in opposing views of how best to maintain the New York City subway

---

SAT Reading Strategies—Keywords, Margin Notes, and the Big Picture Summary

LEARNING OBJECTIVES

After this lesson, you will be able to:

- Identify keywords that promote active reading and relate passage text to the questions
- Create short, accurate margin notes that help you research the text efficiently
- Summarize the big picture of the passage

To read and map a passage like this:

This passage was adapted from an article titled "Millennials and the Market," written by a money management expert in 2018.

During the Golden Age of American manufacturing, it was expected that after putting in 30 to 40 years of tedious labor in a factory, workers
5 would be able to retire around age 65 and enjoy the benefits of retirement comforted by the thought that a pension and the Social Security system they had financed for decades would
10 cover their expenses. Unfortunately for millennials (people born between the early 1980s and late 1990s), prospects look increasingly bleak that they will get a return on their investment at
15 retirement age, despite continuing to fund programs like Social Security and Medicare. Fewer than a quarter of all Fortune 500 corporations still offer some form of pension plan to new
20 hires, and the move from company-funded pension plans to 401(k) plans and IRAs that began in the 1970s shows no sign of slackening. In this financial environment, it might be expected
25 that investment in the stock market would be at an all-time high. An analysis of the data, however, indicates a complicated and even fraught relationship between young adults and
30 the stock market.

The trauma associated with the Great Recession (which began in December 2007 and ended in June 2009) left many investors wary of stock
35 market volatility, and that hesitancy was exacerbated among young people, who saw a considerable portion of their families' wealth erased in short order. A study by Pfeffer, Danziger,
40 and Schoeni published in 2014 posited that the average American household

lost a third of its wealth, approximately $28,000, during the Great Recession. This was at the exact moment when a
45 great many millennials were making decisions about attending college, pursuing post-graduate studies, or entering the workforce. For a median-income family, those decisions were
50 all directly correlated to household wealth. The ripple effects of the Great Recession left many millennials ascribing blame directly to the stock market for missed opportunities.
55 Even with a full awareness that the stock market has rebounded and far exceeded the highs seen prior to the Great Recession, many millennials still feel trepidation about investing in the
60 stock market, preferring to save a larger percentage of their salaries than their parents and grandparents did.

Another factor that has directly impacted the willingness of millennials
65 to invest in the stock market is the seismic shift in the job market brought about by the "gig economy," in which short-term contracts and freelance work have replaced permanent
70 employment. To a large degree, the gig economy is still in its nascent phase, with many of the largest purveyors of jobs only incorporated in the last decade. Research has not adequately
75 kept track of the trend, with estimates of participation in the gig economy ranging from 4% to 40% in the United States. The ability to pick up work on a contingency basis allows
80 millennials to feel a greater level of control over their finances, something a significant number of them believe they cannot achieve through stock market investment. The increased
85 diversity of available methods for

building future wealth has caused many millennials to adopt an a la carte approach to preparing for retirement. But is it possible that this approach
90 has been clouded by some common misconceptions about wealth building?

One persistent, albeit erroneous, view is that real estate is a better investment instrument than a stock market
95 portfolio. While it is true that home equity is the stepping-stone from which most individuals begin to build their personal wealth, statistics make it clear that stock market investments are a more
100 stable and lucrative source of long-term wealth. A London Business School study found that over the same 90-year period, the average rate of return on a real estate investment was 1.3% compared to the
105 9.8% annualized total return for the S&P stock 500 index. Investing the $5,500 IRS-imposed annual limit in an IRA for 25 years would result in a return of over $600,000 based on the annualized
110 return rate. Stock investment requires a smaller overhead than real estate investment, and the liquid nature of stocks makes them ideal for retirement: stocks allocated to retirement accounts

115 remain tax-free until they are drawn on. Despite these pieces of tangible evidence, though, the stigma regarding stock market investment persists in the minds of many millennials.
120 Regardless of their feelings about the stock market, one thing is self-evident: without preparation for retirement, millennials will be a generation adrift in a society without the social "safety
125 nets" available to current retirees. The benchmark for the amount of savings the average retiree needs to live comfortably after retirement, which remained at $1 million for many years,
130 now continues to rise, and exacerbating factors, such as the cost of medical care, continue to increase. Armed with that knowledge, millennials need to be proactive about financial planning. By
135 taking full advantage of their penchant for a hands-on approach to finances and leveraging the various financial technologies and services that were not available to the previous generation,
140 millennials can amass the wealth necessary to retire comfortably and on their own terms.

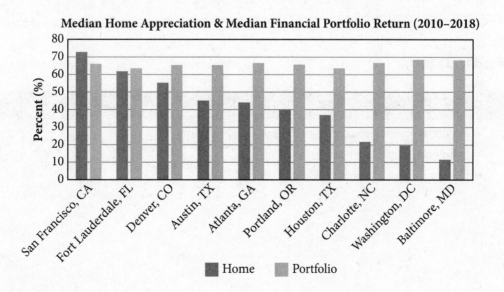

Median Home Appreciation & Median Financial Portfolio Return (2010–2018)

■ Home ■ Portfolio

You need to know this:

- SAT Reading passages are preceded by short blurbs that tell you about the author and source of the passage.
- There are three categories of keywords that reveal an author's purpose and point of view and that unlock the passage's structure:
  - **Opinion and Emphasis**—words that signal that the author finds a detail noteworthy (e.g., *especially, crucial, important, above all*) or has an opinion about it (e.g., *fortunately, disappointing, I suggest, it seems likely*)
  - **Connection and Contrast**—words that suggest that a subsequent detail continues the same point (e.g., *moreover, in addition, also, further*) or that indicate a change in direction or point of difference (e.g., *but, yet, despite, on the other hand*)
    - In some passages, these keywords may show steps in a process or developments over time (e.g., *traditionally, in the past, recently, today, first, second, finally, earlier, since*)
  - **Evidence and Example**—words that indicate an argument (the use of evidence to support a conclusion), either the author's or someone else's (e.g., *thus, therefore, because*), or that introduce an example to clarify or support another point (e.g., *for example, this shows, to illustrate*)
- SAT experts read strategically, jotting down brief, accurate, and useful margin notes next to each paragraph.
- Expert test takers summarize the passage as a whole by paying attention to its big picture:
  - **Main Idea**—the author's primary conclusion or overall takeaway
  - **Purpose**—the author's reason for writing the passage
    - Express this as a verb (e.g., *to explain, to evaluate, to argue, to refute*)

READING PASSAGE AND QUESTION STRATEGY

Why read the passage before reading the questions?

Each SAT Reading passage is accompanied by 10 or 11 questions. Two or three of the questions may ask about the passage as a whole. The others will ask about specific paragraphs, details, or arguments within the passage. SAT experts use deliberate Reading strategies to answer all of the questions quickly and accurately, with a minimum of rereading.

You need to do this:

THE SAT READING PASSAGE STRATEGY

- Extract everything you can from the pre-passage blurb
- Read each paragraph actively
- Summarize the passage's big picture

Extract everything you can from the pre-passage blurb

- Quickly prepare for the passage by unpacking the pre-passage blurb:
  - What does the title and date of the original book or article tell you about the author and her purpose for writing?
  - What information can you glean from the source (nonfiction book, novel, academic journal, etc.)?
  - Is there any other information that provides context for the passage?

Read each paragraph actively

- Note keywords (circling or underlining them may help) and use them to focus your reading on
  - the author's purpose and point of view,
  - the relationships between ideas, and
  - the illustrations or other support provided for passage claims.

KEYWORDS

Why pay attention to keywords?

Keywords indicate opinions and signal structure that make the difference between correct and incorrect answers on SAT questions. Consider this question:

> With which one of the following statements would the author most likely agree?
>
> 1. Coffee beans that grow at high altitudes typically produce dark, mellow coffee when brewed.
> 2. Coffee beans that grow at high altitudes typically produce light, acidic coffee when brewed.

To answer that based on an SAT passage, you will need to know whether the author said:

> Type X coffee beans grow at very high altitudes, *and so* produce a dark, mellow coffee when brewed.

That would make choice (1) correct. But if the author instead said:

> Type X coffee beans grow at very high altitudes, *but* produce a *surprisingly* dark, mellow coffee when brewed.

Then choice (2) would be correct. The facts in the statements did not change at all, but the correct answer to the SAT question would be different in each case because of the keywords the author chose to include.

- As you read, jot down brief, accurate margin notes that will help you research questions about specific details, examples, and paragraphs:
  - Paraphrase the text (put it into your own words) as you go
  - Ask "What's the author's point and purpose?" for each paragraph

---

MARGIN NOTES

Why jot down notes next to each paragraph?

SAT Reading is an open-book test. The answer is always in the passage. Margin notes help you zero in on the details and opinions you need to answer questions like these:

> As used in line 38, "erased" most nearly means

> In the context of the passage as a whole, the question in lines 89–91 primarily functions to help the author

> The passage most strongly implies which of the following statements about the Great Recession?

> In the third paragraph (lines 63–91), the most likely purpose of the author's discussion of the "gig economy" is to

---

Summarize the passage's big picture

- At the end of the passage, pause for a few seconds to summarize the passage's big picture to prepare for Global questions. Ask yourself:
  - "What is the main idea of the entire passage?"
  - "Why did the author write it?"

THE BIG PICTURE

Why summarize the passage's big picture?

Summarizing the big picture prepares you to answer Global questions such as the following:

> Which one of the following most accurately expresses the main point of the passage?

> The passage primarily serves to

Explanation:

This passage was adapted from an article titled "Millennials and the Market," written by a money management expert in 2018.

During the Golden Age of American manufacturing, it was expected that after puttingin 30 to 40 years of tedious labor in a factory, workers
5 would be able to retire around age 65 and enjoy the benefits of retirement comforted by the thought that a pension and the Social Security system they had financed for decades would
10 cover their expenses. Unfortunately for millennials (people born between the early 1980s and late 1990s), prospects look increasingly bleak that they will get a return on their investment at
15 retirement age, despite continuing to fund programs like Social Security and Medicare. Fewer than a quarter of all Fortune 500 corporations still offer some form of pension plan to new
20 hires, and the move from company-funded pension plans to 401(k) plans and IRAs that began in the 1970s shows no sign of slackening. In this financial environment, it might be expected
25 that investment in the stock market would be at an all-time high. An analysis of the data, however, indicates a complicated and even fraught relationship between young adults and
30 the stock market.

Millennials won't have same retirement $

But they don't like stock market

ANALYSIS

Pre-passage blurb: This passage discusses millennials and the stock market. It is written from the perspective of an investment counselor.

SAT Reading Strategy: On the SAT, the pre-passage blurb will always give the author's name, the title of the book or article from which the passage was adapted, and the year it was published. When necessary, the blurb may also include a context-setting sentence with additional information. Train yourself to unpack the blurb to better anticipate what the passage will cover.

¶1: The first opinion keyword is "[u]nfortunately" (line 10). The author explains that, when they retire, millennials will not have the same kinds of pensions and social "safety net" programs that their parents and grandparents had. Then, the author expresses surprise that despite these challenges, millennials are hesitant to invest in the stock market.

SAT Reading Strategy: When an author introduces a surprising or confusing event or condition, expect her to offer some explanation in the following paragraph(s).

The trauma associated with the Great Recession (which began in December 2007 and ended in June 2009) left many investors (wary) of stock

35　market volatility, and that hesitancy was exacerbated among young people, who saw a considerable portion of their families' wealth erased in short order. A study by Pfeffer, Danziger,

40　and Schoeni published in 2014 posited that the average American household lost a third of its wealth, approximately $28,000, during the Great Recession. This was at the exact moment when a

45　great many millennials were making decisions about attending college, pursuing post-graduate studies, or entering the workforce. For a median-income family, those decisions were

50　all directly correlated to household wealth. The ripple effects of the Great Recession left many millennials (ascribing blame) directly to the stock market for missed opportunities.

55　Even with a full awareness that the stock market has rebounded and far exceeded the highs seen prior to the Great Recession, many millennials still feel (trepidation) about investing in the

60　stock market, preferring to save a larger percentage of their salaries than their parents and grandparents did.
　　　(Another factor) that has directly impacted the willingness of millennials

65　to invest in the stockmarket is the seismic shift in the job market brought about by the "gig economy," in which short-term contracts and freelance work have replaced permanent

70　employment. To a large degree, the gig economy is still in its nascent phase, with many of the largest purveyors of jobs only incorporated in the last decade. Research has not adequately

75　kept track of the trend, with estimates of participation in the gig economy

*Reason:
07-09
recession =
millennials
blame the
market*

*Reason 2:
gig economy
= diff. ways
to make $*

¶2: One reason millennials distrust the stock market is that many came of age during the Great Recession. They saw their families' savings wiped out and, right out of high school, they had to make tough decisions about going to college or getting a job.

¶3: A second reason millennials avoid stock market investing is the rise of the "gig economy," in which many people have short-term, freelance jobs. This makes millennials open to different ways of managing their money, but maybe they have a mistaken viewpoint.

SAT Reading Strategy: When the author poses a question, expect her to answer it in the following sentence or paragraph.

ranging from 4% to 40% in the
United States. The ability to pick up
work on a contingency basis allows
80   millennials to feel a greater level of
control over their finances, something
a significant number of them believe
they cannot achieve through stock
market investment. The increased
85   diversity of available methods for
building future wealth has caused
many millennials to adopt an a la carte
approach to preparing for retirement.
But is it possible that this approach
90   has been clouded by some common
misconceptions about wealth building?
One persistent, albeit erroneous, view
is that real estate is a better investment   *Bad think-*
instrument than a stock market   *ing: house >*
95   portfolio. While it is true that home   *stock mkt*
equity is the stepping-stone from which
most individuals begin to build their
personal wealth, statistics make it clear
that stock market investments are a more
100   stable and lucrative source of long-term
wealth. A London Business School study
found that over the same 90-year period,
the average rate of return on a real estate
investment was 1.3% compared to the
105   9.8% annualized total return for the S&P
stock 500 index. Investing the $5,500
IRS-imposed annual limit in an IRA
for 25 years would result in a return of
over $600,000 based on the annualized
110   return rate. Stock investment requires
a smaller overhead than real estate
investment, and the liquid nature of
stocks makes them ideal for retirement:
stocks allocated to retirement accounts
115   remain tax-free until they are drawn
on. Despite these pieces of tangible
evidence, though, the stigma regarding
stock market investment persists in the
minds of many millennials.
120   Regardless of their feelings about the
stockmarket, one thing is self-evident:
without preparation for retirement,

¶4: One mistake millennials make comes from
thinking that owning a home is a better investment than the stock market. Studies show that
this isn't true. There are also tax advantages to
investing in stocks for retirement.

¶5: Feelings aside, millennials will need
investment to have a retirement income.
Money for retirement will get tighter, but if
millennials use a variety of investments, they
can get the wealth they need.

millennials will be a generation adrift
in a society without the social "safety
125 nets" available to current retirees.
The benchmark for the amount of
savings the average retiree needs to live
comfortably after retirement, which
remained at $1 million for many years,
130 now continues to rise, and exacerbating
factors, such as the cost of medical
care, continue to increase. Armed with
that knowledge, millennials need to be
proactive about financial planning. By
135 taking full advantage of their penchant
for a hands-on approach to finances
and leveraging the various financial
technologies and services that were not
available to the previous generation,
140 millennials can amass the wealth
necessary to retire comfortably and on
their own terms.

Millennials need to adapt their thinking to have re-tirement $

Graphic: The graph shows return on investment for homes and for stock portfolios in 10 cities during the 2010s. This relates back to paragraph 4. The graph shows that stocks outperformed home ownership (sometimes by a lot) in 9 of the 10 cities.

SAT Reading Strategy: When an SAT Reading passage is accompanied by one or more charts or graphs, ask the following questions as you read them:

- **What information does the graphic contain?**
- **Why has the author included the graphic?**
- **Which paragraph(s) does this information relate to?**
- **Does the graphic display any trends or relationships that support a point made in the passage?**

In the Reading section, you will not be asked to perform calculations from the data in graphs. You will be asked how they relate to the passage and which claims or arguments they support or refute.

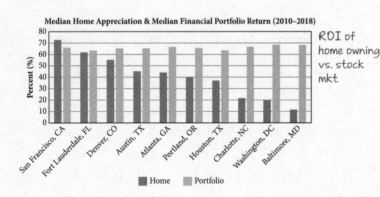

Median Home Appreciation & Median Financial Portfolio Return (2010–2018)

ROI of home owning vs. stock mkt

BIG PICTURE

Main Idea: Millennials are skeptical of investing in the stock market for multiple reasons but will need a variety of investments to be financially secure at retirement.

Author's Purpose: To outline challenges facing millennials in investing for retirement and explain why they are hesitant to invest in the stock market

Now, try another passage on your own. Use the SAT Reading strategies and tactics you've been learning to read and map this passage as quickly and accurately as you can.

Try on Your Own

Directions: Actively read and map the following passage by 1) circling or underlining keywords (from the Opinion and Emphasis, Connection and Contrast, or Evidence and Example categories), 2) jotting down brief, accurate margin notes that reflect good paraphrases of each paragraph, and 3) summing up the big picture. When you're done, compare your work to that of an SAT expert in the Expert Responses.

This passage was adapted from an article titled "Quantum Computing: Where Is It Going?" published in a science magazine in 2018. It discusses the background and potential of quantum computing.

Pharmaceutical companies dream of a time when their research and development process shifts from looking for illnesses whose symptoms
5 can be ameliorated by a specific drug to choosing a disease and creating a drug to eradicate it. Quantum computing may be the key to that goal. The powerful modeling potential
10 unlocked by quantum computing may also someday be employed by autonomous vehicles to create a world free of traffic jams. With plausible applications in so many fields, it is
15 worthwhile to learn a bit about how quantum computing works.

Any understanding of quantum computing begins with its most basic element, the qubit. In classical
20 computing, information is processed by the bit, the binary choice of zero or one. Qubits, on the other hand, allow for infinite superpositions between zero and one and thus can
25 store and process exponentially more complicated values. Imagine showing someone where you live on a globe by pointing only to either the North Pole or the South Pole. While you
30 are likely closer to one pole than the other, you need additional information to represent your specific location. If, however, you could provide your home's latitude and longitude, it could
35 be located without any additional information. The power of quantum

computing lies in the ability to express precise information in a single qubit.

Quantum computing may help
40 scientists and engineers overcome another barrier by reducing energy output while increasing computational speed. The positive correlation between energy output
45 and processing speed often causes classical computers to "run hot" while processing overwhelming amounts of data. Along with their ability to store multiple values simultaneously,
50 qubits are able to process those values in parallel instead of serially. How does processing in parallel conserve energy? Suppose you want to set the time on five separate alarm clocks
55 spaced ten feet apart. You'd have to walk to each clock to change its time. However, if the clocks were connected such that changing the time on one immediately adjusted the other four, you
60 would expend less energy and increase processing speed. Therein lies the benefit of the quantum entanglement of qubits.

While quantum computing has moved beyond the realm of the
65 theoretical, significant barriers still stand in the way of its practical application. One barrier is the difficulty of confirming the results of quantum calculations. If quantum computing
70 is used to solve problems that are impossible to solve with classical computing, is there a way to "check" the results? Scientists hope this paradox may soon be resolved. As a graduate
75 student, Urmila Mahadev devoted over a decade to creating a verification

process for quantum computing. The result is an interactive protocol, based on a type of cryptography called
80 Learning With Errors (LWE), that is similar to "blind computing" used in cloud-computing to mask data while still performing calculations. Given current limitations, Mahadev's protocol
85 remains purely theoretical, but rapid progress in quantum computing combined with further refinement of the protocol will likely result in real-world implementation within the next
90 decade or two.

    It is unlikely that early pioneers in the field, including Stephen Wiesner, Richard Feynman, and Paul Benioff, could have foreseen the rapid progress
95 that has been made to date. In 1960, when Wiesner first developed conjugate coding with the goal of improving cryptography, his paper on the subject was rejected for publication
100 because it contained logic far ahead of its time. Feynman proposed a basic quantum computing model at the 1981 First Conference on the Physics of Computation. At that same conference,
105 Benioff spoke on the ability of discrete mechanical processes to erase their own history and their application to Turing machines, a natural extension of Wiesner's earlier work. A year later,
110 Benioff more clearly outlined the theoretical framework of a quantum computer.

    The dawn of the 21st century brought advancements at an even
115 more impressive pace. The first 5- and 7-qubit nuclear magnetic resonance (NMR) computers were demonstrated in Munich, Germany, and Santa Fe, New Mexico, respectively. In 2006,
120 researchers at Oxford were able to cage a qubit within a "buckyball," a buckminsterfullerene molecule, and

maintain its state for a short time using precise, repeated microwave pulses. The
125 first company dedicated to quantum computing software, 1QB Information Technologies, was founded in 2012, and in 2018, Google announced the development of the 72-qubit Bristlecone
130 chip designed to prove "quantum supremacy," the ability of quantum computers to solve problems beyond the reach of classical computing.

    With progress in quantum
135 computing accelerating, it seems inevitable that within a few decades, the general population will be as familiar with quantum computing as they now are with classical computing. At present,
140 quantum computing is limited by the struggle to build a computer large enough to prove quantum supremacy, and the costs associated with quantum computing are prohibitive to all but
145 the world's largest corporations and governmental institutions. Still, classical computing overcame similar problems, so the future of quantum computing looks bright.

How Much Have You Learned?

Directions: Take five minutes to actively read the following passage by 1) noting the keywords, 2) jotting down margin notes next to each paragraph, and 3) summarizing the big picture. When you're done, compare your work to the Answers and Explanations at the end of the chapter.

This passage was adapted from an article entitled "John Snow Knew Something" published in a popular history magazine in 2018.

Few would deny that doctors use critical thinking to solve problems, but most imagine a difference between the practice of medicine and, say,
5   the methods a police detective might use to solve a case. In fact, medical researchers have long used forensic methods of detection and analysis. The case of John Snow, a
10 19th-century anesthesiologist, is often said to have ushered in the modern era of epidemiology, the branch of medicine that tracks the incidence and distribution of diseases and
15 proposes solutions for their control and prevention.

It would not be until 1861 that Louis Pasteur would propose the link between microorganisms and disease,
20 now known as the germ theory. Before Pasteur's breakthrough, the predominant explanation for the cause of most illnesses was the so-called miasma theory, which held that noxious
25 fumes and pollution—quite literally, as the theory's name implies, "bad air"— were responsible for making people sick. Consequently, during the 1854 outbreak of cholera in Westminster,
30 London, doctors and government officials alike blamed "miasmatic particles" released into the air by decaying organic matter in the soil of the River Thames.

35 Despite the widespread acceptance of the miasma theory, there were those, Snow included, who were skeptical of

this view. Snow would not have known, as doctors do today, that cholera
40 is caused by a bacterial infection, *Vibrio cholerae*. Nevertheless, he was convinced that the spread of the disease was caused by some form of matter passed between individuals, likely
45 through contaminated water.

To demonstrate this, Snow targeted a particularly deadly outbreak in the Soho district of Westminster in London. From August 31 to September
50 3, 1854, 127 people in the area died of cholera. Within a week, that number had risen to over 500. Snow took to the streets. Speaking to residents of the area, he found a commonality among
55 them: most of the victims had used a single public water pump located on Broad Street. Though he was unable to find conclusive proof that the pump was the source of the outbreak, his
60 demonstration of a pattern in the cholera cases prompted authorities to disable the pump by removing its handle. The epidemic quickly subsided.

Soon after the Broad Street pump
65 was shut down, Snow's continued investigation provided additional evidence that contaminated water was the source of the outbreak. Snow created a dot map of the cases of cholera in London
70 and demonstrated that they occurred in areas where water was supplied by two companies that obtained their water from wells near the Thames. Investigation of these wells showed that they had been
75 dug three feet from a cesspit that was leaking sewage into the surrounding soil. Snow also discovered that there were no cases of cholera among workers in a

brewery close to the Broad Street pump.
80 These workers were provided a daily
allowance of beer, which they drank
instead of water, and although the beer
was brewed using the contaminated
water, it was boiled during the brewing
85 process. This revelation provided a
practical solution for the prevention of
future outbreaks.

Snow is now hailed as the "father of
modern epidemiology," and the radical
90 nature of his approach—formulating
a new theory, substantiating it with
verifiable evidence, and proposing
preventative action—is fully
appreciated. At the time, however, not
95 all were convinced, at least publicly, of
Snow's findings. As anxiety over the

outbreak flagged, government officials
replaced the handle on the Broad Street
pump and publicly denounced Snow's
100 conclusions. It seems they felt that the
city's residents would be upset and
disgusted to have the unsettling nature
of the well's contamination confirmed.
It wasn't until 1866, more than a decade
105 after Snow's original investigation and
theory—when another cholera outbreak
killed more than 5,500 residents of
London's East End—that officials
working in public health began to
110 accept the link between contaminated
water and certain kinds of illness and
to take appropriate actions to quell such
outbreaks.

Reflect

Directions: Take a few minutes to recall what you've learned and what you've been practicing in this chapter. Consider the following questions, jot down your best answer for each one, and then compare your reflections to the expert responses on the following page. Use your level of confidence to determine what to do next.

Why do SAT experts note keywords as they read?

_____

_____

_____

What are the three categories of keywords? Provide some examples from each category.

- _____
    - Examples: _____

- _____
    - Examples: _____

- _____
    - Examples: _____

Why do SAT experts jot down margin notes next to the text?

_____

_____

_____

What are the elements of a strong big picture summary?

_____

_____

_____

Expert Responses

Why do SAT experts note keywords as they read?

Keywords indicate what the author finds important, express his point of view about the subject and details of the passage, and signal key points in the passage structure. Keywords are the pieces of text that help test takers see which parts of the passage are likely to be mentioned in questions and help the test taker to distinguish between correct and incorrect answer choices about those parts of the passage.

What are the three categories of keywords? Provide some examples from each category.

- *Opinion and Emphasis*
  - Examples: *indeed, quite, masterfully, inadequate*
- *Connection and Contrast*
  - Examples: *furthermore, plus, however, on the contrary*
- *Evidence and Example*
  - Examples: *consequently, since, for instance, such as*

Why do SAT experts jot down margin notes next to the text?

Margin notes help the test taker research questions that ask about details, examples, and arguments mentioned in the passage by providing a "map" to their location in the text. Margin notes can also help students answer questions about the passage structure and the purpose of a specific paragraph.

What are the elements of a strong big picture summary?

A strong big picture summary prepares a test taker to answer any question about the main idea of the passage or the author's primary or overall purpose in writing it. After reading the passage, SAT experts pause to ask, "What's the main point of the passage?" and "Why did the author write it?"

Next Steps

If you answered most questions correctly in the "How Much Have You Learned?" section, and if your responses to the Reflect questions were similar to those of the SAT expert, then consider strategic reading and passage mapping an area of strength and move on to the next chapter. Come back to this topic periodically to prevent yourself from getting rusty.

If you don't yet feel confident, review the material in "Reading Passage Strategies," then try the questions you missed again. As always, be sure to review the explanations closely.

Answers and Explanations

Try on Your Own

This passage was adapted from an article titled "Quantum Computing: Where Is It Going?" published in a science magazine in 2018. It discusses the background and potential of quantum computing.

Pharmaceutical companies dream of a time when their research and development process shifts from looking for illnesses whose symptoms
5　can be ameliorated by a specific drug to choosing a disease and creating a drug to eradicate it. Quantum computing maybe the (key) to that goal. The (powerful) modeling (potential)
10　unlocked by quantum computing may also someday be employed by autonomous vehicles to create a world free of traffic jams. With plausible applications in so many fields, it is
15　worthwhile to learn a bit about how quantum computing works.

Any understanding of quantum computing begins with its most basic element, the qubit. In classical
20　computing, information is processed by the bit, the binary choice of zero or one. Qubits, (on the other) hand, allow for infinite superpositions between zero and one and thus can
25　store and process (exponentially) more complicated values. Imagine showing someone where you live on a globe by pointing only to either the North Pole or the South Pole. While you
30　are likely closer to one pole than the other, you need additional information to represent your specific location. If, however, you could provide your home's latitude and longitude, it could
35　be located without any additional information. The power of quantum computing lies in the ability to express precise information in a single qubit.

QC: big potential

QC based on qubits – can store more values

Qubit > bit, much more data

ANALYSIS

Pre-passage blurb: Based on the article's title, you can expect to see a discussion of the past and future of quantum computing.

¶1: The author claims that quantum computing may help solve two big problems—new pharmaceuticals and traffic management. Because of this potential, she says, it's good to learn about quantum computing. Expect some of that background information in paragraph 2.

SAT Reading Strategy: Don't panic when confronted with unfamiliar or scientifically advanced subject matter. Pay attention to the author's purpose for discussing it.

¶2: The basis for quantum computing is the qubit, a much more powerful way to store and process information than the bit (which is what we currently use). The author illustrates this with the "globe" example.

SAT Reading Strategy: When you encounter an example or analogy, always ask, "What does this illustrate or explain?"

Quantum computing may help
40 scientists and engineers overcome
another barrier by reducing
energy output while increasing
computational speed. The positive
correlation between energy output
45 and processing speed often causes
classical computers to "run hot" while
processing overwhelming amounts of
data. Along with their ability to store
multiple values simultaneously,
50 qubits are able to process those values
in parallel instead of serially. How
does processing in parallel conserve
energy? Suppose you want to set the
time on five separate alarm clocks
55 spaced ten feet apart. You'd have to
walk to each clock to change its time.
However, if the clocks were connected
such that changing the time on one
immediately adjusted the other four, you
60 would expend less energy and increase
processing speed. Therein lies the benefit
of the quantum entanglement of qubits.

While quantum computing has
moved beyond the realm of the
65 theoretical, significant barriers still
stand in the way of its practical
application. One barrier is the difficulty
of confirming the results of quantum
calculations. If quantum computing
70 is used to solve problems that are
impossible to solve with classical
computing, is there a way to "check"
the results? Scientists hope this paradox
may soon be resolved. As a graduate
75 student, Urmila Mahadev devoted
over a decade to creating a verification
process for quantum computing.
The result is an interactive protocol,
based on a type of cryptography called
80 Learning With Errors (LWE), that is
similar to "blind computing" used in
cloud-computing to mask data while
still performing calculations. Given
current limitations, Mahadev's protocol

*Qubits =
parallel
processing*

*faster AND
cooler*

*One barrier
to QC –
How to
check
results?*

¶3: Another advantage: quantum computing is faster but cooler (current computers overheat). The reason is parallel processing, illustrated by the "five clocks" example.

SAT Reading Strategy: Rhetorical questions help you focus on the author's point in a paragraph and her reason for writing it.

¶4: Here, the passage shifts to obstacles to quantum computing. One problem: when they solve extremely complex problems, regular computers can't check them. One scientist is working on a solution, and the author is optimistic that it will work out in the next 20 years or so.

85 remains purely theoretical, but rapid
progress in quantum computing
combined with further refinement of
the protocol will likely result in real-
world implementation within the next
90 decade or two.

*probably will
get solved*

It is unlikely that early pioneers in
the field, including Stephen Wiesner,
Richard Feynman, and Paul Benioff,
could have foreseen the rapid progress
95 that has been made to date. In 1960,
when Wiesner first developed conjugate
coding with the goal of improving
cryptography, his paper on the
subject was rejected for publication
100 because it contained logic far ahead
of its time. Feynman proposed a basic
quantum computing model at the 1981
First Conference on the Physics of
Computation. At that same conference,
105 Benioff spoke on the ability of discrete
mechanical processes to erase their
own history and their application to
Turing machines, a natural extension
of Wiesner's earlier work. A year later,
110 Benioff more clearly outlined the
theoretical framework of a quantum
computer.

*QC pioneers
- 1960s –
80s*

The dawn of the 21st century
brought advancements at an even
115 more impressive pace. The first 5- and
7-qubit nuclear magnetic resonance
(NMR) computers were demonstrated
in Munich, Germany, and Santa Fe,
New Mexico, respectively. In 2006,
120 researchers at Oxford were able to
cage a qubit within a "buckyball," a
buckminsterfullerene molecule, and
maintain its state for a short time using
precise, repeated microwave pulses. The
125 first company dedicated to quantum
computing software, 1QB Information
Technologies, was founded in 2012,
and in 2018, Google announced the
development of the 72-qubit Bristlecone
130 chip designed to prove "quantum
supremacy," the ability of quantum

*QC sped up
in 2000s*

¶5: The pre-passage blurb indicated that the passage would cover quantum computing's past, and here it is. The point of this paragraph is that early developers of quantum computing (the author names three of them) would be surprised by how quickly it has developed.

¶6: This gives a little more about the past. Progress in quantum computing really took off during the 2000s. The author supports that point with examples of companies that have created and improved quantum computers.

SAT Reading Strategy: The SAT doesn't expect you to know the definitions of technical terms and phrases. The test will ask you why the author has included these details or how they function in the paragraph.

computers to solve problems beyond the reach of classical computing.

With progress in quantum
135 computing accelerating, it seems (inevitable) that within a few decades, the general population will be as familiar with quantum computing as they now are with classical computing. At present,
140 quantum computing is limited by the struggle to build a computer large enough to prove quantum supremacy, and the costs associated with quantum computing are prohibitive to all but
145 the world's largest corporations and governmental institutions. (Still,) classical computing overcame similar problems, so the future of quantum computing (looks bright.)

QC still difficult, but bright future

¶7: The passage ends on a high note: quantum computing will "inevitably" become popular and its future is "bright." The author acknowledges obstacles, but clearly implies that she expects them to be overcome.

BIG PICTURE

Main Idea: Quantum computing has many potential uses despite current obstacles.

Author's Purpose: To explain some fundamental principles of how quantum computing works to show its enormous potential over classical computing and to give a brief history of its development to anticipate how it can overcome current limitations

---

As with the other passages in this chapter, don't worry about whether you used the exact language found in the expert's map and summary. Instead, focus on how the expert used the skills and strategies outlined here to prepare himself to tackle the question set with speed and confidence.

How Much Have You Learned?

This passage was adapted from an article entitled "John Snow Knew Something" published in a popular history magazine in 2018.

Few would deny that doctors use critical thinking to solve problems, (but) most imagine a difference between the practice of medicine and, say,
5 the methods a police detective might use to solve a case. In fact, medical researchers have long used forensic methods of detection and analysis. The case of John Snow, a
10 19th-century anesthesiologist, is often said to have ushered in the modern era of epidemiology, the branch of medicine that tracks the incidence and distribution of diseases and
15 proposes solutions for their control and prevention.

It would not be until 1861 that Louis Pasteur would propose the link between microorganisms and disease,
20 now known as the germ theory. (Before) Pasteur's breakthrough, the predominant explanation for the cause of most illnesses was the so-called miasma theory, which held that noxious
25 fumes and pollution—quite literally, as the theory's name implies, "bad air"— were responsible for making people sick. (Consequently,) during the 1854 outbreak of cholera in Westminster,
30 London, doctors and government officials alike blamed "miasmatic particles" released into the air by decaying organic matter in the soil of the River Thames.
35 (Despite) the widespread acceptance of the miasma theory, there were those, Snow included, who were skeptical of this view. Snow would not have known, as doctors do today, that cholera

Snow's work used investigation, changed medicine

1854 – didn't know about germs; miasma theory

ANALYSIS

Pre-passage blurb: The article is about someone named John Snow, who must be a historical figure of some importance. Beyond that, however, there's not too much to go on in this blurb.

¶1: The author provides some background on John Snow. Today, he is known for changing how doctors track and prevent diseases, apparently by using methods often associated with detectives and investigations. The rest of the passage will illustrate why he was so important.

¶2: This paragraph sets the stage. At the time of the cholera outbreak in 1854, people did not know that germs and bacteria caused the disease.

¶3: The author contrasts (note the keywords "Despite" and "Nevertheless") Snow's theories with the popular ideas of his time. He thought cholera might be passed through contaminated water.

40 is caused by a bacterial infection,
Vibrio cholerae. Nevertheless, he was
convinced that the spread of the disease
was caused by some form of matter
passed between individuals, likely
45 through contaminated water.

*Snow: chol-
era from
contam.
H_2O*

To demonstrate this, Snow targeted
a particularly deadly outbreak in
the Soho district of Westminster in
London. From August 31 to September
50 3, 1854, 127 people in the area died of
cholera. Within a week, that number
had risen to over 500. Snow took to
the streets. Speaking to residents of the
area, he found a commonality among
55 them: most of the victims had used a
single public water pump located on
Broad Street. Though he was unable
to find conclusive proof that the pump
was the source of the outbreak, his
60 demonstration of a pattern in the
cholera cases prompted authorities
to disable the pump by removing its
handle. The epidemic quickly subsided.

*Proof from
interviews
– all used
same pump*

Soon after the Broad Street pump
65 was shutdown, Snow's continued
investigation provided additional evidence
that contaminated water was the source
of the outbreak. Snow created a dot
map of the cases of cholera in London
70 and demonstrated that they occurred in
areas where water was supplied by two
companies that obtained their water from
wells near the Thames. Investigation of
these wells showed that they had been
75 dug three feet from a cesspit that was
leaking sewage into the surrounding soil.
Snow also discovered that there were no
cases of cholera among workers in a
brewery close to the Broad Street pump.
80 These workers were provided a daily
allowance of beer, which they drank
instead of water, and although the beer
was brewed using the contaminated
water, it was boiled during the brewing
85 process. This revelation provided a

*Water from
contam.
wells*

*Boiling first
prevented
disease*

¶4: Snow investigated the area and interviewed people. He demonstrated that a
specific water pump was "ground zero" for the
outbreak and got it turned off.

¶5: Through further investigation, Snow
showed that leaking cesspools were the
source of contamination and used his observations at a nearby brewery to deduce that
boiling water before drinking would prevent
the disease.

practical solution for the prevention of future outbreaks.

Snow is now hailed as the "father of modern epidemiology," and the radical
90 nature of his approach—formulating a new theory, substantiating it with verifiable evidence, and proposing preventative action—is fully appreciated. At the time, however, not
95 all were convinced, at least publicly, of Snow's findings. As anxiety over the outbreak flagged, government officials replaced the handle on the Broad Street pump and publicly denounced Snow's
100 conclusions. It seems they felt that the city's residents would be upset and disgusted to have the unsettling nature of the well's contamination confirmed. It wasn't until 1866, more than a decade
105 after Snow's original investigation and theory—when another cholera outbreak killed more than 5,500 residents of London's East End—that officials working in public health began to
110 accept the link between contaminated water and certain kinds of illness and to take appropriate actions to quell such outbreaks.

¶6: Another contrast: Snow is now seen as a pioneer but wasn't appreciated at the time. It took another epidemic for officials to buy in to his theory.

Snow not accepted at the time

1866 – another epidemic

Reading

BIG PICTURE

Main Idea: John Snow's investigative approach to explaining the cholera epidemic of 1854 ushered in the modern era of epidemiology.

Author's Purpose: To demonstrate how Snow's use of interviews, maps, and data altered the way doctors study the spread and prevention of disease

---

CHAPTER 15

SAT Reading Question Types

LEARNING OBJECTIVES

After completing this chapter, you will be able to:

Unpack SAT Reading question stems by

- distinguishing among six SAT Reading question types, and
- determining if the correct answer is best found by researching the passage text or by consulting your big picture summary

How Much Do You Know?

Directions: In this chapter, you'll learn to unpack SAT Reading question stems (Step 1 of the Method for SAT Reading Questions). Unpacking a question stem means identifying your task (as identified by the question type) and noting where the answer will be found (a specific reference within the passage text or in your big picture summary). You first saw the question types defined in chapter 13. For your reference as you complete this quiz, here they are again:

- **Global**—asks about the big picture
- **Detail**—asks about explicitly stated points
- **Inference**—asks about points that are unstated but strongly suggested
- **Command of Evidence**—asks for evidence to support the answer to a previous question
- **Function**—asks why the author wrote specific parts of the text
- **Vocabulary-in-Context**—asks for the meaning of a word as it is used in the passage

For each of the following question stems, identify the question type, cite the language in the stem that helped you identify it, and indicate where you would begin to research this question: either your big picture summary or a specific part of the text.

Example

The author of the passage would most likely agree with which one of the following statements concerning hydraulic mining?

Question type: *Inference*

Identifying language: *"would most likely agree"*

Research where? *passage, where author discusses hydraulic mining*

1. The passage indicates that non-rush hour commuters

    Question type:
    Identifying language:
    Research where?

2. As used in line 41, "labyrinthine" most nearly means

    Question type:
    Identifying language:
    Research where?

3. According to the passage, which of the following is true of the New York City subway system?

    Question type:
    Identifying language:
    Research where?

4. The fifth paragraph (lines 66–90) serves mainly to

    Question type:
    Identifying language:
    Research where?

5. Which of the following best expresses the primary purpose of the passage?

    Question type:
    Identifying language:
    Research where?

6. Based on the passage, which choice best describes a claim that critics of the current subway maintenance plan would likely make?

    Question type:
    Identifying language:
    Research where?

7. Which choice provides the best evidence for the answer to the previous question?

    Question type:
    Identifying language:
    Research where?

8. With which one of the following statements would the author of the passage be most likely to agree?

    Question type:
    Identifying language:
    Research where?

9. Based on the passage, advocates of the current New York City subway maintenance plan would most likely agree that

    Question type:
    Identifying language:
    Research where?

10. In the third paragraph, the discussion of two specific subway lines (lines 44–49) primarily serves to

    Question type:
    Identifying language:
    Research where?

Check Your Work

1. The passage indicates that non-rush hour commuters

   Question type: Detail

   Identifying language: "indicates"

   Research where? passage, where author discusses non-rush hour commuters

2. As used in line 41, "labyrinthine" most nearly means

   Question type: Vocab-in-Context

   Identifying language: "most nearly means"

   Research where? passage, line 41

3. According to the passage, which of the following is true of the New York City subway system?

   Question type: Detail

   Identifying language: "According to the passage"

   Research where? passage, where author discusses NYC subway system

4. The fifth paragraph (lines 66–90) serves mainly to

   Question type: Function

   Identifying language: "serves mainly to"

   Research where? passage, fifth paragraph

5. Which of the following best expresses the primary purpose of the passage?

   Question type: Global

   Identifying language: "primary purpose of the passage"

   Research where? big picture summary

6. Based on the passage, which choice best describes a claim that critics of the current subway maintenance plan would likely make?

   Question type: Inference

   Identifying language: "Based on the passage," "would likely make"

   Research where? passage, where author discusses critics' views

7. Which choice provides the best evidence for the answer to the previous question?

   Question type: Command of Evidence

   Identifying language: "provides the best evidence"

   Research where? passage, where you went to answer the previous question

8. With which one of the following statements would the author of the passage be most likely to agree?

   Question type: Inference

   Identifying language: "most likely to agree"

   Research where? big picture summary (no specific clues)

9. Based on the passage, advocates of the current New York City subway maintenance plan would most likely agree that

   Question type: Inference

   Identifying language: "Based on the passage," "would most likely agree"

   Research where? passage, where author discusses advocates' views

10. In the third paragraph, the discussion of two specific subway lines (lines 44–49) primarily serves to

    Question type: Function

    Identifying language: "primarily serves to"

    Research where? passage, third paragraph

How to Unpack SAT Reading Question Stems

LEARNING OBJECTIVES

After this lesson, you will be able to:

- Unpack SAT Reading question stems by
  - distinguishing among six SAT Reading question types, and
  - determining if the correct answer is best found by researching the passage text or by consulting your big picture summary

To unpack question stems like these:

1. One central idea of the passage is that

2. Which choice best describes the overall structure of the passage?

3. According to the passage, large corporations are

4. As used in line 38, "erased" most nearly means

5. The passage most strongly implies which of the following statements about the Great Recession?

6. Which choice provides the best evidence for the answer to the previous question?

7. In the third paragraph (lines 63–91), the most likely purpose of the author's discussion of the "gig economy" is to

8. In the context of the passage as a whole, the question in lines 89–91 primarily functions to help the author

9. The passage indicates that investing in the stock market

10. Which of the following statements is supported by the graph?

11. Which statement from the passage is most directly reflected by the data presented in the graph?

You'll need to know this:

- The six kinds of question types, each of which defines a specific task:
  - **Global**—asks about the passage's main idea, the author's primary purpose, or the passage's overall organization

TYPICAL GLOBAL QUESTION STEMS
The central claim of the passage is that
Which choice best summarizes the passage?
The main purpose of the passage is to
Which choice best describes the developmental pattern of the passage?
Which choice best reflects the overall sequence of events in the passage?

o **Detail**—asks about something explicitly stated in the passage

TYPICAL DETAIL QUESTION STEMS

According to the passage, which of the following is true of developmental psychology?

The author indicates that people value solitude because

In the second paragraph (lines 14–27), what does the author claim are key questions the study must answer?

The passage identifies which of the following as a factor that influences economic growth?

o **Inference**—asks for something that follows from the passage without having been stated explicitly in it

TYPICAL INFERENCE QUESTION STEMS

Based on the passage, the author's statement "in response, the Federal Reserve will often lower interest rates" (lines 21–22) implies that

Which concept is supported by the passage and by the information in the graph?

Based on information in the passage, it can reasonably be inferred that

The authors of both passages would most likely agree with which of the following statements?

o **Command of Evidence**—asks you to cite the support offered in the passage for the correct answer to the previous question or for a given statement

TYPICAL COMMAND OF EVIDENCE QUESTION STEMS

Which choice provides the best evidence for the answer to the previous question?

Which choice best supports the claim that the new policy is unlikely to curtail water pollution?

o **Function**—asks about the purpose of a piece of text—why the author included it or how the author has used it

TYPICAL FUNCTION QUESTION STEMS

The sentence in lines 35–37 serves mainly to

The main purpose of the fourth paragraph (lines 42–50) is to

How do the words "must," "necessary," and "imperative" in the third paragraph (lines 35–49) help establish the tone of the paragraph?

The author uses the image of an explorer overlooking a valley (lines 23–28) most likely to

The sentence in lines 74–78 ("After … rest") primarily serves which function in paragraph 7?

o **Vocabulary-in-Context**—asks you to define a word as the author used it in the passage

> ### TYPICAL VOCABULARY-IN-CONTEXT QUESTION STEMS
>
> As used in line 55, "platform" most nearly means
>
> As used in line 29, "substantial" most nearly means

- The kinds of research clues found in SAT Reading question stems:

  o **Line Numbers**—Mentions of "line 53" or "lines 37–40," often in parentheses, tend to stand out and give you a clear place to start your research. (In Command of Evidence questions, line numbers are found in the answer choices.)

  o **Paragraph Numbers**—A reference to "paragraph 5," "the third paragraph," or "the last two paragraphs" is not as precise as a line reference but will still give you an idea of where to look. Start with your margin notes for the paragraph.

  o **Quoted Text**—(often accompanied by line numbers)—Check the context of the quoted term or phrase to see what the author meant by it in the passage.

  o **Proper Nouns**—Names like "Professor James," "World War II," and "Baltimore" will likely stand out in question stems due to the capitalization. If a particular proper noun is discussed in only part of the passage, it narrows the range of text you have to research.

  o **Specific Content Clues**—Sometimes a question stem will repeat terminology used in part of the passage like "federalism" or "action potentials." Use your passage map to direct your research to the right part of the passage.

  o **Whole Passage Clues**—If a question lacks specific content clues but refers to the passage as a whole, or to the author in general, you are likely dealing with a Global question or an open-ended Inference question, which should lead you to your big picture summary rather than to rereading parts of the text.

You need to do this:

The Method for SAT Reading Questions	
Step 1.	Unpack the question stem
Step 2.	Research the answer
Step 3.	Predict the answer
Step 4.	Find the one correct answer

- Unpack SAT Reading question stems by
  - ○ identifying the question type and anticipating how it will need to be answered, and
  - ○ noting research clues that indicate how best to research the correct answer

---

QUESTION TYPES

Why distinguish question types in SAT Reading?

Unpacking the question stem puts you in control. You'll know exactly what the question is asking, where to find the correct answer, and what form the correct answer will take.

- **Global:** The correct answer must take the entire passage into account. A choice that reflects only part of the passage is incorrect.
- **Detail:** The correct answer must be stated in the passage explicitly. A choice that is not directly stated in the passage is incorrect.
- **Inference:** The correct answer will be a conclusion that can be drawn from the passage. A choice that draws too strong a conclusion from the evidence available in the passage is incorrect.
- **Command of Evidence:** The correct answer must directly support the correct answer to the previous question. A choice about the same subject but providing no direct evidence is not good enough.
- **Function:** The correct answer will say *why* a certain detail is included. Look up the detail, then ask yourself what the author was trying to accomplish by putting it there.
- **Vocab-in-Context:** The correct answer will give the meaning of a word as it is used *in the context of the passage.* Choices that give common meanings of the word are often incorrect.

Correct answers to Reading questions are never random or vague. They are tailored to the precise language of the stem, so being able to distinguish the question types will save you time and eliminate confusion during the test.

Answers and Explanations:

1. This is a Global question, as is clear from the phrase "central idea of the passage." Your big picture summary will likely have the answer.

GLOBAL STRATEGY

Start with your big picture summary

Global questions ask for the big picture of the passage, so always start by reviewing your big picture summary. You should generally avoid rereading passage text when tackling a Global question but, if you get stuck, the first and last paragraphs are usually the best places to look.

---

2. The mention of the "overall structure of the passage" indicates that this is also a Global question. In addition to your big picture summary, look for structural trends in your marginal notes (particularly for places where the author changes direction or perspective) when answering a Global question about structure.

3. "According to the passage" is a clear sign of a Detail question. Though this question lacks specific line or paragraph clues, the mention of "large corporations" may help to narrow your research.

DETAIL STRATEGY

Search for the relevant information

Don't expect a lot of precise clues such as line numbers with Detail questions. Your task will usually be to extract the stem's specific content clues and then use your passage map to help you locate that content in the text. If you can't find it within about a minute, consider skipping a Detail question and returning to it after you answer the passage's other questions. Researching them may inadvertently lead you to the detail you need.

4. A question stem that begins with a line reference, quotes a term from the passage, and ends in "most nearly means" is always a Vocab-in-Context question.

VOCAB-IN-CONTEXT STRATEGY

Go back to the context

At a minimum, go to the line cited in a Vocab-in-Context question and reread the entire sentence that contains the word. If that doesn't give you enough context, look for additional help in the surrounding sentences until you have a clear idea of what the author intended.

5. The word "implies" tells you that this is an Inference question. The proper noun "the Great Recession" gives you something to look for in the passage.

INFERENCE STRATEGY

What follows from the text?

Inference questions come in a wider variety of forms than the other question types, but all are united by asking you to identify something that the author only suggests without saying outright. Fortunately for you, these questions are not asking for subtle hints, but for statements that MUST be true given what the author does state. Follow the clues to locate the relevant text, and then ask yourself, "What *must* follow from this?"

6. The vast majority of Command of Evidence questions have this exact wording: "Which choice provides the best evidence for the answer to the previous question?" All Command of Evidence answer choices feature direct quotes with line numbers, which you should use to guide your research.

COMMAND OF EVIDENCE STRATEGY

Use your work on the previous question

The line numbers listed in Command of Evidence answer choices give you four potential locations to look for the correct answer, but preempt this extensive searching by looking first at the lines of text you used to answer the previous question (usually an Inference or Detail). Alternatively, if you're working on a different question and see a Command of Evidence coming up next, you can use the line numbers there to guide your research, increasing your efficiency by answering both questions at once.

---

7. This is a Function question because it asks for the "most likely purpose" of a specific part of the text. To research it, you should look for mentions of the "gig economy" in the third paragraph.

FUNCTION STRATEGY

Why did the author write *that*?

Most Function questions are *why* questions, asking you to explain what the author intended to accomplish with a particular piece of text, usually singled out with precise clues like line or paragraph numbers. Start researching by looking at the appropriate location on your passage map, reviewing what you described as the author's purpose in that part of the text. If that doesn't help, reread the indicated text and ask yourself, "Why did the author include this?"

---

8. The use of "primarily functions" gives this away as a Function question. The cited lines tell you where to start researching.

9. This is a Detail question, as can be garnered from "indicates." The other clues in the stem suggest that you'll need to search the passage for a discussion of stock market investment.

10. This is an Inference question because it asks for a statement that "is supported" by part of the passage—in this case, the graph. To research such a question, look for major takeaways from the data presented in the graph.

11. This is a less common variation of Command of Evidence, which would be more obvious after looking at the answer choices (quotes from the text with line references). To research, follow the line references until you come upon a quote that describes a major takeaway from the data in the graph.

Try on Your Own

Directions: Analyze each of the following question stems by 1) identifying the word or phrase that describes your task, 2) naming the question type, and 3) noting how best to research the correct answer (research the text or consult the big picture summary). Answers are found at the end of the chapter.

1. According to the passage, which one of the following is true of Urmila Mahadev's graduate work?

   Question type:
   Identifying language:
   Research where?

2. Which choice provides the best evidence for the answer to the previous question?

   Question type:
   Identifying language:
   Research where?

3. The author's attitude toward the potential success of quantum computing can best be described as

   Question type:
   Identifying language:
   Research where?

4. Which statement best describes the technique the author uses to advance the main point of the third paragraph (lines 39–62)?

   Question type:
   Identifying language:
   Research where?

5. The primary purpose of the passage is to

   Question type:
   Identifying language:
   Research where?

6. Based on the passage, the author would most likely criticize classical computing because it

   Question type:
   Identifying language:
   Research where?

7. The passage indicates that which of the following factors slowed early developments in the theory of quantum computing?

   Question type:
   Identifying language:
   Research where?

8. In the second paragraph, the discussion of locating a person's home on a globe (lines 26–36) primarily serves to

   Question type:
   Identifying language:
   Research where?

9. Which one of the following does the passage imply about the development of quantum computing in the 21st century?

   Question type:
   Identifying language:
   Research where?

10. As used in line 123, "maintain" most nearly means

    Question type:
    Identifying language:
    Research where?

For any question types that you misidentified, return to the definitions and question stem examples before you try the final question set in this chapter.

How Much Have You Learned?

Directions: Now, complete a similar assessment under timed conditions. Take a few minutes to analyze each of the following question stems by 1) identifying the word or phrase that describes your task, 2) naming the question type, and 3) noting how best to research the correct answer (research the text or consult the big picture summary).

11. The passage primarily serves to

    Question type:

    Identifying language:

    Research where?

12. Which of the following is most analogous to John Snow's discovery of the source of the cholera outbreak?

    Question type:

    Identifying language:

    Research where?

13. Which choice provides the best evidence for the answer to the previous question?

    Question type:

    Identifying language:

    Research where?

14. The passage indicates that the main reason government officials rejected Snow's hypothesis was

    Question type:

    Identifying language:

    Research where?

15. The second paragraph serves mainly to

    Question type:

    Identifying language:

    Research where?

16. It can reasonably be inferred from the passage that scientists in 1855 would have found which of the following solutions to be most practical in dealing with future outbreaks of cholera?

    Question type:

    Identifying language:

    Research where?

17. The author of this passage writes from the perspective of a

    Question type:

    Identifying language:

    Research where?

18. Which of the following is cited as the primary reason Snow suspected the Broad Street pump as the source of the epidemic?

    Question type:

    Identifying language:

    Research where?

19. As used in line 97, the word "flagged" most nearly means

    Question type:

    Identifying language:

    Research where?

20. The author uses the final sentence of the passage ("It wasn't … outbreaks") at least in part to:

    Question type:

    Identifying language:

    Research where?

Reflect

Directions: Take a few minutes to recall what you've learned and what you've been practicing in this chapter. Consider the following questions, jot down your best answer for each one, and then compare your reflections to the expert responses on the following page. Use your level of confidence to determine what to do next.

Why is it important to always unpack the question stem before proceeding?

_____

_____

_____

Can you name the six SAT Reading question types and cite words or phrases that identify each one?

- _____
  - Identifying language: _____
- _____
  - Identifying language: _____
- _____
  - Identifying language: _____
- _____
  - Identifying language: _____
- _____
  - Identifying language: _____
- _____
  - Identifying language: _____

How will you approach SAT Reading question stems differently as you continue to practice and improve your performance in the Reading section? What are the main differences you see between SAT Reading questions and those you're used to from tests in school?

_____

_____

_____

Expert Responses

Why is it important to always unpack the question stem before proceeding?

Knowing the SAT Reading question types makes you a more strategic and efficient reader because the test maker uses the same question types on every test. Fully analyzing each question stem helps you research the text more effectively, predict the correct answer in a way that fits the question stem, and avoid wrong answers made from misreading the question.

Can you name the six SAT Reading question types and cite words or phrases that identify each one?

- *Global*
  - Identifying language: *main idea of the passage, author's primary purpose*
- *Detail*
  - Identifying language: *according to the passage, identifies, claims*
- *Inference*
  - Identifying language: *implies, can be inferred, based on the passage*
- *Command of Evidence*
  - Identifying language: *provides the best evidence, best supports, the answer to the previous question*
- *Function*
  - Identifying language: *is used to, serves mainly to, functions as*
- *Vocabulary-in-Context*
  - Identifying language: *as used in line [number], most nearly means*

How will you approach SAT Reading question stems differently as you continue to practice and improve your performance in the Reading section? What are the main differences you see between SAT Reading questions and those you're used to from tests in school?

There is no one-size-fits-all answer here. Reflect on your own strengths and weaknesses as you consider how to best improve your performance in the SAT Reading section. Depending on the kinds of classes and teachers you've had in high school, the skills rewarded on SAT Reading questions may be more or less familiar, but almost every test taker needs to be aware of her own instincts as a reader, and needs to break certain reading habits, to master this section of the test. The more you give yourself an honest self-assessment, the better prepared you'll be to handle all of the SAT Reading question types confidently.

Next Steps

If you answered most questions correctly in the "How Much Have You Learned?" section, and if your responses to the Reflect questions were similar to those of the SAT expert, then consider identifying Reading question types an area of strength and move on to the next chapter. Come back to this topic periodically to prevent yourself from getting rusty.

If you don't yet feel confident, review the material in "How to Unpack SAT Reading Question Stems," then try the questions you missed again. As always, be sure to review the explanations closely.

Answers and Explanations

1. According to the passage, which one of the following is true of Urmila Mahadev's graduate work?

   Question type: Detail
   Identifying language: "According to the passage"
   Research where? passage, where the author discusses Mahadev's work

2. Which choice provides the best evidence for the answer to the previous question?

   Question type: Command of Evidence
   Identifying language: "provides the best evidence"
   Research where? passage, where you answered the previous question

3. The author's attitude toward the potential success of quantum computing can best be described as

   Question type: Inference
   Identifying language: "can best be described as"
   Research where? passage, where author discusses quantum computing success

4. Which statement best describes the technique the author uses to advance the main point of the third paragraph (lines 39–62)?

   Question type: Function
   Identifying language: "the technique the author uses"
   Research where? passage, third paragraph

5. The primary purpose of the passage is to

   Question type: Global
   Identifying language: "primary purpose of the passage"
   Research where? big picture summary

6. Based on the passage, the author would most likely criticize classical computing because it

   Question type: Inference
   Identifying language: "Based on the passage"
   Research where? passage, where author discusses classical computing

7. The passage indicates that which of the following factors slowed early developments in the theory of quantum computing?

   Question type: Detail
   Identifying language: "indicates"
   Research where? passage, where author discusses early developments

8. In the second paragraph, the discussion of locating a person's home on a globe (lines 26–36) primarily serves to

   Question type: Function
   Identifying language: "primarily serves to"
   Research where? passage, second paragraph

9. Which one of the following does the passage imply about the development of quantum computing in the 21st century?

   Question type: Inference
   Identifying language: "imply"
   Research where? passage, where author discusses 21st-century development

10. As used in line 123, "maintain" most nearly means

    Question type: Vocab-in-Context
    Identifying language: "most nearly means"
    Research where? passage, line 123

11. The passage primarily serves to

    Question type: Global
    Identifying language: "passage primarily serves to"
    Research where? big picture summary

12. Which of the following is most analogous to John Snow's discovery of the source of the cholera outbreak?

    Question type: Inference
    Identifying language: "most analogous"
    Research where? passage, where author discusses Snow's discovery

13. Which choice provides the best evidence for the answer to the previous question?

    Question type: Command of Evidence
    Identifying language: "provides the best evidence"
    Research where? passage, where you went to answer the previous question

14. The passage indicates that the main reason government officials rejected Snow's hypothesis was

    Question type: Detail
    Identifying language: "indicates"
    Research where? passage, where author discusses officials' rejection of Snow

15. The second paragraph serves mainly to

    Question type: Function
    Identifying language: "serves mainly to"
    Research where? passage, second paragraph

16. It can reasonably be inferred from the passage that scientists in 1855 would have found which of the following solutions to be most practical in dealing with future outbreaks of cholera?

    Question type: Inference
    Identifying language: "reasonably be inferred"
    Research where? passage, where author discusses cholera outbreak solutions

17. The author of this passage writes from the perspective of a

    Question type: Global
    Identifying language: "author ... writes from the perspective of a"
    Research where? big picture summary

18. Which of the following is cited as the primary reason Snow suspected the Broad Street pump as the source of the epidemic?

    Question type: Detail
    Identifying language: "is cited as"
    Research where? passage, where author discusses Broad Street pump

19. As used in line 97, the word "flagged" most nearly means

    Question type: Vocab-in-Context
    Identifying language: "most nearly means"
    Research where? passage, line 97

20. The author uses the final sentence of the passage ("It wasn't ... outbreaks") at least in part to:

    Question type: Function
    Identifying language: "uses ... at least in part to"
    Research where? passage, final sentence

Answering SAT Reading Questions

How Much Do You Know?

Directions: In this chapter, you'll learn how best to research, predict, and find the correct answers to SAT Reading questions. For this quiz, first take a couple of minutes to refresh your memory of the passage. Then, for each question 1) research the answer in the passage text or from your big picture summary, 2) predict the correct answer in your own words, and 3) identify the one correct answer.

Questions 1-11 refer to the following passage.

This passage is adapted from a 2018 article summarizing two different proposals for solving problems with maintaining New York City's mass transit system.

The history of the New York City subway system, quickly told: the first stations opened in 1904, and over the next century, it expanded to 472 stations,
5 more than any other subway system in the world, with 850 miles of track. Operating 24 hours a day seven days a week, with an average weekday ridership of approximately 5.7 million, it is the
10 planet's 7th-busiest rapid transit system. While the system is, on many levels, an amazing achievement, it is also beset by a problem that harms both quality of life and economic activity. Such a
15 large system must inevitably suffer from service interruptions and delays; normal wear and tear combined with the sheer age of the system necessitates regular maintenance. However, there
20 is no consensus as to the best way to accomplish the required repairs.

NYC subway: how to repair? diff. views

The current maintenance scheme is designed to minimize service interruptions. A subway line in need
25 of repair will be taken out of service during a comparatively less busy time, such as nights or weekends, while another line is re-routed to cover as many as possible of the missing line's
30 stops. The main advantage to this approach is that trains are not taken out of service during rush hour, when most subway trips occur; subway service generally remains predictable
35 and commuters are, for the most part,

Current approach – night and weekend repairs

able to use the system to get to their destinations on time.

But critics are quick to point out the disadvantages to this approach. Perhaps
40 most obvious is the confusion caused by trains switching lines. The labyrinthine system is hard enough to navigate at the best of times, especially for tourists. A subway rider on the A train naturally
45 expects the train to make stops on the A line. If, instead, it is diverted temporarily to the F line, the rider may find herself miles from her intended destination.
50 While annoying, the confusion arising from route switching is hardly the most serious problem with the current approach to repairs. Because the system runs 24 hours a
55 day, routine maintenance can generally be done only during the temporary closures on nights and weekends. This means that more serious repair and crucial preventative maintenance is
60 often neglected. Problems that could have been fixed or prevented reasonably expeditiously given a slightly longer closure wind up leading to major breakdowns and service interruptions
65 later on.

On rare occasions, such breakdowns have resulted in entire subway lines being shut down for months or even a year. Beginning in 2019, for
70 example, the L Train connecting lower Manhattan to parts of Brooklyn was scheduled to close for as much as 15 months for long overdue service and upgrades. In a city fewer than
75 half of whose households own a car,

Critics: line switch confusion

Even worse – major breakdowns

this can have serious economic impacts.
Residents of the affected area may
face a much longer commute via an
alternate subway line if one is available;
80 or, if there is no alternate subway
service, they may need to take other,
potentially more expensive, modes
of transportation, such as taxis or
ferries. Moreover, studies indicate that
85 increased stress from the commute to
work can lead to lower productivity, and
that businesses near the impacted lines
may see decreased revenue as potential
customers have a harder time getting to
90 them.

One controversial proposal for
reducing breakdowns and the resulting
transit interruptions is to end the
subway's 24-hour service and to shut
95 down for several hours each night.
Proponents of this plan argue that
this would allow time, on a regular
rather than sporadic basis, for more
preventative maintenance. This, they
100 claim, would ultimately lead to more
consistent service; rather than shutting
down entire lines for long periods of
a time, there would merely be shorter
service outages overnight, when fewer
105 people use the subway system. While
this may seem a preferable outcome to
the economic consequences of a total
shutdown resulting from a breakdown,
it has its liabilities as well. While most
110 subway trips may occur during rush
hour, not everyone works during the
daytime. New York is famously known
as the "the city that never sleeps."
Doctors, nurses, bartenders, police
115 officers, and firefighters are just a few
examples of occupations whose workers
need transportation at all hours of
the day and night. Rather than be
subjected to a relatively short period
120 of inconvenience, these workers would
find their commutes irrevocably altered.

Econ. & Soc.
harms of
shutdowns

Alt proposal
– stop
24-hour
service

Pros

Cons

One thing, at least, is clear: the city
must carefully consider many economic
and social factors in designing a subway
125 maintenance plan.

K   417

1. Which of the following best expresses the primary purpose of the passage?

   A) To argue that the New York City subway system maintenance plan should be altered

   B) To explain the effects of the current New York City subway system maintenance plan and a proposed alternative

   C) To discuss the economic and social importance of the New York City subway system

   D) To show how the history of the New York City subway system has resulted in the current maintenance crisis

2. According to the passage, which of the following is true of the New York City subway system?

   A) It is the oldest subway system in the world.

   B) It is the busiest mass transit system in the world.

   C) It has more stations than any other subway system.

   D) A majority of city residents rely on the subway to get to work.

3. Based on the passage, advocates of the current New York City subway maintenance plan would most likely agree that

   A) given its size, the city's subway system is one of the most well maintained in the world.

   B) avoiding service interruptions during rush hour is a paramount consideration when designing a maintenance schedule.

   C) confusion caused by route switching is a minor inconvenience for commuters and tourists.

   D) operating the subway system 24 hours a day seven days a week is untenable given the wear and tear it causes.

4. Which choice provides the best evidence for the answer to the previous question?

   A) Lines 14–19 ("Such a . . . maintenance")

   B) Lines 30–37 ("The main . . . time")

   C) Lines 50–53 ("While . . . repairs")

   D) Lines 96–99 ("Proponents . . . maintenance")

5. Based on the passage, which choice best describes a claim that critics of the current subway maintenance plan would likely make?

   A) The negative impacts that arise from neglecting preventative maintenance outweigh the benefits of minimizing subway service interruptions.

   B) When devising a subway maintenance plan, no factor is more important than avoiding rush hour service interruptions.

   C) The negative impact from subway line closures is greater on commuters than it is on businesses near the affected lines.

   D) Slightly longer periods of scheduled maintenance would help the subway system minimize rush hour service interruptions.

6. Which choice provides the best evidence for the answer to the previous question?

   A) Lines 24–30 ("A subway . . . stops")

   B) Lines 60–65 ("Problems . . . later on")

   C) Lines 69–74 ("Beginning in . . . upgrades")

   D) Lines 84–90 ("Moreover, studies . . . them")

7. As used in line 41, "labyrinthine" most nearly means

   A) subterranean.

   B) mythological.

   C) meandering.

   D) complicated.

8. In the third paragraph, the discussion of two specific subway lines (lines 44–49) primarily serves to

   A) support the contention that line switching has a negative impact on tourism.

   B) illustrate one problem created by the current subway maintenance plan.

   C) underline the importance of minimizing subway service interruptions.

   D) quantify the social costs that arise from extended subway repair schedules.

9. The fifth paragraph (lines 66–90) serves mainly to

   A) illustrate the impact of the current maintenance plan on one subway line.

   B) advocate for increased funding for subway repair and maintenance.

   C) provide support for a proposal to curtail 24-hour subway service.

   D) outline the negative impacts of extended subway line outages.

10. The passage indicates that non-rush hour commuters

    A) would risk losing public transportation options if 24-hour subway service were suspended.

    B) would face only minor inconveniences if 24-hour subway service were suspended.

    C) work primarily in health care and its related fields.

    D) are among the strongest advocates for a change to the current subway maintenance plan.

11. With which one of the following statements would the author of the passage be most likely to agree?

    A) The controversy surrounding New York City's subway system reflects similar issues for mass transit in many American cities.

    B) Without major changes to its subway maintenance plan, New York City will be unable to provide regular service to its 5.7 million weekly riders.

    C) Any plan for maintaining New York City's subway system will entail advantages and disadvantages for commuters.

    D) The social and economic costs resulting from New York City's current subway maintenance schedule justify an end to 24-hour, seven-day subway service.

Check Your Work

1. B

Difficulty: Medium

Category: Global

Strategic Advice: Consult your big picture summary and find the one answer that matches the passage's scope and the author's purpose.

Getting to the Answer: Here, the author does not take a side. He lays out advantages and disadvantages to both the current maintenance plan and one proposal offered by critics of the current plan. That matches **(B)**.

(A) distorts the author's position. He doesn't advocate for the critics of the current plan.

(C) is too narrow. It misses the key subject of subway *maintenance*.

(D) is also too narrow. This answer describes only the first paragraph.

2. C

Difficulty: Medium

Category: Detail

Strategic Advice: The correct answer will be something explicitly stated in the passage.

Getting to the Answer: Start by checking the answers against paragraph 1 where the author provides general facts about the New York City subway. Doing so will lead you to the correct answer, **(C)**.

(A) is unsupported. You're told that the subway opened in 1904, but not whether other subway systems already existed at that time.

(B) is simply incorrect. New York City's subway system is the seventh busiest in the world.

(D) distorts a fact from the passage. The fifth paragraph states that fewer than half of households in the city own a car, but that doesn't mean that everyone in the majority of households that do not own cars takes the subway.

3. B

Difficulty: Hard

Category: Inference

Strategic Advice: The correct answer will follow from the passage text without having been explicitly stated in the text.

Getting to the Answer: The current maintenance plan is outlined in paragraph 3. You're told that its goal is to "minimize service interruptions" and that its main advantage is that trains operate during rush hour. Combining those statements leads to the correct answer, **(B)**.

(A) is too extreme. Everyone seems to agree that maintaining the system is a huge challenge. The debate is over *how* best to implement the necessary repairs.

(C) misuses a detail from the passage. The author says nothing about how serious a problem those who support the current plan consider route switching to be. They might understand that it causes a major inconvenience but still be willing to re-route trains in order to keep the subway open during rush hour.

(D) states a position taken by *critics*, not advocates, of the current plan.

4. B

Difficulty: Medium

Category: Command of Evidence

Strategic Advice: The most common Command of Evidence question stems task you with locating the piece of text that supports the correct answer to the preceding question. Use that answer to direct your research as you evaluate the answer choices.

Getting to the Answer: In this case, the correct answer to the preceding question paraphrased the final sentence in paragraph 3. That sentence covers the lines in **(B)** making that the correct answer here.

(A) cites a sentence from paragraph 1. It contains the phrase "wear and tear," which was part of incorrect answer (D) in the preceding question, but doesn't support the correct answer, **(B)**.

(C) comes from the beginning of paragraph 4. It suggests that there are problems with the current system even bigger than the inconvenience caused by line switching. This choice could be tempting if you chose (C) on the preceding question.

(D) provides evidence for the *critics'* proposal to stop running the subway 24/7. That is not the argument made by advocates of the current system who were the subject of the preceding question.

5. A

Difficulty: Hard

Category: Inference

Strategic Advice: The phrases "[b]ased on the passage" and "would likely" indicate an Inference question. Note that this question asks specifically for the position of the critics of the current plan. The correct answer will be implied by the passage text.

Getting to the Answer: The critics' objections to the current plan are laid out primarily in paragraphs 3 and 4. Quick research shows that they make two arguments. First (paragraph 3), line switching for routine maintenance can be confusing and frustrating for riders. Second (paragraph 4), and worse, the limited time allowed for routine maintenance prevents important preventative maintenance from taking place. That leads to severe service outages that can last for weeks or months. This second criticism accords with the correct answer, **(A)**.

(B) is something that advocates, not opponents, of the current plan might say. See paragraph 2 for this argument.

(C) is an irrelevant comparison. Paragraph 5 lays out the social and economic impacts of extended subway line closures to both riders and businesses, but it doesn't assert that the impacts are worse for one group or the other.

(D) distorts the critics' argument. They contend that slightly longer periods of scheduled maintenance would allow time for preventative maintenance, not that it would reduce rush hour interruptions.

6. B

Difficulty: Medium

Category: Command of Evidence

Getting to the Answer: Here, the correct answer to the preceding question paraphrased the critics' argument in paragraph 4. That paragraph's final sentence, represented by **(B)**, provides the support.

(A) is a sentence from paragraph 2. It explains the rationale behind the current maintenance plan and does not support a criticism of that plan.

(C) contains an example of an extended service outage for one subway line. That's an illustration of the kind of problem the critics hope to avoid, but by itself does not support the claim in the correct answer to the preceding question.

(D) cites a line from the end of paragraph 5. It does not support the correct answer to the preceding question, but might be tempting if you chose (C) there.

7. D

Difficulty: Easy

Category: Vocab-in-Context

Strategic Advice: Check the sentence in which the word was used to determine the author's intended meaning. The correct answer can be substituted for the word without changing the meaning of the sentence.

Getting to the Answer: Here, the author uses *labyrinthine* to describe the New York subway system's complexity. **(D)** fits perfectly.

(A) means *underground*. That is true of the subway system, of course, but it would be redundant for the author to use "labyrinthine" in this way.

(B) plays off the famous labyrinth from Greek mythology, but this definition does not fit the word "labyrinthine" or the context of the sentence.

(C) suggests that the subway system is *random* or *wandering*. While the huge system may be difficult to navigate at times, it isn't random.

8. B

Difficulty: Hard

Category: Function

Strategic Advice: The phrase "serves to" tags this as a Function question, asking for the role a specific detail plays in the passage. Research the lines cited in the question stem to see *why* the author has included this example.

Getting to the Answer: The third paragraph introduces the first disadvantage cited by critics of the current subway maintenance schedule. The detail referenced in the question stem provides an example. That purpose is accurately described in the correct answer, **(B)**.

(A) misuses a detail from the passage. You're told that line switching—the problem being discussed—is particularly difficult for tourists, but that's not the reason the author included this example.

(C) refers to the rationale provided by supporters of the current maintenance plan in paragraph 2.

In (D), the word "quantify" suggests that the example provides numbers to show the impact of the current maintenance plan. That's something the author never does in this passage.

9.   D

Difficulty: Easy

Category: Function

Strategic Advice: In this case, you're asked for the author's purpose for including an entire paragraph. Consult your margin notes to see the role of paragraph 5 in the passage.

Getting to the Answer: Paragraph 5 details some of the social and economic harms caused by shutting down subway lines. That matches **(D)**.

(A) distorts the purpose of the paragraph. The specific line—the L train—is given as an example of an extended shutdown, but the harms described in the paragraph apply to all similar extended service outages.

(B) is outside the scope of the passage. The author does not discuss the need for increased funding.

(C) refers to a proposal from paragraph 6. The author does not endorse that proposal and does not use paragraph 5 to support it.

10.   A

Difficulty: Medium

Category: Detail

Strategic Advice: The phrase "[t]he passage indicates" shows this to be a Detail question. The correct answer will paraphrase a statement made explicitly in the text.

Getting to the Answer: The author discusses non-rush hour commuters in paragraph 5. He lists some examples of these commuters—"doctors, nurses, bartenders, police officers, and firefighters"—and explains that a cessation of 24-hour subway service could permanently alter their commutes. That matches choice **(A)**, the correct answer here.

(B) is the opposite of the what the passage says. The current system creates minor inconveniences for these workers when their subways lines are rerouted or closed for repair, but a suspension of 24-hour service would entail a permanent disruption.

(C) distorts the paragraph. Doctors and nurses are among the non-rush hour commuters, but that doesn't mean they are the majority of them.

(D) is outside the scope of the passage. The author does not discuss which occupations show the strongest support for a change in subway maintenance.

11.   C

Difficulty: Hard

Category: Inference

Strategic Advice: For an open-ended Inference question like this one, predict the correct answer based on your big picture summary. Consider also any thesis statement or conclusion that sums up the author's point of view.

Getting to the Answer: This author outlines both sides of a debate and discusses the advantages and disadvantages to both the current subway maintenance plan and proposed alternatives. His conclusion at the end of the passage is neutral, encouraging the city to carefully consider all factors without advocating for a specific outcome. This matches up with the correct answer, **(C)**.

(A) strays beyond the scope of the passage. Be careful not to bring in bigger issues if the author has not discussed them in the passage.

(B) is too extreme. To be sure, the author considers subway maintenance a major issue but stops short of dire predictions like the one stated in this answer choice.

(D) matches the position of one side in the debate, but not that of the author, who remains neutral throughout.

How to Answer SAT Reading Questions

LEARNING OBJECTIVES

After this lesson, you will be able to:

- Research the answer in the passage or your big picture summary
- Predict the correct answer
- Find the one correct answer choice

To answer questions like these:

Directions: Choose the best answer choice for the following questions.

Questions 1-11 refer to the following passage and supplementary material.

This passage was adapted from an article titled "Millennials and the Market," written by a money management expert in 2018.

During the Golden Age of American manufacturing, it was expected that after putting in 30 to 40 years of tedious labor in a factory, workers
5 would be able to retire around age 65 and enjoy the benefits of retirement comforted by the thought that a pension and the Social Security system they had financed for decades would
10 cover their expenses. Unfortunately for millennials (people born between the early 1980s and late 1990s), prospects look increasingly bleak that they will get a return on their investment at
15 retirement age, despite continuing to fund programs like Social Security and Medicare. Fewer than a quarter of all Fortune 500 corporations still offer some form of pension plan to new
20 hires, and the move from company-funded pension plans to 401(k) plans and IRAs that began in the 1970s shows no sign of slackening. In this financial environment, it might be expected
25 that investment in the stock market would be at an all-time high. An analysis of the data, however, indicates a complicated and even fraught

Millennials won't have same retirement $

But they don't like stock market

relationship between young adults and
30 the stock market.

The trauma associated with the Great Recession (which began in December 2007 and ended in June 2009) left many investors wary of stock
35 market volatility, and that hesitancy was exacerbated among young people, who saw a considerable portion of their families' wealth erased in short order. A study by Pfeffer, Danziger,
40 and Schoeni published in 2014 posited that the average American household lost a third of its wealth, approximately $28,000, during the Great Recession. This was at the exact moment when a
45 great many millennials were making decisions about attending college, pursuing post-graduate studies, or entering the workforce. For a median-income family, those decisions were
50 all directly correlated to household wealth. The ripple effects of the Great Recession left many millennials ascribing blame directly to the stock market for missed opportunities.
55 Even with a full awareness that the stock market has rebounded and far exceeded the highs seen prior to the Great Recession, many millennials still feel trepidation about investing in the
60 stock market, preferring to save a larger percentage of their salaries than their parents and grandparents did.

Reason: 07-09 recession = millennials blame the market

(Another factor) that has directly
impacted the willingness of millennials
65　to invest in the stock market is the
seismic shift in the job market brought
about by the "gig economy," in which
short-term contracts and freelance
work have replaced permanent
70　employment. To a large degree, the gig
economy is still in its nascent phase,
with many of the largest purveyors
of jobs only incorporated in the last
decade. Research has not adequately
75　kept track of the trend, with estimates
of participation in the gig economy
ranging from 4% to 40% in the
United States. The ability to pick up
work on a contingency basis allows
80　millennials to feel a greater level of
control over their finances, something
a significant number of them believe
they cannot achieve through stock
market investment. The increased
85　diversity of available methods for
building future wealth has caused
many millennials to adopt an a la carte
approach to preparing for retirement.
(But) is it possible that this approach
90　has been clouded by some common
misconceptions about wealth building(?)
(One persistent, albeit erroneous, view)
is that real estate is a better investment
instrument than a stock market
95　portfolio. (While) it is true that home
equity is the stepping-stone from which
most individuals begin to build their
personal wealth, statistics make it clear
that stock market investments are a more
100　stable and lucrative source of long-term
wealth. A London Business School study
found that over the same 90-year period,
the average rate of return on a real estate
investment was 1.3% compared to the
105　9.8% annualized total return for the S&P
stock 500 index. Investing the $5,500
IRS-imposed annual limit in an IRA
for 25 years would result in a return of

Reason 2: gig economy = diff. ways to make $

Bad thinking: house > stock mkt

over $600,000 based on the annualized
110　return rate. Stock investment requires
a smaller overhead than real estate
investment, and the liquid nature of
stocks makes them (ideal) for retirement(:)
stocks allocated to retirement accounts
115　remain tax-free until they are drawn on.
(Despite) these pieces of tangible evidence,
though, the stigma regarding stock
market investment persists in the minds
of many millennials.
120　(Regardless) of their feelings about the
stock market, one thing is self-evident(:)
without preparation for retirement,
millennials will be a generation adrift
in a society without the social "safety
125　nets" available to current retirees.
The benchmark for the amount of
savings the average retiree needs to live
comfortably after retirement, which
remained at $1 million for many years,
130　now continues to rise, and exacerbating
factors, such as the cost of medical
care, continue to increase. Armed with
that knowledge, millennials need to be
proactive about financial planning. (By)
135　taking full advantage of their penchant
for a hands-on approach to finances
and leveraging the various financial
technologies and services that were not
available to the previous generation,
140　millennials can amass the wealth
necessary to retire comfortably and on
their own terms.

Millennials need to adapt their thinking to have retirement $

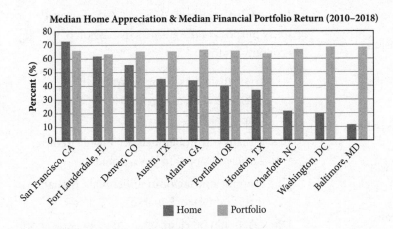

Median Home Appreciation & Median Financial Portfolio Return (2010–2018)

ROI of home owning vs. stock mkt

1. One central idea of the passage is that

    A) changes to social "safety net" programs such as Social Security and Medicare will force millennials to retire later in life than their parents did.

    B) investing in the stock market is the only money management strategy that will allow millennials to amass savings sufficient to retire comfortably.

    C) leveraging opportunities in the "gig economy" has allowed millennials to avoid the risks associated with investing in the stock market.

    D) despite their distrust of the stock market, millennials will need a variety of investment tools and strategies to build adequate retirement savings.

2. Which choice best describes the overall structure of the passage?

    A) A surprising attitude is introduced, two criticisms of it are offered, an alternative attitude is presented, and data proving the alternative is superior is provided.

    B) A surprising attitude is introduced, two reasons for it are described, a mistaken idea associated with it is revealed through data, and its effect on those holding it is assessed.

    C) A previously held attitude is presented, reasons for its rejection are offered, new data is presented, and those rejecting the old attitude are endorsed.

    D) Two reasons for a previously held attitude are presented, both reasons are rejected, and data is presented to introduce an alternative attitude.

3. According to the passage, large corporations are

   A) less likely to offer their employees pension plans than they were in the past.

   B) more likely to invest in the stock market than millennial individuals are.

   C) opposed to the gig economy because it reduces the number of permanent employees.

   D) skeptical that their current employees will receive their full Social Security benefit.

4. As used in line 38, "erased" most nearly means

   A) canceled.

   B) effaced.

   C) laundered.

   D) eradicated.

5. The passage most strongly implies which of the following statements about the Great Recession?

   A) It could have been avoided by continued funding of Social Security and Medicare.

   B) It impacted families with millennial-age children more severely than any other group.

   C) It resulted from misconceptions about the stability of stock market investments.

   D) It caused at least some millennials to forego their educational and career goals.

6. Which choice provides the best evidence for the answer to the previous question?

   A) Lines 10–17 ("Unfortunately . . . Medicare")

   B) Lines 39–43 ("A study . . . Recession")

   C) Lines 48–54 ("For a . . . opportunities")

   D) Lines 89–91 ("But . . . wealth building")

7. In the third paragraph (lines 63–91), the most likely purpose of the author's discussion of the "gig economy" is to

   A) argue that short-term contracts and freelance work are preferable to permanent employment.

   B) explain why millennials are unable to raise sufficient capital to buy a home.

   C) examine one factor in millennials' hesitancy to invest in the stock market.

   D) cast doubt on claims that up to 40 percent of workers hold short-term and freelance jobs.

8. In the context of the passage as a whole, the question in lines 89–91 ("But is . . . wealth building") primarily functions to help the author

   A) establish that millennials are mismanaging their retirement investments.

   B) show how professional money managers diversify their investments to avoid market volatility.

   C) introduce data that reveals a flaw in the premises that influence millennials' investment choices.

   D) call into question opposing opinions about the effects of the gig economy.

9. The passage indicates that investing in the stock market

   A) is the stepping stone from which most individuals begin to build personal wealth.

   B) remains less stable and lucrative than home ownership as a source of wealth.

   C) has tax implications well suited to retirement planning.

   D) is limited by IRS rules to a $5,500 annual maximum.

10. Which of the following statements about the period from 2010 to 2018 is supported by the graph?

   A) Investment in the stock market generated more wealth than home ownership in every market listed in the graph.

   B) The value of a home appreciated by a greater percentage in Portland, Oregon, than in Charlotte, North Carolina.

   C) The return on a median financial portfolio outperformed the value of home ownership by a greater margin in each subsequent year.

   D) Austin, Texas, saw a greater disparity between home value appreciation and return on financial portfolios than Atlanta, Georgia, saw.

11. Which statement from the passage is most directly reflected by the data presented in the graph?

   A) Lines 48–51 ("For a . . . wealth")

   B) Lines 74–78 ("Research . . . United States")

   C) Lines 98–101 ("statistics . . . wealth")

   D) Lines 110–115 ("Stock . . . drawn on")

Reading

You need to know this:

- Use clues to direct your research to a specific portion of the passage or to your big picture summary:

  ○ **Line Numbers**—Reread the indicated text and possibly the lines before and after; look for keywords indicating why the referenced text has been included or how it's used.

  ○ **Paragraph Numbers**—Consult your margin notes to see the paragraph's purpose and scope before rereading the text. Sometimes your passage map alone is enough to find an answer.

  ○ **Quoted Text**—Go back to the passage to read the entire quote if the stem or answer choices use ellipses (. . .). Then check the surrounding context of the quoted term or phrase to see what the author meant by it in the passage.

  ○ **Proper Nouns**—Use your passage map or look for capital letters in the text to find the term and then check the context to see why the author included it in the passage; note whether the author had a positive, negative, or neutral evaluation of it.

  ○ **Specific Content Clues**—Use your margin notes to help you search the passage for terms or ideas mentioned in the question stem; these clues will usually refer to something the author offered an opinion about or emphasized.

  ○ **Whole Passage Clues**—Begin by reviewing your big picture summary, and only go back to the passage if you can't find the information you need. If you do get stuck, the first and last paragraphs are typically the best places to go for global takeaways.

- Predicting what you're looking for in the correct answer saves time and reduces confusion as you read each choice.

- SAT Reading questions always have one correct answer and three incorrect answers:

  ○ The correct answer will match what the passage says in a way that responds to the task set out in the question stem.

  ○ Wrong answers often fall into one of five categories. Not every incorrect choice matches one of these types exactly, but learning to spot them can help you eliminate some wrong answers more quickly.

    - **Out of Scope**—contains a statement that is too broad, too narrow, or beyond the purview of the passage

    - **Extreme**—contains language that is too strong (*all, never, every, none*) to be supported by the passage

    - **Distortion**—based on details or ideas from the passage but distorts or misstates what the author says or implies

    - **Opposite**—directly contradicts what the correct answer must say

    - **Misused Detail**—accurately states something from the passage but in a manner that incorrectly answers the question

You need to do this:

The SAT Reading Question Method	
Step 1.	Unpack the question stem
Step 2.	**Research the answer**
Step 3.	**Predict the answer**
Step 4.	**Find the one correct answer**

- Research the answer:
  - When clues point to a specific part of the passage (line or paragraph numbers, quotations, content discussed only in particular paragraphs), begin by rereading the specified text and immediate context.
    - If the immediate context does not provide enough info to answer the question, gradually expand outward, rereading sentences that come before and after.
  - With whole passage clues or questions that seem to lack clear content clues, begin by reviewing your big picture summary.
  - If you can't figure out where to research the question and your big picture summary doesn't help either, consider using process of elimination, skipping the question and coming back to it later, or just making a guess.
- Predict or characterize what the correct answer will say or suggest:
  - Don't worry about phrasing your prediction as a complete sentence or about repeating exactly the language used in the passage. Just try to answer the question posed in your own words based on your research.
  - If you struggle to predict, use your active reading of the passage to characterize the correct answer, setting expectations about characteristics it must possess.
    - For example, if the author has a negative view of a topic in the question, expect a correct answer with negative language and eliminate choices that suggest a positive or neutral view.
- Find the one correct answer:
  - Identify the choice that matches your prediction, if possible.
    - Don't expect a word-for-word match, but look for a correspondence of ideas. For example, if you predict that the function of a detail is to "provide support for the main idea," an answer choice that says it "supplies evidence for the author's thesis" would likely be correct.

- If there is no clear match, use process of elimination:

  o Eliminate any choice that contradicts your prediction or that clearly falls into one of the five wrong answer categories.

    • Choose the only answer remaining or guess among those you were unable to eliminate.

FINDING THE CORRECT ANSWER

One Correct Choice—Three *Demonstrably* Incorrect Choices

Great SAT test takers know that there is always one correct answer, written to match the meaning of the passage, and three *demonstrably* incorrect ones. The word "demonstrably" underscores that the wrong answers aren't merely worse than the credited choice; they fail, for one or more reasons, to accurately answer the question. SAT experts don't compare answer choices to one another; they evaluate the choices based on the passage. They never ask themselves, "Do I like (B) or (C) more?" Instead, they ask, "Does the second paragraph imply (B)? Why or why not?"

Answers and Explanations

Question	Analysis
1. One central idea of the passage is that A) changes to social "safety net" programs such as Social Security and Medicare will force millennials to retire later in life than their parents did. B) investing in the stock market is the only money management strategy that will allow millennials to amass savings sufficient to retire comfortably. C) leveraging opportunities in the "gig economy" has allowed millennials to avoid the risks associated with investing in the stock market. D) despite their distrust of the stock market, millennials will need a variety of investment tools and strategies to build adequate retirement savings.	**Answer: D** **Difficulty:** Easy **Category:** Global **Strategic Advice:** Answer Global questions based on your big picture summary. Sometimes, the author has already "boiled down" the central idea and summarized it in a sentence, usually near the beginning of or end of the passage. **Getting to the Answer:** The big picture summary captured the author's main point as it is expressed near the end of the passage: "Millennials are skeptical of investing in the stock market for several reasons, but they'll need a variety of investments to be financially secure at retirement." That matches **(D)** perfectly. (A) distorts the author's point. The author doesn't compare millennials' potential retirement *age* with that of their parents' generation. (B) is extreme. The author thinks millennials are too hesitant to use stock market investments, but concludes that their financial stability will come from a variety of financial technologies and services, not from the stock market alone. (C) is too narrow (the gig economy is discussed only in paragraph 3) and misstates the author's point about the gig economy, which is that it has encouraged millennials to "feel a greater level of control over their finances."

Question	Analysis

2. Which choice best describes the overall structure of the passage?

A) A surprising attitude is introduced, two criticisms of it are offered, an alternative attitude is presented, and data proving the alternative is superior is provided.

B) A surprising attitude is introduced, two reasons for it are described, a mistaken idea associated with it is revealed through data, and its effect on those holding it is assessed.

C) A previously held attitude is presented, reasons for its rejection are offered, new data is presented, and those rejecting the old attitude are endorsed.

D) Two reasons for a previously held attitude are presented, both reasons are rejected, and data is presented to introduce an alternative attitude.

Answer: B

Difficulty: Medium

Category: Global

Strategic Advice: Occasionally, a Global question will ask you to outline the overall structure of the passage. To answer a question like this, consult your big picture summary and review the notes you've jotted down next to each paragraph.

Getting to the Answer: In this passage, the author introduces a surprising opinion (millennials distrust the stock market), gives two reasons for their opinion (the Great Recession and the "gig economy"), points out an oversight in this opinion (the stock market is usually a better investment than home ownership), and concludes with an assessment of how that opinion needs to balance with other considerations (millennials will need a variety of investment strategies). That outline matches up nicely with the correct answer, **(B)**.

(A) starts off well but runs into trouble with "two criticisms of [the attitude] are offered." Paragraphs 2 and 3 explain *why* millennials distrust the market; those paragraphs don't criticize millennials for their point of view. The end of choice (A) is also problematic. The author offers data to show why millennials' attitudes toward the market are mistaken, not to prove an alternative opinion.

The beginning of choice (C) may be tempting because the author does provide background on older generations' expectations upon retirement, but the remainder of this choice wanders far from the structure of the passage.

(D) goes off course right from the start. This passage does not open with reasons for rejecting an older point of view on investing.

Question	Analysis

Question

3. According to the passage, large corporations are

A) less likely to offer their employees pension plans than they were in the past.

B) more likely to invest in the stock market than millennial individuals are.

C) opposed to the gig economy because it reduces the number of permanent employees.

D) skeptical that their current employees will receive their full Social Security benefit.

Analysis

Answer: A

Difficulty: Easy

Category: Detail

Strategic Advice: "According to the passage" at the beginning of a question stem signals a Detail question. The correct answer will paraphrase something stated explicitly in the passage.

Getting to the Answer: The author discusses large corporations in paragraph 1. She says that two-thirds of large corporations no longer offer pension plans and indicates that this trend is likely to continue. That supports **(A)**, the correct answer.

(B) is an irrelevant comparison; the author never discusses how large corporations invest.

(C) presents a misused detail; in paragraph 3, the author states that the gig economy has replaced permanent employment with short-term contracts and freelance work, but she does not mention corporate opposition to the gig economy.

(D) distorts the passage; the author expresses concern that individuals will not have enough income at retirement despite their investments in Social Security and Medicare, but she does not ascribe this concern to corporations.

Reading

Question	Analysis
4. As used in line 38, "erased" most nearly means A) canceled. B) effaced. C) laundered. D) eradicated.	**Answer: D** **Difficulty:** Medium **Category:** Vocab-in-Context **Strategic Advice:** To answer a Vocab-in-Context question, examine the sentence in which the word was used for clues about how the author used the word. You can substitute the correct answer into the sentence without changing the sentence's meaning. **Getting to the Answer:** Here, the author uses "erased" to mean *lost* or *destroyed*. **(D)**, *eradicated*, is the best fit for the sentence. (A), *canceled*, carries with it the implication that there was a plan or expected event that was deleted from the calendar before it ever took place. The wealth "erased" by the Great Recession already existed; it wasn't canceled before it was created. (B), *effaced*, usually refers to removing a sign or indication of something. That doesn't fit the context of money in a savings account or investment. (C), *laundered*, may bring to mind the financial crime of "money laundering," but that has no logical connection to the sentence in the passage.

Question	Analysis
5. The passage most strongly implies which of the following statements about the Great Recession? A) It could have been avoided by continued funding of Social Security and Medicare. B) It impacted families with millennial-age children more severely than any other group. C) It resulted from misconceptions about the stability of stock market investments. D) It caused at least some millennials to forego their educational and career goals.	**Answer: D** **Difficulty:** Medium **Category:** Inference **Strategic Advice:** The phrase "most strongly implies" marks this as an Inference question. The correct answer will follow from the passage without having been explicitly stated in the passage. The reference in the question stem to the "Great Recession" points you to paragraph 2. **Getting to the Answer:** Paragraph 2 provides one reason that millennials distrust the stock market. Many millennials were considering college and career options when the market crashed in 2007, leading to the Great Recession. As a result, many of these young people blamed the market for "missed opportunities." This directly supports **(D)**. (A) is outside the scope; the author does not draw a connection between the Great Recession and the two social programs named here. (B) distorts the passage; while the author cites the damage that the Great Recession did to the "average American family," she doesn't compare the effect on families with millennial-age children to that on other groups of people. (C) is outside the scope; the author does not discuss any causes of the Great Recession.

Question	Analysis
6. Which choice provides the best evidence for the answer to the previous question? A) Lines 10–17 ("Unfortunately . . . Medicare") B) Lines 39–43 ("A study . . . Recession") C) Lines 48–54 ("For a . . . opportunities") D) Lines 89–91 ("But . . . wealth building")	**Answer: C** **Difficulty:** Medium **Category:** Command of Evidence **Strategic Advice:** Use the answer from the previous question to evaluate the answer choices here. **Getting to the Answer:** The correct answer to the preceding question focused on how the Great Recession curtailed educational and employment opportunities for young people. That is substantiated by the text in **(C)**. (A) comes from paragraph 1 and cannot be used to support the answer to the preceding question. This choice may have been tempting to test takers who thought (A) was the correct answer to the previous question. (B) cites a study that quantified the harm done by the Great Recession, but that does not directly support the correct answer to the preceding question, which focused on missed opportunities for young adults at the time. (D) contains the rhetorical question at the end of paragraph 3; that's outside the scope of the previous question's correct answer.

Question	Analysis
7. In the third paragraph (lines 63–91), the most likely purpose of the author's discussion of the "gig economy" is to	**Answer: C**
	Difficulty: Medium
A) argue that short-term contracts and freelance work are preferable to permanent employment.	**Category:** Function
	Strategic Advice: Function questions ask you *why* an author included a specific piece of text or *how* she uses it in the passage. In this question stem, the identifying language is "most likely purpose." The research clue sends you back to paragraph 3.
B) explain why millennials are unable to raise sufficient capital to buy a home.	
C) examine one factor in millennials' hesitancy to invest in the stock market.	**Getting to the Answer:** Paragraph 3 opens with a clear-cut topic sentence: this paragraph will examine "[a]nother factor" that leads millennials to distrust the stock market. That factor is the rise of the gig economy and its effects on millennial attitudes toward money management. That leads right to the correct answer, **(C)**.
D) cast doubt on claims that up to 40 percent of workers hold short-term and freelance jobs.	
	(A) distorts the passage; the author expresses no preference for one kind of work or another.
	(B) misuses a detail from paragraph 4; one reason the author gives for considering stock market investment is its lower capital requirements. The author does not explain why millennials would have difficulty raising capital for down payment on a home.
	(D) misuses a detail within paragraph 3; the author cites studies showing a range of gig economy participation, but her purpose is not to cast doubt on the high end of those claims.

Reading

Question	Analysis

8. In the context of the passage as a whole, the question in lines 89–91 ("But is . . . wealth building") primarily functions to help the author

A) establish that millennials are mismanaging their retirement investments.

B) show how professional money managers diversify their investments to avoid market volatility.

C) introduce data that reveals a flaw in the premises that influence millennials' investment choices.

D) call into question opposing opinions about the effects of the gig economy.

Answer: C

Difficulty: Hard

Category: Function

Strategic Advice: Most Function questions use "serves to," but occasionally, they'll be as direct as this question stem, asking what a piece of text "functions to" do. The research clue in this stem points to the final sentence in paragraph 3.

Getting to the Answer: By ending a paragraph with a rhetorical question, the author signals that the following paragraph will provide the answer. Paragraph 4 discusses the flaw in assuming that home ownership is a more stable or profitable investment than the stock market is. The question at the end of paragraph 3 helps the author set up this discussion, so **(C)** is the correct answer.

(A) is extreme; the author questions one assumption underlying millennials' "a la carte" investment approach, but she doesn't accuse them of overall mismanagement.

(B) is outside the scope. The pre-passage blurb suggests that this author is an investment strategist, but nothing in the passage claims to demonstrate professional approaches to reducing risk.

(D) is outside the scope; the author doesn't present or contradict any opposing views in this paragraph.

Question	Analysis
9. The passage indicates that investing in the stock market	**Answer: C**

Difficulty: Medium

Category: Detail

A) is the stepping stone from which most individuals begin to build personal wealth.

B) remains less stable and lucrative than home ownership as a source of wealth.

C) has tax implications well suited to retirement planning.

D) is limited by IRS rules to a $5,500 annual maximum.

Strategic Advice: A question asking for something that the "passage indicates" is a Detail question. The correct answer will paraphrase a fact, opinion, or claim made explicitly in the passage. Broadly speaking, the entire passage is about "investing in the stock market," but the author provides her most detailed analysis in paragraph 4, making it the best place to target your research.

Getting to the Answer: The bulk of paragraph 4 compares investment in the market favorably to home ownership. The author demonstrates the large return on a modest investment and then points out other reasons why they are well suited to retirement income. One of those reasons is the investments' tax-free status (lines 112–115); that matches the correct answer, **(C)**.

(A) is a misused detail; this answer choice virtually quotes the passage, but the piece of text it cites refers to home ownership, not to stock market investments.

(B) says the opposite of what's in the passage; the author demonstrates that the stock market is more stable and lucrative than home ownership is.

(D) misuses a detail contained in paragraph 4; the $5,500 annual cap applies to IRA contributions, not to stock market investments in general.

Reading

Question	Analysis

10. Which of the following statements about the period from 2010 to 2018 is supported by the graph?

A) Investment in the stock market generated more wealth than home ownership in every market listed in the graph.

B) The value of a home appreciated by a greater percentage in Portland, Oregon, than in Charlotte, North Carolina.

C) The return on a median financial portfolio outperformed the value of home ownership by a greater margin in each subsequent year.

D) Austin, Texas, saw a greater disparity between home value appreciation and return on financial portfolios than Atlanta, Georgia, saw.

Answer: B

Difficulty: Medium

Category: Inference

Strategic Advice: When a question stem says that the correct answer is "supported by" something in the passage, you're looking at an Inference question. It's no different when the support comes from a graph or chart at the end of the passage. Use the information in the graph to evaluate the answer choices.

Getting to the Answer: To see what is implied by a graph or chart accompanying an SAT Reading passage, make sure you understand what is being represented and look for trends. Here, the x-axis shows 10 different cities. For each one, the percent increase in value of a median-priced home and a median-size stock portfolio are given on the y-axis. Only in San Francisco did the value of a home outperform the value of a portfolio of investments. Note that, along the x-axis, the cities are arranged from greatest increase in home value to least. The increases in stock portfolios, while all similar, are not in a particular order. Testing the answers against the graph reveals **(B)** as the correct choice. Charlotte is to the right of Portland on the graph, and you know that means its home values appreciated less than those in Portland.

(A) is contradicted by the case of San Francisco, the one market in which home ownership outperformed stock market investments.

(C) is not supported; the graph does not show year-over-year changes in value. This choice might be tempting to a test taker who glanced at the graph and made the unwarranted assumption that the x-axis represents different years instead of different locations.

(D) can be eliminated by comparing the two named locations. Stock portfolios outperformed home ownership in both cities, but the gap is a little smaller for Austin than it is for Atlanta.

Question	Analysis
11. Which statement from the passage is most directly reflected by the data presented in the graph? A) Lines 48–51 ("For a . . . wealth") B) Lines 74–78 ("Research . . . United States") C) Lines 98–101 ("statistics . . . wealth") D) Lines 110–115 ("Stock . . . drawn on")	**Answer: C** **Difficulty:** Hard **Category:** Command of Evidence **Strategic Advice:** This question stem is relatively rare. It is a variation on the Command of Evidence question type. Here, instead of asking you to find the text supporting a previous answer choice, the question provides you with the evidence—in this case, it is the graph at the end of the passage—and asks you to find the text it supports. **Getting to the Answer:** The graph compares the value of home ownership to stock market investment. The author made the same comparison in paragraph 4. Only **(C)** and (D) contain statements from paragraph 4, and a quick check shows that it is the text in **(C)** that follows from the data shown in the graph. (A) comes from paragraph 2, which discusses the impact on millennials of the Great Recession. Don't get tripped up by the word "median" here; the sentence from paragraph 2 mentions median-income families, while the graph represents median-value homes and median-sized portfolios. (B) comes from paragraph 3, which discusses the gig economy. Always check the full reference in the answer choice; a hurried or sloppy test taker might see the words "[r]esearch" and "United States" and think that's enough to connect this answer to the graph. (D) comes from the correct paragraph, but from a point at which the author has moved on from comparing home ownership and is now discussing other advantages of stock market investments as a source of retirement income.

Try on Your Own

Directions: Put the expert question strategies to work on the following passage. First, take a few minutes to refresh your memory of the passage (which you first saw in chapter 14). Then, for each question 1) identify the question type, 2) note where/how you will research the answer, 3) jot down your prediction of the correct answer, and 4) find the one correct answer.

PREDICTIONS

On the real test, you won't have time to write down your full prediction in complete sentences. If you feel the need to write something to help you hold on to your prediction, keep it very brief: a word or two, or even better, a single abbreviation. For example, if you predict that an author is including a detail as support for a broader point, you might just write "suppt" next to the choices.

Directions: Choose the best answer choice for the following questions.

Questions 1-11 refer to the following passage.

This passage was adapted from an article titled "Quantum Computing: Where Is It Going?" published in a science magazine in 2018. It discusses the background and potential of quantum computing.

Pharmaceutical companies dream of a time when their research and development process shifts from looking for illnesses whose symptoms
5 can be ameliorated by a specific drug to choosing a disease and creating a drug to eradicate it. Quantum computing may be the (key) to that goal. The (powerful) modeling (potential)
10 unlocked by quantum computing may also someday be employed by autonomous vehicles to create a world free of traffic jams. With plausible applications in so many fields, it is
15 worthwhile to learn a bit about how quantum computing works.

Any understanding of quantum computing begins with its most basic element, the qubit. In classical
20 computing, information is processed by the bit, the binary choice of zero or one. Qubits, (on the other) hand, allow for infinite superpositions between zero and one and thus can
25 store and process (exponentially) more

QC: big potential

QC based on qubits – can store more values

complicated values. Imagine showing someone where you live on a globe by pointing only to either the North Pole or the South Pole. While you
30 are likely closer to one pole than the other, you need additional information to represent your specific location. If, however, you could provide your home's latitude and longitude, it could
35 be located without any additional information. The power of quantum computing lies in the ability to express precise information in a single qubit.

Quantum computing may help
40 scientists and engineers overcome another barrier by reducing energy output while increasing computational speed. The positive correlation between energy output
45 and processing speed often causes classical computers to "run hot" while processing overwhelming amounts of data. Along with their ability to store multiple values simultaneously,
50 qubits are able to process those values in parallel (instead of) serially. How does processing in parallel conserve energy? Suppose you want to set the time on five separate alarm clocks
55 spaced ten feet apart. You'd have to walk to each clock to change its time.

Qubit > bit, much more data

Qubits = parallel processing

However, if the clocks were connected such that changing the time on one immediately adjusted the other four, you would expend less energy and increase processing speed. Therein lies the benefit of the quantum entanglement of qubits.

> faster AND cooler

While quantum computing has moved beyond the realm of the theoretical, significant barriers still stand in the way of its practical application. One barrier is the difficulty of confirming the results of quantum calculations. If quantum computing is used to solve problems that are impossible to solve with classical computing, is there a way to "check" the results? Scientists hope this paradox may soon be resolved. As a graduate student, Urmila Mahadev devoted over a decade to creating a verification process for quantum computing. The result is an interactive protocol, based on a type of cryptography called Learning With Errors (LWE), that is similar to "blind computing" used in cloud-computing to mask data while still performing calculations. Given current limitations, Mahadev's protocol remains purely theoretical, but rapid progress in quantum computing combined with further refinement of the protocol will likely result in real-world implementation within the next decade or two.

> One barrier to QC – How to check results?

> probably will get solved

It is unlikely that early pioneers in the field, including Stephen Wiesner, Richard Feynman, and Paul Benioff, could have foreseen the rapid progress that has been made to date. In 1960, when Wiesner first developed conjugate coding with the goal of improving cryptography, his paper on the subject was rejected for publication because it contained logic far ahead of its time. Feynman proposed a basic quantum computing model at the 1981 First Conference on the Physics of

> QC pioneers – 1960s – 80s

Computation. At that same conference, Benioff spoke on the ability of discrete mechanical processes to erase their own history and their application to Turing machines, a natural extension of Wiesner's earlier work. A year later, Benioff more clearly outlined the theoretical framework of a quantum computer.

The dawn of the 21st century brought advancements at an even more impressive pace. The first 5- and 7-qubit nuclear magnetic resonance (NMR) computers were demonstrated in Munich, Germany, and Santa Fe, New Mexico, respectively. In 2006, researchers at Oxford were able to cage a qubit within a "buckyball," a buckminsterfullerene molecule, and maintain its state for a short time using precise, repeated microwave pulses. The first company dedicated to quantum computing software, 1QB Information Technologies, was founded in 2012, and in 2018, Google announced the development of the 72-qubit Bristlecone chip designed to prove "quantum supremacy," the ability of quantum computers to solve problems beyond the reach of classical computing.

> QC sped up in 2000s

With progress in quantum computing accelerating, it seems inevitable that within a few decades, the general population will be as familiar with quantum computing as they now are with classical computing. At present, quantum computing is limited by the struggle to build a computer large enough to prove quantum supremacy, and the costs associated with quantum computing are prohibitive to all but the world's largest corporations and governmental institutions. Still, classical computing overcame similar problems, so the future of quantum computing looks bright.

> QC still difficult, but bright future

1. The primary purpose of the passage is to

   A) argue that quantum computing will provide the solution to pressing societal problems.

   B) compare the speed and efficiency of quantum computing to that of classical computing.

   C) explain the progress and potential of quantum computing despite current obstacles.

   D) refute those who argue that quantum computing is too impractical and expensive to succeed.

2. According to the passage, which one of the following is true of Urmila Mahadev's graduate work?

   A) It was focused on ways to improve "cloud computing."

   B) Its results cannot be confirmed by classical computing techniques.

   C) It will likely have applications for the pharmaceutical industry.

   D) It may lead to verification of quantum computing calculations.

3. Which choice provides the best evidence for the answer to the previous question?

   A) Lines 1–9 ("Pharmaceutical . . . goal")

   B) Lines 67–73 ("One barrier . . . results")

   C) Lines 78–83 ("The result . . . calculations")

   D) Lines 84–90 ("Given . . . two")

4. In the second paragraph, the discussion of locating a person's home on a globe (lines 26–36) primarily serves to

   A) contrast the processing power of quantum computing to that of classical computing.

   B) illustrate the rapid progress of research in quantum computing.

   C) argue that quantum computing will allow for exponentially more complicated mapping software.

   D) support the claim that quantum computing will enable autonomous vehicles to navigate.

5. Based on the passage, the author would most likely criticize classical computing because it

   A) has developed more slowly than quantum computing in recent years.

   B) lacks any application for autonomous vehicles.

   C) employs serial processing.

   D) cannot verify quantum computing calculations.

6. Which statement best describes the technique the author uses to advance the main point of the third paragraph (lines 39–62)?

   A) She describes research done by leading scientists and engineers.

   B) She proposes a laboratory experiment that would prove a hypothesis.

   C) She offers a hypothetical example to illustrate a complex comparison.

   D) She cites data demonstrating the superior efficiency of one technique.

7. The passage indicates that which of the following factors slowed early developments in the theory of quantum computing?

   A) Feynman and Benioff were discouraged that their computing models were rejected.

   B) At least one academic journal was reluctant to publish papers containing advanced logic.

   C) Quantum computing was too expensive for colleges and universities to support effectively during the 1980s.

   D) A focus on cryptology in the early 1960s drew the most talented researchers away from quantum computing.

8. Which one of the following does the passage imply about the development of quantum computing in the 21st century?

    A) At least some companies anticipate commercial viability for quantum computing in the future.

    B) Recent advancements in hardware have demonstrated "quantum superiority."

    C) Research into quantum computing led to the discovery of the "buckyball."

    D) It has stalled due to reluctance of major corporations and governments to fund such expensive research.

9. Which choice provides the best evidence for the answer to the previous question?

    A) Lines 115–119 ("The first . . . respectively")

    B) Lines 119–124 ("In 2006 . . . pulses")

    C) Lines 124–133 ("The first . . . computing")

    D) Lines 139–142 ("At present . . . supremacy")

10. As used in line 123, "maintain" most nearly means

    A) sustain.

    B) repair.

    C) resupply.

    D) nurture.

11. The author's attitude toward the potential success of quantum computing can best be described as

    A) skeptical.

    B) resigned.

    C) incredulous.

    D) optimistic.

Reading

How Much Have You Learned?

Directions: Take 13 minutes to read the passage and answer the associated questions. Try to use the various SAT Reading question strategies you learned in this chapter.

Questions 12-22 refer to the following passage.

This passage was adapted from an article entitled "John Snow Knew Something" published in a popular history magazine in 2018.

Few would deny that doctors use critical thinking to solve problems, but most imagine a difference between the practice of medicine and, say,
5   the methods a police detective might use to solve a case. In fact, medical researchers have long used forensic methods of detection and analysis. The case of John Snow, a
10 19th-century anesthesiologist, is often said to have ushered in the modern era of epidemiology, the branch of medicine that tracks the incidence and distribution of diseases and
15 proposes solutions for their control and prevention.

Snow's work used investigation, changed medicine

It would not be until 1861 that Louis Pasteur would propose the link between microorganisms and disease,
20 now known as the germ theory. Before Pasteur's breakthrough, the predominant explanation for the cause of most illnesses was the so-called miasma theory, which held that noxious
25 fumes and pollution—quite literally, as the theory's name implies, "bad air"— were responsible for making people sick. Consequently, during the 1854 outbreak of cholera in Westminster,
30 London, doctors and government officials alike blamed "miasmatic particles" released into the air by decaying organic matter in the soil of the River Thames.
35 Despite the widespread acceptance of the miasma theory, there were those, Snow included, who were skeptical of

1854 – didn't know about germs; miasma theory

this view. Snow would not have known, as doctors do today, that cholera
40 is caused by a bacterial infection, *Vibrio cholerae.* Nevertheless, he was convinced that the spread of the disease was caused by some form of matter passed between individuals, likely
45 through contaminated water.

Snow: cholera from contam. H_2O

To demonstrate this, Snow targeted a particularly deadly outbreak in the Soho district of Westminster in London. From August 31 to September
50 3, 1854, 127 people in the area died of cholera. Within a week, that number had risen to over 500. Snow took to the streets. Speaking to residents of the area, he found a commonality among
55 them: most of the victims had used a single public water pump located on Broad Street. Though he was unable to find conclusive proof that the pump was the source of the outbreak, his
60 demonstration of a pattern in the cholera cases prompted authorities to disable the pump by removing its handle. The epidemic quickly subsided.

Proof from interviews – all used same pump

Soon after the Broad Street pump
65 was shut down, Snow's continued investigation provided additional evidence that contaminated water was the source of the outbreak. Snow created a dot map of the cases of cholera in London
70 and demonstrated that they occurred in areas where water was supplied by two companies that obtained their water from wells near the Thames. Investigation of these wells showed that they had been
75 dug three feet from a cesspit that was leaking sewage into the surrounding soil. Snow also discovered that there were no cases of cholera among workers in a brewery close to the Broad Street pump.

Water from contam. wells

Reading

80　These workers were provided a daily
　　allowance of beer, which they drank
　　instead of water, and although the beer
　　was brewed using the contaminated
　　water, it was boiled during the brewing

Boiling first prevented disease

85　process. This revelation provided a
　　~~practical solution~~ for the prevention of
　　future outbreaks.

　　　　Snow is ~~now hailed~~ as the "father of
　　modern epidemiology," and the radical
90　nature of his approach—formulating
　　a new theory, substantiating it with
　　verifiable evidence, and proposing
　　preventative action—is fully
　　appreciated. At the time, ~~however,~~ not
95　all were convinced, at least publicly, of
　　Snow's findings. As anxiety over the
　　outbreak flagged, government officials
　　replaced the handle on the Broad Street
　　pump and publicly denounced Snow's

Snow not accepted at the time

100　conclusions. It seems they felt that the
　　city's residents would be upset and
　　disgusted to have the unsettling nature
　　of the well's contamination confirmed.
　　It wasn't until 1866, more than a decade
105　after Snow's original investigation and
　　theory—when another cholera outbreak
　　killed more than 5,500 residents of
　　London's East End—that officials
　　working in public health began to

1866 – another epidemic

110　accept the link between contaminated
　　water and certain kinds of illness and
　　to take appropriate actions to quell such
　　outbreaks.

12. The passage primarily serves to

    A) summarize the history of research into the causes and prevention of cholera.

    B) critique government officials for failing to consider evidence that could have prevented further loss of life.

    C) chronicle an episode in the history of medicine that changed the way in which research is conducted.

    D) demonstrate similarities in the methods used by medical researchers and by police detectives.

13. The author of this passage writes from the perspective of

    A) a public health official advocating for improved disease prevention measures.

    B) a journalist narrating medical history to lay readers.

    C) an editorial opinion writer critiquing the actions of local officials.

    D) a medical school professor explaining the techniques of epidemiological research.

14. The second paragraph serves mainly to

    A) suggest a reasonable alternative to a hypothesis presented later.

    B) outline the scientific and historical context for a problem that required a novel solution.

    C) summarize the conditions that led to a recurring public health issue.

    D) criticize the stubbornness of physicians and politicians against considering new evidence.

15. Which of the following is most analogous to John Snow's theory that contaminated water caused the cholera outbreak?

    A) Gregor Mendel described the principles of biological heredity years before the discovery of genes and DNA.

    B) Robert Koch used Louis Pasteur's experiments to develop the postulates of the germ theory of disease.

    C) Rosalind Franklin produced x-ray diffraction images of DNA, which were used by Watson and Crick to describe its structure.

    D) Galileo Galilei promoted a sun-centered model of the solar system but was put on trial because his views conflicted with those of the Spanish Inquisition.

16. Which choice provides the best evidence for the answer to the previous question?

    A) Lines 17–20 ("It would . . . theory")

    B) Lines 38–45 ("Snow would . . . water")

    C) Lines 57–63 ("Though he . . . subsided")

    D) Lines 85–87 ("This revelation . . . outbreaks")

17. The passage indicates that the main reason government officials rejected Snow's hypothesis was

    A) a lack of concrete scientific proof.

    B) a fear of public backlash.

    C) mistrust of Snow's methods.

    D) financial ties to the city's water suppliers.

18. Which choice provides the best evidence for the answer to the previous question?

    A) Lines 35–38 ("Despite the . . . view")

    B) Lines 57–63 ("Though he . . . subsided")

    C) Lines 68–73 ("Snow created . . . Thames")

    D) Lines 100–103 ("It seems . . . confirmed")

19. Which of the following is cited as the primary reason Snow suspected the Broad Street pump as the source of the epidemic?

    A) The discovery of decaying organic matter in soil near the Thames releasing gases into the air

    B) The decline of cases of the disease following the removal of the pump handle

    C) A pattern in the geographical location of cases of the disease

    D) A lack of cases of the disease among those working in a brewery near the pump

20. It can be reasonably inferred from the passage that scientists in 1855 would have found which of the following solutions to be most practical in dealing with future outbreaks of cholera?

    A) Using alcoholic beverages in place of water for all applications

    B) Removing the handles from all water pumps in the affected area

    C) Vaccinating the public against the disease using inactive *V. cholerae* bacteria

    D) Advising the public to boil all water from municipal sources before use

21. As used in line 97, the word "flagged" most nearly means

    A) subsided.

    B) indicated.

    C) penalized.

    D) peaked.

22. The author uses the final sentence of the passage ("It wasn't . . . outbreaks") at least in part to

    A) underscore the assertion that Snow's explanation of the cause of the epidemic was ultimately correct.

    B) demonstrate that an explanation of a phenomenon will not be accepted until after the mechanism behind it is fully detailed.

    C) suggest that there is often a significant delay between medical discovery and its application.

    D) lament the loss of life caused by failing to act on medical recommendations that are reasonably supported by evidence.

Reflect

Directions: Take a few minutes to recall what you've learned and what you've been practicing in this chapter. Consider the following questions, jot down your best answer for each one, and then compare your reflections to the expert responses on the following page. Use your level of confidence to determine what to do next.

Why do SAT experts research and predict the correct answer to Reading questions before reading the answer choices?

_____

_____

_____

What are the types of research clues contained in SAT Reading question stems?

_____

_____

_____

What are the five common wrong answer types associated with SAT Reading questions?

- _____
- _____
- _____
- _____
- _____

How will you approach the process of answering SAT Reading questions more strategically going forward? Are there any specific habits you will practice to make your approach to SAT Reading more effective and efficient?

_____

_____

_____

Expert Responses

Why do SAT experts research and predict the correct answer to Reading questions before reading the answer choices?

Expert test takers know that the correct answer to each SAT Reading question is based on the text of the passage. They research to avoid answering based on memory or on a whim. Predicting the correct answer before reading the choices increases accuracy and speed by helping the test taker avoid rereading, confusion, and comparing answer choices to one another.

What are the types of research clues contained in SAT Reading question stems?

Line numbers, paragraph numbers, proper nouns, quoted text, specific content clues, and whole passage clues

What are the five common wrong answer types associated with SAT Reading questions?

- *Out of scope*
- *Opposite*
- *Distortion*
- *Extreme*
- *Misused detail*

How will you approach the process of answering SAT Reading questions more strategically going forward? Are there any specific habits you will practice to make your approach to SAT Reading more effective and efficient?

There is no one-size-fits-all answer here. Reflect on your own habits in answering SAT Reading questions and give yourself an honest assessment of your strengths and weaknesses. Consider the strategies you've seen experts use in this chapter, and put them to work in your own practice to increase your accuracy, speed, and confidence.

Next Steps

If you answered most questions correctly in the "How Much Have You Learned?" section, and if your responses to the Reflect questions were similar to those of the SAT expert, then consider answering Reading questions an area of strength and move on to the next chapter. Come back to this topic periodically to prevent yourself from getting rusty.

If you don't yet feel confident, review the material in "How to Answer SAT Reading Questions," and then try the questions you missed again. As always, be sure to review the explanations closely.

Answers and Explanations

1.   C

Difficulty: Easy

Category: Global

Strategic Advice: "[P]rimary purpose" indicates a Global question. Consult your big picture summary to predict the correct answer.

Getting to the Answer: The author is convinced that quantum computing has enormous potential despite current obstacles. She explains the basis of quantum computing, outlines its rapid progress, and describes efforts to make it practicable. **(C)** summarizes all of this and is correct.

(A) is too narrow and too strong. The passage opens with examples of problems that quantum computing may *help* solve, but this isn't the author's main point.

(B) is too narrow. The discussion of processing speed and energy output is included in paragraph 3 as one potential advantage of quantum computing.

(D) misstates the author's purpose. The passage was not written to *refute* an opposing point of view, nor does the author contend that anyone else is mistaken in their criticism of quantum computing.

2.   D

Difficulty: Medium

Category: Detail

Strategic Advice: "According to the passage" indicates a Detail question. The correct answer is something stated explicitly in the passage. The research clue, Urmila Mahadev, leads you straight to paragraph 4.

Getting to the Answer: Paragraph 4 is about an obstacle to quantum computing: the paradox that arises from the fact that classical computing cannot be used to verify the results of quantum computing. How does Mahadev figure in here? Mahadev dedicated her graduate studies to trying to resolve this paradox. She has come up with a theoretical solution that the author concludes will likely have real-world application in the coming years. That final statement matches **(D)**, making it the correct answer.

(A) is a faulty use of detail. Part of Mahadev's protocol is similar to techniques used in cloud computing, but nothing indicates that she was trying to improve cloud computing.

(B) distorts the paragraph. It is the results of quantum computing that cannot be confirmed by classical computing, not the results of Mahadev's graduate work.

(C) brings in a detail from paragraph 1; pharmaceutical research is irrelevant to Mahadev's graduate studies.

3.   D

Difficulty: Medium

Category: Command of Evidence

Strategic Advice: Questions that ask you to locate the evidence for the preceding question's correct answer are Command of Evidence questions. Use your research for the preceding question to put your finger on the relevant support from the passage and match that to the correct answer choice here.

Getting to the Answer: The correct answer to the preceding question said that Mahadev's graduate work would likely lead to verification of quantum computing results. That was from the end of paragraph 4, matching **(D)**.

(A) refers back to paragraph 1; this is irrelevant to Mahadev's work, but matches up with choice (C) in the preceding question.

(B) quotes the statement of the problem that Mahadev's work is trying to solve, but doesn't match the correct answer to the preceding question, which stated that her protocol will likely work.

(C) cites the description of Mahadev's protocol; this answer could be tempting if you incorrectly chose (A) on the preceding question.

4.   A

Difficulty: Medium

Category: Function

Strategic Advice: The phrase "serves to" identifies this as a Function question. Check the context of the example cited in the question stem and identify *how* the author uses it.

Getting to the Answer: The second paragraph outlines why qubits (the basis for quantum computing) are so much more powerful than bits (the building blocks of classical computing). The hypothetical case of pinpointing one's house on a globe illustrates this contrast. Thus, **(A)** is correct.

(B) is off topic. The progress of quantum computing research is discussed in the fifth and sixth paragraphs.

(C) contains a distracting reference to "mapping software," which may remind you of a globe, but the author doesn't discuss software applications at all in this paragraph. Another potentially distracting phrase here is "exponentially more complicated," an exact quote from earlier in the paragraph. When evaluating answer choices in SAT Reading, look for the answer that matches the meaning of your correct-answer prediction, not simply for a choice with familiar words.

(D) inappropriately drags in an example—autonomous vehicles—from the first paragraph. The author does not connect that to the globe analogy in any way.

5.   C

Difficulty: Hard

Category: Inference

Strategic advice: "Based on the passage" introduces an Inference question. The correct answer will follow from the passage without having been explicitly stated in the passage. Use the research clues in the question stem to narrow down your search and then consider the implications of what is stated at that point in the passage.

Getting to the Answer: The author compares classical computing unfavorably to quantum computing in paragraphs 2 (quantum computing can handle exponentially more complicated values) and 3 (quantum computing uses parallel processing to run faster with less energy output). Paragraph 3 directly supports the correct answer, **(C)**. Because parallel processing gives quantum computing its advantage, serial processing is the reason classical computing is inferior.

(A) distorts the author's point of view. She describes quantum computing's rapid advancement, but doesn't compare that to classical computing's development.

(B) is extreme. The author doesn't say that classical computing has *no value* for driverless cars, but rather that quantum computing may have great value for this technology in the future.

(C) is a faulty use of detail. This answer choice is true according to paragraph 4, but the author doesn't claim that this is a shortcoming of classical computing.

6.   C

Difficulty: Hard

Category: Function

Strategic Advice: On occasion, the SAT will ask you to describe the way in which the author has made or supported a point in the passage. Research a question like this from the clues in the question stem. Be prepared for somewhat abstract language in the answer choices as they will be worded to describe the author's technique, not to recount the details in the paragraph.

Getting to the Answer: In paragraph 3, the author describes a potential advantage of quantum computing by comparing parallel processing in quantum computing to serial processing in classical computing. She illustrates this with the simple thought experiment about the five clocks. That matches the "complex comparison" and "hypothetical example" described in **(C)**.

(A) distorts the paragraph. Quantum computing, you're told, may help scientists and engineers, but doesn't mention any research by people in those occupations.

(B) distorts the author's example. She doesn't suggest that someone set up the five clocks in a laboratory and test them for efficiency.

(D) misses the paragraph entirely; the author doesn't cite any data here.

7.   B

Difficulty: Medium

Category: Detail

Strategic Advice: The word "indicates" signals a Detail question. The correct answer will be something explicitly stated in the text. The research clue "early developments" should send you to paragraph 5 to research.

Getting to the Answer: Most of the details in paragraph 5 are positive and speak to a slow but consistent advancement in theorizing and modeling quantum computing. The one setback that is mentioned is the rejection of Wiesner's paper by an academic journal hesitant to publish logic that was "ahead of its time." That's described in the correct answer, **(B)**.

(A) distorts the paragraph, which does not suggest that Feynman's and Benioff's models were rejected.

(C) misapplies a detail from paragraph 7; the expense of quantum computing limits research today. You're told nothing about whether schools funded this research in the 1980s.

(D) contradicts the passage; Wiesner's interest in cryptology appears to have promoted his work leading to early quantum computing models.

8. A

Difficulty: Medium

Category: Inference

Strategic Advice: The word "imply" marks this as an Inference question. The correct answer will be supported by something in the passage's discussion of quantum computing's development in the 21st century.

Getting to the Answer: The passage focuses on the 21st century development of quantum computing in paragraph 6, which contains three main details: the demonstration of MNR computers, the Oxford research that caged a qubit, and the emergence of commercial interest in quantum computing. The last of those, as exemplified in the passage by 1QB Information Technologies and Google, supports choice **(A)** as the correct answer.

(B) distorts the paragraph; Google's *Bristlecone* chip is intended to prove quantum superiority, but the passage does not say that it has been used successfully.

(C) distorts what the passage says about the Oxford research; there, researchers used a "buckyball," but you're not told who discovered the molecule or when it was discovered.

(D) misuses a claim from paragraph 7; while it's true that quantum computing is very expensive, the last sentence of paragraph 6 contradicts the statement made in this answer choice.

9. C

Difficulty: Medium

Category: Command of Evidence

Strategic Advice: This is a standard Command of Evidence question asking you to locate the text that supports the correct answer to the preceding question. Use that answer to guide your research.

Getting to the Answer: The final sentence of paragraph 6 demonstrates that companies are pursuing quantum computing research. That matches **(C)**.

(A) comes from paragraph 6 but doesn't support the correct answer to the preceding question.

(B) describes the Oxford research; it might be tempting to a test taker who mistakenly chose (C) on the preceding question.

(D) comes from paragraph 7; it cites a hurdle that quantum computing must overcome.

10. A

Difficulty: Medium

Category: Vocab-in-Context

Strategic Advice: For Vocab-in-Context questions, check the sentence in which the word from the question stem is used to paraphrase its meaning in context. The correct answer could be substituted into the sentence without changing the meaning of the sentence at all.

Getting to the Answer: In the sentence at line 123, scientists have been able to maintain the state of qubit using an oddly named molecule. You don't need to understand the details of the process to get the gist of the sentence. The scientists are keeping the qubit in a constant, or stable, state. That matches the correct answer, **(A)**.

(B) doesn't work here because nothing suggests that the qubit was "broken" in the process.

(C) implies that the qubit loses something and needs to be refreshed or made whole; that doesn't fit the context.

(D) means to care for the development of, which would add information not implied by the sentence.

11. D

Difficulty: Medium

Category: Inference

Strategic Advice: A question about the author's attitude is a variety of Inference question. The correct answer follows from the author's opinions and points of view as they are expressed in the passage.

Getting to the Answer: The author concludes the passage on a high note. While acknowledging ongoing difficulties that quantum computing still needs to overcome, she finds it "inevitable" that it will one day be familiar to most people and explicitly states that the field's future "looks bright." Thus, **(D)** is correct.

(A) is too negative to describe this author's point of view.

(B) is also negative; a "resigned" attitude would indicate an author who has accepted an unfortunate result and has stopped fighting against it.

(C) means "unbelieving." If the author were incredulous, she would deny that quantum computing could actually happen.

12. C

Difficulty: Easy

Category: Global

Strategic Advice: The phrase "primarily serves to" marks this as a Global question. Consult your big picture summary to predict the correct answer.

Getting to the Answer: For this passage, you can summarize the author's purpose as something like: "Narrate the story of how Snow's cholera research changed doctors' understanding and prevention of disease." That leads to the correct answer, **(C)**. The phrase "chronicle an episode" contains a verb that accurately describes the author's journalistic tone and focuses on the correct scope, a single event.

(A) is too broad; the passage does not attempt to sum up the entire history of cholera research.

(B) is too narrow; officials' rejection of Snow's findings the decade after the 1854 cholera outbreak is an unfortunate coda to the story, not the main point of the passage.

(D) is too narrow; the author mentions forensic evidence and investigation in the introduction to familiarize the reader with techniques that will be discussed.

13. B

Difficulty: Medium

Category: Global

Strategic Advice: This is a relatively rare variation on Global questions that asks you to describe the author's perspective. Consider your big picture summary, especially the author's purpose, to determine the role this author most likely fills.

Getting to the Answer: This passage centers on the story of Snow's cholera research to explain its importance for medical research. The author compares epidemiology to criminal investigation to provide context for the general reader. This leads to **(B)** as the correct answer.

(A) suggests a passage that would likely focus on a current problem and would use language intended to persuade the reader to adopt new policies.

(C) describes an article primarily focused on the mistakes of present-day politicians and bureaucrats.

(D) portrays an expert communicating scientific and technical details to an expert reader.

14. B

Difficulty: Medium

Category: Function

Strategic Advice: When a Function question ("serves . . . to") asks about the role of a paragraph, check your margin notes to see why the author wrote the paragraph and how it fits into the rest of the passage.

Getting to the Answer: Your note for paragraph 2 should indicate that this is where the author laid out the state of medical knowledge in 1854: doctors didn't know about germs; people still believed the miasma theory of disease. The author included this to show how innovative Snow's hypothesis and investigation were. That analysis leads to the correct answer, **(B)**.

(A) states the opposite of what the author intended; the beliefs outlined in paragraph 2 were unreasonable and soon rejected.

(C) distorts the passage; the conditions that led to the outbreak, such as wells dug too near cesspits, are discussed later in the passage.

(D) describes details the author introduces in paragraph 6, not paragraph 2.

15. A

Difficulty: Hard

Category: Inference

Strategic Advice: A question asking you to select a scenario "analogous to" one described in the passage is an Inference question. The correct answer follows from the passage without having been stated explicitly in the passage.

Getting to the Answer: The passage says that Snow hypothesized that cholera was spread by contaminated water even though he and his contemporaries were unaware of germs as the cause of diseases. Among the answer choices, the most appropriate analogy is the one described in **(A)**; Mendel described the workings of heredity even though he didn't know about its underlying structures, genes and DNA.

(B) may be tempting because it mentions Louis Pasteur—a scientist also mentioned in the passage—but it gets the analogy backwards; the situation described in this answer choice involves a scientist building on information already discovered.

(C) describes a situation in which a technological breakthrough (x-ray diffraction images) led to the refinement of a scientific theory; that doesn't match Snow's investigation, performed without the aid of technology.

(D) recounts a case in which social pressure was used in an attempt to silence a scientist; after Snow's discovery, some officials ignored his findings, but the passage does not imply that he was persecuted.

16. B

Difficulty: Medium

Category: Command of Evidence

Strategic Advice: This is a standard Command of Evidence question. Your job is to locate the passage text that directly supports the correct answer to the preceding question.

Getting to the Answer: The correct answer to the question immediately before this one suggested that an important aspect of Snow's theory was that he formulated the theory before scientists had discovered the biological mechanism explaining it. The author said this explicitly in the sentence quoted in choice **(B)**.

The sentence quoted in choice (A) discusses the germ theory of disease but does not directly discuss the fact that Snow would not have known about it.

The sentence quoted in (C) focuses on how Snow pinpointed the physical source of the cholera outbreak, not on how he formulated his initial hypothesis.

The text quoted in (D) explains how Snow's research helped find a way to prevent the spread of cholera; the question preceding this one focused on his theory of its cause, not prevention.

17. B

Difficulty: Medium

Category: Detail

Strategic Advice: The word "indicates" signals a Detail question. The correct answer will paraphrase something explicitly stated in the passage. Target paragraph 6 where the author discussed government officials' rejection of Snow's findings.

Getting to the Answer: The question stem asks for the *reason* officials ignored Snow's hypothesis. This is discussed in lines 94–103. The officials feared public outcry ("upset and disgusted") upon finding out that sewage had leaked into their water supply, a concern that **(B)** sums up succinctly.

(A) misuses a detail from paragraph 4: Snow persuaded officials to remove the pump handle despite a lack of "conclusive proof."

(C) distorts the passage; the author says that officials publicly rejected Snow's findings for political reasons but doesn't say that they doubted his methods.

(D) is outside the scope; nothing in the passage suggests that corruption played a role in the officials' decisions.

18. D

Difficulty: Medium

Category: Command of Evidence

Strategic Advice: This is a standard Command of Evidence question. Your job is to locate the passage text that directly supports the correct answer to the preceding question.

Getting to the Answer: The preceding question focused on why officials rejected Snow's findings. That is directly explained by the sentence quoted in choice **(D)**.

(A) quotes the first sentence of paragraph 3; this addresses Snow's rejection of the miasma theory, not officials' rejection of Snow's theory.

(B) quotes the end of paragraph 4 where the author explained that removal of the pump handle curtailed the cholera outbreak. Because this excerpt contains the phrase "unable to find conclusive proof," it may tempt test takers who mistakenly chose (A) in the preceding question.

(C) quotes a sentence from paragraph 5 that details further steps in Snow's research; it is unrelated to the officials' reactions to his findings.

19. C

Difficulty: Hard

Category: Detail

Strategic Advice: This is a Detail question asking for something "cited" in the passage. Direct your research to paragraph 4, where the author explains how Snow narrowed his search for the cause of the cholera outbreak to the Broad Street pump.

Getting to the Answer: According to the passage, Snow interviewed "residents of the area" and discovered that "most of the victims had used a single pump." That is summed up nicely in the correct answer, **(C)**.

(A) restates what those who still held the miasma theory of disease, not Snow, believed to be the outbreak's source.

(B) gets the order of events backwards; Snow's suspicions about the Broad Street pump *led* to the removal of its handle.

(D) also describes a situation Snow discovered *after* the pump handle was removed.

20. D

Difficulty: Hard

Category: Inference

Strategic Advice: The phrase "reasonably inferred" indicates an Inference question. The correct answer will follow from the passage without having been explicitly stated in the passage.

Getting to the Answer: At the end of paragraph 5, the passage states that Snow's "revelation"—that workers at the brewery near Broad Street pump boiled the water before using it to make beer—provided a way to prevent future outbreaks. Thus, **(D)** is the correct answer.

(A) is extreme; while the brewery employees were fortunate to avoid contamination, the passage does not imply that drinks containing alcohol could be universally substituted for water.

(B) is extreme; the result of this recommendation would be that no one in the city would have water, which would be untenable.

(C) might be a reasonable suggestion today, but the passage tells you that the bacteria was unknown in 1855.

21. A

Difficulty: Medium

Category: Vocab-in-Context

Strategic Advice: To answer a Vocab-in-Context question, check the sentence in which the word was used for clues about its meaning. The correct answer can be substituted for the word in the question stem without changing the meaning of the sentence.

Getting to the Answer: If you know that one meaning of "flag," used as a verb, is *decrease* or *lessen*, this question is straightforward. If you are unfamiliar with this definition, the logic of the sentence still leads to **(A)** as the correct answer. Officials would have replaced the pump handle at the point when public anxiety went down.

(B), *indicated*, suggests a use of "flagged" that would be appropriate in a sentence like, "The teacher flagged the error with a sticky note." In the context of the passage, it does not make sense to say that "public anxiety" was flagged in this way.

(C), *penalized*, might remind you of the way "flagged" is used to describe a referee's actions in a sporting event, but it is not appropriate for this sentence in the passage.

(D), *peaked*, meaning "arriving at the highest point," is opposite of the correct meaning; officials certainly would not replace the pump handle at the height of public anxiety.

22. A

Difficulty: Hard

Category: Function

Strategic Advice: A question asking how the author uses a piece of text—in this case, a specific sentence—is a Function question. Research the sentence in the context of the paragraph.

Getting to the Answer: The final paragraph of the passage opens with a statement of how Snow is now appreciated as an innovator. The heart of the paragraph then explains how political expediency led to a temporary rejection of his findings. The paragraph's final sentence brings you back to Snow's ultimate vindication, despite an intervening tragedy. **(A)** accurately describes the final sentence's purpose in the paragraph.

(B) distorts the passage; Snow's explanation was accepted because it was effective in preventing cholera, not because he fully explained the bacteria causing the disease.

(C) contradicts the passage; Snow's discovery was applied immediately when officials removed the handle of Broad Street pump.

(D) refers to the 1866 epidemic for the wrong reason; the author mentions this detail to explain what finally motivated acceptance of Snow's ideas, not to criticize the officials' actions.

PART 4

SAT Writing and Language

CHAPTER 17

The Method for SAT Writing and Language Questions

LEARNING OBJECTIVE

After completing this chapter, you will be able to:

- Efficiently apply the SAT Writing and Language Method

How to Do SAT Writing and Language

The Writing and Language section of the SAT tests a limited number of grammar errors and style or logic issues. You should feel empowered in knowing that you can familiarize yourself with these recurring errors and learn to spot them and address them quickly and efficiently. We'll describe the grammar issues that you're likely to see on test day in the next chapter and the organization and style issues you may encounter in the online Appendix to this book. In this chapter, we'll present a simple series of steps for tackling Writing and Language questions.

Take a look at the passage and questions that follow and think about how you would approach them on test day. Then compare your approach to the recommendations presented.

Questions 1 and 2 refer to the following passage.

Child Expenditures

A report from the United States Department of Agriculture estimates that the average cost of raising a child born in 2015 until age seventeen is over $230,000. This cost includes housing, food, transportation, health care, child care, and education; the overall cost varies considerably from family to family. **1** Therefore, with the average cost of raising a child set at nearly a quarter million dollars, and with additional children in the family raising that financial expenditure accordingly, it becomes clear that parenthood is a major undertaking. When planning a family, **2** financial considerations should be kept in mind by future parents.

1. A) NO CHANGE
    B) However,
    C) Moreover,
    D) Subsequently,

2. A) NO CHANGE
    B) financial considerations should be at the forefront of parents' thinking.
    C) future parents should keep financial considerations in mind.
    D) future parents should consider financial issues to be of paramount importance in the process of their preparations.

There is no need to read the entire passage before you start to answer questions. Instead, answer them as you read. When you see a number, finish the sentence you are reading and then look at the corresponding question. If you can answer the question based on what you've read so far, do so—this will likely be the case if the question is testing grammar. If you need more information—which may happen if the question is testing organization or relevance—keep reading until you have enough context to answer the question.

Sometimes the issue being tested will be obvious to you when you look at the underlined segment. If it isn't, glance at the answer choices to help you determine what the test maker is after. For instance, in question 1, a transition word plus a comma is underlined. Is the question testing the transition or the punctuation? A quick glance at the choices makes it obvious that it's the former, given that they all include the comma but feature different transition words. **Identifying the issue**, using the choices if necessary, is step 1 of the Writing and Language Method.

To find the correct transition, use the surrounding text. The previous sentence addresses the variability of child expenditures, while the sentence that includes the transition word draws a conclusion from the *average* expenditure, not from the variability. The correct transition must highlight this contrast, so the sentence is incorrect as written, and you can eliminate (A). Among the remaining choices, there is only one contrast word: "However." Of the other choices, "Moreover" conveys continuation and "Subsequently" conveys a sequence in time. Neither fixes the error, so eliminate both and choose **(B)** as the correct answer to question 1. **Eliminating answer choices that do not address the issue** is step 2 of the Writing and Language Method.

Sometimes there will be more than one choice that addresses the issue. When that happens, you'll need to base your final response on three considerations: conciseness, relevance, and the potential of a given choice to introduce a new error. Question 2 is an example of a question in which more than one choice addresses the issue. This question features an underlined segment immediately following an introductory phrase—a signal to check for a modification error. Indeed, it is future parents who would be planning a family, so the phrase "future parents" should be right next to the introductory modifying phrase. That eliminates (A) and (B), but you still have to decide between (C) and (D), both of which fix the misplaced modifier. Both of these choices are grammatically correct and relevant to the surrounding context. However, **(C)** is more concise and is therefore the correct answer for question 2. **Choosing the most concise and relevant response from those that are grammatically correct** is step 3 of the Writing and Language method.

Here are the steps we just illustrated:

Method for SAT Writing and Language Questions	
Step 1.	Identify the issue (use the choices if need be)
Step 2.	Eliminate answer choices that do not address the issue
Step 3.	Plug in the remaining answer choices and select the most *correct, concise,* and *relevant* one

Correct, concise, and **relevant** means that the answer choice you select:

- Has no grammatical errors
- Is as short as possible while retaining the writer's intended meaning
- Is relevant to the paragraph and the passage as a whole

Correct answers do *not* change the intended meaning of the original sentence, paragraph, or passage, or introduce new grammatical errors.

Try on Your Own

Directions: Take as much time as you need on these questions. Work carefully and methodically. Practice using the steps that you just learned.

Questions 1-4 refer to the following passage.

Bebop Jazz

For a jazz musician in New York City in the early 1940s, the most interesting place to spend the hours between midnight and dawn was probably a Harlem nightclub called Minton's. After finishing their jobs at other clubs, young musicians like **1** Charlie Parker, Dizzy Gillespie, Kenny Clarke, Thelonious Monk would gather at Minton's and have jam sessions, informal performances featuring lengthy group and solo improvisations. The all-night sessions resulted in the birth of modern jazz as these African American artists together forged a new sound, known as bebop.

Unlike swing, the enormously popular jazz played in the 1930s, bebop was not dance music. It was often blindingly fast, incorporating tricky, irregular rhythms and discordant sounds that jazz audiences had never heard before. Earlier jazz used blue notes but, like much of Western music up to that time, generally stuck to chord tones to create melodies. Bebop, in contrast, relied heavily on chromatic ornamentation and borrowed notes from altered **2** scales. Thereby, it opened up new harmonic opportunities for musicians.

The musicians who pioneered bebop shared two common elements: a vision of the new music's possibilities and astonishing improvisational skill—the ability to play or compose a musical line on the spur

1. A) NO CHANGE
    B) Charlie Parker; Dizzy Gillespie; Kenny Clarke; and Thelonious Monk
    C) Charlie Parker and Dizzy Gillespie, and Kenny Clarke and Thelonious Monk
    D) Charlie Parker, Dizzy Gillespie, Kenny Clarke, and Thelonious Monk

2. Which choice most effectively combines the sentences at the underlined portion?

    A) scales, thereby, it opened up
    B) scales, and thereby opening up
    C) scales, opening up
    D) scales, thereby opening up

of the moment. After all, **3** improvisation, within the context of a group setting, is a hallmark of jazz. Parker, perhaps the greatest instrumental genius jazz has known, was an especially brilliant improviser. He often played double-time, twice as fast as the rest of the band, and his solos were exquisitely shaped, revealing a harmonic imagination that enthralled his listeners.

Like many revolutions, unfortunately, the bebop movement encountered heavy resistance. Opposition came from older jazz musicians initially, but also, later and more lastingly, from a general public alienated by the **4** music's complexity and sophistication. Furthermore, due to the government ban on recording that was in effect during the early years of World War II (records were made of vinyl, a petroleum product that was essential to the war effort), the creative ferment that first produced bebop was poorly documented.

3. A) NO CHANGE
    B) improvisation within the context of a group setting is a hallmark
    C) improvisation within the context of a group setting, is a hallmark
    D) improvisation, within the context of a group setting is a hallmark

4. A) NO CHANGE
    B) musics
    C) musics'
    D) music

Writing & Lang

Answers and Explanations

1.   D

Difficulty: Easy

Category: Sentence Structure: Commas, Dashes, and Colons

Getting to the Answer: Use commas to separate three or more items forming a series or list. This series contains four items. Separate each item with a comma and use a comma with the conjunction "and" to separate the final item from the rest of the series. Choice **(D)** is correct.

2.   C

Difficulty: Hard

Category: Organization: Conciseness

Getting to the Answer: Consider the relationship between the sentences in order to determine how best to combine them. The second sentence contributes useful information regarding the results of using the "chromatic ornamentation" and "altered scales." Making the second sentence a modifying phrase and connecting it to the first with a comma will eliminate unnecessary words and more clearly and smoothly show the relationship between the ideas. Choice **(C)** is correct. Choice (D) is similar and may be tempting, but since "opening up vast new harmonic opportunities" now directly modifies "altered scales," the word "thereby" is redundant.

3.   B

Difficulty: Medium

Category: Sentence Structure: Commas, Dashes, and Colons

Getting to the Answer: When you see a phrase set off by commas, always read the sentence without the phrase to determine if the phrase is nonessential. Although the sentence is still grammatically correct without the information that is set off by the commas, an essential part of the meaning is lost. The author is stating that it is the group setting that characterizes the type of improvisation important to jazz. Choice **(B)** properly removes the commas that set off the phrase.

4.   A

Difficulty: Easy

Category: Agreement: Modifiers

Getting to the Answer: When an underlined section features an apostrophe after a noun, check the noun's number. This sentence is correct as written. Although there are many styles of music, the noun "music" is a collective noun and singular. Choice **(A)** correctly uses the singular possessive.

CHAPTER 18

Spotting and Fixing Errors: Sentence Structure, Punctuation, and Agreement

LEARNING OBJECTIVES

After completing this chapter, you will be able to:

- Determine the correct punctuation and/or conjunctions to form a complete sentence
- Identify and correct inappropriate uses of semicolons
- Identify and correct inappropriate uses of commas, dashes, and colons
- Use punctuation to set off simple parenthetical elements
- Identify and correct verb agreement issues
- Identify and correct pronoun agreement issues
- Identify and correct modifier agreement issues
- Identify and correct inappropriate uses of apostrophes
- Identify and correct expressions that deviate from idiomatic English
- Determine the appropriate word in frequently confused pairs

145/300 SmartPoints®

How Much Do You Know?

Directions: Try the following questions. The "Category" heading in the explanation for each question gives the title of the lesson that covers how to answer it. If you answered the question(s) for a given lesson correctly, you may be able to move quickly through that lesson. If you answered incorrectly, you may want to take your time on that lesson.

Questions 1-6 refer to the following passage.

The Hindenburg

Although they are best known today for their peculiar niche as floating commercials over sports [1] arenas, airships, now more commonly called "blimps," widely used as passenger transportation in the early twentieth century. The most infamous was the *Hindenburg*. When the 804-foot *Hindenburg* was launched in 1936, it was the largest airship in the world. Like most airships, and more specifically zeppelins, of the period, [2] a light gas in the *Hindenburg* filled a simple balloon encased by a solid frame—in this case, hydrogen. In an age when airplanes could carry no more than 10 passengers at a time, [3] they could initially carry 50 passengers, a capacity that was later upgraded to 72. Transatlantic journeys in an airship could cut the travel time in half compared to voyages in ocean liners at the time.

Despite these advantages, the *Hindenburg* was hampered by many of the same drawbacks as other airships. Tickets to fly in the *Hindenburg* were not affordable for most people. The massive amount of fuel needed not only to fill the balloon [4] and to power the propellers made this airship very expensive to operate.

1. A) NO CHANGE
    B) arenas; airships, more commonly called "blimps" today, widely used as
    C) arenas, airships, more commonly called "blimps" today, were widely used as
    D) arenas, airships, more commonly called "blimps" today, widely used to

2. A) NO CHANGE
    B) the *Hindenburg*'s simple balloon was filled with a light gas encased by the solid frame
    C) the solid frame of the *Hindenburg* encased a simple balloon filled with a light gas
    D) the *Hindenburg* was built with a solid frame that encased a simple balloon filled with a light gas

3. A) NO CHANGE
    B) it
    C) the *Hindenburg*
    D) each

4. A) NO CHANGE
    B) but also
    C) and also
    D) nor

Worst of all was the safety concern: hydrogen gas is extremely flammable. Any spark or flame that came near the gas could cause a horrific **5** explosion, which is exactly what happened. On May 6, 1937, in Lakehurst, New Jersey, as the *Hindenburg* **6** landed, it suddenly burst into flames, killing 36 of the 97 passengers and crew on board. By the 1940s, commercial airplanes had advanced in development far beyond the airship's capacity. The airship thus became outdated as a mode of passenger service and acquired its modern-day role as an advertising platform.

5. A) NO CHANGE
    B) explosion; which is
    C) explosion: which is
    D) explosion which—is

6. A) NO CHANGE
    B) had landed
    C) would have landed
    D) was landing

SAT Writing and Language

Check Your Work

1. C

Difficulty: Hard

Category: Sentence Structure: The Basics

Getting to the Answer: The first sentence is long and grammatically complex. Identify the most important pieces and outline the structure. The sentence begins with the word "although," which means that the first clause, "they are best known," is dependent. The following clause, therefore, needs to be independent for the sentence to have a complete, grammatically correct structure. The second clause as written, "airships . . . widely used as passenger transportation," is not an independent clause—it could not stand alone as its own complete sentence. Eliminate (A). Choice (B) is incorrect because the semicolon does not turn the second clause into an independent clause. Similarly, (D) does not make the second clause independent by replacing "as" with "to." Choice **(C)** is correct because "airships . . . were widely used as passenger transportation" is an independent clause: it has a subject "airships" and a predicate verb "were used."

2. D

Difficulty: Hard

Category: Agreement: Modifiers

Getting to the Answer: The phrases that precede the underlined portion are introductory modifiers. The subject of the sentence needs to immediately follow these modifiers. The introductory phrases talk about something that is like most airships; therefore, the subject must be comparable to most other airships. Neither "a light gas," "the *Hindenburg*'s simple balloon," nor the "solid frame" are comparable to "most airships." The *Hindenburg* itself is a specific airship, which can be logically compared to most airships. Only **(D)** correctly places "the *Hindenburg*" immediately after the introductory phrase as the subject of the sentence. Additionally, the underlined portion must end with "a light gas" because the phrase after the dash specifies which gas: hydrogen.

3. C

Difficulty: Medium

Category: Agreement: Pronouns

Getting to the Answer: Complex sentences can often benefit from the use of pronouns, reducing wordiness and repetition. That said, make sure that the use of a pronoun will not introduce ambiguity into the sentence. In a complicated sentence including multiple nouns, it is often better to avoid pronouns to preserve the clarity of the author's claims. Choice **(C)** is correct because it avoids any confusion over what the pronoun refers to.

4. B

Difficulty: Medium

Category: Agreement: Idioms

Getting to the Answer: Check to see if the underlined section is part of an idiomatic expression, such as *either . . . or*. The sentence contains the first half of the idiomatic combination *not only . . . but also*. The use of "and" in this context is incorrect. Choice **(B)**, "but also," is correct.

5. A

Difficulty: Medium

Category: Sentence Structure: Commas, Dashes, and Colons

Getting to the Answer: Commas set off non essential information from the main part of the sentence just as parentheses do. The sentence's concluding phrase "which is exactly what happened" is not necessary for understanding the sentence's main clause, which explains how a spark or flame could ignite the hydrogen and cause an explosion. The use of a semicolon or a colon is not appropriate for setting off non essential information. Eliminate (B) and (C). A dash can replace a comma as a way to emphasize the parenthetical phrase, which would be appropriate here, but (D) misplaces the dash. Choice **(A)** is correct because it uses the necessary punctuation, a comma, in the proper location.

6. D

Difficulty: Hard

Category: Agreement: Verbs

Getting to the Answer: The sentence expresses a main action that occurs once, "burst," while another action is in process, "landed." An action that occurs once in the past should be in simple past tense. An action that is in process in the past—signaled by the word "as"—should be in past progressive tense, ending in *-ing*. Eliminate (A). Only **(D)** gives the verb in past progressive and is correct.

Sentence Structure: The Basics

LEARNING OBJECTIVES

After this lesson, you will be able to:

- Determine the correct punctuation and/or conjunctions to form a complete sentence
- Identify and correct inappropriate uses of semicolons

To answer a question like this:

In the late spring of 1953, New Zealand mountaineer Sir Edmund Hillary and Nepalese Sherpa Tenzing Norgay became the first people to walk on the top of the world. After a grueling expedition that spanned several **1** months. They had finally reached the summit of Mount Everest.

A) NO CHANGE

B) months, and they

C) months; they

D) months, they

You need to know this:

Fragments and run-ons

A complete sentence must have both a subject and a verb and express a complete thought. If any one of these elements is missing, the sentence is a **fragment**. You can recognize a fragment because the sentence will not make sense as written. There are some examples in the table below.

Missing Element	Example	Corrected Sentence
Subject	*Ran a marathon.*	*Lola ran a marathon.*
Verb	*Lola a marathon.*	
Complete thought	*While Lola ran a marathon.*	*While Lola ran a marathon, her friends cheered for her.*

The fragment "While Lola ran a marathon" is an example of a dependent clause: it has a subject (Lola) and a verb (ran), but it does not express a complete thought because it starts with a subordinating conjunction (while). Notice what the word "while" does to the meaning: While Lola ran a marathon, what happened? To fix this type of fragment, eliminate the subordinating conjunction or join the dependent clause to an independent clause using a comma. Subordinating conjunctions are words and phrases such as *since*, *because*, *therefore*, *unless*, *although*, and *due to*.

Writing & Lang

Unlike a dependent clause, an independent clause can stand on its own as a complete sentence. If a sentence has more than one independent clause, those clauses must be properly joined. If they are not, the sentence is a **run-on**: *Lucas enjoys hiking, he climbs a new mountain every summer.* There are several ways to correct a run-on, as shown in the table below.

To Correct a Run-on	Example
Use a period	*Lucas enjoys hiking. He climbs a new mountain every summer.*
Use a semicolon	*Lucas enjoys hiking; he climbs a new mountain every summer.*
Use a colon	*Lucas enjoys hiking: he climbs a new mountain every summer.*
Make one clause dependent	*Since Lucas enjoys hiking, he climbs a new mountain every summer.*
Add a FANBOYS conjunction: For, And, Nor, But, Or, Yet, So	*Lucas enjoys hiking, so he climbs a new mountain every summer.*
Use a dash	*Lucas enjoys hiking—he climbs a new mountain every summer.*

Semicolons

Semicolons are used in two specific ways:

- A semicolon may join two independent clauses that are not connected by a FANBOYS conjunction (also called a coordinating conjunction), just as you would use a period.
- Semicolons may be used to separate items in a list if those items already include commas.

Use semicolons to . . .	Example
Join two independent clauses that are not connected by a comma and FANBOYS conjunction	*Gaby knew that her term paper would take at least four hours to write; she got started in study hall and then finished it at home.*
Separate sub lists within a longer list when the sub lists contain commas	*The team needed to bring uniforms, helmets, and gloves; oranges, almonds, and water; and hockey sticks, pucks, and skates.*

You need to do this:

To recognize and correct errors involving fragments, run-ons, and semicolons, familiarize yourself with the ways in which they are tested:

- Fragments
  - If a sentence is missing a subject, a verb, or a complete thought, it is a fragment.
  - Correct the fragment by adding the missing element.

- Run-ons
  - ○ If a sentence includes two independent clauses, they must be properly joined.
  - ○ Employ one of the following options to properly punctuate independent clauses:
    - Use a period
    - Insert a semicolon
    - Use a comma and a FANBOYS (for, and, nor, but, or, yet, so) conjunction
    - Use a dash
    - Make one clause dependent by using a subordinating conjunction (since, because, therefore, unless, although, due to, etc.)
- Semicolons
  - ○ A semicolon is used to join two independent clauses that are not connected by a comma and FANBOYS conjunction.
  - ○ Semicolons separate sub lists within a longer list. (The items inside the sub lists are separated by commas.)

Explanation:

The sentence before the period in the underlined segment is a fragment; it is a dependent clause that does not express a complete thought. Eliminate (A) because, as written, there is an error. Eliminate (B) because you need only one conjunction to join two clauses, not two. In (B), using both "although" and "and" creates an error. Eliminate (C) because it does not correct the original error: the semicolon serves exactly the same function as the period in the original. Choice **(D)** is correct.

If sentence formation or semicolons give you trouble, study the information above and try these Drill questions before completing the following Try on Your Own questions. Answers can be found on the next page.

Drill

a. Correct the fragment by adding a subject: Brought snacks to the weekend study session.

b. Correct the fragment by completing the thought: After getting to the stadium.

c. Correct the run-on sentence with a punctuation mark: The new arts center just opened it has a crafts room for children under thirteen.

d. Correct the run-on sentence with a punctuation mark: Herodotus is known as one of the first historians he is even called "The Father of History."

e. Make one clause dependent to correct the run-on sentence: Herodotus is sometimes accused of making up stories for his histories, he claimed he simply recorded what he had been told.

Try on Your Own

Directions: Take as much time as you need on these questions. Work carefully and methodically. There will be an opportunity for timed practice at the end of the chapter.

Questions 2-6 refer to the following passage.

The Sun

It is perhaps impossible to overestimate the impact of the Sun on our planet Earth. **2** The Sun is situated roughly 100 million miles away from the Earth, the Sun provides essentially all of Earth's heat. Functioning like a great thermonuclear reactor, **3** the Sun's core temperature of nearly 30 million degrees Fahrenheit. The energy sources we use daily to fuel our cars and heat our homes, resources like oil and coal harvested from deep within the Earth's crust, were produced by the power of the Sun acting upon living organisms millions of years ago. The radiant energy of the Sun is the reason the Earth has **4** light, warmth, and other forms of electromagnetic waves; plants, animals, and all metabolic life; weather patterns, atmospheric movement, and many more of the Earth's natural phenomena. Yet, while the Sun's ability to provide heat and light can be easily felt by simply lying out on a beach or gazing up into a brilliant blue sky, closer inspection of the Sun's dynamic surface through special telescopes has revealed activity capable of affecting the Earth in less obvious ways.

2. A) NO CHANGE
   B) However, the Sun
   C) Not many know that the Sun
   D) Even though the Sun

3. A) NO CHANGE
   B) the Sun has a core temperature
   C) the core temperature of the Sun
   D) the temperature of the Sun's core

4. A) NO CHANGE
   B) light, warmth, and other forms of electromagnetic waves—plants, animals, and all metabolic life—weather patterns, atmospheric movement, and many more of the Earth's natural phenomena.
   C) light, warmth, other forms of electromagnetic waves, plants, animals, all metabolic life, weather patterns, atmospheric movement, and many more of the Earth's natural phenomena.
   D) light, warmth, and other forms of electromagnetic waves, plants, animals, and all metabolic life, weather patterns, atmospheric movement, and many more of the Earth's natural phenomena.

Drill answers from previous page:

Note: These are not the only ways to correct the sentences; your answers may differ.

a. **My friend** brought snacks to the weekend study session.

b. After getting to the stadium, **we went looking for our seats.**

c. The new arts center just opened. **It** has a crafts room for children under thirteen.

d. Herodotus is known as one of the first historians; he is even called "The Father of History."

e. **Although** Herodotus is sometimes accused of making up stories for his histories, he claimed he simply recorded what he had been told.

One of the most curious features of the Sun's violent surface is sunspots, which are dark stormy areas half the temperature of the Sun's surface and as large as 19,000 miles across. They were first viewed by telescope as early as **5** <u>1610 but scientists</u> today know relatively little about them. Scientists have noticed that these spots seem to erupt and fade in 11-year cycles, affecting the Sun's luminosity and, in turn, the Earth's climate. Studies have shown that the charged particles released by solar flares, associated with sunspots, can react with the Earth's magnetic **6** <u>field, the radiation</u> can disrupt satellite communications, radio broadcasts, and even cell phone calls. As scientists continue to carefully observe such occurrences, referred to as "space weather," they gain a greater understanding of the powerful ability of the Sun to impact our lives.

5. A) NO CHANGE
    B) 1610, but scientists
    C) 1610 still scientists
    D) 1610, still scientists

6. A) NO CHANGE
    B) field, however the radiation
    C) field so the radiation
    D) field; the radiation

Sentence Structure: Commas, Dashes, and Colons

> **LEARNING OBJECTIVES**
>
> After this lesson, you will be able to:
>
> - Identify and correct inappropriate uses of commas, dashes, and colons
> - Use punctuation to set off simple parenthetical elements

To answer a question like this:

But climbing Mount Everest may be easier than answering the question posed by decades of non-climbers: Why? Perhaps Mallory said it best in 1923 before his ill-fated **7** climb; "Because it is there."

A) NO CHANGE

B) climb: "Because it is there."

C) climb. "Because it is there."

D) climb "Because it is there."

You need to know this:

Answer choices often move punctuation marks around, replace them with other punctuation marks, or remove them altogether. When underlined portions include commas, dashes, or colons, check to make sure the punctuation is used correctly in context.

Commas

There are two ways in which commas are not interchangeable with any other punctuation: a series of items and introductory words or phrases.

Use commas to . . .	Comma(s)
Set off three or more items in a series	*Jeremiah packed a sleeping bag, a raincoat, and a lantern for his upcoming camping trip.*
Separate an introductory word or phrase from the rest of the sentence	*For example, carrots are an excellent source of several vitamins and minerals.*

Commas and Dashes

In many cases, either a comma or a dash may be used to punctuate a sentence.

Use commas or dashes to . . .	Comma(s)	Dash(es)
Separate independent clauses connected by a FANBOYS conjunction (For, And, Nor, But, Or, Yet, So)	*Jess finished her homework earlier than expected, so she started an assignment that was due the following week.*	*Jess finished her homework earlier than expected—so she started an assignment that was due the following week.*
Separate an independent and dependent clause	*Tyson arrived at school a few minutes early, which gave him time to organize his locker before class.*	*Tyson arrived at school a few minutes early—which gave him time to organize his locker before class.*
Separate parenthetical elements from the rest of the sentence (use either two commas or two dashes, not one of each)	*Professor Mann, who is the head of the English department, is known for assigning extensive projects.*	*Professor Mann—who is the head of the English department—is known for assigning extensive projects*

Colons and Dashes

Colons and dashes are used to include new ideas by introducing or explaining something or by breaking the flow of the sentence. Note that the clause before the colon or dash must be able to stand on its own as a complete sentence.

Use colons and dashes to . . .	Colon	Dash
Introduce and/or emphasize a short phrase, quotation, explanation, example, or list	*Sanjay had two important tasks to complete: a science experiment and an expository essay.*	*Sanjay had two important tasks to complete—a science experiment and an expository essay.*
Separate two independent clauses when the second clauses explains, illustrates, or expands on the first sentence	*Highway 1 in Australia is one of the longest national highways in the world: it circles the entirety of the continent and connects every mainland state capital.*	*Highway 1 in Australia is one of the longest national highways in the world—it circles the entirety of the continent and connects every mainland state capital.*

Writing & Lang

Unnecessary Punctuation

Knowing when punctuation should not be used is equally important. If an underlined portion includes punctuation, take time to consider if it should be included at all.

Do NOT use punctuation to...	Incorrect	Correct
Separate a subject from its verb	*The diligent student council, meets every week.*	*The diligent student council meets every week.*
Separate a verb from its object or a preposition from its object	*The diligent student council meets, every week.*	*The diligent student council meets every week.*
Set off elements that are essential to a sentence's meaning	*The, diligent student, council meets every week.*	*The diligent student council meets every week.*
Separate adjectives that work together to modify a noun	*The diligent, student council meets every week.*	*The diligent student council meets every week.*

Parenthetical Elements

Parenthetical elements may appear at the beginning, in the middle, or at the end of a sentence. They must be properly punctuated with parentheses, commas, or dashes for the sentence to be grammatically correct. A phrase such as *the capital of France* is considered parenthetical if the rest of the sentence is grammatically correct when it is removed. Do not mix and match; a parenthetical element must begin and end with the same type of punctuation.

Parenthetical Element Placement	Parentheses	Comma(s)	Dash(es)
Beginning	*N/A*	*The capital of France, Paris is a popular tourist destination.*	*N/A*
Middle	*Paris (the capital of France) is a popular tourist destination.*	*Paris, the capital of France, is a popular tourist destination.*	*Paris—the capital of France—is a popular tourist destination.*
End	*A popular tourist destination is Paris (the capital of France).*	*A popular tourist destination is Paris, the capital of France.*	*A popular tourist destination is Paris— the capital of France.*

You need to do this:

If the underlined portion includes punctuation, ask yourself:

- Is the punctuation used correctly?

  The punctuation needs to be the correct type (comma, dash, or colon) and in the correct location.

- Is the punctuation is necessary?

  If you cannot identify a reason why the punctuation is included, the punctuation should be removed.

Explanation:

The underlined segment includes a semicolon that is used incorrectly because it neither joins two independent clauses nor separates items containing commas in a series or list. The underlined segment here is intended to emphasize a short quotation, so a colon or dash would be appropriate. **(B)** is correct.

If commas, dashes, and colons give you trouble, study the information above and try these Drill questions before completing the following Try on Your Own questions. Edit each sentence to correct the punctuation issue. Answers can be found on the next page.

Drill

a. For my birthday, I asked for my favorite dessert chocolate pecan pie.

b. The story of Emperor Nero playing the fiddle while Rome burned has been debunked by historians but the saying based on it remains popular.

c. Koalas' fingerprints are nearly indistinguishable from human fingerprints which has occasionally led to mistakes at crime scenes.

d. Invented by Sir John Harrington in 1596 the flush toilet actually precedes modern indoor plumbing.

e. Toni Morrison born Chloe Wofford is one of America's most celebrated writers.

Try on Your Own

Directions: Take as much time as you need on these questions. Work carefully and methodically. There will be an opportunity for timed practice at the end of the chapter.

Questions 8-15 refer to the following passage.

Mauritius

[8] <u>Although, most</u> of the products we buy today are made abroad in places well-known to Americans, such as Mexico and China, a quick check of many clothing labels will reveal the name of a country that might not be so **[9]** <u>familiar. Mauritius.</u> Named in honor of Prince Maurice of Nassau by the Dutch who colonized it in 1638, this small island in the Indian Ocean has a complicated history influenced by several international powers. Since gaining independence in **[10]** <u>1968—Mauritius</u> has emerged as a stable democracy with one of Africa's highest per capita incomes. Mauritius is considered a significant **[11]** <u>player: in the modern global economy one</u> of the few in the Southern Hemisphere.

Yet, before its hard-won economic and political stability, Mauritius underwent several tumultuous phases. After the Portuguese landed on the island in 1511, they hunted a large, slow-moving, native bird known as the dodo into extinction. The Portuguese

8. A) NO CHANGE
   B) Although most
   C) Although; most
   D) Most

9. A) NO CHANGE
   B) familiar and it's Mauritius
   C) familiar: Mauritius
   D) familiar which is Mauritius

10. A) NO CHANGE
    B) 1968; Mauriutius
    C) 1968 as Mauritius
    D) 1968, Mauritius

11. A) NO CHANGE
    B) player in the modern global economy, one
    C) player—in the modern global economy—one
    D) player in the modern, global economy one

Drill answers from previous page:

Note: These are not the only ways to correct the sentences; your answers may differ.

a. For my birthday, I asked for my favorite dessert: chocolate pecan pie.

b. The story of Emperor Nero playing the fiddle while Rome burned has been debunked by historians, but the saying based on it remains popular.

c. Koalas' fingerprints are nearly indistinguishable from human fingerprints—which has occasionally led to mistakes at crime scenes.

d. Invented by Sir John Harrington in 1596, the flush toilet actually precedes modern indoor plumbing.

e. Toni Morrison, born Chloe Wofford, is one of America's most celebrated writers. OR Toni Morrison—born Chloe Wofford—is one of America's most celebrated writers.

were followed by the Dutch, who brought waves of
12 traders, planters, and slaves; and indentured laborers,
merchants, and artisans, whose collective arrival
brought international recognition to Mauritius. In
1715, the island again changed hands, this time to the
French, and in 1810, with a successful invasion during
the Napoleonic Wars, the British became the fourth
European power to rule the island. Yet it was during this
period of changing **13** colonial powers—Mauritius was
traded like a commodity, that the demographics of the
island began to experience important changes with great
political ramifications.

By the time slavery was abolished in 1835, for
example, the growing Indian population, the Creoles
who could trace their roots back to island's sugarcane
plantations, and the Muslim community originating
from present-day Pakistan far outnumbered the
remaining Franco-Mauritian elites. And with these
demographic changes came political change. The first
step toward self-rule came with the legislative elections
of **14** 1947 and in March of 1968, an official constitution
was adopted. Today, Mauritius peacefully balances
the diversity of its multicultural society and flourishes
in international **15** trade through its advantageous
geographic location and large labor force.

12. A) NO CHANGE
    B) traders, planters and slaves, indentured laborers, merchants and artisans,
    C) traders, planters, slaves, indentured laborers, merchants, artisans,
    D) traders, planters, slaves, indentured laborers, merchants, and artisans,

13. A) NO CHANGE
    B) colonial powers—Mauritius was traded like a commodity that
    C) colonial powers—Mauritius was traded like a commodity—that
    D) colonial powers, Mauritius was traded like a commodity that

14. A) NO CHANGE
    B) 1947, and in March
    C) 1947 and, in March
    D) 1947 and in March,

15. A) NO CHANGE
    B) trade, through
    C) trade through,
    D) trade; through

Agreement: Verbs

> **LEARNING OBJECTIVE**
>
> After this lesson, you will be able to:
>
> • Identify and correct verb agreement issues

To answer questions like this:

For example, the editors had their work cut out for them when the part of the book devoted to avalanches and landslides **16** <u>were found</u> to be inaccurate.

A) NO CHANGE

B) was found

C) are found

D) is found

You need to know this:

Verb Tense

Verb tense indicates when an action or state of being took place: in the past, present, or future. The tense of the verb must fit the context of the passage. Each tense can express three different types of action.

Type of Action	Past	Present	Future
Single action occurring only once	Connor **planted** vegetables in the community garden.	Connor **plants** vegetables in the community garden.	Connor **will plant** vegetables in the community garden.
Action that is ongoing at some point in time	Connor **was planting** vegetables in the community garden this morning before noon.	Connor **is planting** vegetables in the community garden this morning before noon.	Connor **will be planting** vegetables in the community garden this morning before noon.
Action that is completed before some other action	Connor **had planted** vegetables in the community garden every year until he gave his job to Jasmine.	Connor **has planted** vegetables in the community garden since it started five years ago.	Connor **will have planted** vegetables in the community garden by the time the growing season starts.

Subject-Verb Agreement

A verb must agree with its subject in person and number:

- Person (first, second, or third)

  ○ First: *I **ask** a question.*

  ○ Second: *You **ask** a question.*

  ○ Third: *She **asks** a question.*

- Number (singular or plural)
  - Singular: *The apple **tastes** delicious.*
  - Plural: *Apples **taste** delicious.*

The noun closest to the verb is not always the subject: *The chair with the lion feet is an antique.* The singular verb in this sentence, *is*, is closest to the plural noun *feet*. However, the verb's actual subject is the singular noun *chair*, so the sentence is correct as written.

When a sentence includes two nouns, only the conjunction *and* forms a compound subject requiring a plural verb form:

- Plural: *Saliyah and Taylor **are** in the running club.*
- Singular: *Either Saliyah or Taylor **is** in the running club.*
- Singular: *Neither Saliyah nor Taylor **is** in the running club.*

Collective nouns are nouns that name entities with more than one member, such as *group*, *team*, and *family*. Even though these nouns represent more than one person, they are grammatically singular and require singular verb forms:

- *The collection of paintings **is** one of the most popular art exhibits in recent years.*
- *The team **looks** promising this year.*

Parallelism

Verbs in a list, a compound, or a comparison must be parallel in form.

Feature	Example	Parallel Form
A list	Chloe **formulated** a question, **conducted** background research, and **constructed** a hypothesis before starting the experiment.	3 simple past verb phrases
A compound	**Hunting** and **fishing** were essential to the survival of Midwestern Native American tribes such as the Omaha.	2 -*ing* verb forms
A comparison	Garrett enjoys **sculpting** as much as **painting**.	2 -*ing* verb forms

Note that parallelism may be tested using other parts of speech besides verbs. In general, any items in a list, compound, or comparison must be in parallel form. For example, if a list starts with a noun, the other items in the list must also be nouns; if it starts with an adjective, the other items must be adjectives, etc.

Incorrect	Correct
Naomi likes **pumpkin pie and to drink coffee** on chilly weekend afternoons.	Naomi likes **pumpkin pie and coffee** on chilly weekend afternoons.
	or
	Naomi likes **to eat pumpkin pie and drink coffee** on chilly weekend afternoons.
Which of the dogs is the **most docile and better behaved**?	Which of the dogs is the **most docile and best behaved**?
	or
	Which of the dogs is the **more docile and better behaved**?

Writing & Lang

You need to do this:

If the underlined portion includes a verb, check that the verb:

- Reflects the correct tense: does it fit the context?
- Agrees with the subject in person and number
- Is parallel in form with other verbs in a series, list, or compound if there is one in the sentence

Explanation:

The subject of the verb "were found" is the noun "part," which is singular. The verb is plural, so there is an error. Rule out (A) and (C). (Note that the test makers like to put prepositional phrases or other descriptive phrases, such as the phrase, "devoted to avalanches and landslides," between the subject and verb to make the subject-verb agreement error trickier to spot.)

To decide between (B) and (D), look at the context defined by the other verb tense in the sentence. The editors "*had* their work cut out for them," so the sentence describes past events. Choice **(B)** is also in the past tense and is consistent with this context. It is the correct answer.

If verbs give you trouble, study the information above and try these Drill questions before completing the following Try on Your Own questions. Edit each sentence to correct the verb issue. Turn the page to see the answers.

Drill

a. Angel audition for the school play next week.

b. The song, with its upbeat rhythm and catchy lyrics, were wildly popular.

c. Either the governor or the lieutenant governor usually present the award.

d. By the time the last runner completed the marathon, the winner has crossed the finish line hours ago.

e. Few people know that Stephen Hawking both revolutionized physics and co-written children's books with his daughter.

Try on Your Own

Directions: Take as much time as you need on these questions. Work carefully and methodically. There will be an opportunity for timed practice at the end of the chapter.

Questions 17-22 refer to the following passage.

SMOM

At 69 Condotti Street in Rome sits what **17** is believed by many to be the smallest country in the world, a country that few have ever heard of. The Sovereign Military and Hospitaller Order of St. John of Jerusalem of Rhodes and of Malta, or SMOM, **18** were an ancient order of knights well known for its humanitarian activities. The order's headquarters in Rome—a mere 6,000 square meters, or about one acre— is considered an independent state by at least 75 nations. How SMOM got to Rome is a story almost a millennium old, spanning as many places as the order's official name suggests.

SMOM began in 1099, during the First Crusade, a large-scale military conflict pitting Christian armies against the Muslim rulers of what is now Israel. The order's task was to protect and defend Christian pilgrims traveling to Jerusalem as well as **19** providing a hospital for their care. Though it began as a religious order, SMOM developed into a military knighthood as a result of the volatile political situation.

First because of the ongoing conflict between Muslims and Christians and, later, Napoleon Bonaparte's expansionist ambitions, the order was forced to move a number of times. After the Muslims had taken Jerusalem in the 1170s, forcing SMOM to relocate first to the Mediterranean island of Cyprus and then to the nearby island of Rhodes, the Ottoman Turks

17. A) NO CHANGE
    B) are believed
    C) is to be believed
    D) are to be believed

18. A) NO CHANGE
    B) was
    C) are
    D) is

19. A) NO CHANGE
    B) to provide
    C) providing them
    D) ensuring availability of

[20] had seized Rhodes in 1522, forcing SMOM to move again, this time to Malta. Then [21] Napoleon drives the order from Malta in 1798, and the island fell into British hands soon after. SMOM wandered from city to city in Italy, finally establishing its current headquarters in 1834.

Today, SMOM [22] will concentrate on providing humanitarian aid to everyone regardless of creed, establishing hospitals and charities in all corners of the world. Its many activities include vaccination programs, refugee relief, and philanthropic works to combat deadly diseases, such as leprosy and malnutrition.

20. A) NO CHANGE
    B) seized
    C) have seized
    D) would have seized

21. A) NO CHANGE
    B) Napoleon drove
    C) Napoleon had driven
    D) Napoleon was driving

22. A) NO CHANGE
    B) will be concentrating
    C) concentrates
    D) concentrates and is concentrating

Drill answers:

Note: These are not the only ways to correct the sentences; your answers may differ.

a. Angel **will** audition for the school play next week.

b. The song, with its upbeat rhythm and catchy lyrics, **was** wildly popular.

c. Either the governor or the lieutenant governor usually **presents** the award.

d. By the time the last runner completed the marathon, the winner **had** crossed the finish line hours ago.

e. Few people know that Stephen Hawking both revolutionized physics and **co-wrote** children's books with his daughter.

Agreement: Pronouns

To answer a question like this:

In their search for Ozark cavefish, the researchers were encouraged by the stability of the caves' ground-water as well as by **23** <u>its</u> length and by the presence of bats.

A) NO CHANGE

B) it's

C) their

D) there

You need to know this:

Pronoun forms

A pronoun is a word that takes the place of a noun. Pronouns can take three different forms, each of which is used based on the grammatical role it plays in the sentence.

Form	Pronouns	Example
Subjective: The pronoun is used as the subject.	I, you, she, he, it, we, they, who	*Rivka is the student **who** will lead the presentation.*
Objective: The pronoun is used as the object of a verb or a preposition.	me, you, her, him, it, us, them, whom	*With **whom** will Rivka present the scientific findings?*
Possessive: The pronoun expresses ownership.	my, mine, your, yours, his, her, hers, its, our, ours, their, theirs, whose	*Rivka will likely choose a partner **whose** work is excellent.*

Note that a pronoun in subjective form can, logically, be the subject in a complete sentence. Pronouns that are in objective form cannot.

When there are two pronouns or a noun and a pronoun in a compound structure, drop the other noun or pronoun to tell which form to use. For example: *Leo and me walked into town*. If you were talking about yourself only, you would say, "I walked into town," not "Me walked into town." Therefore, the correct form is subjective, and the original sentence should read: *Leo and I walked into town*.

Writing & Lang

Pronoun-Antecedent Agreement

A pronoun's antecedent is the noun it logically represents in a sentence. If the noun is singular, the pronoun must be singular; if the noun is plural, the pronoun must be plural.

Antecedent	Incorrect	Correct
selection	*The selection of books was placed in **their** designated location.*	*The selection of books was placed in **its** designated location.*
Addison	*Addison fed the giraffes all of the lettuce **they** had purchased.*	*Addison fed the giraffes all of the lettuce **she** had purchased.*
sapling	*The sapling, along with dozens of flowers, was relocated to where **they** would thrive.*	*The sapling, along with dozens of flowers, was relocated to where **it** would thrive.*
student	*If a student is confused, **they** should ask for clarification.*	*If a student is confused, **he** or **she** should ask for clarification.*

Ambiguous Pronouns

A pronoun is ambiguous if its antecedent is either missing or unclear. When you see an underlined pronoun, make sure you can identify the noun to which it refers.

Ambiguous Pronoun Use	Corrected Sentence
*Anthony walked with Cody to the ice cream shop, and **he** bought a banana split.*	*Anthony walked with Cody to the ice cream shop, and **Cody** bought a banana split.*

You need to do this:

If the underlined portion includes a pronoun, *find the logical antecedent*. If there is no clear antecedent, the pronoun is ambiguous and this error must be corrected. Then check that the pronoun:

- Uses the correct form
  - If the pronoun is the subject of the sentence, use a subjective pronoun such as *I, you, she, he, it, we, they,* or *who.*
  - If the pronoun is an object within the sentence, use an objective pronoun such as *me, you, her, him, it, us, they,* or *whom.*
  - If the pronoun indicates possession, use a possessive pronoun such as *my, mine, your, yours, his, her, hers, its, our, ours, their, theirs,* or *whose.*
- Agrees with its antecedent
  - A singular antecedent requires a singular pronoun; a plural antecedent requires a plural pronoun.

Explanation:

The phrase "its length" logically refers to the caves, not the groundwater. You need the possessive form, but because the word "caves" is plural, you need the plural "their." Choice **(C)** is correct.

If pronouns give you trouble, study the information above and try these Drill questions before completing the following Try on Your Own questions. Edit each sentence to correct the pronoun issue. Answers can be found on the next page.

Drill

a.   Although the teacher gave the student detention after school, she was not angry.

b.   My uncle likes to go bowling with my sister and I.

c.   The box of nails has been moved from their usual place in the shed.

d.   My favorite singer, who I have wanted to see in person for years, will give a concert a week after my birthday.

e.   The cathedral of Notre Dame, with vast vaulted ceilings and intricate carvings, never fails to amaze their visitors.

Try on Your Own

Directions: Take as much time as you need on these questions. Work carefully and methodically. There will be an opportunity for timed practice at the end of the chapter.

Questions 24-29 refer to the following passage.
Akira Kurosawa

What do samurai,[1] cowboys, shogun,[2] gangsters, peasants, and William Shakespeare all have in common? **24** He is just one of the varied influences on the work of Akira Kurosawa (1910–1998), a Japanese film director considered by movie critic Leonard Maltin to be "one of the undisputed giants of cinema." Over his career, Kurosawa's unique blend of Western themes and Eastern settings made **25** them arguably the most important Japanese filmmaker in history.

The most famous example of Kurosawa's style is his 1954 film *Seven Samurai*. Although the setting is medieval Japan, with peasants and samurai, **26** its story is influenced by Western films: a village, terrorized by local bandits, turns to seven down-on-their-luck yet good-hearted samurai for the protection

24. A) NO CHANGE
B) His is just one
C) They are just some
D) Theirs are just some

25. A) NO CHANGE
B) he
C) him
D) his

26. A) NO CHANGE
B) their
C) the film's
D) the setting's

Drill answers from previous page:

Note: These are not the only ways to correct the sentences; your answers may differ.

a. Although the teacher gave the student detention after school, **the student** was not angry.

b. My uncle likes to go bowling with my sister and **me**.

c. The box of nails has been moved from **its** usual place in the shed.

d. My favorite singer, **whom** I have wanted to see in person for years, will give a concert a week after my birthday.

e. The cathedral of Notre Dame, with vast vaulted ceilings and intricate carvings, never fails to amaze **its** visitors.

[1] samurai: noble warriors of medieval Japan, similar to European knights
[2] shogun: military dictators of Japan from 1603 to 1868

27 they need. Like movie cowboys, these samurai are romantic heroes, sure of their morals and battling clear forces of evil. The traditional Japanese version of a samurai was a noble and often distant symbol of Japan's imperial heritage, but Kurosawa considered the main characters differently. To **28** him, the film's samurai were distinctly human characters, each with a conscience and the will to act to correct the wrongs around them.

Although Kurosawa's films enjoy a lofty reputation in the West, many critics and moviegoers in his home country view his films as neither original nor particularly Japanese. His use of Western ideals and themes—even reinterpreting Western authors such as William Shakespeare and Fyodor Dostoyevsky—leads Japanese cinema lovers, many of **29** who see Kurosawa's use of Japanese culture as mere "window dressing" applied to essentially foreign stories, to regard his work with suspicion. Ironically, it was Kurosawa's success that opened the door for other, more "Japanese" directors, such as Yasujiro Ozu and Kenji Mizoguchi, to gain a wider audience.

27. A) NO CHANGE
    B) it needs.
    C) he needs.
    D) you need.

28. A) NO CHANGE
    B) me
    C) you
    D) us

29. A) NO CHANGE
    B) whose
    C) which
    D) whom

Agreement: Modifiers

LEARNING OBJECTIVES

After this lesson, you will be able to:

- Identify and correct modifier agreement issues
- Identify and correct inappropriate uses of apostrophes

To answer a question like this:

30 Called "Mother of the Universe" by the Tibetan people, the lives of George Mallory and Andrew Irvine had already been claimed by Mount Everest, despite its maternal appellation, before Hillary and Norgay finally conquered its icy peak.

A) NO CHANGE

B) Hillary and Norgay, called "Mother of the Universe" by the Tibetan people, finally conquered the icy peak of Mount Everest, which had already claimed the lives of George Mallory and Andrew Irvine, despite its maternal appellation.

C) The lives of George Mallory and Andrew Irvine, called "Mother of the Universe" by the Tibetan people, had already been claimed by Mount Everest, despite its maternal appellation, before Hillary and Norgay finally conquered its icy peak.

D) Called "Mother of the Universe" by the Tibetan people, Mount Everest had already, despite its maternal appellation, claimed the lives of George Mallory and Andrew Irvine before Hillary and Norgay finally conquered its icy peak.

You need to know this:

A **modifier** is a word or phrase that describes, clarifies, or provides additional information about another part of the sentence. Modifier questions require you to identify the part of a sentence being modified and use the appropriate modifier in the proper place.

In order to be grammatically correct, the modifier must be placed as close to the word it describes as possible. Use context clues in the passage to identify the correct placement of a modifier; a misplaced modifier can cause confusion and is always incorrect on test day.

Note that a common way the SAT tests modifiers is with modifying phrases at the beginning of a sentence. Just like any other modifier, the modifying phrase grammatically modifies whatever is right next to it in the sentence. For example, consider the sentence, "While walking to the bus stop, the rain drenched Bob." The initial phrase, "While walking to the bus stop," grammatically modifies "the rain," creating a nonsense sentence; the rain can't walk to the bus stop. The writer meant that Bob was walking to the bus stop, so the sentence should read, "While walking to the bus stop, Bob was drenched by the rain."

Modifier/Modifying Phrase	Incorrect	Correct
nearly	Andre **nearly** watched the play for four hours.	Andre watched the play for **nearly** four hours.
in individual containers	The art teacher handed out paints to students **in individual containers**.	The art teacher handed out paints **in individual containers** to students.
A scholar athlete	**A scholar athlete**, maintaining high grades in addition to playing soccer were expected of Maya.	**A scholar athlete**, Maya was expected to maintain high grades in addition to playing soccer.

Adjectives and Adverbs

Use adjectives only to modify nouns and pronouns. Use adverbs to modify everything else.

- **Adjectives** are single-word modifiers that describe nouns and pronouns: *Ian conducted an **efficient** lab experiment.*
- **Adverbs** are single-word modifiers that describe verbs, adjectives, or other adverbs: *Ian **efficiently** conducted a lab experiment.*

Note that nouns can sometimes be used as adjectives. For example, in the phrase "the fashion company's autumn line," the word "fashion" functions as an adjective modifying "company," and the word "autumn" functions as an adjective modifying "line."

Comparative/Superlative

When comparing similar things, use adjectives that match the number of items being compared. When comparing two items or people, use the **comparative** form of the adjective. When comparing three or more items or people, use the **superlative** form.

Comparative (two items)	Superlative (three or more items)
better, more, newer, older, shorter, taller, worse, younger	best, most, newest, oldest, shortest, tallest, worst, youngest

Possessive Nouns and Pronouns

Possessive nouns and pronouns indicate that something that belongs to someone or something. In general, possessive nouns are written with an apostrophe, while possessive pronouns are not.

To spot errors in possessive noun or pronoun construction, look for . . .	Incorrect	Correct
Two nouns in a row	The **professors lectures** were both informative and entertaining.	The **professor's lectures** were both informative and entertaining.
Pronouns with apostrophes	The book is her's.	The book is **hers**.
Words that sound alike	The three friends decided to ride **there** bicycles to the park over **they're** where **their** going to enjoy a picnic lunch.	The three friends decided to ride **their** bicycles to the park over **there** where **they're** going to enjoy a picnic lunch.

Apostrophes

Use an apostrophe to . . .	Example
Indicate the possessive form of a single noun	My oldest **sister's** soccer game is on Saturday.
Indicate the possessive form of a plural noun	My two older **sisters'** soccer games are on Saturday.
Indicate a contraction (e.g., don't, can't)	**They've** won every soccer match this season.

Note that plural nouns are formed without an apostrophe.

Incorrect	Correct
Sting **ray's** are cartilaginous fish related to **shark's**.	Sting **rays** are cartilaginous fish related to **sharks**.
There are many **carnival's** in this area every summer.	There are many **carnivals** in this area every summer.

To check whether it's is appropriate, replace it in the sentence with it is or it has. If the sentence no longer makes sense, it's is incorrect. The following sentence is correct:

The tree frog blends perfectly into its surroundings. When it holds still, it's nearly invisible.

Note that its' and its's are never correct.

You need to do this:

If the underlined portion includes a modifier, determine whether the modifier:

- Is placed correctly
  - Is it as near as possible to the word it logically modifies?
  - If it is not in the correct place, where should it be moved?
- Agrees with the word or words it is describing
  - Does the sentence require an adjective or an adverb?
  - Does the noun or pronoun show proper possession?

If the underlined portion includes an apostrophe, make sure it correctly indicates either possession or a contraction. If an apostrophe is missing, select the answer choice that places it in the correct location.

Explanation:

The phrase "despite its maternal appellation" indicates that it was Mount Everest that was known in Tibetan culture as the "Mother of the Universe." That means "Mount Everest" must be placed immediately next to the phrase, "[c]alled 'Mother of the Universe' by the Tibetan people." This is not the case in the current sentence, so there is a modification error. The only choice that corrects the error is **(D)**.

If modifiers give you trouble, study the information above and try these Drill questions before completing the following Try on Your Own questions. Edit each sentence to correct the modifier or apostrophe issue. Answers can be found on the next page.

Drill

a. Computers have grown exponential more efficient since their invention.

b. Estella chose to take the route with the most attractively scenery to her destination.

c. The leaf-tailed gecko's amazing natural camouflage enables it to blend perfectly into it's surroundings.

d. Between basketball and baseball, basketball is the most popular sport in the United States.

e. From Edgar Allan Poe to Monty Python, the infamous Spanish Inquisition has provided material for many artists.

Try on Your Own

Directions: Take as much time as you need on these questions. Work carefully and methodically. There will be an opportunity for timed practice at the end of the chapter.

Questions 31-37 refer to the following passage.

Sergei Eisenstein

Considered the father of the montage, a popular cinematic technique that involves a rapid succession of shots, often superimposed, **31** the modern movie has as one of its principal architects Russian director Sergei Eisenstein. Although his career was not particularly prolific—he completed only seven feature-length films—Eisenstein's work contains a clarity and sharpness of composition that make the depth of his plots and the **32** powerfully complexity of his juxtaposed images easily accessible to most viewers. In fact, few filmmakers were **33** most instrumental in pushing the envelope of the established, conservative nineteenth-century Victorian theatre than Eisenstein, whose films helped to usher in a new era of abstract thought and expression in art.

Eisenstein's feature debut, a film entitled *Statchka* (*Strike* in English) released in 1925, was many **34** moviegoer's first experience of montage on the big screen. Based on the contemporary theory of biomechanics and criticizing the mechanical and

31. A) NO CHANGE
   B) the modern movie has Russian director Sergei Eisenstein to thank as one of its principal architects.
   C) the Russian director Sergei Eisenstein was one of the principal architects of the modern movie.
   D) critics name the Russian director Sergei Eisenstein as one of the principal architects of the modern movie.

32. A) NO CHANGE
   B) powerful
   C) power
   D) power of

33. A) NO CHANGE
   B) more instrumental
   C) the best at being instrumental
   D) better at instrumentally

34. A) NO CHANGE
   B) movie's goer
   C) moviegoers
   D) moviegoers'

Drill answers from previous page:

Note: These are not the only ways to correct the sentences; your answers may differ.

a. Computers have grown **exponentially** more efficient since their invention.

b. Estella chose to take the route with the most **attractive** scenery to her destination.

c. The leaf-tailed gecko's amazing natural camouflage enables it to blend perfectly into **its** surroundings.

d. Between basketball and baseball, basketball is the **more** popular sport in the United States.

e. The infamous Spanish Inquisition has provided material for many artists, **from Edgar Allan Poe to Monty Python**.

repetitive movements required of exploited factory workers, [35] <u>Eisenstein's montage consisted of a powerful sequence of conflicting images that were</u> able to abbreviate time spans in the film while introducing new metaphors and allusions to the storyline. Essentially, Eisenstein sought to use the montage to create a cumulative emotional effect that was greater than the sum of the individual shots.

[36] <u>Enormously, it was with the successful technique of montage that Eisenstein's work caught the eye of the new Communist Party leaders</u> in Moscow, who saw in his cinematic style a film for the "common man." His next two films, *Battleship Potemkin* and *October: Ten Days That Shook the World*, were commissioned by party officials in an attempt to use Eisenstein's mass appeal to disseminate Soviet propaganda. As a result, these achievements have been frequently criticized [37] <u>for they're</u> lack of artistic integrity. Yet, in the end, regardless of politics, Eisenstein's films continue to have an undeniably significant and lasting impact on filmmakers.

35. A) NO CHANGE
    B) Eisenstein arranged a powerful sequence of conflicting images into a montage that was
    C) Eisenstein used conflicting images in a powerful sequence, composing a montage that was
    D) Eisenstein created a montage consisting of a powerful sequence of conflicting images that were

36. A) NO CHANGE
    B) It was enormously with the successful technique of montage that Eisenstein's work caught the eye of the new Communist Party leaders
    C) It was with the enormously successful technique of montage that Eisenstein's work caught the eye of the new Communist Party leaders
    D) It was with the successful technique of montage that Eisenstein's work caught the eye of the enormously new Communist Party leaders

37. A) NO CHANGE
    B) therefore
    C) for their
    D) for there

Idioms

To answer a question like this:

38 The goal of the conference was not only to find ways to reduce carbon emissions but to provide information to communities threatened by sea level rise as well.

A) NO CHANGE

B) Not only was the goal of the conference to find ways to reduce carbon emissions, albeit also to provide information to communities threatened by sea level rise.

C) The goal of the conference was not only to find ways to reduce carbon emissions, and to provide information to communities whom sea level rise threatens.

D) The goal of the conference was not only to find ways to reduce carbon emissions but also to provide information to communities threatened by sea level rise.

You need to know this:

An **idiom** is a combination of words that must be used together to convey either a figurative or literal meaning. Idioms are tested in three ways:

1. Proper preposition use in context: the preposition must reflect the writer's intended meaning.

    She waits **on** customers.

    She waits **for** the bus.

    She waits **with** her friends.

2. Idiomatic expressions: some words or phrases must be used together to be correct.

    Simone will **either** bike **or** run to the park.

    Neither the principal **nor** the teachers will tolerate tardiness.

    This fall, Shari is playing **not only** soccer **but also** field hockey.

3. Implicit double negatives: some words imply a negative and therefore cannot be paired with an explicit negative. The words "barely," "hardly," and "scarcely" fall into this category.

    Correct: Janie **can hardly** wait for vacation.

    Incorrect: Janie **can't hardly** wait for vacation.

Frequently Tested Prepositions	Idiomatic Expressions	Words That Can't Pair with Negative Words
at	as . . . as	barely
by	between . . . and	hardly
for	both . . . and	scarcely
from	either . . . or	
of	neither . . . nor	
on	just as . . . so too	
to	not only . . . but also	
with	prefer . . . to	

Commonly Confused Words

English contains many pairs of words that sound alike but are spelled differently and have different meanings, such as *accept* (to take or receive something that is offered) and *except* (with the exclusion of).

Other words, such as *among* (in a group of, or surrounded by, multiple things or people) and *between* (distinguishing one thing from one other thing), do not sound alike but have similar meanings that are often confused.

You'll want to familiarize yourself with the following list of commonly misused words so you can spot them on test day.

Accept: to take or receive something that is offered	*My niece **accepted** her pile of birthday gifts with great enthusiasm.*
Except: with the exclusion of	*All of the presents are toys **except** for a box containing a popular book series.*

Affect: to act on, to have influence on something	*The dreary, rainy weather negatively **affected** Rahul's mood.*
Effect: something that is produced by a cause; a consequence	*A recent study explored the **effects** of weather on mental well-being.*

Lay: to put or place something	*My boss asked me to **lay** the report on her desk before I left for the day.*
Lie: to rest or recline	*After a long day of work, I just want to **lie** down on the couch.*

Writing & Lang

Raise: to build or lift up something; to support the growth of someone	*Many books are dedicated to the topic of **raising** children.*
Rise: to get up	*Ted likes to **rise** early in the morning to exercise before his children wake up.*

Whose: a possessive pronoun	***Whose** uniform shirt is this?*
Who's: a contraction meaning "who is"	***Who's** responsible for ordering new uniforms?*

Their: a possessive pronoun for a plural noun or pronoun	*The college students plan to travel internationally after **their** graduation.*
They're: a contraction for "they are"	***They're** going to visit several countries in East Asia.*
There: at a certain point or place	*The students are excited to experience the foods and cultures **there**.*
There's: a contraction for "there is"	***There's** a tour of an ancient palace that they're looking forward to seeing.*

Among: in a group of, or surrounded by, multiple things or people	*Navya was **among** many doctoral candidates who visited the university.*
Between: distinguishing one thing from one other thing	*Navya had to decide **between** her top two doctoral program choices.*

Amount: sum or quantity of multiple things that cannot be counted	*The **amount** of pollution in the ocean is affecting dolphin populations.*
Number: Sum or quantity of a finite collection that can be counted	*Scientists report that the **number** of dolphins has decreased significantly.*

Less: a smaller extent or amount of things that cannot be counted	*The common supermarket sign "10 items or **less**" is actually incorrect.*
Fewer: of a smaller number, referring to things that can be counted	*Since the items can be counted, the sign should read "10 items or **fewer**."*

Much: great in quantity, referring to things that cannot be counted	*My sister has **much** more patience than I have.*
Many: great in quantity, referring to things that can be counted	***Many** of her friends admire her ability to stay calm in difficult situations.*

Good: satisfactory in quality, quantity, or degree; adjective	*Dakota considered both the **good** and bad effects of wind energy before composing her essay.*
Well: To perform an action in a satisfactory manner; adverb	*Dakota wrote her essay so **well** that her professor used it as an example of excellent persuasive writing.*

You need to do this:

- If the underlined portion includes a preposition, a conjunction, or *barely/hardly/scarcely*, look for a common idiom error.
- If the underlined segment includes a commonly misused word, check the context to determine whether it is used properly.

Explanation:

A sentence that contains the phrase "not only" must also contain the phrase "but also" (and vice versa). The only choice that includes the phrase "but also" is **(D)**, making it the correct answer.

If idioms give you trouble, study the information above and try out these Drill questions before completing the following Try on Your Own questions. Edit each sentence to correct the incorrect idiom. Answers can be found on the next page.

Drill

a. When Fatima returned home from school, she was unpleasantly surprised to find that her hamster had escaped to its cage again.

b. The surgeon took great pride of her work, saying she was honored to be able to help when her patients thanked her.

c. Neither apples or cherries will grow in the Phillipines due to its hot climate.

d. The day after Kumar tried yoga for the first time, he was so sore he couldn't hardly move.

e. The attorney wanted to except the case but couldn't because his caseload was already full.

Try on Your Own

Directions: Take as much time as you need on these questions. Work carefully and methodically. There will be an opportunity for timed practice at the end of the chapter.

Questions 39-44 refer to the following passage.

The Intriguing Opossum

Much maligned as a repulsive nuisance, the opossum is actually one of North America's most interesting animals, exhibiting many notable characteristics. For example, opossums boast an incredible array of 50 razor-sharp teeth, the most of any mammal in the world. Also, because opossums are partially or totally immune, [39] neither rabies or snake venom presents much of a danger to them.

While their beady eyes, pointy snouts, and bald tails might make them seem like a cousin of the rat, opossums are actually closely related to the kangaroo and are the only marsupial native to the continent. One of the most primitive animals, existing since the time of the dinosaurs, opossums have survived for millions of years by adapting to diverse habitats—including dense urban areas—and food supplies. [40] There isn't hardly anything that opossums will not eat; included in their possible diet are rodents, birds, frogs, eggs, insects,

39. A) NO CHANGE

    B) neither rabies nor snake venom presents much of a danger to them

    C) not even rabies nor snake venom presents much of a danger to them

    D) not much of a danger is presented by even rabies or snake venom

40. A) NO CHANGE

    B) There is hardly nothing that opossums will not eat;

    C) There is hardly anything that opossums will not eat;

    D) Opossums will not eat hardly anything;

Drill answers from previous page:

Note: These are not the only ways to correct the sentences; your answers may differ.

a. When Fatima returned home from school, she was unpleasantly surprised to find that her hamster had escaped **from** its cage again.

b. The surgeon took great pride **in** her work, saying she was honored to be able to help when her patients thanked her.

c. Neither apples **nor** cherries will grow in the Phillipines due to its hot climate.

d. The day after Kumar tried yoga for the first time, he was so sore he **could hardly** move.

e. The attorney wanted to **accept** the case but couldn't because his caseload was already full.

snails, slugs, earthworms, plants, tree roots, fruits, and grains. Today, many opossums that live in areas densely populated by humans survive on garbage and small mice, even consuming the bones to satisfy their high need for calcium.

Of course, the opossum does have vulnerabilities. Its average three-year life span is not unusual for its size, typically 41 between two or three feet long. What is unusual is that opossums continue growing throughout their lifetimes. Such a state of constant development is linked with metabolic limitations 42 of the amount of food and energy that can be stored within the opossum's body, requiring that ready food sources be available year-round. In addition, opossums are highly susceptible to the cold, making it rather common to see opossums with frostbitten ears and tails.

Nevertheless, opossums have displayed amazing resilience over the years, often surviving attacks from intimidating predators like dogs and even hawks. While the opossum's first reaction when threatened is to begin running to the nearest tree, their primary defense 43 is an affect of the nervous system that, when sensing danger, throws the opossum's body into a catatonic state that dramatically slows its heart rate. The opossum will then 44 lay still, begin to drool, and appear dead, another trait that only adds to the fascinating nature of these animals.

41. A) NO CHANGE
    B) either two or three
    C) at least two or three
    D) between two and three

42. A) NO CHANGE
    B) on
    C) with
    D) for

43. A) NO CHANGE
    B) is an effect of the nervous system
    C) effects the nervous system so
    D) of the nervous system is an affect

44. A) NO CHANGE
    B) have laid
    C) lie
    D) have lain

How Much Have You Learned?

Directions: For testlike practice, give yourself 9 minutes to complete this question set. Be sure to study the explanations, even for questions you got right. They can be found at the end of this chapter.

Questions 45-55 refer to the following passage.

The Experts of Visual Communication

When people consider different types of **45** communication often, they think of only verbal or written forms. Few, perhaps, think of art as a **46** mode of communication; however, from early cave paintings and the intricate craftwork of ancient civilizations to contemporary, esoteric, abstract works that challenge traditional notions of aesthetic representation, art has played an essential role in visual communication. In the world of business, the intersection of art and communication is graphic design. **47** The explosion of media brought on by the digital age offered a growing platform for art, through graphic design, to express ideas and messages.

There is almost no detail too small, no space too unimportant to escape the attention of a graphic designer. **48** Their work is nearly ubiquitous in modern commercial life: **49** business logos, billboard advertisements; website layouts, T-shirt designs; and even the decorated cardboard of cereal boxes and coffee cups feature graphic design. In a culture increasingly wired for visual communication, graphic designers wield a powerful influence over the ordinary consumer. They craft the formats, styles, images, and symbols that shape how we perceive products, services, and ideas.

45. A) NO CHANGE
    B) communication often, they think of only verbal
    C) communication, often only they think of verbal
    D) communication, often they think of only verbal

46. A) NO CHANGE
    B) mode of communication; however from early cave paintings
    C) mode of communication, however, from early cave paintings
    D) mode of communication, however from early cave paintings

47. A) NO CHANGE
    B) The explosion of media brings on by the digital age offers
    C) The explosion of media brought on by the digital age offering
    D) The explosion of media brought on by the digital age offers

48. A) NO CHANGE
    B) The work of them
    C) The work of graphic designers
    D) The work of theirs

49. A) NO CHANGE
    B) business logos, billboard advertisements, website layouts, T-shirt designs, and even the decorated cardboard of cereal boxes and coffee cups feature graphic design.
    C) business logos, billboard advertisements, website layouts, T-shirt designs, and, even the decorated cardboard of cereal boxes, and coffee cups feature graphic design.
    D) business logos; billboard advertisements; website layouts; T-shirt designs; and even the decorated cardboard of cereal boxes, and coffee cups feature graphic design.

How do these visual innovators navigate a career path? Most **50** began by studying graphic design and earn a bachelor's degree at a four-year college, where they build skills through interactive class settings to hone expertise. These programs are heavily project-based and provide the sort of experience professional work will require. Students gradually compile design portfolios to showcase their best work. Once students have graduated, these portfolios are essential for the job search because **51** it demonstrates the ability and creative potential of designers.

Competition in the job market for graphic designers is **52** rigorous yet the field offers a variety of professional options. Some work in design studios. There they team with other graphic designers, taking on projects for external clients. Others work "in-house" for businesses that staff their own graphic designers to create media on a more frequent basis. Those with more entrepreneurial inclinations can work as freelance graphic designers, doing their own networking and contracting. Trying to expand their possibilities, **53** many graphic designers are also now applying their knowledge to website and web application design, which continues to be a growing field for tech-minded artists.

54 Although the demand for graphic designers persists the highly competitive job market gives some prospective artists pause. The trope of the "struggling artist" holds true, it seems, even in our highly visually oriented society. Still, most graphic designers find their **55** careers both satisfying and also invigorating. Perhaps, for the dedicated artists who seek a career in graphic design, the thrill and beauty of the work yields enough motivation and inspiration to persevere and succeed.

50. A) NO CHANGE
    B) have begun by studying graphic design and earning
    C) begin by studying graphic design and earning
    D) will begin by studying graphic design and will earn

51. A) NO CHANGE
    B) you demonstrate
    C) they demonstrate
    D) theirs demonstrate

52. A) NO CHANGE
    B) rigorous, although the field offers
    C) rigorous; even though the field offers
    D) rigorous, but the field offers

53. A) NO CHANGE
    B) much graphic design knowledge also now applies to website and web application design, which
    C) many graphic designers' knowledge also now applies to website and web application design, which
    D) website and web application design allows many graphic designers to apply their knowledge, which

54. A) NO CHANGE
    B) Yet the demand for graphic designers persists; the highly competitive job market
    C) While the demand for graphic designers persists, but the highly competitive job market
    D) Even though the demand for graphic designers persists, the highly competitive job market

55. A) NO CHANGE
    B) careers neither satisfying or invigorating
    C) careers both satisfying and invigorating
    D) career not only satisfying but invigorating

Reflect

Directions: Take a few minutes to recall what you've learned and what you've been practicing in this chapter. Consider the following questions, jot down your best answer for each one, and then compare your reflections to the expert responses on the following page. Use your level of confidence to determine what to do next.

Name at least three ways to correct a run-on sentence.

_____

_____

_____

How does the SAT test subject-verb agreement and parallelism?

_____

_____

_____

What are the three different pronoun forms? When do you use each one?

_____

_____

_____

What is the difference between an adjective and an adverb?

_____

_____

_____

What are the three ways that apostrophes are tested on the SAT?

_____

_____

_____

Which commonly confused words do you need to be especially careful to look out for?

_____

_____

_____

Expert Responses

Name at least three ways to correct a run-on sentence.

There are a number of ways to fix a run-on sentence on the SAT. The six ways that you are likely to see are:
1) use a period to create two separate sentences, 2) use a semicolon between the two independent clauses, 3)
use a colon between the two independent clauses, 4) make one clause dependent, 5) add a FANBOYS conjunc-
tion after the comma, or 6) use a dash between the two independent clauses.

How does the SAT test subject-verb agreement and parallelism?

A subject and verb must always agree in person (first, second, or third) and number (singular or plural). You
will need to be able to spot subject-verb mismatches and correct them. Parallelism requires that all items in
a list, a compound, or a comparison are in parallel form. The SAT may test lists or comparisons in which one
item is in the wrong form.

What are the three different pronoun forms? When do you use each one?

The three forms are subjective (when the pronoun is the subject), objective (when the pronoun is the object of
a verb or preposition), and possessive (when the pronoun expresses ownership).

What is the difference between an adjective and an adverb?

An adjective is a single word that modifies a noun or a pronoun, while an adverb is a single word that modifies
a verb, an adjective, or another adverb.

What are the three ways that apostrophes are tested on the SAT?

Apostrophes on the SAT are used to 1) indicate the possessive form of a singular noun ('s), 2) indicate the
possessive form of a plural noun (s'), or 3) indicate a contraction (don't = do not).

Which commonly confused words do you need to be especially careful to look out for?

The answer to this question is specific to you. If you have concerns about more than half of the words out of the
list of 24, consider making flash cards to help you practice. The extra effort will ensure that you do not confuse
any of the commonly confused words on test day.

Next Steps

If you answered most questions correctly in the "How Much Have You Learned?" section, and if your
responses to the Reflect questions were similar to those of the SAT expert, then consider sentence structure,
punctuation, and agreement areas of strength and move on to the next chapter. Come back to these topics
periodically to prevent yourself from getting rusty.

If you don't yet feel confident, review those parts of this chapter that you have not yet mastered. In particular,
review punctuation usage in the Sentence Structure: The Basics and Commas, Dashes, and Colons lessons,
as well as how to select the appropriate pronoun or modifier in the Agreement: Pronouns and Agreement:
Modifiers lessons. Then try the questions you missed again. As always, be sure to review the explanations
closely.

Answers and Explanations

1. Review the Explanation portion of the Sentence Structure: The Basics lesson.

2. D

Difficulty: Medium

Getting to the Answer: The sentence as written is a run-on. Two independent clauses are joined incorrectly by a comma. Eliminate (A). Because the comma is not underlined, you cannot fix the run-on by adding a coordinating conjunction or by replacing the comma with a semicolon. Instead, you need to change one of the independent clauses into a dependent clause. Choice **(D)** is correct because it makes the first clause dependent.

3. B

Difficulty: Medium

Getting to the Answer: In the passage, the sentence has a subject but is missing a verb. In other words, there is no main action that "the Sun's core temperature" is performing. Eliminate (A). The correct answer will add a verb to the underlined portion. Choice **(B)** is correct because it is the only answer choice that includes a verb, "has."

4. A

Difficulty: Hard

Getting to the Answer: The underlined portion lists examples of benefits that the Sun provides for the Earth. The list is long, but it is broken up into three main parts: electromagnetic waves, metabolic life, and the Earth's natural phenomena. Each is a category that has two specific items that precede it. When a list has multiple categories, each with its own members, then commas alone are often not sufficient to express the information clearly. Use semicolons to distinguish the main categories, and use commas to separate the items within each category. Choice **(A)** does exactly this and is correct.

5. B

Difficulty: Easy

Getting to the Answer: When two independent clauses are joined by a coordinating conjunction, such as "but," as is the case in this sentence, the conjunction needs to be preceded by a comma. Eliminate (A) and (C). Also eliminate (D) because "still" is not a FANBOYS conjunction. Choice **(B)** is correct.

6. D

Difficulty: Medium

Getting to the Answer: Two independent clauses are joined incorrectly by a comma, so you need to combine them according to correct grammar. Eliminate (A). There are several ways to combine two independent clauses, but only one answer choice offers an acceptable method: **(D)** uses a semicolon to join the two independent clauses and is correct. (B) does not use a FANBOYS conjunction and (C) erroneously omits the comma.

7. Review the Explanation portion of the Sentence Structure: Commas, Dashes, and Colons lesson.

8. B

Difficulty: Medium

Getting to the Answer: When a comma is underlined, check to see if the parts of the sentence before and after the comma need to be separated. In this sentence, the comma separates the subordinating conjunction "although" from the clause it introduces and breaks the link between the dependent clause and the main clause. Choice **(B)** correctly eliminates the unnecessary punctuation.

9. C

Difficulty: Medium

Getting to the Answer: Technically, "Mauritius" is not a complete sentence; there is no verb. Eliminate (A). You need a choice that will either make "Mauritius" a complete sentence or combine it with the first sentence. Choice **(C)** correctly uses a colon to introduce important information. Both (B) and (D) are missing commas after "familiar," making them grammatically incorrect.

10. D

Difficulty: Hard

Getting to the Answer: The beginning of the sentence, "Since gaining independence in 1968," is a short introductory phrase that needs to be set off with a comma. Eliminate (A). Neither a dash nor a semicolon is appropriate in this scenario, so eliminate (B) as well. (C) incorrectly makes the independent clause that begins "Maritius has emerged" dependent. **(D)** correctly uses a comma to separate the introductory phrase from the main clause.

11. B

Difficulty: Hard

Getting to the Answer: When a colon is used to introduce a short phrase, it emphasizes the information in the phrase. A colon that introduces and emphasizes information should be used only if the phrase is not connected to the sentence in another way. In this sentence, the phrase "in the modern global economy" is connected to the main clause with the preposition "in," so the colon is unnecessary. Eliminate (A). Dashes set off unnecessary information, but the phrase "in the modern global economy" is essential to the meaning of the sentence because it describes what kind of player Mauritius is. Eliminate (C). The adjectives "modern" and "global" are cumulative, meaning that their order can change the sense of the phrase. In other words, "modern" describes "global economy," and the phrase "global modern economy" has a different meaning from what is intended. Cumulative adjectives should not have a comma between them, so (D) is incorrect. The sentence's final phrase, "one of the few in the Southern Hemisphere" does need to be set off with a comma because it is a parenthetical phrase that could have been omitted from the sentence. **(B)** is correct.

12. D

Difficulty: Easy

Getting to the Answer: When you have a list of three or more items in a series, separate them with commas, and separate the last two items with a comma and the conjunction "and." This series contains six distinct items. In longer lists, it can be appropriate to use a semicolon to separate the list into logical groups of items. In the underlined portion, however, there is no logical grouping, so a semicolon is unnecessary. Eliminate (A). Choice (B) is incorrect because "and" should appear only between the last and second to last items in the list. (C) is incorrect because it omits "and" altogether. Only **(D)** offers the list correctly.

13. C

Difficulty: Easy

Getting to the Answer: If a dash is used to introduce a break in thought, a second dash must be used to end the parenthetical phrase unless a period ends both the phrase and the sentence. Determine whether the information after the dash is parenthetical by reading the sentence without that information. Although the phrase provides a description of how the "colonial powers" treated Mauritius, the sentence makes logical sense without it. The phrase is therefore parenthetical and must be properly set off. Only choice **(C)** correctly sets off the phrase with both an opening and a closing dash.

14. B

Difficulty: Easy

Getting to the Answer: When two independent clauses are combined with a FANBOYS conjunction, a comma needs to precede the conjunction. Eliminate (A). Only **(B)** places the necessary comma in the appropriate spot.

15. A

Difficulty: Medium

Getting to the Answer: Avoid using unnecessary punctuation. Reread the sentence to determine how its parts are related. This sentence is correct as written because no punctuation is required. The phrase "through its advantageous geographic location and large labor force" completes the thought in the sentence by providing information on how Mauritius "balances" and "flourishes." Choice **(A)** is correct.

16. Review the Explanation portion of the Agreement: Verbs lesson.

17. A

Difficulty: Medium

Getting to the Answer: When a verb is underlined, one of your tasks is to identify its subject to ensure that there is proper subject-verb agreement. The sentence construction is a little unusual, "what is believed," but the vague word "what" is indeed the subject for the verb "is believed." The subject, "what," is singular, so eliminate (B) and (D), which use "are," a verb that goes with a plural subject. The writer is referring to what is believed at the moment, not some time in the future; therefore, eliminate (C). Choice **(A)** is correct because "is" is the correct singular form of the verb and in the correct present tense.

18. D

Difficulty: Medium

Getting to the Answer: Determining whether a subject is singular or plural can be difficult sometimes, especially if the subject refers to many things. Here, "SMOM" is a group of knights, but because it is a single entity, the word functions as a singular. The use of the singular possessive pronoun "its" at the end of the sentence confirms that SMOM is singular. Eliminate (A) and (C). When a verb is underlined, also consider the tense. The entire first paragraph is in present tense and it is clear from the context that SMOM, though an "ancient" order, still exists, so maintain the same tense in this sentence. Choice **(D)** is correct because "is" is a singular verb in present tense.

19. B

Difficulty: Medium

Getting to the Answer: When a subject has multiple verbs, known as compound verbs, they must all be in the same form. The sentence begins with two verbs, both in infinitive form, "to protect" and "to defend." The underlined portion includes a third verb, which needs to be in the infinitive form, as well, to maintain parallelism. **(B)** is correct because it matches the form of the verbs earlier in the sentence.

20. B

Difficulty: Hard

Getting to the Answer: The perfect forms of verbs (i.e. have/has, had, and will have + a past participle) present special challenges in interpretation. It is crucial to determine the order of events. Because the sentence is rather long, focus on the underlined verb "had seized" and the verb in the opening phrase, "had overrun." The past perfect tense of "had overrun" signals that the action happened in the past and was completed in the past before some other action. The word "After" that begins the sentence and the dates show that the seizing of Rhodes happened after the overrunning of Jerusalem was completed. The only verb tense that expresses that temporal relationship is simple past tense. **(B)** is correct.

21. B

Difficulty: Easy

Getting to the Answer: The paragraph describes actions that occurred in the past and uses the simple past tense to do so, so the underlined portion should follow suit. Simple past describes a single event that occurred in the past, which is what Napoleon did. **(B)** is correct.

22. C

Difficulty: Easy

Getting to the Answer: The first word of the last paragraph is "Today," which signals a shift from the past tense of the previous paragraphs to present tense. The following sentence's main verb "include" is in present tense and confirms the shift. **(C)** is correct.

23. Review the Explanation portion of the Agreement: Pronouns lesson.

24. C

Difficulty: Medium

Getting to the Answer: When a pronoun is underlined, identify its antecedent. In the passage's first sentence, the writer gives a list, and in the second sentence, you find that these are the varied influences. The pronoun "He" is singular, but it refers to the plural group of "samurai, cowboys, shogun, gangsters, peasants, and William Shakespeare." Eliminate (A). The plural, third-person, subject pronoun "they" is needed to refer to the list. **(C)** is correct.

25. C

Difficulty: Medium

Getting to the Answer: The underlined portion should refer to "the most important Japanese filmmaker" as stated later in the sentence. "Filmmaker" is singular, but "them" is plural, so eliminate (A). In addition to being singular, the pronoun needs to be in the objective form because it is the "themes" and "settings" that are acting on the filmmaker, the object. The singular, objective (and third-person) pronoun is "him." **(C)** is correct.

26. C

Difficulty: Medium

Getting to the Answer: Pronouns can be in the grammatically correct form, but if they lack a clear referent, they need to be replaced with a specific word. The singular pronoun "its" is underlined and several singular nouns precede it, which makes it ambiguous. Eliminate (A). The underlined pronoun "its" is also possessive, so ask yourself, "whose story is the writer referring to?" The logical answer is "the film's story." **(C)** is correct.

27. B
Difficulty: Hard

Getting to the Answer: When a pronoun's antecedent is far away from the pronoun itself, it can be difficult to identify the antecedent. Checking for agreement between a pronoun and its antecedent is also tricky when the noun being replaced is singular in grammar but plural in concept. Both hurdles are present in this question. The entity seeking protection is the "village," which grammatically is singular. The third-person, singular pronoun "it" is required. **(B)** is correct.

28. A
Difficulty: Medium

Getting to the Answer: The pronoun "him" is replacing the third-person noun "Kurosawa." The end of the previous sentence raises the topic of what the samurai (in the film *Seven Samurai*) meant to Kurosawa. Any other change in person would cause an undesired shift in the passage. **(A)** is correct.

29. D
Difficulty: Hard

Getting to the Answer: In the passage, the word "of" means that the pronoun that follows should be in the objective form. However, the next word, "who," is in the subjective form; therefore, eliminate (A). Choice (B) is incorrect because "whose" is a possessive pronoun, but an objective pronoun is needed. Choice (C) is incorrect because "many" refers to people and "which" is for inanimate objects. Only **(D)** has the right pronoun in objective form and is correct.

30. Review the Explanation portion of the Agreement: Modifiers lesson.

31. C
Difficulty: Hard

Getting to the Answer: The sentence begins with a modifier, "Considered the father of montage," which means that the subject of the sentence must be the father of montage. Typically, the subject will immediately follow the opening modifying phrase, but in this sentence the next phrase, beginning "a popular cinematic technique," is an additional description, not the main clause. The underlined section is where the main clause begins, and the first words need to be the subject, the father of montage, Sergei Eisentstein. **(C)** is correct.

32. B
Difficulty: Easy

Getting to the Answer: Because the underlined word modifies "complexity," a noun, the underlined word needs to be an adjective. Choice **(B)** is correct.

33. B
Difficulty: Medium

Getting to the Answer: When making a comparison, you should note whether it is between two things or among three or more. In this sentence "few filmmakers" are being compared to Eisenstein. Although "filmmakers" is plural, the logic of the sentence treats them as one thing, so there are two things being compared. The comparative form "more" is needed. Choice **(B)** is correct.

34. D
Difficulty: Medium

Getting to the Answer: The qualifier "many" that precedes the underlined word shows that "moviegoers" is meant to be plural. The plural possessive is constructed by adding an apostrophe after the last "s." Choice **(D)** is correct.

35. A
Difficulty: Hard

Getting to the Answer: The sentence opens with an opening modifying phrase. Whatever that phrase modifies must immediately follow it. Ask yourself what is "[b]ased on the contemporary theory of biomechanics." The answer is Eisenstein's montage, so the underlined segment is correct and no change is needed. Choice **(A)** is correct.

Note that while Eisenstein could be using the montage to make a criticism, it does not make sense to say that Eisenstein is based on the theory of biomechanics. Therefore, the correct answer will not have "Eisenstein" as its subject; eliminate (B), (C), and (D). Choice **(A)** is correct because "Eisenstein's montage" is the subject, and the montage can both criticize and be based on the theory of biomechanics.

36. C

Difficulty: Medium

Getting to the Answer: The only difference among the underlined section and the answer choices is the placement of the word "enormously." The word is an adverb, so it needs to modify a verb, an adjective, or another adverb. Also, modifiers need to be placed near the word or phrase that they modify. Choice **(C)** is correct because it provides the closest placement to "successful," the only word that could be logically modified by "enormously."

37. C

Difficulty: Medium

Getting to the Answer: An apostrophe can signal a contraction, a shortening of two words. The underlined "they're" is a contraction of "they are," which does not make sense in the context of the sentence. Eliminate (A). You need a plural possessive pronoun because it refers back to "achievements." Choice **(C)** is correct.

38. Review the Explanation portion of the Idioms lesson.

39. B

Difficulty: Easy

Getting to the Answer: The construction "neither . . . nor" is idiomatic, so a phrase beginning with "neither" must be followed by "nor." Choice **(B)** is correct.

40. C

Difficulty: Easy

Getting to the Answer: The word "hardly" is a negative like "not." Double negatives, like "not hardly," are grammatical mistakes. Eliminate (A). The word "nothing" is another negative, so eliminate (B). Choice **(C)** is correct because it removes the double negative around "hardly."

41. D

Difficulty: Medium

Getting to the Answer: The construction in the underlined section is not idiomatic: "between . . . or" is incorrect. Eliminate (A). The three answer choices are all correct idiomatically, but only one makes logical sense in the sentence. (B) makes it sound as if an opossum cannot be two and a half feet long, which doesn't make sense. Similarly, (C) does not fit in the context of the passage because the word "typically" means that the

opossum length given will be authoritative and precise, not a loose estimation as "at least" suggests. **(D)** is correct because it has the appropriate idiomatic phrase "between . . . and."

42. B

Difficulty: Hard

Getting to the Answer: Make sure that the proper prepositions are being used in the passage. As written, "of" implies that the metabolic limitations belong to the amount of food and energy that can be stored, but the intended meaning is that the metabolic limitations belong to the opossum and put a restriction on the amount of food and energy that can be stored. Eliminate (A). The preposition "on" is correct, given the context because there is a restriction *on* the amount of food that can be stored. Choice **(B)** is correct. If idioms are tricky, think of an analogous situation. A computer's limited warranty has limitations *on* the parts of the computer that are covered if something breaks. It doesn't have limitations *of* or *with* or *for* the parts of the computer.

43. B

Difficulty: Medium

Getting to the Answer: It will help to memorize commonly confused words like "affect" and "effect" and know what they mean and how to use them in various contexts. As written, the underlined portion incorrectly uses "affect," which is almost always a verb, as a noun. Eliminate (A). The intended word is "effect," which means some sort of change brought on by some cause (think *cause and effect*). Choice **(B)** is correct. Choice (C) also uses the word "effect" but incorrectly as a verb. "Effect" is almost always a noun, a thing that happens, but when "effect" is a verb, it means to cause or bring about. The nervous system is not an action that can be caused to happen, so (C) is incorrect.

44. C

Difficulty: Hard

Getting to the Answer: The distinction between "lay" and "lie" is mostly lost in everyday speech, but in formal written English, the difference is important. The word "lay" takes an object; the word "lie" does not. In other words, you lay down your book, but you lie down. Because the opossum is doing the action (the opossum is not, for example, laying down some food it had just picked up), "lie" is the appropriate verb. **(C)** is correct. The word "laid" is the past participle of "lay," and "lain" is the past participle of "lie." Neither (B) nor (D) offer verb tenses that make sense in the context of the sentence.

45. D

Difficulty: Medium

Category: Agreement: Modifiers

Getting to the Answer: Scan the answer choices to see that the difference is the placement of the words "often" and "only." These two words are modifiers, so they need to be placed as closely as possible to words or phrases that they modify. The word "often" tells the frequency with which people think of verbal or written forms; therefore, it needs to be at the beginning of the phrase. Eliminate (A) and (B), which put "often" before the comma so that it incorrectly modifies the previous phrase. The word "only" describes the limits of which forms of communication people think of, so the word needs to be nearest those forms of communication, "verbal and written." **(D)** is correct. (C) incorrectly places "only" so that it modifies "they."

46. A

Difficulty: Medium

Category: Sentence Structure: The Basics

Getting to the Answer: The underlined section is part of a long sentence that has two independent clauses. To join them you need to use a semicolon, a comma and coordinating (i.e., FANBOYS) conjunction, or a dash. The word "however" is not a coordinating conjunction; eliminate (C) and (D). While "however" does help in connecting the ideas of the first and second clauses, the word is not necessary, and should therefore be set off by a comma. **(A)** is correct.

47. D

Difficulty: Medium

Category: Agreement: Verbs

Getting to the Answer: Verb tense should stay consistent unless a certain thought requires a shift. In the underlined portion, the main verb is "offered," which is past tense, but the rest of the paragraph is in present tense. Eliminate (A). The correct verb form is present tense. Eliminate (C) because the *-ing*, or progressive, form is not a main verb. The passive voice "brought" is correct because it is the digital age that is bringing on the explosion of media; **(D)** is correct.

48. C

Difficulty: Medium

Category: Agreement: Pronouns

Getting to the Answer: Pronouns need to agree with their antecedents. In the underlined portion, the plural pronoun "their" incorrectly refers to the singular "a graphic designer" at the end of the previous sentence. Eliminate (A). Also, eliminate (B) and (D) because the pronouns they use are also plural and incorrectly refer to a singular antecedent. (B) is also incorrect because "them" is not possessive. **(C)** is correct because it replaces the pronoun with the correct plural referent.

49. B

Difficulty: Medium

Category: Sentence Structure: Commas, Dashes, and Colons

Getting to the Answer: You can treat the underlined portion after the colon as a long list, but also notice that it is a compound subject. All of the underlined items do the same thing: they feature graphic design. Sometimes, it can be helpful to use semicolons to organize complicated and long lists into groups of items, but in this case, the placement of the semicolons is not logical. There is no obvious reason why website layouts and T-shirt designs should be grouped together, nor why they should belong to a group that is separate from business logos and billboard advertisements. Eliminate (A). Both (C) and (D) are incorrect because the last item in the list is decorated cardboard, not cereal boxes and coffee cups. Placing a comma between "the decorated cardboard of cereal boxes" and "and coffee cups" would mean that the coffee cups are not decorated cardboard. **(B)** is correct because it separates each item in the list with a comma.

50. C

Difficulty: Medium

Category: Agreement: Verbs

Getting to the Answer: Verb tense should remain constant unless there is shift in meaning. The second half of the sentence has "they build," which is present tense. The sentence before and the sentence after also have main verbs in present tense, so the main verb of the underlined clause needs to be in present tense, too. **(C)** is correct.

51. C

Difficulty: Medium

Category: Agreement: Pronouns

Getting to the Answer: Pronouns need to match the noun that they are replacing. In the underlined portion, the singular pronoun "it" is supposed to replace the plural "portfolios," so eliminate (A) and (B). The word "portfolios" is not a possessive like "theirs," so (D) is also incorrect. Only **(C)** is left and is correct because "they" correctly replaces "portfolios."

52. D

Difficulty: Medium

Category: Sentence Structure: The Basics

Getting to the Answer: The sentence as constructed has two independent clauses, so they need to be joined correctly either with a comma and FANBOYS (coordinating) conjunction, or with a semicolon, or with a dash. As written, there is no comma between "rigorous" and "yet," so eliminate (A). Only **(D)** uses a comma and FANBOYS conjunction, so it is correct.

53. A

Difficulty: Medium

Category: Agreement: Modifiers

Getting to the Answer: When a sentence begins with a modifying phrase, whatever follows must be the thing that is modified and is the subject of the sentence. Logically, the modifying phrase "Trying to expand their possibilities" can refer only to the graphic designers. The pronoun "their" is plural and so is "graphic designers." **(A)** is correct.

54. D

Difficulty: Medium

Category: Sentence Structure: The Basics

Getting to the Answer: The word "Although" in the underlined portion signals that the first clause is a dependent clause and the second clause is independent. A comma is required to separate the two, but the sentence as written has no comma. Eliminate (A). A semicolon is not appropriate for subordinating one clause to another, and "yet" is a coordinating (FANBOYS) conjunction, not a subordinating conjunction. Eliminate (B). Choice (C) is incorrect because "while" makes the first clause dependent, and "but" cannot be used to join a dependent and an independent clause. That leaves **(D)**, which is correct because "Even though" subordinates the first clause and uses a comma to separate it from the second clause.

55. C

Difficulty: Medium

Category: Agreement: Idioms

Getting to the Answer: Idiomatic expressions have no logical rules, so they must be memorized. The construction "both . . . and also" is not a valid idiomatic phrase in formal written English. Eliminate (A). The correct construction is "both . . . and," which makes **(C)** correct. (B) is an incorrect form of "neither . . . nor," and it does not make sense in the context of the sentence. The idiom in (D) should be "not only . . . but also," so it is incorrect, too.

PART 5

Countdown to Test Day

CHAPTER 19

Countdown to Test Day

The Week Before the Test

- Focus your additional practice on the question types and/or subject areas in which you usually score highest. Now is the time to sharpen your best skills, not cram new information.

- Make sure you are registered for the test. Remember, Kaplan cannot register you. If you missed the registration deadlines, you can request Waitlist Status on the test maker's website, collegeboard.org.

- Confirm the location of your test site. Never been there before? Make a practice run to make sure you know exactly how long it will take to get from your home to your test site. Build in extra time in case you hit traffic or construction on the morning of the test.

- Get a great night's sleep the two days before the test.

The Day Before the Test

- Review the methods and strategies you learned in this book.
- Put new batteries in your calculator.
- Pack your backpack or bag for test day with the following items:
  - Photo ID
  - Registration slip or printout
  - Directions to your test site location
  - Five or more sharpened no. 2 pencils (no mechanical pencils)
  - Pencil sharpener
  - Eraser
  - Calculator
  - Extra batteries
  - Non-prohibited timepiece
  - Tissues
  - Prepackaged snacks, like granola bars
  - Bottled water, juice, or sports drink
  - Sweatshirt, sweater, or jacket

The Night Before the Test

- No studying!
- Do something relaxing that will take your mind off the test, such as watching a movie or playing video games with friends.
- Set your alarm to wake up early enough so that you won't feel rushed.
- Go to bed early, but not too much earlier than you usually do. You want to fall asleep quickly, not spend hours tossing and turning.

The Morning of the Test

- Dress comfortably and in layers. You need to be prepared for any temperature.
- Eat a filling breakfast, but don't stray too far from your usual routine. If you normally aren't a breakfast eater, don't eat a huge meal, but make sure you have something substantial.
- Read something over breakfast. You need to warm up your brain so you don't go into the test cold. Read a few pages of a newspaper, magazine, or favorite novel.
- Get to your test site early. There is likely to be some confusion about where to go and how to sign in, so allow yourself plenty of time, even if you are taking the test at your own school.
- Leave your cell phone at home. Many test sites do not allow them in the building.
- While you're waiting to sign in or be seated, read more of what you read over breakfast to stay in reading mode.

During the Test

- Be calm and confident. You're ready for this!
- Remember that while the SAT is a three-hour marathon (or four if you opt to do the essay), it is also a series of shorter sections. Focus on the section you're working on at that moment; don't think about previous or upcoming sections.
- Use the methods and strategies you have learned in this book as often as you can. Allow yourself to fall into the good habits you built during your practice.
- Don't linger too long on any one question. Mark it and come back to it later.
- Can't figure out an answer? Try to eliminate some choices and take a strategic guess. Remember, there is no penalty for an incorrect answer, so even if you can't eliminate any choices, you should take a guess.
- There will be plenty of questions you *can* answer, so spend your time on those first.
- Maintain good posture throughout the test. It will help you stay alert.
- If you find yourself losing concentration, getting frustrated, or stressing about the time, stop for 30 seconds. Close your eyes, put your pencil down, take a few deep breaths, and relax your shoulders. You'll be much more productive after taking a few moments to relax.
- Use your breaks effectively. During the five-minute breaks, go to the restroom, eat your snacks, and get your energy up for the next section.

After the Test

- Congratulate yourself! Then, reward yourself by doing something fun. You've earned it!

- If you got sick during the test or if something else happened that might have negatively affected your score, you can cancel your scores by the Wednesday following your test date. Request a score cancellation form from your test proctor or visit the test maker's website for more information.

- Your scores will be available online approximately two to four weeks after your test. The College Board sends scores to colleges 10 days after they are available to you.

PART 6

Practice Test

HOW TO SCORE YOUR PRACTICE TESTS

For each subject area in the practice test, convert your raw score, or the number of questions you answered correctly, to a scaled score using the table below. To get your raw score for Evidence-Based Reading & Writing, add the total number of Reading questions you answered correctly to the total number of Writing questions you answered correctly; for Math, add the number of questions you answered correctly for the Math—No Calculator and Math—Calculator sections.

Evidence-Based Reading and Writing		Math		Evidence-Based Reading and Writing		Math	
TOTAL Raw Score	Scaled Score	Raw Score	Scaled Score	TOTAL Raw Score	Scaled Score	Raw Score	Scaled Score
0	200	0	200	49	490	49	700
1	200	1	220	50	500	50	710
2	210	2	240	51	500	51	720
3	220	3	260	52	510	52	740
4	240	4	290	53	510	53	750
5	260	5	310	54	520	54	760
6	270	6	320	55	520	55	770
7	270	7	330	56	530	56	780
8	290	8	340	57	530	57	790
9	290	9	360	58	540	58	800
10	300	10	370	59	540		
11	300	11	380	60	550		
12	310	12	390	61	550		
13	320	13	400	62	560		
14	320	14	410	63	560		
15	330	15	420	64	570		
16	330	16	430	65	570		
17	340	17	430	66	580		
18	340	18	440	67	580		
19	350	19	450	68	590		
20	350	20	450	69	590		
21	360	21	460	70	600		
22	360	22	470	71	600		
23	370	23	480	72	610		
24	370	24	490	73	610		
25	370	25	500	74	610		
26	380	26	510	75	620		
27	380	27	520	76	620		
28	380	28	530	77	630		
29	380	29	540	78	630		
30	390	30	540	79	640		
31	390	31	550	80	640		
32	400	32	560	81	660		
33	400	33	560	82	660		
34	410	34	570	83	670		
35	410	35	580	84	680		
36	420	36	590	85	690		
37	430	37	600	86	700		
38	430	38	600	87	700		
39	440	39	610	88	710		
40	440	40	620	89	710		
41	450	41	630	90	730		
42	450	42	640	91	740		
43	460	43	640	92	750		
44	460	44	660	93	760		
45	470	45	670	94	780		
46	480	46	670	95	790		
47	480	47	680	96	800		
48	490	48	690				

SAT Practice Test Answer Sheet

You will see an answer sheet like the one below on test day. Review the answer key following the test when finished.

When testing, start with number 1 for each section. If a section has fewer questions than answer spaces, leave the extra spaces blank.

SECTION 1

1. Ⓐ Ⓑ Ⓒ Ⓓ
2. Ⓐ Ⓑ Ⓒ Ⓓ
3. Ⓐ Ⓑ Ⓒ Ⓓ
4. Ⓐ Ⓑ Ⓒ Ⓓ
5. Ⓐ Ⓑ Ⓒ Ⓓ
6. Ⓐ Ⓑ Ⓒ Ⓓ
7. Ⓐ Ⓑ Ⓒ Ⓓ
8. Ⓐ Ⓑ Ⓒ Ⓓ
9. Ⓐ Ⓑ Ⓒ Ⓓ
10. Ⓐ Ⓑ Ⓒ Ⓓ
11. Ⓐ Ⓑ Ⓒ Ⓓ
12. Ⓐ Ⓑ Ⓒ Ⓓ
13. Ⓐ Ⓑ Ⓒ Ⓓ

14. Ⓐ Ⓑ Ⓒ Ⓓ
15. Ⓐ Ⓑ Ⓒ Ⓓ
16. Ⓐ Ⓑ Ⓒ Ⓓ
17. Ⓐ Ⓑ Ⓒ Ⓓ
18. Ⓐ Ⓑ Ⓒ Ⓓ
19. Ⓐ Ⓑ Ⓒ Ⓓ
20. Ⓐ Ⓑ Ⓒ Ⓓ
21. Ⓐ Ⓑ Ⓒ Ⓓ
22. Ⓐ Ⓑ Ⓒ Ⓓ
23. Ⓐ Ⓑ Ⓒ Ⓓ
24. Ⓐ Ⓑ Ⓒ Ⓓ
25. Ⓐ Ⓑ Ⓒ Ⓓ
26. Ⓐ Ⓑ Ⓒ Ⓓ

27. Ⓐ Ⓑ Ⓒ Ⓓ
28. Ⓐ Ⓑ Ⓒ Ⓓ
29. Ⓐ Ⓑ Ⓒ Ⓓ
30. Ⓐ Ⓑ Ⓒ Ⓓ
31. Ⓐ Ⓑ Ⓒ Ⓓ
32. Ⓐ Ⓑ Ⓒ Ⓓ
33. Ⓐ Ⓑ Ⓒ Ⓓ
34. Ⓐ Ⓑ Ⓒ Ⓓ
35. Ⓐ Ⓑ Ⓒ Ⓓ
36. Ⓐ Ⓑ Ⓒ Ⓓ
37. Ⓐ Ⓑ Ⓒ Ⓓ
38. Ⓐ Ⓑ Ⓒ Ⓓ
39. Ⓐ Ⓑ Ⓒ Ⓓ

40. Ⓐ Ⓑ Ⓒ Ⓓ
41. Ⓐ Ⓑ Ⓒ Ⓓ
42. Ⓐ Ⓑ Ⓒ Ⓓ
43. Ⓐ Ⓑ Ⓒ Ⓓ
44. Ⓐ Ⓑ Ⓒ Ⓓ
45. Ⓐ Ⓑ Ⓒ Ⓓ
46. Ⓐ Ⓑ Ⓒ Ⓓ
47. Ⓐ Ⓑ Ⓒ Ⓓ
48. Ⓐ Ⓑ Ⓒ Ⓓ
49. Ⓐ Ⓑ Ⓒ Ⓓ
50. Ⓐ Ⓑ Ⓒ Ⓓ
51. Ⓐ Ⓑ Ⓒ Ⓓ
52. Ⓐ Ⓑ Ⓒ Ⓓ

correct in Section 1

incorrect in Section 1

SECTION 2

1. Ⓐ Ⓑ Ⓒ Ⓓ
2. Ⓐ Ⓑ Ⓒ Ⓓ
3. Ⓐ Ⓑ Ⓒ Ⓓ
4. Ⓐ Ⓑ Ⓒ Ⓓ
5. Ⓐ Ⓑ Ⓒ Ⓓ
6. Ⓐ Ⓑ Ⓒ Ⓓ
7. Ⓐ Ⓑ Ⓒ Ⓓ
8. Ⓐ Ⓑ Ⓒ Ⓓ
9. Ⓐ Ⓑ Ⓒ Ⓓ
10. Ⓐ Ⓑ Ⓒ Ⓓ
11. Ⓐ Ⓑ Ⓒ Ⓓ

12. Ⓐ Ⓑ Ⓒ Ⓓ
13. Ⓐ Ⓑ Ⓒ Ⓓ
14. Ⓐ Ⓑ Ⓒ Ⓓ
15. Ⓐ Ⓑ Ⓒ Ⓓ
16. Ⓐ Ⓑ Ⓒ Ⓓ
17. Ⓐ Ⓑ Ⓒ Ⓓ
18. Ⓐ Ⓑ Ⓒ Ⓓ
19. Ⓐ Ⓑ Ⓒ Ⓓ
20. Ⓐ Ⓑ Ⓒ Ⓓ
21. Ⓐ Ⓑ Ⓒ Ⓓ
22. Ⓐ Ⓑ Ⓒ Ⓓ

23. Ⓐ Ⓑ Ⓒ Ⓓ
24. Ⓐ Ⓑ Ⓒ Ⓓ
25. Ⓐ Ⓑ Ⓒ Ⓓ
26. Ⓐ Ⓑ Ⓒ Ⓓ
27. Ⓐ Ⓑ Ⓒ Ⓓ
28. Ⓐ Ⓑ Ⓒ Ⓓ
29. Ⓐ Ⓑ Ⓒ Ⓓ
30. Ⓐ Ⓑ Ⓒ Ⓓ
31. Ⓐ Ⓑ Ⓒ Ⓓ
32. Ⓐ Ⓑ Ⓒ Ⓓ
33. Ⓐ Ⓑ Ⓒ Ⓓ

34. Ⓐ Ⓑ Ⓒ Ⓓ
35. Ⓐ Ⓑ Ⓒ Ⓓ
36. Ⓐ Ⓑ Ⓒ Ⓓ
37. Ⓐ Ⓑ Ⓒ Ⓓ
38. Ⓐ Ⓑ Ⓒ Ⓓ
39. Ⓐ Ⓑ Ⓒ Ⓓ
40. Ⓐ Ⓑ Ⓒ Ⓓ
41. Ⓐ Ⓑ Ⓒ Ⓓ
42. Ⓐ Ⓑ Ⓒ Ⓓ
43. Ⓐ Ⓑ Ⓒ Ⓓ
44. Ⓐ Ⓑ Ⓒ Ⓓ

correct in Section 2

incorrect in Section 2

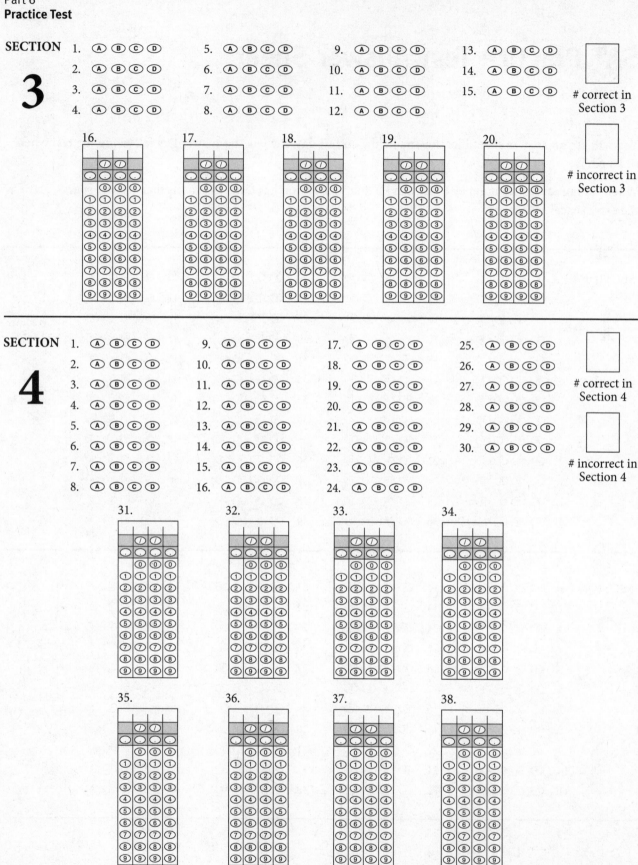

SECTION

3

1. Ⓐ Ⓑ Ⓒ Ⓓ
2. Ⓐ Ⓑ Ⓒ Ⓓ
3. Ⓐ Ⓑ Ⓒ Ⓓ
4. Ⓐ Ⓑ Ⓒ Ⓓ

5. Ⓐ Ⓑ Ⓒ Ⓓ
6. Ⓐ Ⓑ Ⓒ Ⓓ
7. Ⓐ Ⓑ Ⓒ Ⓓ
8. Ⓐ Ⓑ Ⓒ Ⓓ

9. Ⓐ Ⓑ Ⓒ Ⓓ
10. Ⓐ Ⓑ Ⓒ Ⓓ
11. Ⓐ Ⓑ Ⓒ Ⓓ
12. Ⓐ Ⓑ Ⓒ Ⓓ

13. Ⓐ Ⓑ Ⓒ Ⓓ
14. Ⓐ Ⓑ Ⓒ Ⓓ
15. Ⓐ Ⓑ Ⓒ Ⓓ

correct in
Section 3

incorrect in
Section 3

16. 17. 18. 19. 20.

SECTION

4

1. Ⓐ Ⓑ Ⓒ Ⓓ
2. Ⓐ Ⓑ Ⓒ Ⓓ
3. Ⓐ Ⓑ Ⓒ Ⓓ
4. Ⓐ Ⓑ Ⓒ Ⓓ
5. Ⓐ Ⓑ Ⓒ Ⓓ
6. Ⓐ Ⓑ Ⓒ Ⓓ
7. Ⓐ Ⓑ Ⓒ Ⓓ
8. Ⓐ Ⓑ Ⓒ Ⓓ

9. Ⓐ Ⓑ Ⓒ Ⓓ
10. Ⓐ Ⓑ Ⓒ Ⓓ
11. Ⓐ Ⓑ Ⓒ Ⓓ
12. Ⓐ Ⓑ Ⓒ Ⓓ
13. Ⓐ Ⓑ Ⓒ Ⓓ
14. Ⓐ Ⓑ Ⓒ Ⓓ
15. Ⓐ Ⓑ Ⓒ Ⓓ
16. Ⓐ Ⓑ Ⓒ Ⓓ

17. Ⓐ Ⓑ Ⓒ Ⓓ
18. Ⓐ Ⓑ Ⓒ Ⓓ
19. Ⓐ Ⓑ Ⓒ Ⓓ
20. Ⓐ Ⓑ Ⓒ Ⓓ
21. Ⓐ Ⓑ Ⓒ Ⓓ
22. Ⓐ Ⓑ Ⓒ Ⓓ
23. Ⓐ Ⓑ Ⓒ Ⓓ
24. Ⓐ Ⓑ Ⓒ Ⓓ

25. Ⓐ Ⓑ Ⓒ Ⓓ
26. Ⓐ Ⓑ Ⓒ Ⓓ
27. Ⓐ Ⓑ Ⓒ Ⓓ
28. Ⓐ Ⓑ Ⓒ Ⓓ
29. Ⓐ Ⓑ Ⓒ Ⓓ
30. Ⓐ Ⓑ Ⓒ Ⓓ

correct in
Section 4

incorrect in
Section 4

31. 32. 33. 34.

35. 36. 37. 38.

Reading Test

65 Minutes—52 Questions

This section corresponds to Section 1 of your answer sheet.

Directions: Read each passage or pair of passages, then answer the questions that follow. Choose your answers based on what the passage(s) and any accompanying graphics state or imply.

Questions 1-10 are based on the following passage.

This passage is adapted from "Metamorphosis" by Franz Kafka, a famous story that combines elements of fantasy and reality. This excerpt begins with the protagonist realizing he has literally turned into a giant, beetle-like insect.

One morning, when Gregor Samsa woke from troubled dreams, he found himself transformed in his bed into a horrible vermin. He lay on his armor-like back, and if he lifted his head a little
5 he could see his brown belly, slightly domed and divided by arches into stiff sections. The bedding was hardly able to cover it and seemed ready to slide off any moment. His many legs, pitifully thin compared with the size of the rest of him, waved
10 about helplessly as he looked.

"What's happened to me?" he thought. It wasn't a dream. His room, a proper human room although a little too small, lay peacefully between its four familiar walls. A collection of textile samples lay
15 spread out on the table—Samsa was a travelling salesman—and above it there hung a picture that he had recently cut out of an illustrated magazine and housed in a nice, gilded frame. It showed a lady fitted out with a fur hat and fur boa who sat
20 upright, raising a heavy fur muff that covered the whole of her lower arm towards the viewer.

Gregor then turned to look out the window at the dull weather. Drops of rain could be heard hitting the pane, which made him feel quite sad.
25 "How about if I sleep a little bit longer and forget all this nonsense," he thought, but that was something he was unable to do because he was used to sleeping on his right, and in his present state couldn't get into that position. However hard he
30 threw himself onto his right, he always rolled back to where he was. He must have tried it a hundred times,

shut his eyes so that he wouldn't have to look at the floundering legs, and only stopped when he began to feel a mild, dull pain there that he had never felt before.

35 He thought, "What a strenuous career it is that I've chosen! Travelling day in and day out. Doing business like this takes much more effort than doing your own business at home, and on top of that there's the curse of travelling, worries about
40 making train connections, bad and irregular food, contact with different people all the time so that you can never get to know anyone or become friendly with them." He felt a slight itch up on his belly; pushed himself slowly up on his back
45 towards the headboard so that he could lift his head better; found where the itch was, and saw that it was covered with lots of little white spots which he didn't know what to make of; and when he tried to feel the place with one of his legs he drew it quickly
50 back because as soon as he touched it he was overcome by a cold shudder.

He slid back into his former position. "Getting up early all the time," he thought, "it makes you stupid. You've got to get enough sleep. Other
55 travelling salesmen live a life of luxury. For instance, whenever I go back to the guest house during the morning to copy out the contract, these gentlemen are always still sitting there eating their breakfasts. I ought to just try that with my boss; I'd
60 get kicked out on the spot. But who knows, maybe that would be the best thing for me. If I didn't have my parents to think about I'd have given in my notice a long time ago, I'd have gone up to the boss and told him just what I think, tell him everything
65 I would, let him know just what I feel. He'd fall right off his desk! And it's a funny sort of business to be sitting up there at your desk, talking down at your subordinates from up there, especially when you

GO ON TO THE NEXT PAGE

have to go right up close because the boss is hard
70 of hearing. Well, there's still some hope; once I've
got the money together to pay off my parents' debt
to him—another five or six years I suppose—that's
definitely what I'll do. That's when I'll make the big
change. First of all though, I've got to get up, my
75 train leaves at five."

1. According to the passage, Gregor initially believes his transformation is a

   A) curse.
   B) disease.
   C) nightmare.
   D) hoax.

2. As used in line 12, "proper" most nearly means

   A) called for by rules or conventions.
   B) showing politeness.
   C) naturally belonging or peculiar to.
   D) suitably appropriate.

3. The passage most strongly suggests which of the following about Gregor's attitude toward his profession?

   A) He is resentful.
   B) He is diligent.
   C) He is depressed.
   D) He is eager to please.

4. Which choice provides the best evidence for the answer to the previous question?

   A) Lines 14–18 ("A collection…gilded frame")
   B) Lines 22–24 ("Gregor then turned…quite sad")
   C) Lines 54–60 ("Other…the spot")
   D) Lines 66–70 ("And it's…hard of hearing")

5. What central idea does the passage communicate through Gregor's experiences?

   A) Imagination is a dangerous thing.
   B) People are fearful of change.
   C) Dreams become our reality.
   D) Humankind is a slave to work.

6. The passage most strongly suggests that which of the following is true of Gregor?

   A) He feels a strong sense of duty toward his family.
   B) He is unable to cope with change.
   C) He excels in his profession.
   D) He is fearful about his transformation.

7. Which choice provides the best evidence for the answer to the previous question?

   A) Lines 11–14 ("What's happened…familiar walls")
   B) Lines 22–24 ("Gregor then turned…quite sad")
   C) Lines 36–43 ("Doing business…with them")
   D) Lines 70–73 ("Well, there's still…what I'll do")

8. As used in line 33, "floundering" most nearly means

   A) thrashing.
   B) painful.
   C) pitiful.
   D) trembling.

9. The author most likely includes a description of Gregor's itch in lines 43–51 to

   A) remind the reader that Gregor has turned into an insect.
   B) emphasize the disconnect between Gregor's thoughts and his actual situation.
   C) give important details about what Gregor's new body looks like.
   D) show that Gregor's thoughts are focused on the changes to his body.

10. The function of the final sentence of the excerpt ("First of all though, I've got to get up, my train leaves at five") is to

   A) provide a resolution to the conflict Gregor faces.
   B) foreshadow the conflict between Gregor and his boss.
   C) illustrate Gregor's resilience and ability to move on.
   D) emphasize Gregor's extreme sense of duty.

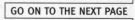 GO ON TO THE NEXT PAGE

Questions 11-20 are based on the following passage.

This passage is adapted from Hillary Rodham Clinton's speech titled "Women's Rights Are Human Rights," addressed to the U.N. Fourth World Conference on Women in 1995.

If there is one message that echoes forth from this conference, it is that human rights are women's rights.... And women's rights are human rights.

Let us not forget that among those rights are the
5 right to speak freely and the right to be heard.

Women must enjoy the right to participate fully in the social and political lives of their countries if we want freedom and democracy to thrive and endure.

It is indefensible that many women in
10 nongovernmental organizations who wished to participate in this conference have not been able to attend—
or have been prohibited from fully taking part.

Let me be clear. Freedom means the right of people to assemble, organize, and debate openly.
15 It means respecting the views of those who may disagree with the views of their governments. It means not taking citizens away from their loved ones and jailing them, mistreating them, or denying them their freedom or dignity because of
20 the peaceful expression of their ideas and opinions.

In my country, we recently celebrated the seventy-fifth anniversary of women's suffrage. It took one hundred and fifty years after the signing of our Declaration of Independence for women to
25 win the right to vote. It took seventy-two years of organized struggle on the part of many courageous women and men.

It was one of America's most divisive philosophical wars. But it was also a bloodless war.
30 Suffrage was achieved without a shot fired.

We have also been reminded, in V-J Day observances last weekend, of the good that comes when men and women join together to combat the forces of tyranny and build a better world.
35 We have seen peace prevail in most places for a half century. We have avoided another world war. But we have not solved older, deeply-rooted problems that continue to diminish the potential of half the world's population.
40 Now it is time to act on behalf of women everywhere.

If we take bold steps to better the lives of women, we will be taking bold steps to better the lives of children and families too. Families rely on mothers and
45 wives for emotional support and care; families rely on women for labor in the home; and increasingly, families rely on women for income needed to raise healthy children and care for other relatives.

As long as discrimination and inequities remain
50 so commonplace around the world—as long as girls and women are valued less, fed less, fed last, overworked, underpaid, not schooled and subjected to violence in and out of their homes— the potential of the human family to create a
55 peaceful, prosperous world will not be realized.

Let this conference be our—and the world's— call to action.

And let us heed the call so that we can create a world in which every woman is treated with respect
60 and dignity, every boy and girl is loved and cared for equally, and every family has the hope of a strong and stable future.

11. What is the primary purpose of the passage?

A) To chastise those who have prevented women from attending the conference

B) To argue that women continue to experience discrimination

C) To explain that human rights are of more concern than women's rights

D) To encourage people to think of women's rights as an issue important to all

12. Which choice provides the best evidence for the answer to the previous question?

A) Lines 4–5 ("Let us...be heard")

B) Lines 9–12 ("It is indefensible...taking part")

C) Lines 37–39 ("But we have...population")

D) Lines 44–48 ("Families...other relatives")

13. As used in line 28, "divisive" most nearly means

    A) conflict-producing.

    B) carefully watched.

    C) multi-purpose.

    D) time-consuming.

14. Based on the speech, with which statement would Clinton most likely agree?

    A) More men should be the primary caregivers of their children in order to provide career opportunities for women.

    B) Women do not need the support and cooperation of men as they work toward equality.

    C) Solutions for global problems would be found faster if women had more access to power.

    D) The American movement for women's suffrage should have been violent in order to achieve success more quickly.

15. Which choice provides the best evidence for the answer to the previous question?

    A) Lines 6–8 ("Women…endure")

    B) Line 30 ("Suffrage…shot fired")

    C) Lines 44–48 ("Families…other relatives")

    D) Lines 49–55 ("As long…realized")

16. As used in line 26, "organized" most nearly means

    A) arranged.

    B) cooperative.

    C) hierarchical.

    D) patient.

17. Which claim does Clinton make in her speech?

    A) The conference itself is a model of nondiscrimination toward women.

    B) Democracy cannot prosper unless women can participate fully in it.

    C) Women's rights are restricted globally by the demands on them as parents.

    D) Women are being forced to provide income for their families as a result of sexism.

18. Clinton uses the example of V-J Day observations to support the argument that

    A) campaigns succeed when they are nonviolent.

    B) historical wrongs against women must be corrected.

    C) many tragedies could have been avoided with more female participation.

    D) cooperation between men and women leads to positive developments.

19. According to lines 35–39, problems that affect women

    A) harm half of the world's women.

    B) are worldwide and long-standing.

    C) could be eliminated in half a century.

    D) are isolated to a few less developed countries.

20. The fifth paragraph (lines 13–20) can be described as

    A) a distillation of the author's main argument.

    B) an acknowledgment of a counterargument.

    C) a veiled criticism of a group.

    D) a defense against an accusation.

Questions 21-31 are based on the following passages and supplementary material.

The following passages discuss the history and traditions associated with tea.

Passage 1

Europe was a coffee-drinking continent before it became a tea-drinking one. Tea was grown in China, thousands of miles away. The opening of trade routes with the Far East in the fifteenth and sixteenth
5 centuries gave Europeans their first taste of tea.

However, it was an unpromising start for the beverage, because shipments arrived stale, and European tea drinkers miscalculated the steeping time and measurements. This was a far cry from
10 the Chinese preparation techniques, known as a "tea ceremony," which had strict steps and called for steeping in iron pots at precise temperatures and pouring into porcelain bowls.

GO ON TO THE NEXT PAGE

China had a monopoly on the tea trade and
15 kept their tea cultivation techniques secret. Yet
as worldwide demand grew, tea caught on in
Europe. Some proprietors touted tea as a cure for
maladies. Several European tea companies formed,
including the English East India Company. In
20 1669, it imported 143.5 pounds of tea—very little
compared to the 32 million pounds that were
imported by 1834.

Europeans looked for ways to circumvent
China's monopoly, but their attempts to grow the
25 tea plant (Latin name *Camellia sinensis*) failed.
Some plants perished in transit from the East. But
most often the growing climate wasn't right, not
even in the equatorial colonies that the British,
Dutch, and French controlled. In 1763, the French
30 Academy of Sciences gave up, declaring the tea
plant unique to China and unable to be grown
anywhere else. Swedish and English botanists grew
tea in botanical gardens, but this was not enough to
meet demand.

35 After trial and error with a plant variety
discovered in the Assam district of India, the
British managed to establish a source to meet the
growing demands of British tea drinkers. In May
1838, the first batch of India-grown tea shipped
40 to London. The harvest was a mere 350 pounds
and arrived in November. It sold for between
16 and 34 shillings per pound. Perfecting production
methods took many years, but ultimately, India
became the world's largest tea-producing country.
45 By the early 1900s, annual production of India tea
exceeded 350 million pounds. This voluminous
source was a major factor in tea becoming the
staple of European households that it is today.

Passage 2

In Europe, there's a long tradition of taking
50 afternoon tea. Tea time, typically four o'clock,
means not just enjoying a beverage, but taking time
out to gather and socialize. The occasion is not
identical across Europe, though; just about every
culture has its own way of doing things.

55 In France, for example, black tea is served
with sugar, milk, or lemon and is almost always
accompanied by a pastry. Rather than sweet
pastries, the French prefer the savory kind, such as
the *gougère*, or puff pastry, infused with cheese.

60 Germans, by contrast, put a layer of slowly melting
candy at the bottom of their teacup and top the tea
with cream. German tea culture is strongest in the
eastern part of the country, and during the week tea
is served with cookies, while on the weekend
65 or for special events, cakes are served. The Germans
think of tea as a good cure for headaches and stress.

Russia also has a unique tea culture, rooted in
the formalism of its aristocratic classes. Loose leaf
black tea is served in a glass held by a *podstakannik*,
70 an ornate holder with a handle typically made from
silver or chrome—though sometimes it may be
goldplated. Brewed separately, the tea is then diluted
with boiled water and served strong. The strength of
the tea is seen as a measure of the host's hospitality.
75 Traditionally, tea is taken by the entire family and
served after a large meal with jams and pastries.

Great Britain has a rich tradition of its own.
Prior to the introduction of tea into Britain, the
English had two main meals, breakfast and a
80 second, dinner-like meal called "tea," which was
held around noon. However, during the middle
of the eighteenth century, dinner shifted to an
evening meal at a late hour; it was then called "high
tea." That meant the necessary introduction of an
85 afternoon snack to tide one over, and "low tea" or
"tea time" was introduced by British royalty. In
present-day Britain, your afternoon tea might be
served with scones and jam, small sandwiches, or
cookies (called "biscuits"), depending on whether
90 you're in Ireland, England, or Scotland.

Wherever they are and however they take it,
Europeans know the value of savoring an afternoon
cup of tea.

**Average Annual Tea Consumption
(Pounds per Person)**

Turkey	6.961
Ireland	4.831
United Kingdom	4.281
Russia	3.051
New Zealand	2.629
Japan	2.133
Netherlands	1.714
Germany	1.524
China	1.248
Switzerland	0.971
India	0.715
Finland	0.539

Data from Euromonitor International and World Bank.

21. Based on the information provided in Passage 1, it can be inferred that

   A) European nations tried to grow tea in their colonies.

   B) European tea growers never learned Chinese cultivation techniques.

   C) Europeans' purpose in opening trade routes with the Far East was to gain access to tea.

   D) Europeans believed tea was ineffective as a treatment against illness.

22. Which choice provides the best evidence for the answer to the previous question?

   A) Lines 6–9 ("However…measurements")

   B) Lines 17–18 ("Some…maladies")

   C) Lines 26–29 ("But…French controlled")

   D) Lines 40–42 ("The harvest…per pound")

23. Based on the information in Passage 1, what would have been the most likely result if the British had not been able to grow tea in India?

   A) Tea would have decreased in price across Europe.

   B) The British would have learned to grow tea in Europe.

   C) Europeans would have saved their tea for special occasions.

   D) China would have produced more tea for the European market.

24. As used in line 23, "circumvent" most nearly means

   A) destroy.

   B) get around.

   C) ignore.

   D) compete with.

25. It can be inferred from both Passage 1 and the graphic that

   A) English botanical gardens helped make the United Kingdom one of the highest tea-consuming countries in the world.

   B) if the French Academy of Sciences hadn't given up growing tea in 1763, France would be one of the highest tea-consuming countries in the world.

   C) Britain's success at growing tea in India in the 1800s helped make the United Kingdom one of the highest tea-consuming nations in the world.

   D) China's production of tea would be higher if Britain hadn't discovered a way to grow tea in India in the 1800s.

26. It is reasonable to infer, based on Passage 2, that

   A) serving tea is an important part of hosting guests in Russia.

   B) Germans generally avoid medicine for stress.

   C) drinking tea in modern Britain is confined to the upper classes.

   D) the usual hour for drinking tea varies across Europe.

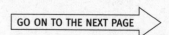
GO ON TO THE NEXT PAGE

27. Which choice provides the best evidence for the answer to the previous question?

    A) Lines 50–52 ("Tea time…socialize")

    B) Lines 65–66 ("The Germans…stress")

    C) Lines 73–74 ("The strength…hospitality")

    D) Lines 84–86 ("That meant…royalty")

28. As used in line 68, "aristocratic" most nearly means

    A) culinary.

    B) political.

    C) rigid.

    D) noble.

29. Compared with France's tradition of tea-drinking, having tea in Germany

    A) is more formal.

    B) involves sweeter food.

    C) requires greater solitude.

    D) is more of a meal than a snack.

30. Which statement is the most effective comparison of the two passages' purposes?

    A) Passage 1's purpose is to describe the early history of tea in Europe, while Passage 2's purpose is to compare European cultural practices relating to tea.

    B) Passage 1's purpose is to argue against the Chinese monopoly of tea, while Passage 2's purpose is to argue that Europeans perfected the art of tea drinking.

    C) Passage 1's purpose is to express admiration for the difficult task of tea cultivation, while Passage 2's purpose is to celebrate the rituals surrounding tea.

    D) Passage 1's purpose is to compare Chinese and European relationships with tea, while Passage 2's purpose is to describe the diffusion of tea culture in Europe.

31. Both passages support which generalization about tea?

    A) Tea drinking in Europe is less ritualized than in China.

    B) Coffee was once more popular in Europe than tea was.

    C) India grows a great deal of tea.

    D) Tea is a staple of European households.

Questions 32-42 are based on the following passage.

The following passage is adapted from an article about the *Spinosaurus*, a theropod dinosaur that lived during the Cretaceous period.

At long last, paleontologists have solved a century-old mystery, piecing together information discovered by scientists from different times and places.

The mystery began when, in 1911, German
5 paleontologist Ernst Stromer discovered the first evidence of dinosaurs having lived in Egypt. Stromer, who expected to encounter fossils of early mammals, instead found bones that dated back to the Cretaceous period, some 97
10 to 112 million years prior. His finding consisted of three large bones, which he preserved and transported back to Germany for examination. After careful consideration, he announced that he had discovered a new genus of sauropod, or a
15 large, four-legged herbivore with a long neck. He called the genus *Aegyptosaurus*, which is Greek for Egyptian lizard. One of these Aegyptosaurs, he claimed, was the *Spinosaurus*. Tragically, the fossils that supported his claim were destroyed during
20 a raid on Munich by the Royal Air Force during World War II. The scientific world was left with Stromer's notes and sketches, but no hard evidence that the *Spinosaurus* ever existed.

It was not until 2008, when a cardboard box
25 of bones was delivered to paleontologist Nizar Ibrahim by a nomad in Morocco's Sahara desert, that a clue to solving the mystery was revealed. Intrigued, Ibrahim took the bones to a university in Casablanca for further study. One specific bone
30 struck him as interesting, as it contained a red line coursing through it. The following year, Ibrahim and his colleagues at Italy's Milan Natural History

Museum were looking at bones that resembled the ones delivered the year before. An important
35 clue was hidden in the cross-section they were examining, as it contained the same red line Ibrahim had seen in Morocco. Against all odds, the Italians were studying bones that belonged to the very same skeleton as the bones Ibrahim received
40 in the desert. Together, these bones make up the partial skeleton of the very first *Spinosaurus* that humans have been able to discover since Stromer's fossils were destroyed.

Ibrahim and his colleagues published a study
45 describing the features of the dinosaur, which point to the *Spinosaurus* being the first known swimming dinosaur. At 36 feet long, this particular *Spinosaurus* had long front legs and short back legs, each with a paddle-shaped foot and claws that
50 suggest a carnivorous diet. These features made the dinosaur a deft swimmer and excellent hunter, able to prey on large river fish.

Scientists also discovered significant aquatic adaptations that made the *Spinosaurus* unique
55 compared to dinosaurs that lived on land but ate fish. Similar to a crocodile, the *Spinosaurus* had a long snout, with nostrils positioned so that the dinosaur could breathe while part of its head was submerged in water. Unlike predatory
60 land dinosaurs, the *Spinosaurus* had powerful front legs. The weight of these legs would have made walking upright like a *Tyrannosaurus rex* impossible, but in water, their strong legs gave the *Spinosaurus* the power it needed to swim quickly
65 and hunt fiercely. Most notable, though, was the discovery of the *Spinosaurus*'s massive sail. Made up of dorsal spines, the sail was mostly meant for display.

Ibrahim and his fellow researchers used both
70 modern digital modeling programs and Stromer's basic sketches to create and mount a life-size replica of the *Spinosaurus* skeleton. The sketches gave them a starting point, and by arranging and rearranging the excavated fossils they had in their
75 possession, they were able to use technology to piece together hypothetical bone structures until the mystery of this semiaquatic dinosaur finally emerged from the murky depths of the past.

32. Which of the following best summarizes the central idea of this passage?

A) Paleontologists were able to identify a new species of dinosaur after overcoming a series of obstacles.

B) Most dinosaur fossils are found in pieces and must be reconstructed using the latest technology.

C) The first evidence of the *Spinosaurus* was uncovered by German paleontologist Ernst Stromer.

D) Fossils of an aquatic dinosaur called the *Spinosaurus* were first found in Egypt in the early twentieth century.

33. According to the passage, the fossils Stromer found in the Egyptian desert were

A) younger and smaller than he expected.

B) younger and larger than he expected.

C) older and smaller than he expected.

D) older and larger than he expected.

34. Based on the information in the passage, the author would most likely agree that

A) aquatic dinosaurs were more vicious than dinosaurs that lived on land.

B) too much emphasis is placed on creating realistic models of ancient dinosaurs.

C) most mysteries presented by randomly found fossils are unlikely to be solved.

D) the study of fossils and ancient life provides important scientific insights.

35. Which choice provides the best evidence for the answer to the previous question?

A) Lines 13–15 ("After careful…long neck")

B) Lines 53–56 ("Scientists also…fish")

C) Lines 59–61 ("Unlike…front legs")

D) Lines 72–78 ("The sketches…past")

GO ON TO THE NEXT PAGE ⟹

36. As used in line 37, the phrase "against all odds" most nearly means

   A) by contrast.

   B) at the exact same time.

   C) to their dismay.

   D) despite low probability.

37. The author uses the phrases "deft swimmer" and "excellent hunter" in line 51 to

   A) produce a clear visual image of the *Spinosaurus*.

   B) show how the *Spinosaurus* searched for prey.

   C) create an impression of a graceful but powerful animal.

   D) emphasize the differences between aquatic and land dinosaurs.

38. The information presented in the passage strongly suggests that Ibrahim

   A) chose to go into the field of paleontology after reading Stromer's work.

   B) was familiar with Stromer's work when he found the fossils with the red lines.

   C) did not have the proper training to solve the mystery of the *Spinosaurus* on his own.

   D) went on to study other aquatic dinosaurs after completing his research on the *Spinosaurus*.

39. Which choice provides the best evidence for the answer to the previous question?

   A) Lines 24–27 ("It was…revealed")

   B) Lines 44–47 ("Ibrahim…swimming dinosaur")

   C) Lines 53–56 ("Scientists also…fish")

   D) Lines 69–72 ("Ibrahim and…skeleton")

40. As used in line 76, "hypothetical" most nearly means

   A) imaginary.

   B) actual.

   C) possible.

   D) interesting.

41. Which statement best describes the relationship between Stromer's and Ibrahim's work with fossils?

   A) Stromer's work was dependent on Ibrahim's work.

   B) Stromer's work was contradicted by Ibrahim's work.

   C) Ibrahim's work built on Stromer's work.

   D) Ibrahim's work copied Stromer's work.

42. Which of the following is most similar to the methods used by Ibrahim to create a life-size replica of the *Spinosaurus*?

   A) An architect using computer software and drawings to create a scale model of a building

   B) A student building a model rocket from a kit in order to demonstrate propulsion

   C) A doctor using a microscope to study micro-organisms unable to be seen with the naked eye

   D) A marine biologist creating an artificial reef in an aquarium to study fish

Questions 43-52 are based on the following passage and supplementary material.

The following passage is adapted from an essay about intricacies and implications of laughter.

Today's technology and resources enable people to educate themselves on any topic imaginable, and human health is one of particular interest to all. From diet fads to exercise trends, sleep studies
5 to nutrition supplements, people strive to adopt healthier lifestyles. And while some people may associate diets and gym memberships with sheer enjoyment, most of the population tends to think of personal healthcare as a necessary but time-consuming,
10 energy-draining, less-than-fun aspect of daily life.

Yet for centuries, or perhaps for as long as conscious life has existed, sneaking suspicion has suggested that fun, or more accurately, *funniness*, is essential to human health. Finally, in recent years
15 this notion, often phrased in the adage, "Laughter is the best medicine," has materialized into scientific evidence.

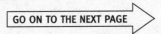

GO ON TO THE NEXT PAGE

K 533

When a person laughs, a chemical reaction in the brain produces hormones called endorphins.
20 Other known endorphin-producing activities include exercise, physical pain, and certain food choices, but laughter's appearance on this list has drawn increasing empirical interest. Endorphins function as natural opiates for the human body,
25 causing what are more commonly referred to as "good feelings." A boost of endorphins can thwart lethargy and promote the mental energy and positivity necessary to accomplish challenging tasks. Furthermore, recent data reveal that the
30 laughter-induced endorphins are therapeutic and stress reducing.

This stress reduction alone indicates significant implications regarding the role of laughter in personal health. However, humor seems to address
35 many other medical conditions as well. One study from Loma Linda University in California found that the act of laughing induced immediate and significant effects on senior adults' memory capacities. This result was in addition to declines
40 in the patients' cortisol, or stress hormone, measurements. Another university study found that a mere quarter hour of laughter burns up to 40 calories. Pain tolerance, one group of Oxford researchers noticed, is also strengthened
45 by laughter—probably due to the release of those same endorphins already described. And a group of Maryland scientists discovered that those who laugh more frequently seem to have stronger protection against heart disease, the illness that
50 takes more lives annually than any other in America. Studies have shown that stress releases hormones that cause blood vessels to constrict, but laughter, on the other hand, releases chemicals that cause blood vessels to dilate, or expand. This dilation
55 can have the same positive effects on blood flow as aerobic exercise or drugs that help lower cholesterol.

Already from these reputable studies, empirical data indicates that laughter's health benefits include heart disease prevention, good physical exertion,
60 memory retention, anxiety reduction, and pain resilience—not to mention laughter's more self-evident effects on social and psychological wellness. Many believe that these findings are only

the beginning; these studies pave the way for more
65 research with even stronger evidence regarding the powerful healing and preventative properties of laughter. As is true for most fields of science, far more can be learned.

As for how laughter is achieved, these studies
70 used various methods to provoke or measure laughter or humor. Some used comedy films or television clips; others chose humor-gauging questionnaires and social—or group—laughter scenarios. Such variance suggests that the means
75 by which people incorporate laughter into their daily routine matters less than the fact that they do incorporate it. However, it should be said that humor shared in an uplifting community probably offers greater benefits than that found on a screen.

80 It is believed that young people begin to laugh less and less as they transition to adulthood. Time-pressed millennials might, in the interest of wellness, choose isolated exercise instead of social- or fun-oriented leisure activities. However,
85 this growing pool of evidence exposes the reality that amusement, too, can powerfully nourish the health of both mind and body. Humor is no less relevant to well-being than a kale smoothie or track workout. But, then, some combination of
90 the three might be most enjoyable (and, of course, beneficial) of all.

Laughter and Its Effect on Pain

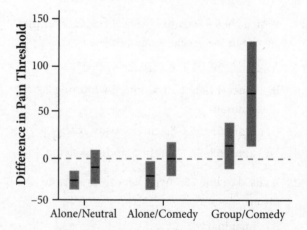

Adapted from I.M. Dunbar, et al., "Social Laughter Is Correlated with an Elevated Pain Threshold." © 2011 by The Royal Society of Biological Sciences.

GO ON TO THE NEXT PAGE

43. The author would most likely characterize the study findings mentioned in the passage as

    A) irrelevant.

    B) very promising.

    C) inconclusive.

    D) mildly interesting.

44. Which choice provides the best evidence for the answer to the previous question?

    A) Lines 4–6 ("From diet...lifestyles")

    B) Lines 14–17 ("Finally,...evidence")

    C) Lines 18–19 ("When a person... endorphins")

    D) Lines 74–77 ("Such variance...incorporate it")

45. Which statement best explains the relationship between endorphin production and mental outlook?

    A) Increasing a person's amount of endorphins encourages a positive state of mind.

    B) The act of laughing produces endorphins, which can offer a person protection against heart disease.

    C) Research indicates that chemical reactions in the brain produce endorphins.

    D) If a person has more endorphins, he or she has a difficult time tolerating pain.

46. As used in line 57, "reputable" most nearly means

    A) honorable.

    B) distinguished.

    C) celebrated.

    D) credible.

47. Which of the following statements can be concluded from the passage?

    A) Laughing alone or in the company of others benefits people's health equally.

    B) There is reason for optimism about future research into laughter's health benefits.

    C) Public support for the idea that laughter is healthy is somewhat limited.

    D) Physical exercise is sufficient to maintain and improve mental health.

48. Which choice provides the best evidence for the answer to the previous question?

    A) Lines 11–14 ("Yet for centuries,...health")

    B) Lines 32–35 ("This stress...well")

    C) Lines 63–67 ("Many believe...of laughter")

    D) Lines 87–91 ("Humor is...of all")

49. Which reason best explains why the author chose to discuss the function of endorphins in lines 23–26 ("Endorphins...good feelings")?

    A) To reach a wider audience without a background in physiology

    B) To support the claim that laughter affects an individual's mental state

    C) To show that laughter is one of several endorphin-producing activities

    D) To demonstrate why scientists have an interest in studying laughter

50. As used in line 15, "adage" most nearly means

    A) remark.

    B) comment.

    C) cliché.

    D) proverb.

51. Which value shown on the graph most closely relates to the idea in line 78 that "humor shared in an uplifting community" increases resilience to pain?

    A) −25

    B) 0

    C) 20

    D) 75

52. The information in the passage strongly suggests that

    A) older adults prefer to laugh in a community setting rather than watch funny movies.

    B) adults who laugh less as they age are at greater risk for heart disease.

    C) millennials are in danger of developing heart disease from too much exercise.

    D) soon doctors will be using laughter to treat most diseases.

Writing and Language Test

35 Minutes—44 Questions

This section corresponds to Section 2 of your answer sheet.

Directions: Each passage in this section is followed by several questions. Some questions will reference an underlined portion in the passage; others will ask you to consider a part of a passage or the passage as a whole. For each question, choose the answer that reflects the best use of grammar, punctuation, and style. If a passage or question is accompanied by a graphic, take the graphic into account in choosing your response(s). Some questions will have "NO CHANGE" as a possible response. Choose that answer if you think the best choice is to leave the sentence as written.

Questions 1-11 are based on the following passage.

From Here to the Stars

Gene Kranz hadn't slept in ages. **1** The flight director, pacing between rows of monitors in NASA's Mission Control Center, an impossible problem weighing heavy in his weary mind: Three astronauts were operating a crippled spacecraft nearly 200,000 miles from Earth. And time was running out.

Kranz was no stranger to **2** issues. After losing his father at an early age, Kranz turned to the stars for guidance—and found inspiration. His high school thesis was about the possibility of **3** space travel; an idea that prompted Kranz to set a path for the stars. Kranz pursued a degree in aeronautical engineering after high school graduation. After the Wright brothers had pioneered powered, controlled flight only half a century earlier, aviation milestones like breaking the sound barrier changed the future of flight. Aeronautical engineering required a thorough understanding of **4** physics—like lift and drag on wings—as well as proficiency in mathematics to determine maximum weight on an aircraft. After graduating from Saint Louis University's Parks College of Engineering, Aviation,

1. A) NO CHANGE
   B) The flight director paced
   C) The pacing flight director
   D) The flight director pacing

2. A) NO CHANGE
   B) adversity.
   C) deadlines.
   D) maladies.

3. A) NO CHANGE
   B) space travel: an idea
   C) space travel, an idea
   D) space travel. An idea

4. A) NO CHANGE
   B) physics; like lift and drag on wings, as well as proficiency
   C) physics like lift and drag on wings, as well as proficiency
   D) physics: like lift and drag on wings—as well as proficiency

GO ON TO THE NEXT PAGE

and Technology, Kranz piloted jets for the Air Force Reserve before performing research and development on missiles and rockets. Kranz later joined NASA and directed the successful *Apollo 11* mission to the moon in 1969.

[5] Without his unusual vest, no one would have noticed Kranz in the crowd. One year after the launch, the mood had drastically changed; there were no cheers, no celebratory pats on the back or teary-eyed congratulations. Coffee and adrenaline fueled the scientists and engineers communicating with the astronauts on *Apollo 13*. [6] Kranz was easy to spot among the avalanche of moving bodies and shifting papers. He was dressed, as ever, in his signature handmade vest. [7] The engineers looked to the calm man in the homemade vest.

Kranz's wife, Marta, had begun making vests at his request in the early '60s. [8] Their was power in a uniform, something Kranz understood from his years serving overseas. The vests served not as an authoritative mark or [9] sartorial flair, but a defining symbol for his team to rally behind. During the effort to save the *Apollo 13* crew, Kranz wore his white vest around the clock like perspiration-mottled battle armor.

5. Which sentence would serve as the most effective introduction to the paragraph?

A) NO CHANGE

B) During the mission, Kranz stood out as a pillar of strength in the chaos of the command center.

C) Kranz earned the badges of honor that now adorned his vest.

D) Kranz possessed more years of experience than anyone in the control center.

6. A) NO CHANGE

B) Among the avalanche of moving bodies and shifting papers, it is easy to spot Kranz.

C) Kranz easily spotted the avalanche of moving bodies and shifting papers.

D) Kranz is easy to spot among the avalanche of moving bodies and shifting papers.

7. Which sentence provides effective evidence to support the main focus of the paragraph?

A) NO CHANGE

B) Many of the men in the Mission Control Center had lengthy military careers.

C) Kranz's thoughts returned to the many tribulations he had experienced.

D) Several engineers joined together as a bastion of calm in a sea of uncertainty.

8. A) NO CHANGE

B) They're was

C) There was

D) They were

9. A) NO CHANGE

B) sanguine

C) military

D) martial

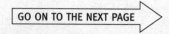

10 <u>Among</u> meetings and calculations, Kranz and the NASA staff hatched a wild plan. By using the gravitational force of the moon, **11** <u>it</u> could slingshot the injured spacecraft back on an earthbound course. It was a long shot, of course, but also their best and only one. And, due to the tireless efforts of support staff on earth and the intrepid spirit of the *Apollo 13* crew, it worked. Six days after takeoff, all three astronauts splashed down safely in the Pacific Ocean.

Questions 12-22 are based on the following passage.

The UK and the Euro

[1] The United Kingdom is a long-standing member of the European Union (EU), a multinational political organization and economic world leader **12** <u>elected</u> over the course of the past half-century. [2] However, there is one key feature of the EU in which the UK does not **13** <u>participate; the monetary</u> union known as the Eurozone, consisting of countries that share the euro as currency. [3] While the nation's public opinion has remained generally supportive of that decision, evidence suggests that the euro's benefits for the UK might, in fact, outweigh the risks. [4] When the EU first implemented the euro in 1999, intending to strengthen the collective economy across the union, Britain was permitted exclusion and continued using the pound instead. [5] This, UK leaders hoped, would shield Britain from financial dangers that the euro might suffer. **14**

10. A) NO CHANGE
    B) In spite of
    C) Despite
    D) Between

11. A) NO CHANGE
    B) he
    C) they
    D) one

12. A) NO CHANGE
    B) determined
    C) advanced
    D) built

13. A) NO CHANGE
    B) participate: the monetary
    C) participate, the monetary
    D) participate. The monetary

14. To make this paragraph most logical, sentence 3 should be placed
    A) where it is now.
    B) after sentence 1.
    C) after sentence 4.
    D) after sentence 5.

Proponents for avoiding the euro point 15 to faltering economies in the Eurozone region throughout the Eurozone. To join a massive, multinational economy would involve surrendering taxable wealth from one's own region to aid impoverished countries that may be some thousands of miles away. If a few economies in the Eurozone suffer, all of the participating nations suffer, too. Other proponents point to details of financial policy such as interest rates and territory responsibilities, fearing loss of agency and political traction. 16 The UK's taxable wealth would decrease if it assisted impoverished countries.

But complications loom: the UK's current EU status may be untenable. In recent years, EU leaders seem to want to transition all members 17 toward the Eurozone, for many reasons, this action appears necessary for protecting nations involved and ensuring the monetary union's long-term success. These conditions may potentially force the UK to choose either the security of its multidecade EU membership, or the pound and all it entails for Britain's economy. Enjoying both may not remain possible. 18 The UK wants to maintain the pound as its currency.

[1] Regarding Britain's intent to be protected from the Eurozone's economic dangers, this hope never quite materialized. [2] The UK saw economic downturns of its own during the euro's problematic years thus far. [3] Many families in the UK still struggle to pay their bills in the face of higher than normal unemployment rates. [4] It seems that regardless of shared currency, the economies of Britain and its Eurozone neighbors are too closely 19 intertwined

15. Which choice best completes the sentence?

A) NO CHANGE

B) to financial dangers that the euro might suffer.

C) to faltering economies in most if not all Eurozone countries.

D) to financial dangers and faltering economies in Eurozone countries throughout Europe.

16. Which statement most clearly communicates the main claim of the paragraph?

A) NO CHANGE

B) Economic independence from impoverished countries would still be possible.

C) The UK would take on significant economic risk if it adopted the euro as its currency.

D) Euro adoption would require subsequent economic assistance on the UK's behalf.

17. A) NO CHANGE

B) toward the Eurozone. For many reasons,

C) toward the Eurozone, for many reasons.

D) toward the Eurozone. For many reasons.

18. Which sentence most effectively concludes the paragraph?

A) NO CHANGE

B) All EU members may soon have to accept the euro.

C) The UK faces a difficult decision regarding its EU membership.

D) All member nations want to ensure the success of the EU.

19. A) NO CHANGE

B) disparate

C) identical

D) relevant

GO ON TO THE NEXT PAGE ⟹

for one to remain unscathed by another's crises. `20`

Perhaps this question of economic security has been the wrong one. Due to Britain's location and long-standing trade relationships with its neighbors, economies will continue to be somewhat reliant on each other, euro or not. `21` Furthermore, political security, power, and protection bear more significance for the future. If the UK hopes to maintain and expand its influential presence in world leadership, its association and close involvement with greater Europe is invaluable. Considering that the euro probably offers a lower risk margin than many have supposed, the benefits of euro `22` adoption: to secure EU membership and strengthen its cause, made Britain carefully reconsider.

Questions 23-33 are based on the following passage.

Coffee: The Buzz on Beans

Americans love coffee. `23` Some days you can find a coffee shop in nearly every American city. But this wasn't always true. How did coffee, which was first grown in Africa over five hundred years ago, come to America?

The coffee plant, from which makers get the "cherries" that `24` is dried and roasted into what we call beans, first appeared in the East African country Ethiopia, in the province of Kaffa. From there, it spread to the Arabian Peninsula, where the coffeehouse, or *qahveh khaneh* in Arabic, was very popular. Like spices and cloth, coffee was traded internationally as European explorers reached far lands and `25` establishing shipping routes. The first European coffeehouse opened in Venice, Italy, in 1683, and

20. Which sentence is least relevant to the central idea of this paragraph?

   A) Sentence 1
   B) Sentence 2
   C) Sentence 3
   D) Sentence 4

21. A) NO CHANGE
    B) Or,
    C) Also,
    D) However,

22. A) NO CHANGE
    B) adoption—to secure EU membership and strengthen its cause—
    C) adoption: to secure EU membership and strengthen its cause—
    D) adoption; to secure EU membership and strengthen its cause,

23. A) NO CHANGE
    B) Many
    C) The
    D) These

24. A) NO CHANGE
    B) are being dried and roasted
    C) are dried and roasted
    D) is being dried and roasted

25. A) NO CHANGE
    B) established
    C) having established
    D) was establishing

not long after London 26 displayed over three hundred coffeehouses.

There is no record of coffee being among the cargo of the *Mayflower*, which reached the New World in 1620. It was not until 1668 that the first written reference to coffee in America was made. The reference described a beverage made from roasted beans and flavored with sugar or honey and cinnamon. Coffee was then chronicled in the New England colony's official records of 1670. In 1683, William Penn, who lived in a settlement on the Delaware River, wrote of buying supplies of coffee in a 27 New York market, he paid eighteen shillings and nine pence per pound. 28

Coffeehouses like those in Europe were soon established in American colonies, and as America expanded westward, coffee consumption grew. In their settlement days, 29 Chicago St. Louis and New Orleans each had famous coffeehouses. By the mid-twentieth century, coffeehouses were abundant. In places like New York and San Francisco, they became 30 confused with counterculture, as a place where intellectuals and artists gathered to share ideas. In American homes, coffee was a social lubricant, bringing people together to socialize as afternoon tea had done in English society. With the invention of the electric coffee pot, it became a common courtesy to ask a guest if she wanted "coffee or tea?"

26. A) NO CHANGE
    B) bragged
    C) highlighted
    D) boasted

27. A) NO CHANGE
    B) New York market and William Penn
    C) New York market so he paid
    D) New York market, paying

28. Which choice best establishes a concluding sentence for the paragraph?

    A) Coffee's appearance in the historical record shows it was becoming more and more established in the New World.
    B) The colonies probably used more tea than coffee because there are records of it being imported from England.
    C) William Penn founded Pennsylvania Colony, which became the state of Pennsylvania after the Revolutionary War with England ended.
    D) The *Mayflower* did carry a number of items that the colonists needed for settlement, including animals and tools.

29. A) NO CHANGE
    B) Chicago, St. Louis, and New Orleans
    C) Chicago, St. Louis, and, New Orleans
    D) Chicago St. Louis and, New Orleans

30. A) NO CHANGE
    B) related
    C) associated
    D) coupled

31 "There were many coffee shops n New York and in Chicago."

However, by the 1950s, U.S. manufacturing did to coffee what it had done to **32** other foods; produced it cheaply, mass-marketed it, and lowered its quality. Coffee was roasted and ground in manufacturing plants and freeze-dried for a long storage life, which compromised its flavor. An "evangelism" began to bring back the original bracing, dark-roasted taste of coffee and spread quickly. **33** In every major city of the world, now travelers around the world, expect to be able to grab an uplifting, fresh, and delicious cup of coffee—and they can.

31. Which choice most effectively concludes the paragraph?
   A) NO CHANGE
   B) Electric coffee machines changed how people entertained at home.
   C) Over time, it was clear that coffee had become a part of everyday American life.
   D) People went to coffeehouses to discuss major issues.

32. A) NO CHANGE
   B) other foods produced
   C) other foods, produced
   D) other foods: produced

33. A) NO CHANGE
   B) Now travelers, in every major city of the world, around the world expect to be able to grab an uplifting, fresh, and delicious cup of coffee—and they can.
   C) Now in every major city of the world, travelers around the world expect to be able to grab an uplifting, fresh, and delicious cup of coffee—and they can.
   D) Now travelers around the world expect to be able to grab an uplifting, fresh, and delicious cup of coffee in every major city of the world—and they can.

Questions 34-44 are based on the following passage and supplementary material.

Predicting Nature's Light Show

One of the most beautiful of nature's displays is the aurora borealis, commonly known as the Northern Lights. As **34** their informal name suggests, the best place to view this phenomenon **35** is the Northern Hemisphere. How far north one needs to be to witness auroras depends not on conditions here on Earth, but on the Sun. **36**

As with hurricane season on Earth, the Sun **37** observes a cycle of storm activity, called the solar cycle, which lasts approximately 11 years. Also referred to as the sunspot cycle, this period is caused by the amount of magnetic flux that rises to the surface of the Sun, causing sunspots, or areas of intense magnetic activity. The magnetic energy is sometimes so great it causes a storm that explodes away from the Sun's surface in a solar flare.

These powerful magnetic storms eject high-speed electrons and protons into space. Called a coronal mass ejection, this ejection is far more powerful than the hot gases the Sun constantly emits. The speed at which the atoms are shot away from the Sun is almost triple that of a normal solar wind. It takes this shot of energy one to three days to arrive at Earth's upper atmosphere. Once it arrives, it is captured by Earth's own magnetic field. It is this newly captured energy that causes the Northern Lights. **38** Scientists and interested amateurs in the

34. A) NO CHANGE
   B) an
   C) its
   D) that

35. A) NO CHANGE
   B) is through the Northern Hemisphere.
   C) is over the Northern Hemisphere.
   D) is in the Northern Hemisphere.

36. Which of the following would most strengthen the passage's introduction?
   A) A statement about the Kp-Index and other necessary tracking tools scientists use
   B) A mention that the National Oceanic and Atmospheric Administration monitors solar flares
   C) An explanation about why conditions on the Sun rather than on Earth affect the Northern Lights
   D) A statement about what scientists think people should study before viewing auroras

37. A) NO CHANGE
   B) experiences
   C) perceives
   D) witnesses

38. A) NO CHANGE
   B) Interested scientists and amateurs
   C) Scientists and amateurs interested
   D) Scientists interested and amateurs

GO ON TO THE NEXT PAGE ⟶

Northern Hemisphere [39] use tools readily available to all in order to predict the likelihood of seeing auroras in their location at a specific time. One such tool is the Kp-Index, a number that determines the potential visibility of an aurora. The Kp-Index measures the energy added to Earth's magnetic field from the Sun on a scale of 0-9, with 1 representing a solar calm and 5 or more indicating a magnetic storm, or solar flare. The magnetic fluctuations are measured in three-hour intervals (12 a.m. to 3 a.m., 3 a.m. to 6 a.m., and so on) so that deviations can be factored in and accurate data can be presented. [40]

Magnetometers, tools that measure the strength of Earth's magnetic field, are located around the world. When the energy from solar flares reaches Earth, the strength and direction of the energy [41] is recorded by these tools and analyzed by scientists at the National Oceanic and Atmospheric Administration, who calculate the difference between the average strength of the magnetic field and spikes due to solar flares. They plot this information on the Kp-Index and [42] update the public with information on viewing the auroras as well as other impacts solar flares may have on life on Earth. [43] While solar flares can sometimes have negative effects

39. A) NO CHANGE
    B) use tools for prediction
    C) use specific tools to predict
    D) use all tools readily available to predict

40. Which of the following, if added to this paragraph, would best support the author's claims?
    A) The speeds of normal solar winds and coronal mass ejections
    B) The strength of Earth's magnetic field
    C) The temperature of normal solar wind
    D) The definition of coronal mass ejection

41. A) NO CHANGE
    B) are
    C) will be
    D) has been

42. A) NO CHANGE
    B) update aurora viewing information
    C) update information on viewing the auroras
    D) update aurora viewing information for the public

43. A) NO CHANGE
    B) However,
    C) Since
    D) Whereas

GO ON TO THE NEXT PAGE

on our communications systems and weather patterns, the most common effect is also the most enchanting: a beautiful light show, such as the solar flare that took place from  3 p.m. to 6 p.m. on September 11.

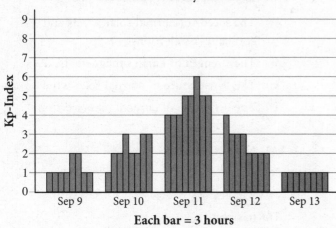

Potential Visibility of an Aurora

Each bar = 3 hours

Data from National Oceanic and Atmospheric Administration.

44. Which choice competes the sentence with accurate data based on the graphic?

A) NO CHANGE

B) 12 a.m. on September 11 to 3 a.m. on September 12.

C) 9 a.m. on September 10 to 12 p.m. on September 12.

D) 9 a.m. on September 11 to 12 a.m. on September 12.

IF YOU FINISH BEFORE TIME IS CALLED, YOU MAY CHECK YOUR WORK ON THIS SECTION ONLY.
DO NOT TURN TO ANY OTHER SECTION IN THE TEST.

STOP

546

Math Test

25 Minutes—20 Questions

NO-CALCULATOR SECTION

This section corresponds to Section 3 of your answer sheet.

Directions: For this section, solve each problem and decide which is the best of the choices given. Fill in the corresponding oval on the answer sheet. You may use any available space for scratch work.

Notes:

1. Calculator use is NOT permitted.
2. All numbers used are real numbers, and all variables used represent real numbers, unless otherwise indicated.
3. Figures are drawn to scale and lie in a plane unless otherwise indicated.
4. Unless stated otherwise, the domain of any function f is assumed to be the set of all real numbers x, for which $f(x)$ is a real number.

Information:

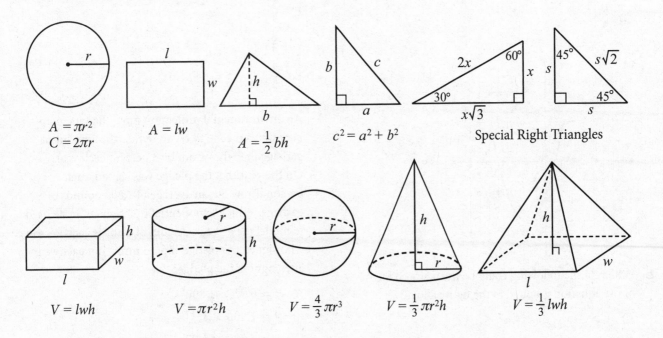

$A = \pi r^2$
$C = 2\pi r$

$A = lw$

$A = \frac{1}{2}bh$

$c^2 = a^2 + b^2$

Special Right Triangles

$V = lwh$

$V = \pi r^2 h$

$V = \frac{4}{3}\pi r^3$

$V = \frac{1}{3}\pi r^2 h$

$V = \frac{1}{3}lwh$

The sum of the degree measures of the angles in a triangle is 180.

The number of degrees of arc in a circle is 360.

The number of radians of arc in a circle is 2π.

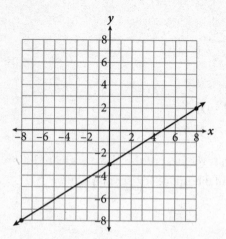

1. What is the average rate of change for the line graphed in the figure above?

   A) $\dfrac{3}{5}$

   B) $\dfrac{5}{8}$

   C) $\dfrac{8}{5}$

   D) $\dfrac{5}{3}$

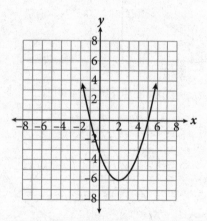

2. Which of the following could be the factored form of the equation graphed in the figure above?

   A) $y = \dfrac{1}{5}(x - 2)(x + 6)$

   B) $y = \dfrac{1}{5}(x + 2)(x - 6)$

   C) $y = \dfrac{2}{3}(x - 1)(x + 5)$

   D) $y = \dfrac{2}{3}(x + 1)(x - 5)$

3. Kinetic energy is the energy of motion. The equation $E_K = \dfrac{1}{2}mv^2$ represents the kinetic energy in joules of an object with a mass of m kilograms traveling at a speed of v meters per second. What is the kinetic energy in joules of an unmanned aircraft that has a mass of 2×10^3 kilograms traveling at a speed of approximately 3×10^3 meters per second?

   A) 9×5^9

   B) 9×10^8

   C) 9×10^9

   D) 1.8×10^{10}

4. $\dfrac{3(k-1)+5}{2} = \dfrac{17-(8+k)}{4}$

   In the equation above, what is the value of k?

   A) $\dfrac{9}{13}$

   B) $\dfrac{5}{7}$

   C) $\dfrac{8}{7}$

   D) $\dfrac{8}{5}$

5. An environmental protection group had its members sign a pledge to try to reduce the amount of garbage they throw out by 3 percent each year. On the year that the pledge was signed, each person threw out an average of 1,800 pounds of garbage. Which exponential function could be used to model the average amount of garbage each person who signed the pledge should throw out each year after signing the pledge?

   A) $y = 0.97 \times 1,800^t$

   B) $y = 1,800 \times t^{0.97}$

   C) $y = 1,800 \times 1.97^t$

   D) $y = 1,800 \times 0.97^t$

GO ON TO THE NEXT PAGE ▷

$$\frac{6x+2}{x+5} - \frac{3x-8}{x+5}$$

6. Which of the following is equivalent to the expression above?

A) $\dfrac{3x-6}{x+5}$

B) $\dfrac{3x+10}{x+5}$

C) $\dfrac{3x-6}{2x+10}$

D) $\dfrac{3x+10}{2x+10}$

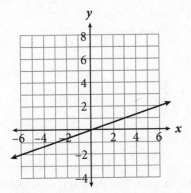

7. If the equation of the line shown in the figure above is written in the form $\dfrac{y}{x} = m$, which of the following could be the value of m?

A) -3

B) $-\dfrac{1}{3}$

C) $\dfrac{1}{3}$

D) 3

8. If $4x^2 + 7x + 1$ is multiplied by $3x + 5$, what is the coefficient of x in the resulting polynomial?

A) 3

B) 12

C) 35

D) 38

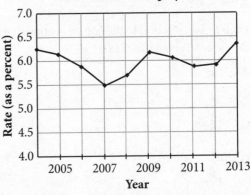

Worldwide Unemployment

9. The figure above shows worldwide unemployment rates from 2004 to 2013. Which of the following statements is true?

A) The graph is decreasing everywhere.

B) The graph is increasing from 2007 to 2010.

C) The graph is decreasing from 2004 to 2007 and from 2009 to 2011.

D) The graph is increasing from 2007 to 2010 and decreasing from 2011 to 2013.

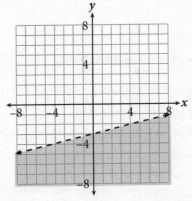

10. The solution to which inequality is represented in the graph above?

A) $\dfrac{1}{4}x - y > 3$

B) $\dfrac{1}{4}x - y < 3$

C) $\dfrac{1}{4}x + y > -3$

D) $\dfrac{1}{4}x + y < -3$

$\frac{1}{2}(4a + 10b) = b$

11. If (a, b) is a solution to the equation above, what is the ratio $\frac{b}{a}$, given that $a \neq 0$?

A) -3

B) -2

C) $-\frac{1}{2}$

D) $-\frac{1}{3}$

$\begin{cases} \frac{1}{3}x + \frac{2}{3}y = -8 \\ ax + 6y = 15 \end{cases}$

12. If the system of linear equations above has no solution, and a is a constant, what is the value of a ?

A) $-\frac{1}{3}$

B) $\frac{1}{3}$

C) $\frac{3}{2}$

D) 3

13. A taxi in the city charges \$3.00 for the first $\frac{1}{4}$ mile, plus \$0.25 for each additional $\frac{1}{8}$ mile. Eric plans to spend no more than \$20.00 on a taxi ride around the city. Which inequality represents the number of miles, m, that Eric could travel without exceeding his limit?

A) $2.5 + 2m \leq 20$

B) $3 + 0.25m \leq 20$

C) $3 + 2m \leq 20$

D) $12 + 2m \leq 20$

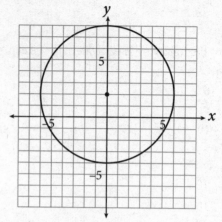

14. If the equation of the circle shown above is written in the form $x^2 + y^2 + ax + by = c$, what is the value of $ab + c$?

A) 6

B) 16

C) 28

D) 32

15. A projectile is any moving object that is thrown near the Earth's surface. The path of the projectile is called the trajectory and can be modeled by a quadratic equation, assuming the only force acting on the motion is gravity (no friction). If a projectile is launched from a platform 8 feet above the ground with an initial velocity of 64 feet per second, then its trajectory can be modeled by the equation $h = -16t^2 + 64t + 8$, where h represents the height of the projectile t seconds after it was launched. Based on this model, what is the maximum height in feet that the projectile will reach?

A) 72

B) 80

C) 92

D) 108

Directions: For questions 16-20, enter your responses into the appropriate grid on your answer sheet, in accordance with the following:

1. You will receive credit only if the circles are filled in correctly, but you may write your answers in the boxes above each grid to help you fill in the circles accurately.
2. Don't mark more than one circle per column.
3. None of the questions with grid-in responses will have a negative solution.
4. Only grid in a single answer, even if there is more than one correct answer to a given question.
5. A **mixed number** must be gridded as a decimal or an improper fraction. For example, you would grid $7\frac{1}{2}$ as 7.5 or 15/2.

   (Were you to grid it as [7 1 / 2 grid], this response would be read as $\frac{71}{2}$.)

6. A **decimal** that has more digits than there are places on the grid may be either rounded or truncated, but every column in the grid must be filled in order to receive credit.

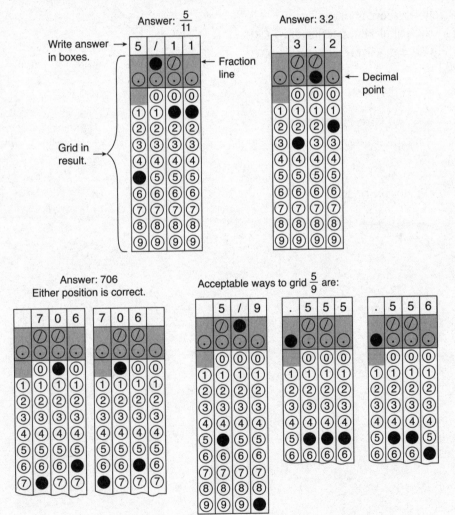

Answer: $\frac{5}{11}$

Write answer in boxes.

Fraction line

Grid in result.

Answer: 3.2

Decimal point

Answer: 706
Either position is correct.

Acceptable ways to grid $\frac{5}{9}$ are:

GO ON TO THE NEXT PAGE

16. If $\frac{3}{4}x + \frac{5}{6}y = 12$, what is the value of $9x + 10y$?

17. How many degrees does the minute hand of an analog clock rotate from 3:20 p.m. to 3:45 p.m.?

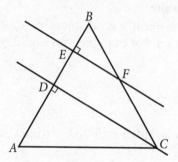

18. Triangle ABC shown above is an equilateral triangle cut by two parallel lines. If the ratio of BF to FC is 3:4 and $EB = 3$, what is the length of DE?

$$\frac{3x^{\frac{3}{2}} \cdot \left(16x^2\right)^3}{8x^{-\frac{1}{2}}}$$

19. What is the exponent on x when the expression above is written in simplest form?

20. An exponential function is given in the form $f(x) = a \cdot b^x$. If $f(0) = 3$ and $f(1) = 15$, what is the value of $f(-2)$?

IF YOU FINISH BEFORE TIME IS CALLED, YOU MAY CHECK YOUR WORK ON THIS SECTION ONLY.
DO NOT TURN TO ANY OTHER SECTION IN THE TEST.

STOP

552

Practice Tests

Math Test

55 Minutes—38 Questions

CALCULATOR SECTION

This section corresponds to Section 4 of your answer sheet.

Directions: For this section, solve each problem and decide which is the best of the choices given. Fill in the corresponding oval on the answer sheet. You may use any available space for scratch work.

Notes:

1. Calculator use is permitted.
2. All numbers used are real numbers, and all variables used represent real numbers, unless otherwise indicated.
3. Figures are drawn to scale and lie in a plane unless otherwise indicated.
4. Unless stated otherwise, the domain of any function f is assumed to be the set of all real numbers x, for which $f(x)$ is a real number.

Information:

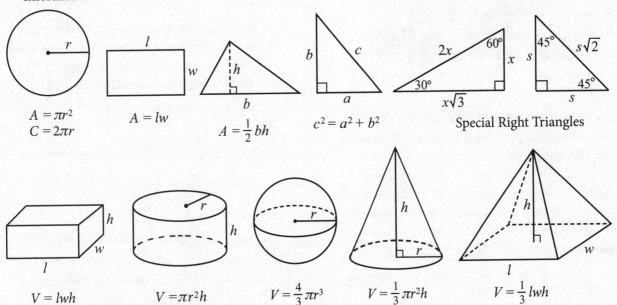

$A = \pi r^2$
$C = 2\pi r$

$A = lw$

$A = \frac{1}{2}bh$

$c^2 = a^2 + b^2$

Special Right Triangles

$V = lwh$

$V = \pi r^2 h$

$V = \frac{4}{3}\pi r^3$

$V = \frac{1}{3}\pi r^2 h$

$V = \frac{1}{3}lwh$

The sum of the degree measures of the angles in a triangle is 180.

The number of degrees of arc in a circle is 360.

The number of radians of arc in a circle is 2π.

1. A home improvement store that sells carpeting charges a flat installation fee and a certain amount per square foot of carpet ordered. If the total cost for f square feet of carpet is given by the function $C(f) = 3.29f + 199$, then the value 3.29 best represents which of the following?

   A) The installation fee

   B) The cost of one square foot of carpet

   C) The number of square feet of carpet ordered

   D) The total cost not including the installation fee

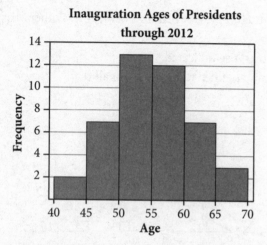

Inauguration Ages of Presidents through 2012

2. The United States Constitution requires that any candidate for the presidency be at least 35 years of age, although no president to date has been that young. The figure above shows the distribution of the ages of the presidents through 2012 at the time they were inaugurated. Based on the information shown, which of the following statements is true?

   A) The shape of the data is skewed to the left, so the mean age of the presidents is greater than the median.

   B) The shape of the data is fairly symmetric, so the mean age of the presidents is approximately equal to the median.

   C) The data has no clear shape, so it is impossible to make a reliable statement comparing the mean and the median.

   D) The same number of 55-or-older presidents have been inaugurated as ones who were younger than 55, so the mean age is exactly 55.

$$\frac{1}{3}(5x - 8) = 3x + 4$$

3. Which value of x satisfies the equation above?

   A) -5

   B) -3

   C) -1

   D) 1

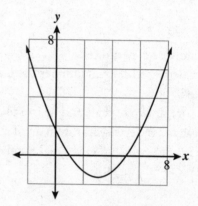

4. The following quadratic equations are all representations of the graph shown above. Which equation could you use to find the minimum value of the function without doing any additional work?

   A) $y = \frac{3}{8}(x - 3)^2 - \frac{3}{2}$

   B) $y = \frac{3}{8}(x - 1)(x - 5)$

   C) $y - \frac{15}{8} = \frac{3}{8}x^2 - \frac{9}{4}x$

   D) $y = \frac{3}{8}x^2 - \frac{9}{4}x + \frac{15}{8}$

5. The farmers market sells apples by the basket. The market charges \$3.00 for the basket itself, plus \$1.97 per pound of apples. A 6 percent sales tax is also applied to the entire purchase. Which equation represents the total cost of p pounds of apples at the farmers market?

   A) $c = (1.97 + 0.06p) + 3$

   B) $c = 1.06(1.97p) + 3$

   C) $c = 1.06(1.97 + 3)p$

   D) $c = 1.06(1.97p + 3)$

GO ON TO THE NEXT PAGE

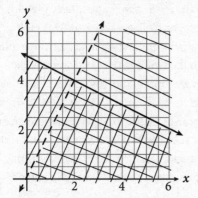

6. Which of the following is a solution to the system of inequalities shown in the figure above?

   A) (1, 5)

   B) (2, 6)

   C) (4, 1)

   D) (5, 4)

7. Marion is a city planner. The city she works for recently purchased new property on which it plans to build administrative offices. Marion has been given the task of sizing the lots for new buildings, using the following guidelines:

   - The square footage of each lot should be greater than or equal to 3,000 square feet, but less than or equal to 15,000 square feet.
   - Each lot size should be at least 30 percent greater in area than the size before it.
   - To simplify tax assessment calculations, the square footage of each lot must be a multiple of 1,000 square feet.

   Which list of lot sizes meets the city guidelines and includes as many lots as possible?

   A) 3,000; 5,000; 10,000; 15,000

   B) 3,000; 4,500; 6,000; 7,500; 10,000; 15,000

   C) 3,000; 4,000; 6,000; 8,000; 11,000; 15,000

   D) 3,000; 3,900; 5,100; 6,600; 8,600; 11,200; 14,600

8. One function of the Environmental Protection Agency (EPA) is to reduce air pollution. After implementing several pollution reduction programs in a certain city, EPA calculated that the air pollution should decrease by approximately 8 percent each year. What kind of function could be used to model the amount of air pollution in this city over the next several years, assuming no other significant changes?

   A) A linear function

   B) A quadratic function

   C) A polynomial function

   D) An exponential function

9. Escape velocity is the speed that a traveling object needs to break free of a planet or moon's gravitational field without additional propulsion (for example, without using fuel). The formula used to calculate escape velocity is $v = \sqrt{\dfrac{2Gm}{r}}$, where G represents the universal gravitational constant, m is the mass of the body from which the object is escaping, and r is the distance between the object and the body's center of gravity. Which equation represents the value of r in terms of v, G, and m ?

   A) $r = \dfrac{2Gm}{v^2}$

   B) $r = \dfrac{4G^2m^2}{v^2}$

   C) $r = \sqrt{\dfrac{2Gm}{v}}$

   D) $r = \sqrt{\dfrac{v}{2Gm}}$

10. A movie rental kiosk dispenses DVDs and Blu-rays. DVDs cost \$2.00 per night and Blu-rays cost \$3.50 per night. Between 5 p.m. and 9 p.m. on Saturday, the kiosk dispensed 209 movies and collected \$562.00. Solving which system of equations would yield the number of DVDs, d, and the number of Blu-rays, b, that the kiosk dispensed during the 4-hour period?

A) $\begin{cases} d + b = 209 \\ 2d + 3.5b = \dfrac{562}{4} \end{cases}$

B) $\begin{cases} d + b = 562 \\ 2d + 3.5b = 209 \end{cases}$

C) $\begin{cases} d + b = 562 \\ 2d + 3.5b = 209 \times 4 \end{cases}$

D) $\begin{cases} d + b = 209 \\ 2d + 3.5b = 562 \end{cases}$

11. The United States Senate has two voting members for each of the 50 states. The 113th Congress had a 4:1 male-to-female ratio in the Senate. Forty-five of the male senators were Republican. Only 20 percent of the female senators were Republican. How many senators in the 113th Congress were Republican?

A) 20

B) 49

C) 55

D) 65

12. According to the *Project on Student Debt* prepared by The Institute for College Access and Success, 7 out of 10 students graduating in 2012 from a four-year college in the United States had student loan debt. The average amount borrowed per student was \$29,400, which is up from \$18,750 in 2004. If student debt experiences the same total percent increase over the next eight years, approximately how much will a college student graduating in 2020 owe, assuming he takes out student loans to pay for his education?

A) \$40,100

B) \$44,300

C) \$46,100

D) \$48,200

13. Annalisa has 10 beanbags to throw in a game. She gets 7 points if a beanbag lands in the smaller basket and 3 points if it lands in the larger basket. If she gets b beanbags into the larger basket and the rest into the smaller basket, which expression represents her total score?

A) $3b$

B) $3b + 7$

C) $30 + 4b$

D) $70 - 4b$

GO ON TO THE NEXT PAGE

Questions 14 and 15 refer to the following information.

In a 2010 poll, surveyors asked registered voters in four different New York voting districts whether they would consider voting to ban fracking in the state. Hydraulic fracturing, or "fracking," is a mining process that involves splitting rocks underground to remove natural gas. According to ecologists, environmental damage can occur as a result of fracking, including contamination of water. The results of the 2010 survey are shown in the following table.

	In Favor of Ban	Against Ban	No Opinion	Total
District A	23,247	17,106	3,509	43,862
District B	13,024	12,760	2,117	27,901
District C	43,228	49,125	5,891	98,244
District D	30,563	29,771	3,205	63,539
Total	110,062	108,762	14,722	233,546

14. According to the data, which district had the smallest percentage of voters with no opinion on fracking?

   A) District A
   B) District B
   C) District C
   D) District D

15. A random follow-up survey was administered to 500 of the respondents in District C. They were asked if they planned to vote in the next election. The follow-up survey results were 218 said they planned to vote, 174 said they did not plan to vote, and 108 said they were unsure. Based on the data from both the initial survey and the follow-up survey, which of the following is most likely an accurate statement?

   A) Approximately 19,000 people in District C who support a ban on fracking can be expected to vote in the next election.

   B) Approximately 21,000 people in District C who support a ban on fracking can be expected to vote in the next election.

   C) Approximately 43,000 people in District C who support a ban on fracking can be expected to vote in the next election.

   D) Approximately 48,000 people in District C who support a ban on fracking can be expected to vote in the next election.

$$\begin{cases} 2x + 4y = 13 \\ x - 3y = -11 \end{cases}$$

16. Based on the system of equations above, what is the value of the sum of x and y ?

   A) $-\frac{1}{2}$
   B) 3
   C) $3\frac{1}{2}$
   D) 4

GO ON TO THE NEXT PAGE

	Bowling Scores		
	Ian	**Mae**	**Jin**
Game 1	160	110	120
Game 2	135	160	180
Game 3	185	140	105
Game 4	135	130	160
Game 5	185	110	135
Mean Score	160	130	140
Standard Deviation	22	19	27

17. Ian, Mae, and Jin bowled five games during a bowling tournament. The table above shows their scores. According to the data, which of the following conclusions is correct?

A) Ian bowled the most consistently because the mean of his scores is the highest.

B) Mae bowled the least consistently because the standard deviation of her scores is the lowest.

C) Mae bowled the most consistently because the standard deviation of her scores is the lowest.

D) Jin bowled the most consistently because the standard deviation of his scores is the highest.

18. Which of the following are solutions to the quadratic equation $(x + 3)^2 = 16$?

A) $x = -19$ and $x = 13$

B) $x = -7$ and $x = 1$

C) $x = -1$ and $x = 1$

D) $x = -1$ and $x = 7$

19. An architect is building a scale model of the Statue of Liberty. The real statue measures 305 feet, 6 inches from the bottom of the base to the tip of the torch. The architect plans to make her model 26 inches tall. If Lady Liberty's nose on the actual statue is 4 feet, 6 inches long, how long in inches should the nose on the model be?

A) $\dfrac{1}{26}$

B) $\dfrac{26}{141}$

C) $\dfrac{18}{47}$

D) $\dfrac{13}{27}$

20. If $f(x) = 3x + 5$, what is $f(6) - f(2)$?

A) 11

B) 12

C) 17

D) 23

GO ON TO THE NEXT PAGE ⟹

**Northern Spotted Owls
West Oregon, 1994–2014**

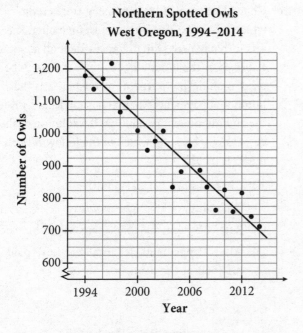

21. The United States Fish and Wildlife Service classifies animals whose populations are at low levels as either threatened or endangered. Endangered species are animals that are currently on the brink of extinction, whereas threatened species have a high probability of being on the brink in the near future. Since 1990, the Northern Spotted Owl has been listed as threatened. The figure above shows the populations of the Northern Spotted Owl in a certain region in Oregon from 1994 to 2014. Based on the line of best fit shown in the figure, which of the following values most accurately reflects the average change per year in the number of Northern Spotted Owls?

A)   −25

B)   −0.04

C)   0.04

D)   25

22. The x-coordinates of the solutions to a system of equations are -4 and 2. Which of the following could be the system?

A) $\begin{cases} y = 2x - 4 \\ y = (x + 4)^2 \end{cases}$

B) $\begin{cases} y = x - 2 \\ y = (x + 4)^2 + 2 \end{cases}$

C) $\begin{cases} y = x - 2 \\ y = (x - 4)^2 - 16 \end{cases}$

D) $\begin{cases} y = 2x - 4 \\ y = (x + 2)^2 - 16 \end{cases}$

Mice Litter Sample Data

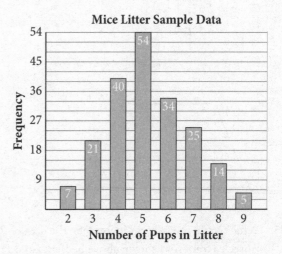

23. The White-footed Mouse, named for its darker body fur and white feet, is primarily found on the east coast of the United States, living in warm, dry forests and brushland. A scientist in Virginia studied a sample of 200 white-footed mice to see how many offspring they had per birth. The results of the study are recorded in the figure above. Based on the data, given a population of 35,000 female white-footed mice living in Virginia, how many would you expect to have a litter of seven or more pups?

A)   3,325

B)   4,375

C)   7,700

D)   15,400

24. Human beings have a resting heart rate and an active heart rate. The resting heart rate is the rate at which the heart beats when a person is at rest, engaging in no activity. The active heart rate rises as activity rises. For a fairly active woman in her 20s, eight minutes of moderate exercise results in a heart rate of about 90 beats per minute. After 20 minutes, the same woman's heart rate will be about 117 beats per minute. If the human heart rate increases at a constant rate as the time spent exercising increases, which of the following linear models represents this same woman's heart rate, r, after t minutes of moderate exercise?

A) $r = 0.15t - 5.3$

B) $r = 0.44t - 32$

C) $r = 2.25t + 72$

D) $r = 6.75t + 36$

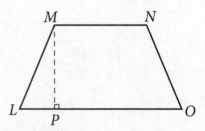

25. What would the percent increase in the area of the isosceles trapezoid shown above be if MN and LO were each multiplied by 4 and MP was reduced by 75 percent?

A) 0

B) 25

C) 100

D) 400

26. Chantal buys new furniture using store credit, which offers five-year, no-interest financing. She sets up a payment plan to pay the debt off as soon as possible. The function $40x + y = 1,400$ can be used to model her payment plan where x is the number of payments Chantal has made and y is the amount of debt remaining. If a solution to the equation is (21, 560), which of the following statements is true?

A) Chantal pays \$21 per month.

B) Chantal pays \$560 per month.

C) After 21 payments, \$560 remains to be paid.

D) After 21 payments, Chantal will have paid off \$560 of the debt.

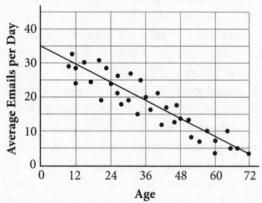

27. Which of the following equations best represents the trend of the data shown in the figure above?

A) $y = -2.4x + 30$

B) $y = -1.2x + 40$

C) $y = -0.8x + 40$

D) $y = -0.4x + 36$

28. The graph of $f(x)$ passes through the point (5, 1). Through which point does the graph of $-f(x + 3) - 2$ pass?

A) $(-2, -1)$

B) $(2, -3)$

C) $(2, 1)$

D) $(8, -3)$

GO ON TO THE NEXT PAGE ⟹

Practice Tests

29. When a certain kitchen appliance store decides to sell a floor model, it marks the retail price of the model down 25 percent and puts a "Floor Model Sale" sign on it. Every 30 days after that, the price is marked down an additional 10 percent until it is sold. The store decides to sell a floor model refrigerator on January 15th. If the retail price of the refrigerator was $1,500 and it is sold on April 2nd of the same year, what is the final selling price, not including tax?

    A) $820.13

    B) $825.00

    C) $911.25

    D) $1,012.50

30. When New York City built its 34th Street subway station, which has multiple underground levels, it built an elevator that runs along a diagonal track approximately 170 feet long to connect the upper and lower levels. The angle formed between the elevator track and the bottom level is just under 30 degrees. What is the approximate vertical distance in feet between the upper and lower levels of the subway station?

    A) 85

    B) 98

    C) 120

    D) 147

Directions: For questions 31-38, enter your responses into the appropriate grid on your answer sheet, in accordance with the following:

1. You will receive credit only if the circles are filled in correctly, but you may write your answers in the boxes above each grid to help you fill in the circles accurately.

2. Don't mark more than one circle per column.

3. None of the questions with grid-in responses will have a negative solution.

4. Only grid in a single answer, even if there is more than one correct answer to a given question.

5. A **mixed number** must be gridded as a decimal or an improper fraction. For example, you would grid $7\frac{1}{2}$ as 7.5 or 15/2.

   (Were you to grid it as [7 | 1 | / | 2], this response would be interpreted as $\frac{71}{2}$.)

6. A **decimal** that has more digits than there are places on the grid may be either rounded or truncated, but every column in the grid must be filled in order to receive credit.

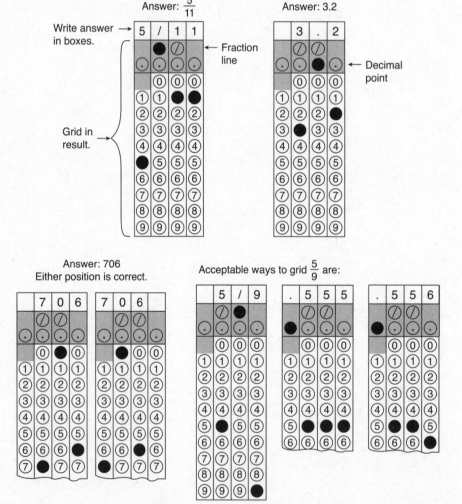

GO ON TO THE NEXT PAGE

31. If $-\frac{3}{2} < 3 - \frac{a}{5} < -\frac{1}{4}$, what is the maximum possible whole number value of a ?

Boeing Jets	Coach	Business	First Class
747-400	310	52	12
767-300	151	26	6
777-200	194	37	16
777-300	227	52	8

32. The table above shows the seating configuration for several commercial airplanes. The day before a particular flight departs, a travel agent books the last seat available for a client. If the seat is on one of the two Boeing 777s, what is the probability that the seat is a Business Class seat, assuming that all seats have an equal chance of being the last one available?

33. Heating water accounts for a good portion of the average home's energy consumption. Tankless water heaters, which run on natural gas, are about 22 percent more energy efficient on average than electric hot water heaters. However, a tankless hot water heater typically costs significantly more. Suppose one tankless water heater costs $160 more than twice as much as a conventional hot water heater. If both water heaters cost $1,000 together, how many more dollars does the tankless water heater cost than the conventional one?

34. Medically speaking, remission is a period in which the symptoms of a disease or condition subside or, for some diseases, a period during which the condition stops spreading or worsening. In a certain drug trial in which a drug designed to treat cancer was tested, exactly 48 percent of patients experienced remission while take the drug. What is the fewest number of patients who could have participated in this trial?

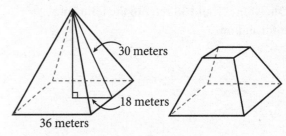

30 meters

18 meters

36 meters

35. When the top of a pyramid (or a cone) is cut off, the remaining bottom part is called a frustum. Suppose the top third (based on the height) of the square pyramid shown above is cut off and discarded. What will be the volume, in cubic meters, of the remaining frustum?

36. After a surface has been cleaned, bacteria begin to regrow. Because bacteria reproduce in all directions, the area covered is usually in the shape of a circle. The diameter of the circle in millimeters can give scientists an idea of how long the bacteria have been growing. For a certain kind of bacteria, the equation $d = 0.015 \times \sqrt{h - 24}$ can be used to find the number of hours, $h \geq 24$, that the bacteria have been growing. If the diameter of a circle of these bacteria is 0.12 millimeters, how many hours have the bacteria been growing?

Questions 37 and 38 refer to the following information.

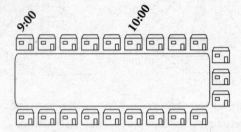

Daniel works for a pest control company and is spraying all the lawns in a neighborhood. The figure above shows the layout of the neighborhood and the times that Daniel started spraying the lawns at two of the houses. Each lawn in the neighborhood is approximately 0.2 acres in size and takes the same amount of time to spray.

37. How many minutes will it take Daniel to spray all of the lawns in the neighborhood?

38. Daniel uses a mobile spray rig that holds 20 gallons of liquid. It takes 1 gallon to spray 2,500 square feet of lawn. How many times, including the first time, will Daniel need to fill the spray rig, assuming he fills it to the very top each time? (Note: 1 acre = 43,560 square feet.)

Essay Test

50 Minutes

You will be given a passage to read and asked to write an essay analyzing it. As you write, be sure to show that you have read the passage closely. You will be graded on how well you have understood the passage, how clear your analysis is, and how well you express your ideas.

Your essay must be written on the lines in your answer booklet. Anything you write outside the lined space in your answer booklet will not be read by the essay graders. Be sure to write or print in such a way that it will be legible to readers not familiar with your handwriting. Additionally, be sure to address the passage directly. An off-topic essay will not be graded.

As you read the passage, think about the author's use of

- evidence, such as statistics or other facts.

- logic to connect evidence to conclusions and to develop lines of reasoning.

- style, word choice, and appeals to emotion to make the argument more persuasive.

Adapted from Royal Dixon, *The Human Side of Animals*. © 1918 by Frederick A. Stokes Company, New York.

1   The trouble with science is that too often it leaves out feeling. If you agree that we cannot treat men like machines, why should we put animals in that class? Why should we fall into the colossal ignorance and conceit of cataloging every human-like action of animals under the word "instinct"? Man had to battle with animals for untold ages before he domesticated and made servants of them. He is just beginning to learn that they were not created solely to furnish material for stories, or to serve mankind, but that they also have an existence, a life of their own.

2   Man has long claimed dominion over animals and a right to assert that dominion without restraint. This anthropocentric conceit is the same thing that causes one nation to think it should rule the world, that the Sun and moon were made only for the laudable purpose of giving light unto a chosen few, and that young lambs playing on a grassy hillside, near a cool spring, are just so much mutton allowed to wander over man's domain until its flavor is improved.

3   It is time to remove the barriers, once believed impassable, which man's egotism has used as a screen to separate him from his lower brothers. Our physical bodies are very similar to theirs except that ours are almost always much inferior. Merely because we have a superior intellect which enables us to rule and enslave the animals, shall we deny them all intellect and all feeling?

4   It is possible to explain away all the marvelous things the animals do, but after you have finished, there will still remain something over and above which quite defies all mechanistic interpretation. An old war horse, for instance, lives over and over his battles in his dreams. He neighs and paws, just as he did in real battle.... This is only one of the plethora of animal phenomena which man does not understand. If you are able to explain these things to humanity, you will be classed as wise indeed. Yet the average scientist explains them away, with the ignorance and empty words of the unwise.

5   By a thorough application of psychological principles, it is possible to show that man himself is merely a machine to be explained in terms of neurons and nervous impulses, heredity and environment and reactions to outside stimuli. But who is there who does not believe that there is more to a man than that?

GO ON TO THE NEXT PAGE

6   Animals have demonstrated long ago that they not only have as many talents as human beings but that, under the influence of the same environment, they form the same kinds of combinations to defend themselves against enemies, to shelter themselves against heat and cold, to build homes, to lay up a supply of food for the hard seasons. In fact, all through the ages man has been imitating the animals in burrowing through the earth, penetrating the waters, and now, at last, flying through the air.

7   There are also numerous signs, sounds and motions by which animals communicate with each other, though to man these symbols of language may not always be understandable. Dogs give barks indicating surprise, pleasure and all other emotions. Cows will bellow for days when mourning for their dead.

8   In their reading of the weather, animals undoubtedly possess superhuman powers. Even squirrels can predict an unusually long and severe winter and thus make adequate preparations. Some animals act as both barometers and thermometers.

9   There is no limit to the marvelous things animals do. The ape or baboon who puts a stone in the open oyster to prevent it from closing, or lifts stones to crack nuts, or beats other apes with sticks…in all these actions is actual reasoning. Indeed, there is nothing which man makes with all his ingenious use of tools and instruments, of which some suggestion may not be seen in animal creation.

Write an essay that analyzes the author's approach in persuading his readers that animals and humans have much in common and humans should treat animals with more respect. Focus on specific features, such as the ones listed in the box above the passage, and explain how these features strengthen the author's argument. Your essay should discuss the most important rhetorical features of the passage.

Your essay should not focus on your own opinion of the author's conclusion, but rather on how the author persuades his readers.

Answer Key

Reading Test

1. C	14. C	27. C	40. C
2. D	15. D	28. D	41. C
3. A	16. B	29. B	42. A
4. C	17. B	30. A	43. B
5. D	18. D	31. D	44. B
6. A	19. B	32. A	45. A
7. D	20. C	33. D	46. D
8. A	21. A	34. D	47. B
9. B	22. C	35. B	48. C
10. D	23. C	36. D	49. B
11. D	24. B	37. C	50. D
12. D	25. C	38. B	51. D
13. A	26. A	39. D	52. B

Writing and Language Test

1. B	12. D	23. D	34. C
2. B	13. B	24. C	35. D
3. C	14. D	25. B	36. C
4. A	15. B	26. D	37. B
5. B	16. C	27. D	38. B
6. A	17. B	28. A	39. C
7. A	18. C	29. B	40. A
8. C	19. A	30. C	41. B
9. A	20. C	31. C	42. B
10. D	21. D	32. D	43. A
11. C	22. B	33. D	44. D

Math Test—No-Calculator

1. B	6. B	11. C	16. 144
2. D	7. C	12. D	17. 150
3. C	8. D	13. A	18. 4
4. B	9. C	14. D	19. 8
5. D	10. A	15. A	20. 3/25 or .12

Math Test—Calculator

1. B	11. B	21. A	31. 22
2. B	12. C	22. D	32. 1/6 or .166 or .167
3. A	13. D	23. C	33. 440
4. A	14. D	24. C	34. 25
5. D	15. A	25. A	35. 9984
6. C	16. B	26. C	36. 88
7. C	17. C	27. D	37. 252
8. D	18. B	28. B	38. 4
9. A	19. C	29. C	
10. D	20. B	30. A	

Answers and Explanations

Reading Test

Suggested passage map notes:

¶1: Gregor woke up not himself
¶2: description of Gregor's room, job
¶3: thought sleep would make him normal, couldn't roll over
¶4: thought job stress was to blame for how he was
¶5: thinks he needs more sleep, wants more luxury but has to help parents

1. C

Difficulty: Easy

Category: Detail

Getting to the Answer: Skim the passage to locate Gregor's first reaction to his transformation. The first sentence states that Gregor woke "from troubled dreams." He only realizes "it wasn't a dream" (lines 11–12) after he has examined his new body and looked around his room to orient himself. Choice **(C)** is the correct answer. "Nightmare" describes a dream that is "troubled."

2. D

Difficulty: Hard

Category: Vocab-in-Context

Getting to the Answer: Use context clues and tone to help determine the meaning of the word. Use the surrounding text to paint a mental picture of descriptive words. Finally, make sure the answer choice does not alter the meaning of the sentence when inserted. The paragraph in which the word appears describes an average room appropriate for a person. Therefore, **(D)** is the correct answer. "Proper" means "suitably appropriate" in this context.

3. A

Difficulty: Medium

Category: Inference

Getting to the Answer: Look for Gregor's thoughts and statements about work. Use this as evidence of his attitude. Paragraphs 4 and 5 are essentially rants about Gregor's dissatisfaction with his job. He dislikes travelling, feels that he works much harder than others, and expresses anger toward his boss. Gregor feels that it is unfair that other salesmen have a life of "luxury" while he has to wake up early. Choice **(A)** is the correct answer. Gregor is resentful and bitter about his job.

4. C

Difficulty: Medium

Category: Command of Evidence

Getting to the Answer: Review your answer to the previous question. Decide which lines of text give clues to how Gregor feels about his job. Choice **(C)** offers the best support. These lines describe Gregor's bitterness and the unfairness he perceives. He feels he works much harder than the other salesmen, but that he would be fired if he asked for better treatment or less work.

5. D

Difficulty: Hard

Category: Global

Getting to the Answer: Ask yourself what purpose the author has in writing the passage. What main point does the majority of the excerpt support? The events in the passage show that despite a dramatic physical transformation, Gregor still plans to go to work. Gregor consistently expresses unhappiness and bitterness about his job but ignores his transformation into an insect because he feels he must still go to work or he will be fired. In this situation, **(D)** is the correct answer. Gregor's duty to his job overrides reason and sense when he plans to attend work despite the physical transformation that has left him inhuman and helpless.

6. A

Difficulty: Medium

Category: Inference

Getting to the Answer: Reread the text, looking for evidence to support each of the answer choices. Examine Gregor's thoughts and statements for clues about his personality. Based on Gregor's statements about his work, it is clear that he continues to work at a job he dislikes in order to support his parents. He largely ignores his physical transformation, and there is no evidence as to whether he excels at his work. Choice **(A)** is the correct answer.

7. D

Difficulty: Medium

Category: Command of Evidence

Getting to the Answer: Review your answer to the previous question. Read each choice and figure out which one provides specific support for that answer. Choice **(D)** provides the best support. These lines show that Gregor thinks it may be best to quit the job he hates, but he will continue to work until he can pay off his parents' debt.

8. A

Difficulty: Medium

Category: Vocab-in-Context

Getting to the Answer: Use context clues from the target sentence and surrounding sentence. Predict the meaning of the word and look for a match in the answer choices. Gregor is attempting to turn over in his bed, but finds his legs and body are useless and unable to turn him over into his preferred position. Choice **(A)** is the nearest match to the meaning of "floundering" in this context.

9. B

Difficulty: Medium

Category: Function

Getting to the Answer: Think about where the description of Gregor's itch is placed in the story. Look at the lines before and after it and consider why the author chose to include it at that particular point in the narrative. The description of the itch comes in the middle of Gregor's thoughts about his job. After attempting and failing to relieve the itch, Gregor immediately goes back to thinking about his job-related concerns. This shows that Gregor is so preoccupied with his job that he is unable to recognize the seriousness—and absurdity—of his situation. The correct answer is **(B)**.

10. D

Difficulty: Medium

Category: Function

Getting to the Answer: Contrast Gregor's thoughts with the dark tone of the rest of the excerpt. Think about how this phrase adds to or supports the interpretations you made in previous questions. The author ends the excerpt with Gregor completely disregarding the fact that he is now an insect. Gregor plans to go to work as he always does, and the author draws attention to the absurdity of this decision. Choice **(D)** is the correct choice. The author uses the matter-of-fact tone in the sentence to emphasize that Gregor will ignore his physical condition and go to work because he has such a strong sense of duty to his family.

Suggested passage map notes:

¶1–3: women are equal and deserve to be treated as such

¶4: what freedom is

¶5–6: history of women fighting for equality

¶7–8: men and women do great things when they work together

¶9–13: must help women in other countries achieve equality and fight discrimination

11. D

Difficulty: Easy

Category: Global

Getting to the Answer: Consider the word choices Clinton uses throughout her speech. Notice any recurring themes. Choice **(D)** is the correct answer. Clinton says that working to improve the lives of women will improve others' lives as well.

12. D

Difficulty: Medium

Category: Command of Evidence

Getting to the Answer: Beware of answer choices that are only vaguely related to Clinton's point. The correct answer will follow her purpose closely. Clinton indicates that women's rights issues affect more than just women. Choice **(D)** is the best fit. These lines from the text provide concrete examples of how improving the lives of women improves their families' lives as well.

13. A

Difficulty: Medium

Category: Vocab-in-Context

Getting to the Answer: Sometimes you can recognize similarities between the word in question and a more familiar word. "Divisive" is similar to "divide" and "division," both of which have to do with things being split or made separate. Clinton is saying that though suffrage produced great conflict and divided people more than other philosophical wars, it was "bloodless." Choice **(A)** is correct; "divisive" means "conflict-producing."

14. C

Difficulty: Hard

Category: Inference

Getting to the Answer: You're being asked to decide which statement Clinton is most likely to agree with. Because the statement isn't explicitly mentioned in the speech, you must infer, or make a logical guess, based on information in the speech. Clinton states that the world would be improved if women were able to contribute more. She provides specific examples of her vision for an improved world. Choice **(C)** is correct as it suggests that if women did not experience discrimination and had more power, the world would be better off.

15. D

Difficulty: Medium

Category: Command of Evidence

Getting to the Answer: Try paraphrasing the answer you chose for the previous test item. Then, decide which quote from the speech supports this idea. Choice **(D)** provides the best evidence. This quote notes that women are discriminated against and that it is not just women who suffer from this discrimination; there are global problems that could benefit from women's ideas.

16. B

Difficulty: Hard

Category: Vocab-in-Context

Getting to the Answer: A word like "organized" can have several meanings, depending on the context. Beware of choosing the most common meaning, as it may not fit this situation. Choice **(B)** successfully conveys the idea of the women's suffrage movement being one in which many different people worked together over a long period of time.

17. B

Difficulty: Hard

Category: Detail

Getting to the Answer: Be careful to assess not only what topics are mentioned but also how Clinton discusses them. Choice **(B)** is supported by the passage, which claims in lines 6–8: "Women must enjoy the right to participate fully in the social and political lives of their countries if we want freedom and democracy to thrive and endure."

18. D

Difficulty: Medium

Category: Detail

Getting to the Answer: Notice how the stem of the question doesn't ask you to find evidence for an argument; it instead gives you the evidence (the example of V-J Day) and then asks you to figure out what argument this evidence supports. Choice **(D)** is correct. Clinton mentions V-J Day as an example of something that resulted from cooperation between men and women.

19. B

Difficulty: Medium

Category: Detail

Getting to the Answer: Pay close attention to the words Clinton uses in the cited lines to describe problems that affect women. Clinton states that the problems that "diminish the potential" (line 38) of women are "older" (line 37) and "deeply-rooted" (line 37), making **(B)** the correct answer.

20. C

Difficulty: Medium

Category: Function

Getting to the Answer: Notice how the question is asking you to figure out how the paragraph functions in relation to other parts of the speech. Clinton goes into specific detail in this paragraph to provide examples of freedom. She very specifically states what she means by freedom and accuses some of failing to respect others' freedom. Therefore, **(C)** is the correct answer.

Suggested passage map notes:

Passage 1

    ¶1: history of tea, Europe and China

    ¶2: tea not received well in Europe at first

    ¶3: China controlled tea production

    ¶4: Europe wanted to produce tea

    ¶5: finally had tea growing success in India

Passage 2

    ¶1: history of tea time in Europe

    ¶2: tea in France served with savory

    ¶3: tea in Germany served with sweet

    ¶4: tea in Russia sign of class

    ¶5: tea in GB

21. A

Difficulty: Medium

Category: Inference

Getting to the Answer: Be careful to choose an answer that is clearly supported by the information in the passage. The passage states that the climate was not right for growing tea "even in the equatorial colonies"

(line 28). Choice **(A)** is the correct answer. Clearly, European tea-drinking nations tried to grow tea in their equatorial colonies; that's how they learned that the climate there wasn't right.

22. C

Difficulty: Medium

Category: Command of Evidence

Getting to the Answer: The correct answer will be the reason you were able to make the inference in the previous question. Choice **(C)** works logically. Europeans knew that tea would not grow well in their colonies; this leads to the conclusion that they tried.

23. C

Difficulty: Medium

Category: Inference

Getting to the Answer: When a question refers to only one of the paired passages, be sure to focus on the correct passage. Find where Passage 1 discusses Great Britain's attempts to grow tea in India. Eliminate any answer choices that are not supported by information in this section of the passage. The last sentence of Passage 1 states that the large quantities of tea imported from India allowed tea to become a "staple" (line 48) in European households. You can infer that if the British had not succeeded in growing tea in India, Europeans would have had tea less often. Choice **(C)** is correct.

24. B

Difficulty: Medium

Category: Vocab-in-Context

Getting to the Answer: You should be able to replace the original word with the correct answer in the sentence. The passage states that in order to "circumvent" the monopoly, European growers tried growing their own tea. It makes sense that Europeans' attempt at growing their own tea was a way to "get around" the Chinese monopoly. Therefore, **(B)** is the best choice.

25. C

Difficulty: Hard

Category: Inference

Getting to the Answer: Keep in mind that the graphic focuses on tea consumption, not tea production. The last paragraph of Passage 1 describes Britain's great success growing tea in India, which resulted in great increases in the amount of tea arriving in London. Therefore, **(C)** is a reasonable conclusion that may be drawn by synthesizing information in Passage 1 and the graphic.

26. A

Difficulty: Hard

Category: Inference

Getting to the Answer: Be careful to deduce only information that can reasonably be inferred from the passage. It can logically be inferred that hosting guests in Russia generally involves tea. Passage 2 emphasizes that Russian hosts are judged based on the strength of their tea, and that Russians have elaborate tea-making equipment. Choice **(A)** is the correct answer.

27. C

Difficulty: Medium

Category: Command of Evidence

Getting to the Answer: Identify the country associated with the correct answer to the previous question and see what evidence fits. The passage states that Russian tea ceremonies are highly formal and that hosts are judged on their tea making. Choice **(C)** is the correct answer. The referenced lines support the conclusions about Russia.

28. D

Difficulty: Medium

Category: Vocab-in-Context

Getting to the Answer: Look for other words in this sentence that offer clues to the word's meaning. A noble, or high-ranking, class is likely to have associations with formalism, so **(D)** is the correct answer.

29. B

Difficulty: Easy

Category: Inference

Getting to the Answer: Make sure to compare only the two countries being asked about. Choice **(B)** is correct. The passage notes that cookies and cakes are served with tea in Germany, while foods served with tea in France are "savory" and include puff pastry with cheese.

30. A

Difficulty: Easy

Category: Inference

Getting to the Answer: Look for true statements about Passage 1. Then, do the same for Passage 2. Choice **(A)** is correct. Passage 1 focuses on an earlier period in European history, while Passage 2 compares different cultures within Europe.

31. D

Difficulty: Medium

Category: Synthesis

Getting to the Answer: For this question, you're looking for a statement that is reflected in both passages. Choice **(D)** is the only choice supported by both passages.

Suggested passage map notes:

¶1: Stromer discovered dinosaur fossils in Egypt, new genus, fossils destroyed in WWII, notes and sketches survived
¶2: Ibrahim rediscovered similar fossils, able to make partial skeleton
¶3: description of *Spinosaurus*
¶4: *Spino* unique—lived on land, hunted in water
¶5: Ibrahim used digital model and Stromer sketches to create replica

32. A

Difficulty: Easy

Category: Global

Getting to the Answer: Look for the answer choice that describes an important idea that is supported throughout the text rather than a specific detail. The passage is mostly about how the mystery of the *Spinosaurus* fossils was decoded. Choice **(A)** is the best summary of the central idea of the passage.

33. D

Difficulty: Medium

Category: Detail

Getting to the Answer: Locate the information about the fossils Stromer expected to find and the fossils he actually found, particularly those fossils' sizes and ages. The passage explains that Stromer expected to find fossils of early mammals, but instead found fossils that "dated back to the Cretaceous period" (line 9). This indicates that the fossils were older than he expected. Eliminate choices (A) and (B). Because the *Spinosaurus* was larger than any mammal, **(D)** is correct.

34. D

Difficulty: Medium

Category: Inference

Getting to the Answer: Think about the overall message of the passage and consider why the author would choose to write about this topic. The author's tone, or attitude, toward the topic of the passage demonstrates the point of view that the study of fossils and ancient life has value. Choice **(D)** is the correct answer. The evidence in the passage supports the idea that the author thinks the study of fossils and ancient life is important.

35. B

Difficulty: Medium

Category: Command of Evidence

Getting to the Answer: Some answer choices may seem important. However, if they don't support your answer to the previous question, they aren't what you should choose. Choice **(B)** is correct. The author's use of the word "significant" in this quote shows that he or she thinks the study of fossils and ancient life is important.

36. D

Difficulty: Medium

Category: Vocab-in-Context

Getting to the Answer: Though more than one answer choice might seem acceptable, one comes closest to meaning the same as the phrase in question. Earlier in the paragraph, the author explains that two different bones gathered at different times both had a red line coursing through them. This means that the bones were from the same animal. Choice **(D)** fits best. "Against all odds" most nearly means "despite low probability."

37. C

Difficulty: Medium

Category: Function

Getting to the Answer: Be careful to avoid answers that don't make sense in the context of the paragraph. These phrases help the author describe the animal in a generally positive way. Choice **(C)** is the correct answer.

38. B

Difficulty: Hard

Category: Inference

Getting to the Answer: Be careful of answers that make sense but are not implied by the information presented in the passage. Choice **(B)** is correct. The passage does not explicitly state how Ibrahim became familiar with Stromer's work, but it is implied that he was familiar with Stromer's work when he found the fossils with the red lines and used Stromer's sketches to aid with the modern digital models as mentioned in the last paragraph.

39. D

Difficulty: Hard

Category: Command of Evidence

Getting to the Answer: Eliminate any answer choices that have nothing to do with your answer to the previous question. Choice **(D)** is correct. It directly supports the inference that Ibrahim was familiar with Stromer's work, showing that he used Stromer's sketches to aid in creating his life-size replica of the *Spinosaurus*.

40. C

Difficulty: Easy

Category: Vocab-in-Context

Getting to the Answer: Ibrahim and his fellow researchers didn't know how the bones went together. They were making an educated guess with the help of technology and Stromer's sketches. Choice **(C)** is correct. "Hypothetical" in this sentence means "possible."

41. C

Difficulty: Easy

Category: Inference

Getting to the Answer: Think about the order in which Stromer and Ibrahim's work with the fossils occurred. Choice **(C)** is correct. Ibrahim used Stromer's sketches to create his models of the *Spinosaurus*. He built on Stromer's work to complete his own.

42. A

Difficulty: Hard

Category: Inference

Getting to the Answer: Think about the process described in each answer choice and compare it to how Ibrahim went about building his replica of the *Spinosaurus*. Choice **(A)** is the correct choice. An architect creating a model of a building would use tools and methods similar to those used by Ibrahim, such as drawings and digital technologies.

Suggested passage map notes:

¶1: people willing to try anything to be healthy
¶2: laughter important part of health
¶3: what happens to body when you laugh
¶4: humor helps many medical conditions, laugh more = better health
¶5: benefits of laughter
¶6: various methods to provoke laughter, best achieved in person, not through watching shows
¶7: laughter decreases with age

43. B

Difficulty: Easy

Category: Inference

Getting to the Answer: When a question asks you about the point of view of an author, look for words and phrases in the passage that hint at the author's feelings or attitude toward the topic. Choice **(B)** is the correct answer because the author speaks quite positively of the studies throughout the passage.

44. B

Difficulty: Medium

Category: Command of Evidence

Getting to the Answer: Reread each quote in the context of the passage. Consider which one is the best evidence of the author's point of view toward laughter research. The word "finally" in line 14 helps demonstrate that the author finds laughter research worthwhile. Choice **(B)** is the best answer.

45. A

Difficulty: Medium

Category: Inference

Getting to the Answer: Think about the connection the passage makes between laughter and the ability to accomplish challenging tasks. Choice **(A)** is correct. The passage notes that endorphin production is associated with "mental energy and positivity" (lines 27–28).

46. D

Difficulty: Medium

Category: Vocab-in-Context

Getting to the Answer: Notice that all of the answer choices are related to the word "reputable," but the correct answer will reflect the specific context in which the word is used. "Reputable" in this case indicates that the studies are official and are based on empirical data (data based on observation and experiment). This makes **(D)**, "credible," the correct choice.

47. B

Difficulty: Hard

Category: Inference

Getting to the Answer: Eliminate any answer choices that are not suggested in the passage. Choice **(B)** is correct because early results of studies into laughter and health all seem to strengthen the relationship between the two.

48. C

Difficulty: Medium

Category: Command of Evidence

Getting to the Answer: Avoid answer choices like (D) that may not support a general conclusion you could take from the passage. Choice **(C)** is the correct answer. The author expects future research will yield stronger evidence in support of laughter's health benefits.

49. B

Difficulty: Hard

Category: Function

Getting to the Answer: Look at the verbs provided in each of the answer choices. Decide whether the author wanted to "reach," "support," "justify," or "show" by discussing the function of endorphins. After asserting that laughter produces endorphins, the author explains their function in order to help the reader understand why a positive mental state may result. Choice **(B)** is the correct answer.

50. D

Difficulty: Medium

Category: Vocab-in-Context

Getting to the Answer: Look carefully at the paragraph's context to help you decide on the correct answer choice. The phrase "Laughter is the best medicine" (lines 15–16) is an example of an adage, or proverb. Therefore, **(D)** is correct.

51. D

Difficulty: Hard

Category: Inference

Getting to the Answer: Decide whether the phrase "uplifting community" is a reference to a person alone or a group of people. Choice **(D)** is correct. The graph shows that shared humor with others most significantly increased pain tolerance in individuals.

52. B

Difficulty: Medium

Category: Inference

Getting to the Answer: Watch out for answer choices that seem plausible but are not directly supported by information in the passage. The passage states that laughter seems to provide protection from heart disease and that young people laugh less as they get older. You can infer from this information that as young people age, they have less protection from heart disease and are therefore more at risk. Choice **(B)** is correct.

Writing and Language Test

1. B

Difficulty: Medium

Category: Sentence Structure: The Basics

Getting to the Answer: Read the sentence and determine whether it is grammatically complete. To form a grammatically complete sentence, you must have an independent clause prior to a colon. As written, the text that comes before the colon is not grammatically complete because it lacks an independent clause with a subject and predicate. Choice **(B)** correctly adds a verb to the clause before the comma. It also correctly uses the past tense to match with the tense of "hadn't" in the first sentence of the passage.

2. B

Difficulty: Medium

Category: Development: Precision

Getting to the Answer: Read the sentences surrounding the word to look for context clues. Watch out for near synonyms that are not quite correct. The word "issues" is not precise and does a poor job of conveying the meaning of the sentence. A better word, such as **(B)**, "adversity," more precisely conveys hardship, difficulties, or painful situations.

3. C

Difficulty: Medium

Category: Sentence Structure: The Basics

Getting to the Answer: Determine whether a clause is independent or dependent to decide between a comma and a semicolon. The clause is dependent, as it contains only a noun ("an idea") and a relative clause to modify it. A semicolon is used to separate two independent clauses, so it cannot be used here. A comma is the appropriate punctuation mark to separate the dependent clause from the independent clause in the sentence. Choice **(C)** is the correct answer.

4. A

Difficulty: Medium

Category: Sentence Structure: Commas, Dashes, and Colons

Getting to the Answer: Figure out the role of the underlined phrase in the sentence to find the correct punctuation. "Like lift and drag on wings" is a parenthetical element provided as an example. The sentence is correctly punctuated as written because it uses dashes to set off the parenthetical element. The answer is **(A)**.

5. B

Difficulty: Hard

Category: Development: Introductions and Conclusions

Getting to the Answer: Read the paragraph and summarize the main idea to predict an answer. Then, look for an answer that matches your prediction. Choice **(B)** correctly establishes that Kranz stood out as a leader in a time of crisis.

6. A

Difficulty: Easy

Category: Agreement: Verbs

Getting to the Answer: Read the paragraph to establish the correct verb tense for the sentence. Other verbs in the paragraph, such as "were" and "fueled," are past tense and indicate that another past tense verb is needed for this sentence. Choice **(A)** is correct because it uses the past tense "was" and logically transitions into the explanation about Kranz's vest making him easy to spot.

7. A

Difficulty: Hard

Category: Development: Introductions and Conclusions

Getting to the Answer: Quickly summarize the main idea of the paragraph. Eliminate choices that may be accurate but do not support this primary focus. Choice **(A)** clearly supports the main focus of the paragraph by drawing attention to Kranz's role as a leader in Mission Control.

8. C

Difficulty: Easy

Category: Agreement: Idioms

Getting to the Answer: Be careful with homophones. Figure out the part of speech and what the target word refers to if it is a pronoun. "Their" is a possessive pronoun indicating ownership. "There" is a pronoun that replaces a place name. "They're" is a contraction that is short for "they are." Choice **(C)**, "There," is the correct choice.

9. A

Difficulty: Hard

Category: Development: Precision

Getting to the Answer: When faced with unfamiliar words, eliminate clearly incorrect answers first. The paragraph indicates that Kranz did not intend for the vest to be stylish. Kranz wore the vest as a military type of symbol, but the correct answer will need to be in contrast to that idea. Choice **(A)** is the correct answer. The word "sartorial" means "having to do with clothing."

10. D

Difficulty: Medium

Category: Organization: Transitions

Getting to the Answer: Think about the commonly confused pair between/among. Consider which preposition is usually used to reference two distinct objects. Choice **(D)** appropriately selects the word "between" because the objects "meetings" and "calculations" are two distinct items. "Among" is used for more than two distinct items.

11. C

Difficulty: Medium

Category: Agreement: Pronouns

Getting to the Answer: Read the target sentence and the sentence before it. Figure out whom or what the pronoun refers to and make sure it matches the antecedent in number. The plural antecedent is found in the previous sentence ("Kranz and the NASA staff") and is clearly plural. Choice **(C)** correctly uses a plural pronoun to refer to a plural antecedent.

12. D

Difficulty: Medium

Category: Development: Precision

Getting to the Answer: Read carefully to identify the context of the underlined word. Then, choose the word that best fits the content of the sentence. You're looking for a word that suggests that the organization has developed over time, as is stated in the last part of the sentence. "Built," **(D)**, best fits the context of the sentence.

13. B

Difficulty: Medium

Category: Sentence Structure: Commas, Dashes, and Colons

Getting to the Answer: Read the entire sentence to get a better sense for which punctuation would be correct. A colon will introduce an explanation of the "key feature," allowing the rest of the sentence to elaborate on the preceding clause. Choice **(B)** is correct. In this case, the colon prompts the reader to see that the part of the sentence after the colon defines the phrase "key feature."

14. D

Difficulty: Medium

Category: Organization: Sentence Placement

Getting to the Answer: Watch out for any choices that would make the sentence seem out of place. Choice **(D)** is correct. Sentence 3 offers a transition to a specific discussion of those risks in the next paragraph.

15. B

Difficulty: Medium

Category: Organization: Conciseness

Getting to the Answer: Avoid choices that are redundant, or use more words than necessary to communicate an idea. All of the choices communicate the same idea, but one does so with a greater economy of language. Choice **(B)** uses a minimal number of well-chosen words to revise the text.

16. C

Difficulty: Hard

Category: Development: Introductions and Conclusions

Getting to the Answer: Watch out for answer choices that correctly identify supporting points but do not explain the main claim. The paragraph contains evidence, including decreased taxable wealth and decreased control over interest rates, to support the main claim. Choice **(C)** is correct. It expresses the main claim of the paragraph and is supported by the evidence.

17. B

Difficulty: Medium

Category: Sentence Structure: The Basics

Getting to the Answer: Read the text carefully. Notice that the existing structure creates a run-on sentence. Then, consider which answer choice will create two complete sentences. Choice **(B)** revises the run-on sentence to create two grammatically complete sentences.

18. C

Difficulty: Medium

Category: Development: Introductions and Conclusions

Getting to the Answer: Find the main claim in the paragraph and then come back to the question. The statement found in **(C)** best supports the paragraph statements that maintaining the current status may not be an option and moving to the Eurozone may be in the best interest of the UK.

19. A

Difficulty: Easy

Category: Development: Precision

Getting to the Answer: Watch out for choices that imply little relationship between the EU and the UK. "Intertwined" most accurately reflects the content of the text, because it implies a complex economic relationship between the UK and the Eurozone. Therefore, **(A)** is correct. No change is necessary.

20. C

Difficulty: Hard

Category: Development: Relevance

Getting to the Answer: Find the central idea of the paragraph and then come back to the question. The central idea in the paragraph is that economic downturns in the Eurozone also affect the UK. Choice **(C)** is correct.

21. D

Difficulty: Easy

Category: Organization: Transitions

Getting to the Answer: Decide which transition word makes the most sense in the context of the sentence by reading each choice in the sentence. The correct choice should connect the two sentences as the text transitions from economic concerns to those of "security, power, and protection." The word "however" is the best transition because it provides a logical contrast between the ideas in the passage. Choice **(D)** is the correct answer.

22. B

Difficulty: Medium

Category: Sentence Structure: Commas, Dashes, and Colons

Getting to the Answer: Consider which punctuation will correctly set off the parenthetical information in this sentence. Dashes are often used to offset parenthetical sentence elements. Choice **(B)** is correct.

23. D

Difficulty: Easy

Category: Organization: Precision

Getting to the Answer: Review each answer choice and decide which makes the most sense in terms of what the first sentence says. Choice **(D)** is the correct answer. "These days" contrasts with the next sentence's use of "this wasn't always true."

24. C

Difficulty: Medium

Category: Agreement: Verbs

Getting to the Answer: Make sure that verbs agree with the subject. Check back and figure out what the subject is and then see if it agrees. The word "cherries" requires a plural verb. Choice **(C)** is the correct answer.

25. B

Difficulty: Medium

Category: Agreement: Verbs

Getting to the Answer: Read the complete sentence carefully whenever you see a shift in tense or verb form. Decide whether this change is logically correct in the sentence. The verbs in a sentence need to be in parallel form. Choice **(B)** is in parallel form with the first verb "reached," so it is the correct answer.

26. D

Difficulty: Medium

Category: Development: Precision

Getting to the Answer: Beware of some answer choices that may have similar meanings but do not fit into the context of this sentence. The word "boasted" is the best fit for the context of the sentence, so **(D)** is the correct answer.

27. D

Difficulty: Medium

Category: Sentence Structure: The Basics

Getting to the Answer: Pay close attention to commas to ensure that they do not create run-on sentences. Notice that this sentence contains two complete thoughts. Choice **(D)** is the correct answer because it combines the two complete thoughts into one sentence in the best way.

28. A

Difficulty: Hard

Category: Development: Introductions and Conclusions

Getting to the Answer: To find the best conclusion, look for the choice that summarizes the main points of the paragraph and best completes the paragraph. The paragraph begins by talking about the lack of record of coffee as cargo on the Mayflower and then introduces when it was first referenced. Choice **(A)** does the best job of retelling what the paragraph is about, therefore providing an effective conclusion.

29. B

Difficulty: Easy

Category: Sentence Structure: Commas, Dashes, and Colons

Getting to the Answer: Study the words in the series and see where commas might need to be placed or eliminated. Choice **(B)** is the correct answer.

30. C

Difficulty: Medium

Category: Development: Precision

Getting to the Answer: Replace the word with the other answer choices. See which word works best in the context of the sentence. One answer choice indicates the correct relationship between coffeehouses and counterculture, and that is **(C)**. "Associated" works best within the context of the sentence.

31. C

Difficulty: Medium

Category: Development: Introductions and Conclusions

Getting to the Answer: To find the main topic of a paragraph, identify important details and summarize them in a sentence or two. Then, find the answer choice that is the closest to your summary. Choice **(C)** is the correct answer. The sentence best explains the increasing popularity of coffee in American life, the main topic of the paragraph.

32. D

Difficulty: Medium

Category: Sentence Structure: Commas, Dashes, and Colons

Getting to the Answer: Determine the relationship between the two parts of this sentence, and then consider the purpose of the various forms of punctuation. A colon indicates that the rest of the sentence will be a list or an explanation. Choice **(D)** is the correct answer as it shows the correct relationship between both parts of the sentence.

33. D

Difficulty: Hard

Category: Agreement: Modifiers

Getting to the Answer: Read the complete sentence carefully and look for sections that do not seem to follow logically. The modifiers need to be in the proper order so the sentence's meaning is clear. Choice **(D)** is correct.

34. C

Difficulty: Medium

Category: Agreement: Pronouns

Getting to the Answer: Recall that a pronoun must agree with its antecedent, or the word to which it refers. Begin by identifying the antecedent of the pronoun. Then, check each choice against the antecedent to find the best match. The antecedent for the pronoun "their" is "this phenomenon," which appears in the main clause. The antecedent and its pronoun do not currently agree as "this phenomenon" is singular and "their" is plural. Although the "s" in "Lights" implies many lights, it is still considered a singular phenomenon and so requires a singular pronoun. Choice **(C)** is the correct answer.

35. D

Difficulty: Medium

Category: Agreement: Idioms

Getting to the Answer: Read each answer choice carefully to determine the correct preposition. Choice **(D)** is the correct answer because it correctly uses the preposition "in."

36. C

Difficulty: Medium

Category: Development: Introductions and Conclusions

Getting to the Answer: Choice **(C)** is the correct answer because it provides additional information regarding how people are able to view auroras.

37. B

Difficulty: Hard

Category: Agreement: Verbs

Getting to the Answer: When choosing the correct verb, note how it alters the relationship between the subject, the "sun," and the stated action, in this case "storm activity." Choice **(B)** is correct. The verb "experiences" is the only one that states a direct action upon the subject, the sun, rather than the sun "observing" an action occurring externally, as suggested by the other verbs.

38. B

Difficulty: Easy

Category: Agreement: Modifiers

Getting to the Answer: The placement of the adjective has a great effect upon the intention of the noun. Read the sentence carefully to determine where the adjective makes the most sense. By placing the adjective before the nouns, **(B)** ensures that only those scientists and amateurs interested in the topic at hand use the specific tools mentioned in this passage.

39. C

Difficulty: Hard

Category: Organization: Conciseness

Getting to the Answer: Generalized statements with inexact definitions that border on opinion have no place in a scientific essay. The tone and style must exhibit a reliance on verifiable statements. Because "readily available" cannot be quantified and implies the author's opinion, using the word "specific" in **(C)** creates a more exact statement that precedes the information on the precise tools used.

40. A

Difficulty: Medium

Category: Development: Relevance

Getting to the Answer: Reread the paragraph to understand the author's claims. Which answer choice provides a fact that would best support these claims? Make sure the answer choice does not digress from the progression of ideas. The speed of the solar flare is referenced as being three times the speed of normal solar winds, but neither exact speed is given. To make a stronger case for the author's statements, both speeds should be stated. Therefore, **(A)** is the correct answer.

41. B

Difficulty: Medium

Category: Agreement: Verbs

Getting to the Answer: Read closely to find the subject of the verb. Sometimes, the closest noun is not the subject. The subject of the sentence is "strength and direction," not "energy." Choice **(B)** is the correct answer because it matches the subject in number and maintains a consistent tense with the rest of the passage.

42. B

Difficulty: Hard

Category: Organization: Conciseness

Getting to the Answer: Eliminate extraneous and redundant information ("the public") and needless prepositions. Then, reorder the verb and nouns to achieve the most efficient language possible. Making adjustments to the passage language as shown in **(B)** results in the most concise phrasing.

43. A

Difficulty: Hard

Category: Organization: Transitions

Getting to the Answer: Consider the meanings of each introductory word carefully. Use the context clues in the rest of the sentence to choose the correct word. The context clues in the rest of the sentence reveal that the Northern Lights can create communication and weather problems and yet are still beautiful. Keeping the word "While" makes the most sense in this context, so **(A)** is the correct answer.

44. D

Difficulty: Hard

Category: Graphs

Getting to the Answer: Reread paragraph 4 for information that will help you understand how to read the graphic. Use that information to calculate the precise start and end time for the solar flare as indicated in the graphic. The passage states that a solar flare is represented by any Kp-Index of 5 or higher. While there is one three-hour period where the Kp-Index reached 6, there is a consistent period where the chart shows readings of level 5 or higher. Choice **(D)** is the correct answer. This choice gives the complete time period showing a reading of level 5 or higher, according to the chart.

Math Test—No-Calculator

1. B

Difficulty: Easy

Category: Heart of Algebra/Linear Equations

Getting to the Answer: The average rate of change for a linear function is the same as the slope of the line. Find the slope of the line by either using the slope formula or by counting the rise and the run from one point to the next. If you start at $(0, -3)$, the line rises 5 units and runs 8 units to get to $(8, 2)$, so the slope, or average rate of change, is $\frac{5}{8}$.

2. D

Difficulty: Easy

Category: Passport to Advanced Math/Quadratics

Getting to the Answer: A root of an equation is an x-value that corresponds to a y-value of 0. The x-intercepts of the graph, and therefore the roots of the equation, are $x = -1$ and $x = 5$. When $x = -1$, the value of $x + 1$ is 0, so one of the factors is $x + 1$. When $x = 5$, the value of $x - 5$ is 0, so the other factor is $x - 5$. The equation in **(D)** is the only one that contains these factors and is therefore correct.

3. C

Difficulty: Easy

Category: Passport to Advanced Math/Exponents

Getting to the Answer: Substitute the values given in the question into the formula. Then, simplify using the rules of exponents. Remember, when raising a power to a power, you multiply the exponents:

$$
\begin{aligned}
KE &= \frac{1}{2}\left(2 \times 10^3\right)\left(3 \times 10^3\right)^2 \\
&= \frac{1}{2}\left(2 \times 10^3\right)\left(3^2 \times 10^{3 \times 2}\right) \\
&= \frac{1}{2} \times 2 \times 10^3 \times 9 \times 10^6 \\
&= 9 \times 10^{3+6} \\
&= 9 \times 10^9
\end{aligned}
$$

Choice **(C)** is correct.

4. B

Difficulty: Medium

Category: Heart of Algebra/Linear Equations

Getting to the Answer: Choose the best strategy to answer the question. You could start by cross-multiplying to get rid of the denominators, but simplifying the numerators first will make the calculations easier:

$$
\begin{aligned}
\frac{3(k-1)+5}{2} &= \frac{17-(8+k)}{4} \\
\frac{3k-3+5}{2} &= \frac{17-8-k}{4} \\
\frac{3k+2}{2} &= \frac{9-k}{4} \\
4(3k+2) &= 2(9-k) \\
12k+8 &= 18-2k \\
14k &= 10 \\
k &= \frac{10}{14} = \frac{5}{7}
\end{aligned}
$$

Choice **(B)** is correct.

5. D

Difficulty: Medium

Category: Passport to Advanced Math/Functions

Getting to the Answer: Whenever a quantity repeatedly increases or decreases by the same percentage (or fraction) over time, an exponential model can be used to represent the situation. Choice (B) is not an exponential equation, so you can eliminate it right away. The amount of garbage is decreasing, so the scenario represents exponential decay and you can use the form $y = a \times (1 - r)^t$, where a is the initial amount, r is the rate of decay, and t is time in years. The initial amount is 1,800, the rate is 3%, or 0.03, and t is an unknown quantity, so the correct equation is $y = 1,800 \times (1 - 0.03)^t$, which is equivalent to the equation $y = 1,800 \times 0.97^t$. **(D)** is correct.

6. B

Difficulty: Medium

Category: Passport to Advanced Math/Rational Expressions

Getting to the Answer: The terms in the expression have the same denominator, $x + 5$, so their numerators can be subtracted. Simply combine like terms and keep the denominator the same. Don't forget to distribute the negative to both $3x$ and -8:

$$\frac{6x + 2}{x + 5} - \frac{3x - 8}{x + 5} = \frac{6x + 2 - (3x - 8)}{x + 5}$$
$$= \frac{6x + 2 - 3x - (-8)}{x + 5}$$
$$= \frac{6x - 3x + 2 + 8}{x + 5}$$
$$= \frac{3x + 10}{x + 5}$$

Choice **(B)** is correct.

7. C

Difficulty: Medium

Category: Heart of Algebra/Linear Equations

Getting to the Answer: The slope-intercept form of a line is $y = mx + b$. In this question, the graph passes through the origin, so b is 0. Because b is 0, the equation of this line in slope-intercept form is $y = mx$, which can be rewritten as $\frac{y}{x} = m$. Count the rise and the run from the origin, (0, 0), to the next point, (3, 1), to get a slope of $m = \frac{1}{3}$. This matches **(C)**.

8. D

Difficulty: Medium

Category: Passport to Advanced Math/Polynomials

Getting to the Answer: When multiplying polynomials, carefully multiply each term in the first factor by each term in the second factor. This question doesn't ask for the entire product, so check to make sure you answered the correct question (the coefficient of x). After performing the initial multiplication, look for the x terms and add their coefficients. To save time, you do not need to simplify the other terms in the expression:

$$\left(4x^2 + 7x + 1\right)(3x + 5)$$
$$= 4x^2(3x + 5) + 7x(3x + 5) + 1(3x + 5)$$
$$= 12x^3 + 20x^2 + 21x^2 + \underline{35x + 3x} + 5$$

The coefficient of x is $35 + 3 = 38$, which is **(D)**.

9. C

Difficulty: Medium

Category: Passport to Advanced Math/Functions

Getting to the Answer: A graph is *decreasing* when the slope is negative; it is *increasing* when the slope is positive. Eliminate (A) because there are some segments on the graph that have a positive slope. Eliminate (B) because the slope is negative, not positive, between 2009 and 2010. Choice **(C)** is correct because the slope is negative for each segment between 2004 and 2007 and also between 2009 and 2011.

10. A

Difficulty: Medium

Category: Heart of Algebra/Inequalities

Getting to the Answer: Don't answer this question too quickly. The shading is below the line, but that does not necessarily mean that the symbol in the equation will be the less than symbol ($<$). Start by writing the equation of the dashed line shown in the graph in slope-intercept form. Then, use the shading to determine the correct inequality symbol. The slope of the line shown in the graph is $\frac{1}{4}$ and the y-intercept is -3, so the equation of the dashed line is $y = \frac{1}{4}x - 3$. The graph is shaded below the boundary line, so use the $<$ symbol. When written in slope-intercept form, the inequality is $y < \frac{1}{4}x - 3$. The inequalities in the answer choices are given in standard form ($Ax + By = C$), so rewrite your answer in this form. Don't forget to reverse the inequality symbol if you multiply or divide by a negative number:

$$y < \frac{1}{4}x - 3$$
$$-\frac{1}{4}x + y < -3$$
$$\frac{1}{4}x - y > 3$$

Choice **(A)** is correct.

11. C

Difficulty: Medium

Category: Heart of Algebra/Linear Equations

Getting to the Answer: When you're given only one equation but two variables, chances are that you can't actually solve the equation (unless one variable happens to cancel out), but rather that you are going to need to manipulate it to look like the desired expression (which in this question is $\frac{b}{a}$). This type of question can't be planned out step-by-step—instead, start with basic algebraic manipulations and see where they take you. First, distribute the $\frac{1}{2}$ on the left side of the equation to get $2a + 5b = b$. There are two terms that have a b,

so subtract $5b$ from both sides to get $2a = -4b$. You're hoping for plain b in the numerator, so divide both sides by -4 to get $\frac{2a}{-4} = b$. Finally, divide both sides by a to move the a into a denominator position under b. The result is $\frac{2}{-4} = \frac{b}{a}$, which means the ratio $\frac{b}{a}$ is $-\frac{2}{4}$, or $-\frac{1}{2}$, making **(C)** correct.

12. D

Difficulty: Hard

Category: Heart of Algebra/Systems of Linear Equations

Getting to the Answer: Graphically, a system of linear equations that has no solution indicates two parallel lines, or in other words, two lines that have the same slope. So, write each of the equations in slope-intercept form ($y = mx + b$) and set their slopes (m) equal to each other to solve for a. Before finding the slopes, multiply the top equation by 3 to make it easier to manipulate:

$$3\left(\frac{1}{3}x + \frac{2}{3}y = -8\right) \rightarrow x + 2y = -24 \rightarrow y = -\frac{1}{2}x - 12$$
$$ax + 6y = 15 \rightarrow 6y = -ax + 15 \rightarrow y = -\frac{a}{6}x + \frac{15}{6}$$

The slope of the first line is $-\frac{1}{2}$ and the slope of the second line is $-\frac{a}{6}$. Now, set the slopes equal to each other and solve:

$$-\frac{1}{2} = -\frac{a}{6}$$
$$-6(1) = -a(2)$$
$$-6 = -2a$$
$$3 = a$$

Choice **(D)** is correct.

13. A

Difficulty: Hard

Category: Heart of Algebra/Inequalities

Getting to the Answer: Pay careful attention to units, particularly when a question involves rates. The taxi charges \$3.00 for the first $\frac{1}{4}$ mile, which is a flat fee, so write 3. The additional charge is \$0.25 per $\frac{1}{8}$ mile, or $0.25 \times 8 = \$2.00$ per mile. The number of miles after the first $\frac{1}{4}$ mile is $m - \frac{1}{4}$, so the cost of the trip, not including the first $\frac{1}{4}$ mile is $2\left(m - \frac{1}{4}\right)$. This means the cost of the whole trip is $3 + 2\left(m - \frac{1}{4}\right)$. The clue "no more than \$20" means that much or less, so use the symbol $\leq$. The inequality is $3 + 2\left(m - \frac{1}{4}\right) \leq 20$, which simplifies to $2.5 + 2m \leq 20$, **(A)**.

14. D

Difficulty: Hard

Category: Additional Topics in Math/Geometry

Getting to the Answer: First, find the center and the radius of the circle: each grid line represents one unit on the graph, so the center is (0, 2), and the radius is 6. Substitute these values into the equation for a circle, $(x - h)^2 + (y - k)^2 = r^2$, and then simplify until the equation looks like the one given in the question:

$$(x - 0)^2 + (y - 2)^2 = 6^2$$
$$x^2 + (y - 2)^2 = 36$$
$$x^2 + (y - 2)(y - 2) = 36$$
$$x^2 + y^2 - 4y + 4 = 36$$
$$x^2 + y^2 - 4y = 32$$

There is no x term, so $a = 0$. The coefficient of y is -4 and $c = 32$, so $ab + c = (0)(-4) + 32 = 32$, which matches **(D)**.

15. A

Difficulty: Hard

Category: Passport to Advanced Math/Quadratics

Getting to the Answer: The quadratic equation is given in standard form, so use the method of completing the square to rewrite the equation in vertex form. Then, read the value of k to find the maximum height of the projectile:

$$\begin{aligned} h &= -16t^2 + 64t + 8 \\ &= -16\left(t^2 - 4t + \underline{}\right) + 8 - \underline{} \\ &= -16\left(t^2 - 4t + 4\right) + 8 - (-16 \times 4) \\ &= -16(t - 2)^2 + 8 - (-64) \\ &= -16(t - 2)^2 + 72 \end{aligned}$$

The vertex is (2, 72), so the maximum height is 72 feet, **(A)**.

16. 144

Difficulty: Easy

Category: Heart of Algebra/Linear Equations

Getting to the Answer: There is only one equation given and it has two variables. This means that you don't have enough information to solve for either variable. Instead, look for the relationship between the left side of the equation and the other expression that you are trying to find. Start by clearing the fractions by multiplying both sides of the original equation by 12. This yields the expression that you are looking for, $9x + 10y$, so no further work is required—just read the value on the right-hand side of the equation:

$$\frac{3}{4}x + \frac{5}{6}y = 12$$
$$12\left(\frac{3}{4}x + \frac{5}{6}y\right) = 12(12)$$
$$9x + 10y = 144$$

17. 150

Difficulty: Medium

Category: Additional Topics in Math/Geometry

Getting to the Answer: There are 360 degrees in a circle. You need to figure out how many degrees each minute on the face of a clock represents. There are 60 minutes on the face of an analogue clock. This means that each minute represents $360 \div 60 = 6$ degrees. Between 3:20 and 3:45, 25 minutes go by, so the minute hand rotates $25 \times 6 = 150$ degrees.

18. 4

Difficulty: Medium

Category: Additional Topics in Math/Geometry

Getting to the Answer: Start by marking up the figure with the information you're given. You know the length of *EB*, which is 3. You also know the triangle is equilateral, which means all three sides are congruent and all three angles are 60 degrees. This means angles *A* and *B* are both 60 degrees, which further means that triangles *BEF* and *ADC* are 30-60-90 triangles, and therefore similar by the AAA theorem. Now, recall that 30-60-90 triangles always have side lengths in the ratio $x:x\sqrt{3}:2x$, which means if *EB* is 3, then *BF* (the hypotenuse) is $2(3) = 6$. Now, because you know the ratio of *BF* to *FC*, you can find the length of *FC*:

$$\frac{3}{4} = \frac{6}{FC}$$
$$3(FC) = 24$$
$$FC = 8$$

Now you can find the length of each side of the original equilateral triangle: $6 + 8 = 14$, which is the length of *AC*, the hypotenuse of triangle *ADC*. This means side *AD*, being the shorter leg of triangle *ADC*, is $14 \div 2 = 7$. You now have enough information to find the length of *DE*, which is $AB - (AD + EB) = 14 - (7 + 3) = 4$.

19. 8

Difficulty: Hard

Category: Passport to Advanced Math/Exponents

Getting to the Answer: Read the question carefully to determine what part of the expression you need to simplify and what part you don't. Sometimes, you can work a simpler question and still arrive at the correct answer. The question only asks for the exponent on *x*,

so you do not have to simplify the coefficients. Rewrite the expression without the coefficients and simplify using the rules of exponents:

$$\frac{3x^{\frac{3}{2}} \cdot \left(16x^2\right)^3}{8x^{-\frac{1}{2}}} \rightarrow \frac{x^{\frac{3}{2}} \cdot \left(x^2\right)^3}{x^{-\frac{1}{2}}}$$
$$= x^{\frac{3}{2} - \left(-\frac{1}{2}\right)} \cdot x^{2 \times 3}$$
$$= x^{\frac{3}{2} + \frac{1}{2}} \cdot x^6$$
$$= x^2 \cdot x^6$$
$$= x^8$$

The exponent on *x* is **8**.

20. 3/25 or .12

Difficulty: Hard

Category: Passport to Advanced Math/Functions

Getting to the Answer: When a question involving a function provides one or more ordered pairs, substitute them into the function to see what information you can glean. Start with $x = 0$ because doing so often results in the elimination of a variable:

$$f(x) = a \cdot b^x$$
$$f(0) = a \cdot b^0$$
$$3 = a \cdot b^0$$
$$3 = a \cdot 1$$
$$3 = a$$

Now you know the value of *a*, so the equation looks like $f(x) = 3 \cdot b^x$. Substitute the second pair of values into the new equation:

$$f(x) = 3 \cdot b^x$$
$$f(1) = 3 \cdot b^1$$
$$15 = 3 \cdot b^1$$
$$15 = 3b$$
$$5 = b$$

The exponential function is $f(x) = 3 \cdot 5x$. The final step is to find the value being asked for, $f(-2)$. Substitute -2 for *x* and simplify:

$$f(-2) = 3 \cdot 5^{-2} = \frac{3}{5^2} = \frac{3}{25}$$

Grid this in as **3/25 or .12**.

Math Test—Calculator

1. B

Difficulty: Easy

Category: Heart of Algebra/Linear Equations

Getting to the Answer: The total cost consists of a flat installation fee and a price per square foot. The installation fee is a one-time fee that does not depend on the number of feet ordered and therefore should not be multiplied by f. This means that 199 is the installation fee. The other expression in the equation, $3.29f$, represents the cost per square foot (the unit price) times the number of feet, f. Hence, 3.29 must represent the cost of one square foot of carpet, **(B)**.

2. B

Difficulty: Easy

Category: Problem Solving and Data Analysis/Statistics and Probability

Getting to the Answer: Quickly read each answer choice. Cross out false statements as you go. Stop when you arrive at a true statement. There is no long "tail" of data on either side, so the shape is not skewed and you can eliminate (A). The shape of the data *is* symmetric because the data is fairly evenly spread out, with about half of the ages above and half below the median. When the shape of a data set is symmetric, the mean is approximately equal to the median so **(B)** is correct. Don't let (D) fool you—the *median* is 55, not the *mean*.

3. A

Difficulty: Easy

Category: Heart of Algebra/Linear Equations

Getting to the Answer: Think about the best strategy to answer the question. If you distribute the $\frac{1}{3}$, it creates messy numbers. Instead, clear the fraction by multiplying both sides of the equation by 3. Then, use inverse operations to solve for x:

$$\frac{1}{3}(5x - 8) = 3x + 4$$
$$5x - 8 = 3(3x + 4)$$
$$5x - 8 = 9x + 12$$
$$-4x = 20$$
$$x = -5$$

Choice **(A)** is correct.

4. A

Difficulty: Easy

Category: Passport to Advanced Math/Quadratics

Getting to the Answer: The minimum value of a quadratic function is equal to the y-value of the vertex of its graph, so vertex form, $y = a(x - h)^2 + k$, reveals the minimum without doing any additional work. Choice **(A)** is the only equation written in this form and therefore must be correct. The minimum value of this function is $-\frac{3}{2}$.

5. D

Difficulty: Easy

Category: Heart of Algebra/Linear Equations

Getting to the Answer: Organize information as you read the question; the total cost includes the per-pound rate, the cost of the basket, and the 6% tax on the entire purchase. If a customer buys p pounds of apples, the total cost is the per-pound rate, $1.97, multiplied by the number of pounds, p, plus the $3.00 fee for the basket, or $1.97p + 3$. This expression represents the untaxed amount of the purchase. To calculate the amount that includes the 6% tax, multiply the untaxed amount by 1.06. The equation is $c = 1.06(1.97p + 3)$, which is **(D)**.

6. C

Difficulty: Easy

Category: Heart of Algebra/Inequalities

Getting to the Answer: The intersection (overlap) of the two shaded regions is the solution to the system of inequalities. The point (4, 1) lies within the intersection of the two shaded regions, so it is a solution to the system shown in the figure. None of the other points lie within the intersection, so **(C)** is correct.

7. C

Difficulty: Medium

Category: Problem Solving and Data Analysis/Rates, Ratios, Proportions, and Percentages

Getting to the Answer: Start with the smallest possible lot size, 3,000 square feet. The next lot must be at least 30% larger, so multiply by 1.3 to get 3,900 square feet. Then, round up to the next thousand (which is not necessarily the nearest thousand) to meet the tax assessment requirement. You must always round up because rounding down would make the subsequent lot size less than 30% larger than the one before it. Continue this process until you reach the maximum square footage allowed, 15,000 square feet:

$$3,000 \times 1.3 = 3,900 \rightarrow 4,000$$
$$4,000 \times 1.3 = 5,200 \rightarrow 6,000$$
$$6,000 \times 1.3 = 7,800 \rightarrow 8,000$$
$$8,000 \times 1.3 = 10,400 \rightarrow 11,000$$
$$11,000 \times 1.3 = 14,300 \rightarrow 15,000$$

Choice **(C)** is correct.

8. D

Difficulty: Medium

Category: Problem Solving and Data Analysis/Functions

Getting to the Answer: Determine whether the change in the amount of pollution is a common difference (linear function) or a common ratio (exponential function), or if it changes direction (quadratic or polynomial function). Each year, the amount of pollution should be $100 - 8 = 92\%$ of the year before. You can write 92% as $\frac{92}{100}$, which represents a common ratio from one year to the next. This means that the best model is an exponential function, **(D)**, of the form $y = a \cdot (0.92)^x$.

9. A

Difficulty: Medium

Category: Passport to Advanced Math/Radicals

Getting to the Answer: Don't spend too much time reading the scientific explanation of the equation. Solve for r using inverse operations. First, square both sides of the equation to remove the radical. Then, multiply

both sides by r to get the r out of the denominator. Finally, divide both sides by v^2:

$$v = \sqrt{\frac{2Gm}{r}}$$
$$v^2 = \frac{2Gm}{r}$$
$$v^2 r = 2Gm$$
$$r = \frac{2Gm}{v^2}$$

This matches **(A)**.

10. D

Difficulty: Medium

Category: Heart of Algebra/Systems of Linear Equations

Getting to the Answer: One equation should represent the total *number* of rentals, while the other equation represents the *cost* of the rentals. The number of DVDs plus the number of Blu-rays equals the total number of rentals, 209. Therefore, one equation is $d + b = 209$. This means you can eliminate choices (B) and (C). Now, write the cost equation: cost per DVD times number of DVDs ($2d$) plus cost per Blu-ray times number of Blu-rays ($3.5b$) equals the total amount collected (562). The cost equation is $2d + 3.5b = 562$. Don't let (A) fool you. The question says nothing about the cost *per hour* so there is no reason to divide the cost by 4. Choice **(D)** is correct.

11. B

Difficulty: Medium

Category: Problem Solving and Data Analysis/Rates, Ratios, Proportions, and Percentages

Getting to the Answer: Break the question into short steps. *Step 1*: Find the number of female senators. *Step 2*: Use that number to find the number of female Republican senators. *Step 3*: Find the total number of Republican senators.

Each of the 50 states gets 2 voting members in the Senate, so there are $50 \times 2 = 100$ senators. The ratio of males to females in the 113th Congress was 4:1, so 4 parts male plus 1 part female equals a total of 100 senators. Write this as $4x + x = 100$, where x represents one part and therefore the number of females. Next, simplify and solve the equation to find that $x = 20$ female senators. To find the number of female senators that were Republican, multiply 20% (or 0.20) times 20 to get 4. Finally, add to get 45 male plus 4 female = 49 Republican senators in the 113th Congress, **(B)**.

12. C

Difficulty: Medium

Category: Problem Solving and Data Analysis/Rates, Ratios, Proportions, and Percentages

Getting to the Answer: Find the percent increase by dividing the amount of change by the original amount. Then, apply the same percent increase to the amount for 2012. The amount of increase is $29,400 - 18,750 = 10,650$, so the percent increase is $10,650 \div 18,750 = 0.568 = 56.8\%$ over 8 years. If the total percent increase over the next 8 years is the same, the average student who borrowed money will have loans totaling $29,400 \times 1.568 = 46,099.20$, or about $46,100. Choice **(C)** is correct.

13. D

Difficulty: Medium

Category: Heart of Algebra/Linear Equations

Getting to the Answer: Write the expression in words first: points per large basket (3) times number of beanbags in large basket (b), plus points per small basket (7) times number of beanbags in small basket. If there are 10 beanbags total and b go into the larger basket, the rest, or $10 - b$, must go into the smaller basket. Now, translate the words to numbers, variables, and operations: $3b + 7(10 - b)$. This is not one of the answer choices, so simplify the expression by distributing the 7 and combining like terms: $3b + 7(10 - b) = 3b + 70 - 7b = 70 - 4b$. This matches **(D)**.

14. D

Difficulty: Easy

Category: Problem Solving and Data Analysis/Statistics and Probability

Getting to the Answer: To calculate the percentage of the voters in each district who had no opinion on fracking, divide the number of voters in *that* district who had no opinion by the total number of voters in *that* district. Choice **(D)** is correct because $3,205 \div 63,539 \approx 0.05 = 5\%$, which is a lower percentage than in the other three districts that were polled (District A = 8%; District B = 7.6%; District C = 6%).

15. A

Difficulty: Medium

Category: Problem Solving and Data Analysis/Statistics and Probability

Getting to the Answer: Scan the answer choices quickly to narrow down the amount of information in the table that you need to analyze. Each choice makes a statement about people from District C who support a ban on fracking that can be expected to vote in the next election. To extrapolate from the follow-up survey sample, multiply the fraction of people from the follow-up survey who plan to vote in the upcoming election $\left(\dfrac{218}{500}\right)$ by the number of people in District C who support a ban on fracking (43,228) to get 18,847.408, or approximately 19,000 people. Choice **(A)** is correct.

16. B

Difficulty: Medium

Category: Heart of Algebra/Systems of Linear Equations

Getting to the Answer: Solve the system of equations using substitution. Then, check that you answered the right question (find the sum of x and y). First, solve the second equation for x to get $x = 3y - 11$, then substitute this expression into the first equation to find y:

$$2x + 4y = 13$$
$$2(3y - 11) + 4y = 13$$
$$6y - 22 + 4y = 13$$
$$10y - 22 = 13$$
$$10y = 35$$
$$y = \frac{7}{2}$$

Now, substitute the result into $x = 3y - 11$ and simplify to find x:

$$x = 3\left(\frac{7}{2}\right) - 11$$
$$= \frac{21}{2} - 11$$
$$= -\frac{1}{2}$$

The question asks for the sum, so add x and y to get $-\frac{1}{2} + \frac{7}{2} = \frac{6}{2} = 3$, which is **(B)**.

17. C

Difficulty: Medium

Category: Problem Solving and Data Analysis/Statistics and Probability

Getting to the Answer: The keyword in the answer choices is "consistently," which relates to how spread out a player's scores are. Standard deviation, not mean, is a measure of spread so you can eliminate choice (A) right away. A lower standard deviation indicates scores that are less spread out and therefore more consistent. Likewise, a higher standard deviation indicates scores that are more spread out and therefore less consistent. Notice the opposite nature of this relationship: lower standard deviation = more consistent; higher standard deviation = less consistent. Choice **(C)** is correct because the standard deviation of Mae's scores is the lowest, which means she bowled the most consistently.

18. B

Difficulty: Medium

Category: Passport to Advanced Math/Quadratics

Getting to the Answer: Notice the structure of the equation. The expression on the left side of the equation is the square of a quantity, so start by taking the square root of both sides. After taking the square roots, solve the resulting equations. Remember, $4^2 = 16$ and $(-4)^2 = 16$, so there will be *two* equations to solve:

$$(x + 3)^2 = 16$$
$$\sqrt{(x + 3)^2} = \sqrt{16}$$
$$x + 3 = \pm 4$$

$$x + 3 = 4 \rightarrow x = 1$$
$$x + 3 = -4 \rightarrow x = -7$$

Choice **(B)** is correct.

19. C

Difficulty: Medium

Category: Problem Solving and Data Analysis/Rates, Ratios, Proportions, and Percentages

Getting to the Answer: Pay careful attention to the units. You need to convert all of the dimensions to inches, and then set up and solve a proportion. The real statue's height

is $305 \times 12 = 3,660 + 6 = 3,666$ inches; the length of the nose on the real statue is $4 \times 12 = 48 + 6 = 54$ inches; the height of the model statue is 26 inches; the length of the nose on the model is unknown. Now set up and solve your equation:

$$\frac{3,666}{54} = \frac{26}{x}$$
$$3,666x = 26(54)$$
$$3,666x = 1,404$$
$$x = \frac{1,404}{3,666} = \frac{18}{47}$$

Choice **(C)** is correct.

20. B

Difficulty: Medium

Category: Passport to Advanced Math/Functions

Getting to the Answer: When evaluating a function, substitute the value inside the parentheses for x in the equation. Evaluate the function at $x = 6$ and at $x = 2$, and then subtract the second output from the first. Note that this is not the same as first subtracting $6 - 2$ and then evaluating the function at $x = 4$:

$$f(6) = 3(6) + 5 = 18 + 5 = 23$$
$$f(2) = 3(2) + 5 = 6 + 5 = 11$$
$$f(6) - f(2) = 23 - 11 = 12$$

Choice **(B)** is correct.

21. A

Difficulty: Medium

Category: Problem Solving and Data Analysis/ Scatterplots

Getting to the Answer: Examine the graph, paying careful attention to units and labels. Here, the years increase by 2 for each grid line and the number of owls by 25. The average change per year is the same as the slope of the line of best fit. Find the slope of the line of best fit using the slope formula, $m = \frac{y_2 - y_1}{x_2 - x_1}$, and any two points that lie on (or very close to) the line. Using the two endpoints of the data, (1994, 1,200) and (2014, 700), the average change per year is $\frac{700 - 1,200}{2014 - 1994} = \frac{-500}{20} = -25$, which is **(A)**. Pay careful attention to the sign of the answer—the number of owls is decreasing, so the rate of change is negative.

22. D

Difficulty: Medium

Category: Passport to Advanced Math/Quadratics

Getting to the Answer: The solution to a system of equations is the point(s) where their graphs intersect. You could solve this question algebraically, one system at a time, but this is not time efficient. Instead, graph each pair of equations in your graphing calculator and look for the graphs that intersect at $x = -4$ and $x = 2$. The graphs of the equations in (A) and (B) don't intersect at all, so you can eliminate them right away. The graphs in (C) intersect, but both points of intersection have a positive x-coordinate. This means **(D)** must be correct. The graph looks like this:

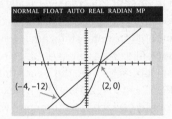

23. C

Difficulty: Medium

Category: Problem Solving and Data Analysis/Statistics and Probability

Getting to the Answer: Read the question, identifying parts of the graphic you need—the question asks about litters of 7 or more pups, so you'll only use the heights of the bars for 7, 8, and 9 pups. Start by finding the percent of the mice in the study that had a litter of 7 or more pups. Of the 200 mice in the sample, $25 + 14 + 5 = 44$ had a litter of 7 or more pups. This is $\frac{44}{200} = \frac{22}{100} = 22\%$ of the mice in the study. Given the same general conditions (such as living in the same geographic region), you would expect approximately the same results, so multiply the number of female mice in the whole population by the percent you found: $35,000 \times 0.22 = 7,700$. Choice **(C)** is correct.

24. C

Difficulty: Medium

Category: Heart of Algebra/Linear Equations

Getting to the Answer: You'll need to interpret the information given in the question to write two ordered pairs. Then you can use the ordered pairs to find the

slope and the y-intercept of the linear model. In an ordered pair, the independent variable is always written first. Here, the heart rate depends on the amount of exercise, so the ordered pairs should be written in the form (time, heart rate). They are (8, 90) and (20, 117). Use these points in the slope formula, $m = \frac{y_2 - y_1}{x_2 - x_1}$, to find that $m = \frac{117 - 90}{20 - 8} = \frac{27}{12} = 2.25$. Then, substitute the slope (2.25) and either of the points into slope-intercept form and simplify to find the y-intercept:

$$90 = 2.25(8) + b$$
$$90 = 18 + b$$
$$72 = b$$

Finally, write the equation using the slope and the y-intercept that you found to get $r = 2.25t + 72$. Note that the only choice with a slope of 2.25 is **(C)**, so you could have eliminated the other three choices before finding the y-intercept and saved yourself a bit of time.

25. A

Difficulty: Medium

Category: Additional Topics in Math/Geometry

Getting to the Answer: The formula for finding the area of a trapezoid is $A = \frac{1}{2}h(b_1 + b_2)$. This particular formula is not given on the formula page; memorizing it prior to test day will save you a bit of time (rather than having to find the sum of the areas of the triangles and the rectangle that make up the trapezoid).

You could pick numbers to represent the lengths of the bases and height, and then find the area of the trapezoid before and after the indicated changes. Or, you might happen to notice that reducing the height by 75% means the new height is $\frac{1}{4}$ of the original height, which is likely to cancel nicely with the 4 that the bases are being multiplied by. Using the second strategy, the formula for the area of the new trapezoid becomes $A = \left(\frac{1}{2}\right)\left(\frac{1}{4}h\right)(4b_1 + 4b_2)$. If you factor 4 out of the bases, you can cancel it with the 4 in the denominator of the new height: $A = \left(\frac{1}{2}\right)\left(\frac{1}{\cancel{4}}h\right)\cancel{4}(b_1 + b_2)$.

The resulting equation is $A = \frac{1}{2}h(b_1 + b_2)$, the same as the original equation, which means the area has not changed, and therefore the percent increase is 0%. Choice **(A)** is correct.

26. C

Difficulty: Medium

Category: Heart of Algebra/Linear Equations

Getting to the Answer: Pay careful attention to what the question tells you about the variables. The x-value is the number of payments already made and the y-value is the amount of debt remaining (not how much has been paid). If a solution is (21, 560), the x-value is 21, which means Chantal has made 21 payments already. The y-value is 560, which means $560 is the amount of debt *left to be paid*, making **(C)** correct.

27. D

Difficulty: Hard

Category: Problem Solving and Data Analysis/Scatterplots

Getting to the Answer: A line that "represents the trend of the data" is another way of saying line of best fit. The trend of the data is clearly linear because the path of the dots does not turn around or curve, so draw a line of best fit on the graph. Remember, about half of the points should be above the line and half below.

Emails per Day by Age

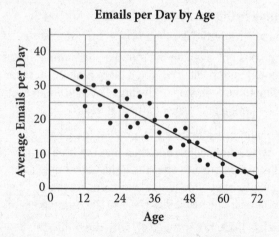

If you draw your line of best fit all the way to the y-axis, you'll save yourself a step by simply looking at the scatterplot to find the y-intercept. For this graph, it's about 35. This means you can eliminate choices (B) and (C). Next, find the approximate slope using two points that lie on (or very close to) the line. You can use the y-intercept, (0, 35), as one of them to save time and estimate the second, such as (72, 4). Use the slope formula to find the slope:

$$m = \frac{y_2 - y_1}{x_2 - x_1} = \frac{4 - 35}{72 - 0} = \frac{-31}{72} \approx -0.43$$

The equation that has the closest slope and y-intercept is **(D)**. (Note that if you choose different points, your line may have a slightly different slope or y-intercept, but the answer choices will be far enough apart that you should be able to determine which is the *best* fit to the data.)

28. B

Difficulty: Hard

Category: Passport to Advanced Math/Functions

Getting to the Answer: Transformations that are grouped with the x in a function shift the graph horizontally and, therefore, affect the x-coordinates of points on the graph. Transformations that are not grouped with the x shift the graph vertically and, therefore, affect the y-coordinates of points on the graph. Remember, horizontal shifts are always backward of what they look like. Start with $(x + 3)$. This shifts the graph left 3, so subtract 3 from the x-coordinate of the given point: $(5, 1) \rightarrow (5 - 3, 1) = (2, 1)$. Next, apply the negative in front of f, which is not grouped with the x, so it makes the y-coordinate negative: $(2, 1) \rightarrow (2, -1)$. Finally, -2 is not grouped with x, so subtract 2 from the y-coordinate: $(2, -1 - 2) \rightarrow (2, -3)$, which is **(B)**.

29. C

Difficulty: Hard

Category: Problem Solving and Data Analysis/Rates, Ratios, Proportions, and Percentages

Getting to the Answer: Draw a chart or diagram detailing the various price reductions for each 30 days.

Date	Percent of Most Recent Price	Resulting Price
Jan 15	100 − 25% = 75%	$1,500 × 0.75 = $1,125
Feb 15	100 − 10% = 90%	$1,125 × 0.9 = $1,012.50
Mar 15	100 − 10% = 90%	$1,012.50 × 0.9 = $911.25

You can stop here because the refrigerator was sold on April 2, which is not 30 days after March 15. The final selling price was $911.25, **(C)**.

30. A

Difficulty: Hard

Category: Additional Topics in Math/Geometry

Getting to the Answer: Organize information as you read the question. Here, you'll definitely want to draw and label a sketch.

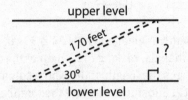

The lower level, the vertical distance between levels, and the diagonal elevator track form a 30-60-90 triangle, where the elevator track is the hypotenuse. The vertical distance is opposite the 30° angle so it is the shortest leg. The rules for 30-60-90 triangles state that the shortest leg is half the length of the hypotenuse, so the vertical distance between levels is approximately $170 \div 2 = 85$ feet, **(A)**.

31. 22

Difficulty: Medium

Category: Heart of Algebra/Inequalities

Getting to the Answer: You don't need to separate this compound inequality into pieces. Just remember, whatever you do to one piece, you must do to all three pieces. Don't forget to flip the inequality symbols if you multiply or divide by a negative number. Here, the fractions make it look more complicated than it really is, so start by clearing the fractions by multiplying everything by 20:

$$20\left(-\frac{3}{2}\right) < 20\left(3 - \frac{a}{5}\right) < 20\left(-\frac{1}{4}\right)$$
$$-30 < 60 - 4a < -5$$
$$-30 - 60 < 60 - 60 - 4a < -5 - 60$$
$$-90 < -4a < -65$$
$$\frac{-90}{-4} > \frac{-4a}{-4} > \frac{-65}{-4}$$
$$22.5 > a > 16.25$$
$$16.25 < a < 22.5$$

The question asks for the maximum possible whole number value of a, so the correct answer is **22**.

32. 1/6 or .166 or .167

Difficulty: Easy

Category: Problem Solving and Data Analysis/Statistics and Probability

Getting to the Answer: This question requires concentration, but no complicated calculations. First, you need to identify the rows that contain information about the seating on the 777s, which are the bottom two rows. To find the probability that the seat is a Business Class seat, find the total number of seats in that category (in only the bottom two rows), and divide by the total number of seats on the planes (in only the bottom two rows):

$$P(\text{Business Class}) = \frac{37 + 52}{194 + 37 + 16 + 227 + 52 + 8}$$
$$= \frac{89}{534} = \frac{1}{6} = 0.1\overline{6}$$

Grid in your answer as **1/6 or .166 or .167**.

33. 440

Difficulty: Medium

Category: Heart of Algebra/Systems of Linear Equations

Getting to the Answer: Translate from English into math to write a system of equations with $t =$ the cost of the tankless heater in dollars, and $c =$ the cost of the conventional heater in dollars. First, a tankless heater (t) costs $160 more (+160) than twice as much ($2c$) as the conventional one, or $t = 2c + 160$. Together, a tankless heater (t) and a conventional heater (c) cost $1,000, or $t + c = 1,000$. The system is:

$$\begin{cases} t = 2c + 160 \\ t + c = 1,000 \end{cases}$$

The top equation is already solved for t, so substitute $2c + 160$ into the second equation for t and solve for c:

$$2c + 160 + c = 1,000$$
$$3c + 160 = 1,000$$
$$3c = 840$$
$$c = 280$$

Be careful—that's not the answer! The conventional hot water heater costs $280, so the tankless heater costs $2(280) + 160 = \$720$. This means the tankless heater costs $\$720 - \$280 = \$440$ more than the conventional heater.

34. 25

Difficulty: Medium

Category: Problem Solving and Data Analysis/Rates, Ratios, Proportions, and Percentages

Getting to the Answer: The key to answering this question is reading carefully—the word "exactly" is very important because it tells you that there cannot be a portion of a patient, so you are looking for the smallest whole number of which 48 percent is also a whole number. Every percent can be written as a number over 100 (because *per cent* means *per hundred*), so start by writing 48 percent as a fraction and reducing it: $\frac{48}{100} = \frac{12}{25}$. The denominator of this fraction **(25)** gives the least possible number of patients who could have participated in the trial because it is the first number that will cancel when multiplied by the fraction.

35. 9984

Difficulty: Hard

Category: Additional Topics in Math/Geometry

Getting to the Answer: Don't be too quick to answer a question like this. You can't simply find two-thirds of the volume of the pyramid because the top is considerably smaller than the bottom. Instead, you'll need to find the volume of the whole pyramid and subtract the volume of the top piece that is being discarded.

The figure shows a right triangle inside the pyramid. The bottom leg is given as 18 and the slant height, or hypotenuse of the triangle, is given as 30. You might recognize this as a multiple of the Pythagorean triplet, 3-4-5, which is in this case 18-24-30. This means the height of the original pyramid is 24. You now have enough information to find the volume of the original pyramid:

$$V = \frac{1}{3}\,lwh$$

$$V = \frac{1}{3}\,(36)(36)(24)$$

$$V = \frac{1}{3}\,(31,104)$$

$$V = 10,368$$

To determine the dimensions of the top piece that is cut off, use similar triangles:

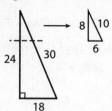

One-third of the original height is $24 \div 3 = 8$, resulting in a 6-8-10 triangle, making the length of the smaller leg 6, which means the length of the whole cutoff pyramid is $6 \times 2 = 12$. Substitute this into the formula for volume again:

$$V = \frac{1}{3}\,lwh$$

$$V = \frac{1}{3}\,(12)(12)(8)$$

$$V = \frac{1}{3}\,(1,152)$$

$$V = 384$$

Thus, the volume of the frustum is $10,368 - 384 = 9,984$ cubic meters.

36. 88

Difficulty: Hard

Category: Passport to Advanced Math/Radicals

Getting to the Answer: When you're asked to solve an equation that has two variables, the question usually gives you the value of one of the variables. Read carefully to see which variable is given and which one you're solving for. You are given the diameter (0.12), so substitute this value for d in the equation and then solve for the other variable, h. Before dealing with the radical, divide both sides of the equation by 0.015:

$$0.12 = 0.015 \times \sqrt{h - 24}$$

$$8 = \sqrt{h - 24}$$

$$8^2 = \left(\sqrt{h - 24}\right)^2$$

$$64 = h - 24$$

$$88 = h$$

37. 252

Difficulty: Medium

Category: Problem Solving and Data Analysis/Rates, Ratios, Proportions, and Percentages

Getting to the Answer: Break the question into steps. First, find how long it took Daniel to spray one lawn, and then use that amount to find how long it took him to spray all the lawns. According to the figure, he started the first house at 9:00 and the sixth house at 10:00, so it took him 1 hour, or 60 minutes, to spray 5 houses. This gives a unit rate of $60 \div 5 = 12$ minutes per house. Count the houses in the figure—there are 21. Multiply the unit rate by the number of houses to get $12 \times 21 = 252$ minutes to spray all the lawns.

38. 4

Difficulty: Hard

Category: Problem Solving and Data Analysis/Rates, Ratios, Proportions, and Percentages

Getting to the Answer: This part of the question contains several steps. Think about the units given in the question and what you need to convert so that you can get to the answer. The total acreage of all the lawns in the neighborhood is $21 \times 0.2 = 4.2$ acres. This is equivalent to $4.2 \times 43,560 = 182,952$ square feet. Each gallon of spray covers 2,500 square feet, so divide to find that Daniel needs $182,952 \div 2,500 = 73.1808$ gallons to spray all the lawns. The spray rig holds 20 gallons, so Daniel will need to fill it **4** times. After he fills it the fourth time and finishes all the lawns, there will be some spray left over.

Essay Test Rubric

The Essay Demonstrates. . .

4—Advanced	• **(Reading)** A strong ability to comprehend the source text, including its central ideas and important details and how they interrelate, and effectively use evidence (quotations, paraphrases, or both) from the source text. • **(Analysis)** A strong ability to evaluate the author's use of evidence, reasoning, and/or stylistic and persuasive elements and/or other features of the student's own choosing; make good use of relevant, sufficient, and strategically chosen support for the claims or points made in the student's essay; and focus consistently on features of the source text that are most relevant to addressing the task. • **(Writing)** A strong ability to provide a precise central claim; create an effective organization that includes an introduction and conclusion, as well as a clear progression of ideas; successfully employ a variety of sentence structures; use precise word choice; maintain a formal style and objective tone; and show command of the conventions of standard written English so that the essay is free of errors.
3—Proficient	• **(Reading)** Satisfactory ability to comprehend the source text, including its central ideas and important details and how they interrelate, and use evidence (quotations, paraphrases, or both) from the source text. • **(Analysis)** Satisfactory ability to evaluate the author's use of evidence, reasoning, and/or stylistic and persuasive elements and/or other features of the student's own choosing; make use of relevant and sufficient support for the claims or points made in the student's essay; and focus primarily on features of the source text that are most relevant to addressing the task. • **(Writing)** Satisfactory ability to provide a central claim; create an organization that includes an introduction and conclusion, as well as a clear progression of ideas; employ a variety of sentence structures; use precise word choice; maintain an appropriate formal style and objective tone; and show control of the conventions of standard written English so that the essay is free of significant errors.
2—Partial	• **(Reading)** Limited ability to comprehend the source text, including its central ideas and important details and how they interrelate, and use evidence (quotations, paraphrases, or both) from the source text. • **(Analysis)** Limited ability to evaluate the author's use of evidence, reasoning, and/or stylistic and persuasive elements and/or other features of the student's own choosing; make use of support for the claims or points made in the student's essay; and focus on relevant features of the source text. • **(Writing)** Limited ability to provide a central claim, create an effective organization for ideas, employ a variety of sentence structures, use precise word choice, maintain an appropriate style and tone, or show command of the conventions of standard written English, resulting in certain errors that detract from the quality of the writing.

1—Inadequate	• **(Reading)** Little or no ability to comprehend the source text or use evidence from the source text.
	• **(Analysis)** Little or no ability to evaluate the author's use of evidence, reasoning, and/or stylistic and persuasive elements; choose support for claims or points; or focus on relevant features of the source text.
	• **(Writing)** Little or no ability to provide a central claim, organization, or progression of ideas; employ a variety of sentence structures; use precise word choice; maintain an appropriate style and tone; or show command of the conventions of standard written English, resulting in numerous errors that undermine the quality of the writing.

Essay Response #1 (Advanced Score)

In "The Human Side of Animals," Royal Dixon makes the argument that animals are complex beings with thoughts and feelings that deserve the same respect as humans. When Dixon first makes his argument, he probably realizes that he faces an uphill climb. Most people are meat-eaters, and it is likely that much of Dixon's audience consists of people whose lifestyle depends on the domination and consumption of animals. In order to build a strong argument in the face of such opposition, Dixon effectively uses persuasive techniques that include emotional language and imagery, appeals to his audience's intelligence, and persuasive reasoning and evidence.

Dixon uses emotionally laden language and imagery to persuade his audience of the humanity of animals. First, he conjures the heartwarming image of "young lambs playing on a grassy hillside," only to give his audience an unpleasant jolt when he abruptly turns the lambs into cold, impersonal "mutton." Dixon uses a similarly emotional image later in the passage when he describes cows "[bellowing] for days when mourning for their dead." By including these powerful images that are likely to upset people, Dixon makes it difficult for his audience to maintain the position that humans should have no feeling for animals.

Dixon also uses appeals to his audience's intelligence to sway them to his side. In the first paragraph, he asks the rhetorical question, "Why should we fall into the colossal ignorance and conceit of cataloging every human-like action of animals [as] instinct?" By associating disrespect of animals with ignorance, Dixon leads his audience, who wants to feel intelligent, into agreeing with his views. In the second paragraph, Dixon uses the analogies of fascism and primitive religion to compare dominion over animals to other misguided ideas. Later, he labels the views of the average scientist as ignorant and "empty," encouraging his audience to align themselves with his views instead.

Dixon, however, relies on more than just stylistic elements and emotional appeals to make his case. He also uses persuasive reasoning and evidence to support his point that animals are worthy of the same respect as humans. To critics who would argue that animals' abilities are due to instinct and neurological impulses, Dixon counters that humans, too, are ruled by the same forces, and yet we allow a level of compassion and feeling for humans that we deny to animals. He also makes the point that physically, humans and animals are very similar to each other, and in fact, animals are physically superior to humans in most cases. The major difference, he says, is that we have a superior intellect. By pointing out how much we have in common with animals, Dixon removes the barrier between us and them, making it harder for his opposition to argue that animals have neither intellect nor feeling.

He continues this line of reasoning by pointing out that human and animal behaviors are similar, and that "man has been imitating the animals" by flying, tunneling, and exploring Earth's waters. Dixon uses a variety of examples to provide evidence for his case: animals organizing themselves against enemies, building shelter, storing food, and making and using tools, just like humans. He also cites animal communication as a marker of intelligence and different emotional states, even if humans don't understand what they are hearing. An especially vivid piece of evidence is the example of a dreaming war horse who "lives over and over his battles," just as humans re-live their exploits in their dreams. Time and again, Dixon proves humans and animals share common experiences, and are therefore worthy of mutual respect.

By presenting the evidence of commonalities between humans and animals, as well as evidence of animals' feeling and intellect, Dixon makes an effective case that we should cease our dominion over them. He bolsters his case with appeals to his audience's intelligence and emotional imagery, both of which make his audience less resistant to his claims. While Dixon may not persuade every member of his audience that animals are worthy of respect, his use of these features makes his argument much more effective than it would be without them.

Essay Response #2 (Proficient Score)

Royal Dixon makes the argument in "The Human Side of Animals" that animals and humans should be treated with the same respect. He uses appeals to emotion, rhetorical questions, and evidence of animals' thoughts and feelings to make his case.

Knowing that most people who eat meat would disagree with his claims, Dixon uses emotional language to break down their resistance. It is hard to argue that animals have no feelings when Dixon describes cows mourning for days for their dead. Dixon gives other examples of animals having strong emotions, like when a war horse acts out its former battles in its sleep. These examples remind people of themselves; which is Dixon's goal: to break down the barriers between animals and humans.

He also uses rhetorical questions to persuade his audience to agree with ideas that may be new to them. In the first paragraph he asks, "If you agree that we cannot treat men like machines, why should we put animals in that class?" Since most people would agree with the first part of the statement, they are more likely to agree with the second part as well. The next rhetorical question in the paragraph asks people if they want to "fall into the colossal ignorance" of thinking that all animal behavior is due to instinct, the answer is obviously no. By carefully constructing these questions, Dixon puts his audience in a position in which they will be more likely to agree with his claims.

For readers who still may doubt that animals and humans have much in common, Dixon offers many examples of how animal behavior is like human behavior. Animals build shelter, make tools, and do other things that are just like the things humans do. With these examples, and others, Dixon shows that animals and humans are so similar that it makes no sense for one to dominate the other. In fact, he points out, some animal abilities are superhuman, like their ability to predict the weather. By giving examples of animals' traits and abilities that are similar to and even better than ours, Dixon causes the audience to feel respect for animals.

In conclusion, Dixon uses different ways of getting his audience to agree that animals are worthy of respect in "The Human Side of Animals." The use of emotional appeals, rhetorical questions, and evidence of animals' "humanity" helps him to persuade an audience that may be resistent at first to hearing his ideas.